Cognitive Disability and Its Challenge to Moral Philosophy

T0355670

⚭ METAPHILOSOPHY

METAPHILOSOPHY SERIES IN PHILOSOPHY

Series Editors Armen T. Marsoobian, Brian J. Huschle,
and Eric Cavallero

Cognitive Disability and Its Challenge to Moral Philosophy

Edited by

Eva Feder Kittay and Licia Carlson

WILEY-BLACKWELL

A John Wiley & Sons, Ltd., Publication

This edition first published 2010

Originally published as Volume 40, Nos. 3–4 (July 2009) of *Metaphilosophy* except for "Developmental Perspective on the Emergence of Moral Personhood," by James C. Harris, and earlier versions of the following three chapters: "The Limits of the Medical Model: Historical Epidemiology of Intellectual Disability in the United States," by Jeffrey P. Brosco, published as "More Than the Names Have Changed: Exploring the Historical Epidemiology of Intellectual Disability in the United States," chapter 8 of *Healing the World's Children: Interdisciplinary Perspectives on Child Health in the Twentieth Century*, edited by Cynthia Comacchio, Janet Golden, and George Weisz (Montreal: McGill-Queen's University Press, 2008); "Caring and Full Moral Standing Redux," by Agnieszka Jaworska, published as "Caring and Full Moral Standing" in *Ethics* 117 (April 2007): 460–97; and "Cognitive Disability, Paternalism, and the Global Burden of Disease," by Daniel Wikler, published as "Paternalism and the Mildly Retarded," *Philosophy and Public Affairs* 8, no. 4 (1979): 377–92.

Blackwell Publishing was acquired by John Wiley & Sons in February 2007. Blackwell's publishing program has been merged with Wiley's global Scientific, Technical, and Medical business to form Wiley-Blackwell.

Registered Office

John Wiley & Sons Ltd, The Atrium, Southern Gate, Chichester, West Sussex, PO19 8SQ, United Kingdom

Editorial Offices

350 Main Street, Malden, MA 02148-5020, USA
9600 Garsington Road, Oxford, OX4 2DQ, UK
The Atrium, Southern Gate, Chichester, West Sussex, PO19 8SQ, UK

For details of our global editorial offices, for customer services, and for information about how to apply for permission to reuse the copyright material in this book please see our website at www.wiley.com/wiley-blackwell.

Library of Congress Cataloging-in-Publication Data

Cognitive disability and its challenge to moral philosophy/edited by Eva Feder Kittay and Licia Carlson.
     p. cm. – (Metaphilosophy series in philosophy)
  Originally published as volume 40, nos. 3-4 (July 2009) of Metaphilosophy.
  Includes bibliographical references and index.
  ISBN 978-1-4051-9828-8 (pbk. : alk. paper) 1. Cognition disorders. 2. Ethics. I. Kittay, Eva Feder. II. Carlson, Licia, 1970- III. Metaphilosophy.
  RC553.C64C6277 2010
  616.8001–dc22

                                                         2009045860

A catalogue record for this book is available from the British Library.

Set in 10pt Times
By Macmillan India Ltd

01 2010

In Memoriam

Heather Ann McElory
February 3, 1971–May 19, 2009

Her life was a shining example of what is possible.

CONTENTS

CONTENTS

EDITORS' ACKNOWLEDGMENTS

This volume has been a collaborative effort, involving not only the outstanding group of scholars who have contributed their essays but also the many individuals and institutions who made possible the conference on which the volume is based. The early collaboration was between Eva Kittay and Sophia Wong. When other commitments compelled Sophia Wong to leave the project, Licia Carlson stepped in to fill the breach. We want to acknowledge the important role Sophia Wong played in shaping the arc of the project.

The conference, "Cognitive Disability: A Challenge to Moral Philosophy," held at Stony Brook University, Manhattan, from September 16 to 18, 2008, was two years in the planning and was materially supported by many institutions and individuals whom we'd like to acknowledge. At Stony Brook we had the support of the Department of Philosophy, where we give special thanks to Robert Crease for his early encouragement and willingness to make departmental resources and staff time available to us and a thank-you goes to Alissa Betz; to Provost Eric Kaler for his recognition of the importance of this work and for generous support in financially tight circumstances; and to the Office of the Vice President for Research. We also acknowledge the support of the Stony Brook Humanities Institute, the Dean of the Liberal Arts and Sciences, the Templeton Lecture Series, and the Office of the President, who offered encouragement and help in locating financial support.

Armen Marsoobian, editor in chief of *Metaphilosophy* and coeditor of the *Metaphilosophy* Series in Philosophy, was centrally important to the project. His was the first offer of financial support, and from the inception of the project to its conclusion Armen Marsoobian, Wiley-Blackwell, and Otto Bohlmann were generous with time as well as resources.

William Ruddick of the NYU Bioethics Center was also an early and enthusiastic supporter. We thank the Center and NYU for their generosity and hospitality in hosting the opening session of the conference.

A number of other organizations provided helpful grants, among them Forest Laboratories, the New York Association for Retarded Citizens, and the Alzheimer's Association. Deep thanks go to Donald Sussman for his always boundless generosity. The artistic beauty of the conference materials was the work of The Abelson Company, especially Dan Abelson and Nette Gaastra, who contributed their labor, as did our dear friend and outstanding portrait photographer Philippe Vermes, whose photographs grace the book's cover.

Even with all this wonderful assistance, we would not have been able to carry out the project without the indispensible support of Patrick Dollard and all the amazing people at the Center for Discovery.

Mention of the help we received from the philosophy graduate students at Stony Brook requires virtually a volume in itself. Cara O'Connor was our right hand. She was integral to every aspect of the project, from the conceptual and the artistic to the organizational. We are thankful for her philosophical knowledge, her administrative skills and organizational intelligence, and the joyfulness and graciousness with which she handled every task. Our other hand was Michael Roess, providing indispensable technical assistance with all the computer-related intricacies any contemporary project involves and adding his good nature and his philosophical and organizational skills to those of Cara O'Connor. Danae McLeod was that third hand many of us long to have as a permanent appendage. Her fiscal responsibility kept the project on track and in the black. Others too many to name helped in one form or another, and are all part of the project that has culminated in this volume.

Our final joint thanks go to our terrific and distinguished contributors for their willingness to be pioneers in a rich project that may forever alter some basic assumptions in the discipline of philosophy—a discipline we treasure too much not to challenge.

Separately, Licia Carlson would especially like to thank her colleagues at the Harvard Writing Program for their support, and to offer her deepest gratitude to Eva Kittay for inviting her to be a part of this incredible project. And to her beloved Jeremiah and Julian, whose love and inspiration make her work possible: "this is for you."

Eva Kittay, in turn, wants to express her gratitude to Licia Carlson for stepping in and helping her realize a project that holds special significance for her. To her family, Sesha, Leo, Kim, Micah, Asa, Ezra, and especially Jeffrey: thanks for supporting me through every step and cheering me along at each turn.

NOTES ON CONTRIBUTORS

Michael Bérubé is Paterno Family Professor in Literature at Penn State University, where he is an affiliate of the Program in Science, Technology, and Society and codirector of the Disability Studies Program. His most recent book is *The Left at War* (New York University Press, 2009).

Jeffrey P. Brosco completed an M.D. and a Ph.D. in the history of medicine at the University of Pennsylvania. He teaches and practices general pediatrics and developmental pediatrics as professor of clinical pediatrics at the University of Miami Miller School of Medicine. He is Associate Director of LEND (which is related to the Mailman Center) and he is Associate Professor of clinical pediatrics. His previous research includes an analysis of the organization of health care for children in the early twentieth century, and his current work focuses on public policy trends in health care for people with developmental disabilities.

Licia Carlson received her Ph.D. in philosophy from the University of Toronto and is assistant professor of philosophy at Providence College. The primary focus of her research has been on philosophy and intellectual disability, and she has published numerous articles on disability in the context of bioethics, feminist philosophy, phenomenology, and the work of Michel Foucault. Her book *The Faces of Intellectual Disability: Philosophical Reflections* will be published by Indiana University Press in 2010.

Leslie P. Francis is Distinguished Professor of Law and Philosophy and Alfred C. Emery Professor of Law at the University of Utah. She is also chair of the philosophy department. Along with legal and philosophical articles on ethics and disability, her other recent work includes the coauthored *Patient as Victim and Vector: Ethics and Infectious Disease* (Oxford, 2009) and "Privacy and Confidentiality: The Importance of Context" (*Monist* January, 2008). She cochairs the Security, Privacy, and Confidentiality Subcommittee of the National Committee on Vital and Health Statistics.

Ian Hacking is professor emeritus, Collège de France, where he held the chair of the philosophy and history of scientific concepts, and also

University Professor Emeritus, University of Toronto. He is the author of books on many subjects, including experimental physics, probability, mental illness, and "social construction." His *Historical Ontology* is a collection of essays that indicates some of the ways in which he does philosophy. He received the Holberg International Memorial Prize in 2009.

James C. Harris, M.D., is professor of psychiatry and behavioral sciences, pediatrics, and mental hygiene at the Johns Hopkins University School of Medicine. He is a former member of PCMR and a recipient of the AACAP George Tarjan Award for outstanding leadership and continuous contributions in the field of mental retardation, and the Agnes Purcell McGavin Award for Distinguished Career Achievement in Child and Adolescent Psychiatry from the APA. His textbook *Developmental Neuropsychiatry* was chosen medical book of the year of its publication.

Agnieszka Jaworska is associate professor of philosophy at the University of California, Riverside. She received her B.S.E. from Princeton University and her Ph.D. from Harvard University, and previously worked at Stanford University and the Department of Bioethics at the National Institutes of Health. She has published in *Ethics, Philosophy and Public Affairs*, and *Philosophy and Phenomenological Research*. Her contribution to this book is part of a larger project entitled "Ethical Dilemmas at the Margins of Agency."

Bruce Jennings is director at the Center for Humans and Nature, a private operating foundation that studies philosophical and ethical questions in environmental and health policy. He also teaches at the Yale University School of Public Health and is a senior consultant at the Hastings Center. He has written widely on issues in bioethics, political theory, and public policy. He is currently completing a book on dementia and the ethics of long-term care.

Eva Feder Kittay is Distinguished Professor of Philosophy and Women's Studies, and senior fellow, Center for Medical Humanities, Compassionate Care, and Bioethics, Stony Brook University/SUNY. Her major publications include "On the Margins of Moral Personhood" (in *Ethics*); *Love's Labor: Essays on Women, Equality, and Dependency*; *Blackwell Studies in Feminist Philosophy* (with Linda Alcoff); *Theoretical Perspectives on Dependency and Women* (with Ellen Feder); and *Women and Moral Theory* (with Diana T. Meyers). She is the mother of a woman with intellectual disabilities.

Hilde Lindemann is professor of philosophy at Michigan State University, a fellow of the Hastings Center, and was president of the American

Society for Bioethics and Humanities. She is the former editor of *Hypatia* and the author of *Damaged Identities, Narrative Repair* and *An Invitation to Feminist Ethics*. Her ongoing research interests are in narrative approaches to bioethics, feminist ethics, the ethics of families, and the social construction of persons and their identities

Victoria McGeer holds a research position in the University Center for Human Values at Princeton University and lectures in the Department of Philosophy. Her published work focuses on topics in moral psychology, the development of agential capacities and its impairments (especially with regard to autism), the nature of folk-psychological explanation, problems of self-knowledge, and the metaphysics of mind.

Jeff McMahan is professor of philosophy at Rutgers University and author of *The Ethics of Killing: Problems at the Margins of Life* (Oxford, 2002) and *Killing in War* (Oxford, 2009).

James Lindemann Nelson is professor of philosophy at Michigan State University and teaches primarily in bioethics and moral theory, with occasional forays into issues in the philosophy of mind and of language. The author most recently of *Hippocrates' Maze* (Rowman, 2003), he is currently working on two books: one concerns ethical issues in human organ procurement, and the other, the contributions of Jane Austen to moral psychology.

Martha Nussbaum is the Ernst Freund Distinguished Service Professor of Law and Ethics at the University of Chicago, appointed in law, philosophy, and divinity. Her books include *Cultivating Humanity*, *Upheavals of Thought*, *Hiding from Humanity*, *Frontiers of Justice*, *Liberty of Conscience*, and *From Disgust to Humanity* (forthcoming).

David Shoemaker is an associate professor at Tulane University, teaching in both the Murphy Institute and the Department of Philosophy. His publications have primarily been on agency and moral responsibility, as well as on the relation between personal identity and ethics. His current research is on the intersection of moral responsibility, personal identity, disability, and irrationality.

Anita Silvers, professor and chair of philosophy at San Francisco State University, writes on social/political philosophy, ethics/bioethics, and feminist/disability studies, among other topics. She has published eight books and more than 150 articles and chapters in philosophy journals, medical journals, law reviews, encyclopedias, collections, and magazines. During a long career as a disability advocate, she has worked to open higher education to people with disabilities and will chair the APA's Inclusiveness Committee starting in 2010.

Peter Singer is Ira W. DeCamp Professor of Bioethics in the University Center for Human Values at Princeton University and Laureate Professor at the University of Melbourne. His books include *Animal Liberation, Practical Ethics, Rethinking Life and Death, One World,* and most recently, *The Life You Can Save.*

Cynthia A. Stark is associate professor of philosophy at the University of Utah. She works on political philosophy (especially social contract theory), ethical theory, and feminist philosophy. Her recent publications include "How to Include the Severely Disabled in a Contractarian Theory of Justice" in the *Journal of Political Philosophy* and "Contractarianism and Cooperation" in *Politics, Philosophy, and Economics.*

Anna Stubblefield (Ph.D. Rutgers–New Brunswick, 2000) is chair of the Department of Philosophy at Rutgers–Newark; affiliate faculty of the American Studies and Urban Systems doctoral programs, the Department of African and African-American Studies, and the Women's Studies program; and faculty adviser to the Disability Services Office. She is the author of *Ethics Along the Color Line* (Cornell University Press, 2005) and serves as ethics consultant to agencies that provide services to people with developmental disabilities.

Daniel Wikler is Mary B. Saltonstall Professor of Population Ethics in the Department of Global Health and Population at the Harvard School of Public Health. He earlier served as the first "staff ethicist" at the World Health Organization in Geneva and taught bioethics and philosophy at the University of Wisconsin. His current research agenda includes ethical issues in population and global health, and the use of human subjects in international health research.

Jonathan Wolff is professor of philosophy and director of the Centre for Philosophy, Justice and Health at University College London, and a member of the Nuffield Council on Bioethics. His most recent book is *Disadvantage* (Oxford, 2007), cowritten with Avner de-Shalit. He is currently writing a book on political philosophy and public policy.

Sophia Isako Wong received her Ph.D. in philosophy from Columbia University and is associate professor at Long Island University in Brooklyn, New York. Her research interests include the ethics of prenatal genetic testing and sex selection, reproductive autonomy and preimplantation genetic diagnosis, moral personhood, and distributive justice. She is currently writing a book about siblings of people with intellectual disabilities.

INTRODUCTION:
RETHINKING PHILOSOPHICAL PRESUMPTIONS IN LIGHT OF
COGNITIVE DISABILITY

LICIA CARLSON AND EVA FEDER KITTAY

Why Philosophy and Cognitive Disability?

Philosophers conceive of the mark of humanity as the ability to reason.[1] It is to humans that we extend the mantles of equality, dignity, justice, responsibility, and moral fellowship. Reason, in philosophical accounts, is generally taken to be the ground for human dignity, hence the special accord and moral status we attribute to humans. But people with cognitive disability are individuals who have, at best, a diminished capacity for rational deliberation. Yet they are human. How should we think about these individuals? In what way do they present challenges to some of philosophy's most cherished conceptions of personhood, agency, responsibility, equality, citizenship, the scope of justice, and human connection?

In posing philosophical questions about cognitive disability, philosophers focus on numerous ethical problems. Some address the moral status of individuals with cognitive disabilities, and ask: Are those with cognitive disabilities due the same respect and justice due to those who have no significant cognitive impairments? Are the grounds of our moral obligation different when a human being may lack certain cognitive faculties that are often understood as the basis for moral personhood? Are those with significant cognitive impairment moral persons? What sort

---

[1] A note on terminology: We employ the terms "mental retardation" and "cognitive disability," recognizing that both are problematic. Despite the fact that the (former) American Association for Mental Retardation has now changed its name to the American Association for Intellectual and Developmental Disabilities and many in the advocacy and professional communities have rejected the term, we speak of "the mentally retarded," as the term picks out a specific group commonly discussed in philosophical literature. We've chosen the term "cognitive disability," under which we include conditions like autism, dementia, Alzheimer's, and mental retardation, rather than "intellectual disability." The former is broader. Also, some forms of cognitive disability do not imply diminished intellectual capacity (e.g., autism.)

of moral responsibility is it appropriate to expect of people with differing degrees and sorts of cognitive disabilities? Are the distinctions between mild and severe impairment morally relevant? Are the people with cognitive disabilities, especially those labeled as "mentally retarded," distinct, morally speaking, from nonhuman animals?

Other philosophers take our moral obligations to those with cognitive disabilities as a given and consider the challenges that they pose to existing moral theories and concepts. If we take these obligations as a given, then people with cognitive disabilities offer an opportunity to explore the nature and limits of concepts like justice, rights, respect, care, and responsibility. We also are faced with the difficult question of how we realize these conceptions in practice given the challenges presented by those with cognitive disabilities.

Animal rights theorists have paid special attention to those with cognitive disabilities. Some have averred that we need to parse our moral universe so that "normal" human and nonhuman beings who possess the capacity for reason constitute one category, while nonhuman animals and intellectually subpar humans together constitute another. If these philosophers are right, then people who are lacking the capacity (or possess it but not to the threshold level) for rational deliberation cannot be our equals—they are nonpersons. Thus they should be denied the entitlements of a just society, a society composed of persons. Their moral claims are subordinated to those of persons. And they do not possess dignity and the moral status that we associate with persons. How definitive are these arguments, and what consequences follow? The controversy indicates the extent to which the moral status of individuals with cognitive disabilities remains unsettled, as does a consensus about the approach to their care and treatment.

These issues and debates were the subject of a conference, held at Stony Brook University in September 2008 that, for the first time brought together philosophers and ethicists in other disciplines as well as physicians and medical historians from across North America, Europe, and Australia.[2] The conference focused on three groups who all face the challenges of functioning in a society that requires proficiency in certain cognitive abilities: those with intellectual and developmental disabilities (IDD) (formerly identified as "mental retardation"), autism, and Alzheimer's disease. There are overlapping philosophical and practical concerns raised by these three conditions, as we will see below. These conditions were chosen to constrain the discussion, but many issues are pertinent to other cognitive disabilities, such as brain injury, other forms of senile dementia, and other developmental disabilities.

As people with cognitive disabilities appear to present the few exceptions to the standard philosophical conception of the person, their outlier status may justify the marginal importance of the questions they raise for philosophy. It is true that there are very few who have severe cases of IDD and that the entire group of people with IDD constitutes only about 2.5 percent of the general population. But the "normal" adults who will become cognitively disabled with old age are numerous, with up to 20 percent of adults older than seventy-five suffering from Alzheimer's and other forms of dementia.[3] Moreover, there has been (for no known reason) a vast increase in the number of children diagnosed with autism, a condition that involves cognitive, perceptual, and behavioral anomalies, setting these children and adults apart from the norm. Furthermore, medical advances have permitted people who would otherwise die of brain injury to survive, albeit with diminished cognitive abilities, and have kept people living longer, increasing the likelihood of them developing dementia. Finally, while new technologies have enabled younger and younger premature infants to survive, a number of whom will experience significant cognitive impairments, earlier and more reliable prenatal testing and pre-implantation embryo selection have presented prospective parents with the dilemma of whether or not to bring such children into the world.

When we consider the aged adults we may become or need to care for, the decisions we or our children may have to make as prospective parents, the possibility that we, our children, friends, or others close to us may have a child diagnosed with autism, and that at any moment, through illness or accident, we or those we love may develop a significant cognitive impairment, we see that cognitive disability has a reach into the lives of many and can touch the lives of all. This realization should compel us to view cognitive disability as a feature of the human condition that philosophers should take seriously. Once we do so, a number of fundamental philosophical presumptions and received views are up for reconsideration, including the centrality of rational thought to our conception of humanity and moral standing, the putative universality of philosophical discourse, and the scope and nature of moral equality.

Historical Overview

Although the subject of cognitive disability remains somewhat marginal in philosophical discourse, there are historical precedents to a discussion of the topic. While people with cognitive disabilities rarely appear in historical philosophical texts, when they are mentioned they are referenced only to be discounted as irrelevant, or as exceptions that prove the rule. For example, as early as Plato's *Republic* (460c) we find references to the abandonment of "defective infants." When John Locke, in his *Two Treatises on Government*, a foundational work in modern political philosophy, explains that what makes one a "Free Man" is maturity,

---

[3] See Hebert et al. 1995 and www.dementiacarefoundation.org

he notes that "[i]f through defects that may happen out of the ordinary course of Nature, any one comes not to such a degree of Reason, wherein he might be supposed incapable to know the Law . . . he is *never capable of being a Free Man,* he is never let loose to the disposure of his own Will. . . . And so Lunaticks and Ideots are never set free from the Government of their Parents" (1824, 2: §60). Not being "Free Men", those "Ideots" can never be citizens and cannot be due justice, only charity. For justice, says Locke, gives "every man a Title to the product of his honest Industry," while charity gives "every man a Title to so much out of another's Plenty, as will keep him from extreme want, where he has no means to subsist otherwise" (1: §42). The view that those with cognitive impairments are not subject to the same basic rights and protections may also be inferred in Kant's philosophy. Kant is generally taken to be the locus situ of the intimate connection between personhood, dignity, and autonomy. He writes: "Autonomy then is the basis of the dignity of human and of every rational nature" (1959, 59). It is thought that only *persons* can make autonomous decisions and ought not to be treated paternalistically. But this view of autonomy suggests that those with cognitive disability have no autonomy that needs protection (see Agich 1995; Kittay 2006; O'Neill 1984; Wikler 1979).

In the wake of the increased attention paid to it in a political and social context, due to the emerging parental and self-advocacy movements and the public discourse surrounding deinstitutionalization in the 1960s and 1970s, cognitive disability emerged as an object of philosophical inquiry and ethical discourse in its own right. Philosophers in different traditions began examining the nature and moral status of individuals with cognitive disabilities, and addressing both theoretical and practical questions. Here we find ethicists and bioethicists grappling with questions of justice, respect, personhood, and autonomy, and with concerns regarding the treatment of persons with cognitive disabilities in a variety of philosophical contexts (Kopelman and Moskop 1984; Khuse and Singer 1985). In the theological realm, some argued against the dehuman-ization and diminished status accorded to persons with cognitive dis-abilities, and noted important resonances between these philosophical arguments and concrete practices like Jean Vanier's development of the L'Arche communities (Veatch 1986; Hauerwas 1986; Reinders 2008).

At the same time, however, we find a number of places where the "cognitively disabled" are addressed *indirectly,* as a tactical move in an unrelated philosophical argument. Most notable is the increased presence of cognitive disability on the philosophical stage as part of certain arguments addressing the moral status of nonhuman animals. A clear example of this can be found in arguments against speciesism, and in animal rights literature that utilizes the "severely cognitively impaired" as a group to bolster the case for this other marginalized group (Singer 1995; Regan and Singer 1989; Tooley 1984; Rachels 1990). Peter Singer and Jeff

McMahan, both of whom are represented in this collection, each argue that to grant human beings higher moral status than nonhuman animals with what they call "comparable" intellectual ability is arbitrary and unjustified (Singer 1995; McMahan 1996, 2003).

More recently there has been a significant shift in the philosophical discourse surrounding cognitive disability. A number of philosophers have begun to problematize the very category "cognitive disability" and have raised critical questions regarding the nature, status, and treatment of persons with disabilities, both in political contexts and in academic and philosophical scholarship. In part, this shift in the mode of questioning and scope of analysis is symptomatic of broader changes on the disability landscape over the past few decades. The burgeoning disability rights movement, the Americans with Disabilities Act, and the explosion of work in the interdisciplinary field of disability studies have all provided a very different stage upon which philosophers can speak about disability.

New philosophical questions have emerged against the backdrop of "the social model of disability," whereby people with disabilities have argued that it is not so much the person who needs fixing but the environment that needs adaptation if people with disabilities are to lead flourishing lives.[4] Some philosophers and disability scholars question whether cognitive disability, or its various instantiations such as the category of "mental retardation," is a self-evident and unproblematic "natural kind" (Hacking 1999; Carlson forthcoming), and they problematize the very notion of "normalcy" (see Amundson 2000; Carlson 2003; Davis 1997; Kittay 2006). Rather than taking an ahistorical approach to the topic, many are exploring the sociopolitical foundations of the oppression of persons with cognitive disabilities, both now and in the past (Stubblefield 2007; Carlson 2001 and forthcoming). Finally, philosophers are unmasking the discriminatory and erroneous assumptions that underlie certain philosophical treatments of disability. This growing body of work has emerged from multiple philosophical sites, including ethics and political philosophy (Kittay 1999; Reinders 2000; Nussbaum 2006; MacIntyre 1999; Mahowald 1998; Byrne 2000; Francis and Silvers 2000; Silvers, 1995, 1996), feminist philosophy (Wendell 1989; Kittay 1999; Wong 2002; Silvers 1999; Tremain 2006), philosophy of

---

[4] This is but a crude gloss on the social model. Rich discussion of this model can be found in numerous places: in disability memoirs, in academic texts, in expressions of disability culture in the media and the arts, in grassroots political movements such as the independent living movement and the self-advocacy movement, and in its legal embodiment, the Americans with Disabilities Act. See Oliver 1990; Wendell 1996, 1989; Lane 1995; Morris 1991; Davis 1997; Thomson 1997; Conners, Browne, and Stern 1985; Silvers 1998. This list is hardly complete, as there are far too many discussions of the social model to include in this list. But note that most of the work is about physical disability. More needs to be said about the social model and cognitive disability. See Tremain 2002; Carlson forthcoming; Reinders 2008.

science, bioethics (Kittay 1999; Asch and Parens 2000; Goering 2003; Reinders 2002), and postmodern theory (Tremain 2002, 2005; Davis 2002).

Despite this new critical philosophical orientation, the general issue of disability sometimes overshadows the particularity of cognitive disability within both critical disability theory and traditional moral theory. In contrast, the chapters in this collection give cognitive disability a central place in this changing philosophical and political landscape and reveal the broad range of arguments and issues that have surfaced. Surely physical disability has presented a challenge to many philosophical conceptions. But because philosophy has long taken reason and other aspects of cognition as central to its very project, it is cognitive disability that is "the philosopher's nightmare" (Carlson forthcoming, chap. 1). Therefore it is this form of disablement that provides the opportunity for a radical set of reflections about philosophy itself.

Discussion of Themes and the Chapters

The chapters in this collection begin with a historical overview of the medical approach to intellectual disability and the limitations of that perspective. The rest of the chapters are grouped according to five themes. The first of these deals with *justice*, asking how a theory of justice can accommodate those with cognitive disabilities and what such accommodation requires in terms of political participation. *Care* is the second theme discussed and raises the problem of whether the care and treatment of people with cognitive disabilities is commensurate with their just treatment. We then consider aspects of *agency,* inquiring how we might construe agency in people who do not demonstrate or enact agency in typical ways. The next set of chapters interrogate the *language and representation of cognitive disability*. They ask how the agency and status of the disabled subject come to be defined and understood, and what historical and contextual considerations are relevant. The collection concludes with chapters on the vexing issue of *personhood*, taking up the question of moral status head-on. These chapters grapple with the challenge to the moral personhood of people with disabilities and the challenge to modes of philosophizing in which people with cognitive disabilities are rendered nonpersons.

Intellectual Disability: The Medical Model and Beyond

This part of the book contains two essays by physicians who are specialists in intellectual and developmental disabilities, and who articulate the importance of critically revisiting and moving beyond a narrow medical model of cognitive disability. Taken together, these two chapters offer an important backdrop for the philosophical discussions that follow, as they situate the categories of intellectual and developmental disabilities in both medical and historical contexts. Jeffrey Brosco, a pediatrician and medical historian, lays out a rich historical epidemiology of intellectual disability. Beginning with a question posed by Sargent Shriver in 2002 regarding what progress has been made in addressing intellectual disability, Brosco lays out an intricate account of why there is not a straightforward and easy answer to even the most basic questions regarding the prevalence and causes of intellectual disability. He charts changes in definitions, public health measures, and diagnostic tools, all of which highlight the complex intersection of the political and the social with the medical. While he acknowledges that there have been significant advances on many fronts in the past century, Brosco argues that we must resist appeals to facile explanations that are reductionist in defining intellectual disability and its causes, or that rely on simplistic arguments regarding heredity, intelligence, and IQ.

In his chapter "Developmental Perspective on the Emergence of Moral Personhood," psychiatrist James Harris provides an overview of definitions, prevalence, and etiology of intellectual disability as an entry point into more specific questions regarding the individual's moral, cognitive, and emotional development. Whereas Brosco's chapter demonstrates the insights that can be gained by expanding the medical model to include a public health perspective, Harris's developmental account of moral personhood in persons with intellectual disabilities illustrates what is lost if we reduce cognitive *disability* to cognitive *impairment*, that is, if we take a physiological impairment as definitive of the extent to which capacities and functioning within a society are impeded. If we recognize the significance of neuroplasticity and the bonds that form between infants and parents, Harris argues that even the most severely disabled individuals are capable of important forms of development. He concludes by pointing to some of the ethical questions regarding autonomy and treatment that emerge in a new light once the possibility of moral and emotional development is acknowledged, topics that are taken up by many of the philosophers in subsequent chapters.

Justice

Of the many indignities suffered by people with disabilities, the denial of their claims to justice (or claims made on their behalf) has been especially serious and particularly acute for people with *cognitive* disabilities. Through the Americans with Disabilities Act, people with disabilities have demanded and have been granted legal protections against discrimination in civic and political life. But people with severe cognitive disabilities appear unable to participate in the workplace on a competitive basis and may not be able to exhibit the understanding and judgment needed for political participation. With Locke, many philosophers and lay people have presumed that while charity is appropriately bestowed on people who cannot function as rational agents in the public domain, these individuals have no claim to just treatment. Were we able to count on each other to be magnanimous to those unlikely to return our favors, worries about justice for the cognitively disabled might be of less concern. But justice entitles us to protections and provisions, and those who have to be at the mercy of another's charity live precarious lives and are most likely to suffer poverty, neglect, and abuse. This surely has been the history of all whose claims to just treatment have been denied, and people with cognitive disabilities have suffered as much as any, and more than most.

Yet, finding a justification for including people with cognitive disabilities in extant theories of justice is a challenge. To adopt the language of the political philosopher John Rawls, they are frequently unable to share the burdens of social cooperation. If they do not, does this imply that they have no claim on the benefits of social cooperation? If not, are they then to be deprived of any claims to justice, as well as all forms of political participation? Today, for example, people with significant cognitive disabilities do not vote, and there are currently debates about how to deal with elderly persons who may have always have had the right to vote, but whose current dementia now makes it easy to manipulate them when they do go to the polls.

Martha Nussbaum has been a prominent voice among those who have questioned the ability of dominant theories of justice to include people with disabilities. In her important work *Frontiers of Justice* (2006), Nussbaum, building on previous work of disability theorists, argues that contractarian theories such as those of Rawls (1971, 1992) fail as a conception of justice for animals, people in poor distant lands, and people with disabilities, especially cognitive disabilities. She proposes the capability theory, with an enumeration of ten central capabilities that all governments should guarantee all citizens, including those with cognitive disabilities, as an important corrective to a Rawlsian position. In the chapter she has contributed to this collection, she discusses the various requirements, including access to medical care, education, and so forth, needed to guarantee that people with cognitive disabilities are treated as citizens with equal dignity. But she wants to go beyond the obvious entitlements and insist that in a capability theory justice for people with cognitive disabilities extends to their political participation in voting and jury duty. Either through direct participation or via a guardian each individual with cognitive disabilities, no matter how severe or extensive, should have a vote. She also envisions the possibility of an arrangement whereby people with cognitive disabilities, or a surrogate such as a guardian, can serve on juries, and she argues that such functions are essential to being fully included within society.

Michael Bérubé expresses his strong agreement with Nussbaum, even with respect to the question of surrogacy. But surrogacy, he argues, poses an important challenge to disability studies because of the disability community's insistence that there be "nothing about me, without me." That is, people in the disability community have fought a hard-won battle to be heard and to be heard in their own voice. And yet such a requirement leaves out those who cannot communicate effectively and those who may not be able to cognize effectively. Bérubé's contribution also reflects on an interchange with Peter Singer (begun at and pursued after the Stony Brook conference) concerning the limitations of people with Down syndrome.

Although Bérubé defends Nussbaum's capability view, another contributor, Cynthia Stark, raises questions about her solution to the question of justice for people with cognitive disability. In a related paper (Stark 2007), she defends Rawls and argues that there are good reasons for excluding all but the fully functioning, free, and equal parties in choosing the principles of justice in the original position. But this exclusion does not preclude full representation of people with cognitive disabilities at the Constitutional stage; that is, at the stage when citizens establish the framework of laws and protections, and so guarantee the recognition of their claims to justice. In her contribution to this collection, Stark argues that in trying to accommodate the requirements of justice for those left out by the contractual approach, Nussbaum fails to respect the dignity of rational agents adequately. Given that the social contract is the device by which the coercive power of the state is justified, to give up contractarianism is to lose the central means by which the dignity of rational agents is respected in political arrangements.

Sophia Wong also looks for a way to preserve the central insights and the contractual structure of Rawls's theory of justice. She indicates openings in the theory that allow us to conceive of parties in the original position as representing not only *actualized* fully functioning individuals but also those with the *potential* to develop the two moral powers (namely, a sense of justice and an ability to form and revise one's own conception of the good). Furthermore, she argues that given the history of mistaken (and self-fulfilling) prophecies of physicians regarding the capacities of the disabled, we cannot presume an unalterable moral incompetence on the part of any given human being. If we take seriously this epistemic caution, and if Rawls's theory embraces all those with the potential to acquire the two moral powers, then society has an obligation to provide what she calls "the enabling conditions" to acquire these moral powers.

Care

These enabling conditions require resources devoted to the care of people with disabilities, care that would enable those with cognitive disabilities to develop a flourishing life. As questions of justice are intimately bound up with questions of equality and resources, and as the distribution of resources and the need to treat people with their due measure of equality are indispensible for good care, we need to ask what arrangements will be both just and support good care. What we see is that questions of justice and care are not necessarily opposed and can be more than complementary. Each can be viewed as foundational for the other. A just society that meets the requirements of each citizen to flourish needs good social technologies of care; a truly caring society must be one in which resources and the fruits of social cooperation are fairly distributed. The authors of the next three chapters engage in different aspects of what good care requires in a society that treats all its citizens with justice.

People with significant cognitive disabilities are often dependent on others for help in caring for themselves and negotiating their way in the world. Those who give care will frequently find that the burdens are substantial. Often, caregiving is carried out by family members at great cost to themselves, financially, medically, and professionally. Paid care-givers are generally poorly paid, and the work lacks high social status. At the same time, caregivers tend to form deep and abiding relationships with people with cognitive disabilities, relationships that give their work and their life a heightened sense of meaning. Such significant relationships indicate one way that people with disabilities enhance their communities in ways that cannot be measured by economic standards.[5]

How we conceive of care and obligations that fall upon caregivers and the wider society are linked to the quality of life we believe people with cognitive disabilities are capable of having. If we think that the best that can be done is custodial care, or a measure of hedonic well-being, duties may be discharged with relatively minimal effort. But if we believe that even those with very significant cognitive disabilities are capable of a greater degree of agency, one that requires a more meaningful sense of flourishing, then the demands are more rigorous.

Beginning with the presumption that citizens with intellectual and developmental disabilities (IDD) are equal citizens that have the capacity to live a fulfilling life, yet recognizing that good care can be costly, Jonathan Wolff considers what sorts of models of care would at once serve people with IDD and their families well—giving people with IDD maximal autonomy and avoiding excessive demands on the

---

[5] The health toll on caregivers has recently been brought to the attention of the mainstream media (see LeRoy 2007). For discussion by and about long-term caregivers see Levine 2004. For studies on the effects of long-term care of parents of people with mental retardation see Seltzer and Krauss 1994; Birenbaum 1971; Darling 1979; Krauss and Seltzer 1993; McDonnell 1991. These are important issues which are not discussed in the present collection of chapters but which require a thorough treatment. See Kittay 2001, 1999; Fein 1995; Rimer 1998. For a further discussion of caregivers, see narratives of parents (Kittay 2000, 1999, chaps. 7 and 8; Bérubé 1996; McDonnell 1991.

family—and still be cost-effective to the state. His recommendations are based on experimental models in the United Kingdom that deploy a strategy of "targeted resource enhancement." Families and people with IDD are granted cash transfers that are targeted for expenditures on care, habilitation, and education. People with IDD and their families can use the resources in ways that best meet their needs for such goods.

Bruce Jennings and Hilde Lindemann are each concerned with the obligations that fall to the caregivers or guardians to represent appropriately the needs and capacities of those whose cognitive disabilities result from Alzheimer's disease and other forms of progressive dementia. Lindemann considers a form of care that has not been much discussed in bioethics. She calls this "holding one in personhood," that is, helping another in the construction and retention of his or her identity. This is an activity that parents engage in with their children, but it is also a form of care required for those with Alzheimer's. Such holding, notes Lindemann, can be done well, or badly, or clumsily. But even when it is done clumsily, it can perform a service and be a form of caring. Furthermore, we need to recognize that those whose personal identity seems to be slipping away from them can also contribute to holding another in personhood, again, well, badly, or, as dementia progresses, clumsily. Acknowledging this as a contribution that a person with dementia still makes to family and friends allows all involved to construe that life as one that retains meaning.

A person whose life retains meaning is one with "semantic agency," a form of agency that Jennings thinks is critical to recognize in people with Alzheimer's disease and other forms of progressive dementia. Such acknowledgment of semantic agency allows caregivers to provide care that goes beyond the meeting of hedonic needs and desires. Jennings launches a critique of a hedonic conception of the quality of life. He believes it is at once limiting and untrue. It blocks an accurate and respectful way to conceive of the personhood of people with Alzheimer's and other forms of progressive dementia. His original conceptions of memorial personhood and semantic agency are not only contributions to the way we think of care for this population, they also complement the discussions of agency and personhood that follow.

Other chapters in the collection address caregiving more obliquely. Eva Kittay talks about the efforts to get others to recognize her cognitively disabled daughter as a person as itself a form of care. Anna Stubblefield demonstrates the appalling lack of care Americans have provided African Americans who have been labeled with cognitive disabilities. Peter Singer questions the cost to parents in providing care to the cognitively disabled. And one may consider the various discussions of surrogacy, trusteeship, and guardianship as presenting different aspects of care.

Agency

The next four chapters hone in on the question of the agency of people with cognitive disabilities. Lindemann already shows not only that those who care for the cognitively disabled discharge obligations to people with cognitive disabilities, but also that people with these disabilities will be involved in a form of moral engagement that holding another in person-hood involves. This more active side of moral agency on the part of the cognitively disabled is an aspect explored both by Daniel Wikler and by David Shoemaker. Wilker asks what justifies the paternalism we exert on those who have an attenuated but nonetheless recognizable agency characteristic of those with mild intellectual disabilities. While we may view paternalism in legal and medical matters as consistent with a standard of care for those with limited cognitive capacities, Wikler invites us to reconsider the usual answer, which is that those with mild ID do not fully understand the consequences of their decisions. For this answer only raises more questions. Few of us are fully able to understand the consequences of our actions, and we do not regard another's superior intelligence as warranting paternalistic behavior toward those of average intelligence. Usually typical intelligence suffices for the degree of understanding we require to function in society as it is currently constructed. Thus, were we to simplify certain institutional arrangements sufficiently to reduce the burden of mild cognitive deficiencies, paternalistic behavior toward those with intellectual disabilities might not be required to protect their interests. This, however, may reduce the efficiency of institutions that are so modified. What are the obligations of a just society, asks Wikler, to accommodate the agency of the intellectually disabled by modifying its institutions? To make such an assessment, we may need to assess "the overall burden of mild and moderate cognitive disability within a comprehensive measure of the global burden of disease," a question that refers us back to the sort of assessments Brosco attempts in his chapter.

Shoemaker asks why we regard the person with mild cognitive disabilities as a member of our moral community even as we are wary of holding her morally responsible for her actions. He contrasts these sets of intuitions with those that we attach to psychopaths, whom we view as outside the moral community in many respects, even as we hold them responsible for their actions. The investigation brings to light many intriguing relationships between cognition, moral responsibility, and emotional responsiveness, especially empathy. The ability to empathize is a capacity that is unimpaired in many with cognitive disabilities and is dangerously absent in the psychopath, and it appears to be criterial for membership in a moral community, more so even than the ability to understand the consequences of our actions.

Those with mild cognitive disabilities exhibit unquestionable signs of agency, even if they are not fully capable of understanding the consequences of their actions. But those whose impairments are more pronounced are less easily viewed as agents, especially when agency is thought to require the capacity to conceive of one's own good and to act on it oneself. The second two chapters in this grouping set out to develop conceptions of agency that are not dependent on the autonomous actions conceived and executed by a singular individual, but rather are more social and relational. In making use of the concepts of trusteeship, surrogacy, and guardianship Nussbaum, Jennings, and Wolff implicitly invoke such relational models. These theories, along with the one developed by Anita Silvers and Leslie Francis in their chapter may implicitly call into question what in philosophy has been known as the "internalist theory of mind"—namely, that our terms and our thoughts are individuated by us alone, independent of the social understanding of these terms.

James Nelson takes the "bull by the horns" and argues that we need to move away from a purely internalist conception of mind when thinking about dementia: the way in which we treat people with dementia must reflect that the meaning of concepts and even the beliefs we hold are individuated by facts about the world and social understandings independently of those who hold the beliefs. In adducing the instance of a woman with moderate dementia who is a devout Jehovah's Witness and who comes down with an illness treatable by a blood transfusion, Nelson asks us to imagine that during the time she developed dementia, the Jehovah's Witnesses altered their view that blood transfusions violated the biblical prohibition against "eating blood" and reversed the prohibition. Nelson argues that providing the transfusion would not violate her beliefs even though the woman fails to grasp that the prohibition has been ended. This is because her own belief about blood transfusion no longer contains the same content it previously had—not because she has changed, but because the social understanding has altered. If the beliefs we hold are "not in our heads," and what constitutes the human mind is more than the sum of the cognitive and psychological capacities of our brains, then there is an important sense in which the limitations of cognitive capacities are not as determinative of the meaning we attribute to the words, actions, and beliefs of those with these disabilities. Our minds are underwritten and constituted in part by the social as well as the physical world that is external to us. Some may worry that applying an externalist theory of mind to the concerns of people with cognitive disability may fail to give due consideration to desires, fears, and needs as the individuals themselves experience them.

The chapter by Francis and Silvers is especially interesting to consider in the light of these questions, for they make a case for the idea that for people with serious cognitive impairments the formulation and articulation of such desires and understandings of one's own good may require the assistance of others, and moreover that such collaboration in formulating and articulating a conception of the good is continuous with the way we all form our conceptions of the good.

They insist that liberal theories, with their commitment to pluralism regarding conceptions of the good, contain a curious breach of pluralistic thinking. These theories, Rawls's in particular, hold that one of the two moral powers is the power to form and revise a conception of the good. But according to Francis and Silvers, liberalism is less pluralistic when it considers the cognitive processes whereby people form these conceptions. The assumption is that these must be formed and maintained by the individuals themselves. Silvers and Francis make the case for including conceptions of the good that are formulated, validated, and maintained in a collaborative fashion, where a person, because of cognitive impairments, is unable to engage in these processes without the prosthetic-like assistance of another. Whether an externalist conception of the mind is either necessary or useful for this idea of "prosthesis," the idea presented by Silvers and Francis coheres with that of Nelson, Lindemann, Wolff, Jennings, and others in the volume who argue for a conception of agency such that the formulation and execution of the agentic features of an individual are not all located within the limits of an individual body. The various chapters in the collection help draw a picture of a more collaborative conception of agency, one that is, in reality, appropriate to all, but especially useful to consider when we speak of those with cognitive disabilities.

Speaking About Cognitive Disability

As the chapters on agency reveal, there is a close relationship between the theoretical frameworks within which we conceive of agency, and the ways in which we then articulate conceptions of the good, the necessity for care, and the demands of justice in relation to the individual with cognitive disabilities. Yet underlying these particular philosophical concerns is a deeper metaphilosophical issue that must be addressed: how and why we speak about cognitive disability at all. The chapters in the next group situate our philosophical discussions in a broader context in the following ways: by exposing the historical contingency and permeability of the categories themselves; by examining the ways academic and nonacademic voices can shape how cognitive disabilities are defined and experienced; by considering the presumptions and theoretical commitments that underlie our understanding of these conditions; and finally, by problematizing the positions that we, as philosophers, occupy when speaking about cognitive disability as an object of inquiry.

While this task of contextualizing cognitive disability can be done in broad theoretical terms, the chapters collected here point to the importance of taking up these issues with greater specificity, and focus on two specific conditions: autism and "mental retardation." Both of these categories have been and continue to be contested, though for different reasons and in distinct ways. Mental retardation as a category has gone through many incarnations, and with the advent of genetic research we find that it has become an increasingly fractured category (Carlson forthcoming). Moreover, vocal self-advocacy and the disability rights movement have challenged the very term "mental retardation," and many professional groups have moved away from this terminology. Finally, as Stubblefield shows, the very concept of the "intellect" must be critically revisited.

The contemporary debates surrounding autism have taken on a slightly different hue, though similar questions regarding the nature and causes of this condition are being raised. First, the overlap and connections *between* mental retardation and autism have changed dramatically; thus, while some forms of autism are accompanied by intellectual and developmental disabilities, there are many individuals with autism that would not qualify as "mentally retarded." Like "mental retardation," however, the term "autism" is becoming increasingly heterogeneous. It refers to multiple conditions, and we now speak about disorders along the "autism spectrum" rather than assuming that individuals can be characterized with a single label. Even the metaphor of the spectrum is being challenged, however. Ian Hacking, in his chapter for this collection, suggests that it is inapt because it betrays our linear thinking, whereas "autism is a many-dimensional manifold of abilities and limitations."

While we have moved beyond the idea of the "refrigerator mother" as the cause of autism, there is currently a deep polarization between some in the scientific and parental advocacy groups regarding the causes of autism. Yet beyond these etiological debates, there has been what might be called a discursive explosion surrounding autism. As the chapters by Ian Hacking and Victoria McGeer reveal, the new genre of autistic autobiography and fiction that has emerged over the past decade is having a profound effect on how to think and talk about autism.

Hacking has given considerable attention to questions of language and classification in a variety of contexts (including child abuse, transient mental illness, and multiple personality disorder), and though his work has not explicitly centered on disability, he offers rich philosophical resources for philosophers and scholars interested in disability. In this collection, he turns his attention to the growth of a new genre of autistic fiction, and argues that this new "language game" is significant in that it is creating a new way for autistic individuals to exist in the world of "neurotypicals." Hacking introduces us to myriad characters and tropes: the autistic individuals themselves are represented in forms ranging from alien and hero to nerd and savant; those around them include a variety of heroes (from parents to psychiatrists), and "neurotypicals" for whom the autistic character provides a path to *self*-discovery. These forms of fiction range from mysteries and biographies-cum-novels, to "incidental autism" stories, where autism is not the centerpiece but does play an important role. While some of these books, in Hacking's estimation, can be misguided, poorly written, and even dangerous insofar as they misrepresent autism, in these stories we find new ways of articulating the relationship between the autistic individual and the "neurotypical," between parents and children, and between the normal and the abnormal.

McGeer picks up Hacking's thread and critically considers the two theses that she finds in his work on autistic fiction and autobiography: the *informative thesis*, which argues that autistic narratives can offer us insight into the world of autism, and the more controversial *transformative thesis*, namely, that these narratives can actually reshape the very way that the autism spectrum is constituted. Ultimately, she argues that the theory of mind deficit hypothesis can only offer "thin" descriptions of the lives of autistic individuals, and she defends the "form of life hypothesis," an alternate model that resonates with earlier discussions of agency that call for a more robust and relational conception of selfhood (Nelson and Jennings in this collection).

While Hacking and McGeer's work brings philosophical considerations to bear on autistic fiction, Anna Stubblefield and Licia Carlson are interested in the possible fictions that attend historical and philosophical accounts of cognitive disability. Stubblefield's chapter traces the multiple intersections between race and cognitive disability, a topic that has been grossly neglected in philosophical discussions of disability. Given the close historical connections between racist ideologies and definitions of cognitive disability, she argues that it is both politically and philosophically irresponsible to reify the "intellect" and "mental retardation." Her exploration of the intricate ways in which racist assumptions and practices shape the definitions and treatment of cognitive disability suggests that the very status of "cognitive disability" as a condition cannot be abstracted from the political and social forces that shape its boundaries. Stubblefield submits that we must consider the ways in which these categories and subcategories (like the distinction between "mild" and "severe") are themselves socially constructed and bear the mark of various racialized assumptions and institutions. Furthermore, she maintains that neither people of color who, because of racism, have been condemned to inferior educations and inferior life prospects nor those deprived, again because of racism, of needed services to ameliorate the disadvantage of disability will be adequately served until we recognize the entwinement of cognitive disability and racism.

Carlson directly addresses the nature and limits of *philosophical* discourse surrounding cognitive disability. Taking certain concrete historical and contemporary figures as a model (for example, the superintendent of the institution, the genetic counselor, the nonhuman animal, the parent or advocate), she offers a taxonomy of philosophers of intellectual disability. In doing so, she brings philosophical questions regarding power, authority, and voice to the surface and suggests that it is as important for philosophers to recognize their *own* limitations and ignorance as it is to consider the limits that define cognitive disability. Ultimately, these concerns are significant not only insofar as they force a critical evaluation of the philosophical discourse that we produce but also because the ways in which we philosophize about cognitive disability reveal deeper assumptions regarding the personhood, agency, and moral status of individuals who bear this label. Thus, in problematizing the ways that philosophers animalize cognitive disability, we must confront the final question that this collection takes up: namely, how we define the boundaries of personhood and the moral community when we consider both the human and nonhuman.

Moral Personhood

We come finally to the chapters that focus specifically on the question of personhood. Personhood grants us special moral standing. We generally believe that killing persons is morally different from killing nonpersons. McMahan (2003), for example, makes the point that killing a nonperson is viewed as morally less serious than killing a person, one of "us."

When it comes to defining the philosophical conception of personhood, the discussion has largely been dependent on conceptions of psychological capacities associated with the human ability to reason. But were we to concede that a human being with sufficiently significant cognitive deficits (however we come to construe these) ought not to be considered a person, would we not then be committed to the view that this individual would be deprived of equal moral standing in a community and may justifiably be treated like an animal, a plant, or even an inanimate object? At its most benign such a view would justify serious cutbacks on spending for the care, education, and habilitation of people labeled with these disabilities. A more sinister possibility is that removing such protections could be (and historically has been) used to justify experimentation that will not benefit and may lead to the suffering or death of individuals with cognitive disabilities (see Beauchamp and Childress 2001). At its extreme, depriving the cognitively disabled of the inviolability of persons can license policies such as those of the Nazi regime in which physicians exterminated "life not worthy of living" in the name of racial hygiene. While such practices will strike all decent people today as highly abhorrent, they were, surprising as it may seem, not very far from what advocates of eugenics (a respectable movement of citizens, doctors, and scientists in the United States and elsewhere in the earlier part of the twentieth century) recommended: namely, ridding the population of those "elements" who are drags on the gene pool and on resources (Proctor 1988; Lifton 2000).

Those with significant cognitive disabilities, however, are not the only human beings who fall short of many traditional philosophical criteria for personhood. Fetuses, infants, those in advanced stages of progressive dementia, people with some serious forms of mental illness, and even young children fall short as well. Had we been writing in a different century, we might have included women, slaves, people of African descent, "savages," and so forth, as Stubblefield's discussion of race reminds us. If philosophical conceptions of personhood argue against including people with significant cognitive disabilities, and if such arguments have the potential to cause much mischief, then these need very careful evaluation.

One group that has steadfastly remained outside the boundaries set by personhood is nonhuman animals. Some philosophers question our treatment of nonhuman animals by using, as a ploy, current intuitions against treating the cognitively disabled as nonpersons. Singer and McMahan, in previous writings and in their contributions to this collection, have asked whether there is any warrant for treating human beings with cognitive disabilities significantly better than the way we treat animals, given what they claim are the "comparable" cognitive capacities of individuals in each of these groups. As Singer puts it, people with severe cognitive disabilities cannot do many of the things that many nonhuman animals can, and so seem to lack the cognitive processes that he claims are the only nonprejudicial bases for the special moral consideration we give to persons. To base such moral status on species membership, he insists, is "speciesist" and prejudicial in favor of our own species in much the same way that racism is prejudicial to those of one's own race. There is no reason to claim that *all* humans are superior to *all* nonhuman animals, and so our treatment of the cognitively disabled, relative to other humans and to nonhuman animals, is unwarranted. Singer believes that we should be able to kill severely disabled neonates if the parents are willing, although he would insist that neither the severely mentally disabled nor animals should be mistreated, caused to suffer pain, or gratuitously killed.

McMahan, in his book *The Ethics of Killing* and in other articles, has argued a similar position, namely, that animals should be treated much better than we currently treat them and that people with severe mental impairment should be given a lesser status than those with normal cognitive capacities. That is, the moral status of nonhuman animals and those with severely impaired cognition should converge. This means that some humans are not due justice, and that they have a lesser level of inviolability than persons.

In light of the historical and contextual contingency of the categories of cognitive disabilities, this is a chilling prospect for anyone who might be vulnerable to being construed as being significantly cognitively deficient. But even with the best safeguards in place to assure that only those who "genuinely" are "radically cognitively impaired" are so labeled, we may have reason to be concerned.

Adrienne Asch summarized many of the concerns when she asked during Singer's session at the Stony Brook conference why McMahan and Singer's position is not just another form of an "ethics of exclusion." She and many others questioned Singer and McMahan on the use and moral demotion of cognitively disabled humans for the purpose of advancing what all agree is otherwise a morally worthy project, namely, calling attention to the unwarranted suffering humans cause nonhuman animal. Both Singer and McMahan responded that they were not only directing their positions at advancing the cause of animals but were also responding to other important concerns, such as the suffering of parents who have a very severely disabled child (Singer) and the consistency between accepting a high moral standing for severely cognitively disabled humans while adopting permissive views on the killing of fetuses (McMahan).[6]

In his contribution to this collection, McMahan elaborates additional motivations for his position on "radical cognitive impairment." But not before he sets out a challenge to the defenders of the equal moral worth of people with severe cognitive impairments: give up the practice of eating meat. The major portion of the chapter, however, tries to explore further the moral status of people with radical cognitive impairments by contemplating the possibility of enhancing human cognitive capacities and by considering the violability of fetuses and the moral status of cognitively enhanced "supra-persons."

First, with respect to abortion, he asks us to contemplate the harm of aborting a cognitively normal fetus relative to the harm of withholding enhancement to a cognitively impaired fetus in utero. Although inconclusive, this comparison is intended to indicate the difficulties of bringing into alignment intuitions about the treatment of the radically cognitively impaired and the abortion of normal fetuses. The second thought experiment involves supra-person humans whose cognitive capacities are as significantly above our own as the cognitive capacities of normal humans are above those of nonhuman animals.

Agnieszka Jaworska asks us to consider a particular conception of personhood that does *not* center on rational capacities, whether they be normal or enhanced, but instead is based on an individual's affective capacities, particularly the capacity to care. Such a conception has the possibility of including within personhood many individuals who would

---

[6] This dialogue is available at http://www.stonybrook.edu/sb/cdconference/podcasts. shtml. See especially the podcasts of Singer's remarks at https://podcast.ic.sunysb.edu// blojsom_resources/meta/phicdc/16-PETER_Singer_Q%26A.mp4; Asch's question and McMahan's response at https://podcast.ic.sunysb.edu//blojsom_resources/meta/phicdc/36-KITTAY %3AMcMAHAN_Q%26A.mp4.

fall short of the traditional views adopted by Singer and McMahan. In making her case for the central role of the capacity to care as a sufficient condition for full moral standing, Jaworska echoes some of the arguments and conceptions of agency we find in the essays by Shoemaker, Lindemann, and Jennings. But unlike those essays (all of which accept the full moral standing of people with cognitive disabilities), which depend on human examples, and unlike the invocation of actual nonhuman animals deployed by Singer or the cognitively enhanced conjured up by McMahan (both of whom argue against the full moral standing of many cognitively disabled individuals), Jaworska's essay invokes innovative scenarios involving various imaginary nonhuman agents modeled on nonstandard forms of human agency. In this way, Jaworska hopes to establish a criterion for personhood that does not depend on species membership but will embrace more human beings than the rationalistic criteria do. Her exploration of our intuitions regarding these imaginary figures appears to warrant full moral standing for individuals with cognitive disabilities who retain a sufficiently robust capacity to care.

Eva Kittay, who has the last word in this collection, does not want to abandon the importance of species membership. In a thought experiment that is similar to the exercise McMahan puts us through, Bernard Williams (2008) imagines being confronted with the prospect that such enhanced beings think they have the right to dominate us, use us to their own purposes, and perhaps eat us. Williams avers that a human who agrees with such supra-persons, because these beings are, after all, so vastly superior to us, would be greeted by other humans with the question, "Well, whose side are you on?" Williams uses this exercise to justify what he calls "the human prejudice," an assessment that would not be warranted by the cognitivist antispeciesism of McMahan or Singer.

Kittay, however, sides squarely with Williams. Elsewhere she has argued (Kittay 2006, 2008) that favoring giving all within one's own species an equal status is not akin to racism. She has argued emphatically (if not persuasively enough to convince either Singer or McMahan) that moral status should not be based on the possession of some given property or properties, and that species membership itself should be sufficient (if not necessary) for equal moral standing. In this collection, however, she responds in a very personal voice, speaking of what it is like, as the mother of a child with the sorts of disabilities[7] of which Singer and McMahan speak, to have her child compared to a nonhuman animal, to try to counter their arguments philosophically, and to be heard not just as a subjectively involved mother but as a fellow philosopher. In charting her course in this dual role, she makes explicit the issues of moral and

---

[7] We use the term "disabilities" even though McMahan has tried to argue that severe cognitive impairment is not a disability. See McMahan 2009 and the Kittay chapter in this collection (footnote 2).

epistemic authority raised by Carlson. Her reflections lead her, ironically, to see how central to the *argument itself* is her passionate attachment to her daughter and its manifestation in the context of philosophical engagement. She concludes that her efforts to get her colleagues to recognize the profundity of her relationship to her disabled daughter is but another way of arguing that this relationship is no different from the attachment of any loving mother to her child. The abstract arguments about personhood threaten to obscure the reality at stake in the personhood debate. The philosophical demonstration then has to be just that, a demonstration, a showing of the concrete reality of cognitive disability and its place in the human family.

Concluding Remarks

Historian of medicine Ellen Dwyer states, "[J]ust as legislators and taxpayers often have relegated 'defective dependents' to the back wards of state institutions, scholars have relegated them to the back wards of history" (Dwyer 2004, 258). We believe that the conference and this ensuing collection of chapters demonstrate that philosophers cannot continue to ignore, or relegate to a footnote or afterthought, a numerically and conceptually significant portion of human beings, those who have cognitive disabilities and who stand in actual or potential relationship to us all. We hope that philosophers and people in the humanities more broadly will see how much is lost to us if we turn away from giving full consideration to the neglected or misused members of the population who are or are thought to be cognitively disabled. Neither justice nor care is served by the legislator's neglect. Nor is truth or goodness served by the scholar's turning away. We believe that the conference and the chapters provide a much needed addition to philosophical scholarship, and we hope that they will be a spur to further work in this underexplored terrain.

References

Agich, George J. 1995. "Actual Autonomy and Long-Term Care Decision Making." In *Long-Term Care Decisions: Ethical and Conceptual Dimensions*, edited by Laurence B. McCullough and Nancy L. Wilson, 113–36. Baltimore: John Hopkins University Press.

Amundson, Ron. 2000. "Against Normal Function." *Studies in History and Philosophy of Biological and Biomedical Sciences* 31, no. 1:33–53.

Asch, Adrienne, and Erik Parens, eds. 2000. *Prenatal Testing and Disability Rights*. Washington, D.C.: Georgetown University Press.

Beauchamp, Tom L., and James F. Childress. 2001. *Principles of Biomedical Ethics*. New York: Oxford University Press.

Bérubé, Michael. 1996. *Life as We Know It: A Father, a Family, and an Exceptional Child*. New York: Random House.

Birenbaum, Arnold. 1971. "The Mentally Retarded Child in the Home and in the Family Cycle." *Journal of Health and Social Behavior* 11:55–65.

Byrne, Peter. 2000. *Philosophical and Ethical Problems in Mental Handicap.* New York: St. Martin's Press.

Carlson, Licia. 2001. "Cognitive Ableism and Disability Studies: Feminist Reflections on the History of Mental Retardation." *Hypatia* 16, no. 4:124–46.

———. 2003. "Rethinking Normalcy, Normalization, and Cognitive Disability." In *Science and Other Cultures: Issues in the Philosophy of Science and Technology,* edited by Sandra Harding and Robert Figueroa, 154–71. New York: Routledge.

———. Forthcoming. *The Faces of Intellectual Disability: Philosophical Reflections.* Bloomington: Indiana University Press.

Conners, Debra, Susan Browne, and Nanci Stern, eds. 1985. *With the Power of Each Breath: A Disabled Women's Anthology.* Pittsburgh: Cleis Press.

Darling, Rosalyn Benjamin. 1979. *Families Against Society: A Study of Reactions to Children with Birth Defects.* Beverly Hills: Sage.

Davis, Lennard J., ed. 1997. *The Disability Studies Reader.* New York: Routledge.

Davis, Lennard J. 2002. *Bending Over Backwards: Essays on Disability and the Body.* New York: New York University Press.

Dwyer, Ellen. 2004. "The State and the Multiply Disadvantaged: The Case of Epilepsy." In *Mental Retardation in America,* edited by Steven Noll and James Trent, 258–80. New York: New York University Press.

Fein, Ester B. 1995. "The packaging of personal care: In the new cluster concept one attendant serves many." *New York Times,* February 27, sec. B, p. 1, col. 1.

Francis, Leslie Pickering, and Anita Silvers, eds. 2000. *Americans with Disabilities: Exploring the Implications of the Law for Individuals and Institutions.* New York: Routledge.

Goering, Sarah. 2003. "Conformity Through Cosmetic Surgery: The Medical Erasure of Race and Disability." In *Science and Other Cultures: Issues in the Philosophy of Science and Technology,* edited by Sandra Harding and Robert Figueroa, 172–88. New York: Routledge.

Hacking, Ian. 1999. *The Social Construction of What?* Cambridge, Mass: Harvard University Press.

Hauerwas, Stanley. 1986. *Suffering Presence.* South Bend, Ind.: University of Notre Dame Press.

Hebert, Liesi E., Paul A. Scherr, Laurel A. Beckett, Marilyn S. Albert, David M. Pilgrim, Marilyn J. Chown, Harris H. Funkenstein, and Denis A. Evans. 1995. "Age-Specific Incidence of Alzheimer's Disease in a Community Population." *JAMA* 273:1354–69.

Kant, Immanuel. 1959. *Foundations of the Metaphysics of Morals*. Edited and translated by Lewis White Beck. Indianapolis: Bobbs-Merrill.

Khuse, Helga, and Peter Singer. 1985. *Should the Baby Live? The Problem of Handicapped Infants*. Oxford: Oxford University Press.

Kittay, Eva Feder. 1999. *Love's Labor: Essays in Women, Equality and Dependency*. New York: Routledge.

———. 2000. "At Home with My Daughter." In *Americans with Disabilities*, edited by Leslie Pickering Francis and Anita Silvers, 64–80. New York: Routledge.

———. 2001. "When Care Is Just and Justice is Caring: The Case of the Care for the Mentally Retarded." *Public Culture* 13, no.3:557–79 (special issue entitled *The Critical Limits of Embodiment: Reflections on Disability Criticism*). Reprinted in *The Subject of Care: Feminist Perspectives on Dependency*, edited by Eva Feder Kittay and Ellen K. Feder, 257–76. Lanham, Md.: Rowman and Littlefield, 2002.

———. 2006. "On the Margins of Moral Personhood." *Ethics* (October):100–131.

———. 2008. "Ideal Theory Bioethics and the Exclusion of People with Severe Cognitive Disabilities." In *Naturalized Bioethics: Toward Responsible Knowing*, edited by Hilde Lindemann, Marian Verkerk, and Margaret Walker, 218–37. Cambridge: Cambridge University Press.

Kopelman, Loretta, and John C. Moskop, eds. 1984. *Ethics and Mental Retardation*. Dordrecht: D. Reidel.

Krauss, Marty Wyngaarten, and Marsha Mailick Seltzer. 1993. "Long-Term Caring: Family Experiences over the Life Course." Paper read at "Down Syndrome, Living, and Learning in the Community" meeting, New York.

Lane, Harlan. 1995. "Constructions of Deafness." *Disability and Society* 10, no. 2:171–89.

LeRoy, Andree. 2007. *Exhaustion, Anger of Caregiving Get a Name*. International CNN.com//health 2007 (cited August 24, 2007). Available from http://edition.cnn.com/2007/HEALTH/conditions/08/13/caregiver.syndrome/index.html

Levine, Carol, ed. 2004. *Always on Call: When Illness turns Families into Caregivers*. New York: Vanderbilt University Press.

Lifton, Robert Jay. 2000. *The Nazi Doctors: Medical Killing and the Psychology of Genocide*. New York: Basic Books.

Locke, John. 1824. *Two Treatises on Government*. London. (Original 1690.)

MacIntyre, Alasdair. 1999. *Dependent Rational Animals*. Chicago: Open Court.

Mahowald, Mary B. 1998. "A Feminist Standpoint." In *Disability, Difference, Discrimination: Perspectives on Justice in Bioethics and Public Policy*, by Anita Silvers, David Wasserman, and Mary B. Mahowald, 209–52. Lanham, Md.: Rowman and Littlefield.

McDonnell, Jane Taylor. 1991. "Mothering an Autistic Child: Reclaiming the Voice of the Mother." In *Narrating Mothers: Theorizing Maternal Subjectivities*, edited by B. O. Daly and M. T. Reddy, 58–75. Knoxville: University of Tennessee Press.

McMahan, Jeff. 1996. "Cognitive Disability, Misfortune, and Justice." *Philosophy and Public Affairs* 25, no. 1:3–35.

———. 2003. *The Ethics of Killing: Problems at the Margins of Life*. Oxford: Oxford University Press.

———. 2009. "'Our Fellow Creatures' and 'Radical Cognitive Limitation'." In *Disability and Disadvantage*, edited by Kimberley Brownlee and Adam Cureton, 240–59. Oxford: Oxford University Press.

Morris, Jenny. 1991. *Pride and Prejudice: Transforming Attitudes to Disability*. Philadelphia: New Society.

Nussbaum, Martha. 2006. *Frontiers of Justice: Disability, Nationality, Species Membership. The Tanner Lectures on Human Values.* Cambridge, Mass.: Belknap Press of Harvard University Press.

Oliver, Michael. 1990. *The Politics of Disablement*. London: Macmillan.

O'Neill, Onora. 1984. "Paternalism and Partial Autonomy." *Journal of Medical Ethics* 10:173–8.

Proctor, Robert. 1988. *Racial Hygiene: Medicine Under the Nazis*. Cambridge, Mass.: Harvard University Press.

Rachels, James. 1990. *Created From Animals: The Moral Implications of Darwinism*. New York: Oxford University Press.

Rawls, John. 1971. *A Theory of Justice*. Cambridge, Mass.: Belknap Press of Harvard University Press.

———. 1992. *Political Liberalism*. New York: Columbia University Press.

Regan, Thomas, and Peter Singer, eds. 1989. *Animal Rights and Human Obligations*. Englewood, N.J.: Prentice Hall.

Reinders, Hans. 2000. *The Future of the Disabled in Liberal Society*. Notre Dame, Ind.: University of Notre Dame Press.

———. 2002. "The Good Life for Citizens with Intellectual Disability." *Journal of Intellectual Disability Research* 46, no. 1:1–5.

———. 2008. *Receiving the Gift of Friendship: Profound Disability, Theological Anthropology and Ethics*. Grand Rapids, Mich.: Eerdmans.

Rimer, Sara. 1998. "Blacks carry load of care for their elderly." *New York Times*, March 15, pp. 1, 22.

Seltzer, Marsha Mailick, and Marty Wyngaarden Krauss. 1994. "Aging Parents with Coresident Adult Children: The Impact of Lifelong Caregiving." In *Life Course Perspectives on Adulthood and Old Age*, 3–18. Washington, D.C.: American Association on Mental Retardation.

Silvers, Anita. 1995. "Reconciling Equality to Difference: Caring (f)or Justice for People with Disabilities." *Hypatia* 10, no. 1:30–55.

———. 1996. "(In)Equality, (Ab)Normality, and the Americans with Disabilities Act." *Journal of Medicine and Philosophy* 21:209–24.

———. 1999. "On Not Iterating Women's Disability: A Crossover Perspective on Genetic Dilemmas." In *Embodying Bioethics*, edited by Anne Donchin and Laura Purdy, 177–202. Lanham, Md.: Rowman and Littlefield.

Silvers, Anita, David Wasserman, and Mary B. Mahowald. 1998. *Disability, Difference, Discrimination: Perspectives on Justice in Bioethics and Public Policy*. Lanham, Md.: Rowman and Littlefield.

Singer, Peter, ed. 1993. *A Companion to Ethics*. Cambridge, Mass.: Blackwell.

———. 1995. *Animal Liberation*. London: Pimlico.

Stark, Cynthia. 2007. "How to Include the Severely Disabled in a Contractarian Theory of Justice." *Journal of Political Philosophy* 15, no. 2:127–45.

Stubblefield, Anna. 2007. "'Beyond the Pale': Tainted Whiteness, Cognitive Disability, and Eugenic Sterilization." *Hypatia* 22, no. 2:162–81.

Thomson, Rosemarie Garland. 1997. *Extraordinary Bodies*. New York: Columbia University Press.

Tooley, Michael. 1984. *Abortion and Infanticide*. New York: Oxford University Press.

Tremain, Shelley. 2002. "On the Subject of Impairment." In *Disability/Postmodernity*, edited by Marian Corker and Tom Shakespeare, 32–47. New York: Continuum.

———. 2005. *Foucault and the Government of Disability*. Ann Arbor: University of Michigan Press.

———. 2006. "Reproductive Freedom, Self-Regulation, and the Government of Impairment in Utero." *Hypatia* 21, no. 1:35–53.

Veatch, Robert. 1986. *The Foundations of Justice: Why the Retarded and the Rest of Us Have Claims to Equality*. New York: Oxford University Press.

Wendell, Susan. 1989. "Toward a Feminist Theory of Disability." *Hypatia* 4, no. 2:104–24.

———. 1996. *The Rejected Body: Feminist Philosophical Reflections on Disability*. New York: Routledge.

Wikler, Daniel. 1979. "Paternalism and the Mildly Retarded." *Philosophy and Public Affairs* 8, no. 4:377–92.

Williams, Bernard. 2008. "The Human Prejudice." In *Philosophy as a Humanistic Discipline*, 135–54. Princeton: Princeton University Press.

Wong, Sophia. 2002. "At Home with Down Syndrome and Gender." *Hypatia* 17, no. 3 (Summer):89–117.

2

THE LIMITS OF THE MEDICAL MODEL: HISTORICAL EPIDEMIOLOGY OF INTELLECTUAL DISABILITY IN THE UNITED STATES

JEFFREY P. BROSCO

Introduction

Few people have devoted more attention to improving public policy for persons with disabilities than Eunice and Sargent Shriver. When John F. Kennedy was president, his sister Eunice and brother-in-law Sargent used their informal political clout and personal resources to ensure that the federal government invested substantial resources in programs for persons with intellectual and other developmental disabilities. In part because Eunice and John's sister Rose had a neurodevelopmental disability, the entire Kennedy family has focused its considerable financial and political might on developmental disability issues over the past five decades (Berkowitz 1980). It was not surprising, then, that at a board meeting in 2002, the still-active Sargent Shriver would ask whether their work had made any difference. Using the scientific terminology for mild intellectual disability (ID) common in the early twentieth century, Shriver asked, "What happened to the morons? What have we done for the morons?"[1]

Perhaps Shriver's questions were merely personal—a public servant reflecting on decades of service. As a historian and developmental pediatrician, however, I was fascinated by the policy implications of his questions. Although the disability rights movement began with local grassroots efforts by families as early as the 1930s, Shriver sensed correctly that it was the Kennedy administration that instituted major federal involvement in developmental disabilities (Shapiro 1994; Berkowitz 1987). In the early 1960s, Kennedy appointed a Panel on Mental Retardation, which recommended an emphasis on training a special

---

[1] Personal communication, Best Buddies Board Meeting, Miami, Fl., May 2002. In this essay, I have chosen to use the term "intellectual disability," though there is not yet consensus on its use to replace the more familiar American English term "mental retardation." "Developmental disability" refers to a broader category of disabling conditions that do not necessarily include impaired cognitive ability, such as cerebral palsy and autism.

education workforce and investing in scientific research. The panel boldly predicted that their recommendations would lead to a 50 percent reduction in the number of persons with ID by the year 2000. Since 1960 the number of federal ID programs has grown to more than fifty, with overall spending topping $40 billion per year (figures 1 and 2). Our nation's investment in the research laboratory has led to specific medical interventions to prevent ID, but what was the overall impact on the number of persons with ID?

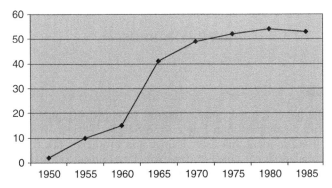

FIGURE 1. Number of United States federal programs for persons with developmental disabilities

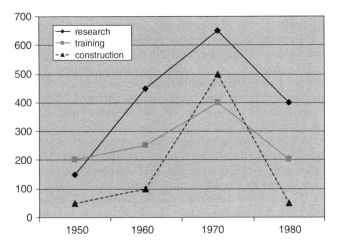

FIGURE 2. Federal spending for persons with developmental disabilities (in thousands of U.S. dollars, 1980)
Note: The peak in construction funds reflects the building of dozens of "University Affiliated Facilities," institutions devoted to research, training, technical assistance, and policy development.

Shriver's seemingly simple question is not so easily answered. Exploring the historical epidemiology of ID in the United States over the past century is not merely a question of counting persons with ID then and now. It also requires understanding why investment in science to prevent ID made sense in the mid-twentieth century, how definitions of medical conditions reflect broader historical trends in U.S. history, and how investments in public health, educational, and economic programs may have had a greater impact on the prevalence of ID. In some ways, Shriver was asking a much broader question: Is the U.S. health care system's traditional focus on technologically sophisticated medical interventions delivered at the hospital bedside or doctor's office the best approach to improving child health or addressing the needs of people with developmental disabilities? This essay offers one preliminary answer to this key public policy question.

There is a limit to using historical epidemiology to answer Shriver's question, and it is implied in his use of the antiquated meaning of the word "moron" to mean mild ID. Since the 1960s the disability rights movement has led to dramatic improvements in the lives of persons with a developmental disability, and changes in our attitudes, laws, and practice are surely more important than the prevalence of any one condition. Nonetheless, investigating the historical epidemiology of ID reveals much about the history of medicine in the twentieth century. As Charles Rosenberg and others have argued, the boundaries of specific medical diagnoses are constructed by a complex interaction of social, political, and scientific factors (Rosenberg and Golden 1992). Exploring the historical epidemiology of ID in the United States reveals the complex interaction between science and politics, and provides a historical platform for future policy discussions on the relative value of scientific medicine.

Investing in Science: Child Health and U.S. Medicine in the Twentieth Century

Intellectual disability was primarily an issue for families and local governments in the United States until the early 1800s, when states opened institutions where persons with ID could live if their families were unable to care for them. Hundreds of these large institutions were built with public funds in the nineteenth century when physicians and advocates convinced politicians and philanthropists that ID could be cured with the proper environmental treatment. Short stays and dramatic improvements were the exception, however, and by 1900 chronic underfunding meant that most of these institutions became warehouses where persons unable to care for themselves lived for decades, neglected and maltreated. Reports of deplorable conditions in large state-funded institutions began in the 1880s and continued through the twentieth century (Grob 1991).

One solution was to avoid the institutions, and in the 1930s families across the United States began to advocate for home supports for their children with ID. By 1951 there were more than 125 local parent organizations in the United States and Canada, loosely held together by the desire for peer support and the conviction that the public schools had a responsibility to aid children with disabilities (Trent 1994). The National Association of Parents and Friends of Mentally Retarded Children (later NARC) was founded in 1950 to advocate for disability rights on the state and national level. The disability rights movement grew throughout the twentieth century, and one key battle has been to support community living options for persons with developmental disabilities. Though nearly all of the large state institutions for persons with ID have now closed, in the 1960s more than five hundred thousand persons still lived in such facilities, and state governments were still grappling with the enormous financial and human costs of custodial care (Trent 1994).

Scientific medicine seemed to provide an answer: the prevention of ID through early detection and treatment of medical conditions could both improve health and eventually reduce the need for state institutions (Paul 2000). Phenylketonuria (PKU) was an instructive example. In 1934 Asjborn Folling reported that an inborn error of metabolism characterized by high levels of phenylpyruvic acid in urine could cause ID, and several years later George Jervis reported finding the same substance in the urine of fifty persons with ID at the Village State School in Thiells, New York. Treatment could prevent the neurological impairment associated with PKU, but only if started in the newborn period. In 1961 universal infant newborn screening became practical when microbiologist and pediatrician Robert Guthrie introduced a semiquantitative phenylalanine assay that could be applied to a drop of dried blood. Advocacy groups like NARC lobbied state governments to implement newborn screening programs for PKU, and by the mid-1960s nearly every state had one in place—even before there was widespread evidence of the effectiveness of such programs (Brosco, Seider, and Dunn 2006). Although PKU was relatively rare, many experts believed that it was simply one example of how investing in scientific medicine would reveal the causes—and cures—of ID.

It is hardly surprising that ID was viewed as a problem to be solved primarily by science and technology. Discoveries in the laboratory had helped the military victory in World War II and, it seemed in 1962, would soon put a man on the moon. Scientific medicine in particular seemed to offer unlimited hope for the future. The emergence of wonder drugs such as penicillin in the 1940s and vaccines against polio of the mid-1950s confirmed decades of faith that science would deliver better health. The

Salk and Sabin vaccines in particular were critical to the public understanding of the power of the laboratory to prevent disease and improve health. For the first half of the twentieth century, families lived in fear of the summer epidemics of polio. Communities across the United States closed swimming pools and quarantined the ill in hopes that what started as mild viral illness would not become a local epidemic of death and disability. By the late 1950s, polio epidemics had disappeared, and medical science was credited in headlines across the United States (Rothman 1997).

The more general decline in childhood mortality also seemed to confirm the value of scientific medicine. The so-called mortality transition describes the dramatic epidemiological shift in the United States and Europe from the early 1800s to the late 1900s. In this two-hundred-year period, early childhood deaths due to infectious diseases decreased, while deaths from cancer and heart disease later in life increased. For example, in 1900 the infant mortality rate was still well over one hundred deaths per thousand live births in most U.S. cities, and nearly every family knew the tragedy of childhood death. By 1960 the infant mortality rate in the United States was less than thirty per thousand births, and childhood deaths were relatively rare (Meckel 1990). The net effect of the mortality transition was an increase in average life span from less than fifty years to greater than seventy, and the trend continues today. Some authors have noted the relatively small role of antibiotics and vaccines in the decline of infant and child mortality (McKeown 1976; McKinlay and McKinlay 1977), and debate continues on the contribution of improved nutrition, education, and sanitary practices in the mortality transition more generally (Szreter 2002; Link and Phelan 2002; Colgrove 2002). There is no doubt, however, that the remarkable improvement in child health meant that, by the mid-twentieth century, families and physicians no longer faced daily deaths caused by infectious diseases. U.S. society could thus consider investing large-scale resources in relatively rare conditions such as PKU, which affected fewer than one in ten thousand individuals.

President Kennedy's Panel on Mental Retardation 1962 report included many recommendations beyond investing in scientific medicine to prevent ID. Education, public awareness, clinical and social services, and a new legal and social definition of ID were among its 112 recommendations. Unlike the fate of many government commissions, the Panel's recommendations were generally carried out, largely due to the efforts of Eunice and Sargent Shriver, as well as pediatrician Robert Cooke (Shorter 2000). Investment in prevention and cure, however, was the primary focus of the federal government's efforts, as symbolized in the creation of the National Institute for Child Health and Human Development in 1962. With the help of political leaders such as Representative John Fogarty of Rhode Island, federal investment in understanding the biology of ID rose dramatically in the second half of the twentieth century (Braddock 1987).

The Impact of Specific Medical Interventions

There have been many specific medical interventions designed to prevent ID in the past fifty years, including newborn screening programs, vaccines, and advances in nutritional and pharmacologic treatments. Table 1 includes more than a dozen medical conditions that commonly lead to ID, as well as treatments, which can reduce the chances that an individual with those conditions would meet criteria for ID. A number of other conditions can be detected through prenatal or preconceptional screening; in these cases the family can elect therapeutic abortion (table 2). As Duane Alexander points out in his review of the benefits of biomedical interventions to prevent ID, not all of these treatments have their origins in federal research funding, but all have benefited from our national decision to focus on biomedical research (Alexander 1998).

TABLE 1. Causes of ID with specific medical interventions

♦ Congenital syphilis (screening and antimicrobial therapy)
♦ Measles encephalitis (vaccination)
♦ Kernicterus (maternal treatment for Rh incompatibility)
♦ Bacterial meningitis (vaccination, antibiotics)
♦ Congenital hypothyroidism (newborn screen/treatment)
♦ Phenylketonuria (newborn screening/treatment)
♦ Congenital rubella syndrome (vaccination)
♦ Galactosemia (newborn screening/treatment)
♦ Tuberculosis meningitis (nutrition, antibiotics)
♦ Whooping cough (vaccination)
♦ Fetal hydantoin syndrome (no phenytoin during pregnancy)
♦ Pelvic irradiation (limited X-rays during pregnancy)
♦ HIV encephalitis (reduced perinatal transmission)
♦ Stroke in sickle cell disease (transfusion therapy)
♦ Brain tumors (reduced radiation therapy)
♦ Metabolic disorders (transplant/gene therapy)

TABLE 2. Causes of ID with available prenatal/preconceptional screening

♦ Down syndrome
♦ Neurofibromatosis
♦ Tuberous sclerosis
♦ Fragile X syndrome
♦ Tay-Sachs disease
♦ Maple syrup urine disease
♦ Duchenne muscular dystrophy
♦ Other genetic abnormalities

Two colleagues and I selected seven conditions to study in detail: congenital syphilis (CS), Rh hemolytic disease of the newborn (Rh disease), measles, Haemophilus influenza type b meningitis (H. flu), congenital hypothyroidism (CH), phenylketonuria (PKU), and congenital rubella syndrome (CRS) (Brosco, Mattingly, and Sanders 2006). We chose these seven conditions for several reasons: (1) all were recognized in the 1950s as specific causes of ID with a high probability of finding or implementing a cure (Heber 1970; Stern 1963; Levinson and Bigler 1960; Alexander 1998); (2) they account for all of the relatively high-incidence conditions noted in table 1; (3) they are the commonly discussed "success" stories in the prevention of ID (Moser 1992; Alexander 1998; Brockley 1999; Centerwall and Centerwall 2000; Crocker 1985; Lakin, Braddock, and Smith 1994; Scheerenberger 1987); and (4) interventions for these conditions depend largely on care provided through the individual doctor-patient relationship, that is, they exemplify the traditional biomedical approach of preventing disease of complications in each individual patient.

Tracing the historical epidemiology of these conditions is difficult because there are no longitudinal research programs that track the condition-specific incidence of ID over the past fifty years in the United States. However, there have been cross-sectional studies of each condition at different points in time; taken together, these disparate studies allow us to construct estimates of the incidence over time. Although our specific data sources varied for each condition, in general we used a common set of variables to construct estimates of the condition-specific prevalence of ID over the past fifty years: (1) the incidence of the condition, (2) the number of cases of ID likely to arise from that condition (natural history), (3) the efficacy of the intervention to cure the condition, and (4) the population-wide availability of the intervention.

As depicted in figure 3, congenital syphilis and Rh disease are the most significant acquired causes of ID that have a specific medical intervention. Although the trends for congenital syphilis, measles, and CRS have been cyclical, ID due to these infections has fallen dramatically over the past fifty years. The peak number of cases of ID due to CRS was 450/million in the epidemic years 1964–65. Rh disease, H. flu, CH, and PKU also cause many fewer cases of ID than they did in the 1950s. The net effect of medical interventions in these seven conditions is a significant decrease in the number of cases of ID.

To gauge the impact of medical interventions on the seven disease-specific causes of ID, we compared the prevalence of these conditions to the overall prevalence of ID. In figure 4, the seven disease-specific causes of ID are combined and compared to one estimate of the prevalence of ID in the U.S. school-age population, 2.27/1,000 children. Because the prevalence of each of these disease-specific conditions is relatively low, together they account for a relatively small proportion of the total

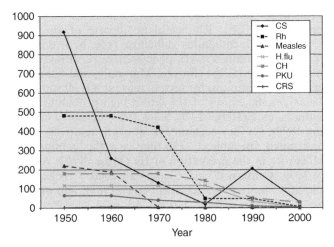

FIGURE 3. Estimated prevalence of ID in the United States by selected causes (per million children)

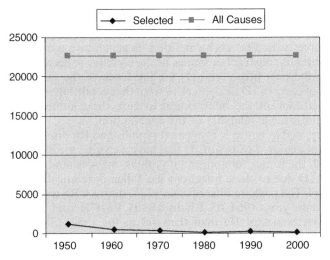

FIGURE 4. Cases of ID expected to arise by ten years of age from selected and all causes (per million births)

number of cases of ID (approximately 10 percent). If other preventable conditions that cause ID are considered (see table 1), the impact would be only marginally greater given that these other conditions have such a low prevalence. We did not consider causes of ID for which prenatal or preconceptional screening is available (see table 2). We chose not to consider these conditions (e.g., Down syndrome) because there is a difference between the unambiguous good of a medical intervention that prevents ID in an otherwise healthy individual, and the more controversial intervention, which prevents the birth of an individual likely to have ID. Furthermore, our initial data review did not suggest substantial changes in the incidence of Down syndrome over the past fifty years.

Based on these seven conditions, one might conclude that the impact of specific medical interventions is a small but significant decrease to the number of persons with ID. There are more factors to be investigated, however, before reaching conclusions about the general impact of medical interventions. Medical interventions over the past fifty years may also have contributed to a rise in the prevalence of ID. The increased life span of persons with ID, for example, increases the prevalence of ID: children with Down syndrome now live well into adulthood (Yang, Rasmussen, and Friedman 2002). Furthermore, the clinical successes of neonatalogists and cardiothoracic surgeons, among other clinicians, mean that many children who would have died in infancy one or two generations ago, now survive to school age and are frequently diagnosed with ID and other neurodevelopmental disabilities (Aylward 2002; Wernovsky, Shillingford, and Gaynor 2005). Our preliminary data suggest that the dramatic rise in the survival of the smallest infants ($< 1,500$ grams) over the past fifty years has increased the prevalence of MR approximately 5 percent, if the overall prevalence of ID is assumed to be 2.27 percent (Brosco et al. 2007). Based on our investigation of specific conditions, it appears that medical interventions have lowered the prevalence of ID approximately 5 percent over the past fifty years.

The Changing Definition of ID

Given the difficulty of tracking the incidence of dozens of specific medical conditions, perhaps the best way to answer Shriver's question is to look at the overall prevalence of ID. Have we attained the Kennedy panel's goal of a 50 percent reduction in the number of persons with ID? The astute reader will have been rightly suspicious of figure 4, as we implied that the prevalence of ID has been constant over the past 50 years. We chose a single number only to simplify the comparison of the disease-specific causes of ID to the total prevalence of ID.[2] In fact, there were no

[2] 2.27 percent represents the number of persons that would be predicted to score two standard deviations below the mean on a standardized IQ test. This definition of ID—an IQ less than 70—is the one used by authors of most studies of the seven specific medical conditions. Furthermore, estimates of the prevalence of ID from studies that meet current epidemiological standards have ranged between 1 percent and 3 percent for the U.S. school-age population.

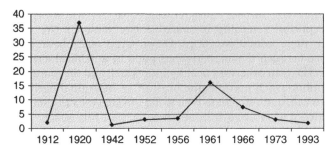

FIGURE 5. Cross-sectional estimates of the prevalence of ID in the United States (per 1,000 persons)

longitudinal studies of ID prevalence until recently, and even these studies differ on the exactly how many people meet criteria for ID (Institute on Community Integration, University of Minnesota 2000; Larson et al. 2001; Boyle et al. 1996; Yeargin-Allsopp et al. 1995). If for our comparison we had used the different estimates of the prevalence of ID in specific communities over the past century, our graph would have looked like figure 5, with prevalence estimates for ID ranging from 1 percent to more than 30 percent of the total population.

Why have estimates varied so dramatically over the past one hundred years? When determining the prevalence of any medical condition, there are methodological issues that significantly affect outcomes (Heber 1970; Fryers 1984; Lipkin 1996). Prevalence is the number of persons that have a condition (the numerator) within a certain population (the denominator) at a certain point in time. The denominator is usually straightforward: how many people are in the population at risk for the condition. Inaccuracy in this number, however, can certainly affect the prevalence. For example, the decrease in the infant mortality rate in the early twentieth century occurred in part because birth registries improved: as the denominator increased, the rate of infant deaths per thousand births decreased (Meckel 1990; Brosco 1999).

The numerator is affected principally by case ascertainment and case definition. Case ascertainment refers to the methods used to find all the persons with the condition, and can be based on administrative databases, clinic attendance, or active case finding. The resources devoted to case ascertainment can dramatically affect the prevalence, especially for low prevalence conditions.[3] Case ascertainment of ID was a particularly

---

[3] If the predicted prevalence is 5/1,000 and five new cases are found, that would double the prevalence. If the predicted prevalence were 500/1,000, five new cases would make only a slight difference.

significant variable in the prevalence of ID early in the twentieth century because ID was thought to be a low prevalence condition and there was no easy way to find persons with ID. Although many lived in institutions and some attended public schools, many more persons with ID were cared for by families at home and did not come to "official" attention—in part because of the stigma of having ID and also because there were not many federal or state programs supporting children living at home (Braddock 2002).

Although there are many other factors that can influence prevalence, I argue that case definition is the most important factor in the wide variation in prevalence estimates of ID. Case definition is simply the criteria used to determine whether a person truly has the condition; the criteria for ID have changed significantly over the past one hundred years. For example, the most recent edition of *Mental Retardations* (2002) is the tenth attempt by the American Association on Intellectual Disability (AAID) to define Intellectual Disability since 1908 (American Association on Mental Retardation 2002a and 2002b). The American Psychiatric Association's *Diagnostic and Statistical Manual* has also offered different definitions since the first DSM in 1952 (American Psychiatric Association, Committee on Nomenclature and Statistics 1952). The federal government currently uses a functional definition of developmental disability—though not all government programs use the same definition, and states do not necessarily use the federal definitions. The one constant over the past one hundred years has been change: From *feeble-minded, moron*, and *idiot* in the early 1900s, through *mental defect* and *mental retardation* in mid-century, to the *levels of support* model informed by today's disability perspective, each generation has struggled to choose terms and define boundaries.

In general, there have been three broad approaches to defining ID: medical conditions, cognitive ability or IQ (intelligence quotient), and adaptive/social functioning (Zenderland 1998; Mercer 1992). Each approach has been used in some way since the early twentieth century, and each approach has affected estimates of the prevalence of ID. Published reports of ID prevalence before 1910 typically came from physicians who worked in institutions and schools for persons with ID. They were experts in specific medical conditions such as Down syndrome or "cretinism" (hypothyroidism), and they believed that experienced clinicians could detect findings of ID on physical examination. Indeed, some argued that they could see ID in the faces of children as they strolled through schools of supposed "normal" children. The earliest estimates of the prevalence of ID were based on institutional populations and clinical diagnoses by experienced physicians, and were in the range of 5/1,000 children. The medical approach to ID continues today with physicians who seek to discover "underlying conditions" causing ID and administer medical treatment—such as thyroid hormone replacement—for persons with ID.

With the discovery of Fragile X and other specific genetic causes of ID in the past five decades, the number of routine laboratory and imaging studies continues to increase, thus emphasizing the continuing role of the physician in the diagnosis of ID.

Psychologists have long argued that intelligence can be measured by standardized IQ tests, and that persons who score well below the mean—usually defined by two standard deviations or 70 on most tests—meet the cognitive criteria to qualify for a diagnosis of ID (figure 6). Current measures of IQ began with the work of Alfred Binet in the late nineteenth century. Binet was a French educator who hoped to identify young children who had difficulty learning and therefore needed special education. He tried using head measurements, the standard quantitative approach of the time, but failed to find significant correlations between head size and school performance. He next devised a series of simple tasks that could typically be performed by children of certain ages, such as drawing a circle or placing blocks in a pattern. Binet did not believe that ability to perform these tasks measured intelligence, but he concluded that children who could not do them needed more attention from teachers. He explicitly *warned* against using his tests to make comparisons between children or to make judgments regarding a child's potential for learning or achieving as an adult (Gould 1996).

American psychologists and physicians adopted Binet's testing techniques but ignored his warnings about the limits of measuring intelligence. Instead they agreed with Charles Spearman's belief that intelligence was a single unitary process with a biologic reality to be found in the substance of the brain. In 1904 Spearman argued that

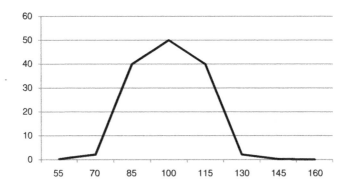

FIGURE 6. Bell curve demonstrating normal distribution

Note: Most IQ tests are constructed such that mean score is 100. Approximately 16 percent of the population taking the test will score 85 or below (one standard deviation), and 2.3 percent will score 70 or below (two standard deviations).

statistical correlations among various kinds of test proved the existence of a single, underlying cognitive ability, named g. Simply put, people who scored well on one kind of cognitive test (e.g., remembering digits) tend to do well on other kinds of tests (e.g., arranging patterns). Each of us, Stanford University professor Louis Terman and other psychologists argued, has a certain amount of general intelligence—a single, measurable capacity that changes little if any over time. In the early twentieth century, Terman applied his "Stanford-Binet" test to enough children to believe that he had a statistically sound measure of intelligence. Henry Goddard used such tests to discover a new entity, the "moron"—an individual who appeared to be normal but in fact had very low cognitive ability as measured by standardized tests. Using such tests on school children, Goddard argued that ID was much more common than in previous estimates by physicians (Zenderland 1998). When Yale professor Robert Yerkes used an IQ test on thousands of U.S. military recruits during World War I, he found astonishing results: approximately a third of these young men could be classified as morons, and thus met the definition of ID. This accounts for the high prevalence estimate in figure 5 in 1920. As Stephen J. Gould has demonstrated, however, these early tests of IQ were obviously culturally biased, which accounts for the poor performance of the recruits, many of whom were illiterate or recent immigrants to the United States (Gould 1996).

Herein lies one key to the relationship between the definition of ID and the prevalence of ID. Estimates of the prevalence of ID by physicians were relatively low because they focused on moderate and severe ID, or "idiots" and "imbeciles" in the scientific terminology of the time. The prevalence of moderate-severe ID has been relatively constant over the past one hundred years (in and outside the United States), at a rate of approximately 5/1,000 (Fryers 1984). With the advent of IQ tests and the discovery of the "moron" came estimates of the number of persons with mild ID that ranged between 70 and 370/1,000. Because of this large difference in rates between mild and moderate-severe ID, variation in estimates of total prevalence in the last century is largely explained by the difficulty in distinguishing between "normal" individuals and those with mild ID (figure 7). For example, even if IQ scores constitute a more objective measure of intelligence, changes in cut-off scores contribute to the wide variation in prevalence: shifting from 70 to 75, a difference within the known accuracy of such tests, doubles the number of persons with ID. When Rick Heber wrote for the AAID in 1959 that one standard deviation below the mean (a score of 85) should be considered instead of two standard deviations (70), the number of persons with ID potentially rose to 16 percent of the population (see figure 6) (Heber 1959).

Heber and the AAID committee were arguing for a new definition of ID, however, one that included consideration of a person's ability to function in everyday life. Clinical experience suggested that some

JEFFREY P. BROSCO

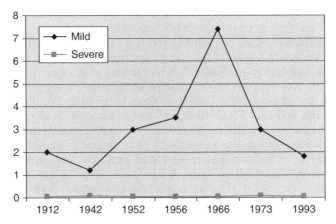

FIGURE 7. Moderate-severe vs. mild ID: Cross-sectional estimates in the United States (per 100 persons)

individuals with IQ scores in the 60s seemed generally indistinguishable from their higher-scoring peers, while other individuals with scores in the 70s needed significant support with everyday activities. Rather than use an arbitrary cut-off of 70, Heber and his colleagues believed that ID could be considered in any individual who had below-average cognitive ability (less than 85) but who also had substantial difficulty in adaptive functioning. This "adaptive/social" model of defining ID has been used informally for over a century, although it has been overshadowed by scholarly reports using the medical and IQ approaches. In the nineteenth-century institutions for persons with ID, for example, physicians focused on medical aspects of the condition, but other personnel were more interested in an individual's ability to function, and in particular what support a person needed in his or her daily life (Zenderland 1998). Historian Molly Ladd-Taylor has argued that family court judges in the 1940s gave this functional definition of ID at least as much weight as medical diagnosis or psychological testing (Ladd-Taylor 2003).

Adding a measure of adaptive functioning can dramatically alter the estimated prevalence of ID. For example, in the early 1970s, Jane Mercer and colleagues compared rates of ID in three populations in Southern California: whites, blacks, and Mexican Americans (Eckberg 1979). Based on a measure of cognitive ability alone, 4.4 percent of blacks and 14.9 percent of Mexican Americans had IQ scores in the ID range, compared to fewer than 2 percent of whites. However, when persons scoring in the ID range were tested according to behavioral skills such as how to take a bus, hold a job, stay in school, do one's own shopping, or read books and magazines, the percentage of blacks and Mexican

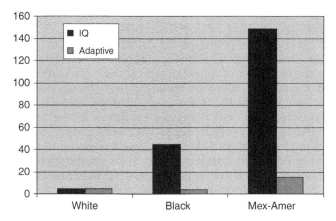

FIGURE 8. Effect of adaptive functioning on prevalence of IQ (per 1,000 persons)

Americans scoring in the ID range dropped dramatically, while the rate for whites did not change (figure 8).

As might be surmised from the previous example, estimating rates of ID in specific populations has social and political consequences. Over the past century, some U.S. scholars have argued that there are important differences in the intelligence of specific ethnic/racial groups, that these differences are genetically determined, and that our educational and political policy must conform to these facts. In his study of U.S. military recruits for World War I, for example, Yerkes concluded that recent immigrants from southern and eastern Europe scored 10 to 15 points lower than "native" Americans (northern Europeans who had emigrated to the United States before 1870). African Americans on average scored even lower than recent immigrants did, and both groups therefore had high rates of ID. Political leaders used these reports to make calls for a host of policies such as immigration restriction (Kraut 1988; Gould 1996). IQ testing of World War II recruits provided similar evidence when nearly half of the 716,000 men rejected by the military because of "mental deficiency" were nonwhites—a rate six times higher for nonwhites over whites (Shuey 1958). In 1969, Arthur Jensen emphasized reports that the average African American scored 15 IQ points below the average Caucasian; he concluded that remedial education should be abandoned (Jensen 1969). More recently, Richard Herrnstein and Charles Murray concluded their 1994 book, *The Bell Curve*, with a series of policy statements based on their interpretation of the evidence linking race and average group intelligence (Herrnstein and Murray 1994). Each generation has seen scholars from a variety of disciplines dispute such arguments and fault the authors for presenting political views as "scientific" facts (Block and Dworkin 1976; Kagan 1969; Kamin 1974; Gould 1996; Zenderland 1997; Neisser 1998).

More generally, the politics of the projected prevalence of ID in turn affects the definition of ID. Indeed, a number of scholars have pointed out how the definition of a developmental disability can only be understood in the context of social welfare policy (Stone 1984; Berkowitz, Johnson, and Murphy 1976). For example, broad definitions leading to high prevalence rates suited eugenic reformers in the early twentieth century because they could argue that immigration restriction and sterilization of persons with ID were a logical response to the alarmingly high rates of ID among immigrants and to the genetic roots of ID. In the 1960s, ironically, advocates for persons with ID were eager to accept Rick Heber's expanded definition of ID. Unlike eugenic scholars in the early twentieth century, they believed that environmental intervention could prevent or improve ID: the high prevalence of ID helped them argue for federal resources for ID programs (President's Panel on Mental Retardation 1962). In contrast, disability policy experts within the U.S. government have sometimes pushed for narrow definitions to limit the number of persons eligible for services. Thus definitions of ID were narrow in the 1930s when the Great Depression severely limited available funds (Berkowitz 1987). In the 1980s, conservative politicians within the Reagan administration argued that government programs had grown out of control, and a more narrow definition of ID again prevailed, at least for certain federal programs (Erkulwater 2006) (see figure 5).

Given the challenges in defining ID, it seems impossible to determine whether there has been a true change in the number of persons with ID: no study has used a consistent definition of ID over the past fifty years, so any reported changes in prevalence cannot be attributed solely to "true" changes in the numbers of persons with ID. We can conclude that the definition of ID cannot be divorced from the political and social consequences of choosing any one definition. Indeed, the relationship between definition and policy is made explicit in the AAID's most recent report defining ID: an entire chapter is devoted to explaining the consequences of its proposed definition on eligibility for various educational and financial support programs (Stein et al. 1993; American Association on Mental Retardation 2002a and 2002b; Westbrook, Silver, and Stein 1998; Stein, Westbrook, and Bauman 1997). From the historians' point of view, each generation's choice of how to define ID also defines contemporary attitudes and approach to persons with developmental disabilities.

The "Flynn Effect" and the Impact of Improved Public Health

One way to avoid difficulties with changing definitions over time is retrospectively to apply a single, seemingly objective definition, such as

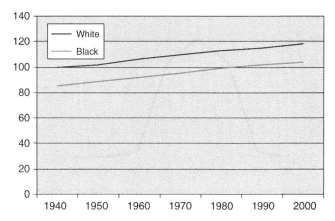

FIGURE 9. The Flynn effect: Mean IQ scores
Note: If mean IQ scores of blacks and whites are plotted over the past sixty years using a test standardized in 1940, scores have risen at least 3 points per decade. There has been little change in the relative mean scores of blacks and whites, though achievement scores for blacks have risen more dramatically than those of whites in the past fifty years (not shown).

"two standard deviations below the mean on a standardized measure of cognitive ability (e.g., IQ <70)." Although this approach is used to define ID for longitudinal medical studies, there is strong evidence that even this approach cannot provide consistency over decades. According to the so-called Flynn effect, IQ scores have been steadily rising since the early twentieth century. In the 1980s James R. Flynn and others reported an increase of at least 3 IQ points per decade among diverse populations in the twenty nations where IQ trends have been studied (figure 9) (Neisser 1998). For example, all 18-year-old men in the Netherlands take a specific IQ test as they enter compulsory military service; using scores from the last half-century, Flynn calculates that the mean IQ of Dutch men has increased more than 20 points (Flynn 1998). Indeed, IQ tests are periodically re-standardized—deliberately devised to be a little bit "harder" than the previous version—in order to keep the mean at 100.

This shifting of the IQ distribution curve has important implications for the prevalence of ID. In Figure 10, we compare a hypothetical "Year 2000" cohort with a "Year 1950" one. When the entire distribution of IQ scores is shifted a modest 15 points, one can see that many fewer persons in the Year 2000 cohort would fall below the IQ cut-off point for ID if given the IQ test devised in 1950—whether we used one or two standard deviations below the mean (figure 10). Thus, one way to interpret the Flynn effect is to consider that some persons who currently qualify as ID would not if given an older, simpler version of an IQ test. Indeed, Tomoe Kanaya and colleagues conducted such an experiment and found this to

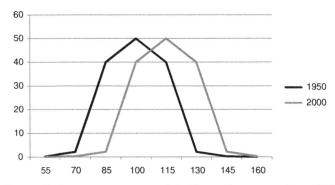

FIGURE 10. Apparent consequence of the Flynn effect on prevalence of IQ
Note: As the mean IQ shifts 15 points higher, the number of persons in the Year 2000 taking
a 1950 standardized exam who score below 85 decreases from 16 percent to 2.3 percent; the
number scoring below 70 approaches 0.

be true: school children were more likely to be diagnosed as ID when
given the WISC IV test than when the same children took the early,
"easier," version of the test. Flynn estimates that the number of American
children eligible to be classified as mentally retarded might have decreased
from 8.8 million to 2.6 million in the period from 1948 to 1977 (Flynn
1998).

Such reductions are not apparent, of course, because IQ tests are
adjusted periodically to ensure that there is a normal distribution, and
therefore 2.27 percent of the population always scores two deviations
below the mean. If ID is defined principally by scoring substantially
below the mean in cognitive ability, even if the entire population shifts, a
small minority of the population will always qualify as having ID. This is
true for any condition, such as hypertension or obesity, which relies on
quantitative differences from peers as the principle component of diagnosis. Indeed, herein lies the argument for a public health approach to
such conditions: if we apply clinical solutions (e.g., reduced salt in diet,
increased exercise) across an entire population and "shift the curve," it is
possible to reduce the burden of disease more greatly than focusing on
interventions for high-risk individuals.

Is it possible that similar reasoning can be applied to the prevalence of
intellectual disability? Although there is substantial debate on the causes
of the Flynn effect, some scholars argue that it is related to population-
level changes in health and environment over the past century. Poverty,
early home environment, malnutrition, discrimination, cultural values,
and inferior educational opportunities are all remediable causes of lower
achievement on standardized tests (table 3). In the U.S. since the 1960s, a
number of federal, state, and philanthropic programs have sought to

TABLE 3. Causes of ID with potential public health interventions

♦ Child abuse/neglect (public education and intervention)
♦ Fetal alcohol effects (public health education)
♦ Iron-deficiency anemia (nutrition programs)
♦ Lead intoxication (environmental intervention)
♦ Malnutrition (nutrition programs)
♦ Neural tube abnormalities (folic acid before pregnancy)
♦ Traumatic brain injury (child restraint systems)
♦ Near-drowning (water safety instruction; pool enclosures)

TABLE 4. Examples of U.S. federal programs that aid children growing up in poverty

♦ Medicaid (health insurance)
♦ Head Start (early education program)
♦ WIC (nutrition for Women, Infants, Children)
♦ Aid to Families with Dependent Children (AFDC, now TANF, provides income support)
♦ Earned Tax Credit (provides income support)
♦ School lunch program (nutrition)
♦ Housing Urban Development programs (improved housing; lead abatement)
♦ Department of Education (improved education, especially for children with ID)
♦ Civil rights legislation and judicial decisions (improved education, housing, etc.)

improve the general environment for growing children (table 4). These broad-based public health and education programs may have helped shift the IQ curve higher, and thus reduced the number of persons who would meet criteria for ID.

For example, nutrition is associated with cognitive ability: low overall caloric or protein intake, as well as absence of micronutrients such as iron in the diet, all cause lower performance on tests of cognitive ability (Lozoff et al. 2000; Behrman, Kliegman, and Jenson 2004). In general, increases in IQ over the past century are matched by increases in mean height, and some scholars have linked the simultaneous rise to improvements in nutrition (Lynn 1998; Sigman and Whaley 1998). More recently in the United States, school-lunch programs have helped reduce the prevalence of hunger among children, and there is evidence that the prevalence of iron-deficiency anemia has decreased since the introduction of iron in baby formulas and the existence of programs such as WIC (Women, Infants, Children), which provides nutritional supplements for pregnant women and their young children (Miller 1985). Direct relationships are difficult to prove, however, and some scholars point to inconsistent evidence that improvements in nutrition largely account for the Flynn effect (Sigman and Whaley 1998; Martorell 1998).

Ingestion of lead is also clearly associated with impaired cognitive development. As Christian Warren and others have reported, the amount of lead in U.S. homes and neighborhoods steadily decreased throughout the twentieth century (Warren 2000; English 2001). For example, nearly half of the children living in some U.S. cities in the 1960s had lead levels above 40 μg/dL; today most children have levels less than 5 μg/dL, though even small amounts of lead are considered to affect IQ scores (Warren 2000). Perhaps the steady decline in lead exposure helps account for population shift in IQ in the United States; given higher lead levels in poor and minority neighborhoods, this explanation may also help explain more precisely why poverty and race/ethnicity are related to lower IQ scores. It is likely that reduced lead exposure is part of the explanation for rising IQ scores; however, there has been a similar increase in IQ scores in nations where lead was largely eliminated from the environment in the early 1900s.

Family income and maternal education are two of the most reliable predictors of IQ scores, and improvements in these areas may also account for the Flynn effect. Overall, it appears that there have been gains in economic well-being across the U.S. population over the past fifty years, though the data on child poverty are mixed. According to the U.S. Census Bureau, the poverty rate for children in 1959 was 27 percent, and after the 1960s war on poverty it had fallen to just below 15 percent by 1970. However, the child poverty rate climbed above 20 percent in the 1980s, fell to 15 percent in the 1990s, and in 2005 was 17.6 percent (U.S. Census Bureau 2008). The quality of education of a population is even more difficult to measure, and high school graduation rates remain fairly low in the United States (Williams 1998). On the other hand, since the 1960s there have been efforts to improve the quality of education for children living in poverty or segregated by race, and children with developmental disabilities in particular have benefited from federal laws and courtroom decisions that together provide a strong legal base for a free and appropriate education.

No simple relationship between specific environmental factors and IQ should be expected, based on current models of cognitive development. The complex interplay of genetic and environmental factors suggests that having one or two "risk factors" for low cognitive achievement may not affect IQ much, but with each additional risk factor, IQ scores are likely to decline (Behrman, Kliegman, and Jenson 2004). It is tempting to lump together all the positive changes in children's early environment and conclude that public health and antipoverty programs have shifted the IQ curve and reduced the prevalence of ID. However, while IQ scores have risen over the past fifty years, standardized measures of achievement have not risen as quickly. In general, such tests of math, reading, or other specific academic skills (e.g., the SAT) are more closely associated to a child's home and educational environment than nonverbal IQ scores.

Paradoxically, rises in IQ scores are principally due to subtests that measure the components of cognitive ability that are considered by many scholars to be least affected by education and environment. The term "fluid intelligence" refers to activities that do not require language or prior knowledge, such as pattern recognition; in contrast, "crystallized intelligence" captures the store of knowledge that each of us learns over time. Some scholars—including Flynn himself—have interpreted the large gains in scores of fluid intelligence and smaller gains in crystallized intelligence to conclude that rising IQ scores do not represent true gains in cognitive ability (Neisser 1998).

Other scholars have argued that fluid intelligence depends on abstract reasoning, cognitive flexibility, and rapid decision-making—all traits that emerge from specific cultures and educational practices. For example, research in Africa in 1970s demonstrated cultural practices that emphasized social intelligence, compliance with society, and slow deliberation in decision-making; these traits would lead to lower scores on most tests of fluid intelligence (Greenfield 1998). Carmi Schooler has argued that increasing environmental complexity such as urbanization and educational opportunities are empirically associated with increasing IQ scores (Schooler 1998; Williams 1998). Patricia Greenfield and others have looked specifically at the increasing visual complexity of industrialized environments—movies, TV, computers—and concluded that it is not surprising that scores on pattern recognition tests are rising (Greenfield 1998).

In sum, then, the Flynn effect provides suggestive but not conclusive evidence that there has been a reduction in the number of persons with ID over the past fifty years. It does provide definitive evidence, on the other hand, against simplistic arguments about hereditarian differences in group mean IQ scores. As Ulric Neisser has argued, IQ scores either do or do not accurately reflect innate intelligence. If they do not, arguments based on group IQ scores are suspect. If IQ scores do truly measure innate intelligence, the rapid rise in scores over the past six decades demonstrates the critical importance of environment, because such large, complex genetic changes could not occur in less than a century (Neisser 1998).

Conclusion

In a 1964 speech, Sargent Shriver recalled the work of the Kennedy administration in the early 1960s: "For the first time in history mental retardation—the least understood, most feared and most neglected scourge of mankind—came under the guns of the chief executive of the most powerful government in the world" (Shorter 2000). Since then the U.S. federal government has devoted substantial resources to laboratory research, medical interventions, and workforce education to prevent ID and improve the lives of persons living with developmental disabilities.

The mid-twentieth century attention to ID was partly a response to epidemiologic shifts in child health in the U.S.: the dramatic decrease in infant and child mortality allowed the nation to focus on low-incidence conditions such as ID. The choices of the Kennedy and Johnson administrations in their approach to "combating mental retardation" reflected optimism that medical science and government programs could prevent many cases of ID and improve the lives of persons with developmental disabilities. What, Shriver asked nearly forty years later, has been the outcome of this investment in science and medical intervention?

As demonstrated in this essay, applying laboratory findings to specific medical conditions did indeed prevent thousands of individuals in the United States from developing ID over the past fifty years. Preliminary research suggests, however, that medical interventions have also led to more individuals with ID, and that overall medical interventions for specific conditions have had a relatively small impact on the general prevalence of ID. This does not mean that the nation's faith in science was misplaced: thousands of lives have been saved, and the astonishing complexity of neurodevelopment is slowly being revealed. The potential for preventing ID in many more individuals remains, though it may now center on the elusive promise of gene therapy and other extraordinary interventions.

Perhaps more important, scientific understanding of neurodevelopment has led to public health interventions to improve nutrition and housing and to reduce exposure to toxins such as lead and alcohol. Furthermore, federal programs to alleviate poverty and hunger may have had a greater impact on the number of persons with ID than specific medical interventions, a finding not unlike that of Thomas McKeown's work on the mortality transition (McKeown 1979). Indeed, if the Flynn effect represents a true increase in cognitive ability over the past half century, the U.S. federal government of the 1960s and 1970s may deserve more credit for the war on poverty than for specific developmental disabilities programs. The irony is that the medical profession has remained firmly focused on specific medical interventions, despite calls from a vocal minority calls for the medical profession to focus on issues of poverty, education, nutrition, and psychosocial issues (Haggerty 1968; American Academy of Pediatrics' Committee on Psychosocial Aspects of Child and Family Health 2001).

This brief exploration of the historical epidemiology of ID is clearly based on a medical model, which assumes that one of our most important goals is to prevent ID. Obviously this is but one, very limited, approach, and indeed is subordinate to providing appropriate supports and services to persons with disabilities. The Kennedy panel itself called for investment in education and social support for persons with developmental disabilities. While it may be difficult to measure the cognitive impact of deinstitutionalization and special education programs, individuals with disabilities and their advocates have convinced the nation of the fundamental soundness of the disability rights movement. The past five decades have been characterized by a spectacular change in attitudes toward persons with disabilities, and laws such as the Americans with Disabilities Act of 1990 and the reauthorization of the Individuals with Disabilities Education Improvement Act in 2004 enjoy broad popular support. Surely this is the most salient change for persons with ID in the United States over the past fifty years, and the best answer to Shriver's questions.

References

Alexander, Duane. 1998. "Prevention of Mental Retardation: Four Decades of Research." *Mental Retardation and Developmental Disabilities Research Reviews* 4, no. 1:50–58.

American Academy of Pediatrics' Committee on Psychosocial Aspects of Child and Family Health. 2001. "The New Morbidity Revisited: A Renewed Commitment to the Psychosocial Aspects of Pediatric Care." *Pediatrics* 108:1227–1230.

American Association on Mental Retardation. 2002a. *Mental Retardation: Definition, Classification, and Systems of Supports.* 10th ed. Washington, D.C.: American Association on Mental Retardation.

———. 2002b. *Mental Retardation: Definition, Classification, and Systems of Supports: Workbook.* 10th ed. Washington, D.C.: American Association on Mental Retardation.

American Psychiatric Association, Committee on Nomenclature and Statistics. 1952. *Mental Disorders; Diagnostic and Statistical Manual.* Washington, D.C.: American Psychiatric Association.

Aylward, Glen P. 2002. "Cognitive and Neuropsychological Outcomes: More Than IQ Scores." *Mental Retardation and Developmental Disabilities Research Reviews* 8:234–40.

Behrman, Richard E., Robert Kliegman, and Hal B. Jenson. 2004. *Nelson Textbook of Pediatrics.* 17th ed. Philadelphia, Penn.: Saunders.

Berkowitz, Edward D. 1980. "The Politics of Mental Retardation During the Kennedy Administration." *Social Science Quarterly* 61:128–43.

———. 1987. *Disabled Policy: America's Programs for the Handicapped.* Cambridge: Cambridge University Press.

Berkowitz, Monroe, William G. Johnson, and Edward H. Murphy. 1976. *Public Policy Toward Disability.* New York: Praeger.

Block, N. J., and G. Dworkin, eds. 1976. *The IQ Controversy.* New York: Pantheon Books.

Boyle, C. A., M. Yeargin-Allsopp, N. S. Doernberg, P. Holmgreen, C. C. Murphy, and D. E. Schendel. 1996. "Prevalence of Selected Developmental Disabilities in Children 3–10 Years of Age: The Metropolitan

Atlanta Developmental Disabilities Surveillance Program, 1991."
    *Morbidity and Mortality Weekly Report Centers for Disease Control
    Surveillance Summary* 45, no. 2:1–14.
Braddock, David, ed. 2002. *Disability at the Dawn of the 21st Century and
    the State of the States.* Washington, D.C.: American Association on
    Mental Retardation.
———. 1987. *Federal Policy Toward Mental Retardation and Develop-
    mental Disabilities.* Baltimore: Paul H. Brookes.
Brockley, J. A. 1999. "History of Mental Retardation: An Essay
    Review." *History of Psychology* 2, no. 1:25–36.
Brosco, Jeffrey P. 1999. "The Early History of the Infant Mortality Rate
    in America: 'A Reflection upon the Past and a Prophecy of the
    Future'." *Pediatrics* 103, no. 2:478–85.
Brosco, J. P., M. Mattingly, and L. M. Sanders. 2006. "Impact of
    Specific Medical Interventions on Reducing the Prevalence of Mental
    Retardation." *Archives of Pediatrics and Adolescent Medicine* 160,
    no. 3:302–9.
Brosco, J. P., M. I. Seider, and A. C. Dunn. 2006. "Universal Newborn
    Screening and Adverse Medical Outcomes: A Historical Note."
    Mental Retardation Developmental Disability Research Review 12,
    4:262–69.
Brosco, Jeffrey P., Lee M. Sanders, Monica Dowling, and Guez Gilly.
    2007. "Impact of Medical Interventions on the Prevalence of
    Mental Retardation." In *Pediatric Academic Societies' Annual Meeting.*
    Toronto.
Centerwall, S. A., and W. R. Centerwall. 2000. "The Discovery of
    Phenylketonuria: The Story of a Young Couple, Two Retarded
    Children, and a Scientist." *Pediatrics* 105, no. 1, part 1: 89–103.
Colgrove, James. 2002. "The McKeown Thesis: A Historical Controversy
    and Its Enduring Influence." *American Journal of Public Health* 92,
    no. 5:725–29.
Crocker, Allen. 1985. "Prevention of Mental Retardation." *Annual of the
    New York Academy of Sciences* 477:329–37.
Eckberg, Douglas Lee. 1979. *Intelligence and Race: The Origins and
    Dimensions of the IQ Controversy.* New York: Praeger.
English, Peter C. 2001. *Old Paint: A Medical History of Childhood Lead-
    Paint Poisoning in the United States to 1980.* New Brunswick, N.J.:
    Rutgers University Press.
Erkulwater, Jennifer L. 2006. *Disability Rights and the American Social
    Safety Net.* Ithaca, N.Y.: Cornell University Press.
Flynn, James R. 1998. "IQ Gains over Time: Toward Finding the
    Causes." In *The Rising Curve,* edited by Ulric Neisser, 25–66.
    Washington, D.C.: American Psychological Association.
Fryers, Tom. 1984. *The Epidemiology of Severe Intellectual Impairment:
    The Dynamics of Prevalence.* London: Academic Press.

Gould, Stephen Jay. 1996. *The Mismeasure of Man*. Rev. and expand ed. New York: Norton.

Greenfield, Patricia M. 1998. "The Cultural Evolution of IQ." In *The Rising Curve*, edited by Ulric Neisser, 81–104. Washington, D.C.: American Psychological Association.

Grob, Gerald N. 1991. *From Asylum to Community: Mental Health Policy in Modern America*. Princeton: Princeton University Press.

Haggerty, R. J. 1968. "Community Pediatrics." *New England Journal of Medicine* 278, no. 1:15–21.

Heber, Rick F. 1959. "A Manual on Terminology and Classification in Mental Retardation." *American Journal of Mental Deficiency* 64 (Monograph Suppl.).

———. 1970. *Epidemiology of Mental Retardation*. Springfield, Ill.: Thomas.

Herrnstein, Richard J., and Charles A. Murray. 1994. *The Bell Curve: Intelligence and Class Structure in American Life*. New York: Free Press.

Institute on Community Integration, University of Minnesota. 2000. "Prevalence of Mental Retardation and/or Developmental Disabilities: Analysis of the 1994/1995 NHIS-D." *MR/DD Data Brief* 2, no. 1.

Jensen, Arthur. 1969. "How Much Can We Boost IQ and Scholastic Achievements?" *Harvard Educational Review* 39:1–121.

Kagan, Jerome. 1969. "Inadequate Evidence." *Harvard Educational Review* 39:269–87.

Kamin, Leon. 1974. *The Science and Politics of IQ*. Potomac, Md.: Lawrence Erlbaum.

Kraut, Alan M. 1988. "Silent Travelers: Germs, Genes, and American Efficiency, 1890–1924." *Social Science History* 12:377–94.

Ladd-Taylor, Molly. 2003. "Who Is 'Defective' and Who Decides? The 'Feebleminded' and the Courts." Paper read at American Association for the History of Medicine, May 2, 2003, at Boston, Mass.

Lakin, K. C., D. Braddock, and G. Smith. 1994. "Trends and Milestones." *Mental Retardation* 32, no. 5:381.

Larson, S. A., K. C. Lakin, L. Anderson, N. Kwak, J. H. Lee, and D. Anderson. 2001. "Prevalence of Mental Retardation and Developmental Disabilities: Estimates from the 1994/1995 National Health Interview Survey Disability Supplements." *American Journal on Mental Retardation* 106:231–52.

Levinson, Abraham, and John Bigler. 1960. *Mental Retardation in Infants and Children*. Chicago: The Year Book Publishers.

Link, Bruce G., and Jo C. Phelan. 2002. "McKeown and the Idea That Social Conditions Are Fundamental Causes of Disease." *American Journal of Public Health* 92, no. 5:722–25.

Lipkin, Paul H. 1996. "Epidemiology of the Developmental Disabilities." In *Developmental Disabilities in Infancy and Childhood*, edited by

Arnold J. Capute and Pasquale J. Accardo, 35–61. Baltimore: Brookes.

Lozoff, B., E. Jimenez, J. Hagen, E. Mollen, and A. W. Wolf. 2000. "Poorer Behavioral and Developmental Outcome More Than 10 Years After Treatment for Iron Deficiency in Infancy." *Pediatrics* 105, no. 4:E51.

Lynn, Richard. 1998. "In Support of the Nutrition Theory." In *The Rising Curve*, edited by Neisser Ulric, 207–18. Washington, D.C.: American Psychological Association.

Martorell, Reynaldo. 1998. "Nutrition and the Worldwide Rise in IQ Scores." In *The Rising Curve*, edited by Ulric Neisser, 183–206. Washington, D.C.: American Psychological Association.

McKeown, Thomas. 1976. *The Modern Rise of Population*. London: Edward Arnold.

———. 1979. *The Role of Medicine: Dream, Mirage, or Nemesis?* Princeton: Princeton University Press.

McKinlay, J. B., and S. M. McKinlay. 1977. "The Questionable Contribution of Medical Measures to the Decline of Mortality in the United States in the Twentieth Century." *Milbank Memorial Fund Quarterly Health Society* 55, no. 3:405–28.

Meckel, Richard. 1990. *Save the Babies: American Public Health Reform and the Prevention of Infant Mortality*. Baltimore: Johns Hopkins University Press.

Mercer, Jane R. 1992. "The Impact of Changing Paradigms of Disability on Mental Retardation in the Year 2000." In *Mental Retardation in the Year 2000*, edited by Louis Rowitz, 15–38. New York: Springer.

Miller, Virginia. 1985. "Impact of the WIC Program on the Iron Status of Infants." *Pediatrics* 75, no. 1:100–105.

Moser, Hugo W. 1992. "Prevention of Mental Retardation (Genetics)." In *Mental Retardation in the Year 2000*, edited by Louis Rowitz, 140–48. New York: Springer.

Neisser, Ulric. 1998. *The Rising Curve: Long-Term Gains in IQ and Related Measures*. 1st ed., APA science volumes. Washington, D.C.: American Psychological Association.

Paul, Diane. 2000. "A Double-Edged Sword." *Nature* 405, no. 6786: 515–15.

President's Panel on Mental Retardation. 1962. *National Action to Combat Mental Retardation*. Washington, D.C.: U.S. Government Printing Office.

Rosenberg, Charles E., and Janet Lynne Golden. 1992. *Framing Disease: Studies in Cultural History, Health, and Medicine in American Society*. New Brunswick, N.J.: Rutgers University Press.

Rothman, David J. 1997. *Beginnings Count: The Technological Imperative in American Health Care*. New York: Oxford University Press.

Scheerenberger, R. C. 1987. *A History of Mental Retardation: A Quarter Century of Promise*. Baltimore: Brookes.

Schooler, Carmi. 1998. "Environmental Complexity and the Flynn Effect." In *The Rising Curve*, edited by Ulric Neisser, 67–80. Washington, D.C.: American Psychological Association.

Shapiro, Joseph P. 1994. *No Pity: People with Disabilities Forging a New Civil Rights Movement*. New York: Times Books.

Shorter, Edward. 2000. *The Kennedy Family and the Story of Mental Retardation*. Philadelphia: Temple University Press.

Shuey, Audrey M. 1958. *The Testing of Negro Intelligence*. Lynchburg, Va.: J. P. Bell.

Sigman, Marian, and Shannon E. Whaley. 1998. "The Role of Nutrition in the Development of Intelligence." In *The Rising Curve*, edited by Ulric Neisser, 155–82. Washington, D.C.: American Psychological Association.

Stein, R. E., L. J. Bauman, L. E. Westbrook, S. M. Coupey, and H. T. Ireys. 1993. "Framework for Identifying Children Who Have Chronic Conditions: The Case for a New Definition." *Journal of Pediatrics* 122, no. 3:342–47.

Stein, R. E., L. E. Westbrook, and L. J. Bauman. 1997. "The Questionnaire for Identifying Children with Chronic Conditions: A Measure Based on a Noncategorical Approach." *Pediatrics* 99, no. 4: 513–21.

Stern, Edith M. 1963. "Mental Retardation." In *The Encyclopedia of Mental Health*, edited by A. Deutsch and H. Fishman, 1180–93. New York: Franklin Watts.

Stone, Deborah A. 1984. *The Disabled State*. Philadelphia: Temple University Press.

Szreter, Simon. 2002. "Rethinking McKeown: The Relationship Between Public Health and Social Change." *American Journal of Public Health* 92, no. 5:722–25.

Trent, James W. Jr. 1994. *Inventing the Feeble Mind: A History of Mental Retardation in the United States*. Medicine and Society, 6. Berkeley: University of California Press.

U.S. Census Bureau. 2008. *Poverty*. Available at http://www.census.gov/hhes/www/poverty/poverty.html (last updated August 26, 2008; last accessed July 11, 2009).

Warren, Christian. 2000. *Brush with Death: A Social History of Lead Poisoning*. Baltimore: Johns Hopkins University Press.

Wernovsky, G., A. J. Shillingford, and J. W. Gaynor. 2005. "Central Nervous System Outcomes in Children with Complex Congenital Heart Disease." *Current Opinions in Cardioliology* 20, no. 2:94–99.

Westbrook, L. E., E. J. Silver, and R. E. Stein. 1998. "Implications for Estimates of Disability in Children: A Comparison of Definitional Components." *Pediatrics* 101, no. 6:1025–1030.

Williams, Wendy M. 1998. "Are We Raising Smarter Children Today? School- and Home-Related Influences on IQ." In *The Rising Curve*, edited by Ulric Neisser, 105–40. Washington, D.C.: American Psychological Association.

Yang, Q., S. A. Rasmussen, and J. M. Friedman. 2002. "Mortality Associated with Down's Syndrome in the USA from 1983 to 1997: A Population-Based Study." *Lancet* 359, no. 9311:1019–1025.

Yeargin-Allsopp, M., C. D. Drews, P. Decoufle, and C. C. Murphy. 1995. "Mild Mental Retardation in Black and White Children in Metropolitan Atlanta: A Case-Control Study." *American Journal of Public Health* 85, no.3:324–28.

Zenderland, Lela. 1997. "The Bell Curve and the Shape of History." *Journal of the History of the Behavioral Sciences* 33, no. 2:135–39.

———. 1998. *Measuring Minds: Henry Herbert Goddard and the Origins of American Intelligence Testing*. Cambridge: Cambridge University Press.

3

DEVELOPMENTAL PERSPECTIVE ON THE EMERGENCE OF MORAL PERSONHOOD

JAMES C. HARRIS

Introduction

Historically, attitudes toward intellectual disability have ranged from compassionate concern to ostracism and neglect. During the eugenics era in the early twentieth century sterilization was routinely practiced in the United States and other countries with the goal of eradicating the "menace" of degeneracy (Scheerenberger 1983). In the Nazi era in Germany "involuntary euthanasia" was practiced; more than sixty thousand people with intellectual disability and/or mental illness were gassed—in some instances, to conduct research on their brains afterward (Burleigh 1994; Roelcke, Hoendorf, and Rotzoll 2001; Harris 2006a). During the war years there were those in the United States who proposed "involuntary euthanasia" (mercy killing) of people with intellectual disability, a proposition that was formally debated in 1942 in the *American Journal of Psychiatry*. A prominent neurologist, Foster Kennedy at Columbia University, proposed to deal with the social control of the congenitally defective through education, sterilization, and, for the most severely involved, possibly euthanasia (Kennedy 1942). An anonymous editorial in the same issue of the journal generally supported Kennedy's position and suggested that it was an empirical question whether there was, in some parents, a morbid parental attachment to their children that might require psychiatric treatment (Anonymous 1942). Leo Kanner, director of child psychiatry at Johns Hopkins University, who was to publish the first description of infantile autism the following year, opposed euthanasia; he called for better services for those affected and their families. He spoke of parents' fondness for their children and did not view attachment to them as morbid; throughout his career he provided advice to parents about how to care for their children with intellectual disability (Kanner 1953). Kanner (1942) advised psychiatrists to "be friendly planners and helpers rather than carping critics and whining would-be protectors of future generations." He went on to write: "We shall thus exonerate ourselves by exonerating the feebleminded" (Kanner 1942, 22). This is the position I will examine in this essay—that when we seek to facilitate the emergence of personhood in people with intellectual disabilities, we not only enrich their lives but also enrich our own lives and those of others around us.

As knowledge of involuntary euthanasia in Germany to eliminate "life unworthy of life" (Burleigh 1994, 20) and evidence of unethical medical experimentation became widespread after World War II, attitudes began to change toward people with intellectual disabilities in the United States. Ethical guidelines for research were established at Nuremberg after the war to protect research subjects with intellectual disability while allowing for participation in meaningful life saving research. By the mid-twentieth century a series of legal decisions requiring early identification, treatment, and humane care for them in community programs were established. Legal challenges resulted in legislation requiring that appropriate services be provided based on ethical principles from early life to old age. Concurrent with this legislation there have been changes in societal attitudes toward affected children and their families leading to greater recognition of their personhood. The goal of care is normalization of the lives of each affected person and, to the extent possible, self-efficacy and support in individual decision making. The goal of facilitation is to reach one's potential within one's cognitive capacity.

This essay offers a developmental perspective on the emergence of moral personhood. The first part provides an overview of intellectual disability, reviews causation, discusses changes in diagnostic terminology that are increasingly less stigmatizing, and describes intelligence tests and cognitive developmental thresholds. Throughout the focus is on a developmental model that emphasizes the emergence of personhood as the consequence of the maturation of the brain, facilitating environment experiences, and the mastery of developmental tasks. The importance of empathy, moral development, and developmental task mastery is central to this emergence and in facilitating self-efficacy (Sands and Wehmeyer 1996). Having discussed the emergence of moral personhood, I focus in the second part of the essay on respect for the individual that moral personhood confers. I consider societal challenges to autonomy and ethical issues that arise in participation in treatment decisions and in participation in research.

Definition of Disability

Persons diagnosed with an intellectual disability will encounter many obstacles in their lifetime because of limitations in their adaptive abilities based on underlying impairments in bodily or mental functioning. There may be specific limitations in the types of activities that they can undertake. But they also may have limited opportunities to participate in other activities that they could engage in, because the environment is not supportive. An impairment is an underlying disorder—such as low IQ, brain injury, blindness, deafness, or depression—that limits an individual's adaptive ability; it may have been acquired as a result of illness, trauma, or inherited disorder. However, disability is socially and environmentally defined—that is, the term "disability" refers to how others interpret the individual's impairment and to how they make or do not make accommodations to support that person's needs. Impairment is a physical fact, a medical or developmental condition, but often disability is a barrier created by the societal response to impairment. For example, paralysis is an impairment, but a society that does not provide curb cuts in sidewalks or ramps to buildings essentially turns that impairment into a disability by preventing a wheelchair-bound person from independently gaining access to a sidewalk or a building. Without such supports an individual is rendered disabled from active participation in life. Thus, the extent of disability is defined at the threshold of a biomedically based impairment and the environment accommodation that is made for its remediation. An appreciation of the personhood of each individual recognizes that threshold and dictates that barriers be removed.

Causes of Intellectual Impairment

People with intellectual disability make up 1 percent of the general population in the United States. There are many causes for their intellectual disability. These are generally categorized as prenatal (onset in utero), perinatal (onset at the time of birth), and postnatal (onset after birth) (Harris 2006b, 104–6). Prenatal causes of intellectual disability are most commonly genetic disorders; intellectual disability is associated with more than 750 genetic disorders. These include chromosomal disorders, inborn errors of metabolism, and developmental disorders of brain formation. Of the known genetic disorders, about a quarter have their primary effect in the brain, while others may secondarily affect the brain. But environmental causes act in utero as well. For example, use of alcohol by the pregnant mother (gestational substance abuse) may cause intellectual disability. Malnutrition, rubella, glandular disorders such as diabetes, cytomegalovirus disease, and many other illnesses affecting the mother during pregnancy may result in intellectual disability. Perinatal causes are more frequent in those born prematurely and in those born at term with low birth weight. Perinatal causes are linked to birth injury that may result from physical causes or metabolic ones. Postnatal causes of intellectual disability include preventable childhood diseases such as whooping cough, chicken pox, and measles and specific infections resulting in meningitis and encephalitis. Ingested substances such as lead and mercury that do damage to the brain and nervous system may lead to intellectual disability. Other postnatal causes are traumatic brain injury from accidents, particularly head injury, and near drowning. One of the most preventable causes of intellectual disability is maternal substance abuse, especially alcohol abuse, during gestation.

Evolving Terminology for Intellectual Impairment

Over the past hundred years the terminology used to describe intellectual impairment has evolved as each earlier attempt at naming has eventually been deemed pejorative and been discarded. Earlier terms that have been abandoned include idiocy, imbecility, and feeble-mindedness, mental defect, mental deficiency, and the most recent designation, mental retardation. An alternative term, cognitive developmental disability, also has been considered for consistency with other development disability designations. However, "intellectual disability" is the term that has been chosen and is enshrined by the federal government in the naming of the committee that advises the director of the Department of Health and Human Services and the U.S. government, the President's Committee for People with Intellectual Disability. In 2007 the American Association on Mental Retardation (AAMR) changed its name to the American Association on Intellectual and Developmental Disabilities (AAIDD) (Schalock et al. 2007). The term "intellectual disability" will be formally used in the 2011 edition of the association's definition manual. The current AAMR definition of intellectual disability is this: "Mental retardation (intellectual disability) is a disability characterized by significant limitations both in intellectual functioning and in adaptive behavior as expressed in conceptual, social and practical adaptive skills. This disability originates before age 18" (AAMR 2002, 1). The *Diagnostic and Statistical Manual of Mental Disorders*, fourth edition, text revision (DSM-IV-TR), of the American Psychiatric Association (2000) uses criteria for diagnosis similar to those used by the AAIDD.

Even though the diagnosis of an intellectual disability indicates that there is brain dysfunction, the general category "intellectual disability" is not in itself a specific disease or pathology; there are many causes, as noted above. Moreover, intellectual disability may not be permanent for those with mild intellectual disability; even if the underlying brain pathology persists, there is the potential for some compensation for such deficits. The brain continues to develop into the thirties; its development is not fixed and immutable. Thus, because of the possibility for continued adaptation the AAIDD refers to intellectual disability as a state of human functioning in society. The extent of disability varies according to the availability of supports that are provided for an individual. The AAIDD multidimensional model of human functioning emphasizes taking into account all the dimensions that may affect functioning in everyday life when planning supports (Wehmeyer et al. 2008). These include an individual's intellectual abilities, adaptive behavior, physical and emotional health, impairments that limit participation in everyday community life, environmental features, and personal characteristics. The assessment of intellectual disability determines the individual's strengths, talents, and weaknesses. For example, many people with intellectual disability have interest in music. Although not part of the standard intelligence test battery, music is one of the multiple intelligences that in the model proposed by Howard Gardner (1999) have proved helpful to educators.

The Bell Curve and IQ: Levels of Intellectual Disability

There are varying degrees of severity of intellectual disability, ranging from profound to severe to moderate to mild (American Psychiatric Association 2000). Using the standardized bell curve, intellectual disability is defined as two standard deviations from the mean using an IQ test score where 100 is the mean score and one standard deviation is 15 IQ points. Thus mild intellectual disability refers to an IQ of 55–70, moderate 40–55, severe 25–40, profound less than 25. For those who cannot cooperate with standard testing the category "severity unspecified" is used. Categorization in one of these categories can be complicated, because skills can be uneven. Intelligence tests have both verbal and performance components, and there may be considerable variability within them. For example, at least two-thirds of children with a diagnosis of autism have an intellectual impairment. In autism there can be a 30–40 point or greater discrepancy between verbal and performance IQ scores; performance IQ is substantially higher than verbal ability. Moreover, an IQ test is a measure of general intelligence. Where there are broad discrepancies on IQ subtest items, referred to as test scatter, then individual neuropsychological testing is needed to fully develop the legally required individualized treatment plan (IEP). Because neurodevelopmental deficits or damage to developing brain regions may vary among the various intellectual disability syndromes, it is the task of neuropsychological testing to determine the full neurocognitive profile. Such profiles may also be utilized to develop an IEP. Neuropsychological testing measures specific brain functions, such as executive functioning and spatial cognition.

Individualized testing is carried out in recognition of the personhood of each individual with an intellectual disability to determine an individual's specific cognitive and developmental profile. To address unique learning and emotional needs, it provides assessment guidelines to determine levels of support needed for persons to grow and develop. The AAIDD recognizes the importance of ranking intellectual disability according to severity and accepts the current levels of severity (ten classifications) in the *Diagnostic and Statistical Manual of Mental Disorders*, fourth edition, text revision (DSM-IV-TR) (American Psychiatric Association 2000), and the International Classification of

Diseases (ICD). The AAIDD's focus on supports rather than IQ levels is meant to emphasize the importance of individualizing treatment to meet the needs of each individual; it is not intended to ignore differences in severity of intellectual disability. Those with severe impairment have greater need for supports.

Cognitive Developmental Thresholds

One of the chief objections to the term "mental retardation," which contributed to its demise as the preferred designation, is that conceptually this naming inherently diminishes the person by emphasizing impairment rather than acknowledging potential. Families and their affected family member supported a name change too because the derivative term "retard" was pejorative. To address individual potential there is an increasing emphasis on a prospective approach that emphasizes the supports needed for cognitive progression over time. Having determined an individual's cognitive and communicative capabilities, the goal is to maximize them through systematic intervention. Whether or not each of the levels of severity (profound, severe, moderate, and mild) represents an individual's cognitive developmental threshold is an important empirical question for developmental psychiatry. To the extent that there are thresholds based on each severity category, the goal is to facilitate each person's progress to reach his or her potential by approximating his or her cognitive threshold as much as possible.

Supports are not only tailored to an impaired child's needs, they must also be provided for family members who live day to day with the child. It can be a long and difficult road for parents to understand and then acknowledge their child's developmental level. Most families adapt with support, but in doing so each family member may pass through phases where there is denial of the extent of impairment, emotional turmoil, blaming of themselves and/or blaming of others, and in some instances passive dependency on others (Harris 2006b). It is only when their child is fully accepted by them that parents, along with other family members, can be entirely engaged in supporting the child's treatment. It is only then that recognition of their child's ability threshold can be reassuring to them. Knowing what can be realistically expected increasingly allows them to feel pride in their child's slow but gradual progress. Such acknowledgment facilitates a strong bond between parent and child.

Recognizing and discussing developmental thresholds such as these allows the therapist to be optimistic with parents by helping them to appreciate that by acknowledging both their child's limitations and his or her potential they can participate in their child's incremental gains (Harris 2006a). There is an inherent satisfaction that comes from mastering cognitive and emotional challenges. Supports are needed for people with intellectual disability to experience such satisfaction.

Intellectual Disability and the Brain: Fluid and Crystallized Intelligence

When intellectual abilities are measured, both fluid intelligence and crystallized intelligence are assessed. Fluid, eductive, or directed intelligence refers to the ability to find meanings in complex situations and solve newly encountered problems. It is the basis of the ability to draw inferences and understand the relationships among various concepts. This understanding is independent of previously acquired knowledge. Rather than acquired knowledge, it refers to a person's own engagement in problem solving, new learning, pattern recognition, and abstract reasoning. Short-term memory and executive functions are integral to fluid intelligence. The executive functions include higher-order reasoning capacities—for example, selective attention, anticipatory planning, self-regulation, response inhibition, and the manipulation of information held in short-term memory to solve problems. It is the higher-order forms of reasoning that are most affected in people with intellectual disability and must be facilitated in program planning. Fluid intelligence involves the dorsolateral prefrontal cortex, the anterior cingulate gyrus, and other brain systems related to attention and short-term memory.

Crystallized intelligence is known information that is available for use based on past learning. It refers to the ability to use skills, knowledge, and experience that have been previously acquired. It should not be equated with memory, although it does rely on accessing information from long-term memory. Crystallized skills based on knowledge and past experience are tested on IQ test items such as the vocabulary, general information, and analogy subtests. Crystallized intelligence appears to be a function of brain regions that are involved in the storage and usage of long-term memories, such as the hippocampus. Despite the enormous importance attributed to the evolution of primate brain size, the conviction remains that size alone is not enough to account for the observed diversity in primate behavior and that circuitry, neurochemistry, and subsystems (modules) were reorganized within brains to accommodate evolving behavioral repertoires (such as those entailed in language).

Neuroplasticity in Brain Development

Those brain regions that are the most recently evolved seem most vulnerable to developmental perturbations and environmentally based injury. Brain size has increased substantially in human evolution, especially in the expansion of the frontal neocortex and its "association" areas. Moreover, different cognitive abilities have matured in relation to the maturation of specific underlying networks. After birth, the primate brain continues to enlarge through proliferation of glial cells, elaboration of synapses and axons, and myelination of nerve fiber tracts. The phases of synaptic proliferation and pruning both continue through the age of sixteen years (Rapoport 1999).

The basic structure of local brain circuits is not specified by genetics but depends instead on epigenetic factors that effect gene expression in the developing brain through mechanisms other than changes in the underlying DNA sequence. For example, these circuits can be stabilized by life experiences. Brain development is stimulated after birth by "bottom-up" sensory stimulation from life experiences and by "top-down" directed learning experiences that involve fluid intelligence. Thus higher-order "thought" processes can directly activate and modify widespread brain regions. Such thought processes involve attention, memory, complex communication, symbolic manipulation of images, and, as the child matures, the use of words. Visuospatial processing, planning, and "self-awareness" also lead to changes in brain association areas through such top-down mechanisms. Areas in the frontal lobe, parietal cortex, anterior cingulate gyrus, basal ganglia, thalamus, midbrain, and cerebellum make up an "attentional" network. While we sleep, dreaming consolidates what has been learned or experienced during waking life, potentially stabilizing essential brain "association" circuits within the immature brain. The language regions of the brain have evolved concurrently with the emergence of speech and language.

Life experiences are stabilized through learning and stimulation that allows the brain to keep developing past birth. Such learning is possible because of the remarkable neuroplasticity of the human brain. Thanks to neuroplasticity, environmental enrichment can facilitate the elaboration of brain circuits subserving higher-order cognitive processes. Recognition of neuroplasticity and the impact of experience calls for early infant stimulation programs for people with intellectual disability where genetic abnormalities have resulted, for example, in Fragile X syndrome, where there is abnormal synaptic growth, or abnormal pruning during maturation. Early intervention is particularly important for people with autism and other developmental disorders where there are limitations in social understanding. Research using mouse models of Fragile X syndrome and other syndromes raises the possibility of new medical and environmental interventions.

Developmental Perspective on Intellectual Disability: Cognitive Developmental Thresholds

People with intellectual disability, like all other people, will continue to develop throughout their lifetimes. Their personal development continues despite underlying neurodevelopmental deficits. From a development perspective the maturation of the brain, personal experiences, and the capacity to master developmentally appropriate tasks must all be taken into account in gauging progress from infancy to old age (Harris 2006a).

As noted earlier, brain maturation is facilitated though the richness of personal experiences at home, in school, and in the community as, to some extent, life experience sculpts the brain. Personal mastery of developmental challenges and tasks brings satisfaction to people with neurodevelopmental disabilities just as it does to typically developing children. Successfully completing a learning task or handling a social situation effectively produces its own intrinsic rewards.

People with intellectual disability follow the same stages as typically developing children so far as problem solving is concerned, but they fail to make expected progress in their learning and understanding. In comparison to typically developing children, they are "developmentally delayed," but also different in the way they solve problems. There is a slower speed of information processing so that they are less mentally efficient in solving problems at a given chronological age (Demetriou et al. 2002).

The failure to progress in learning and reasoning suggests that there are cognitive developmental thresholds that may be ascribed to each of the levels of intellectual disability. A failure of progression from learning by trial and error in the first year and a half of life to mastery of the subsequent stage of problem solving using representational thinking and imaginative play is associated with profound intellectual disability. A failure to move beyond symbolic thinking that uses early working memory for problem solving in preschool children is linked to severe intellectual disability. A failure to move beyond the capacity to carry out reversible mental operations such as subtraction in mind is linked to moderate intellectual disability. Finally, a failure to progress beyond concrete operational thinking and problem solving is linked to mild intellectual disability.

To determine cognitive thresholds tests are administered to determine how well an individual can solve reasoning tasks that require different degrees of thinking or reasoning abilities. These tests are based on measures of the speed and ability of information processing (reasoning efficiency); of working memory (the ability to keep information in mind as one persists in mastering a task); and of the ability to maintain attention by focusing on a task until the task is solved (task mastery). Individual intervention, using a developmental approach that posits cognitive developmental thresholds, focuses on analyzing why a particular child is failing to progress from one cognitive stage to the next and seeks to find the best way to help the child advance in problem-solving abilities according to his or her ability level.

Moral Development

A developmental perspective involves cognitive development, emotional development, and the development of the person. The emergence of the moral personhood may begin in infancy as the infant becomes aware that the nurturant caregiver and the restrictive caregiver are the same person. From this emerges a capacity for concern that leads to the inhibition of aggression toward the caregiver. A sense of continuity in being is established as an attachment to an adult caregiver is established (Bowlby 1988, 1999). The security that this early relationship provides results in emotional self-regulation and differentiation of one's own feelings, the emergence of self-awareness, adaptive task mastery through imaginative problem solving, interaction with peers, and the establishment of a personal identity in adolescence. Attachment has an evolutionary basis and is biologically related to mirror neurons in the brain that are activated when observing others actions. Mirror neurons are activated in the observer analogous to those needed to conduct the observed task oneself. Attachment requires the affective attunement of the infant with the caregiver and the release of oxytocin, a hormone recently linked to trust (Carter, Harris, and Porges 2009).

Attachment theorists emphasize that children have a need for a secure relationship with adult caregivers, without which normal social and emotional development will not occur. Insecure attachment may lead to personality patterns characterized by social withdrawal, rejection sensitivity, or compulsive self-reliance (Holmes 1993). In the context of typical close attachment children begin to emotionally self-regulate with adult guidance. Children who are securely attached are more curious and self-reliant (Sands and Wehmeyer 1996) and more readily explore their surroundings. By around the age of three and a half years a sense of the personal emerges, and by four and a half to five and a half years children are sufficiently self-aware to have a sense of personal coherence. By this age typical children establish autobiographical memory and spontaneously talk about their recent experiences. When they enter middle childhood the sense of competence increases as they increasingly master age-appropriate developmental tasks and interact with peers. In adolescence they become increasingly autonomous while maintaining connectedness to adults for guidance. Children with neurodevelopmental disabilities progress slowly through these early stages of development, reaching milestones concomitant with their mental age and ongoing life experiences. A person who is severely intellectually disabled (IQ 25–40) is expected to reach a mental age of about four to six years by the age of sixteen years and thus can be expected to establish self-awareness and make choices based on his or her understanding, but will have less flexibility in thinking than a typically developing child of that mental age.

Empathy and Development

Children with intellectual disability progress in their emotional and moral development as children typically do, but at a different pace. At birth typically developing infants show passive emotional engagement through affective resonance with their parents. By the second month, there is social smiling and regulation of face-to-face exchanges with caretakers. The infants engage in imitation and reciprocal games by six months and at that age are surprised if an object moves on its own but not if a person does so. At about nine months they are better able to share their attention with an adult. Empathic engagement is beginning to advance beyond simple face-to-face engagement. At twelve months an infant shows its displeasure by shaking its head to indicate "no." At that age infants respond to an object as an intentional agent in its relationship to themselves. By around fourteen months children can identify themselves as unique and recognize themselves in a mirror. Now they can begin to identify with or project themselves into others, a kind of projective empathy. By eighteen months they have established a sense of we-ness, and jointly the infant and adult look together at an object. Mental zing progresses with the ability to track the speaker's intention when learning words from an adult. Distress expressions and motor actions that alleviate the stress of another become coordinated with the emergence of mirror self-recognition.

Insight is mediated by the empathic response itself; self-objectification is the only real precondition for empathy: it draws a clear-cut distinction between self and others. Thus there are not two processes—that is, a vicarious emotional process and a cognitive perspective-taking process—but instead there is an integrated linking of affect and cognition. In one study involving thirty-six girls and boys aged fourteen to twenty-two months, in two separate sessions the individuals participated in tests for self-recognition and were concurrently confronted with a person in need, who demonstrated grief. Only those individuals who recognized themselves in a mirror tried to help others; non-self-recognizers were indifferent (Harris 2007).

By twenty-four months of age, children begin to manifest self-conscious emotions, including embarrassment, and at this age engage in systematic comparisons and eventually in conceptualization of the self in relation to other people. They begin to understand how they should feel based on how others might feel about them. Other self-conscious emotions, such as pride and shame, begin to emerge too. Toward the third year, children begin to understand that they can know something that someone else does not know. The emergence of self also leads to further development of the self-conscious emotions, shame, guilt, and pride. These emotions are basic to forming relationships with others.

Between the ages of four and six years children normally develop greater awareness of mental states and how the mind can be used to explain and predict others' behavior, and they begin to distinguish objective from subjective thoughts. From now on, children become more capable of recognizing the emotional state of others in relation to their own. Thus, cognitive empathy is linked to the emergence of self-awareness.

By the age of eight affect is increasingly linked to reasoning. It is increasingly possible, in one's imagination, to consider how the other might feel. At adolescence emotions are more intense, and there is a deepening of friendships. With continuing maturation empathy plays a central role in moral development with regard to social justice and mercy toward others in distress.

These studies of empathy focus on typically developing young children. What about empathy in people with intellectual disability? In one study the empathetic response to distress in others was evaluated in thirty children with Down syndrome who were compared to twenty-two children with nonspecific causes for intellectual disability and to twenty-two typically developing children (Kasari, Freeman, and Bass 2003). In comparison to the other groups of children, those with Down syndrome responded to distress in others by looking more toward them and offering them more comfort in the form of helping pro-social behaviors (that is, comforting them). However, children with Down syndrome seemed less likely to feel the same emotion as that experienced by the person who was emotionally upset than were typically developing children of the same mental age. Children with Down syndrome differed from those with nonspecific causes in their greater response to distress in others, whereas those with nonspecific causes were more similar to age-matched typically developing children. Another example demonstrating empathy among persons with intellectual disability occurred at the Seattle Special Olympics. Nine children, all with physical or mental disability, stood at the starting line for the hundred-yard dash. When the gun sounded, all started out with the intention of winning the race. However, one boy stumbled and fell on the asphalt, turned over several times, and began crying. The other eight children heard him cry, slowed down, and looked back toward him. One child, a girl with Down syndrome, turned around and walked back to him. Bending down she kissed him and told him that should make it better. Soon the other children came to check on him too. Then all nine linked arms with him and walked together to the finish line as everyone in the stadium stood up and cheered.

Cognitive and Affective Development

For people with intellectual disability, their understanding of societal norms is based on the extent of their cognitive impairment, but their behavior toward others depends on their life experiences. There are two primary models for moral development in the child development literature. One emphasizes moral judgment and tests how moral dilemmas are solved through moral reasoning—what conceptually is the just, right, or fair thing to do in a particular situation (Kohlberg 1968, 1969). Lawrence

Kohlberg's model is a cognitive developmental one. It addresses the structure of conscious moral beliefs as they are reflected through one's reasoning in response to hypothetical moral dilemmas. Over time, Kohlberg proposes, moral reasoning evolves through three levels and five or six stages. Each stage differs from the prior one in regard to its logical inclusiveness, universality, concepts of justice, and the worth of human life. In this model, education involves exposing people to reasoning at levels higher than their own. Kohlberg's model is akin to classical philosophical models of rational moral decision making. When considering moral choice and moral personhood for people with intellectual disability, however, Kohlberg's model is problematic because of its exclusive focus on rational reflection.

The second model of moral development (Hogan 1973; Hogan, Johnson, and Emler 1978) emphasizes empathy and mercy rather than justice. It focuses on what people actually do when confronted with another person in distress. Are they sensitive to the plight of another person and willing to help that person in distress, as was the girl with Down syndrome in the Seattle race? This approach has its origins in models of evolutionary adaptiveness based on humans evolving in social groups and, in keeping with Bowlby (1988), their biological proneness to respond to others in distress.

The cognitive developmental model proposed by Kohlberg (doing the right or just thing) depends on moral reasoning and is linked to mental age. However, moral development based on affective developmental models such as Hogan's (1973) places greater emphasis on emotional responsiveness to others in distress—a sense of mercy—and is not necessarily so tightly linked to mental age and cognitive level. The emphasis is not so much on what people say they will do but rather on what they actually are observed doing in a stressful situation. For example, as previously noted, we know that typically developing children show empathy in the second year of life, long before they can reason and explain their actions.

Thus, moral behavior based on empathy (Harris 2007; Carter, Harris, and Porges 2009) rather than strictly based on reasoning for solving moral dilemmas is the more pertinent of the two models of moral development when considering moral personhood in persons with intellectual disability. Successful moral education for people with an intellectual disability utilizes emotional sensitivity to provide a sense of membership in a viable family or social group. Emotional empathy is a developmental process in which individuals come to respond to the emotional states of others. The consequences of emotional empathy are compassionate behavior toward others, moral agency, and pro-social behavior. Thus, moral development must be considered as it relates to socialization and empathy, not to reasoning alone.

In summary, moral personhood emerges in people with intellectual disability in the context of a secure attachment relationship, a sense of self-awareness, regulation of emotion, role-play, and affective development. In intellectual disability empathy, mercy, and pro-social behaviors may play a larger role in moral agency than traditional moral reasoning.

Implications of Recognizing Personhood and Autonomy

As people with intellectual disability mature and become more self-aware, issues arise as to the extent that they can be involved in personal decision making. Increasingly, treatment programs are moving away from a strict operant conditioning approach that may lead to overprogramming and limited opportunities for making personal choices to encouraging decision making and greater autonomy. Progress is being made with greater respect for autonomy and individual rights. However, in advocating for individual choice it is critical to understand the characteristic features of each syndrome thoroughly. Focusing too rigidly on individual autonomy without taking into account individual needs can cause a great deal of harm. A case in point is the occurrence of behavioral phenotypes in certain neurogenetic syndromes. Geneticists and specialists working with individuals with intellectual disability now recognize that genetic syndromes may have characteristic physical phenotypes and behavioral features that are specific to a genetic syndrome. A behavioral phenotype is a characteristic pattern of behavior that is consistently associated with a neurodevelopmenal disorder

Two examples of how behavioral phenotypes must be considered in program planning are pertinent to Lesch-Nyhan syndrome and Prader-Willi syndrome. These syndromes raise issues about the routine use of restraints and about food restriction. Because of the long history of misuse of restraints there are very strict regulations about their use for people with intellectual disability. Moreover, there are questions about the importance of appropriate feeding protocols because of the history of nutritional neglect and forced feeding in institutional settings.

William Nyhan introduced the term "behavioral phenotype" (Harris 1998) to describe self-injury leading to self-mutilation in the syndrome named for him, Lesch-Nyhan syndrome. Compulsive self-mutilation occurs in affected individuals despite the fact that sensory systems are intact and the individual feels pain. People with this syndrome require and request physical restraint to prevent them from injuring themselves; they ask for assistance from others to prevent them from harming themselves. When relaxed in a secure environment they will ask for the restraints to be removed to allow participation in activities. Unfortunately, because of general guidelines in group homes to release restraints regularly using a restraint protocol, several injuries with amputation of fingers have occurred when this behavioral phenotype was not appreciated.

Another example is the unrestrained eating with lack of satiation that is characteristic in Prader-Willi syndrome. This syndrome is a neurodevelopmental disorder characterized by obesity, short stature, intellectual disability, and compulsive overeating. Because of their severe obesity, people with the syndrome have an increased risk for diabetes, heart disease, and excessive daytime sleepiness (Harris 1998). The behavioral phenotype includes unusual food-related behavior, including compulsive food seeking, hoarding, and gorging, low frustration tolerance, and aggressiveness around feeding. Because of the biologically driven overeating with failure of satiation, food intake must be restricted. This may include using refrigerator locks and careful monitoring of food intake. Yet in group home settings, because food availability is a right, life-threatening overeating has occurred in those with Prader-Willi syndrome (Dykens et al. 1998).

In both instances appropriate respect for autonomy requires an understanding of the underlying genetic disorder and resulting medical condition. A focus on the rights of the individual with an intellectual disability must be based on careful assessment of the person and an individually based treatment program.

Participation in Research

An important issue that arises from recognition of personhood when considering participation in research is respect for the autonomy of people with intellectual disability. Because of past abuses and misuse of people with disabilities in research projects—especially in Nazi Germany during World War II—guidelines have been developed to protect the rights of research participants with intellectual disability. The Nuremberg code to regulate biomedical research, developed after the war, is the basis for later ethical guidelines for research involving humans (Weindling 2001). The first of the code's ten points is the requirement for voluntary consent. Current guidelines for research pertinent to people with intellectual disability stem from the "Belmont Report," issued in 1979 by the National Commission for the Protection of Human Subjects of Biomedical and Behavioral Research as *Ethical Principles and Guidelines for the Protection of Human Subjects of Research*. The report provides the framework for current research protections and established ethical guidelines. The Institute of Medicine has updated ethical guidelines for children (Field and Behrman 2004). There are three basic principles stipulating that persons with diminished autonomy are entitled to protections, including:

1. *Respect for persons.* Any research requires informed consent and assent (from those who cannot consent) that respects the autonomy of the person.
2. *Beneficence.* Beneficent actions maximize possible benefits to the person and minimize possible harm. Put another way, all research requires discussion of the risk-benefit ratio for participants.

3. *Justice or fairness.* Who will receive the benefits of the research and bear its burdens? On balance, the research must have a benefit that comes to the person or to a group with a disorder. This principle is especially critical when asking a person to participate in research.

Consent and Assent

The Institute of Medicine Committee on Clinical Research Involving Children (Field and Behrman 2004) has summarized research guidelines that apply to children and to people with intellectual disability. The report comprehensively discusses conflicting objectives of scientific research that involves children—ensuring that children benefit from the progress in medical care made possible by such research while concurrently minimizing the risks from their participation. The requirements are that both parental consent and children's assent to participate be obtained. The participant must knowingly agree to be part of any research project. Because people with intellectual disability may not have the legal capacity to enter into this agreement, permission from their caregivers is needed to allow them to participate in a research project. A signed informed consent form and, if full consent cannot be obtained, an assent form must be completed before the individual can participate in a research project. Research forms offer a detailed explanation of the research protocol, and to be finalized they must show the caregiver's written consent and the participant's written or verbal assent. To be fully informed, research subjects must be allowed time to ask questions and obtain detailed explanations. It must also be determined whether the prospective participant always says "yes" or always says "no" to any question to ensure that assent is informed. For research involving younger children or those with more severe forms of intellectual disability, basic information about what will happen at each step of the research is essential, especially if the research may not result in a direct benefit for them. It is essential that they understand that they can voluntarily withdraw from the research protocol at any time.

Summary

A focus on moral personhood considers that limitations in reasoning, working memory, and cognitive efficacy do not mean that people with intellectual disability are lacking in empathy and all capacity for moral action. Moreover, they reciprocate when treated with interpersonal warmth and tenderness regardless of their developmental level and demonstrate the capacity for empathic action toward others, particularly if sufficient emotional support is provided to establish a secure emotional attachment. Understanding brain evolution and development, cognitive thresholds, and fluid and crystallized intelligence allows programs to be adapted to allow each person to approximate his or her own potential. Empathic engagement with others and individual development of task mastery are important to the emergence of moral personhood and self-efficacy. When considering moral development, models based on affective empathy and mercy are more predictive of ethical behavior than strictly cognitive ones in people with intellectual disability. Recognizing the status that moral personhood brings, even to those with the most severe cognitive impairments, means acknowledging their autonomy. Acknowledgment of that autonomy as a feature of moral personhood is essential when planning participation in medical research.

References

American Association on Mental Retardation. 2002. *Mental Retardation: Definition, Classification and Systems of Support*. Tenth edition. Washington, D.C.: AAMR.

American Psychiatric Association. 2000. *Diagnostic and Statistical Manual of Mental Disorders*. Fourth edition, text revision. Washington, D.C.: APA.

Anonymous. 1942. "Euthanasia." *American Journal of Psychiatry* 99:141–43.

Bowlby, John. 1988. *A Secure Base: Parent-Child Attachment and Healthy Human Development*. London: Routledge.

———. 1999. *Attachment*. Volume 1 of *Attachment and Loss*. Second edition. New York: Basic Books.

Burleigh, Michael. 1994. *Death and Deliverance: "Euthanasia" in Germany c. 1900–1945*. Cambridge: Cambridge University Press.

Carter, C. Sue, James C. Harris, and Stephen W. Porges. 2009. "Neural and Evolutionary Perspectives on Empathy." In *The Social Neuroscience of Empathy*, edited by Jean Decety and William Ickes, 199–214. Cambridge Mass.: MIT Press.

Demetriou, Andreas, C. Christou, G. Spanoudis, and M. Platsidou. 2002. "The Development of Mental Processing: Efficiency, Working Memory, and Thinking." *Monographs of the Society for Research in Child Development* 67, no. 1:i–viii, 1–155.

Dykens, Elizabeth M., Barbara J. Goff, Robert M. Hodapp, Lisa Davis, Pablo Devanzo, Fran Moss, Jan Halliday, Bhavik Shah, Matthew State, and Bryan King. 1997. "Eating Themselves to Death: Have 'Personal Rights' Gone too Far in Treating People with Prader-Willi Syndrome?" *Mental Retardation* 35:312–14.

Field, Marilyn J., and Richard E. Behrman. 2004. *Ethical Conduct of Clinical Research Involving Children*. Washington, D.C.: National Academies Press.

Gardner, Howard. 1999. *Intelligence Reframed: Multiple Intelligences for the 21st Century*. New York: Basic Books.

Harris, James C. 1998. *Assessment, Diagnosis and Treatment of the Developmental Disorders.* New York: Oxford University Press.

———. 2006a. "The *Wurgengel.*" *Archives of General Psychiatry* 63: 1066–67.

———. 2006b. *Intellectual Disability: Understanding Its Development, Causes, Classification, Evaluation, and Treatment.* Oxford: Oxford University Press.

———. 2007. "The Evolutionary Biology, Emergence, and Facilitation of Empathy." In *Empathy in Mental Illness*, edited by Tom F. D. Farrow, 169–86. Cambridge: Cambridge University Press.

Hogan, Robert. 1973. "Moral Conduct and Moral Character." *Psychological Bulletin* 79:217–32.

Hogan, Robert, J. A. Johnson, and N. P. Emler. 1978. "A Socioanalytic Theory of Moral Development." *Journal of Moral Education* 2:1–8.

Holmes, Jeremy. 1993. *John Bowlby and Attachment Theory.* London: Routledge.

Kanner, Leo. 1942. "Exoneration of the Feebleminded." *American Journal of Psychiatry* 99:17–22.

———. 1953. "Parents' Feelings About Retarded Children." *American Journal of Mental Deficiency* 57:375–83.

Kasari, C., S. F. Freeman, and W. Bass. 2003. "Empathy and Response to Distress in Children with Down Syndrome." *Journal of Child Psychology and Psychiatry* 44, no. 3:424–31.

Kennedy, Foster. 1942. "The Problem of Social Control of the Congenital Defective: Education, Sterilization, Euthanasia." *American Journal of Psychiatry* 99:13–16.

Kohlberg, Lawrence. 1968. "The Child as Moral Philosopher." *Psychology Today* (September): 45–56.

———. 1969. "Stage and Sequence: The Cognitive-Developmental Approach to Socialization." In *Handbook of Socialization Theory and Research*, edited by D. A. Goslin, 347–480. Chicago: Rand McNally.

Rapoport, Stanley I. 1999. "How Did the Human Brain Evolve? A Proposal Based on New Evidence from In Vivo Brain Imaging During Attention and Ideation." *Brain Research Bulletin* 50:149–65.

Roelcke, Volker, Gerrit Hoendorf, and Maike Rotzoll. 2001. "Psychiatric Research and 'Euthanasia': The Case of the Psychiatric Department at the University of Heidelberg, 1941–1945." *Psychoanalytic Review* 88:275–94.

Sands, Deanna J., and Michael L. Wehmeyer. 1996. *Self-Determination Across the Life Span: Independence and Choice for People with Disabilities.* Baltimore: Brookes.

Schalock, Robert L., R. A. Luckasson, K. A. Shogren, S. Borthwick-Duffy, V. Bradley, W. H. Buntinx, D. L. Coulter, et al. 2007. "The Renaming of Mental Retardation: Understanding the Change to the

Term Intellectual Disability." *Intellectual and Developmental Disabilities* 45, no. 2 (April): 116–24.

Scheerenberger, Robert C. 1983. *A History of Mental Retardation.* Baltimore: Brookes.

Wehmeyer, Michael L., Wils H. E. Buntinx, Yves Lachapelle, Ruth A. Luckasson, Robert L. Schalock, Miguel A. Verdugo, Sharon Borthwick-Duffy, Valerie Bradley, et al. 2008. "The Intellectual Disability Construct and Its Relation to Human Functioning." *Intellectual and Developmental Disabilities* 46, no. 4 (August): 311–18.

Weindling, Paul. 2001. "The Origins of Informed Consent: The International Scientific Commission on Medical War Crimes, and the Nuremberg Code." *Bulletin of the History of Medicine* 75:37–71.

4

THE CAPABILITIES OF PEOPLE WITH COGNITIVE DISABILITIES

MARTHA NUSSBAUM

1. *Frontiers of Justice* and the Challenge of Disability

The presence of people with cognitive disabilities in our societies poses a twofold challenge to philosophical theories of justice. First, it poses a direct challenge. Here are some of our fellow citizens, and fellow participants in human dignity. Their needs, real and important, have not been adequately addressed by previous theories of justice. So the direct challenge asks us to design theories that address these needs and offer good normative guidance for societies seeking to do justice to them. Second, it poses an indirect challenge, by offering a test we can apply to all candidate theories of justice. We ask of each of the theories how the principles they suggest would treat the entitlements of people with cognitive disabilities, and we find fault with theories that, however attractive in other respects, cannot handle that issue well. By the same token, the ability of a theory to handle it well is at least one point in favor of such a theory.

In *Frontiers of Justice* (2006), I focused primarily on the second question. Using the issue of disability as one test to apply to theories of justice that employ the idea of a social contract, I argued that such theories—even John Rawls's, the most subtle and adequate of them all—cannot fully pass the test. That is, its treatment of this one area is not fully adequate. If we can find a theory that does as well in other areas and better in this one, we ought to prefer that theory. I then argued that my version of the "capabilities approach" does well (at least) in other areas and better in this one, though it was beyond my purpose to argue that it does as well as Rawls's in the other areas, and certainly I have not yet argued that it does better. That question was left for a further inquiry.

The direct challenge was relevant to my argument, because one could hardly show that the capabilities approach did better than Rawls's theory on the proposed test without saying quite a lot about what it recommends, and how it argues for its recommendations. Large parts of the direct challenge, however, remained unaddressed. I focused on education of children, and said relatively little about other areas of human capability and functioning. The present chapter aims to fill that gap by showing in much greater detail how my capabilities approach argues in this area and what specific policies it recommends, for both children and adults. (I continue, as in the book, to focus on cognitive disability, because that is the focus of the present collection of chapters, but I am aware that there is a great deal that I shall ultimately need to say about emotional disturbances and mental illnesses of many types, as well as the easier case of physical disability.)

A central job of my chapter will be to return to the difficult question of what equal respect for citizens as persons requires, and to what extent it requires equalizing the relevant capabilities. The capabilities approach, as I have articulated it, is a social-minimum approach, and I have always said that for this reason it is but a partial theory of social justice: it doesn't say what should be done about inequalities above its rather ample threshold. Nonetheless, even in pursuit of a decent social minimum we need to ask when a decent minimum of respect for persons requires full equality of the relevant capabilities and when it requires only something like adequacy. I began to face that task in the chapters of *Frontiers of Justice* devoted to global justice, but I did not connect that analysis back to the earlier analysis of disability. I must also, then, fill that gap.

Confronting the direct challenge will have some theoretically interesting results. For I shall argue that the area of the capabilities approach that is in general the most controversial and difficult in the American context—its strong emphasis on social and economic entitlements—is the easiest and simplest to apply to the case of cognitive disability; nobody should be surprised by my conclusions in that area. Education is some-what more complicated and controversial, since equal respect recommends policies that are very expensive. Here, however, law has gotten in ahead of us, and the analysis I recommend is already not just statutory law, under the Individuals with Disabilities Education Act (IDEA), but is also supported by constitutional law, which used the idea of equal protection to compel a remedy like IDEA, and which has recently interpreted IDEA in an expansive and generous light. The surprising results will come in the area that usually looks so simple that we can basically take it for granted: the area of political and civil liberties. For I shall argue that showing equal respect for the dignity of citizens with cognitive disabilities requires giving them an equal right to vote, to serve on juries, and so forth—just as it entails that equal entitlement for everyone else. And I shall make a surprising and controversial use of notions of guardianship in this connection.

2. The General Approach of *Frontiers of Justice*

The general task of *Frontiers of Justice* was to continue a project I began in *Women and Human Development* (2000), confronting my version of the capabilities approach with the strongest alternatives offered by the philosophical tradition. In *Women and Human Development*, in keeping with my focus on development policy, I focused on the Utilitarian antagonist. In *Frontiers of Justice* I turned to a different and far more subtle opponent, the social contract tradition. Arguing that John Rawls's theory of justice casts that tradition in its best and most persuasive form, I chose to focus on Rawls's work.

I argued that Rawls's work does very well indeed in handling the most familiar issues of political justice: economic justice, justice between people of different religions, races, and classes, and even (though with some modifications suggested in *Women and Human Development*) justice for women and justice in the family. There were, however, four areas that Rawls himself identified as areas where his theory has grave difficulty: justice across generations; transnational justice; the just treatment of people with disabilities; and justice for nonhuman animals. (I use the term "justice" in this last case, but Rawls did not.) Rawls solved the first problem quite well by my lights, so I saw no reason to revisit it. He spent considerable time on the second, but I believe that *The Law of Peoples* (1999) is not a good solution, so I resolved to return to that set of issues. Regarding the third and fourth questions, Rawls expressed grave doubt: these look like questions on which justice as fairness "may fail."

Following Rawls's own invitation, I resolved to probe these issues, searching for the roots of all three remaining difficulties in Rawls's strong allegiance to the social contract tradition, with its image of the parties to the contract as "free, equal, and independent," and as possessing a roughly equal amount of both physical and mental capacity. I argued in detail that although Rawls's principles are in themselves very attractive, he cannot, consistently with several deep commitments in his theory, do justice to the claims of people with cognitive and even physical disabilities; nor, I argued, could he solve the other two problems well. The reason in all three cases was the presence of a large asymmetry of power between the parties, which makes it no longer mutually advantageous for them to be included as fully equal parties to the social contract. I argued that Rawls would ultimately need to jettison the idea of rough equality in power and the related idea of mutual advantage as the aim of the social contract, were he to be able to do full justice to the claims of people with disabilities.

Most of the first of my two chapters on disability was spent analyzing the details of Rawls's argument, in order to show that his theory could not handle the case in any easy or straightforward way, for example, by adding to the account of the Veil of Ignorance the fact that the parties are ignorant of whether they have a disability or not. This would violate the deep commitment to similarity of power, with its associated idea of mutual advantage. In the case of mental disability this problem would be compounded by the need to suspend any determinate account of the rationality of the parties. Rawls was correct in thinking that he could not handle this problem without a major overhaul of his theory.

I then turned, in chapter 3, to my own capabilities approach, showing how it addressed the case of disability, and arguing that it did pretty well—better, for this case at least, than Rawls's theory. Focusing on the education of children with severe cognitive disabilities, I showed some examples of what the theory would yield in practice.

Frontiers of Justice, then, focused on what I've called the indirect challenge. The case of disability was seen as important in its own right, but my central argument was that, on account of its importance, it was a major problem for Rawls's theory that it could not address it. A theory that could do better had an advantage, and the capabilities approach looked like such a theory. My discussion of the direct challenge was confined to the question of education, with a brief discussion of guardianship. Even the education discussion was relatively brief. I left the direct challenge for others, and for myself in the future.

3. Equality and Adequacy

Sometimes people understand the capabilities approach to recommend something like equalizing all the capabilities for everyone.[1] No supporter of a capability-centered approach has ever said anything like this, to my knowledge. Amartya Sen does say that insofar as equality is our goal, the most pertinent space within which to think about and measure equality is that of capabilities (see Sen 1992). But he never says that our goal ought to be equality in all of them. Indeed, as Ronald Dworkin argues, such a social goal would be truly bizarre, and would have absurd entailments.

My own approach is different from Sen's in that it uses a specific list of the "Central Human Capabilities" as its benchmark for the definition of a social minimum.[2] Even here, however, the approach recommends, as a necessary condition of social justice,[3] bringing all citizens above a rather ample threshold on each of the ten capabilities, not complete equalizing of all the capabilities. That, however, is not the end of the matter, as it turns out: the idea of equality crops up again in thinking about the threshold, for at least some of the capabilities. I broached this question in chapter 5 of *Frontiers of Justice*, but the present chapter will press much further, so I must begin by recapitulating the position I took there.

The capabilities approach uses the idea of a threshold: for each important entitlement, there is some appropriate level beneath which it seems right to say that the relevant entitlement has not been secured. The intuitive idea of a life with human dignity already suggests this: people are

---

[1] See Ronald Dworkin's criticism of Amartya Sen in Dworkin 2000.

[2] See the exploration of that difference in my 2003.

[3] Not a sufficient condition, since mine is only a partial account of social justice.

entitled not only to mere life but to a life compatible with human dignity, and this means that the relevant goods must be available at a sufficiently high level. So far, the approach insists only on the idea of adequacy or sufficiency, and has stated that the question of what to do with inequalities above this minimum threshold is a further question that the approach has not yet answered. It is in that way as yet incomplete.

It seems crucial, however, to say more if we can: for we must indicate where, and to what extent, equality is part of the very idea of sufficiency. The list itself suggests that there are some instances in which we will not tolerate inequality of the relevant capabilities. Capability 7B, for example, speaks of "[h]aving the social bases of self-respect and non-humiliation; being able to be treated as a dignified being whose worth is equal to that of others." And it connects this idea to the idea of nondiscrimination. It seems crucial to go further at this point, spelling out the role of an idea of *equal* entitlement in the approach.[4] (Notice that in this area I also make my one concession to paternalism: for I say that people should not be permitted to be humiliated by government, even if they want to be. In that case, we should not shoot simply for the capability to be treated as a dignified being, we should shoot for the actual functioning.)[5]

The touchstone should always be, I believe, the idea of human dignity and the closely related idea of the social bases of self-respect and nonhumiliation. Equality of capability is an essential social goal where the absence of equality would be connected with a deficit in dignity and self-respect. We have seen that the idea of dignity is spelled out from the beginning in terms of equality: it is the *equal dignity* of human beings that demands recognition. Here the idea of equality is essential: we must add it to the bare idea of dignity in order to articulate the goal in an adequate way.

This idea, that equal dignity is what we must protect and promote, has implications for many of the capabilities on the list. For it appears—and a long tradition of Western political philosophy agrees on this point—that all of the political, religious, and civil liberties can only be *adequately* secured if they are *equally* secured. To give some groups of people unequal voting rights, or unequal religious liberty, is to set them up in a position of subordination and indignity vis-à-vis others. It is to fail to recognize their equal human dignity. Large stretches of the U.S. tradition of constitutional law reflect such thinking.[6]

On the other side, there are other capabilities, closely connected with the idea of property or instrumental goods, where what seems appropriate is *enough*. For example, an *adequate* house or other shelter seems to be inherent in the idea of human dignity, and it seems right that constitutions

---

[4] I am exceedingly grateful to Charles Larmore for pushing me to confront this question, and for his suggestions about how it might be confronted.

[5] See the discussion in my 2000, 34–110.

[6] See my 2007. On equality in the area of religious liberty, see my 2008, 115–74.

all over the world are beginning to recognize the right to housing as a constitutional entitlement, following the creative lead of South African jurisprudence. It is not at all clear, however, that an *equal* house is required by the very idea of human dignity or even of equal human dignity; for indeed a mansion may not be better for a human being than a modest house. House size above a certain threshold does not seem intrinsically related to equal human dignity.

Insofar as envy and competition make people *feel* that an unequal house is a sign of unequal dignity, we might wonder whether these judgments are not based on an excessive valuation of material goods, which a just society might decide not to honor. The case is not clear. As Adam Smith observed, what is compatible with human dignity may itself vary from society to society. In England, the ability to appear in public without shame requires a shirt; in some other nations it does not. We might add that the ability to sit in the front of the bus is connected to human dignity not timelessly but through a set of social norms and practices. Thus the fact that house size is connected to dignity through social norms does not suffice to undermine the connection. It does, however, prompt a further inquiry. At least sometimes we may find that excessive valuation of competitive goods lies behind a social norm, and a just society could decide not to honor that valuation. This is surely one area where different nations with their different traditions will need to work out the problem for themselves through ample public deliberation.

In some areas that appear to fall on the "material" side, however, it does seem clear that grossly unequal shares fail to meet the adequacy condition. If education, for example, is arranged as it currently is in the United States, in such a way that students in a rich school district may have as much as seventy-five or a hundred times as much spent on them as is spent on students in a poor district, this does seem to be, in and of itself, a violation of equal dignity and equal political liberty.[7] At least where primary and secondary education are concerned, adequacy does appear to require something close to equality, or at least a very high minimum (perhaps allowing for divergences in aspects of education that are not firmly linked to basic opportunity and political participation). The same is true of basic essential health care. Whether higher education and nonessential health care are matters in which we may accept unequal shares as compatible with the threshold of adequacy, remains a question that societies will have to hammer out.

Harry Frankfurt influentially argues that equality all on its own is not a distinct political value; it becomes important when it affects some other capacity, such as the capacity for speech, or self-respect, or a life with dignity, or for relationships not predicated on hierarchy (see Frankfurt

[7] Cf. Justice Marshall's dissenting opinion in *San Antonio School District v. Rodriguez*, 411 U.S. 1, 70-133 (1973) (Marshall, J., dissenting).

1998). Apart from its connection to the content of these values, it remains a bare formal notion. How should the proponent of a capabilities approach respond to Frankfurt's challenge?

The matter is very difficult to think about, and all statements ought to be tentative. We should begin by insisting, again, that equality is important at the very base of the theory: for it is not just human dignity that must be respected, it is equal human dignity. Equality is not just a proxy for some other value, it is a constituent part of the basic value to be respected and promoted. This role for equality, however, does not entail that equality is a reasonable goal with regard to all the central capabilities.

Some capabilities must be secured to citizens on a basis of equality, or equal dignity has not been respected. Others, however, do not seem to have this intrinsic relationship to dignity; with these, the capabilities approach supplies a threshold of adequacy. Some nations and individuals may prefer a more egalitarian solution with these capabilities as well. But it seems likely that if we want a political conception that can achieve an overlapping consensus among people who differ in their comprehensive ethical and religious doctrines, especially when we are considering transnational trans- fers of wealth, this conception is more likely to prove broadly acceptable than one that insists on equality in all the central capabilities. Individuals whose comprehensive doctrine is more exigent can at least recognize the political conception as compatible with their own doctrine, though it does not deliver everything that they would favor.[8]

What this means is that we need to take the capabilities one by one and ask whether adequacy or equality is the relevant threshold goal in this area, and what, more concretely, that goal entails. And we must do this in a way that is sensitive to social norms—for we don't want to forget that social norms profoundly affect what is and isn't compatible with equal human dignity (our example of riding in the back of the bus shows this), without being unduly deferential to fads and preferences (for if people feel bad because they don't have a mansion, that should not lead us to write mansions into the definition of the social minimum).

When we deal with the capabilities of people with cognitive disabilities, a preference-based approach is particularly likely to offer bad guidance, because we are well aware that many if not most social preferences in this area are deformed by ignorance, stigma, and fear. That likelihood should give us a preference for capability-equality, where we can't give any good reason against it. Here we should take a lesson from U.S. constitutional law. Under the Equal Protection Clause of the Fourteenth Amendment, when- ever a classification is particularly likely to be infected by prejudice, there is a strong case for according that classification some type of *heightened*

---

[8] Note that income and wealth are not on the list at all, since they are not capabilities; thus the frequently discussed issue of equality in income and wealth is touched on only indirectly, through commitments concerning the central capabilities.

scrutiny; in other words, any differential treatment of that group must be justified by an unusually strong state interest, which is called "compelling." Although people with cognitive disabilities have been said not to be a "suspect class," warranting heightened scrutiny,[9] I have argued that heightened scrutiny is appropriate in their case (see Nussbaum forthcoming). Here, then, I apply something like that test: if people with cognitive disabilities have unequal capabilities in some area on my capabilities list, that can be justified only by a compelling state interest.

4. Social and Economic Entitlements

The United States is not consistently supportive of the capabilities of citizens on the side of what are standardly called "social and economic rights" (see Nussbaum 2007). Other nations do much better. As I argued in the previous section, however, entitlements such as entitlements to housing and to health care and others in that group require a high threshold of *adequacy*, rather than complete equality, for their fulfillment. Should people with cognitive disabilities have the same entitlements in these areas as so-called normal people? By and large, we already agree that the answer is yes. There are defects in health care schemes and in subsidized housing where there is subsidized housing. Our nation in particular does far too little to support the labor of care involved in securing the capabilities (health, mobility, bodily integrity) of both people with disabilities and elderly people, as Eva Kittay has so eloquently argued (see Kittay 1998). The argument that people with cognitive disabilities deserve the same level of care as people without cognitive disabilities (for example, physically infirm elderly people) is an easy one to make, and the argument that remains concerns the level of care that a decent society would provide. The debate about mental illness is actually a much more difficult debate in this area, because people still tend to blame mental illness on the ill person, and thus to be reluctant to grant him or her adequate medical support. (Much the same goes for alcoholism and drug addiction.) People with cognitive disabilities, like elderly people, aren't blamed for the care they need, so the debate about care in their case is not marred by false belief and inappropriate stigma. What needs to be done here is to convince all Americans to support a higher level of health care, nursing care, housing support, and so forth, for all, but the situation of people with cognitive disabilities does not appear to raise special problems.

[9] *City of Cleburne v. Cleburne Living Ctr., Inc.*, 473 U.S. 432 (1985). Here, however, the U.S. Supreme Court found in favor of people with cognitive disabilities, since it found that the law in question (a zoning ordinance that denied a permit for a home for people with mental retardation) didn't even pass the weaker rational basis test, being motivated by mere fear and animus.

5. Equality in Education

One might suppose that education for people with cognitive disabilities is also a threshold matter that raises issues about capability-equality, but not about capability-adequacy. In *Frontiers of Justice*, however, discussing equality and adequacy, I suggested that education was an area so central to matters of citizenship and self-respect that we should not tolerate a situation in which everyone comes up to some reasonable threshold but gross inequalities remain. The U.S. approach through constitutional law has never accepted this principle fully, but it has always been recognized that education is an area of fundamental importance in relation to citizenship, so gross inequalities are unconstitutional if the disadvantaged do not come up to a rather ample threshold. Dissenting opinions have suggested that the protection of equality ought to be stronger, given the role played by education in relation to the freedom of speech.[10]

When educational disadvantages are not simply due to de facto economic segregation but track an imposed segregation or exclusion of a group, however, the Constitution's Equal Protection Clause has been held to give the disadvantaged group an enforceable right to educational equality of a kind, meaning, at least, the removal of segregation and an equal openness of local school classrooms to members of the disadvantaged group. Thus *Brown v. Board of Education* used the Equal Protection Clause to argue that legally mandated segregation was unconstitutional.[11] *United States v. Virginia*, similarly, used the Equal Protection Clause to open the doors of the Virginia Military Institute to women, arguing that the separate women's program did not give students equal skills and job opportunities.[12] The analysis in *Brown* was borrowed in the case that ultimately opened the public schools to children with a wide range of disabilities.

In 1972, in *Mills v. Board of Education*,[13] the U.S. District Court for the District of Columbia ruled in favor of a group of children with mental disabilities who challenged their exclusions from the District of Columbia public schools.[14] In an analysis that self-consciously set out to apply *Brown*, the court held that the denial of free suitable public education to the mentally disabled is an equal protection violation.[15] (Notice that the

[10] Refer to *Plyler v. Doe*, 457 U.S. 202 (1982), *San Antonio*, and discussion in my 2007; also refer to Michelman 1969.

[11] 347 U.S. 483 (1954).

[12] 518 U.S. 515 (1996).

[13] 348 F. Supp. 866 (D.D.C. 1972).

[14] A case decided in the same year, *Pennsylvania Association for Retarded Children v. Pennsylvania*, 334 F. Supp. 1257 (E.D. Pa. 1971), reached a similar result.

[15] Technically, because of the legally anomalous situation of the District, the court held that it was a due process violation under the Fifth Amendment and that the equal protection clause in its application to education is "a component of due process binding on the District."

opinion understands *Brown* to be about the difference between exclusion and inclusion, not about a ban on special affirmative remedies: indeed, it understands the *Brown* framework to suggest, very strongly, the need for such affirmative remedies. (Children with disabilities, the court holds, will need to be given special support in order to be fully integrated into the public schools.) Moreover, very important for our purposes, the court held that this equal protection violation could not be reasoned away by saying that the system had insufficient funds and these children were unusually expensive to include. "The inadequacies of the District of Columbia Public School System, whether occasioned by insufficient funding or administrative inefficiency, certainly cannot be permitted to bear more heavily on the 'exceptional' or handicapped child than on the normal child," the opinion argues. Significantly, at this point the opinion cites the U.S. Supreme Court case of *Goldberg v. Kelly*[16] to make the point that the state's interest in the welfare of its citizens "clearly outweighs" its competing concern "to prevent any increase in its fiscal and administrative burdens." The court quotes the resonant reflections of Justice Brennan in *Goldberg* to make this point:

> From its founding the Nation's basic commitment has been to foster the dignity and well-being of all persons within its borders. We have come to recognize that forces not within the control of the poor contribute to their poverty.... Welfare, by meeting the basic demands of subsistence, can help bring within the reach of the poor the same opportunities that are available to others to participate meaningfully in the life of the community.... Public assistance, then, is not mere charity, but a means to "promote the general Welfare, and secure the Blessings of Liberty to ourselves and our Posterity."[17]

Similarly, reasons the court, the District of Columbia's interest in the education of these excluded children "clearly must outweigh its interest in preserving its financial resources." Like *Goldberg*, the opinion emphasizes that the inclusion is not a matter of charity but one of entitlement and basic justice.

As a result of *Mills*, in 1975, Congress passed the Education for All Handicapped Children Act (EAHCA), which turned the *Mills* decision into federal law, giving a wide range of mentally disabled children enforceable rights to free suitable public education, and making funds available to the states to help them meet their constitutional obligation. This law was slightly modified and elaborated in 1997 in the form of the Individuals with Disabilities Education Act (IDEA).

The guiding idea of the Act is that children with disabilities are individuals, equal in dignity to "normal" children, and that, in consequence, education should be based on a careful individualized consideration of a child's educational needs. The central vehicle of this idea is the

---

[16] 397 U.S. 254 (1970).

[17] *Id.* at 264–65 (quoting the preamble of the United States Constitution).

Individualized Education Program (IEP), "a written statement for each child with a disability that is developed, reviewed, and revised." The Act requires that states affirmatively undertake to identify and locate all children with disabilities whose needs have not been addressed. It also requires that districts establish extensive procedural safeguards to give parents input in decisions regarding the evaluation and placement of their children, as well as access to records and rights to participation in due process hearings and judicial review. In general the Act obliges states to educate children with disabilities in the "least restrictive environment" appropriate to meet their needs. It thus urges "mainstreaming" of these children. But the underlying recognition of individuality is paramount: thus if a child will profit more from special education than from mainstreaming, the state is obliged to support a special placement, which sometimes will have to be in a tuition-charging private school.

Thus the remedy can often be very expensive for the state. My nephew Art, whose education I discussed in *Frontiers of Justice*, just graduated from high school and is currently thriving in a community college. For about eight years, the state he lives in supported his placement in a special school for people with Asperger's syndrome, and the educational result has been superb. Art not only is in college (and has already held a job), he also has a circle of friends whom he enjoys, and he is a happy kid. This is basically what I think the capability approach requires: affirmative measures to support the education of children with cognitive disabilities, so that they will have no education-related disadvantages as they prepare to enter society.[18] So, not just adequacy but equal concern and equal protection. Not every child with a cognitive disability will have educational attainments at Art's high level, but IDEA, if implemented well, will ensure that something like this equal concern has been shown, by the very fact of considering the child's educational needs individually and designing a program to develop his or her human potential.

IDEA has noble aspirations, and yet its implementation has been fraught with difficulty. For one thing, the funds were not appropriated for a long time, and even now the funding is not complete. Another major problem, however, is the IEP process, in which parents must negotiate with school committees who are not always well educated about the child's specific disability and who often try to save money, even at the cost of not supporting a special placement for a child who clearly needs one. Autism-spectrum disorders often pose particular problems, making mainstreaming difficult. A whole range of human capabilities, from citizenship to intellectual and emotional development, are at stake in the IEP process, making adequate representation

---

[18] I realize that Asperger's and other autism-spectrum disabilities are both cognitive and affective, but for that reason I am somewhat skeptical of the usual way of classifying these disabilities, as I discuss in my 2006.

crucial.[19] The Supreme Court considered this problem in 2007, interpreting the statute in a way that makes it clear that parents, as well as children, have rights under the Act. This interesting opinion further fleshes out what equal protection means in this context (*Winkelman v. Parma City School District*, 2007).

Many poor parents cannot afford to hire a lawyer. If they are denied the right to represent themselves, the already striking inequities of the Act, which clearly favors educated and articulate parents, become yet more striking. When discussions with the Parma, Ohio, school district led to an impasse, the Winkelmans, availing themselves of IDEA's administrative review procedures, filed a complaint, appealing to a state-level review officer; after losing that appeal, they appealed to the U.S. District Court for the Northern District of Ohio. The District Court found for the school district, so they appealed again, to the Sixth Circuit. The Sixth Circuit held that IDEA does not grant parents independent rights, and that, in consequence, the Winkelmans could not proceed unless they hired a lawyer. The Supreme Court reversed. In *Winkelman v. Parma City School District*, the Court held that IDEA gives rights to parents, as well as children, in respect of their children's education, thus permitting parents of children with disabilities to represent themselves in court when challenging a child's IEP (Individualized Education Program).[20] The statute, carefully read, is not ambiguous, and thus their victory breaks no new legal ground. It does, however, illustrate an ongoing dialogue and partnership between legislative and judicial action that has resulted in the protection of human capabilities for many of our most vulnerable young citizens.

I've said that equal protection and equal respect do not require equality of educational outcomes. In that sense, the approach in education has a good deal in common with the approach in the area of mobility, and thus it might seem to be an adequacy approach, not an equality approach. The whole point of the approach, however, is to ensure that no special disadvantages accrue to children with disabilities in virtue of their disability. They are equally placed in the education process, and equally supported—which, in their case, requires a lot of affirmative measures and extra expense. After that, like all children, they will achieve at different rates and attain different levels. So the equality is in the concern, and the strenuous requirements it imposes.

6. Equality in Political Entitlements

Now to the difficult and controversial case. Where core political entitlements are concerned, we typically have no difficulty in concluding that

[19] See the analysis in my 2006, 155–223, where I also address the unusual difficulties of "mainstreaming" for autism-spectrum children.

[20] 550 U.S. 516 (2007).

adequacy of capability requires equality of capability. We do not hesitate a minute in thinking that the right to vote, the right to participate in the political process, and other basic civil rights such as those of free speech and association, must be delivered to citizens on a basis of equality if the nation in question is to claim even minimal justice. Suppose each woman or African American had a vote that counted as only half a vote, while white men each had a full vote: we immediately see that these policies would be profoundly wrong. Even if someone were to claim that women and African Americans still have "enough" voting rights, we would say, "Surely not. For to have enough voting rights just means to have equal voting rights." Similarly, the exclusion of women and African Americans from jury service, such a large feature of relatively recent political life, is now taken to be obviously and uncontroversially wrong. Why? It seems to express unequal respect for citizens, and politics must express equal respect as a very central and basic value.

It is instructive to observe how deeply this insistence on equality of entitlement enters into law even in the United States, in many respects a profoundly inegalitarian society. Take the freedom of religion. Our constitutional tradition has understood the entitlement to religious liberty to be an entitlement to *equal* liberty. (The words "equal rights of conscience" were used in many of the constitutional debates, and if they do not turn up in the final text that is because they were by that time taken for granted.)[21] What that means is quite interesting. It means that minorities often receive "accommodations," or special dispensations from laws of general applicability, because only an accommodation would render their religious free exercise fully equal to that of the majority. Laws are always made by majorities. Majority preferences determine what workdays will be chosen, what holidays will be observed, what intoxicants will be legal, and so on. Well then, if minorities come up against such laws, even when the laws themselves express no hostile intent, they may face special burdens to their religious practice. They may be fired for refusing Saturday work. They may be told that they must serve in the military, even though their religion forbids that. They may be forbidden to use a hallucinogen in their sacred ceremony, even when the majority is allowed to use alcohol in its sacred ceremonies. The concept of accommodation is the idea that in such instances the minority should not have to shoulder that special burden: they should be exempt from the law. In a 1789 letter to the Quakers, who refused military service, George Washington wrote: "I assure you very explicitly, that in my opinion the conscientious scruples of all men should be treated with great delicacy and tenderness: and it is my wish and desire, that the laws may always be

---

[21] See my 2008 on the role of ideas of equality at the founding (72–114) and their role in the interpretation of the Free Exercise Clause (115–74) and the Establishment Clause (224–305).

as extensively accommodated to them, as a due regard for the protection and essential interests of the nation may justify and permit." Washington did not require the Quakers to perform military service, and he also did not require them to pay a fine or go to prison for breaking the law.

In a famous 1963 case, *Sherbert v. Verner*, the U.S. Supreme Court reasoned that accommodation was constitutionally required, in the absence of a "compelling state interest," and required for reasons of equality.[22] To say that Mrs. Sherbert should not receive unemployment compensation because she refused jobs that required Saturday work was tantamount, they said, to fining someone for Saturday worship. In other words, minorities may not be required to face any substantial disadvantage in their religious lives that majorities do not also have to bear—absent a compelling state interest. Thus the requirements of equal respect are extremely exigent: they brook no compromise except in the gravest of cases.

Let's now turn to the case of people with cognitive disabilities. In fact, there are three such cases.

In Case A, the person is both cognitively and physically capable of voting, serving on a jury, and making religious choices, but because of stigma and majority social arrangements, really enabling the person to do that—putting that person in a position of *combined capability*—will require special efforts and expense. There are many ways in which people with a range of physical disabilities—who are blind, deaf, or wheelchair users, for example—used to be excluded from these functions. These exclusions are gradually being corrected. In the case of cognitive disability, exclusions are more subtle and persistent. People with limited ability to read, people who easily become confused or fearful in a new setting, may be excluded from voting and jury service *de facto*, even though sensitive thought about how to include them could prove just as successful in these settings as it has in education.

In Case B, the person cannot exercise these functions on his or her own, even with special arrangements, but is able to communicate his or her preferences to a guardian, who can then exercise the function on his or her behalf. Here I am thinking about cases in which the person may not be able to speak or express thoughts in a way that is comprehensible to the world at large, or which could easily be adapted to the typical structure of the jury or the polling place, but the person is agreed to have views and to be able to communicate them to a small group of trusted individuals.[23]

In Case C, the person's disability is so profound that he or she is unable to perform the function in question, even to the extent of forming a view and communicating that view to a guardian. In honor of Eva

---

[22] 374 U.S. 398 (1963).
[23] I say "agreed" in order to bracket the controversy about "facilitated communication" in the case of autism.

Kittay, the founder of this field of philosophical research, we might take Sesha Kittay, so thoroughly and movingly described by Eva, as our example in this category.

I note that the other two people with cognitive disabilities who figured in *Frontiers of Justice*, Jamie Bérubé and my nephew Art, are in category A if they are in any category at all. (At least it seems to me that Jamie is in this category.) It seems likely that both can unproblematically go in and vote on their own, but if they need any special arrangements, they would be of the type A variety—thanks to the excellent education made available to them under the IDEA. (Art, as I've mentioned, is a freshman in a community college, Jamie is a flourishing and delightful young adult.)

To simplify, I shall just assume that things are on a par with respect to the whole range of political capabilities I've identified, although that might not be the case in life: some people might be able to make religious choices but not to vote, and so forth.

Case A is extremely easy. Equal respect for the person with a disability requires spending the money required to facilitate that person's full inclusion in the functions of citizenship, including voting, jury service, and so on. This is just like the case of religion that I discussed above: a minority may not be given a diminished entitlement because of majority arrangements or majority preferences. And it is exactly the way in which disability issues in education have already been treated in the court cases and, ultimately, under IDEA.

Case A is, I said, easy, but its implications are still radical for the way voting and jury service are to be constructed and their requirements understood. The Help America Vote Act in 2002 made some progress: polling places must have equipment that allows voters with disabilities to vote privately and independently. Selection of voting equipment should be made with input from the local disability community, with the aim of including as many people with different types of disabilities as possible, but this goal is not always achieved in practice. People with physical disabilities still face such obstacles as unpaved parking lots, election officials who do not know how to operate the wheelchair-accessible equipment, denials of assistance for people who do not bring an assistant with them. More problematic still are the impediments for people with cognitive disabilities. Various jurisdictions impose time limits for marking a ballot, despite the fact that the Americans with Disabilities Act entitles voters with disabilities to a reasonable accommodation in this case. The Voting Rights Act guarantees a right of assistance to voters who need help going through a ballot or through the voting process, but often election personnel refuse the voter assistance from persons of choice, saying that only election workers can assist the voter—and this assistance is often inadequate, given that election workers typically lack training and experience in working with people with disabilities. Signatures may also be refused if the voter uses an X or some other nontraditional signature. Voters' need for assistance understanding complex language and instructions is not always honored, or is met in a stigmatizing and disrespectful way.

All jurisdictions need to address these problems, above all by training election workers to offer respectful assistance to people with disabilities, including allowing them to use the assistance of persons of choice. Such changes are implicit in existing law. Making them reality is difficult in practice, but easy in theory.

Jury service in Case A is more difficult than voting, but still conceptually easy. If jury service is a fundamental symbol of one's equal citizenship, citizens with cognitive disabilities who can follow the trial and make a judgment should not be excluded. Including them, however, will require special aid and special explanations in many cases. Courts should be prepared to provide such assistance.

Case B is also, conceptually, relatively easy. If the person can form a view about whom to vote for but can't exercise that function in person by reason of a disability, then it seems obvious that a guardian ought to be entitled to exercise the function on that person's behalf. With voting this may seldom be necessary, since on-line voting and absentee ballots facilitate the inclusion of such people. (Even in such cases, some state laws require the person to be able to sign his or her name, and a person may be able to form a view about whom to vote for but be unable to sign a name.) Where those solutions are not possible the problems I have pointed out for Case A are even greater. The person may be denied consultation with a person of choice, or may be denied sufficient time, or may be refused on the ground of inability to write a signature. Indeed, Case A and Case B form a continuum: when a person with a disability needs assistance understanding the ballot, that case already requires a kind of guardian-like intervention, so the difference between A and B is one of degree, not kind. In both cases, that role is best played by a person of choice, whether a legally official guardian or not, though it is also good to have trained election officials who can assist those unable to bring a guardian and who can help ensure that the individuals are not being coerced or manipulated.

Now let's think about jury service in Case B. In case B, like Case A, the person ideally should be present in the room taking part personally in the process, but it is obvious that his or her ability to interact with other jurors will be more limited, and the role of the guardian will be correspondingly larger. Many people with a disability who currently do not serve on juries might be able to exercise this important civic function were a guardian entitled to be present with them, as an intermediary in their conversations with the other jurors. How exactly the consultative arrangement would be worked out would be a matter for much debate, and much would remain to be determined about how we would ascertain what the person understands about the proceedings and about the law; but that is a debate that should and must take place, whereas now it is not taking place.

Let us now, however, turn to the most difficult case, Case C. Here the person's cognitive disability is so profound that she cannot communicate her wishes about whom to vote for to a guardian; indeed, in many such cases he or she cannot form such view. Nor can she exercise religious choices, or serve on a jury even in the sense of delegating a guardian to represent her judgments. What does equal respect require in this case? I would argue that it requires that the person's guardian be empowered to exercise the function on that person's behalf and in her interests, just as guardians currently represent people with cognitive disabilities in areas such as property rights and contract.

What is the alternative? That, as at present, a large group of citizens are simply disqualified from the most essential functions of citizenship. They do not count. Their interests are not weighed in the balance. That, to me, means that they are not regarded as fully equal citizens with a dignity commensurate with that of others. The bottom line is, I think, that "one person, one vote" is the right idea, an idea with deep expressive and symbolic meaning, and it currently is not being observed where people with profound cognitive disabilities are concerned. If a concerned parent or other guardian votes in the interests of a person with a disability, she still has but a single vote, hers, and yet there are two people with that interest, not one. (It would be important to compare the case of the adult with senile dementia: Are these people disadvantaged in a similar way?)

Naturally it will be said that there is room for corruption in this process: the guardian may just vote his or her preferences and ascribe them to the person with a disability, thus doubling the guardian's own vote. It should be clear on reflection, however, that this is no more a problem for voting than it is in many other areas where we currently permit surrogate arrangements: property rights, health decisions. A decent guardian will be able to keep those interests apart. Sometimes a candidate's positions will favor certain interests of the guardian that are not shared with the person with a disability, and the guardian should be able to see this. (Once again, law would need to protect the person against the sort of coercion and manipulation that group home settings make possible.) By contrast, the candidate may have certain disability-friendly policies that affect the interests of the person with a disability but not those of the guardian. Again, a good guardian will see this. Many guardians won't be good, but what else is new? Every day, people vote because their parents are voting that way, or their spouse, or their pastor. Often, too, they vote one way because their parents or spouses are voting the opposite way. We do not assess people for independence of mind when we give them the franchise, nor should we. If a person announced that he or she would decide whom to vote for by tossing a coin, or by closing his or her eyes and sticking a pointer randomly into the voting card, we might think that person irresponsible, but there would be no basis for removing the franchise from that person. Indeed, with lesser and local offices, many people vote with no more information than that all the time, and this, though disturbing, is hardly illegal.

So the claim that the guardian may do his or her job badly or incompletely, not fully representing independent interests of the person with a disability, is not a particular objection to my proposal, and we have never thought that it is, in other areas where guardianship is used. Instead, we design procedures to authorize guardianship that try to weed out the incompetent or the selfish. If we were to take this objection to heart, we might be led all the way to something like Mill's suggestion that educated people should have more votes than noneducated people. We know that we do not approve of that suggestion. Why don't we approve of it? Because it does not express equal respect for all citizens. So too here: the current system, under which citizens in class C are denied the franchise for life is disrespectful and wrong.

In terms of constitutional law, my proposal lacks strong grounding. The right to vote has been recognized as a fundamental right inherent in the Equal Protection Clause, and the case law seems to establish that only a "compelling state interest" can ever justify any abridgment of that right.[24] Resonant statements have been made about the importance of this right for equal citizenship. For example, in *Reynolds v. Sims*, a case concerning legislative apportionment, Chief Justice Warren wrote, "[T]he right of suffrage is a fundamental matter in a free and democratic society [and] is preservative of other basic civil and political rights. ... [To] the extent that a citizen's right to vote is debased, he is that much less a citizen."[25]

In practice, however, the Court has been relatively deferential to states. The perpetual controversy over racially gerrymandered districts shows that there is no consensus about whether an equal right to vote entails giving minorities an equally meaningful or effective vote. More pertinent for our purposes, the Court's willingness to allow states to exclude convicted felons from the franchise[26] indicates that they would also very likely defer to the states in this area, upholding the exclusion of people who have to vote via a surrogate in the sense of Case C.

My proposal is, then, an ethical proposal that has little chance of being recognized by the courts right now, although perhaps the legislative route offers some hope. What is important, however, is to see that it *ought* to prevail in the courts. There is no bona fide compelling state interest that justifies the exclusion of these people. Any reason that can be offered in

---

[24] *Dunn v. Blumstein*, 405 U.S. 330 (1972) (ruling long-term residency requirements unconstitutional unless the State can show that they are necessary to protect a compelling governmental interest).

[25] 377 U.S. 533, 561, 567 (1964).

[26] *Richardson v. Ramirez*, 418 U.S. 24 (1974).

this connection would also be a reason to exclude docile and deferential people, people who vote without knowing anything about the candidates, and so forth. We have opted for an understanding of the franchise that is nonelitist and inclusive, rejecting Mill's educational oligarchy. We have also accepted surrogate decision-making for people with severe cognitive disabilities across a wide range of areas of entitlement: property, bodily integrity, and so forth. There is no good reason to refuse a surrogate arrangement in this area, and very strong reasons to accept it.

Jury service is also a recognized hallmark of fully equal citizenship, exclusion from which is stigmatizing. Though a duty that may be burdensome, it is also a badge of civic equality. But jury service in Case C is different from the consultative arrangement that I've proposed for case B. It means, simply, that the guardian is the surrogate for the person she represents. There is no point in bringing that person along into the jury room. Moreover, since personal interests are supposed to be excluded from juror deliberations, there is no easy way to distinguish being a juror for oneself from being a juror representing a person with a disability. There will be differences, perhaps, in the voir-dire process. When jurors are questioned about their background, the surrogate will have to disclose her own background, because it is her own judgment she is using, and the possible biases in that judgment have to be elicited. But since she is representing a person with a disability, she needs to describe that relationship as well, in case any biases would emerge from that description. For example, suppose the case involved sexual violence against a person with a disability. If the representing guardian spoke only about her own experience of sexual violence, or lack of it, the lawyers for both sides would fail to be informed about a crucial factor that might bias the guardian's judgment. Once selected, however, the surrogate would use her own judgment. What would be the point of that? The all-important point that the person with a disability has her name in the pool, has an equal chance to perform that civic function.

So, let the guardian vote in that person's interest and serve on a jury when that person's name comes up. The very presence of the surrogate, known to be the surrogate for a person with a cognitive disability, serves to give due recognition to the person with a disability, and to people with disabilities more generally. Religious and associational liberties are easier, and right now we basically do permit guardians to make key choices in these areas on the person's behalf and in that person's interest.

I said in section 3 that any inequality in the political entitlements of people with disabilities should be examined under a very stringent standard of judicial review, and therefore could be justified only by something that would rise to the level of a "compelling state interest." What might such an interest be? Administrative expense and complexity has traditionally not counted as such an interest, except in the most extreme cases—for example, the refusal of an Amish employer with many employees to pay social security tax for any of them, something that would not just harm the system but would inflict a penalty on the employees. In this case, the difficulty of establishing who the certified guardian is would not be very great, once states had established reasonable systems of certification. Preventing corruption in the voting process will surely be cited, but, as I've already argued, that reason is not compelling, and if we should accept it we will be led down the dangerous road of seeking only qualified or independent voters, something we have long rejected.

In short: people with cognitive disabilities are equal citizens, and law ought to show respect for them as full equals. To do so, law must provide such people with equal entitlements to medical care, housing, and other economic needs. That is the easy part. But law must also go further, providing people with disabilities truly equal access to education, even when that is costly and involves considerable change in current methods of instruction. Even that, our society has begun to realize. Now we must take the most controversial step of all, giving people with cognitive disabilities political and civil rights on a basis of genuine equality. What that requires, and why it requires something that seems at first look so odd, has been the central theme of this chapter. Let the debate begin.

Acknowledgments

I would like to thank Eva Kittay and Licia Carlson for organizing the wonderful *Cognitive Disability: The Challenge to Moral Philosophy* conference, in September 2008, and the participants in the conference for their searching questions. I am very grateful to my University of Chicago Law School colleagues for a stimulating roundtable discussion of these issues, and to Alex Kolod for superb technical assistance.

References

Dworkin, Ronald. 2000. *Sovereign Virtue: The Theory and Practice of Equality*. Cambridge, Mass.: Harvard University Press.

Frankfurt, Harry G. 1998. "Equality and Respect." In *Necessity, Volition, and Love*, edited by Harry G. Frankfurt, 146–54. New York: Cambridge University Press.

Kittay, Eva. 1998. *Love's Labor: Essays on Women, Equality and Dependency*. New York: Routledge.

Michelman, Frank I. 1969. "The Supreme Court, 1968 Term—Foreword: On Protecting the Poor Through the Fourteenth Amendment." *Harvard Law Review* 83, no. 1 (November): 7–59.

Nussbaum, Martha C. 2000. *Women and Human Development: The Capabilities Approach*. New York: Cambridge University Press.

———. 2003. "Capabilities as Fundamental Entitlements: Sen and Social Justice." *Feminist Economics* 9, nos. 2–3 (July): 33–59.

————. 2006. *Frontiers of Justice: Disability, Nationality, Species Member-ship*. Cambridge, Mass.: Harvard University Press.

————. 2007. "The Supreme Court, 2006 Term—Foreword: Constitutions and Capabilities: 'Perception' Against Lofty Formalism." *Harvard Law Review* 121, no. 1 (November): 4–97.

————. 2008. *Liberty of Conscience: In Defense of America's Tradition of Religious Equality*. New York: Basic Books.

————. Forthcoming. *From Disgust to Humanity: Sexual Orientation and Constitutional Law*. New York: Oxford University Press.

Rawls, John. 1999. *The Law of Peoples with "The Idea of Public Reason Revisited."* Cambridge, Mass.: Harvard University Press.

Sen, Amartya. 1992. *Inequality Reexamined*. Cambridge, Mass.: Harvard University Press.

5

EQUALITY, FREEDOM, AND/OR JUSTICE FOR ALL: A RESPONSE TO MARTHA NUSSBAUM

MICHAEL BÉRUBÉ

In this reply to Martha Nussbaum's "The Capabilities of People with Disabilities," I will start by picking up the gauntlet where Nussbaum has thrown it. "People with cognitive disabilities are equal citizens," she writes. "Now we must take the most controversial step of all, giving people with disabilities political and civil rights on a basis of genuine equality.... Let the debate begin." In this chapter, I want to move the debate forward in two ways: first, by largely agreeing with Nussbaum's argument, even where it is most controversial—that is, at the end, where Nussbaum calls for a robust conception of surrogacy that would extend even to such matters as voting and serving on juries (though I have some reservations about jury service, which I'll explain below); second, by noting that this conception of surrogacy poses an underrecognized challenge to disability studies. But I would be remiss if I did not remark at the outset that Nussbaum's willingness to take cognitive disability as a challenge for moral philosophy has been exemplary. A decade ago, Eva Kittay and I were complaining to each other that philosophy had so little to say on the subject—except, of course, when philosophers busy themselves with finding reasons why people with cognitive disabilities do not meet their standards for entities entitled to something called human dignity. So for some years now, I've been in the position of saying to my colleagues in philosophy, "Your silence with regard to cognitive disability is most dismaying," followed in short order by "Actually, your undervaluation of the lives of people with cognitive disabilities is even more dismaying. I liked you all better when you were silent."

My first response to Nussbaum, accordingly, is simply to say that I'm grateful for her work on disability, grateful for the way she has taken the subject as a challenge to the capabilities approach to theories of justice, and grateful that she even has taken the example of my son, Jamie, as one of the foundations for the argument she elaborates in *Frontiers of Justice*. I'm grateful also for the chance to offer an update on the ways Jamie challenges our thinking about cognitive disability. In his 1994 book,

Rethinking Life and Death, Peter Singer famously claimed that "to have a child with Down syndrome is to have a very different experience from having a normal child. It can still be a warm and loving experience, but we must have lowered expectations of our child's ability. We cannot expect a child with Down syndrome to play the guitar, to develop an appreciation of science fiction, to learn a foreign language, to chat with us about the latest Woody Allen movie, or to be a respectable athlete, basketballer or tennis player" (Singer 1994, 213). Back in 1994, when Jamie was only three, I might have been persuaded by this; I once believed—and wrote—that Jamie would not be able to distinguish early Beatles from late Beatles or John's songs from Paul's, and now he knows more about the Beatles' oeuvre than most people who don't study the Beatles for a living (Bérubé 2006). His interest in *Star Wars* and *Galaxy Quest* has given him an appreciation of science fiction, just as his fascination with Harry Potter has led him to ask questions about innocence and guilt. He is learning a foreign language, having mastered the "Est-ce que tu" question form in French and being able to (a) fool the dog by saying "Nous allons faire une promenade avec Lucy" rather than "We'll take Lucy for a walk," which gets the poor dog too excited, and (b) charm young women at the cheese counters of French super-markets by saying "Je voudrais du fromage de chèvre, s'il vous plait." Jamie has a better memory for the gender of nouns than I do, even though he did not grow up speaking a language in which nouns have gender. Lastly, I confess that neither of us has the least interest in chatting about the latest Woody Allen movie; but it might interest Singer to learn that Jamie and I have had a running conversation over the past five years about the film *Babe*, which introduced Jamie not only to the question of whether it is right to eat animals but also to the fact that there are various theories out there as to why humans eat some animals and not others.

But I don't have to tell this to Martha Nussbaum—she already gets it. She has not merely taken up the challenge offered by thinkers like Eva Kittay; she has returned to Kittay's arguments time and again, usually to endorse them. In her 2001 review of Kittay's *Love's Labor*, for instance, Nussbaum argued that Kittay had misguidedly jettisoned liberal social-contract theories of justice root and branch, and she demurred from Kittay's insistence that, in Nussbaum's words, "we are all 'some mother's child,' and that we exist in intertwined relations of dependency, should be the guiding image for political thought. Such a care-based theory, she thinks, will be likely to be very different from any liberal theory, since the liberal tradition is deeply committed to goals of independence and liberty" (Nussbaum 2001, 35). This position, Nussbaum wrote, sat uneasily with Kittay's commitment to greater independence and liberty for people who serve as caretakers for people with disabilities. But in her more recent work Nussbaum has taken on board

Kittay's major premise, that the social-contract tradition cannot adequately accommodate people with cognitive disabilities, and has augmented it. It is not merely that the tradition imagines contracting agents that are "free, equal, and independent," in Locke's phrase; after *Love's Labor*, that's relatively low-hanging fruit for anyone who seeks to put cognitive disability at the center of political philosophy. More damagingly, Nussbaum argues, the tradition imagines that we enter into the social contract for mutual advantage; and for people with cognitive disabilities and their guardians, this isn't a bug in the social-contract software—it's a feature of the program. It has no way to build into its foundations an account of why we should agree to create forms of social organization that will support and nourish some people who will never be capable of repaying the favor. Following Kittay, then, Nussbaum takes aim at the heart of John Rawls's account of the Original Position, namely, the conviction that "the fundamental problem of social justice arises between those who are full and active and morally conscientious participants in society, and directly or indirectly associated together throughout a complete life" (Rawls 1980, 546). And she insists that we place front and center what Rawls relegates to the margins, because, to coin a phrase, the margins *are* in fact the center:

> The parties are being asked to imagine themselves as if they represent citizens who really are "fully cooperating . . . over a complete life," and thus as if citizens have no needs for care in times of extreme dependency. This fiction obliterates much that characterizes human life, and obliterates, as well, the continuity between the so-called normal and people with lifelong impairments. It skews the choice of primary goods, concealing the fact that health care and other forms of care are, for real people, central goods making well-being possible. . . . More generally, care for children, elderly people, and people with mental and physical disabilities is a major part of the work that needs to be done in any society, and in most societies it is a source of great injustice. Any theory of justice needs to think about the problem from the beginning, in the design of the basic institutional structure, and particularly in its theory of the primary goods.
>
> (Nussbaum 2006, 127)

I couldn't have put it better myself—and I've tried: in the final chapter of *Life as We Know It*, I wrote: "The society that fosters Jamie's independence *must* start from an understanding of his dependencies, and any viable conception of justice has to take the concrete bodies and 'private,' idiosyncratic interests of individuals like Jamie into account, or it will be of no account at all" (Bérubé 1996, 248). But I like Nussbaum's version better, for two reasons. First, she's much better than I am at getting the liberal political tradition on the same page with Amartya Sen's capabilities approach and Aristotle's sense of people as social animals. Second, she doesn't make the foolish mistake I made in the closing pages of my book, namely, resting part of the argument on the capacity for reciprocal recognition. For as parents of children with autism have (gently) pointed out to me, my argument reinstates a performance criterion for being human. And any performance criterion—independence, rationality, capacity for mutual cooperation, even capacity for mutual recognition—will leave some mother's child behind. It will create a residuum of the abject, a fraction of the human family that is to be left out of the accounting. Faced with that prospect, it is not enough to say that we should presume competence when confronted by cognitive disability: because sooner or later we will have to come to terms with people who truly are incapable of understanding what it means to come to terms. And then will we write them into the social contract, or will we write them off?

At this point, I can imagine someone suggesting that this desire to include all humans in a theory of justice is hopelessly utopian. The United States doesn't even provide health care to all its citizens, and its health "system" ties health *insurance* to employment even though so many people with disabilities are unemployed; the country has managed to pass a national disability rights law, but its courts rule against disabled plaintiffs more than 95 percent of the time. That is the social backdrop against which Nussbaum and I offer the spectacle of a philosopher and a literary critic picking apart various ways of realizing the human dignity of people with severe and profound cognitive disabilities. As a practical matter, we face the overwhelming temptation to say, in the face of stark social injustice, that the social-contract tradition is *good enough*. It may not cover everyone—and here the structural analogy to debates over universal health care is directly apposite—but it covers *almost* everyone, and that should suffice for now. Surely, if you asked people with disabilities (and their advocates and guardians) if they would consent to be governed by a U.S. administration that operated according to the Difference Principle, which permits inequalities in the distribution of goods only if those inequalities benefit the least well-off, they would take the deal and do so happily. And to the objections lodged by Kittay, Sen, and Nussbaum—that Rawls privileges people with "sufficient intellectual powers to play a normal part in society" (Rawls 1980, 546), defers consideration of disability to the legislative phase, and calibrates the difference principle by means of a reductive, unidimensional reliance on wealth as the measure of well-being—many reasonable people might respond with the famous final line of Billy Wilder's *Some Like It Hot*: well, nobody's perfect. Better to have *some* people with disabilities provided with reasonable accommodation while philosophers and literary critics argue about how to design ideal deck chairs for people with disabilities on a hypothetically egalitarian ocean liner that hasn't been built yet. Anything remotely well-meaning will do—justice as fairness, spheres of justice, frontiers of justice, *they're all good*. We'll take any form of justice at all, just so long as it shores up this eviscerated neoliberal welfare state.

I mention "spheres of justice" because Nussbaum's critiques of Rawls sent me back to Michael Walzer's book of that name, which critiques Rawls from quite another angle. For Walzer, "there is no single set of primary or basic goods conceivable across all moral and material worlds—or, any such set would have to be conceived in terms so abstract that they would be of little use in thinking about particular distributions" (Walzer 1983, 8). Accordingly, Walzer argues that "the principles of justice are themselves pluralistic in form; that different social goods ought to be distributed for different reasons, in accordance with different procedures, by different agents; and that all these differences derive from different understandings of the social goods themselves—the inevitable product of historical and cultural particularism" (Walzer 1983, 6). Nussbaum does not address Walzer's pluralistic account of justice in *Frontiers of Justice*, and Walzer, for his part, says next to nothing about disability. But there's a critical resonance between these spheres and frontiers; in his closing pages, Walzer writes: "'One citizen/ one vote' is the functional equivalent, in the sphere of politics, of the rule against exclusion and degradation in the sphere of welfare, of the principle of equal consideration in the sphere of office, and of the guarantee of a school place for every child in the sphere of education. It is the foundation of all distributive activity and the inescapable framework within which choices have to be made" (Walzer 1983, 305–6). Needless to say, this has interesting implications for Nussbaum's argument about surrogacy. Still, I imagine that Nussbaum would reject Walzer's account precisely because of its deference with regard to historical and cultural particularism; what is wanted, after all, in the capabilities approach is a *universal* theory of the conditions for human flourishing, one that can achieve what Nussbaum calls "an *overlapping consensus* among citizens who otherwise have different comprehensive views" (Nussbaum 2006, 163). And yet Nussbaum wants to make ample room for the "private," idiosyncratic interests of individuals; it is, notably, the reason she favors "capability" over "functioning" with regard to most social goods—because it allows people to choose *not* to make use of all their rights. In the chapter included in this collection, Nussbaum writes: "Even in pursuit of a decent social minimum we need to ask when a decent minimum of respect for persons requires full equality of the relevant capabilities and when it requires only something like adequacy"; similarly, in *Frontiers of Justice*, she wrote: "With items such as political participation, religious functioning, and play, it seems obvious that it is the capability or opportunity to engage in such activities that is the appropriate social goal. To dragoon all citizens into functioning in these ways would be dictatorial and illiberal. . . . Only in the area of self-respect and dignity itself do I think that actual functioning is the appropriate aim of public policy" (Nussbaum 2006, 171–72). The problem here—and it is hardly unique to Nussbaum or to Walzer—is how to reconcile equality with freedom in our conceptions of justice, and in what areas of human life one values equality more than freedom (or vice versa) and why. And I want to stress that this isn't simply a matter of redistributing goods and resources so as to make life better for people with disabilities; it isn't simply a question of pitting *their* claims to equality over against *our* claims to freedom. On the contrary, as Nussbaum's preference for capability over functioning suggests, we need a theory of justice that can accommodate (to cite my very favorite essay subtitle in all of academe) the rights of people with developmental disabilities to eat too many donuts and take a nap. In other words, promoting the equality of people with developmental disabilities also involves promoting their freedom, which may also involve promoting their freedom to make some unhealthy choices, which might in turn pose some troubling ethical questions for their legal guardians.

Which brings me to my polemical conclusion. I'd like to end where Nussbaum did, on the question of surrogacy and guardianship—and I'd like to point out that her argument here poses a challenge not only for moral philosophy but also for disability studies. It's about time disability studies started reexamining a few of its founding premises—including what is arguably *the* founding premise, the "social model" of disability that sees disability as an effect of built environments and social relations rather than as a matter of individual bodies and minds. Tom Shakespeare, one of the people responsible for elaborating the social model in the United Kingdom, recently wrote that the social model "has now become a barrier to further progress" (Shakespeare 2006, 202) in advancing disability rights—partly because it fails to account adequately for people with cognitive disabilities. It is easier, in other words, to speak of a "barrier-free environment" when one is speaking of wheelchairs and ramps than when one is speaking of significant cognitive disabilities. Shakespeare's argument may be overdrawn or premature, for all the instruments agree that most people and most social institutions haven't yet *gotten to* the social model of disability; but then, recognizing the limits of that model is not an argument for jettisoning it altogether. Relatedly, disability studies in the United States has drastically undertheorized surrogacy and guardianship, emphasizing the self-representation of people with disabilities and overlooking the position of people with disabilities whose only substantial hope of representation lies in having their wishes—insofar as we can know their wishes—represented by another. The reasons for this undertheorization are numerous: disability studies theorists have tended subtly to emphasize physical over cognitive disabilities, particularly severe cognitive disabilities, in part because you don't find a lot of people with severe cognitive disability holding academic positions; autonomy and self-representation remain an alluring ideal even (or especially) for people with disabilities; too strong an emphasis on guardianship seems to entail the further infantilization of people with cognitive disabilities; and in my wing of the humanities, where we have been post-something for quite some time, we are still too accustomed to think in terms of the "indignity of speaking for others," as Gilles Deleuze put it in an oft-cited interview with Michel Foucault (Foucault 1977, 209). We are, as a result, too reluctant to acknowledge that with regard to people with severe cognitive disabilities, the surest way of recognizing their dignity is to recognize their guardians as people with the right and the responsibility of speaking for others. If those of us in disability studies are to meet the challenge of cognitive disability, then, we will need to think harder about the limits of the social model—and we will need to think more seriously about the roles of guardians.

The problems with this polemical conclusion should be obvious. For who wants to return to the politics of paternalism? Perhaps, to some scholars in disability studies and some disability-rights advocates, an emphasis on surrogacy and the ethics of guardianship seems to cede too much ground, or to threaten to return us to the days of institutionalization and worse—when, for example, every well-meaning parent understood that involuntary sterilization was the best course of action with regard to their children with cognitive disabilities. Certainly, no one advocates involuntary sterilization as an ethical form of guardianship today. But as was recently demonstrated by the case of Ashley, the "pillow angel" whose parents asked doctors to devise a series of treatments to keep their daughter sexually immature and small in size, there is no consensus as to what constitutes an ethical form of guardianship with regard to children with severe disabilities. I will permit myself but one brief comment on this exceptionally difficult case: one could hardly imagine a more mystifying and infantilizing term than "pillow angel," which has led many observers to conclude that Ashley's parents are acting out of a paternalism that is both vicious and maudlin at once, as if they seek to render their child a kind of Hummel figurine. But when one learns that Ashley's parents were primarily concerned about bedsores and mobility, with regard to Ashley's size, and concerned about Ashley's susceptibility to rape, with regard to her sterilization, the picture becomes considerably more complicated, and the possibility arises that the parents were indeed acting out of a good-faith attempt to imagine Ashley's best interests.

My own situation with Jamie is far less complex; it partakes merely of the ordinary perplexity attending any parent-child relationship. For example: at one point during the cognitive disability conference at which Nussbaum and I presented our papers, Jamie suggested that I hire a limousine to take us to Times Square so that we could play in the arcade at ESPN Zone. (Jamie does not usually have such extravagant tastes; he requested a limo only because it's a form of transportation he's never taken.) I refused this request, just as I refuse any number of less bizarre requests every day. For it is one thing to support, in theory, the right of people with developmental disabilities to eat too many donuts and take a nap; it is quite another to permit your teenager with Down syndrome to drink four cans of soda in the space of two hours. When Jamie did so, at the age of thirteen (admitting, because he is as honest as the day is long, that the four cans in the basement trash were indeed all his), his parents spoke sharply to him and instituted a "two-soda" rule that Jamie has since internalized to the point at which he now refuses soda refills at restaurants whenever he knows he's already consumed his quota for the day. More seriously, we have had to make medical decisions for Jamie—no major crises, just treatments for very crooked teeth, in one case, and pneumonia, in another—without taking his wishes into consideration. Such are the perils of paternalism for any parent, which is why some of the most difficult cases in American law involve parents who seek to withhold medical treatment for their children on religious grounds; but the ethical stakes are a bit higher still when one is dealing with children with developmental disabilities, for whom paternalism seems at once vitally necessary and potentially dangerous.

And when those children grow up, when they attain some forms of legal maturity, how are their surrogates to proceed? What kind of political and civil rights can we hope to realize for them? It is here that I'd like to take some distance from Nussbaum's formulation of this question. For while I agree with Nussbaum about surrogacy voting, and with Walzer that the principle of one person, one vote "is the foundation of all distributive activity and the inescapable framework within which choices have to be made," I do not agree that Jamie is an "easy" case when it comes to jury service. I remarked above that his understanding of the concepts of "guilt" and "innocence" was enhanced wonderfully by the Harry Potter series, most notably by the revelation, in *Harry Potter and the Prisoner of Azkaban*, that Sirius Black was framed and wrongfully imprisoned for thirteen years, and that Peter Pettigrew was in fact responsible for the betrayal of Harry's parents and the murder of a dozen innocent people. But I am not confident that Jamie is capable of applying this insight in a court of law. More specifically (and after discussing the matter repeatedly with Jamie and his mother), I have serious doubts as to whether Jamie can attend carefully, over the course of many hours, to the details of a trial proceeding; he is capable of sitting through academic lectures of sixty to ninety minutes, but would not do well in a setting that demands his sustained and undivided attention for a full day—over a series of days. Nor am I confident, quite apart from my reservations with regard to Jamie's attention span, that he is capable of understanding the nuances of the law, whether the case is a traffic accident or the murder of a dozen innocent people; the difference between manslaughter and murder, for example, like the various degrees of murder, seems to elude him. (I mention his attention span first and his comprehension of the law second because this corresponds to his responses to my questions: he was intrigued by the possibility of being on a jury and adjudicating guilt and innocence until he learned that it entailed sitting in a courtroom all day.) It is possible, of course, that a surrogate could explain such things to Jamie each day, as the need arose, and if Jamie had paid careful attention to the court proceedings he might learn something over the course of the trial about criminal and civil procedure. But this seems to me fertile ground for misunderstanding—and, very likely, for a mistrial.

More important, I am not convinced that jury duty should occupy quite so prominent a place in Nussbaum's argument. The idea that the interests of cognitively disabled adults should be expressed by the votes of guardians and surrogates seems unassailable to me, and an important means of combating everyone and everything that would seek to deny people with cognitive disabilities the full status of political personhood; but I do not see why jury service should be number 2 on the list. Jamie's most pressing needs as a citizen, once he turns twenty-one and is no longer eligible for the support services he now enjoys, will involve employment and health care; he will very likely need a job coach for the first and a knowledgeable guardian to manage the second. Jamie is very fortunate to have a mother who is both a Ph.D. and an R.N., a former cardiac intensive-care nurse; but as Nussbaum would surely agree, his access to quality health care should not depend on such happy accidents of birth. And although I strongly believe that Jamie would make a wonderful employee at an aquarium or zoo, and is capable not only of informing visitors about various shark species but also, possibly, of assisting with animal training and feeding, I know he will need assistance to stay on task and to establish a work routine. I have always hoped that Jamie would be his own best representative, and in many ways—as the people who have met him can attest—he is. But even as my wife and I, and his teachers, try to enhance his independent living skills (making his own breakfast, shopping for food, getting ready for bed), we know that in some contexts he will always need a little help from his friends and a little kindness from strangers. In that respect, we worry less about Jamie's prospects as a juror than about Jamie's access to employment and health care; and we note that despite the virtues of the Americans with Disabilities Act, these aspects of Jamie's life are much less secure—and his access to these social goods much more contested—than Nussbaum's argument suggests.

Postscript: Exchange with Peter Singer

On September 29, 2008, I restarted my personal blog by posting a few brief excerpts from this essay (Bérubé 2008b), along with an account of the "Cognitive Disability: A Challenge to Moral Philosophy" conference as a whole; I also cross-posted the account to the academic group blog *Crooked Timber* (Bérubé 2008a). Within about six weeks, Peter Singer wrote by e-mail to say he'd come across my blog post; he said he was delighted to hear that my son Jamie has a wide range of abilities, intrigued to learn that Jamie understands a range of theories about why humans eat some animals and not others, but sorry that neither Jamie nor I appreciate Woody Allen movies—though he admitted that the recent ones have been disappointing.

But Singer wrote chiefly to take issue with the idea that my reply to his discussion of Down syndrome in *Rethinking Life and Death* constitutes a decisive rebuttal of that discussion, for it takes more than a couple of exceptional children here and there to challenge the general rule. After all, Singer's passage speaks of expectations, and although people do win the lottery now and again, it would be unreasonable to buy a lottery ticket and expect to win. Singer then asked me to direct him to some evidence that would indicate that Jamie is not anomalous—and, he said, this is not an idle challenge: if he is mistaken about Down syndrome, he will correct himself in the future.

I wrote back a few days later. And then, after we'd exchanged another round of e-mails, I asked Singer if it would be all right with him if I posted my initial reply (but not his initial e-mail) as a follow-up blog post.[1] I believe it's important to go public with arguments about what we can and can't expect from people with Down syndrome, because those expectations play such a large role in debates over prenatal testing, reproductive rights, and "selective" abortion.

This was my reply:

Dear Professor Singer,

Many thanks for noticing that blog post, and for taking the time to write. Thanks also for your kind words about Jamie. I do, in fact, enjoy a handful of Woody Allen movies here and there; *Broadway Danny Rose* is a wonderful piece of work, and I'm fond of *Bullets over Broadway* as well. But I do think "we cannot expect a child with Down syndrome to chat with us about the latest Woody Allen film" instates a distinctly Upper West Side-y performance criterion, and is worth critiquing on those grounds alone. More seriously, I note that in the 1920s we were told that people with Down syndrome were incapable of learning to speak; in the 1970s, we were told that people with Down syndrome were incapable of learning how to read. OK, so now the rationale for seeing these people as somewhat less than human is their likely comprehension of Woody Allen films. Twenty years from now we'll be hearing "sure, they get Woody Allen, but only his early comedies—they completely fail to appreciate the breakthrough of *Interiors*." Surely you understand my

---

[1] Of course, I didn't have to ask permission to post my own words, but I don't believe in replying to someone's private e-mail by making a blog post out of it (even if I don't publish the contents of the e-mail). Singer thanked me for asking, noting that some people would have simply gone ahead and posted his letter along with the reply. I acknowledged that I've dealt with some of those people (that's one reason why I eventually got a blog of my own).

sense that the goalposts are being moved around here in a rather arbitrary fashion.

I do appreciate the fact that you're not issuing an idle challenge. I don't think you would do that. I have three responses to it.

The first is nitpicky, and has to do with the meaning of "we cannot expect." You apparently take your phrase to mean "we have no reason to expect" X, any more than we can expect to win the lottery. I take it to mean—and, unfortunately, all too many people take it to mean—that a child with Down syndrome *will not be able* to do any of the things you mention. (This matters, of course, when it comes to the kind of information prospective parents receive after getting a positive result on an amniocentesis.) I think there's all the difference in the world between saying "we cannot expect" and "we should not expect"; the former suggests absolute certainty, and the latter suggests the kind of probabilism you want to convey. Accordingly, I take the former to be falsifiable by any person with Down syndrome who demonstrates one of the abilities you say we cannot expect him or her to have. If you do want to revise the passage ever so slightly, you could always say, "there will no doubt be exceptions that prove the rule, but as a rule, we should not expect etc."

The second is more substantial. The larger point of my argument with your claim is that we cannot (I use the term advisedly) know what to expect of children with Down syndrome. Early-intervention programs have made such dramatic differences in their lives over the past few decades that we simply do not know what the range of functioning looks like, and therefore do not rightly know what to expect. That, Professor Singer, is the real challenge of being a parent of a child with Down syndrome: it's not just a matter of contesting other people's low expectations of your child, it's a matter of recalibrating your own expectations time and time again—and not only for your own child, but for Down syndrome itself. I'll never forget the first time I saw a young man with Down syndrome playing the violin—quite competently, at that, with delicacy and a sense of nuance. I thought I was seeing a griffin. And who could have imagined, just forty or fifty years ago, that the children we were institutionalizing and leaving to rot could in fact grow up to become actors? Likewise, I recently remarked to Jamie, on our way to an appointment at which we would arrive a bit late, that time is so strange that nobody really understands it, that we can't touch it or see it even though we watch the passing of every day, and that it only goes forward like an arrow, and Jamie brightly replied, "except with Hermione's Time-Turner in Harry Potter." I was so stunned I nearly crashed the car. I take issue with your passage, then, not because I'm a sentimental fool or because I believe that one child's surprising accomplishments suffice to win the argument, but because as we learn more about Down syndrome, we honestly—if paradoxically—don't know what constitutes a "reasonable expectation" for a person with Down syndrome.

The third goes to the premise of your argument. You're looking for things people with Down syndrome can't do, and I'm looking for things they can. We each have our reasons, of course. But I don't accept the premise that cognitive capacity is a useful criterion for reading some people out of the human community, any more than you would accept the premise that we should grant rights to animals on the basis of whether humans think they do or don't taste good with barbeque sauce. I stand by what I said at the end of that September 29 blog post: I hope we have learned enough from our own history to understand why it's a bad idea to read anyone out of the human community. (This doesn't mean, by the way, that we have to extend life support to people like Terri Schiavo against the wishes of their legal guardians. One point of my remarks about surrogates and guardians, in my response to Martha Nussbaum's talk, was to challenge people in the disability-rights community who would strip guardians of the right to determine whether their charges would in fact want to be sustained in such fashion.) Better, I think, to add some animals to the category of rights-bearing entities without kicking any humans out. It needn't be a zero-sum affair.

Oh yes, evidence that might change your mind if the above paragraphs won't. The National Down Syndrome Society is full of useful information about what we can and can't expect, and online, the Riverbend Down Syndrome Parent Support Group is an amazing resource for everything from research on language and math skills of people with DS. Finally, there's the book *Count Us In* by Jason Kingsley and Mitchell Levitz (1994). The book includes, among many other things, one of Jason's high-school essays, written when he was seventeen; the topic is his mother's obstetrician, who in 1974 had advised the Kingsley family to institution-alize Jason because he would never grow up to have a "meaningful thought." Of this obstetrician Jason writes:

> He never imagined how I could write a book! I will send him a copy ... so he'll know. I will tell him that I play the violin, that I make relationships with other people, I make oil paintings, I play the piano, I can sing, I am competing in sports, in the drama group, that I have many friends and I have a full life.
>
> So I want the obstetrician who will never say that to any parent to have a baby with a disability any more. If you send a baby with a disability to an institution, the baby will miss all the opportunities to grow and to learn ... and also to receive a diploma. The baby will miss relationships and love and independent living skills. ...
>
> I am glad that we didn't listen to the obstetrician. ... He will never discriminate with people with disabilities again.
>
> And then he will be a better doctor.
>
> (Kingsley and Levitz 1994, 28)

Anecdotal evidence—but good to think with, all the same. And just for the record, Jason's not the young man I saw playing the violin.

All best wishes,

Michael Bérubé

References

Bérubé, Michael. 1996. *Life as We Know It: A Father, a Family, and an Exceptional Child*. New York: Pantheon.

———. 2006. "Was I Ever Wrong." In *Rhetorical Occasions: Essays on Humans and the Humanities*, 328–32. Chapel Hill: University of North Carolina Press.

———. 2008a. "More Untimely Stuff About Disability." *Crooked Timber*. Blog. 29 Sept. http://crookedtimber.org/2008/09/29/more-untimely-stuff-about-disability/ (last accessed 15 Mar. 2009).

———. 2008b. "Wandering Back In." *American Airspace*. Blog. 29 Sept. http://www.michaelberube.com/index.php/weblog/wandering_back_in/ (last accessed 15 Mar. 2009).

Foucault, Michel. 1977. "Intellectuals and Power." In *Language, Counter-Memory, Practice*, edited by Donald Bouchard, translated by Donald Bouchard and Sherry Simon, 205–17. Ithaca: Cornell University Press.

Kingsley, Jason, and Mitchell Levitz. 1994. *Count Us In: Growing Up with Down Syndrome*. New York: Houghton Mifflin.

Nussbaum, Martha. 2009. "The Capabilities of People with Disabilities." Essay included in this collection.

———. 2001. "Disabled Lives: Who Cares?" *New York Review of Books*, 11 Jan., 34–37.

———. 2006. *Frontiers of Justice: Disability, Nationality, Species Membership*. Cambridge, Mass.: Harvard University Press.

Rawls, John. 1980. "Kantian Constructivism in Moral Theory: The Dewey Lectures." *Journal of Philosophy* 77:515–71.

Singer, Peter. 1994. *Rethinking Life and Death: The Collapse of Our Traditional Ethics*. New York: St. Martin's Griffin.

Shakespeare, Tom. 2006. "The Social Model of Disability." *The Disability Studies Reader*, 2nd edition, edited by Lennard Davis, 197–204. New York: Routledge.

Walzer, Michael. 1983. *Spheres of Justice: A Defense of Pluralism and Equality*. New York: Basic Books.

6

RESPECTING HUMAN DIGNITY:
CONTRACT VERSUS CAPABILITIES

CYNTHIA A. STARK

One idea commonly associated with liberal justice is the idea of justifiability to all. This is the notion that just political principles are those that can be justified to all who are subject to those principles. Underlying this notion is an assumption about the nature of citizens: they are regarded as capable of being justified to. To be so capable, they must be able to understand and act for reasons. Indeed, this ability is not only required for individuals to comprehend justifications, it also stands as the normative ground for the requirement that they be *given* a justification. In liberal theory, one's ability to act for reasons—one's "rational agency"—is regarded as valuable. It is something that should be nurtured and cherished. It gives one a special worth or status, often called "dignity," which renders one inviolable. This inviolability places restrictions upon coercion. In the political realm, it places restrictions upon state coercion. The idea is, because one's rational agency is valuable and should be preserved, one harms someone if one forces her to act against her own reasons. By subjecting her, then, *only* to political authority that she has reason to accept, one refrains from such harm and hence from violating her dignity. It follows that political principles are just only in the case where they can be justified to everyone subject to their authority.

The idea of justifiability to all is typically expressed through the device of the social contract. By establishing which political principles appropriately idealized agents would "contract for" under appropriately idealized circumstances, social contract theories tell us which principles actual citizens have reason to accept, and hence which principles are just.[1] The general idea, absent many important details, is that individuals have reason to accept political principles that they would choose if they were reasonable, rational, informed of all relevant facts, and shielded from all irrelevant facts.

The ideal of justification I have described is in tension with another ideal, which says that all members of society are owed justice regardless of

---

[1] Some have argued that this method of justification fails. See Dworkin 1989. For a critique of Dworkin, see Stark 2000.

whether they are or ever will be capable of rational agency. By associating justice with justifiability to all, and confining the "all" to rational agents, social contract theory seems to imply that only rational agents are subjects of justice.[2] Hence it seems to imply either that severely cognitively impaired adults with a limited rational capacity are not owed justice or that what they *are* owed as a matter of justice is a derivative issue.[3] There seems to be a conflict, then, between social contract theory's standard of justification and our judgment that severely cognitively impaired individuals are equal subjects of justice.

In light of these considerations, Martha Nussbaum has argued that we should abandon social contract theory in favor of the capabilities view (Nussbaum 2006, 24–25). One advantage of the capabilities view, according to Nussbaum, is that it does not use the social contract apparatus in order to fulfill the liberal standard of justification. Nussbaum's approach to dissolving the tension I described above is to excise one of the aspects of liberalism that is responsible for the exclusion of the severely cognitively impaired— the social contract and its attendant view of the citizen—and to assign the work done by the social contract—establishing justifiability to all—to another theoretical mechanism, namely, the possibility of "overlapping consensus."

My argument is that Nussbaum's approach does not adequately fulfill the liberal principle of justification.[4] This constitutes a weakness in her proposal for dissolving the tension described above. Hence we have reason to look for a different way to ensure the full inclusion of the severely cognitively impaired under the umbrella of liberal justice.

I begin by briefly summarizing Nussbaum's capabilities view. I then outline Rawls's account of political justification as background for understanding Nussbaum's account of political justification, which draws heavily upon Rawls.[5] Then, after explaining Nussbaum's own account, I set out to assess what she loses by discarding the social contract mechanism. What she loses, I argue, is the ability of her theory fully to

---

[2] The issue is in fact more complicated. As Barry (1989) and Nussbaum (2006) have argued, Rawls's social contract theory excludes the cognitively impaired also by its reliance upon Hume's account of the circumstances of justice, upon the idea of justice as mutual advantage and upon the assumption that all citizens are fully cooperating members of society. Nussbaum also argues that the contractarian's view of the citizen as "free, equal and independent" is troublesome from the point of view of including the cognitively impaired. See also Hartley 2009, Hartley forthcoming, Stark 2007, and Stark 2009.

[3] See Nussbaum 2006 and Kittay 1999. For an argument that Rawlsian contractarianism does not have this implication, see Freeman 2006, Curaton 2008, and Wong 2009,which is included in this collection. See also Wong 2007 and Wong unpublished.

[4] For discussion of whether or not Nussbaum's view is in fact a type of liberalism (or if it is, what type it is), see Barclay 2003, Cudd 2004, and Phillips 2001. See also Nussbaum 2003a.

[5] For a critique of Nussbaum's approach to justification, see Okin 2003. For Nussbaum's response, see Nussbaum 2004.

recognize human dignity.[6] As long as the inherent worth of human beings who are capable of rationality is partly grounded in this capability—as Nussbaum thinks it is—the requirement of justifiability to all is binding.[7] This requirement cannot be fulfilled by establishing the possibility of overlapping consensus, I argue; and so, we have a reason to retain the social contract apparatus.

Justifying the Capabilities Approach

Summary of the Capabilities View

Like John Rawls's account, from which she borrows, Nussbaum's view of political justification is subtle and complex, as is the theory of justice she seeks to justify. The fundamentals of that theory are these. At the theory's center is a list of ten human capabilities. These are regarded as entitlements and are to provide the basis for political principles, which, in turn, are to provide the basis for constitutional guarantees (Nussbaum 2000, 35; 2003b, 40; 2006, 70). The list includes such items as being able to live to the end of a human life of normal length, being able to move freely from place to place, being able to be free from sexual assault, being able to use imagination and thought in connection with experiencing and producing works and events of one's own choice, being able to have attachments to things and people outside of ourselves, being able to form a conception of the good and to engage in critical reflection about the planning of one's life, having the social bases of self-respect and nonhumiliation, being able to live in relation to the world of nature, and so forth (2000, 78–80; 2003b, 41–42; 2006, 76–80).[8]

The capabilities approach, Nussbaum says, represents a minimal theory of justice—governments are required at least to ensure a threshold level of capabilities for each citizen.[9] The approach is silent on, for example, issues of distributive justice that arise once the threshold has been met (2000, 75). Though the view is outcome-oriented, rather than proceduralist, it is nonaggregative (2006, 82). What must be secured is a threshold level of capabilities for each citizen—total or average capability levels are not the goal. Moreover, trade-offs among the capabilities are not permitted (2000, 74; 2006, 85). One cannot reach the minimum threshold by having, for instance, an abundance of opportunity to live in relation to nature, while enjoying no freedom of movement. Underlying Nussbaum's prohibition on aggregation and trade-offs is a conception of the human being as an end

---

[6] Nussbaum defends her account of human dignity in Nussbaum 2008. See also Weithman 2008.

[7] Some have argued that the inherent worth of human beings does not depend at all upon the capacity for rationality. See, for example, Kittay 2005.

[8] The list has been modified over time.

[9] For a critique of the sufficientarian aspect of Nussbaum's view, see Arneson 2006.

(2000, 74). Human beings, on Nussbaum's account, have dignity. This status, however, is grounded not merely in our rational agency but in our animality as well (2006, 159–60).

Rawls's Approach to Political Justification

Let us look, now, at Rawls's account of political justification.[10] His view has three components: the device of the social contract, the idea of an overlapping consensus, and the method of reflective equilibrium. Consider, first, the social contract. Rawls claims that whatever principles would be chosen by parties regarded solely as free and equal persons in circumstances that are fair, are just (1999a, 310). (Hence "justice as fairness" as the label for his view.) Rawls models this criterion by means of the "original position"—his version of the classical contractarian's state of nature. The parties in the original position deliberate behind a "veil of ignorance" that deprives them of certain knowledge, such as their class position and natural abilities, in order to ensure that the agreement reached, upon principles of justice, is not affected by social fortune or natural accident.

Rawls argues that the parties to the original position would choose two principles of justice for distributing "primary social goods"—goods that all citizens need, despite their differences, as free and equal persons (1993, 180).[11] Roughly, the first principle mandates a wide distribution of equal rights and liberties. The second mandates that differences in wealth be permitted only if they, first, arise under conditions of fair equality of opportunity and, second, maximally benefit the least well off (1971, 302–3).

Now consider the idea of an overlapping consensus. Once we have established which principles are just, we must determine whether or not the conception of justice containing those principles is stable. That is, can a society governed by that conception reproduce itself over time? One aspect of this problem concerns whether a conception of justice can be supported by all citizens given the "fact of reasonable pluralism"—given, that is, that citizens in democratic cultures tend to hold a variety of incompatible but reasonable "comprehensive doctrines"—views about the good, about the meaning of life, and so on. Rawls argues that justice as fairness can be supported by the reasonable comprehensive doctrines likely to gain adherents in a democratic society. Each reasonable view can support justice as fairness for its own sake, or on its own merits (1993, 148). This type of support constitutes an overlapping consensus. Justice as fairness, on this account, is a "freestanding" view; it is not justified by appeal to any particular comprehensive doctrine. It is, as such, a "political conception" of justice.[12]

---

[10] I draw heavily here upon Freeman 2003, Scanlon 2003, and Neiman unpublished manuscript. See also Weinstock 1994.

[11] The primary goods include basic rights, liberties, opportunities, income, wealth, and the social bases of self-respect (1993, 5–6).

[12] For discussion of the plausibility of political liberalism, see Saenz unpublished.

Rawls distinguishes stability founded on an overlapping consensus from stability founded on a modus vivendi. The latter is a mere balance of power. The former, says Rawls, constitutes "stability for the right reasons" (1996, xxxix). A society characterized by an overlapping consensus of reasonable comprehensive doctrines meets the "liberal principle of legitimacy," which says, "the exercise of political power is fully proper only when it is exercised in accordance with a constitution the essentials of which all citizens as free and equal may reasonably be expected to endorse in the light of principles and ideals acceptable to their common human reason" (1993, 137).

Finally consider the method of reflective equilibrium (1971, 17–22, 46–53; 1999b, 288–90).[13] Rawls introduces this as a method for characterizing the contractual situation. He observes that the principles yielded by that situation will differ according to how that situation is described (1971, 17–18). So, one needs a justification for one's favored description. The method of reflective equilibrium fulfills this justificatory role. Briefly, it works as follows. Initially we describe the contractual situation by appeal to commonly shared presumptions about the conditions under which principles of justice should be chosen (1971, 18). (These presumptions include, for example, the idea that one should not be able to tailor principles to one's own particular circumstances.)

Next we determine what principles of justice are generated by this description of the initial situation. Then we check to see whether those principles account for our considered judgments about justice. These are judgments made with full information about the relevant facts, where one has no personal stake in the answer and is not distraught or otherwise distracted (1971, 47). They are judgments which tend to be stable over time and about which we are confident. And, they vary as to their degree of generality (1993, 28; 1999b, 289).

We seek to establish whether the principles produced by the choice situation capture the firmest of these judgments and give us guidance where our judgments are less certain. If they do not, we must revise. In doing so, we "work from both ends"—we can either modify the account of the initial situation or modify our considered judgments, conforming them to the principles given by the initial situation. Reflective equilibrium is achieved when we reach a description of the contractual situation that yields principles that match our considered judgments, duly modified (1971, 20). One achieves *wide* reflective equilibrium when one has determined what principles to accept after evaluating other plausible views and their supporting grounds (1993, 28; 1999b, 289).

Rawls conjectures that the original position is the contractual situation we would end up with if we were to achieve reflective equilibrium. That is, the principles generated by the original position are, compared to

---

[13] For discussion of this feature of Rawls's theory, see Daniels 1979.

principles that would be generated by some other choice situation, the ones that best match our considered judgments about justice.

Nussbaum's Approach to Political Justification

Nussbaum's view of political justification makes use, in modified and supplemented forms, of the ideas of overlapping consensus and of reflective equilibrium. The list of capabilities, she says, matches the intuitive ideas of truly human functioning and of human dignity. It specifies what is necessary for truly human functioning and so what is required to respect the dignity inherent in human beings as such (2000, 76–83; 2006, 70). The harmony between the list and our intuitions about human dignity represents, Nussbaum claims, a state of reflective equilibrium.[14] So, where Rawls introduces reflective equilibrium as a means for justifying his description of the contractual situation, Nussbaum relies on it as a method for justifying her list of capabilities. Furthermore, Nussbaum compares the capabilities approach to various types of subjective welfarism and to Rawlsian contractarianism, arguing that the capabilities approach better accounts for many of our firm considered judgments than do those views. This comparison is designed to reach toward *wide* reflective equilibrium (2000, 111–66; 2006, 9–153).[15]

Ancillary to justification through reflective equilibrium are considerations based upon informed desire. The content of the list of capabilities is determined not only by appeal to considered judgments but also by discussion with others—academics and lay persons from a variety of cultures. The list is, in part, a compilation of what people want, where their wants have been subjected to a certain kind of screening to prevent the influence of adaptive preferences.[16] (For instance, Nussbaum draws upon discussions with women *in women's groups that affirm the values of equal dignity and nonhierarchy* (2000, 151).) So, the list of capabilities is justified primarily by the fact that it is in harmony with our considered judgments about justice but also by the fact that it reflects people's informed desires.

The list represents a *stable* conception of justice, Nussbaum claims, because it can be the object of an overlapping consensus. Indeed, where Rawls claims that justice as fairness can be the object of an overlapping consensus within one society, Nussbaum asserts that her list of capabilities can be the object of overlapping consensus across national boundaries. Like justice as fairness, the list of capabilities is not derived from

---

[14] It is evident that Nussbaum thinks that our intuitions about human dignity are very firm and so not likely to be given up in the effort to achieve reflective equilibrium. She claims, for instance, that the idea of truly human functioning is "intuitively powerful" (2000, 101).

[15] Nussbaum does not use the phrase "wide reflective equilibrium." However, her description of the method of reflective equilibrium suggests that she has wide notion in mind. She characterizes reflective equilibrium as follows: "[W]e lay out the arguments for a given theoretical position, holding it up against the 'fixed points' in our moral intuitions; we see how those intuitions both test and are tested by the conceptions we examine" (2000, 101).

[16] For an account of adaptive preferences, see Nussbaum 2003b, 34.

any particular comprehensive doctrine—instead, as we saw, it comes from the intuitive idea of human dignity. This idea, says Nussbaum, has deep cross-cultural and transnational resonance (2000, 72). The fact that the list has been shaped through transnational discussion further shows that it can be accepted by people with widely differing comprehensive doctrines (2000, 76, 151). In keeping with Rawls, then, Nussbaum justifies her account of justice by arguing, first, that its normative imperatives match our considered judgments and, second, that it is stable in a way that meets the liberal principle of legitimacy.

Justification and the Value of Rational Agency

But what about the idea of justifiability to all? As we saw above, Rawls incorporates this idea though the social contract. He argues that *reflective equilibrium obtains when our considered judgments are balanced with principles that would be the outcome of a particular hypothetical choice situation.* It follows that "the most appropriate principles of justice" are, on Rawls's view, principles that can be justified to everyone. Having extracted the hypothetical choice situation from the overall framework of reflective equilibrium, it appears that Nussbaum has eliminated the idea that just principles must be justifiable to all who are governed by them and so has dispensed with a key feature of liberal justice.

At this point it may seem that I am begging the question against Nussbaum. Surely she can reject the idea of justifiability to all as a criterion of justice. Indeed, this is just what we might expect, since she rejects proceduralism (or at least *pure* proceduralism) in favor of a substantive good view of justice. Surely, then, it does not count as an argument *against* her to note that she has failed to use a particular *procedure* to justify her list of capabilities.

But things are not so simple, for Nussbaum is not prepared to abandon proceduralism completely, as her appeal to informed desire indicates, nor is she prepared to abandon the idea of reasonable agreement as a feature of justification (2000, 152–57; 2006, 153). Her theory, she says, uses the idea of rational acceptability common to social contract theories but locates it at a "rather different, and later, point in the theory" (2006, 68). So, it seems that she is indeed concerned to include the notion of justifiability to all in her account of political justification.

As I read her, she presents a two-pronged argument in response to proceduralist worries about her view. First, she argues that the capabilities approach converges in important ways with the contract approach, without relying on the contract (2006, 148, 153). So, perhaps the device of the contract is not as important as proceduralists think. Second, she argues that her view in fact captures the demand for justifiability to all through the idea of an overlapping consensus (2006, 153).

In what follows, I offer objections to both prongs of Nussbaum's argument. First, I show that the contract view, unlike the capabilities approach, allows us to capture fully the value of practical reason. It follows that the contract view better captures Nussbaum's own view of human dignity than does the capabilities approach. Second, I explain why displacing the justificatory work of the contract onto the notion of overlapping consensus cannot mitigate this problem.

Nussbaum emphasizes the similarities between her view and contractarianism in the context of discussing whether social contract theory can be modified to include the severely cognitively disabled (2006, 145–54). We need to answer this question because, if social contract theory can be so modified, then, given its strength, we may be wasting our time developing an alternative, such as the capabilities approach. What modifications of social contract theory would be necessary? Nussbaum argues that a suitably revised theory cannot, as Rawls's theory does, invoke the ideas of rough equality of ability, mutual advantage, or mutual independence. Nor can it, as Rawls's theory does, regard resources as the proper objects of distribution. Instead, it would have to include something like the list of capabilities. What would be *retained* is the hypothetical choice situation and the idea of individuals as ends in themselves—the former because we are looking for a form of contractarianism, and the latter because it grounds the justice claims of people with severe cognitive impairments.

It turns out, though, that the contract device forces us to adopt the problematic notion of the citizen as rational agent. This is because only rational agents can be parties to a contract, and, inasmuch as the parties are to represent citizens, it follows that only rational agents can be citizens. Those lacking the capacity for rationality are relegated to the margins of the theory. So, we must, in the end, reject contractarianism.

This is not a serious loss, suggests Nussbaum, because the capabilities approach contains much of what a revised contract theory would include. In other words, if we retain the strengths of social contract theory, and replace its weaknesses—the parts of the theory that exclude the severely cognitively impaired—with inclusive notions, we will end up with something that looks a lot like the capabilities view (2006, 153). The main difference, Nussbaum claims, is that the capabilities view approaches the question of justice "from a different vantage point," starting with a robust theory of the good and a more expansive account of the person (2006, 153).

Despite this postulated convergence between a suitably revised contractarianism and the capabilities view, it is still worth pressing, it seems to me, the question of whether we lose anything important when we eliminate the contract device so as to include the severely cognitively impaired. I claim that we do. The contract approach, unlike the capabilities approach, allows us to recognize fully the dignity of human beings who are capable of practical reasoning. In other words, by rejecting the contract apparatus in order to recognize the dignity of human beings who lack the capacity for practical reasoning, Nussbaum ends up with a view that fails to recognize fully the dignity of humans who possess the capacity for practical reasoning.

To see this, consider how Nussbaum's view pays tribute to the value of rational agency. The list of capabilities, remember, is given by our intuitions about human dignity in both its animal and its rational manifestations. One of the items on the list is the capacity for practical reasoning. So, in a just society, each person is guaranteed the freedom and opportunity to exercise this capacity to the extent that he has it. Moreover, this capacity enjoys a special status among the capabilities in that it constrains the shape of principles and policies designed to ensure any of the other capabilities (2000, 82). It is clear, then, that the *substance* of the capabilities approach mandates respect for the capacity for practical reasoning. And, to a limited degree, the *form* of the approach also exhibits this respect insofar as provisions for advancing the other capabilities must be compatible with advancing the capability for practical reasoning.

The manner in which the capabilities approach itself is *justified*, however, does not exhibit proper respect for practical reason. The list is simply laid out, as we saw, by the theorist, on the basis of intuitions about human dignity, along with a certain sort of empirical investigation— checking the list against people's actual informed desires. But if rational agency is indeed valuable—if it is a source of human dignity—it follows that political principles backed by coercion must be justifiable to those capable of rational agency. In other words, those individuals must be shown to have reason to abide by such principles; otherwise they are merely *subjected* to those principles. Their capacity for practical reason is, in this case, neglected, and their dignity is violated. It is not enough that the content of principles of justice respect the capacity for practical reasoning. The principles themselves must be justified in a way that respects that capacity. And so we need an approach, such as the social contract approach, that can establish which principles rational agents, as such, have reason to accept.

But perhaps none of this matters, for Nussbaum has the following argument to fall back on. The list of capabilities, she tells us, can be the object of an overlapping consensus. If that is so, then it can be the object of reasonable agreement. And if it can be the object of reasonable agreement, it is justified in a way that recognizes the value of rational agency (2000, 76; 2006, 163–64, 182). And so we can dispense with the contract apparatus at little or no cost. In fact we *should* dispense with it because of what we gain; we make liberalism inclusive of people with severe cognitive impairments.

I have two worries about this move. The first concerns the appropriate depth of an overlapping consensus. Is the appropriate focus of an overlapping consensus the principles endorsed by a conception of justice?

Or, is the appropriate focus the principles and the ideas that underlie them? Or, is the appropriate focus the principles, their underlying ideas and the conception's method? If it turns out that legitimacy requires overlapping consensus on principles of justice *and their justification*, then establishing that the list of capabilities (or the principles derived from it) can be the object of overlapping consensus cannot serve as a justification for the list, because the justification for the list must itself be the object of overlapping consensus. My second worry is that Nussbaum's appeal to overlapping consensus as a method of justification reintroduces the problem that the removal of the contract device was designed to solve, namely, the exclusion of severely cognitively impaired individuals from the domain of citizenship.

Consider, first, the issue of the appropriate depth of an overlapping consensus.[17] It is fairly clear from the text that Rawls takes the proper focus of overlapping consensus to be the whole of a conception of justice. He says, "[T]he consensus goes down to the fundamental ideas within which justice as fairness is worked out. It supposes agreement deep enough to reach such ideas as those of society as a fair system of cooperation and of citizens as reasonable and rational, and free and equal" (1993, 149). Rawls also says that forms of political liberalism (including justice as fairness) are constructivist conceptions. As such, they represent principles of justice as the outcome of a procedure of construction. In the case of justice as fairness, principles are represented as the outcome of the deliberation of the parties in the original position.

The constructivist aspect of justice and fairness (and other political liberalisms), says Rawls, is essential to the ability of justice as fairness (and other political liberalisms) to be the object of overlapping consensus. This is because political constructivism can be neutral about the truth of constructivism as a general metaethical position. Political constructivism, so as to be consistent with comprehensive doctrines that countenance a mind-independent moral order, does not say that the procedure of construction *produces* the order of moral values. Rather it claims "that its procedure represents an order of political values proceeding from the values expressed by the principles of practical reason, in union with conceptions of society and person, to the values expressed by certain principles of justice" (1993, 95). In other words, political constructivism can *represent* principles of justice as constructed without *denying* that they are *more than* constructed—that is, without denying that they may also correspond to an independent order of moral values.

Now, it makes sense that Rawls would hold that a conception of justice, and not merely its principles, must be the object of overlapping consensus. After all, in a society characterized by reasonable pluralism, people disagree not only about the truth or falsity of moral principles but also about the

---

[17] For discussion of this issue, see Hill 2000, 255, and Mandle 1999, 96–98.

metaphysical status of moral propositions and the proper way to justify those propositions. So, in order for reasonable people to agree on a political conception of justice, that conception must be amenable not merely to the moral substance of various comprehensive doctrines but to those doctrines' metaethical and justificatory commitments as well.

If a conception of justice as a whole is the proper focus of overlapping consensus, it follows that overlapping consensus, as least as Rawls understands and utilizes that idea, cannot serve to fully justify principles of justice. Those principles must be justified by appeal to a constructivist procedure that itself is the object of overlapping consensus. So, at least so far as she understands overlapping consensus along Rawlsian lines, Nussbaum cannot rely on overlapping consensus as method for justifying her list of capabilities.

Overlapping consensus is constituted, as we have seen, by reasonable agreement. Exactly what is involved in the notion of reasonableness, in this context, is a matter of debate.[18] Reasonableness is, however, in this context, bearing considerable weight: Rawls says, "[R]easonable persons will think it unreasonable to use political power, should they possess it, to repress comprehensive views that are not unreasonable, though different from their own" (1993, 60). So, "reasonable" applies to persons and to comprehensive doctrines.[19] The exact relationship between reasonable persons and those who hold reasonable comprehensive doctrines is also a matter of controversy (see Mandle 1999). This much is clear, however: reasonable persons tend to hold reasonable comprehensive doctrines. So, an overlapping consensus of reasonable comprehensive doctrines tends to be a consensus among reasonable persons.

A reasonable person, on Rawls's account, is one who is committed to the ideal of society as a fair system of cooperation among free and equal persons, who recognizes the "burdens of judgment," and who accepts the duty of civility (1993, 54). The details of this conception of a reasonable person are not important for my purposes. I merely wish to establish that severely cognitively impaired individuals are not reasonable persons in Rawls's sense; they lack the cognitive capabilities to be classed "reasonable." The idea of overlapping consensus, then, seems to rely, like the social contract, upon an ideal of the citizen as one who is capable of acting for reasons. But this ideal of the citizen is one of the features of social contract theory that, according to Nussbaum, leads that theory to neglect or demote the interests of the severely cognitively impaired. So, if the device of the contract and the mechanism of overlapping consensus essentially entail the same notion of the citizen, why does not the idea of overlapping consensus also exclude the interests of the severely cognitively impaired?

[18] For discussion of this issue see Boettcher 2004, Mandle 1999, and O'Neill 1997.

[19] It also applies to conceptions of justice and limits on the procedure of construction. See Mandle 1999. Rawls's account of reasonable comprehensive doctrines is at 1993, 59.

Perhaps the idea is this: because the "parties" to the overlapping consensus are not idealized as "disinterested," as are (typically) the parties to the social contract, many will take an interest in other people's interests. Hence they are in a position to ratify principles of justice that take account of the interests of, for example, cognitively impaired individuals. Where the contract device ensures that the group that chooses principles is identical with the group for whom the principles are chosen, the method of overlapping consensus, perhaps the reasoning goes, allows for the latter group to be more expansive (Nussbaum 2006, 137).[20]

This line of reasoning is not open to Nussbaum, however, because it invokes a notion of trusteeship that Nussbaum rejects in discussing possible modifications of social contract theory. Some have suggested that this theory could be made more inclusive if the parties to the contract were regarded as trustees for dependent members of society (Hartley 2009). Nussbaum sees two problems with this approach. First, it cannot adequately model equality: the interests of dependents is taken into account only because the parties represent members of society who happen to care about the interests of dependents, not because the dependents are "citizens with rights" who are "equal ends in themselves" (2006, 138).

Second, the trusteeship solution reinforces the Kantian split between the rational agent and the rest of nature. "[O]nly people with Kantian powers in their full-fledged normal form can be fully included, and party to the social contract." It follows that the interests of cognitively impaired individuals are, on the trusteeship view, "worthy of concern only derivatively, in relation to those parties interests" (2006, 138). "Are we not in effect saying," asks Nussbaum, "that the full range of human and animal powers will get support only insofar as it is an object of concern for Kantian rational beings? And doesn't this slight the dignity and worth that needy human animals surely possess?" (2006, 138).

As we can see, Nussbaum maintains that in the case where rational beings are charged with representing the interests of nonrational humans, the interests of nonrational humans are necessarily demoted. Consequently, the dignity of nonrational humans is slighted. Now, if this result precludes trusteeship in the case of the parties to the social contract, then it should also preclude trusteeship in the case of the "parties" to the overlapping consensus. The reasonable persons who accept the list of capabilities (or the principles it implies) cannot, then, accept the list (or the principles) on behalf of nonrational humans. If this is so, it is not clear how Nussbaum's reliance upon overlapping consensus renders her view more inclusive than social contract theory of the severely cognitively impaired.

---

[20] Thanks to Eva Kittay for pressing me on this point.

Conclusion

It is critical that we adjust liberal political theory so that it can address the claims of those whose capacity for rational agency is compromised. This is necessary to acknowledge the worth of such individuals, which worth obviously has a source other than their rational agency. We are ill advised, I have argued, to make this adjustment by rejecting the device of the social contract and placing the burden of justifiability to all on the idea of overlapping consensus. Such a modification will cause us to neglect the dimension of human dignity that *does* reside in the capacity for rational agency. Moreover, the resulting theory proves, in the end, to be no more inclusive of the cognitively impaired than is social contract theory. We should, then, find another way to widen the scope of liberal justice.[21]

Acknowledgments

I would like to thank Licia Carlson, Eva Kittay, and Christopher Lowry for helpful feedback on earlier versions of this chapter.

References

Arneson, Richard. 2006. "Distributive Justice and Basic Capability Equality: 'Good Enough' Is Not Good Enough." In *Capabilities Equality: Basic Problems and Issues*, edited by Alexander Kaufman, 17–43. New York: Routledge.

Barclay, Linda. 2003. "What Kind of Liberal Is Martha Nussbaum?" *Sats—Nordic Journal of Philosophy* 4, no. 2:5–24.

Barry, Brian. 1989. *Theories of Justice*. Los Angeles: University of California Press.

Boettcher, James W. 2004. "What Is Reasonableness?" *Philosophy and Social Criticism* 30, nos. 5–6:597–621.

Cohen, Andrew I. 2007. "Contractarianism, Other-Regarding Attitudes, and the Moral Standing of Nonhuman Animals." *Journal of Applied Philosophy* 24, no. 2:188–201.

Cudd, Anne E. 2004. "The Paradox of Liberal Feminism: Preference, Rationality and Oppression." In *Varieties of Feminist Liberalism*, edited by Amy R. Baehr, 37–62. Lanham, Md.: Rowman and Littlefield.

Curaton, Adam. 2008. "A Rawlsian Perspective on Justice for the Disabled." *Essays in Philosophy* 9, no. 1:1–27.

Daniels, Norman. 1979. "Wide Reflective Equilibrium and Theory Acceptance in Ethics." *Journal of Philosophy* 76, no. 5:256–62.

---

[21] I have offered a suggestion along these lines in Stark 2007. See also, Cohen 2007.

Dworkin, Ronald. 1989. "The Original Position." In *Reading Rawls*, edited by Norman Daniels, 16–53. Stanford: Stanford University Press.

Freeman, Samuel. 2003. "Congruence and the Good of Justice." In *The Cambridge Companion to Rawls*, edited by Samuel Freeman, 227–315. Cambridge: Cambridge University Press.

———. 2006. "Frontiers of Justice: The Capabilities Approach vs. Contractarianism." *Texas Law Review* 85:385–431.

Hartley, Christine. 2009. "Justice for the Disabled: A Contractualist Approach." *Journal of Social Philosophy* 40, no. 1:17–36.

———. Forthcoming. "An Inclusive Contractualism: Obligations to the Mentally Disabled." In *Disability and Disadvantage: Re-examining Topics in Moral and Political Philosophy*, edited by Kimberly Brownlee and Adam Cureton. Oxford: Oxford University Press.

Hill, Thomas E. Jr. 2000. *Respect, Pluralism and Justice: Kantian Perspectives*. Oxford: Oxford University Press.

Kittay, Eva Feder. 1999. *Love's Labor: Essays on Women, Equality and Dependency*. New York: Routledge.

———. 2005. "At the Margins of Moral Personhood." *Ethics* 116, no. 1:100–31.

Mandle, Jon. 1999. "The Reasonable in Justice as Fairness." *Canadian Journal of Philosophy* 29, no. 1:75–108.

Neiman, Paul. Unpublished manuscript. "Practical Reflective Equilibrium in Rawls's *A Theory of Justice*."

Nussbaum, Martha C. 2000. *Women and Human Development: The Capabilities Approach*. Cambridge: Cambridge University Press.

———. 2003a. "Political Liberalism and Respect: A Response to Linda Barclay." *Sats—Nordic Journal of Philosophy* 4, no. 2:25–44.

———. 2003b. "Capabilities as Fundamental Entitlements: Sen and Social Justice." *Feminist Economics* 9, nos. 2–3:33–59.

———. 2004. "On Hearing Women's Voices: A Reply to Susan Okin." *Philosophy and Public Affairs* 32, no. 2:193–205.

———. 2006. *Frontiers of Justice*. Cambridge, Mass.: Harvard University Press.

———. 2008. "Human Dignity and Political Entitlements." In *Human Dignity and Bioethics: Essays Commissioned by the President's Council on Bioethics*. Available at http://www.bioethics.gov/reports/human_dignity/chapter14.html

Okin, Susan Moller. 2003. "Poverty, Well-Being and Gender: What Counts? Who's Heard?" *Philosophy and Public Affairs* 31, no. 3:280–316.

O'Neill, Onora. 1997. "Political Liberalism and Public Reason: A Critical Notice of John Rawls *Political Liberalism*." *Philosophical Review* 106, no. 3:411–28.

Phillips, Anne. 2001. "Feminism and Liberalism Revisited: Has Martha Nussbaum Got It Right?" *Constellations* 8, no. 2:249–66.

Rawls, John 1971. *A Theory of Justice*. Cambridge, Mass.: Harvard University Press.

———. 1993. *Political Liberalism*. New York: Columbia University Press.

———. 1996. *Political Liberalism*, paperback edition. New York: Columbia University Press.

———. 1999a. "Kantian Constructivism in Moral Theory." In *John Rawls: Collected Papers*, edited by Samuel Freeman, 303–58. Cambridge, Mass.: Harvard University Press.

———. 1999b. "The Independence of Moral Theory." In *John Rawls: Collected Papers*, edited by Samuel Freeman, 286–302. Cambridge, Mass.: Harvard University Press.

Saenz, Carla. Unpublished manuscript. "Is Political Liberalism Plausible?"

Scanlon, T. M. 2003. "Rawls on Justification." In *The Cambridge Companion to Rawls*, edited by Samuel Freeman, 139–67. Cambridge: Cambridge University Press.

Stark, Cynthia A. 2000. "Hypothetical Consent and Justification." *Journal of Philosophy* 97, no. 6:313–34.

———. 2007. "How to Include the Severely Disabled in a Contractarian Theory of Justice." *Journal of Political Philosophy* 15, no. 2: 125–47.

———. 2009. "Contractarianism and Cooperation." *Politics, Philosophy and Economics* 8, no. 1:73–99.

Weinstock, David. 1994. "The Justification of Political Liberalism." *Pacific Philosophical Quarterly* 75:165–85.

Weithman, Paul. 2008. "Two Arguments from Human Dignity." In *Human Dignity and Bioethics: Essays Commissioned by the President's Council on Bioethics*. Available at http://www.bioethics.gov/reports/human_dignity/chapter17.html

Wong, Sophia. 2007. "The Moral Personhood of Individuals Labeled 'Mentally Retarded': A Rawlsian Response to Nussbaum." *Social Theory and Practice* 33:579–94.

———. 2009. "Duties of Justice to Citizens with Cognitive Disabilities." Included in this collection.

———. Unpublished manuscript. "Rights for People with Cognitive Disabilities."

7

DUTIES OF JUSTICE TO CITIZENS WITH COGNITIVE DISABILITIES

SOPHIA ISAKO WONG

When resources are limited, a theory of distributive justice helps us decide how to allocate the goods produced by members of society in common. Is it permissible to ration health care services according to age or health status? Would it violate any duties of justice to conserve resources for some groups by denying life-saving treatment to other groups, such as infants diagnosed with "severe" cognitive disabilities or elderly people in the end stages of dementia? In allocating funds for public education, is it permissible to segregate students based on test scores? Should citizens live together under similar conditions, or should they be eligible for segregated housing according to their diagnosed abilities as determined by psychologists and physicians? Is it permissible for some forms of religious or cultural life to exclude some citizens based on their physical or cognitive functioning? These are the questions that a theory of justice helps us to answer.

A successful theory of distributive justice should be able to specify its scope by identifying the group of individuals to which its principles apply. If a theory draws distinctions among those individuals, thereby creating subgroups who are to be treated differently, the theory should also provide a justification for dividing up individuals in that manner. There is a growing, though not yet universal, consensus that distinctions based on religion, race, sexual orientation, gender, and physical disability are no longer acceptable reasons to exclude any human being from the scope of a theory of justice. However, theorists today disagree about whether it is justified to treat living beings differently based on their age (or stage of biological development/ degeneration), cognitive or intellectual ability, or species membership.

Current social practices indicate that many individuals labeled with cognitive disabilities are being treated very differently from their non-disabled peers. In the words of Eugene Richards, photographer and volunteer for the human rights group Mental Disability Rights International, "The cruelty and mistreatment I witnessed in one place I witnessed in all . . . as if there is a global agreement that you can do things to people classified mentally or developmentally disabled that you couldn't possibly do to other people" (Richards 2005).

FIGURE 1. Jorge in Asunción, Paraguay (Richards 2008)

Abandoned at birth, Jorge was held for six years in a tiny cell with a hole in the floor for a toilet and no electricity. His food was passed through openings in the barred doors. Richards took the photograph below when Jorge was seventeen (figure 1).[1]

Although Jorge lives in Paraguay, individuals labeled with cognitive disabilities do not always fare much better when they live in the United States. In 2003, after seven years on the waiting list for in-home care, sixteen-year old Morgan Dooley spent three months in the Austin State School. His mother described it as a place of "dingy yellow floors and patients running around without any clothes on." During his time there, he "did nothing but lay in bed" and was occasionally found sitting in his own excrement (Ramshaw 2008). If a theory of justice does not include within its scope individuals labeled with cognitive disabilities, its principles of justice may tacitly endorse or simply ignore the social institutions that continue to shape the lives of Jorge, Dooley, and the millions of others who have been similarly labeled.

Many theorists have claimed that the needs of those labeled with cognitive disabilities do not raise for Rawls issues of justice but rather fall

---

[1] Thanks to Eugene Richards for his permission to reprint his photo of Jorge (last name withheld upon request) (Wong and Richards 2009). Jorge was released from his cell as a result of the publication of the photograph and the relentless activism of the human rights organization Mental Disability Rights International. He is now living with his family.

outside the scope of justice. After all, Rawls thinks that some "scattered individuals" fail to qualify as persons who are owed justice because they lack the moral capacities to some essential minimum degree; it has been suggested that "people with severe mental impairments" are the very individuals to whom Rawls is referring (Nussbaum 2006, 65). If one accepts such a reading, one might conclude that Rawls's theory of justice (and similar contract-based theories) should be rejected: "No theory of this kind can fully include people with severe mental impairments as people for whom, in the first instance, principles are being framed" (Nussbaum 2006, 66).

I argue that Rawls's theory of justice should not be interpreted as treating citizens labeled with cognitive disabilities differently from the "nondisabled." I will present the following argument:

1. *All* citizens should be regarded as having the *potential* for the two moral powers, and therefore as moral persons, even those labeled as having cognitive disabilities.
2. Justice requires that citizens' basic needs be met. According to Rawls, this duty is lexically prior to both the liberty and the equality principle.
3. Enabling Conditions (the circumstances that allow citizens to develop and exercise the two moral powers) should be included in our understanding of the basic needs of all citizens.
4. Structuring basic social institutions to deny citizens the Enabling Conditions blocks their developmental pathways toward becoming moral persons (fully cooperating members of society) and is therefore unjust by Rawls's own lights.
5. Conclusion: citizens labeled with cognitive disabilities are owed the same duties of justice as other citizens. Rawls's theory implies one specific duty of justice to citizens labeled with cognitive disabilities: to provide them with the Enabling Conditions until they become fully cooperating members of society.[2]

In offering this argument, I part company with many who defend the view that any Rawlsian theory of justice must treat citizens labeled with cognitive disabilities differently from other citizens (see Kittay 1999; Brighouse 2001; Nussbaum 2006; Richardson 2006; Stark 2007; Hartley 2009). Although I will not address the nuances of each theorist's position, I will focus on two key points used to justify the exclusion of people labeled with cognitive disabilities. The first point addresses the scope of moral personhood, while the second involves the fully cooperating assumption. I conclude by considering and rebutting two major objections to my argument.

---

[2] Thanks to Chris Lowry for helping me clarify the structure of my argument.

Defining the Term "Citizens Labeled with Cognitive Disabilities"

James Harris and Jeffrey Brosco have amply demonstrated that the diagnosis and labeling of cognitive disabilities have fluctuated extensively over the years, and still often vary depending on race and socioeconomic status (see Harris 2008; Brosco 2008). Recent studies in the United States indicate that black students are still 2.9 times as likely as white students to be identified as having mental retardation and be placed in segregated classrooms. In wealthier districts, contrary to researchers' expectations, black children, especially males, were more likely to be labeled mentally retarded. This is surprising because usually poverty correlates with poor prenatal care, low birth rates, and other factors and therefore an increased risk for disabilities, while wealth usually correlates with a decreased risk. The research suggests that the observed racial, ethnic, and gender disparities are the result of many complex and interacting factors, including: unconscious racial bias on the part of school authorities; large resource inequalities (such as the lack of high-quality teachers) that run along lines of race and class; unjustifiable reliance on IQ and other evaluation tools; educators' inappropriate responses to the pressures of high-stakes testing; and power differentials between minority parents and school officials (Losen and Orfield 2002; see also Stubblefield 2009).

Bearing this in mind, we should exercise extreme caution in accepting any one particular labeling of an individual who is thought to belong to this category. Hence, when I refer to "citizens labeled with cognitive disabilities" I mean those individuals who were labeled with a diagnosis of cognitive or intellectual disability shortly after birth or during childhood. Examples include people diagnosed with traumatic brain injury, pervasive developmental delay, autism, mental retardation, or Down syndrome.[3]

The Scope of Moral Personhood: The Potentiality View

Let me start by closely examining the Rawlsian ideal of moral personhood. According to Rawls, human beings count as free and equal persons when they have the moral powers necessary to engage in social cooperation. The first moral power is *the capacity for a sense of justice*, by which Rawls means reasonableness, understood as the ability to regard others as equal citizens and to engage with others on terms they could imagine others could accept (Rawls 1993, 19). Having the second moral power, *the capacity for a conception of the good*, means that persons are rational in

---

[3] Some conditions classified as "developmental disabilities" do not affect cognitive functioning; hence, "developmental disability" is not a synonym for cognitive or intellectual disability. I owe this distinction to scholars with cerebral palsy and autism at the Society for Disability Studies meeting in 2008, who assured me that their conditions affect their sensory and motor functioning but not their cognitive functioning.

the sense of being able to determine their goals and take the most useful steps toward those goals (Rawls 1993, 19).

Martha Nussbaum claims that on Rawls's view "people with severe mental impairments" lack the moral capacities to some essential minimum degree, and that therefore, they fail to qualify as equal moral persons (Nussbaum 2006, 133). In making this argument, Nussbaum relies on the implicit premise that Rawls's conception of moral personhood requires the *actual* exercise of the two moral powers. Thus, the argument in full runs as follows:

1. First Premise: Citizens labeled with severe mental impairments lack the two moral powers to some essential minimum degree.
2. *(Implicit Premise): Personhood requires the actual exercise of the two moral powers.*
3. Conclusion: Therefore, citizens labeled with severe mental impairments fail to qualify as equal moral persons.

On Nussbaum's reading of Rawls, citizens who have not yet acquired the two moral powers are therefore excluded from the discussion of equal treatment. Hence, she argues, Rawls's theory of justice should be rejected. My question, however, is whether the two moral powers must be actualized, or could they be understood as merely *potential*? Rawls writes, "One should observe that moral personality is here defined as a *potentiality* that is ordinarily realized in due course. It is this potentiality which brings the claims of justice into play" (1999, 442, emphasis added).

In Rawls's view, all citizens are equally protected by the scope of justice regardless of their abilities: "While individuals presumably have varying capacities for a sense of justice, this fact is not a reason for depriving those with a lesser capacity of the full protection of justice" (1999, 443). Hence, for Rawls, possession of the moral powers is sufficient for equal justice. But is it necessary? Here is Rawls's reply: "Whether moral personality is also a necessary condition I shall leave aside. . . . Even if the capacity were necessary, it would be unwise in practice to withhold justice on this ground. The risk to just institutions would be too great" (1999, 442–43). In other words, Rawls accords justice to all citizens with the potential for the two moral powers, even when they are labeled as having cognitive disabilities. I call this the Potentiality View.

The Fully Cooperating Assumption

Rawls's theory contains an idealizing assumption which is known as the fully cooperating assumption. In *Political Liberalism*, he states: "I have assumed . . . that while citizens do not have equal capacities, they do have, at least to the essential minimum, the moral, intellectual and physical capabilities that enable them to be fully cooperating members of society over a complete life" (1993, 183). Cynthia Stark interprets this passage as meaning that for Rawls citizens with cognitive disabilities do not count as fully cooperating members of society. She believes that Rawls is concerned "to set aside cases of disability that are in a certain sense absolute; they render persons unable to cooperate given a society's particular level of technological advancement, even if that society is committed to making accommodations for the disabled." Stark suggests that "people with severe brain or spinal cord injuries whose motor or communication skills are severely limited" might fall into this category (2007, 131).

If we accept Stark's reading, then Rawls has bracketed the issue of distributing goods to the noncooperating. She argues that if all citizens are imagined as fully cooperating, then the parties in the original position represent only the fully cooperating. Noncontributors are not included in deliberations about the design of the basic structure of society. Hence, the fully cooperating assumption sets aside the problem of distributing health care and material goods to the noncooperating (Stark 2007, 134).

Stark's proposal is to retain the fully cooperating assumption in the original position but drop it at the constitutional stage of the theory. In order to do this, she relies on the assumption that citizens can be neatly divided into two groups: the cooperating and the noncooperating. This presents a puzzle. For Stark, only impaired adults count as noncooperating. Her reasoning is that in the normal life cycle, the unimpaired elderly have already participated in social cooperation, while unimpaired children will someday engage in social cooperation (Stark 2007, 131). Hence, they do not belong to the group of individuals who are noncooperating. Note that the claim about the elderly is an empirical claim about the past actions of this group (assuming that all nondisabled adults contribute to society during their middle-age years, which is not always the case), while the claim about children purports to predict the future actions of that group, when in fact some nondisabled children do encounter accidents, injuries, and other circumstances that result in their not being able to participate in cooperation. It is unclear whether individuals who start out as nondisabled children and subsequently become disabled adults thus count as cooperating or noncooperating. A similar problem exists for adults who have contributed to social cooperation during part of their lives but then become impaired through dementia or degeneration at the end of their lives. Are they to be counted as cooperating for the first part of their lives but not the second part?

In order to bring together the discussion of these two points, let me clarify how the two moral powers are related to social cooperation. For Rawls, the capacity for a conception of the good enables people to see the point of social cooperation and thus to be *willing* to engage in it (Rawls 2001, 6.) The sense of justice enables people to be committed to reciprocity—which involves a commitment to abide by agreed-upon fair terms of cooperation even when doing so contradicts one's own advantage—and thus to be *able* to engage in fair social cooperation. While Stark's account raises the puzzle of distinguishing the cooperating from the noncooperating, my proposal avoids this puzzle by acknowledging that all citizens are located somewhere along a developmental pathway between noncooperating and fully cooperating. I will discuss this developmental pathway shortly.

How Are the Two Moral Powers Acquired?

In Rawls's account of moral development, citizens learn to exercise the two moral powers gradually. This is a scalar process, not a binary process. Readers who are parents or caregivers will understand what this means: there is no clear dividing line between individuals who have acquired a sense of justice and those who have not yet acquired it, and someone who starts exercising the moral powers at one point may fail to exercise them at a later date. Rawls is aware that we cannot view the talents and abilities of individuals as fixed natural gifts. He recognizes explicitly that "these abilities and talents cannot come to fruition apart from social conditions." He writes further that "an ability is not, for example, a computer in the head with a definite measurable capacity unaffected by social circumstances. Among the elements affecting the realization of natural capacities are social attitudes of encouragement and support and the institutions concerned with their training and use" (1993, 270). When Rawls construes the two moral powers as potential properties, he is asserting that a given individual will develop a conception of the good and a sense of justice, *provided that certain* circumstances obtain. I call these circumstances "Enabling Conditions."

The Enabling Conditions

Seeds require moist soil, light, and nutrients to develop into plants. Similarly, human beings also need specific Enabling Conditions in order to develop the two moral powers. Examples of Enabling Conditions are (1) belonging to social groups like families or religious communities; (2) interacting with adults who are already exercising the two moral powers; (3) developing relationships with family members, classmates, friends, and co-workers, and (4) taking ample time to develop their capacities. Note that some human beings require years, even decades, to develop the two moral powers, given the appropriate Enabling Conditions. For example, Jenn Seybert, a person on the autism spectrum, learned to type after living for twenty-four years without access to communication technologies. In her keynote address to the Maryland Coalition for Inclusive Education, she stated: "Learning to learn was and is a process for me as it is for everyone. It began with sitting and watching how others interacted" (Seybert 2002). Sitting and watching others interact was a crucial first step in her learning process; in other words, being included in educational and social contexts for two and a half decades was one of the Enabling Conditions for Seybert.

Personhood as Requiring Enabling Conditions

In his chapter on caring for people with dementia, included in this collection, Bruce Jennings (2009) describes how family members can engage with their loved ones in order to preserve what he calls "memorial personhood." Jennings writes: "To be a memorial person is to be a self in the imagination and memory of others; which, on this view, is just what it is to be a self. It is to be a self whose identity and life must be honored and acknowledged by those who can [do so]. . . . And to be a person of any type—including a memorial person—is to be a self to whom, as Arthur Miller puts it in *Death of a Salesman*, 'attention must be paid' " (page 176 of this volume). He emphasizes that memorial persons or selves are moral subjects, not objects. He writes, "If I am a moral subject, I cannot rightfully be ignored, abandoned, or exiled from the space of connection between selves that we call the moral community" (page 177 of this volume). Jennings captures the difference by stating that as an object of moral concern or kindness, even love, "a moral object may be well cared for" (ibid.) By contrast, "a moral subject calls forth and commands care by dint of his or her identity, status, and agency" (ibid.) in a space of moral recognition extending backward and forward in time.

In the case of citizens who have not yet started to exercise the moral powers, we could think of the Enabling Conditions as fostering personhood along the lines that Jennings suggests for memorial persons. When a citizen appears to have a severe disability and does not currently communicate with us, it is vital that we continue to treat that individual as a moral subject rather than an object. What Jennings states about memorial persons is true of all persons: to be a person is to be a self to whom attention must be paid. In Seybert's case, her family members' expectation that she would one day communicate with her peers was their way of recognizing her as a person. This expectation enabled her to start communicating through typing. Furthermore, to be a person is to be a self in the imagination of others. Being treated as a person during the twenty-four years before she started to communicate was an essential precondition to Seybert's developing the ability to communicate.

Another illustration of the importance of Enabling Conditions can be found in the development of Jamie Burke, who is now a junior at Syracuse University. Originally thought to be nonverbal for the first twelve years of his life, Burke learned to type independently over a period of years and has started to speak as well. "Yes, I understood everything, but people thought I was lost in the reverie of autism," he writes. "I screamed at the idiots who treated me like a kid that was invisible"

(*Syracuse Post-Standard* 2006). As part of the inclusive education process, teacher Marilyn Chadwick spent thirteen years training teachers to be prepared to work with Burke, playing an integral role in his educational journey. Burke now works with five facilitators at Syracuse University whose work makes it possible for him to be a part of group discussions and speak during class (Simmons 2007). It seems that Burke's agency was originally overlooked because he needs a team of people around him who enable his agency to be revealed.

In a similar vein, in her chapter included in this collection Hilde Lindemann (2009) refers to the activity of holding a person in her or his identity, or holding someone in personhood, which describes the Enabling Conditions very aptly. Lindemann presses the claim that close family members have a special responsibility to hold onto a demented person's identity for her by treating her in a way consistent with backward-looking stories about her life. Furthermore, forward-looking stories in childhood are just as important as backward-looking stories near the end of life; Lindemann argues that families are the primary sites for identity formation, and that forward-looking stories play an important role in this respect. In describing the practice of holding an infant or child in personhood, Lindemann states that the child understands who she is by means of the stories that her parents and other family members use to construct her identity.

In Lindemann's account, one set of stories that closes down opportunities (rather than opening them up) are the hateful or dismissive master narratives used by the members of a dominant social group to justify their oppression of another, less powerful group. These identities (for example, black men as violent drug dealers, gay men as pedophiles) unjustly constrict the agency of those who bear them, keeping them from pursuing desirable opportunities and from enjoying their fair share of the goods society has to offer.

Blocking Developmental Pathways to Moral Personhood

Let us apply Lindemann's description of oppressive narratives to the case of Suzy Gray. When she was a child, her parents, their doctors, and state experts recommended admitting her to Indiana's Muscatatuck State Hospital so she would be kept away from society for "everyone's best interest." As a result, close family members were convinced by the medical diagnosis to construct Gray's identity so that her agency was significantly constricted during her early childhood and adolescence. In 1970, Suzy Gray was admitted to Indiana's Muscatatuck State Hospital. The photograph below was her admission photo (figure 2).[4]

---

[4] Thanks to Sherry Gray, the legal guardian of Suzy Gray, for her permission to reprint this photo (Wong and Gray 2009).

FIGURE 2. Suzy Gray, Muscatatuck State Hospital admission photo, Indiana, 1970

Lindemann's account raises the possibility that there may be a causal relationship between the claim that Gray would be best off institutional-ized and her subsequent moral development (or lack thereof). Consider what her life was like in that state hospital: she was "watched over constantly, only ate at fixed times, and was taken to and from activities and examinations without warning, and certainly no choice in the matter" (Gray 2007). Under such conditions, imagine how difficult it would be for anyone to develop a conception of the good—in other words, to become rational in the sense of being able to determine her goals and take the most useful steps toward those goals. Furthermore, consider Gray's opportunities to observe instances of adults treating each other with justice and fairness: "She had no privacy and only temporary possession of any personal things. If she wanted more cake, she had to steal from her neighbor in the dining room. If she wanted attention, she found it more useful to throw something than be nice, as nice girls were ignored." Under such conditions, it would have been challenging for anyone to develop her capacity for a sense of justice, or what Rawls calls "reasonableness," understood as the ability to regard others as equal citizens and to engage with others on terms they could imagine others could accept.

On the basis of his conception of memorial personhood, Jennings argues that both caregivers and social institutions (including public policy for long-term care) have an obligation to provide the environment, resources, services, and human presence necessary to sustain and conserve semantic agency and memorial personhood during the course of life with dementia (Jennings 2009). Similarly, Lindemann notes that families are not the only agents responsible for holding their loved ones in personhood (Lindemann 2009). Societies too have a role to play in helping us hold one another, and she suggests that social institutions and practices could be arranged so that the goods of living at home are integrated into the other forms of care. Later in this chapter I will extend Jennings's claim to argue that Rawlsians have a duty of justice to provide the Enabling Conditions to citizens with disabilities over the course of a complete lifetime.

In *Political Liberalism*, Rawls characterizes the project of extending justice to people with disabilities as a "problem of extension" along with justice for future generations, for international peoples, and for animals and the rest of nature. He states clearly that he is agnostic as to whether justice as fairness covers these problems; as he puts it, "Perhaps we simply lack the ingenuity to see how the extension may proceed" (1993, 21). So far, I have argued that all citizens should be regarded as having the potential for the two moral powers, and therefore as moral persons, even when they are labeled as having cognitive disabilities. If I am correct in arguing that all citizens may be regarded as *potential* possessors of the two moral powers, then surely citizens labeled with cognitive disabilities are owed the same duties of justice as other citizens. I have introduced the idea of Enabling Conditions to refer to those things that people need in order to develop and exercise the two moral powers, and have argued that Enabling Conditions should be included in our understanding of the basic needs of all citizens.

Rawls recognizes that in order to develop the two moral powers, people labeled with cognitive disabilities (like all people) need more than the primary goods alone; they also need access to social and cultural opportunities. He even articulates a Principle of Need requiring that citizens' basic needs be met before the two principles of justice are applied. He writes, "The first principle covering the equal basic rights and liberties may easily be preceded by a *lexically prior principle requiring that citizens' basic needs be met*, at least insofar as their being met is necessary for citizens to *understand* and to be able fruitfully to *exercise* those rights and liberties. Certainly any such principle must be assumed in applying the first principle" (1993, 7, emphasis added). The Principle of Need suggests that the structure of society should be changed to make it more inclusive, while the two principles of justice are concerned with distributing the primary goods. In other words, the Enabling Conditions will be concerned with improving the accessibility of our social, cultural, educational, and residential environments. Food, shelter, and the Enabling Conditions are basic needs because they are jointly necessary conditions for the possibility of exercising other rights, such as Rawls's basic rights and liberties.

The Causal Relationship Between Epistemic Claims and the Concrete Lives of People with Disabilities

It is impossible for medical professionals to predict which individuals will "certainly" develop the two moral powers, and which individuals will "never" do so. To the contrary, a brief survey of the history of medicine demonstrates that the predictions of physicians have been disproved by later discoveries, just as in other scientific fields. For example, in the nineteenth century, people with epilepsy were institutionalized in asylums along with the insane (Rothman 1971). Throughout history, many deaf people have been misdiagnosed as having mental retardation, with severe consequences. They grew up in institutions—homes for the retarded or mentally ill—without access to language. By the time they were discovered to be deaf, not cognitively impaired, it was often too late for them to salvage what was left of their lives. Although misdiagnoses may be rarer in the twenty-first century, they still occur in the United States as well as globally. As recently as 1994, a child who had been labeled "mentally retarded" was found to have a moderate hearing loss instead (Berke 2007). In each of these cases, because they did not have the means to communicate successfully with those who misdiagnosed them, these citizens were institutionalized and denied essential educational opportunities.

To structure society so that it excludes some citizens from the community (at birth or in early childhood) is to deny them the opportunity to develop the two moral powers and hence to become fully cooperating members of society. To illustrate this, I draw an analogy with voting requirements. Imagine a society that specifies a minimum level of literacy as a prerequisite for being able to vote. If the social institutions in that society are structured so that a certain economically oppressed minority are denied access to education, then the basic structure will ensure that all members of this group will be automatically excluded from participating in the political process, because it is impossible (or at least extremely difficult) for them to acquire the minimum criterion for voting rights. If no members of the economically oppressed minority are ever admitted into the group of those who make laws for the society as a whole, it is unlikely that voters will think of verifying whether any of the economically oppressed are actually capable of reading, when allocated enough resources and access to education.[5]

Similarly, as long as society is structured so that it denies certain citizens the Enabling Conditions they require in order to develop the two

---

[5] Martha Nussbaum addresses this very issue in her contribution to this collection.

moral powers, keeping them excluded and isolated, we will never know how much progress they might make if social institutions were transformed to include them. Given our continuing inability to predict which individuals will remain at the level of "noncooperating" and which ones will eventually engage in social cooperation, structuring basic social institutions to deny these citizens the Enabling Conditions blocks their developmental pathways toward becoming moral persons (fully cooperating members of society) and is therefore unjust by Rawls's own lights. Hence, Rawls's theory implies one specific duty of justice to citizens labeled with cognitive disabilities: to provide them with the Enabling Conditions over a complete lifetime, or until they become fully cooperating members of society. Many individuals will need continuing support to communicate and participate in society; so the Enabling Conditions then become something like "supporting conditions."

First Objection: Responding to the Epistemic Difficulty

There are two objections to the Potentiality View, which defines moral personhood as requiring only the potential for (but not the actual exercise of) the two moral powers. The first is what I call the Epistemic Difficulty. The Potentiality View depends on our ability to ascertain which human beings have the potential to develop the two moral powers. The myriad case histories similar to the lives of Jenn Seybert and Jamie Burke demonstrate that when it comes to the history of predicting cognitive development, it has been notoriously difficult to make reliable claims about the future. Nobody can accurately predict who will develop the two moral powers over the course of a complete lifetime, because scientists lack reliable knowledge about the developmental pathways and the specific Enabling Conditions that individuals need in order to start demonstrating their abilities. Still, many would assert that we now have strong evidence that some people will never develop a sense of justice; similarly for a conception of the good— people in persistent vegetative states, for example. Even if we cannot know for certain right now, there may come a time in the future when medical science is developed enough to say for certain who can develop these moral capacities.[6]

Suppose that in certain cases the best prediction we can make is that certain human beings will *not* develop the two moral powers, under any sorts of conditions, no matter how many resources we devote to them. This is the hard case that deserves close attention. Imagine that some brave society decides to devote a portion of its resources over the next fifty years to transforming social institutions so that all citizens have the Enabling Conditions for participating, and that their best scientists also pursue extensive research into encouraging new developmental pathways

[6] Thanks to Christian Perring for raising this objection.

for individuals with conditions that are not yet well understood. Suppose further that after living in this fully inclusive society for fifty years, there is a certain group of noncommunicating citizens (NC for short) who still fail to exercise the two moral powers in any way that we can detect. It would seem reasonable for the Rawlsian theory to specify in this case that society has fulfilled its duty to establish an inclusive society, and has no further duties of justice to members of that group.

Granting that NC would continue to exist even in the most inclusive society with technological solutions to every imaginable barrier to communication, we would be left with two possibilities: (1) NC consists of human beings who utterly lack the two moral powers, or (2) NC consists of citizens possessing the potential for the two moral powers, while lacking the ability to communicate, or attempting to communicate with us in ways that we cannot decipher. It is possible that members of NC might be able to understand others even though they cannot express themselves through speech or any other means (for examples, see Grandin and Scariano 1996; Bauby 1998). As Eva Kittay writes in her description of cognitive disability, "Those who cannot speak must depend on others to speak for them. . . . Perhaps there is no more disabling disablement" (2002, 258).

We can subdivide NC into two subgroups, as shown in figure 3. Either they are people with whom we have communicated in the past, or people with whom we have not yet communicated at all. When considering those who at some point in their lives exercised the two moral powers and communicated with us, we may rely on their previous assertions about what they valued in life to extrapolate what kinds of lives they would like to live in the present and the future. Even these extrapolations are unreliable, however, because people's desires and ideas change as they experience and adjust to different circumstances (see Jaworska 2008).

As for people with whom we have not yet communicated at all, however, we have absolutely no access to their first-person perspective. We are faced with an unpleasant choice concerning their point of view. The first possibility is that we can discount their interests, deciding *a priori* that since they cannot participate in the dialogue they are not worthy of moral consideration. In so doing, we run the risk of erring on the side of doing grievous moral wrong, possibly on the order of the historical injustices of sexist and racist exclusions. To minimize the risk of error, we may choose instead the second possibility; we may commit ourselves to some account of interest, however provisional or well founded, and endeavor to speak on behalf of the voiceless. This alternative runs the risk of erring on the side of overextending moral status to a realm much broader than necessary. In this case, a theory might mistakenly ascribe moral status to all living creatures, or even to trees, rocks, rivers, and glaciers. Such a theory could still distinguish among levels of moral status, but would surely draw criticism for being overly inclusive. As

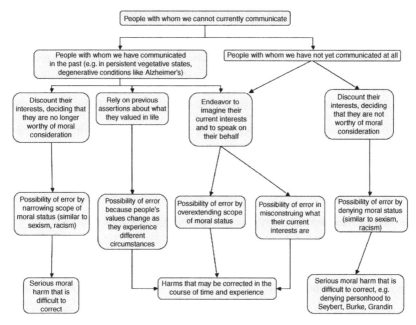

FIGURE 3. Possible ways of treating the voiceless

Rawls has argued, however, the best account of a person's sense of justice is not usually the one that fits her judgments before she takes time to examine any conception of justice (1999, 43). Rather, because moral philosophy is a Socratic enterprise, we may want to change or revise our current moral judgments once we have reflected on their regulative principles.

I would rather err on the side of being overinclusive, given the lessons of history. We are at the first stages of seeking intellectual and moral consensus about the permissibility of excluding certain human beings from moral consideration, just as our European predecessors first started to question the social practices of slavery. It is especially important to guard against bias whenever the parties whose voices are most privileged in a debate are precisely those who stand to benefit from the policies determined by the outcome of that debate. Rawls's principles of justice, if construed in a certain way, have the power to exclude individuals from the scope of personhood with all its attendant rights and advantages; these principles should not be constructed so that they permit some nondisabled persons to benefit materially by excluding those considered nonpersons because of their disability status. The difficulties in implementing the Americans with Disabilities Act indicate the extent to which many nondisabled citizens resist fulfilling their duties of justice to citizens with physical disabilities, even though these citizens clearly count as moral persons. When it comes to citizens labeled with cognitive disabilities, the opportunities for exclusion are even greater.

Considering the possibilities of error as mapped in figure 3, we should endeavor to imagine the interests of people who cannot communicate with us and to speak on their behalf. They should be included in the scope of justice in order to avoid the more serious moral wrong of excluding them. The boundary between moral persons and nonpersons is indistinct and difficult to judge; we should therefore include all human beings without trying to determine exactly where they are on the spectrum of cognitive functioning. The possibility of mistakenly denying someone's personhood is a moral error far more troubling than the difficulty of establishing a society that includes all citizens.

Second Objection: The Argument from Marginal Cases

The second objection to the Potentiality View is that it implies a conclusion which some theorists find unacceptable: that Rawlsians should also extend the scope of morality to include nonhuman animals. There are several variations on the Argument from Marginal Cases (see Singer 1993; Dombrowski 1997; and Rowlands 2002).[7] Scott Wilson defends the following version:

1. If we are justified in attributing the potential for the two moral powers to human "marginal cases" such as infants, senile adults, and people with cognitive disabilities, then we are likewise justified in attributing the potential for the two moral powers to nonhuman animals.
2. According to the Potentiality View, we are justified in attributing the two moral powers to the human marginal cases.
3. Therefore, we are likewise justified in attributing the two moral powers to nonhuman animals (see Wilson 2001).

My reply to the Argument from Marginal Cases is *the Argument from Species-Potential*. People who have actually interacted closely with these individuals in person (in addition to reviewing medical case histories and reading books about them) know that dealing with human beings labeled with cognitive disabilities is in no way equivalent to dealing with nonhuman animals with approximately the same level of cognitive functioning. The important and morally relevant difference is that the human being is a member of a species that has evolved to have certain capacities, and possesses cortical structures that we all share as human beings. When a certain individual's species-potential has gone awry or been thwarted by circumstances, he is still a being who is "wired for language" but cannot

---

[7] Thanks to Nathan Nobis for recommending these references.

speak, a being whose capacities have been limited. By contrast, a nonhuman animal belongs to a species that has not yet evolved to use human language or to participate in human societies, and therefore its level of cognitive functioning is entirely appropriate to its species, rather than a deficiency that requires attention.[8]

If the above argument can be shown to be fatally flawed, it may well turn out that some interpretations of Rawls's theory imply that nonhuman animals are owed duties of justice. For example, one such theory might require that we humans structure our societies to allow nonhuman animals (insofar as they are directly affected by our laws) to pursue their own conceptions of the good life, which would probably include not being killed for food or subjected to painful experiments from which they draw no benefit. This result, while surprising and counterintuitive to many, is not necessarily a weakness of my argument. I see no reason why Rawlsians cannot advocate treating our fellow human citizens with the dignity they deserve while also recognizing that we have obligations to treat justly all the nonhuman animals whose lives are shaped by our actions.

Conclusion

I have argued that rejecting Rawlsian contractualism is premature because Rawlsians do not need to exclude citizens labeled with cognitive disabilities from the scope of justice. I have provided reasons to believe that it is central to Rawls's theory to regard all citizens as moral persons as long as they have the potential for developing the two moral powers. Perhaps my most provocative claim has been that structuring basic social institutions to deny citizens the Enabling Conditions is unjust because it blocks their developmental pathways toward becoming fully cooperating members of society. The result of this Rawlsian investigation is that a just society must provide citizens labeled with cognitive disabilities with the Enabling Conditions until they become fully cooperating members of society.

Acknowledgments

Thanks to Amy Baehr, Licia Carlson, Sanjay Cherubala, Laura Franklin-Hall, Susan Grundberg, Andrew Hall, Eva Kittay, Christopher Lowry, Christian Perring, Thomas Pogge, Cynthia Stark, and Bonnie Talbert for helpful comments on earlier versions of this chapter.

[8] Thanks to Jeremy Waldron and Philip Kitcher for valuable discussion of this point.

References

Bauby, Jean-Dominique. 1998. *The Diving Bell and the Butterfly: A Memoir of Life in Death*. New York: Vintage.

Brighouse, Harry. 2001. "Can Justice as Fairness Accommodate the Disabled?" *Social Theory and Practice* 27, no. 4:537–60.

Brosco, Jeffrey. 2008. "Limits of the Medical Model: Historical Epidemiology of Cognitive Disabilities in the U.S." Conference presentation at *Cognitive Disability: A Challenge to Moral Philosophy*. Stony Brook University, Sept. 20. Podcast accessed on Mar. 29, 2009, at https://podcast.ic.sunysb.edu/blojsom_resources/meta/phicdc/29-BROSCO_JeffreyP.mp4

Berke, Jamie. 2007. "Deaf, Not Retarded: When Misdiagnoses Are Made, Everyone Pays." About.com, updated Dec. 18. Accessed Mar. 22, 2009, at http://deafness.about.com/cs/featurearticles/a/retarded_2.htm

Dombrowski, Daniel. 1997. *Babies and Beasts: The Argument from Marginal Cases*. Urbana: University of Illinois Press.

Grandin, Temple, and Margaret N. Scariano. 1996. *Emergence Labeled Autistic*. Navato, Calif.: Arena Press.

Gray, Sherry. 2007. "Suzy's Mug Shot." *Access Press* 18, no. 2 (Feb. 10). Accessed on Mar. 2, 2009, at http://www.accesspress.org/archive/2007/02/story_suzy%27s_mug_shot.htm

Harris, James. 2008. "A Developmental Perspective on the Emergence of Moral Personhood." Conference presentation at *Cognitive Disability: A Challenge to Moral Philosophy*. Stony Brook University, Sept. 19. Podcast accessed on Mar. 2, 2009, at https://podcast.ic.sunysb.edu//blojsom_resources/meta/phicdc/14-HARRIS_JamesC.mp4

Hartley, Christie. 2009. "Justice for the Disabled: A Contractualist Approach." *Journal of Social Philosophy* 40, no.1:17–36.

Jaworska, Agnieszka. 2008. "The Ethics of Treatment of Individuals Whose Status as Persons Is Thought to Be Compromised or Uncertain." Conference presentation at *Cognitive Disability: A Challenge to Moral Philosophy*. Stony Brook University, Sept. 20. Podcast accessed on Mar. 29, 2009, at https://podcast.ic.sunysb.edu//blojsom_resources/meta/phicdc/08-JAWORSKA_Agnieszka.mp4

Jennings, Bruce. 2009. "Agency and Moral Relationship in Dementia." Included in this collection.

Kittay, Eva Feder. 1999. *Love's Labor: Essays on Women, Equality, and Dependence*. New York: Routledge.

———. 2002. "When Caring Is Just and Justice Is Caring: Justice and Mental Retardation." In *The Subject of Care: Feminist Perspectives on Dependency*, edited by Eva Feder Kittay and Ellen K. Feder, 257–76. New York: Rowman and Littlefield.

Lindemann, Hilde. 2009. "Holding One Another (Well, Wrongly, Clumsily) in a Time of Dementia." Included in this collection.

Losen, Daniel J., and Gary Orfield. 2002. *Racial Inequity in Special Education.* Cambridge, Mass.: Harvard Education Press.

Nussbaum, Martha. 2006. *Frontiers of Justice: Disability, Nationality, Species Membership.* Cambridge, Mass.: Harvard University Press.

Ramshaw, Emily. 2008. "Families facing tough choice to place disabled relatives in institutions." *Dallas Morning News,* Jan. 12. Accessed on Mar. 18, 2009, at http://www.dallasnews.com/sharedcontent/dws/news/healthscience/stories/011208dntexwaitlist.2c69bcb.html

Rawls, John. 1993. *Political Liberalism.* New York: Columbia University Press.

———. 1999. *A Theory of Justice,* revised edition. Cambridge, Mass.: Harvard University Press.

———. 2001. *Justice as Fairness: A Restatement.* Edited by Erin Kelly. Cambridge, Mass.: Belknap Press of Harvard University Press.

Richards, Eugene. 2005. "A Procession of Them." Artist's statement for Moving Walls 10 photo exhibit, March 16, 2005, to October 28, 2005, Open Society Institute in New York. Accessed on Mar. 2, 2009, at http://www.soros.org/initiatives/photography/movingwalls/10/richards_artist

———. 2008. "Photograph of seventeen-year-old Jorge in Asunción, Paraguay." In *A Procession of Them.* Austin: University of Texas Press.

Richardson, Henry S. 2006. "Rawlsian Social-Contract Theory and the Severely Disabled." *Ethics* 10:419–62.

Rothman, David. 1971. *The Discovery of the Asylum.* Boston: Little, Brown.

Rowlands, Mark. 2002. *Animals Like Us.* London: Verso Press.

Seybert, Jenn. 2002. "Inclusion ... Finally!" Keynote address to the Maryland Coalition for Inclusive Education, Baltimore, 2002. In *Sharing Our Wisdom: A Collection of Presentations by People Within the Autism Spectrum,* edited by Gail Gillingham and Sandra McClennen. Durham, N.H.: Autism National Committee, 2003. The book is available only through www.autcom.org. Purchasing information accessed on July 3, 2009, at http://www.iodbookstore.org/products/Sharing-Our-Wisdom%3A-A-Collection-of-Presentations-by-People-Within-the-Autism-Spectrum.html

Simmons, Christina. 2007. "SU student shares experiences, hardships from life with autism." *Daily Orange,* Apr. 25. Accessed on May 25, 2009, at http://media.www.dailyorange.com/media/storage/paper522/news/2007/04/25/Feature/Su.Student.Shares.Experiences.Hardships.From.Life.With.Autism-2879172.shtml

Singer, Peter. 1993. *Practical Ethics.* Cambridge: Cambridge University Press.

Stark, Cynthia. 2007. "How to Include the Severely Disabled in a Contractarian Theory of Justice." *Journal of Political Philosophy* 15, no. 2:127–45.

Stubblefield, Anna. 2009. "The Entanglement of Race and Cognitive Dis/ability." Included in this collection.

Syracuse Post-Standard. 2006. "Jamie finds his voice—but facilitated communication remains controversial." 31 July. Accessed on Mar. 19, 2009, at http://www.autismconnect.org/news.asp?section=00010001 &itemtype=news&id=5841

Wilson, Scott. 2001. "Carruthers and the Argument from Marginal Cases." *Journal of Applied Philosophy* 18, no. 2:135–47.

Wong, Sophia, and Sherry Gray. 2009. Personal correspondence concerning permission to reprint photo of Suzy Gray, March 2–4.

Wong, Sophia, and Eugene Richards. 2009. Personal correspondence concerning permission to reprint photo of Jorge (last name withheld upon request), Mar. 2.

8

COGNITIVE DISABILITY IN A SOCIETY OF EQUALS

JONATHAN WOLFF

It is common among disability activists to remark that disability presents a "challenge" (Hunt 1998). It is also said, although much less commonly, that disability can be a "blessing," both at a theoretical and at a practical level.[1] This may sound like an extraordinary idea, but behind it is the notion that if a society is able to think through and successfully confront issues of disability, doing so will make it more compassionate, more secure in its sense of community, and more understanding both of human vulnerability and dependence and of human nature and potential. If the challenge is shirked, the blessing will be lost, and this will affect how society treats all of its members, disabled or able-bodied (MacIntyre 2001).

Egalitarian political philosophy has been slow to take up the challenge of disability, although the picture, thankfully, is changing fairly rapidly. One obstacle to progress has been the relatively rigid framework within which some leading egalitarian theorists have approached questions of justice and, by implication, disability. For a certain group of theorists the main issue for egalitarianism is that of deciding what the "currency" of justice should be; whether it should be a resource-based metric of income and wealth, or a welfare-based metric of preference satisfaction or welfare. But to view matters this way seems to commit one to the following proposition: injustice is a matter of having too few resources or too little welfare. Therefore, it seems, justice requires transfer of resources from one person or group to another, either because resources are the currency of justice or because they are a good way of generating welfare or preference satisfaction. Accordingly, despite their differences, many contemporary theories of justice seem to have the consequence that injustice is to be corrected by cash compensation. Whatever its appeal in other situations, the idea that financial compensation is the appropriate way of remedying disability seems blinkered, in that it fails to capture, and thereby to address, the reasons why the claims of disabled people have a particular social salience. Although many disabled people lack money, it seems implausible to say that social policy in respect of disability should consist purely of monetary transfers.

---

[1] Simon Duffy, in conversation. As will become evident, I owe much of what follows to discussions with Simon.

My task, then, is to look at the possibilities for social policy regarding cognitive disability, and to consider their possible philosophical under-pinnings or justifications. The question I want to address here is not so much how to understand cognitive disability in itself, or in its variations, but to consider the range of possible policy options that are available if we wish to treat people with disabilities as equal members of society, and of these, which are most appropriate and feasible for people with cognitive disability. Of course, the prospects for incorporating people with dis-abilities—especially cognitive disabilities—into society as "full equals" may be somewhat bleak, at least in the short term. Both resources and goodwill are limited, and many people will argue for other priorities. Nevertheless, it may well be possible to do better than we commonly do at present, and progress may well be more likely if the issue is framed in terms of the aspiration to create a society of equals, encompassing all.

Consequently, rather than starting with a theory of justice that, by implication, suggests that compensation, in some form or other, should be our policy goal, I would like to proceed in a different way: by considering what it is that disabled people so often lack, at least without further help and support, and what, therefore, should be the orientation of social policy. In a discussion of what he calls the phenomenological model of disability, the social theorist Gareth Williams proposes that people with disabilities need to "re-negotiate their place in the world," or in an alternative phrase "re-establish their place in the world" (Williams 1998, 240). Assuming that "place in the world" means "worthwhile place in the world" and that the issue for those born, rather than becoming, disabled is one of establishing, rather than re-establishing, a place in the world, the question, then, is what it would be for a disabled person to establish a worthwhile place in the world. By "worthwhile" I mean worthwhile to the individual concerned, rather than "valuable to society," although for many people, of course, what it is to have a worthwhile life will involve being able to contribute to the lives of others, whether that contribution is modest or extensive.

But if disability presents a challenge to egalitarian theories of justice, then cognitive disability amplifies it. Although there are several important exceptions, a high proportion of philosophical writing on disability, as well as social policy, has concentrated on physical disability, and within physical disability on reduced mobility. It is not clear that attempts to show how justice can be achieved for people with problems of physical disability will have much relevance to cognitive disability. But before exploring this, it is necessary to put some theoretical machinery in place.

In my own previous work on disability I have set out a conceptual framework in which different types of policy approaches to disability can be classified, and their advantages and disadvantages explored (Wolff 2002, 2009a, 2009b). Ultimately in this chapter I shall attempt to apply the framework to issues of cognitive disability, relying heavily on some innovative policies recently introduced in parts of the United Kingdom. First, though, the framework. As a preliminary I need to set out in schematic form a simple social theory that will help illuminate the issues I need to explore here. Let us begin by considering any given individual, whatever her disability status. What will determine the opportunities that this person has for finding a worthwhile place in the world? Crudely, there are two sorts of factors we need to enter into the calculations: first, what the person has at her disposal; and, second, what she can do with it.

The first of these categories we can call "resources"; this category includes external resources, such as money, control over parts of the external world, family support, and so on, as well as "internal resources," which include a person's skills, talents, and abilities, and crucially in this case, cognitive powers. However, you cannot "read off" from an individual's resources his chances of leading a life he values. You also need to know facts about the social structures within the society in which he lives; the influence of tradition, religion, language, culture, and other social norms (such as what counts, within that society, as an acceptably "normal" life); the configuration of the material and natural environment, and perhaps other things too. Somewhat misleadingly, I shall refer to all of this as "social structure," even though it has material, legal, cultural, and "attitudinal" aspects too. Thus the overall formula comes to this: the interaction of your resources with the social structure within which you find yourself determines your opportunities to find a worthwhile place in the world. A crude example: in some agricultural societies a man is more likely to have opportunities to live a life he values if he is physically very strong; in technically advanced societies physical strength becomes of more marginal significance. Both resources and social structures determine an individual's chances of being able to find a worthwhile place in the world.

Against this framework we can see that what is commonly called the medical model of disability suggests that people with disabilities have a less extensive set of internal resources than others, and recommends that society act to boost this set largely by medical means. By contrast, the social model prefers to say that social structures discriminate against people with certain resource bundles, and thus we need to change social structures to eliminate such discrimination. But what we can see is that the question of whether the medical model or the social model is the "correct" account of disability is misplaced. Disability is at least in part a matter of a lack of fit between a person and the world in which she lives. The medical model suggests that changes to the person are the correct way of attempting to achieve a better fit, while the social model suggests that the world, rather than the person, should change. What we need to explore, however, is what reasons there are for preferring one or other strategy. But we should also notice that "changing the person" (what I call "personal enhancement") and "changing the world" (what I call "status enhancement") are not the only possible approaches to increasing an individual's opportunity to find a worthwhile place in the world. It is also possible to transfer resources to someone to boost her opportunities.

In one way, of course, we have been here before; the notion of compensation is that of providing individuals with a resource of a particular kind: money. And I have already suggested that I do not find this an appealing way of attempting to address the disadvantage of disability, at least if it is adopted as a complete approach. However, not all transfer of resources is compensation in the sense of giving an individual full private property rights over the object transferred. Consider, for example, governments that provide wheelchairs for those with mobility problems. Although the issue rarely, if ever, arises, typically such wheelchairs are not given as private property. For example, if the person recovers mobility he would be expected to return the wheelchair, and not to sell it. Not only should it not be sold, it should not be dismantled to make a go-cart for his children. The wheelchair is given for certain purposes and not others, and there are limits to its use. The situation is even more obvious with respect to the social policy of providing state-funded carers for disabled or elderly people. In such a case it is quite obvious that the carers are not provided as individual private property: they are not slaves to do the bidding of their owners, whatever it is. Rather, they are provided in order to perform certain services and not others. For example, a disabled person could not require his carer to work as a banker rather than as a carer, even if doing so would create enough extra cash to employ another carer with money to spare.

Just as property can be provided with strings attached as to its use, so can money. For example, in some U.K. universities visually impaired students are given an extra budget to spend on computers or for people to read to them. They cannot spend the money on beer, even if they promise to spend less on beer than they would be permitted to spend on computers, thereby saving the university cash. The point is that the money is given for certain purposes and not others, and it would be considered an abuse to use it for something else, even if that were preferred. This type of intervention I call a "targeted resource enhancement," in that the resources provided are targeted towards a certain purpose. There is, however, I admit, something puzzling about this type of policy—familiar though it is—which Ronald Dworkin has brought out very well in an example of a paraplegic violinist. Suppose we offer this person a very expensive mobility device, but she replies, "That's very kind of you, but if you are to spend so much money on me I'd much rather have a new violin" (Dworkin 1981, 243). I think most of us will be pulled in two directions: the only reason why we are offering anything is because of limited mobility, and therefore there seems to be something almost exploitative to use the resources in some other way. But on the other hand, if the violin is no more expensive, it just seems mean or spiteful to refuse. This is a troubling example, and I shall return to it towards the end of the chapter.

To sum up this part of the discussion, we now have four policy options that can be used to attempt to address the disadvantage of disability. The first is "compensation": providing disabled people with cash, or goods in kind, in the form of full liberal private property, to make up for the disadvantage of disability. The second is "personal enhancement": to take steps to improve the internal resources of the disabled person, whether through surgery, medicine, education, or training. The third is "targeted resource enhancement": to provide resources for the disabled individual, whether money or other goods, but with some sort of strings attached, so not in the form of free private property. Finally there is "status enhancement": to change the social, material, or cultural structure so that individuals are able to do more with the resources they have, rather than provide them with extra resources of some kind.[2]

As already noted, the social model of disability favours status enhancement as a response to disability, and it is easy to see why. Changing the world rather than the person is a way of accepting individuals in their differences, rather than making them adapt to the world. Hence it respects individuals and communicates a message of acceptance and inclusion. It is also, typically, non-stigmatising, in that no one need be identified as disabled in order to benefit from social policies of status enhancement. For example, once hotel rooms and other buildings are made fully accessible, no wheelchair user will need to ask for special treatment. Hence, especially in cases of physical disability, policies of status enhancement often seem appealing. Rather than spend resources to "act on the impaired body" we can spend resources changing the world so that more types of bodies no longer seem impaired in any way that interferes with the person's chances of finding a worthwhile place in the world. This, after all, is the point of the disability legislation we now see throughout the developed world. It would be naïve, however, to say that status enhancement is always to be preferred. Where medical intervention is cheap, quick, safe, and effective it seems the obvious way to address disability. Furthermore, status enhancements can be very expensive, and have other costs. For example, changing building codes could mean that some formerly public buildings will have to close. But still, status enhancement is often an attractive approach for physical disability (Wolff 2009b).

It is far less clear, however, that status enhancement is even possible for cognitive disability. What would it be to change the world so that people with cognitive disabilities and other people were equally able to

---

[2] I concede that it is not always easy to classify particular interventions under one head or another, but nevertheless the distinction between categories is useful for a number of purposes. For further discussion see Wolff 2009a.

find a worthwhile place in the world? Can we even imagine what this would be? In fact, one philosopher who has tried to imagine such a thing is Dan Wikler, at least in some limited contexts. Considering the question of whether people who are "mildly retarded" have sufficient foresight, and other intellectual abilities, to be bound by contracts, Wikler considers the possibility of changing the legal regime so that legal contracts are no longer binding in the way they are at present, in order that the mildly retarded could then make the same sort of legal commitments as others, and thereby avoid paternalism. This would be a status enhancement in my terminology: the mildly retarded would be given a new opportunity through changes to the legal structure. Wikler, however, appears to reject such a suggestion on the reasonable grounds of the enormous social cost. The fact is that much of what makes modern life possible now relies on binding and enforceable contracts that in turn assume a particular level of intellectual competence. To change the world so that such a bar is lowered would have tremendous costs (Wikler 1979).

What, then, is to be done for people with cognitive disabilities if status enhancement—the remedy of choice for physical disability—is not possible? Of course, various forms of personal enhancement—training, education—are highly appropriate remedies, yet in many cases there are limits to what can be achieved. What can be done to give people with cognitive disabilities a greater chance of finding a worthwhile place in the world?

It will be helpful to start by considering the opposite: the way in which such people are so often denied such a place, and I want to do this by means of taking a detour through the recent history of disability policy in the United Kingdom, which I am sure must have echoes elsewhere. It is, of course, well known that until fairly recently it was standard practice for people labelled as disabled—especially, but not only, those said to have mental disabilities—to spend their lives in special institutions, often in semi-rural settings or on the edges of towns, where they lived with other people in similar conditions and with those who were there to take care of them. Unless they had first established a life elsewhere they would have been unlikely to have friends outside the institution, and visits from family members would typically have been special occasions, such as weekend afternoons, rather than built into the fabric of everyday life. Such places were often called "asylums," as if they were places of special retreat and protection. In the analysis of some critics, though, the reverse is true: they allowed members of mainstream society to take refuge from those people who were disturbing to deal with. Thus, it is claimed, the main function of homes for disabled people was to ensure that the rest of us need have little to do with them. In the worst cases they were likened to prisons, with inmates having no rights to leave.

This changed during the 1980s with the Conservative government policy of introducing "care in the community," strengthening individual rights, and closing down many such facilities. No doubt there were economic motives behind such changes, but whether intended or unintended, the changes have done a certain amount to bring disabled people into contact with broader society. Yet the transition is only half made. In many cases disabled people see few people other than family members, service professionals, and other disabled people at day centres. To some degree, day centres have taken the place of homes for the disabled, in that they keep disabled people occupied, but away from non-disabled people. Imagine yourself in the shoes of a person who attends a day centre. It is likely that you would be collected by a coach or mini-bus, which then winds round town for an hour or two picking up others. On arrival at the day centre there may be a visit from reluctant school children, required to help out as part of a social education programme, or from volunteers or others who will engage you on a variety of levels, but often tending towards the patronising end of the spectrum, and watching television fills the empty spaces. You would be fed a meal of a quality you almost certainly would have not have paid for, followed by an afternoon of cursory activities, under the heading of "occupational therapy," which is half-way between nursery school and the hospital ward. Then back into the coach for a couple of hours, before being dropped off to watch some more television in your parents' home.

This is a caricature, perhaps, but not a wild one. Probably many ordinary citizens have given very little thought to what happens at a day centre, unless a story of abuse makes the newspapers. But the broader concern is not the possibility of abuse, it's the mundane, dreary routine of it all. Although there are no doubt many exceptions and examples of good practice, the danger is that such arrangements turn a person into a passive subject: a consumer rather than a producer; a recipient rather than a provider; someone who needs to be kept occupied or entertained and has little to contribute to others except as an employment opportunity or for "doing good." Individual life becomes an epiphenomenon of other people's decisions. Although the idea of complete independence is a myth, near complete dependence isn't, hence the movement within disability activism towards "independent living" (see, e.g., Brissenden 1998). But the main point is that even in these times of "care in the community" disabled people can still lack opportunities for a worthwhile place in the world.

Against this background, it is fascinating and highly encouraging to see new policy options developing. In particular, I want to lay out an experimental approach that has been used in the United Kingdom for the social care of teenagers and young adults with intellectual and developmental disabilities. Previously many of these people were living in group homes, away from their families, or spending their days at day centres, having very little option as to the services available to them. In some locations, such care has been replaced with an approach called "self-directed support," which revolves around the idea of providing disabled people with their own individual budget and giving them control over how it is spent. Here, from the agency's report on its services, are the key steps involved:

- **Step 1**—Everyone is told their level of entitlement—their Individual Budget—and they decide what level of control they wish to take over their budget.
- **Step 2**—People plan how they will use their Individual Budget to get the help that's best for them; if they need help to plan then advocates, brokers or others can support them.
- **Step 3**—The local authority helps people to create good Support Plans, checks they are safe and makes sure that people have any necessary representation.
- **Step 4**—People control their Individual Budget to the extent they want; there are currently 6 distinct control options, from direct payment to having a service commissioned by your local authority.
- **Step 5**—People can use their Individual Budget flexibly; they can use statutory services (the cost of which is taken out of the Individual Budget) and other forms of support; if they change their minds they can quickly re-direct their Individual Budget.
- **Step 6**—People can use their Individual Budget to achieve the outcomes that are important to them in their context of their whole life and their role and contribution within the wider community.
- **Step 7**—The authority continues to check people are okay, shares what is being learned and can change things if people are not achieving the outcomes they need to achieve. (Waters and Duffy 2007, 9)

Of course, those with very severe cognitive disability many not be able exercise much choice; but very often they can exercise some, when supported by family members or social workers. And some choice is better than none. In saying this I am not assuming that having choice is always better than not having it, for clearly there can be circumstances in which offering individuals choice can make their lives worse. For example, those without resources to make a good choice might be better off when their options are severely restricted. Equally, for all of us there are cases where choices can be bewildering or overwhelming or use mental resources that we would rather reserve for other purposes. My point is the far more restricted one that, for almost all people, having some level of choice will, with suitable support, improve their lives. I am not supposing that for all people at all times increasing choice is always a benefit.[3]

It is clear that the scheme just sketched out has a number of very obvious advantages over more centralised services (Poll and Duffy 2008). First, giving individuals control over their budget may well mean that the money is used more efficiently than it would have been by the local authority, in the sense that people will have an incentive to find the most cost-effective ways of achieving their ends. Rather than relying on

---

[3] I thank Henry Richardson for encouraging me to clarify this point.

suppliers who have a central procurement contract, for example, they can seek out cheaper ways of achieving what they want. They can stop the supply of things they don't want or need but might come as part of a standard care package. And if they get things wrong and make mistakes, soon there will be a new payment, and lessons will have been learned.

Equally, the agency can learn from the experience of individuals too. If one person finds a novel way of achieving a goal, or even dreams up a new goal, the agency will learn about it and can pass on advice to others for general benefit.

But perhaps most interesting of all, even if the money is spent badly, giving individuals with cognitive disabilities such control over their budget is a way of bringing much more autonomy into their lives, which would otherwise be virtually disempowered. As I put it above, their lives would be the epiphenomena of other people's decisions. With self-directed support this is no longer true, or at least a measure of independence is provided, and in many cases a good deal of control over one's environment becomes possible, breaking through much of the paternalism of central support services.

There are, however, some obvious worries. On first hearing about this scheme I was concerned that, given that it is based on the transfer of financial resources, it is a form of compensation for disability, which, as I suggested above, is an inappropriate remedy. At first I felt that I would have either to withdraw my objection to compensation or dogmatically to disapprove of what seems to me an extremely promising social policy. In discussion with the designers of these services, however, I became convinced that the scheme is not one of compensation but, in my terms, one of targeted resource enhancement. The money is not handed over as private property but is given for specific purposes and is subject to scrutiny and audit. In cases of failure the agency can refuse to approve certain expenditures, although I am told that so far this rarely, if ever, happens in practice. The people involved understand the scheme well enough not to abuse it and to seek help if they are in difficulties. And the agency is keen to allow people to experiment. If it goes badly you can spend the money a different way next time. The agency would not allow the money to used for anything that was illegal or endangered the health and safety of the individual (whether through action or neglect), but the strings, though present, are very light. The agency itself is keen to avoid the term "compensation" and, echoing my own terminology of "targeted resource enhancement," now refers to it as "conditional resource entitlement."

A second concern is that the scheme appears to place a heavy burden on carers. When given the choice of paying to go to a day centre or using the money for other things, the day centre is used significantly less than before, and money is spent on other activities or on care at home. Does this mean, then, that parents, especially mothers, have a much higher burden of care? So far it appears that this concern is not shared by the carers themselves. In some cases a mother is quite happy to be paid enough so as not to have to take a job, or to reduce to part-time work, in order to be able to spend more time with her child. In other cases care is shared among members of an extended family. Within an extended family there is also sometimes a relative who has difficulty finding steady work, yet would be very happy, and find it rewarding, to act as a part-time paid carer. Most families report that self-directed services have made an improvement to everyone's life, including increasing contact and support from volunteer non-family members, which is something of a welcome surprise. So this particular objection seems misplaced. It has to be admitted, however, that if it turned out that the burden on carers increased in a way that reduced the quality of the carers' own lives, there would be good reason for discussing whether the scheme simply replaces one form of disadvantage or injustice with another, which could even be more severe.

A third concern is that of the likely decline of public goods like day centres. If most of the disabled people in my town choose not to spend their money on the day centre, what will happen? Most likely it will close down, and those who enjoyed going there will not be able to. Indeed, this is a traditional objection to giving individuals control over their own decisions with respect to public amenities, such as libraries and public swimming pools: there can be collective action problems that require collective solutions. The agency has a number of replies, however. Suppose it is true that a number of people might want to continue to go to the day centre, but that the centre disappears after the move to self-directed support. This would be a pity, but is it such a pity that it justifies forcing many people to use services they don't want so that some can get access to what they want? It is not even clear that it would be justified to give a minority no choice about how money is spent on their behalf even if the majority wanted to continue. Perhaps the answer is—in part—to rely on the logic of the market: if day centres are to continue, they have to be made good enough to survive competition with other ways of spending scarce cash. And the fragility of such public goods provides an argument for extra public subsidy to facilitate quality, as in the case of libraries and community centres. In practice, however, it appears that individuals do choose to continue going to day centres, but for fewer days each week than before. This is easy to understand, of course. Many people will appreciate the variety of a number of different ways of spending their time, and repetition can be stultifying whether it takes place inside or outside the home.

Finally, we need to return to Dworkin's example of the paraplegic violinist. It appears that if self-directed support is applied to his case, then the first step is that he will be assessed on the basis of his need and be given a particular budget. If he then chooses to spend it on a violin, that will be his business. The question, then, is whether self-directed support should be extended to physical disability. The case, I think, is arguable. There is a very important difference between those with cognitive disability and those with physical disability but no cognitive disability. Typically, those with cognitive disabilities have very little scope in their lives for agency or autonomous decision-making. Hence self-directed support provides them with something new and extra, with a good that they wouldn't otherwise have in terms of a measure of control over the environment. Those with physical disability may or may not be in this position, but it is less likely that giving physically disabled people control over their budget opens up a whole new avenue of value and experience. Of course, it is likely to have other advantages, but they do not seem so overwhelming. Consequently, accepting self-directed support for the cognitively disabled does not entail accepting it for other cases of disability (although the arguments do not exclude it either).

In making the arguments in defence of self-directed support as a form of targeted resource enhancement I do not want to be interpreted as assuming that agency or autonomy has some sort of lexical priority among values, and that everything should be done to advance individual autonomy. While, of course, I do have views about the place of autonomy in the scheme of values (see Wolff and de-Shalit 2007) nothing in this chapter is intended to presuppose a specific theory of well-being or of value. Rather, I need only to make some reasonably uncontroversial assumptions that, I believe, will be acceptable from a wide range of viewpoints. First, that generally speaking individual agency is valuable. Second, that people with cognitive disability very often have little scope for the exercise of agency in their lives. And finally, that other things being equal it is very good to increase the agency of those who currently have very little. Others may wish to make greater claims for the importance of agency or autonomy, but that is not my purpose, and not necessary, here.

I need also to make a remark about resource allocation. Nothing I have said in this chapter takes a stand on the question of how important it is to address the claims of people with cognitive disabilities when there are also other urgent demands on scarce social resources. I do not wish to give the impression that I believe that such claims will always be the most important when in competition with others, or that it would be wrong or inhuman to discuss questions of resource allocation when thinking about what society ought to do for people with disabilities. In thinking through public policy approaches, much will depend on the urgency of other claims and the resources society has to meet them. I take this issue very seriously and have discussed it elsewhere (Wolff 2009b), but I shall not repeat that discussion here.

The form of targeted resources enhancement discussed here, so it appears, provides an important policy option and a likely advance on other existing forms of support, which are of course targeted resource enhancements of a different type. There remains the question, however, of how far something like self-directed support would achieve the goal of creating an inclusive society of equals for people with cognitive disabilities. It seems clear that whatever improvements it can bring to the lives of people with cognitive disabilities in helping them find a worthwhile place in the world, it still hardly guarantees that we shall have created a society in which all are valued as equals. Accordingly, it is worth revisiting the question of the possibility of status enhancements for people with cognitive disability. Now, earlier in the chapter I endorsed Wikler's argument against the status enhancement of, say, reducing the cognitive demands necessary to enter a binding legal contract. The argument was that the type of changes that would lead to a fully inclusive social policy would have intolerable broader social costs in terms of making certain sorts of important legal and business relations impossible.

I do not want to withdraw my endorsement of that argument, but it is worth noticing that it is an argument against one very specific form of status enhancement, and it would be hasty to assume that it applies with equal force against all forms of status enhancement. For example, one of the factors that people with cognitive disabilities face is the prejudicial, even hostile, attitudes of others. Attempting to change this, through education and collective reflection, should be an urgent priority of social policy. Yet such a change is, in my terms, a status enhancement, as would be changes to the law to strengthen the rights of people with cognitive disabilities and to remove forms of discrimination. And there does not seem to be any natural extension of Wikler's argument to show that such policies would have intolerable costs; indeed, the opposite seems to be the case. Hence although, as we have seen, there are limits to the extent to which status enhancement can be used to provide improvements, it by no means follows that only targeted resource enhancement should be used in social policy towards people with cognitive disabilities. It appears that some forms of status enhancement remain essential, as does personal enhancement in the form of education, training, and certain forms of therapy. In sum, there is no single, simple route to equality, and indeed no combination of policies will be guaranteed to achieve it. Yet an imaginative set of policies, adopted in the spirit of experiment rather than dogma, and with the explicit aim of doing our best to move in the direction of equality, could achieve a good deal, even within the financial resources currently at our disposal.

Acknowledgments

An earlier version of this chapter was prepared for the Stony Brook conference on cognitive disability in September 2008. I am very grateful to the organisers, Eva Kittay, Licia Carlson, and Sophia Wong, for the invitation to speak, and for their comments on my presentation. I am also very pleased to thank Henry Richardson for his stimulating response to the paper I delivered, which led to several improvements, as well as other members of that audience. The paper was also presented at a seminar at the University of Melbourne, and I am very grateful to the participants on that occasion as well.

References

Brissenden, Simon. 1998. "Independent Living and the Medical Model of Disability." In *The Disability Reader*, edited by Tom Shakespeare, 20–27. London: Continuum.
Dworkin, Ronald. 1981. "What Is Equality? Part 1: Equality of Welfare." *Philosophy and Public Affairs* 10, no. 3:185–246.
Hunt, Paul. 1998 [1966]. "A Critical Condition." In *The Disability Reader*, edited by Tom Shakespeare, 7–19. London: Continuum.
MacIntyre, Alisdair. 2001. *Rational Dependent Animals*. Revised edition. Chicago: Open Court.
Poll, Carol, and Simon Duffy, eds. 2008. *A Report on In Control's Second Phase Evaluation and Learning 2005–2007*. London: In Control.
Waters, John, and Simon Duffy. 2007. *Individual Budget Integration*. London: In Control, for the [U.K.] Department of Health.
Wikler, Daniel. 1979. "Paternalism and the Mildly Retarded." *Philosophy and Public Affairs* 8, no. 4 (Summer): 377–92.
Williams, Gareth. 1998. "The Sociology of Disability: Towards a Materialist Phenomenology." In *The Disability Reader*, edited by Tom Shakespeare, 234–44. London: Continuum.
Wolff, Jonathan. 2002. "Addressing Disadvantage and the Human Good." *Journal of Applied Philosophy* 19, no. 3:207–18.
———. 2009a. "Disability Among Equals." In *Disability and Disadvantage*, edited by Kimberlee Brownlee and Adam Cureton, 112–37. Oxford: Oxford University Press.
———. 2009b. "Disability, Status Enhancement, Personal Enhancement and Resource Allocation." *Economics and Philosophy* 25, no. 1:49–68.
Wolff, Jonathan, and Avner de-Shalit. 2007. *Disadvantage*. Oxford: Oxford University Press.

9

HOLDING ONE ANOTHER (WELL, WRONGLY, CLUMSILY) IN A TIME OF DEMENTIA

HILDE LINDEMANN

When I was very little, my Granny, who has lived in the Deep South all her life, used to sing me the Dixie version of "Froggie Went A-Courtin." When she got to the refrain, her glittery-ringed hands with their fascinating long red fingernails would beat out "Straddle-laddle laddle laddle, Laddle bobaringtum, Ringtum bottom getchee cumbo!" and we would both dissolve in a puddle of giggles. Granny was too bossy to let anybody into her kitchen, but she would allow me to sit at the counter and watch her cook, and pass me a bite when she thought my mom wasn't looking.

Like many other women of her time and place, Granny was a law not only unto herself but unto the rest of us too. She'd light into Gramps for tracking dirt on the carpet or threaten to go after the next youngun who left the front door open, and my daddy regularly got the Come to Jesus lecture about his not bringing us all to see her more often. When she wasn't laying down the law, though, she was a great one for laughing. Best of all was when she would try to tell a story against herself, because she would invariably crack herself up so badly as she went along that she couldn't finish.

Granny loved Gramps, of course, and my Aunt Biz and my mom and all the grandchildren, but my daddy was the apple of her eye. "Are they being good to you up there in that office," she'd ask, "and not working you too hard? You look kind of peaky to me." Dad would assure her he was fine, but she'd shake her head and say, "Well, that's all right but you can't get good boiled peanuts up there like you can here. I fixed you some for after supper." And sure enough, after the dishes were done and the stories were over and Mom told us it was time for bed, Granny would get out the bowl of cold boiled peanuts and plenty of newspapers for the shells, and Dad would sit cross-legged on the floor by Granny's chair, shelling and eating them while she scritched his head as if he were a cat. We could almost see him purr.

Flash forward many years to when the personality of the woman I am calling Granny suddenly begins to unravel as the result of what is probably a multi-infarct dementia. Then the narrator of my story, her father and mother, and the other members of Granny's family become responsible for her care. In this chapter I take a close look at a particular kind of care that is best provided by family members rather than professional caregivers: I call it holding the person in her identity. Because strangers cannot well provide this kind of care, I argue that family members have a special responsibility to hold on to the person's identity for her, and I offer some criteria for doing this morally well or badly. But then I consider how even those who most need to be held can hold others in their identities, albeit clumsily, and I suggest that this kind of holding too can have great moral worth.

Familial Responsibility to Hold

In the sense in which I am using the term, an identity is a representation of a self. It consists of a tissue of stories, constructed from not only first-person but also many third-person perspectives, depicting the more important acts, experiences, relationships, and commitments that characterize a person and so allows that person and those around him to make sense of who he is. Because we change over time, some stories in the narrative tissue cease to depict us faithfully and—ideally—recede into the background, to be replaced with newer narratives that—again ideally—represent us more accurately (Nelson 2001).

Families are the primary sites for identity formation, which often begins even before birth, as the pregnant woman and other family members call the baby-to-be into personhood (Lindemann 2009). They do this through material practices (such as borrowing a crib or knitting tiny garments) that welcome the child into the family, but they also do it by weaving around the expected infant the stories that form its proto-identity. Mostly, these will be stories of relationship—narratives that identify the child to come as a member of *this* family, the son or daughter of *these* people. But the tissue of stories will also contain master narratives—the familiar stories permeating our culture that serve as summaries of socially shared understandings. These are the stories the family will likely draw on to make sense of the fact that the child will be a girl, or Irish American, or deaf, and so on.

As the child grows out of infancy she *becomes* who she is through the mutual process of accommodating herself to her family and being accommodated by it (Minuchin 1974, 47–48), but she *understands* who she is—acquires the self-conception out of which she acts—by means of the stories which her parents and other family members use to constitute her identity, and which they tacitly or explicitly teach her to apply to herself. Two kinds of stories are required to represent selves that are continually growing and changing even as in some respects they remain the same. The first kind is backward-looking; these stories depict who someone is by offering a causal explanation ("She's feisty, all right. Even in the womb she kicked like she meant it"). The second is forward-looking; these set the person's future field of action ("When you're older you'll be a good speller just like Charlotte, only without the web"). While later the child will almost certainly challenge some of these third-person stories, as a young child she does not yet possess the critical skills necessary for challenges of that sort. It is third-person contributions, then, that first form a person's identity.

All this is to say that families do the work of constructing their children's identities, but not yet to explain why this is morally important work, and why families bear a special responsibility for doing it well. Our identities matter morally because they function as counters in our social transactions, in that they convey understandings of both what we are expected to do and how others may or must treat us. Because I am your mechanic, I am expected to know why your car is making that funny sound; because you are the mayor, you get to say how the city is run. However, if families impose identities on their children that stunt their emotional, intellectual, or physical growth ("You'll never amount to anything"; "You're too clumsy to try out for Little League"), they unfairly constrict their children's agency and diminish their self-respect, and unless the children later manage to contest and repair these damaged identities, their lives will go badly for them. Because they are so well positioned to shape their children's self-concepts and so much rides on the outcome, it is morally incumbent on family members to get the process of identity formation off to a good-enough start.

Just as families are primarily responsible for initially constructing the child's identity, so too are they primarily responsible for holding the child in it. They do this by treating him in accordance with their narrative sense of him, and in so doing they reinforce those stories. But identity maintenance also involves weeding out the stories that no longer fit and constructing new ones that do. It's in endorsing, testing, refining, discarding, and adding stories, and then acting on the basis of that ongoing narrative work, that families do their part to keep the child's identity going.

As she grows, of course, the child contributes more and more to this process herself, as do her playmates, teachers, neighbors, and the others she encounters in her life. And just as important, these others challenge her, interrupt certain patterns of behavior, encourage self-transformations of various kinds, help or force her to grow in particular directions (Kukla 2007, 399). But when the kids at school call her names, when her older brother tells her she's adopted, when she doesn't pass the exam—when, in short, her grip on herself is temporarily shaky, what she needs most is to be *held* in her identity. It is then that the adults in her immediate family have the special job of reminding her, by how they interact with her, of who she really is.

It's not only other people who hold us in our identities. Familiar places and things, beloved objects, pets, cherished rituals, one's own bed or favorite shirt, can and do help us to maintain our sense of self. And it is no accident that much of this kind of holding goes on in the place where our families are: at home. "The home," observes Iris Marion Young, "is an extension of and mirror for the living body in its everyday activity," and thus is "the materialization of identity" (Young 1997, 150). Our homes *manifest* who we are at the same time as they provide the physical scaffolding that *supports* who we are. They are the solidly familiar axes around which our changing world revolves. I won't develop this notion any further here, as the primary focus of my chapter is on the narrative activity at the heart of person-to-person holding. Nevertheless, home-to-person holding can be enormously important, as we shall see later.

Good and Bad Holding

There are times when all of us need to be held in our identities, even after we are old enough to do much of this work for ourselves. Indeed, some identities require others to hold us in them continually: I can't be your wife if you stop being my husband, for example. However, just as there are morally admirable as well as morally culpable ways of being a husband or wife, so too are there both admirable and culpable ways of holding each other in these—and all other—identities.

For an identity to be properly yours, the backward-looking stories that constitute it have to pick out something about you that is importantly *true* (Arras 1997, 81–82). If you never went to med school, aren't licensed to practice, and don't see patients, then you aren't a doctor, and neither I, nor your doting mother, nor God himself can hold you in that identity. This is not to say, of course, that one can never be held in an identity that is not properly one's own. Con artists and swindlers count on getting their victims to do just that, as might decent people in dire circumstances whose lives or safety depend on their ability to deceive their enemies. In these cases (by contrast to the case of the would-be doctor who never sees patients), deceivers *act* the part, and this makes it possible for others' identifying stories to represent something that resembles the person the imposter claims to be. The point I want to press, though, is that occasions on which it is morally good to hold people in identities that are not their own are very rare. Good holding almost always requires stories that depict something actual about the person, so if your stories portray him as you wish to see him rather than as he actually is, you are very likely holding him wrong.

Truth is generally necessary but not sufficient for good holding. The stories one uses to constitute the other's identity must also get the proportions right. It may be perfectly true, for example, that your co-worker told a lie, but that by itself does not license your seeing her as a liar. For her to be fairly held in the "liar" identity, the lies must be habitual and serious enough to count as something other than polite euphemisms. Getting the proportions right might also mean taking into account who the person has been, and constructing a credible story of why a particular characteristic that formerly contributed relatively little to the overall shape of the identity is now so prominent a part of who she is. Or it might require discarding a story as too heavily focused on a characteristic that used to be important but no longer matters very much.

In addition to truth and proportionality, good holding also usually requires that the stories constituting the identity keep open the person's field of action, for this is how the narrative tissue captures the way in which selves are continually moving targets. One set of stories that closes down that field are the hateful or dismissive master narratives used by the members of a dominant social group to justify their oppression of another, less powerful group. These identities—black men as violent drug dealers, gay men as pedophiles, women as lovable nitwits, and so on—unjustly constrict the agency of those who bear them, keeping them from pursuing desirable opportunities and from enjoying their fair share of the goods that society has to offer. Good holding requires us to weed out these oppressive narratives from the stories we use to identify *any*one.

There is another set of stories that constrict people's agency. By contrast to morally degrading master narratives that misrepresent entire *classes* of people, *individually* constricting stories might be both true and correctly proportionate but fail to hold well because they look only backward and never ahead. When we interact with someone solely on the basis of these stories, we impede the person's ability to change. As Rebecca Kukla puts it, "In order to let a loved one show herself as herself, we often need to do more than perceive her as she really, already is; we need to offer material assistance and uptake that enable her to *become* ... who she is" (Kukla 2007, 398; my emphasis.). Often, this becoming involves some kind of growth: the stories in the narrative tissue must acknowledge that your teenager really is a slob but leave room for him to reform. At other times, though, the change is in the other direction: the stories that constitute your sister as invariably well dressed still capture something important about her, but now that she is in the grip of Alzheimer's disease, you may have to help her adjust—and adjust yourself—to a more relaxed standard. The only instance that comes to mind where an identity properly consists solely of backward-looking stories is when the person becomes permanently incapable of interacting in any way with those around her. People in the persistent vegetative state or in the end stages of dying are held badly when their loved ones draw on master narratives of miracle cures or mysterious awakenings that project the person into a future she cannot possibly inhabit.

Clumsy Holding

A distinction can be made between wrongful holding and clumsy holding. To make it, I continue the story with which I began.

When Dad called to tell me that Aunt Biz couldn't take care of Granny by herself anymore and there was no money for a home health aide, he sounded upset. "Biz is frazzled and at the end of her rope. She found a nice nursing home," he told me, "but she wants me to come down there to help her convince Mama she's got to go to it. And considering that Mama isn't thinking straight these days and always was pig-headed, there's going to be no reasoning with her."

I knew my duty as a daughter, and I did it. "I'll meet you down there," I said.

As it happened, Granny grew so frail in the three days before I arrived that she put up no resistance to being moved. She couldn't make sense of where she was, and kept referring to the nursing home as "that woman's house," as if she were a guest and trying to be polite about it but was clearly ready for the visit to end. Worse were the paranoid delusions, which mostly concerned enemies out to get, not her, but Dad or sometimes Gramps, now dead for many years. Sometimes she would recognize Aunt Biz and Dad and me, though often she would call me by her sister's name or think Dad was her husband. And sometimes she would just cry quietly and wonder what she had done to make everybody so mad that they wouldn't come see her anymore.

One day I gave her a manicure and pedicure, and I think we both felt better when her fingernails were shiny red again. Dad played his guitar for her, and that helped to steady her a little too. Mostly, though, we just sat with her, listening to her disjointed stream-of-consciousness observations, coaxing her to eat a few bites, and watching over her as she slept. On the final day of our stay, she wasn't quite sure who we were except that we were family, but she grasped that we were saying goodbye.

"Now, I'm going to be brave and not cry until after y'all leave me," she told us. "Come here, Buddy—Earl—Jasper, and let me scritch you before you go."

So Dad sat down again in the chair by her bed and Granny scritched his head for a while. When she finished, his hair was standing on end so she asked me for a comb and began to smooth it down. After she'd fixed it to her satisfaction we kissed her goodbye, and drove to the airport without talking very much and flew home.

There are many kinds of holding going on here, beginning with the narrator's decision to join her father, by which she holds him and her grandmother as well. By coming when he is needed, the father holds his mother and Biz. The manicure is an act of holding; the guitar playing could be another. By the criteria I've just offered, both father and daughter hold well, acting on the basis of backward-looking stories that are still relevant and accurately supplying forward-looking stories that make room for the grandmother's current fear, progressive disorientation, and increasing helplessness.

The most striking form of holding, of course, is the grandmother's of the father. In this Southern-style pietà, Granny holds Dad not well but clumsily, out of a fragmented and chaotic self-concept and an equally chaotic narrative understanding of who this man is. Her grip—on her son, on herself, on reality—is wobbly and unsure, yet for all its clumsiness, I submit, her holding is nevertheless a genuine exercise of her moral agency. It doesn't matter that she is no longer capable of rational reflection or of understanding her own situation. It doesn't even matter that she is no longer clear about whose identity, exactly, she is maintaining. Those considerations keep her from being able to hold well, but they don't stop her from holding clumsily. It is enough that she places this Buddy—Earl—Jasper fellow somewhere in the vicinity of her son, so that although her stories have disintegrated and her words have failed her, the holding still goes more or less where she intends.

I earlier referred to holding as a particular kind of care, and so it is: it is a part of the work of preserving, maintaining, and nurturing people. Joan Tronto has argued that morally good caring requires: (1) attentiveness to the needs of the (potential) recipient of care; (2) taking or accepting responsibility for meeting those needs; (3) competence in performing the tasks of care; and (4) responsiveness of the recipient to the care (Tronto 1993, 127–37). If these are the right characteristics, then presumably bad caring is inattentive, irresponsible, incompetent, and not attuned to the recipient's response.

Notice, though, that clumsy holding can be characterized in these ways as well. Although the grandmother in my story is attentive, she doesn't exactly know whom she is attending. She can scarcely be held responsible for anything she does these days, and she certainly is not competent in any legal or moral sense of the term. Furthermore, something has gone seriously wrong with how responsiveness is supposed to work here. Tronto writes, "Responsiveness suggests . . . that we consider the other's position as that other expresses it. Thus, one is engaged from the standpoint of the other, but not simply by presuming that the other is exactly like the self" (1993, 136). If engagement from the standpoint of the other is the mark of responsiveness, the grandmother doesn't even begin to qualify.

Nevertheless, although she meets none of the criteria for ethical caring, the grandmother's way of holding her son in his identity has tremendous moral worth. The elements Tronto has identified do indeed mark the difference between caring badly and caring well in many ordinary interactions, as between health professionals and patients, for instance, or teachers and students, or parents and young children. But the devastating beauty of the grandmother's action suggests that there are other sources of goodness that can make caring morally valuable—sources that do not require the levels of cognition presupposed by Tronto's list. In holding her son as she does, I believe, the grandmother draws on the long history of her relationship with him from infancy to adulthood, through tantrums and tenderness, fear and fair weather, sorrow, pride, and all the rest. Their entwined lives have held enough goodness so that now, when cognition is largely gone and little but habits of feeling remain, she still has a way to express how much she values her son.

A final thought: societies too have a role to play in helping us hold on to one another. If the familiar places and objects of home importantly hold us, it is better for us, all things being equal, to stay in our homes as long as we possibly can. However, when home care for people with progressive dementia is left almost entirely to family members, the familial capacity for care may be exhausted well before the benefits to the demented person of living at home have come to an end. In the United States, a nursing home then becomes the only option for many people, as Medicare covers home health care only on a part-time or intermittent basis (Medicare 2007, 3) and most private health insurers offer only very limited coverage as well. This state of affairs is not inevitable. Had the grandmother in my story been able to remain in her home, with adequate professional help and a carefully structured daily routine, she might not have gone downhill so rapidly. Social institutions and practices could be arranged so that the goods of home were integrated into the other forms of care. Eventually, nothing will keep the selves of progressively demented people from coming completely undone, but until then, they and their caregivers need the rest of us to hold them—if not as well as we can, then at least better than we do.

Acknowledgments

Thanks to Jim Nelson for first suggesting the distinction between (morally) bad and clumsy holding, to Marian Verkerk for reminding me to make use of Tronto's four ethical elements of care, and to Sara Ruddick for helping me to think more clearly about the holding capabilities of home. Thanks too to the originals of the characters in my story; you know who you are.

References

Arras, John. 1997. "Nice Story, but So What? Narrative and Justification in Ethics." In *Stories and Their Limits: Narrative Approaches to Bioethics*, edited by Hilde Lindemann Nelson, 65–88. New York: Routledge.
Kukla, Rebecca. 2007. "Holding the Body of Another." *Symposium: Canadian Journal of Continental Philosophy* 11, no. 2:397–408.
Lindemann, Hilde. 2009. "But *I* Could Never Have One . . . : The Abortion Intuition and Moral Luck." *Hypatia* 24, no. 1 (Winter): 41–55. Special issue in honor of Claudia Card.
Medicare. 2007. "Medicare and Home Health Care." http://www.medicare.gov/Publications/Pubs/pdf/10969.pdf
Minuchin, Salvador. 1974. *Families and Family Therapy*. Cambridge, Mass.: Harvard University Press.

Nelson, Hilde Lindemann. 2001. *Damaged Identities, Narrative Repair.* Ithaca, N.Y.: Cornell University Press.
Tronto, Joan. 1993. *Moral Boundaries: A Political Argument for an Ethic of Care.* New York: Routledge.
Young, Iris Marion. 1997. *Intersecting Voices: Dilemmas of Gender, Political Philosophy, and Policy.* Princeton: Princeton University Press.

10

AGENCY AND MORAL RELATIONSHIP IN DEMENTIA

BRUCE JENNINGS

In this chapter I examine the goals of care and the exercise of guardianship authority in the long-term care of persons with Alzheimer's disease and other forms of chronic, progressive dementia. I develop a specific conception of the quality of life and offer a critique of hedonic conceptions of quality of life and models of guardianship that are based on a hedonic legal standard of "best interests." (By "hedonic" I mean standards that give moral privilege to physical safety and to the subjective experience of comfort and pleasant sensation.) As an alternative, I offer a conception of quality of life based on the notions of "semantic agency" and "memorial personhood," and a model of trusteeship based on the conservation of agency and on right relationship and right recognition. To be sure, the questions of right (ethically justified) relationship and recognition are posed by any conception of personhood. The specific aspects of personhood in the context of dementia calls for a special conception that I am calling memorial personhood; "memorial" because it falls to others to sustain continuity of the demented self over time by recalling the self that has been when the individual cannot do that alone. But then, who among us can really do that alone?

The chapter is intended to operate on two levels. First, I am interested, from a sociological and historical point of view, in the conceptual framing and function of our public and private—policy, clinical, and familial—discourse concerning dementia. Second, from a philosophical point of view, I am interested in the substantive conceptual content of that discourse. I perceive dementia itself as a hermeneutic problem and dementia care as a hermeneutic process, a form of interpretive practice. I want to bring to the foreground key concepts of meaning, agency, the subject of care, and the ethics of recognition and memory, using these concepts to displace the prevailing discourse of meaninglessness, passivity, objectification, and loss. In too much dementia care today we ask how to come to terms with a diminished thing, when instead we should seek to attain a re-placed plenitude (MacIntyre 1999; Kitwood 1997).

Bioethics in a New Key

In the fields of bioethics and moral philosophy, the ethics of dementia care—and, indeed, all forms of cognitive impairment and chronic long-term care—has been marginal, despite its social, institutional, economic, indeed sheer human, implications (Nussbaum 2002 and 2006; Kittay 2002). Dementia—and conditions of severe brain impairment like it, such as traumatic brain injury—call for a bioethics and a moral philosophy in a new key. This chapter is a quest for the appropriate metaphors, resonance, sensibility, and moral imagination with which to comprehend the goals of care and the responsibilities of caregiving in the context of the generic kind of impairment that dementia represents (Jennings 2000, 2001, and 2006).

Dementia care is a form of reminding. It is reminding in the ordinary sense of recalling to mind something that has been forgotten; in dementia care a person's memory of past abilities and experiences can be nurtured and used therapeutically, and the loss of short-term memory and behavioral control can (to some extent) be mitigated and compensated for. But it is also "re-minding" in the more radical sense of reconstructing the subject, the person.

Dementia care involves the ordeal of reminding, or "re-minding" since this takes place against the background of the erosion of the mind or the person who was acting prior to the effects of the dementia. An important part of the point I wish to make in this chapter is that we should be carefully self-conscious about our terminology here. Reminding is a process, not an event. Similarly, mind is a performance, not an accomplished status or mental state. Reminding then is the rediscovering and refashioning of mind, but not exactly "a" mind of an individual, nor "the" mind of one. The first formulation suggests that we are dealing with one mental state in a series of such states; the second formulation suggests the notion that one such state is the essence or true mind of the individual. Neither formulation orients us properly for thinking about what is going on with mind, self, and action in the context of dementia, and these formulations lead to a good deal of argument over the priority among successive states or over whether the essential self has been lost or is still "there."

I hope to find a way to keep the dynamic, dialogic, or relational aspects of mind and agency (the gerund form, minding) at the center of our thinking about dementia care. It is necessary to focus on the conditions conducive to producing and reproducing a mind, not having or losing or being a mind. Such conditions are relational. Minding and reminding come through interaction that is at bottom about the exchange of meaning—the expression, offering, interpretation, and reception of meaning. To have a mind is to be in correspondence, somehow and to some degree, perhaps not very deeply or richly, with other minds.

Moreover, it is not necessary to draw a sharp distinction between personal and social mind when dealing with dementia, just as it is not requisite to draw a sharp line between minding in the past and minding in the present (remembering and intending).

So, reminding is the rediscovering and refashioning of mind both within the self and among selves. Or (should we say?) it is the process in and through which the individual who receives care, those who provide care, and the environment within which caring occurs each take part in doing this. Reminding is changing the environment and the external support system that surrounds the person so that *different* abilities do not become *the absence of* abilities. Reminding, as the play on words suggests, is remembering who one is, most fundamentally—as a relational human subject, person, agent—a maker and a interpreter of meaning. Once more, I am using this particular terminology deliberately and with some care. I do not believe that these concepts are out of place or inappropriate in application to individuals with dementia (across most of its spectrum). The tragedy of dementia is not so much that it alters brain function and changes what people can think and do; the real tragedy occurs when and if we allow those changes to objectify persons, reducing them to their impaired body and altered behavior, rather than working with them to re-mind themselves and to be re-membered among us (Kitwood 1993; Kittay 1999; Sabat and Harré 1992).

Two questions: (1) Why is this conception I have just sketched so difficult to make plausible? And (2) What follows from this ethics of dementia, from this bioethics in a new key?

(1) Why is it hard to believe this conception? One of the most powerful assumptions in our habitual way of thinking and feeling about dementia is that the erosion and loss of brain function precludes relationality in a deep sense and hence precludes being a social persona and having a social identity. Closely allied with this is the assumption that the impairment of brain function must of necessity erase the ability to make meaning and erode one's membership in the human moral community. We need to reexamine several aspects of the symbolic and emotional economy of our response to brain injury and self-transformation. These are the paradigms, icons, and idioms, inherited from our tradition, with which we most habitually perceive, imagine, think, and feel. They inform our assumptions, attitudes, and reactions to dementia. They are the stuff of its imagined reality. They are our first line of defense when dementia arrives, a most unwelcome visitor, and enters our families. Part of the ordeal of reminding for members of a family is to discover that the conceptual and symbolic resources of their cultural tradition are not sufficient or fully serviceable.

My contention is that generally in our society today, these ready-made patterns of perception and expectation are not reliable, nor are these patterns equal to the task presented by the unique symptoms, disabilities, and needs of an individual who has sustained dementia and now must live with and in spite of it. All too often family members (and other caregivers) have to fashion new patterns and new structures of meaning for themselves (Bayley 1999; Bernlef 1988; DeBaggio 2002 and 2003; Cooney 2003; Davidson 1997; McGowin 1993; and Mitchell 2002). Depending upon the stage of the progressive dementia and the extent of loss of capacity, the person living with dementia may assimilate and take such patterns of response into his or her own work of reminding and healing, and in the process will have to refashion expectations about dementia previously drawn from the culture as well.

(2) What follows from the denial of these assumptions, definitions, and paradigms, from a bioethics in a new key? Nothing short of a revolution in our understanding of what ethics truly requires of long-term care public policy and caregiving practices. In particular, a revolution in our understanding of crucial concepts for long-term care ethics, "quality of life" and "best interests."

I believe that we must abandon the (now predominant) notion that quality of life (or "best interests") for persons with moderate to severe cognitive and behavioral impairments from dementia involves primarily security, comfort, and the fulfillment of immediate, experiential interests. An alternative conception of quality of life, for which I argue, holds that the preservation and restoration of capacities for human communicative relations and an honoring of the identity of the person with dementia define the appropriate goals of care.

I also contend that the notion of best interests, which sets a legal and ethical standard for guardians and other caregivers, must be reconceptualized away from a hedonic conception of good quality of life and a preoccupation with security, comfort, and the fulfillment of immediate, experiential interests (Dresser 1986). An alternative conception is that the ethically (and legally) appropriate standard for caregivers is to create the social ecology and the relational skills and practices that are effective for the preservation of the agency and identity of the individual with dementia receiving care.

Relationship and Recognition in Dementia Care

To fix ideas, I am working with the following general characterization of Alzheimer's disease as the paradigm case of dementia: Alzheimer's disease is a progressive and degenerative brain disorder that gradually undermines cognitive function and emotional control. The disease lends itself to the mapping of various stages of impairment and dysfunction, although the manifestation of behavioral symptoms varies significantly among individuals. In addition to the loss of short-term memory and disorientation in relation to everyday activities, dementia also progressively manifests changes in the individual's personality, the onset of psychiatric conditions such as depression, paranoia, and hallucinations, erosion of executive functions regarding such things as personal hygiene, apparel, and social etiquette, and loss of self-control in the presence of strong feelings such as anger, frustration, and fear. Fine motor function, judgment, and physical response time may also be affected during the course of the disease. Other forms of dementia differ in some ways, but not so as to be significant for my discussion in this chapter.

Alzheimer's disease is both a disease of the brain and a malady of the mind. As a disease, dementia is an attack on the brain, upsetting its enormously complex and delicate chemistry and circuitry. Beyond that, Alzheimer's disease is a human catastrophe because it disrupts and distorts the mind, confounding and eventually overwhelming its remarkable durability and resiliency. It is primarily in the former domain that most of our recent, exciting knowledge in the field of dementia has come (Damasio 1994; Souren and Franssen 1994). The human brain is finally beginning to yield its secrets. Yet new knowledge, new perspectives, and new insights are no less necessary in the realm of the mind and the self—in the realm of phenomenological understanding, interpersonal transaction, self-consciousness, memory, and judgment. New insight is also needed in the realm of reflexive self-monitoring, self-control, and the determinants of culturally and situationally appropriate behavior. When the social and transactional capacities begin to erode and to deteriorate markedly over time, a difficult threshold of personal, ethical, social, and legal questions arises.

The appropriate goals of care in dementia should be those of *rehabilitation* in the broad and etymological sense of the word—to bring the person back to the conditions of the living of a life. Earlier I alluded to the distinction between "guardianship" and "trusteeship" as models of caregiving and surrogacy. Guardianship is a model centered around the preservation of comfort and safety for a profoundly vulnerable and disabled individual. Trusteeship is a model centered on the preservation of an enabling environment for agency in the face of vulnerability and impairment. Rehabilitation is the work of trusteeship, not guardianship; it is a form of conserving, an endeavor of sustaining. It is the sustaining of the integrity of the person, through a meaningful self-identity; the sustaining of effective, albeit different and non-normal capacity for communicative and relational agency; and the sustaining of the individual's identity as a moral subject, as a being worthy of memory and respect and regard. Healing, wholeness, and human flourishing, even in the labyrinth of dementia, come from (1) the exercise of semantic agency, albeit in new ways and with new strategies and forms of assistance that outwit impairment; and (2) being re-membered or recognized as a self who is a subject rather than an object and as a self who is (once more and still) a member of an ongoing social web of meaningful communicative relationships.

Semantic agency refers to the capacity to communicate, to engage in meaning-sending and meaning-receiving relationships (that is, transactional relationships) with others, and to evince understanding and evaluation of such communication. I argue on hermeneutic and clinical grounds that this capacity persists *in properly structured, supportive caregiving environments* even when high-level cognitive, speech, executive, and short-term memory functioning have been impaired. Semantic agency is the capacity for engaging in the activity of making and experiencing meaning, where meaning taps a level or circuit of communication between human beings that goes beyond unilateral sensation or sensate experience (Jaworska 1999). Of course, communication here does not mean verbal or even semiotic communication, for the capacity to manipulate previously learned semiotic systems may be lost with some dementia patients. But touch, gesture, facial expression, posture, eye contact, even control of body movements in order to permit prolonged physical closeness, like sitting together, can conceivably be media of semantic agency, and these may endure even when memory, speech, functional capacities for activities of daily living and self-care, and other capacities are compromised.

For those who provide care for individuals living with dementia, there is also a primary duty to sustain as much as possible the individual's status as a moral subject, a member of a fabric of moral relationships and community. I seek to explore this by deploying the concept of "memorial personhood." Memorial personhood refers to the status of the demented individual within the moral life world of semantic agents and those engaged in the form of moral agency constituted by the giving of care. This particular type and status of personhood is not often recognized as such (Harré and Gillett 1994; Harré 1998). It does not derive from the capacities of the individual, even the capacity for semantic agency. It derives instead from three components of the individual's ontological situation: need, vulnerability, and the duty called forth by remembered identity. To be a memorial person is to be a self in the imagination and memory of others; which, on this view, is just what it is to be a self. It is to be a self whose identity and life must be honored and acknowledged by those who can, even if it can no longer be by the person himself or herself. And to be a person of any type—including a memorial person—is to be a self to whom, as Arthur Miller puts it in *Death of a Salesman*, "attention must be paid."

The notion of memorial personhood is not unique to dementia or Alzheimer's disease, although it seems to fit naturally enough there, since memory loss is one of the salient manifestations of the disease. Yet it seems fitting in other contexts of cognitive impairment as well, whenever a person has difficulty bridging past and present in his or her activity of minding and meaning. It involves the invoking of a self with a life history, an archaeological site for the work of memory, as it were, and therefore it may not hold well for cases of profound cognitive impairment with very early onset. There the work of imagination by others rather than the exercise of memory by others may be more crucial to the fabric of moral personhood which must be recognized and to which attention must be paid. The moral work done by memory and imagination in situations of caring or interrelational agency perhaps is very similar.

However that may be, memorial personhood underscores the neglected place of memory in moral theory and practice; it reaffirms, even in the face of disability and impairment, the continuing recognition of individuals living with dementia as members of a human moral community, a community of constant re-naming and re-membering. On the basis of these conceptions, I argue that both caregivers and social institutions (including public policy for long-term care) have an obligation to provide the environment, resources, services, and human presence necessary to sustain and conserve semantic agency and (memorial) personhood during the course of life with dementia.

The basic idea here is that maintaining, sustaining, and creating relationships—connections and commitments—with the impaired subject is itself an ethical obligation for other individuals in the moral person's environment. If I am a moral subject, I cannot rightfully be ignored, abandoned, exiled from the space of connection between selves that we call the moral community. Moreover, to relate to someone as a moral subject is different from relating to him or her as a moral object, as an object of moral concern, affection, empathy, kindness, even love. A moral object may be well cared for; a moral subject calls forth and commands care by dint of his or her identity, status, and agency in a shared skein of subject status, a moral commons or space of moral recognition (cf. Darwall 2006).

Quality of Life and Agency

A philosophical conception of quality of life is an account of those capacities that are constitutive of the human good or the realization of full humanity and an account of the circumstances (freedoms, powers, rights, and resources) that are most conducive to the actualization or realization of these components of the good in an individual's life and experience. The more fully the human good is realized, the greater the quality of human life. Most philosophical theories of quality of life fall into three basic categories (Brock 1993; McCormick 1978; Parfit 1984, 493–502; Scanlon 1993).

Hedonic or satisfaction conceptions. These accounts identify quality of life with states of awareness, consciousness, or experience of the individual. Happiness or pleasure, however those terms are precisely to be defined, are the sine qua non of quality of life. This allows for considerable individual variation in assessing good quality of life because different things make different people happy, but it also allows for some kind of common metric (at least on the negative side) because there are seemingly universal negative states of pain or suffering or unhappiness that all (normal) persons avoid. An interesting question, when applying this type of theory to the case of dementia, is whether it is necessary for the person to realize he or she is happy in order to be happy. In other words, is the kind of happiness (or pleasure) that makes for a good quality of life a direct, unmediated sensation, or is it a psychic state that results from some act of self-interpretation? If it is the former, then it would seem to follow that a person locked in a cell with an electrode implanted in a pleasure center of the brain would be experiencing the highest quality of life. That conclusion must be mistaken and counts against the theory. On the other hand, if the pleasure or happiness the theory requires some form of cognitive mediation and secondary interpretation, then persons who have serious cognitive deficits will automatically be judged to have a poor quality of life by definition, and that view seems unduly biased against nonintellectual goods in life.

Rational desire or preference conceptions. The second type of theory defines quality of life in terms of the actual realization of a person's rational desires or preferences. I don't have time to discuss this conception any further in this context. My impression is that it has less direct bearing on the ethics of dementia care and long-term care.

Agency conceptions. This type of philosophical theory attempts to base our understanding of the good life on an account of those functions, capacities, and excellences that are most fully and constitutively human. It is within this general conception that I wish to locate my own work. To the extent that we attain and master those capacities, and to the extent that we negate those conditions that would stunt or undermine those capacities, we flourish as human beings. Theories of this type also usually have a developmental component built into them, for those most fully human capacities are ones that are not mastered at birth or automatically expressed by instinct but must be developed and nurtured by education, interaction with others, and practice over the course of a lifetime. To the extent, then, that the individual continues to grow and develop throughout his or her life, the quality of life is enhanced thereby (Nussbaum 2000).

Once again, accounts of these most fully human capacities differ among philosophers, but as a generalization we can say that philosophical accounts of this type usually emphasize the human capacity to express and to experience meaning in social relationships of intimacy, friendship, and cooperation; the capacity to use reason and to develop and follow a life plan of self-fulfillment and self-realization; the capacity for independence and self-reliance; and the human need for an appropriate social and cultural environment that provides the individual with various types of resources—material, symbolic, spiritual—necessary to live a developmentally human life and to meet both basic and secondary needs.

In the literature on quality of life and dementia (and also in the literature on the legal authority of guardianship) the most commonly adopted philosophical perspective is the hedonic (Cantor 2005). And in these fields and in the literature of moral philosophy it is commonly assumed that only the hedonic conception can apply to those with dementia and other severe forms of cognitive disability; the agency conception is inappropriate or irrelevant.

I disagree with that view. I contend that it is the communicative and semantic aspects of human capabilities, not the stress on high-level cognitive skills, that represents what is most worthwhile and defensible in agency or human flourishing theories, or at least in the version of such a theory that we should develop today. Making sense together, remembering a distant past and self, making judgments and expressing evaluations, even though nonverbally through emotional responses and bodily, kinetic gestures—these are some of the constituent elements or capabilities of a quality life, whatever the degree of one's other abilities in short-term memory processing and ratiocination. Those without the impairments of dementia do these, and other, things in many different ways with an audience of others or with an audience of various "selves" or perspectives within their own minds. Those with the impairments of dementia do them differently, more tenuously, and they need different kinds of audiences and help, but they do them, sometimes for remarkably long into the progress of the disease. *Life lived with and in spite of dementia, then, even well into its later stages, can be explicated by drawing on conceptions of human agency and flourishing, and it need not be assessed only in the most directly sensate, hedonic terms.*

I offer this proposition partly as a normative claim and partly in the spirit of a testable hypothesis. If we try to work with broader and richer notions of quality of life, we will in fact be rewarded with more insightful findings for both public policy and clinical practice (Albert and Logsdon 2000). But I also argue for it because I believe the consequences of not doing it, and adhering to the hedonic approach exclusively, are ethically unacceptable.

If we thought that a person with dementia had the capacity for semantic agency or if we remembered his or her identity and status as a subject rather than an object—if we did that, why would we ever be content to say that he or she has a good quality of life merely if her pleasurable sensations outnumber her painful ones? Surely we would look instead at the surrounding conditions that the person is living in and ask how the range of his or her exercise of (remaining) capacity for semantic agency can be enhanced and facilitated. And ask: How could caregivers be given a better opportunity to mend and maintain those relationships and interactions appropriate to the recognition and honoring of moral subject status? Pleasant sensations or feelings will come through the exercise of semantic agency and with the recognition by others of oneself as a subject, to be sure, but agency and recognition, not the sensations per se, are the sum and substance of one's quality of life.

Tragically, with dementia we may actually have to choose between happiness and agency, for to slow the progress of the disease in its early or middle stages and to extend the period of capacity and agency is also to extend the suffering that accompanies the awareness of ongoing and impending loss. Hedonic conceptions of quality of life would not necessarily view drugs that have this effect as beneficial. Moreover, if the hedonic conception of quality of life sets the bar too low for caregivers and policy makers in the early and middle stages of dementia, it also gives the wrong kind of guidance in the late stages. It offers only a thin, inadequate conception of palliative care for those dying with dementia—that is, comfort care and symptom management. In fact, the components and aims of palliative care, rightly understood, go well beyond a hedonic conception of quality of life and aspire to at least some of the elements of human flourishing. The philosophy of palliative care that has been newly emerging in the past decade has primarily to do with the (re)structuring of the environment of caregiving so that the meaning-making and relational human powers of the self may be sustained as long as possible; sustained in new forms of expression as neurological function deteriorates, to be sure, but as long as possible in some form nonetheless.

Caring that disables agency in the service of contemporaneous comfort and existential interests undermines its own ethical rationale and vitiates its moral potential as a practice of human enrichment. Caring that is only loving and not discerning and respecting fails in its recognition of the care recipient as a subject, and it fails to elicit the most worthy moral identity of the caregiver as well. For caring as a practice implicates the caregiver's own identity as a moral subject (Kittay 1999). This is true both at the intimate, personal level of caring and at a more communal and public level, where the ethics of intimate, personal care should be reflected in the larger mirror of public purpose. Aside from the well-being of the person who has entered the long, narrowing path of dementia, and in addition to the health of the moral community of family, caretakers, and friends, the broader health of our shared civic and human community is inextricably bound up with how well we meet the ethical goals of dementia care.

If it does nothing else, the agency notion of quality of life and the concepts of semantic agency and memorial personhood should increase our awareness of new possibilities for family, professional, and community caring for persons with dementia.

Let us affirm the principle that in dementia there is a kind of agency that seems devoid of meaning and lacking in humanness, not because it really is, but only because we do not know how to interpret it.

And let us affirm the principle that curtailing semantic agency and memorial personhood in dementia for the sake of safety, comfort, or expediency is not the path of morally responsible caregiving or prudent public policy. Agency and selfhood of any kind eventually fade all too rapidly in the face of dementia. Let us not hasten their demise prematurely through a kind of inadvertent hermeneutic and moral blindness.

References

Albert, Steven M., and Rebecca G. Logsdon, eds. 2000. *Assessing Quality of Life in Alzheimer's Disease.* New York: Springer.
Bayley, John. 1999. *Elegy for Iris.* New York: St. Martin's Press.
Bernlef, J. 1988. *Out of Mind.* London: Farber and Farber.
Brock, Dan. 1993. "Quality of Life Measures in Health Care and Medical Ethics." In *The Quality of Life,* edited by Martha C. Nussbaum and Amartya Sen, 95–139. New York: Cambridge University Press.
Cantor, Norman L. 2005. *Making Medical Decisions for the Profoundly Mentally Disabled.* Cambridge, Mass.: MIT Press.
Cooney, Eleanor. 2003. *Death in Slow Motion: My Mother's Descent into Alzheimer's.* New York: HarperCollins.
Damasio, Antonio R. 1994. *Descartes' Error: Emotion, Reason, and the Human Brain.* New York: G. P. Putnam's Sons.
Darwall, Stephen. 2006. *The Second-Person Standpoint: Morality, Respect, and Accountability.* Cambridge, Mass.: Harvard University Press.
Davidson, Ann. 1997. *Alzheimer's, a Love Story: One Year in My Husband's Journey.* Secaucus, N.J.: Carol.
DeBaggio, Thomas. 2002. *Losing My Mind: An Intimate Look at Life with Alzheimer's.* New York: Free Press.
———. 2003. *When It Gets Dark: An Enlightened Reflection on Life with Alzheimer's.* New York: Free Press.
Dresser, Rebecca S. 1986. "Life, Death and Incompetent Patients: Conceptual Infirmities and Hidden Values in the Law." *Arizona Law Review* 28:373–405.
Harré, Rom. 1998. *The Singular Self.* Thousand Oaks, Calif.: Sage.
Harré, Rom, and Grant Gillett. 1994. *The Discursive Mind.* Thousand Oaks, Calif.: Sage.
Jaworska, Agnieszka. 1999. "Respecting the Margins of Agency: Alzheimer's Patients and the Capacity to Value." *Philosophy and Public Affairs* 28, no. 2 (Spring): 105–38.
Jennings, Bruce. 2000. "A Life Greater Than the Sum of Its Sensations: Ethics, Dementia, and the Quality of Life." In *Assessing Quality of Life in Alzheimer's Disease,* edited by Steven M. Albert and Rebecca G. Logsdon, 165–78. New York: Springer.
———. 2001. "Freedom Fading: On Dementia, Best Interests, and Public Safety." *Georgia Law Review* 35, no. 2 (Winter): 593–619.

———. 2006. "The Ordeal of Reminding: Traumatic Brain Injury and the Ethics of Care." *Hastings Center Report* 37, no. 2 (March/April): 29–37.

Kittay, Eva Feder. 1999. *Love's Labor: Essays on Women, Equality, and Dependency*. New York: Routledge.

———. 2002. "Can Contractualism Justify State-Supported Long-Term Care Policies? Or, I'd Rather Be Some Mother's Child." In *Ethical Choices in Long-Term Care: What Does Justice Require?* edited by the World Health Organization, 77–83. Geneva: WHO.

Kitwood, Tom. 1993. "Towards a Theory of Dementia Care: The Interpersonal Process." *Ageing and Society* 13:51–67.

———. 1997. *Dementia Reconsidered*. Buckingham: Open University Press.

MacIntyre, Alasdair. 1999. *Dependent Rational Animals*. Chicago: Open Court.

McCormick, Richard. 1978. "The Quality of Life, the Sanctity of Life." *Hastings Center* 8, no. 1 (February): 30–36.

McGowin, Diana Friel. 1993. *Living in the Labyrinth: A Personal Journey Through the Maze of Alzheimer's*. New York: Delta Books.

Mitchell, Marilyn. 2002. *Dancing on Quicksand: A Gift of Friendship in the Age of Alzheimer's*. Boulder, Colo.: Johnson Books.

Nussbaum, Martha C. 2000. *Women and Human Development*. Cambridge: Cambridge University Press.

———. 2002. "Long-Term Care and Social Justice: A Challenge to Conventional Ideas of the Social Contract." In *Ethical Choices in Long-Term Care: What Does Justice Require?* edited by the World Health Organization, 31–66. Geneva: WHO.

———. 2006. *Frontiers of Justice*. Cambridge, Mass.: Harvard University Press.

Parfit, Derek. 1984. *Reasons and Persons*. Oxford: Oxford University Press.

Sabat, Steven R., and Rom Harré. 1992. "The Construction and Deconstruction of Self in Alzheimer's Disease." *Ageing and Society* 12:443–61.

Scanlon, Thomas M. 1993. "Value, Desire, and Quality of Life." In *The Quality of Life*, edited by Martha C. Nussbaum and Amartya Sen, 185–200. New York: Cambridge University Press.

Souren, Liduin, and Emile Franssen. 1994. *Broken Connections: Alzheimer's Disease*, part 1. Lisse: Swets and Zeitlinger.

11

COGNITIVE DISABILITY, PATERNALISM, AND THE GLOBAL BURDEN OF DISEASE

DANIEL WIKLER

As Kittay, Nussbaum, and others have noted, contemporary political philosophy—particularly in the contractarian tradition—tends to view social justice primarily as a set of principles established by and for human adults who enjoy average or better cognitive function. Each sub-population that fails to qualify for membership in this elite group—be they children, those born with serious cognitive disability, or once-competent adults suffering from progressive dementia—thus constitutes a problem case for any general theory that must be worked out in a matter consistent with the particular theory's guiding principles. For the most part, theorists of social justice have given little attention to these tasks. These sub-populations deserve better, and not only to enhance the comprehensiveness and elegance of these theories. Together they constitute a substantial share of any society's citizens; and, lacking the ability to protect themselves against neglect and abuse, their treatment by the cognitively unimpaired has often been unjust. Any serious effort to understand the tasks that must be undertaken by a society that wishes to be viewed as just must ensure that its theory extends to the principal groups of cognitively impaired and provides a reasoned and humane prescription for their care and for their relationship with their fellow citizens.

One group that presents distinctive challenges to theories of social justice are individuals whose level of cognitive functioning, while strong enough to permit a rich understanding of life's challenges and joys, is decisively inferior to that of average adult human beings. With IQ (and related measures) below two standard deviations from the mean, but still able to conduct conversations and to indicate preferences in many daily choices, these adults function just below the cusp of "normalcy," as we have chosen to define it. While efforts may be made to honor a substantial range of their choices, such as food preferences and, where feasible, living arrangements, they are often denied a number of the decision-making powers that accrue to the cognitively unimpaired upon reaching the age of majority. In many of the American states, they must submit to the guidance of competent persons or authorities in deciding whether and whom to marry, whether to have children, to enter into financial contracts, and to live alone.[1] Generally speaking, adults of normal intelligence may make these decisions without obtaining the consent of anyone, and they value this autonomy. When persons of normal intelligence, acting through the state, take custody of the cognitively disabled, they do not seek the consent of the cognitively disabled, who acquire protection but lose their legal rights. If we claim that relative intellectual superiority justifies restricting the liberties of the cognitively disabled, could not exceptionally gifted persons make the same claim concerning persons of normal intelligence? I propose to examine the moral importance of relative intellectual superiority, and to consider whether it can serve as adequate grounds for denying full citizenship to the mildly cognitively disabled.

The question of cognitive "competence" and decision-making authority arises in attempting to understand the position of this cognitively challenged population in a just society. My suggestion is that the question of civil liberties for this group is closely linked to the general problem of determining the extent of the obligation of cognitively unimpaired individuals to construct a society which might reduce the burden of cognitive disability for the mildly impaired but which would also reduce the efficiency of certain social institutions and practices for others. The present essay closes with a brief remark on a second theoretical issue in this vein: how we may best assess the overall burden of mild and moderate cognitive disability within a comprehensive measure of the global burden of disease.

The Case for Restricting the Civil Liberties of the Cognitively Disabled

The standard reason for denying full freedom of decision to the mildly cognitively disabled is the alleged danger to themselves and to others. Each of these grounds may be disputed. The latter is often recognized as dubious, and the former probably exaggerated.[2] One might even argue that the danger posed by the mildly cognitively disabled person to himself is less serious than that posed by a paternalistic bureaucracy endowed

---

[1] The term "guidance" is not strictly accurate in describing the relation of a legally incompetent person to his or her legal guardian. Technically, cognitively disabled persons are (usually) denied the right to make the decisions at all; for example, contracts made by these persons are void, and marriages entered into by them may be annulled. The differences among these legal arrangements do not affect the present argument. See Michael Kindred, "Guardianship and Limitations upon Capacity," in *The Mentally Disabled Citizen and the Law*, edited by Michael Kindred et al. (New York: Free Press, 1976), 63–87.

[2] Partly because many persons labeled cognitively disabled are in fact not mentally deficient, having been mislabeled by inaccurate testing and sorting processes (see Jane Mercer, *Labeling the Mentally Retarded* [Berkeley: University of California Press, 1973]); and partly because the wide range of support services available to many cognitively disabled persons enables them to function adequately on their own.

with broad powers, questionable wisdom, and inconstant motivation. Still, it seems likely that there exist at least some mildly cognitively disabled persons who would in fact damage their own interests if given full civil liberties and who would be protected from this harm by restrictions.

In the liberal tradition, the expectation of doing harm to oneself is certainly part of any strong argument for a paternalistic denial of liberties (doing so merely to impose a benefit would be harder to defend).[3] Still, again within that tradition, an expectation is not itself sufficient to make a case for restrictions. Persons of normal intelligence may also pose a danger or risk to their own interests. They can make impulsive contracts, enter into disastrous marriages, and choose occupations in which they are likely to perform poorly. Despite this, they insist on freedom of choice in such matters; not only freedom to make good choices but also freedom to fail. Though it is not absolute, a standard liberal principle allows us to do as we please as long as the interests of others are not unfairly threatened. The fact that we are about to act against our own interests is not (generally) enough excuse to restrict us.[4]

Thus, the fact that some cognitively disabled persons pose a threat to their own welfare is not in itself sufficient reason to deny them the liberty to do so. This denial derives from an exception clause in the liberal principle. While it would be wrong to place restrictions on a normal person posing exactly the same threat to her own interests, restrictions on a cognitively disabled person would seem to be justified by her mental disability. Some persons of normal intelligence, however self-destructive, are capable of making their decisions on their own; they have the capacity to understand what is at stake, to weigh the alternatives, and to take responsibility for the result. The mildly cognitively disabled, however, by virtue of their retardation, cannot. We normal people must decide for them, just as we must for the temporarily insane, the comatose, and others unable to reason.

Or so the argument goes. As it stands, it is vulnerable to criticism at several points. One is the vagueness of the concept of "retardation." "General" intelligence is not easily characterized, let alone tested and measured. And even so, the fact that a person has been labeled "cognitively disabled" through our social sorting mechanisms is by no means a sure guide to his intellectual abilities. But I do not want to press these

---

[3] See Joel Feinberg, "Legal Paternalism," *Canadian Journal of Philosophy* 1, no. 1 (1971): 105–24.

[4] It must be reemphasized that this claim is not absolute and that there will be occasions on which it is fair to restrict persons of normal intelligence out of concern for their own interests. But since normal persons claim a prima facie right to do as they please, why should not the mildly cognitively disabled also claim this right? Although our behavior toward normal persons is occasionally paternalistic, toward the mildly cognitively disabled it is routinely so.

objections here.[5] Rather, I want to examine the presupposition that there are but two possible statuses, however uncertain their boundary: one of impaired and one of unimpaired intellect, the one lacking a right to self-direction, the other possessing it. For even if we recognize an intellectual deficit in the mildly disabled person when compared to the person of normal ability, there is no obvious and compelling reason to attach such moral significance to it. The moderately cognitively disabled have this deficit when compared with the mildly cognitively disabled; and the normal person might have the same when compared with the gifted. We may recognize, then, an array of such cognitive statuses. Do these differences correspond to a large number of distinct moral statuses? If the average, now deemed "normal," is "impaired from the point of view of those of higher intellectual status, are persons of average intelligence for this reason subject to a paternalistic denial of civil liberties?

It would seem that if the intellectual superiority of normal persons legitimates their controlling the decisions of the mildly cognitively disabled, the same difference in intellect would justify their being regulated by the gifted.[6] Our right to self-direction, however, is a right to be free from constraint by any person whether of normal, subnormal, or high intelligence. It is supposed to hold even when our decisions are poor and when others happen to know better. We are in the position, then, of using relative intellectual superiority as our rationale for regulating the cognitively disabled, while rejecting the possibility of this same rationale being imposed upon us. Unless the apparent inconsistency is resolved, we shall have to either find new foundations for our paternalistic policy toward the mildly cognitively disabled or abandon it.

---

[5] The lack of attention to these points in the present essay is not meant to suggest that they are unimportant. Indeed, as recent case law has shown, they are themselves sufficient arguments against public policies which fail to distinguish between degrees of retardation, which rely solely on group IQ tests, and which fail to take into account the particular abilities and social resources a cognitively disabled individual may possess. Such policies thus extend the protection of the legal status of "cognitively disabled person" to people without regard to their real needs. More important, it also extends the burden of that status, stigmatizing the individual and legitimating the segregation and discrimination that have historically been the lot of those placed in this category. Thus one powerful argument for granting civil liberties to the mildly cognitively disabled is that such equal treatment helps to avoid stigmatization and its adverse consequences. This gain may offset the risks involved. The argument appeals to our concern for the cognitively disabled person's welfare, rather than to any right of self-direction, and it stands (or falls) independently of the issue addressed in this essay.

[6] Robert Nozick poses a related question in his *Anarchy, State and Utopia* (New York: Basic Books, 1974). His concern is with a policy of "Utilitarianism for animals, Kantianism for people," in which beings of higher status may use beings of lower status as means and not as ends. The issue discussed in my essay concerns only behavior toward an individual for his own good, whether it is paternalist benevolence or respect for autonomy; but perhaps the latter is a particularly Kantian moral attitude. Nozick's own resolution, incidentally, seems open to the objections raised below.

Two Conceptions of Competence

The inconsistency of claiming immunity from paternalism on the part of our superiors while claiming the right to impose it on our inferiors rests, I believe, upon a certain conception of mental capacity.[7] On this view, which I will call relativism, mental capacity is an attribute admitting of "more" and "less." The mildly cognitively disabled have less capacity than normal persons, who, in turn, are less endowed than gifted persons might be. No categorization of a group as "mentally impaired" makes sense, on this view, except when understood as relative to the perspective from some other level. Normal persons, those of average intellectual powers, are impaired relative to the gifted, and the mildly cognitively disabled are well endowed relative to the severely cognitively disabled. Intelligence, like wealth, is open-ended. As there is no point at which one is "fully wealthy," only more so and even more so, no one can be "fully intelligent." We may be able to distinguish various levels of mental ability through tests, but any line drawn between mentally "impaired" and mentally "unimpaired" is arbitrary. The line could be drawn anywhere else on the scale with equal justification.

The point of this relativist view can be illustrated by reference to the specific components of what are thought to make up the cognitively disabled person's deficit. The mildly cognitively disabled person, according to one authority, is unable to think about and deal with more than one or two aspects of a complex situation.[8] She is unable to defer gratification so as to make choices most likely to be of benefit over the longest run, and to foresee long-term consequences of present acts. Similarly she will be markedly less adept than a normal person in handling abstract concepts, and in making the kinds of judgments conducive to smooth social functioning.

The average or "normal" person does somewhat better at all of these tasks. But it is plain that normal performance could be improved. An exceptionally gifted individual may have the ability to consider nearly all

---

[7] This conception of competence, and that which follows it below, have structural similarities to the "statistical" and the "pathological" models of normality, respectively, of Jane Mercer's *Labeling the Mentally Retarded.*

[8] Travis Thompson, in an address to the Behavior Control Group, Hastings Center, New York, 1977. Some of Thompson's observations were published in his article "The Behavioral Perspective," *Hastings Center Report* 8, no. 3 (June 1978): 29–32. Thompson's claim that the mildly cognitively disabled have recognizable intellectual and behavioral deficits is quite controversial. One reason is that the faulty labeling process produces such a heterogeneous population within the social category of "cognitively disabled person" that few nontrivial general observations can be made; the present essay concerns those who are "really" cognitively disabled. Another reason is that admitting to group differences between the cognitively disabled and the rest of the populace is seen as a political act, legitimating and even causing unequal treatment in areas having little relation to such actual deficits as a cognitively disabled individual may have (see my note 5 above).

the aspects of a very complex situation, to defer gratification as needed, to look far into the future, and to be at home with the loftiest of abstractions. "Normal," in this context, then, will mean no more than "average" and "unimpaired" simply means as good as most others.

Any definition of normality in mental capacity which is based upon IQ scores is susceptible to a relativist interpretation. According to the American Association of Mental Deficiency,

> A person's mental capacity usually is determined by reference to whether he has the ability to manage his affairs with ordinary or reasonable prudence, is of sound mind, has demonstrated rational understanding or intellectual comprehension, is capable of making a full deliberation of matters presented to him, has the mental capacity to make choices and to formulate requisite judgments about those choices, has demonstrated an ability to engage in meaningful intellectual process, has sufficient intellectual capacity to grasp concepts, or has substantial capacity to understand and appreciate the nature and the consequences of a specified matter or to give intelligent consent to a specified procedure.[9]

These criteria could not be met even by very bright men and women if we set high standards for "full deliberation" or "consent." Nor does this passage indicate why "ordinary or reasonable prudence" should be enough. On the relativist conception, there is nothing intrinsic to average status which earns its rights vis-à-vis its superiors that other levels will lack vis-à-vis theirs. Average mental capacity, which normal persons conveniently label "full" capacity, is simply what happens to be typical for our species at this moment in its evolutionary history. On this view, there can be nothing to convince the gifted that normal capacity is "unimpaired" or "full." As a consequence, our liberal principle, that a person of unimpaired intellect must be free to place his welfare at risk if he so chooses, loses its apparent reasonableness.

The inconsistency could be resolved by abandoning our liberal principle. We could accept the rule that superiors may impose their paternalist guidance upon inferiors who may be mildly cognitively disabled, normal, or even bright persons, depending on the circumstances. It is not *immediately* clear that we do not accept this view now. As Robert Nozick observes, we must reflect on our principles to determine whether they do in fact give such rights to superiors; the difference between such rules and the liberal principle cited above is not evident in our dealings with the cognitively disabled. We would be forced to choose between them in practice only if confronted by some race of supermen.

Ought we to endorse this benevolent hierarchy? No definitive judgment on paternalism by the gifted can be made independently of a comprehensive moral theory. Still, some education of our intuitions might be in

---

[9] *Consent Handbook*, Special Publication No. 3 (Washington, D.C.: American Association on Mental Deficiency, 1977), 7.

order. It is important not to confuse the value (to normal persons) of the advice proffered by those with superior minds with the propriety of that advice of being imposed whether accepted or not. Many normal persons might consent to a regime in which the gifted made important decisions for them. Others, perhaps noting that the lives of the cognitively disabled have not been rendered blissful by the intervention of *their* intellectual superiors, might not. Does the relative intellectual inferiority of normal persons to the gifted exempt the former from the protection of the liberal principle? I presume not; there is little difference, in a given instance, between a gifted person better able to deduce future consequences of a present decision and a normal person who knows these consequences through access to the relevant information. Both know better what the future will bring than does a normal person lacking the genius or the data or both. The liberal principle restricts paternalism on the part of governments composed of normal persons who may know better; presumably it does the same for gifted persons who know better.

Any persisting intuition that the gifted would be justified in imposing their opinions on the non-gifted might be a product of the following reasoning. The normal person is capable of understanding that the gifted person is more intelligent than she is; hence she would, if rational, accept advice from the gifted person; hence, any person of normal intelligence who did not consent to follow the prescriptions of the gifted would have to be suffering from mental disability. Were this true, then even normal persons would be suitable targets for paternalism under the liberal principle's "exception clause." Any non-optimal decision would be taken as the product of an incompetent mind, and the liberal principle would have much less scope.

In any case, we can reject the benevolent hierarchy, save the liberal principle, and still keep our rationale for paternalist restriction of the cognitively disabled by countering the relativist view of mental capacity itself. This requires that "full" mental capacity be understood as a "range property,"[10] one which is possessed in equal measure by all who possess it. Such a conception requires us to determine a non-arbitrary threshold, so that all standing above it are equally endowed and all falling below it are unendowed. The point of the relativist argument is that there can be no such line when the property in question is general intelligence. We need not dispute this claim; rather, we may seek a different (though related) property that, unlike intelligence, has the bipolar structure we require. The idea involved is simple and familiar, and will already have occurred to the reader. Mental capacity ought to be seen not as a matter of intellect but as one of *competence:* intellect's power in meeting a challenge. A given challenge may be wholly and fully met by the use of a certain amount of

---

[10] John Rawls, *A Theory of Justice* (Cambridge, Mass.: Harvard University Press, 1971), 508.

intelligence, if the challenge is not too great. Though a person may have more intelligence than another, he will be no more competent at performing certain tasks; his added power is simply unused surplus. Those lacking enough intelligence for the task will be incompetent to perform it; while those having sufficient intelligence will be equally competent however great the difference in their intellectual levels.

We have, then, a non-relative kind of mental impairment, at least as concerns tasks for which superior intelligence is of, at most, marginal additional advantage. There is a similar kind of threshold for other tasks. It will often be the case that, though added intelligence may increase the benefit to be derived from a given task or opportunity, a lesser talent is all that is needed to understand how to avoid harm. Geniuses may be no more adept than normal persons in determining the safest investments on the stock market, though they may be in better position to get rich. The threshold here distinguishes those unable to comprehend and avoid the "downward" risks from those who can; and all in the latter category are equal in this respect. Relativism applies, in such a case, only to capacity for realizing "upward" gain.

This conception of mental impairment and competence seems to support some use of the liberal principle. In the case of challenges for which a given level of intelligence is wholly sufficient, persons of superior intelligence are not of superior competence. Hence, they could not use the principle's exception, which covers the case of impairment, to justify the assumption of decision-making power. The same will hold even for the second sort of challenge mentioned above, in which added intellect assists one only in realizing gain. For as we noticed in the first section, the strongest argument for paternalism applies when the aim is to protect from harm rather than to ensure a benefit. If a given level of intelligence is sufficient to avoid danger in a given task, those of greater intellect cannot use this principle to restrict a person's liberty in hopes of increasing his gain.[11]

If the foregoing is correct, we have shown the possibility, relative to certain sorts of tasks, of a threshold dividing the mentally impaired from those of full capacity and competence. If this is to help in justifying our restriction of civil liberties of the cognitively disabled, we need to show that the threshold happens to fall precisely at the level of intelligence just below what we consider normal. The relativist, we recall, finds no reason to suppose that the level of intelligence currently typical of our population is just the level of intelligence required to master the key tasks a person

---

[11] No general distinction between "benefit" and "harm" need be insisted upon here. The harms in question in this discussion can be enumerated: they are those visited upon people who engage in unwise exercise of those liberties denied to the mildly cognitively disabled. The seriousness of these harms (not "harms" in general) is what makes paternalism a plausible policy in the areas mentioned in the introduction.

faces.[12] Without such assurance, it will continue to seem arbitrary to pick average mental capacity as that to which a general right to self-direction attaches.

There is a natural-sounding response to this query that, though mistaken, deserves mention. This is that our capacities are suited to our tasks because of natural selection. It would be pointless for the relativist to ask why it should be that we have just enough lung capacity to serve us in our typical pursuits, or why we have just enough blood cells to avoid fatigue most of the time. The answer in both cases, of course, is that neither is an accident. Both traits are admirable adaptations to our environment and its challenges. There is, with most such characteristics, a certain threshold below which the organism is unable to thrive and above which additional increments do not usually aid in avoiding destruction. The same process which ensures that the average human will have just enough of the necessary physical capacities might be expected to shape her intellectual endowment.

However successful in explaining why we have the lung capacity we do, natural selection does not resolve the problem of mental competence. The complexity and difficulty of the challenges facing the intellect in modern society are largely reflections of society itself. The magnitude of that part of human intelligence which is inheritable was presumably fixed, however roughly, before the challenges that now typically occupy us in society were set. Evolution might have endowed us with the mental means to design and build shelter, or to distinguish poisonous berries from nutritive ones, but it cannot have been supple enough to set our abilities at precisely the level required to fill out Form 1040 of the Internal Revenue Service.

These reflections, however, do suggest what must be the correct reply to the relativist's query. The threshold of competence in our society falls at or just below the average because, first, the level of difficulty involved in key life tasks is in large part socially determined; and, second, society stands to gain by setting this level so as to render the average person competent.

The social component of a task like that of completing a tax form is obvious. We need not marvel at the invisible hand of evolution for making us bright enough to compute our own tax deductions; those who designed the form are charged with the responsibility of gearing its difficulty to the level of intelligence that evolution and environment

---

[12] Different tasks, of course, require different levels of intellectual ability for their successful completion. Any adequate social policy of paternalism vis-à-vis the cognitively disabled will employ a notion of "selective competence" in which the cognitively disabled person is judged incompetent with respect to specific tasks and (perhaps) competent in other respects. The present, general argument rests on an assumption that many of the important liberties denied the mildly cognitively disabled require about the same level of intelligence. The argument does not apply to the liberties that do not.

happen to have provided. Importantly for our purposes, this social component is prominent in most of the decisions that are denied to the mildly cognitively disabled under laws restricting their civil liberties. For example, a person who enters into a financial contract assumes an obligation to fulfill his part of the bargain and forswears certain kinds of excuses for not doing so. If he is buying an appliance on the installment plan, he obligates himself to send in payments and cannot default because of inconvenience, second thoughts, or even moderate hardship. At the same time, there are certain excuses that he does not forswear; the safeguards represented by bankruptcy laws may be seen as part of this complex transaction. These socially defined characteristics of contracts set the level of intelligence needed to understand and assume responsibility for risk. Insufficient intellect will prevent a person from foreseeing the difficulties involved and thus to risk overextending himself. At the same time, however, the severity of the penalties is kept within certain limits by the bankruptcy laws and by consumer-interest laws.

Essentially conventional, these arrangements might have been different. Society might have instituted rules allowing persons to annul contracts if they proved inconvenient or if the contractor misjudged her resources at the time of bargaining. Similarly, the burden of a decision to procreate would have been lighter had custom not assigned to parents the responsibility for caring for their offspring. Under these conditions, persons whose mental powers are much weaker than the average would be competent to enter contracts, marry, and make other important decisions without regularly risking serious reverses that they could not predict and understand. The threshold of competence and mental impairment would be set that much lower.

If it is, in theory, within society's power to arrange itself so as to render the mildly cognitively disabled fully competent, why does it not do so? Mere prejudice, a society made up mostly of persons of normal intelligence concerned only for themselves, need not be the answer. There is considerable social utility, at least for normal persons, in setting the threshold about where it is. Contracts that are void when misunderstood or inconvenient would not facilitate the exchange of goods. An appliance seller hands over the product in exchange for a piece of paper because he believes that payments will follow. If such expectation were lacking, no one, regardless of competence, would have a way of obtaining appliances without cash. The value of contracts and other arrangements, the very ones subject to control in our paternalist restriction of the cognitively disabled, depends on their having features that make them hazardous to those with limited ability. Normal persons make the world safe for normality, but not necessarily safe for retardation.

The same holds true with respect to other abilities and capacities. The strength a person must have to be "unimpaired" is set not by biological limits but by the demands of society. It is, then, no surprise that those who design manual gearshift mechanisms and who set the size of grocery bags manufacture products that presuppose something like the average amount of strength. The majority of normal persons in the society benefit (in a purely economic sense) by having the requirements this high. We could make do with levers and containers that even the very weak could handle; but these would undoubtedly be of less use to us. It is also worth noting that current practice sets the threshold for physical competence, and thus renders equal all those at or above the threshold. Those of average strength are just as competent as the very strong in moving gearshift levers; the advantages of exceptional strength lie in other, more esoteric pursuits. Increments of strength, like increments of intelligence, are important if they put one over the socially defined threshold of "full" or "unimpaired" performance. Superiority past that point counts much less, both for the individual's welfare and for our moral theorizing about her.

Of course, the average requirements, whether for intelligence or for physical strength, could also be set much higher than they currently are. A society designed by and for persons who are by present standards gifted would be a risk-laden environment for persons of merely normal intelligence.[13] They would find themselves unable to understand the nature of the contracts and other social arrangements to which they would be parties and probably would be branded incompetent. This seems, after all, to find for the relativist: the argument that is supposed to show that we may restrict the liberties of the mildly cognitively disabled would also show that the gifted have the right to impose restraints upon us, provided, however, that the environments in question also differ in relative difficulty.

Does this argument in fact undermine the standard grounds—need together with incompetence—for denying liberties to the cognitively disabled? Only if, as before, we insist that the gifted would not have the right to deny liberties to normal persons in the gifted society. Those who support our present treatment of the cognitively disabled on the basis of the liberal principle might wish to abandon this insistence, thereby removing any appearance of inconsistency in their approach to the two groups. But I do not think the liberal can abandon it. The intuition behind the liberal principle remains firm: we have a right to make unconstrained choices, shoulder risks, and even court disaster; and we have this right because of our rational faculty. Being placed in a demanding environment, such as a society designed for the gifted, does not diminish our intellectual endowment. To accept paternalistic treat-

---

[13] Calvin Trillin suggests that something of this sort played a role in the financial crisis of 2007–8: prospects of enormous enrichment diverted the brightest people from physics and similar pursuits to financial firms, where they devised instruments that no one else could understand or safely use. See his "Wall Street Smarts," *The New York Times*, October 14, 2009, p. A27.

ment of normal persons in the gifted society because of the severity of the challenges would commit us to accept also paternalistic denial of liberty in our present society in those circumstances in which a normal person meets a strenuous challenge. Since this is exactly what the liberal rejects, he must refuse to endorse paternalistic treatment of the normal person by the gifted person.

The liberal should argue instead that the normal person who finds herself in a society created for the gifted would realize that her powers are inadequate for achieving an understanding and mastery of the tasks besetting her. She would, therefore, seek out guidance from a friendly gifted person; or if she did not, she would at least be in a position to assess the risks attendant on making her own decisions. While, by hypothesis, she is incompetent to make many kinds of decisions that society requires her to make, she remains fully competent to recognize her limitations and to decide to seek help. On the liberal view, her intellectual powers will be sufficient to allow her to shoulder responsibility for what might happen, and this is enough to render a paternalistic denial of liberty to those of normal intelligence unjustified.

Again, however, the relativist has a response to the liberal. He can claim that humility, the disposition to recognize one's own limitations, emerges not with a given level of intelligence but with certain traits of character and temperament (indeed, it *is* such a trait). Besides, the cognitively disabled person is often capable of understanding the principle "seek guidance when you need it." His alleged problem is in knowing when it is needed;[14] and the same might well afflict the person of average intelligence who finds himself in the troubling environment of the society of the gifted. The notion that a right to self-direction attaches to those of a given level of intelligence, simply because of that mental ability and regardless of environmental circumstances, seems impossible to defend. Attempts to found such a moral right on the metaphysical properties of *persons* offers no help to average human beings (or cognitively disabled ones); for in these theories "person" is an ideal, the maximally rational reflective agent. As Daniel Dennett has argued, few if any human beings are "persons" in the sense which Kant and Rawls seem to require.[15] Human beings of average intellect, living in their own society, can insist on autonomy not because they are "persons" in this ideal sense but because, with respect to the challenges they have fashioned for themselves, they are nearly on a par with persons.

Before we apply these conclusions to the moral issue of civil liberties for the cognitively disabled, it will be useful to review and summarize the

[14] See Travis Thompson, "Behavioral Perspective," *Hasting Center Report* 8, no. 3 (June 1978): 31–32.
[15] Daniel Dennett, "Conditions of Personhood," in *The Identities of Persons*, edited by Amelie Rorty (Berkeley: University of California Press, 1976), 175–96.

arguments presented thus far. Restrictions on the mildly cognitively disabled are usually justified by citing the dangers the person can inflict on herself. This, in turn, is thought to legitimate paternalistic intervention because the cognitively disabled person, being mentally deficient, does not have the right to self-direction claimed by the normal person. We may grant that many so-called cognitively disabled persons are in fact normal and that many of those who are not are capable of living freely and independently without unacceptable risk to their welfare. The question that remains, then, is whether restrictions are defensible for those who are in fact cognitively disabled and who do seem likely to encounter trouble if granted full citizenship. If the right to take risks is to be denied the cognitively disabled by normal persons on the basis of the latter's intellectual superiority, one would think it legitimate for exceptionally gifted persons to do the same to normal persons. The right to self-direction claimed by normal persons, however, seems to be a claim of immunity against the paternalistic interventions even of those who are more gifted.

I have sought to relieve this apparent inconsistency, and to show that, for certain important tasks, the person of merely normal intelligence is fully the equal of his intellectual superior. But the moral issue is not yet settled. My argument, while showing that the threshold between mental incompetence and competence is not arbitrary,[16] also shows it to be set by society. As such, it could also be changed. Arrangements could be made to create the conditions under which the cognitively disabled would be in the same position to claim autonomy as those of normal and superior intelligence. We would need to show that fairness does not compel us to make these changes before we could regard the restriction of liberties of the cognitively disabled as justified.

There is no simple solution to the problem. We may say at once that society, through consumer laws, for example, ought to make its institutions, customs, and practices as safe as possible insofar as it can do so without compromising their utility. This would serve to make the risks involved understandable to those with limited intelligence and hence in some matters give them the status of competent persons with a right to make their own decisions. To change society so that mild mental retardation would be no handicap in any of the tasks in question might reduce the economic and social value of the relevant practices, thereby shifting hardships from the cognitively disabled onto those of normal and high intelligence. I have no way of estimating the degree of hardship at stake. If it is substantial enough to seriously impede economic and social

---

[16] The boundary is, of course, a vague one. The decision to draw the line at some precise point between average intelligence and severe retardation is arbitrary. What is nonarbitrary, according to my argument, is the drawing of the line at some point below the average rather than above it.

functioning, perhaps the majority, which consists of normal persons, would have no obligation to change present practices so radically. *Some* redistribution of burdens, however, is undoubtedly in order.

The fairness of denying civil liberties to the mildly cognitively disabled depends, then, on the legitimacy of giving higher priority to general social welfare than to doing what is necessary to achieve equal liberty for all. Given our concern that the mildly cognitively disabled not be pushed out into a dangerous world in which they may come to ruin, we have two choices. We may change the world so as to render it safer for all. Or we may refrain from allowing the cognitively disabled access to it. The morality of paternalism reduces to a question about distributive justice.

Further Topics

I would like to supplement my discussion of competence and the civil liberties of the moderately cognitively disabled with brief remarks on two further topics.

Civil Liberties in an Era of Biotechnological Enhancement

Some people anticipate the development of interventions—perhaps genetic, perhaps pharmaceutical—that will greatly enhance the cognitive capacity of ordinary human beings. Recall Leon Trotsky: "Man will become immeasurably stronger, wiser and subtler; his body will become more harmonized, his movements more rhythmic, his voice more musical. The average human type will rise to the heights of an Aristotle, a Goethe, or a Marx. And above these heights, new peaks will rise."[17] Trotsky was writing about socialism rather than about genetic or biotechnological enhancement, but the sentiment is the same.

Let's suppose for the sake of argument that enhancement of human intellectual performance becomes feasible. Thus Nozick's question ceases to be science fiction. What would my analysis entail for the civil liberties of those who have not yet achieved enhancement?

I think it depends on how many fellow citizens have made the plunge and what they have done thereafter. If the movement toward genius is a trickle, my civil liberties should be secure. It will be true that these already-enhanced could do a better job of running some of my affairs, but my performance is already good enough to permit me to fend off any efforts, however well intentioned, to force this help on me when I don't want it.

But suppose that the trend toward cognitive enhancement becomes a flood. If I remain behind, I will find fewer and fewer peers. My much smarter neighbors, meanwhile, will certainly realize that our common

[17] Leon Trotsky, *Literature and Revolution* (Ann Arbor: University of Michigan Press, 1960 [originally published 1924]), 255–56.

social environment would serve their interests much better if a very high level of cognitive functioning were a prerequisite for everyday social navigation. They will have to decide whether those efficiencies justify raising the bar in such a way that people like me will be rendered incompetent. It should be obvious that this is not a matter of stigma; it might develop, but the problem will be present even if it does not. Everyday life will require one to think faster than I can; to keep more ideas in one's head at a time than I'm capable of; to remember much more than I tend to do; to grasp subtle connections between ideas that are now entirely beyond me. I will not do well in this environment. My experience will be akin to the elderly person experiencing progressive dementia. She might have kept her full citizenship in an earlier, simpler age, but today she will soon be separated from her money and may soon come to grief in managing her drug regimen. Guardianship will soon be inevitable.

This is a fairly obvious extension or application of my argument. I am not claiming that I would necessarily be wronged if my cognitively enhanced fellow citizens change the social environment so as to render me incompetent. You can't stand in the way of progress. The smarter majority, especially if they are a large majority, do not owe it to those of us left behind to pass up the benefits that could result from changing society to suit their talents, if these are very large relative to the distress experienced by the newly incompetent. I offer no theoretically compelling argument for this claim, but I doubt that it is one that only utilitarians would make. Regardless of one's moral theory, no one is going to insist that everyone crawl so that babies are not left behind. It's not a matter of whether to render some people incompetent in order to deliver efficiencies and other advantages to the more able, but when and by how much. Here moral theories may diverge.

Measuring the Contribution of Causes of Cognitive Functioning to the Global Burden of Disease

The most widely used classifications of cognitive disability count those with IQs of 70 or above as non-disabled. Some refer to differences in capacity for cognitive performance above that level as differences in "talent." Intuitively, a "talent" enables one to perform unusually well, whereas a deficit or impairment makes it harder to perform ordinarily well. The boundary is not always clear, nor is the nature of the distinction. A child with an IQ of 120 is more talented in this respect than one with an IQ of 75, and the latter will not qualify as cognitively disabled, but is the latter simply less talented?

These questions arise in attempting to measure and map the global "burden of disease." This phrase designates a set of units, measures, and concepts that have been under development for some time, both in academia and at the World Health Organization. The burden of disease is understood as a deficit from a theoretical maximum amount of population health and is computed by cause. Burden of disease data document the harm due to each disease or treatable condition; the development of rigorous and objective methods for collecting and analyzing health data helps to prevent exaggeration by competing groups of advocates. This in turn makes each group very interested in ensuring that the full burden of the disease that it cares about is fully represented in the burden-of-disease tables.

Large numbers of people, concentrated in the poorest regions of the world, are robbed of some of their potential for cognitive functioning by exposure to conditions that are largely and inexpensively avoidable, such as low intake of iodine and other micronutrients, and infestation by roundworm and other parasites. It costs little to supply sufficient iodine, and low-cost medicines, administered twice yearly, can keep children from having to share their meals with worms. These problems occur mostly in countries in which spending on health is minimal, and competition for all resources is fierce. It is not enough that the cost of prevention is low; the burden and the potential improvement in population health must be sufficiently high.

The IQ 70 threshold in the classification of cognitive disability presumably reflects some of the same considerations that underlie the threshold of competence that I have discussed above. In a classification of disabilities, this makes sense; yet it still seems reasonable to view a person above that threshold whose IQ has been lowered by ten or fifteen points by malnutrition or parasites as one who has not merely lost a chance for additional talent. And from a population-level perspective, the cumulative total of the effects of worms, malnutrition, and other IQ-robbing conditions may be staggering. It would be unfortunate, therefore, if that burden should register as zero simply because the affected individuals still remained above the IQ 70 threshold. This would be low in priority, in competition with other health needs. Put differently, money spent in preventing these tragic losses in cognitive potential would be counted as hugely expensive, yielding insufficient gain per dollar to be justified.

The Global Burden of Disease methodology is a large-scale, international enterprise involving extensive surveys and data analysis by medical specialists in every field, economists, and a host of others, even including a few philosophers. A new version, GBD 2005, is currently under development under the leadership of the World Health Organization and a Gates-sponsored organization, the Institute for Health Metrics and Evaluation, which are attempting to respond to criticisms of earlier versions and to extend its scope.

The methodology for accounting for the burden of IQ-robbing diseases and conditions is not yet determined. One proposal will convey some of the flavor of the discussion. One school of thought posits that the conditions favorable to cognitive functioning track those favorable to stature. Those living in very poor regions in Africa, for example, where stunting is common, tend also to be victimized by malnutrition and infestation by worms. Perhaps the cumulative deficit of these populations could be expressed by adding up the measured IQ of its people and subtracting this from the measured IQ of the world's tallest people (who, in 2008, are the Dutch). Even if few of the affected individuals have IQs below 70, this method might be able to represent the cost, in cognitive functioning, of these cruel conditions, and thus to warrant the expenditures needed for amelioration. If successful, this would ensure that the burden-of-disease tables would reflect the intuitive judgment that iodine supplements, drugs for roundworm, and the like are easily worth their costs in view of the harm they prevent.

If I were to try to link the topics discussed in here in a single remark, it might be this: though impairment underlies the thresholds we cite in classifying the cognitively disabled, the thresholds reflect social conventions, and they do not, in themselves, delimit the location of the problem of the burden that produced the impairment. The point I would like most to make, however, is that ethical issues arising in connection with cognitive disability may profitably be addressed from a population health perspective. Geoffrey Rose's *The Strategy of Preventive Medicine*,[18] summarizing decades of research, contrasted a "medical" approach that focused on the most extreme cases (e.g., people with very high blood pressure) to a public health approach that sought to reduce the risk of harm for everyone. The non-intuitive result, in the cases that Rose discussed, would be a greater improvement in population health. The reason—here is why intuition fails—is that even if the few people at the extreme, in the tail of the bell curve, are at greatest risk, most people who will experience problems are people with average risk. There are so many more of them.

If cognitive disability, as a problem of public health, fits this pattern, our marching orders are clear: do not fail to address causes of mild cognitive disability and avoidable causes of mild loss of cognitive functioning, even among those who are not classified as disabled. And be prepared to advocate for social justice, if this turns out to be a more effective strategy than interventions on individuals using highly skilled professionals and expensive drugs.

Editor's Note

We recognize that some of the terminology and references in this chapter are outdated today (e.g., the American Association of Mental Deficiency). However, they were appropriate in 1979 when the first portion of this chapter appeared.

[18] Oxford: Oxford University Press, 1992.

12

RESPONSIBILITY, AGENCY, AND COGNITIVE DISABILITY

DAVID SHOEMAKER

"Moral community" is a term of art in philosophy, but it's often taken to refer to the collection of moral agents, that is, those agents eligible for assessments of moral responsibility.[1] Discovering the boundaries of the moral community—as well as the conditions for membership in it—has thus typically involved two steps: (a) identifying the ways in which paradigm members like you and me are in fact assessed as responsible, and (b) identifying the conditions distinguishing such members from paradigm examples of agents *exempted* from assessments of responsibility.[2] But of course all we may learn from this exercise is what makes you and me *paradigm* members of the moral community and what makes the exempted agents *paradigm* nonmembers. We may thus learn less about the actual boundaries of the moral community—and thus the necessary conditions for entry into it—than we learn simply about the

---

[1] Some take "moral community" instead to refer to the collection of moral *patients*, those entities with nonnegligible moral status to which some degree of moral consideration is owed. This is a wide reading of the phrase. Those attracted to this view should consider my usage a narrow reading of the phrase. In conversation and in his book manuscript in progress on the nature of moral responsibility, Michael McKenna advocates a slightly more restricted understanding of the term "moral agents," reserving it for those capable of actions morally evaluable as good or bad, right or wrong, virtuous or vicious. Consequently, there may be moral agents who are not eligible for assessments of moral *responsibility*. The example McKenna favors is of Lenny, from *Of Mice and Men*, who knows he "done a bad thing," but whose cognitive disability is such that he's rendered ineligible for moral responsibility insofar as he's not an appropriate target of blame. It's not clear to me, though, that Lenny, while certainly an agent, is a *moral* agent, insofar as the goodness or badness of his conduct fails to play any role in his deliberations. So he's capable of an action that's evaluable as good or bad, but so is a dog. I thus prefer to tie moral agency to eligibility for moral assessment *of one's agency* (rather than merely one's actions). Nevertheless, this does not make for a huge difference between McKenna and me generally.

[2] To address (a) most often involves appeal to, and discussion of, the Strawsonian reactive attitudes. See Strawson 2003. For some examples of theorists following more or less in this vein, see Wallace 1994, Watson 2004, 219–59, Darwall 2006, and Russell 1995. To address (b), many theorists appeal to the examples of young children, the insane, and the mentally ill. See again Wallace 1994 and Watson 2004, but also see Greenspan 2003, Fine and Kennett 2004, Russell 2004, McKenna 2005, Dwyer 2003, and Shoemaker 2007.

sufficient conditions for *full-fledged* membership or nonmembership. This is why I believe we can actually learn more about the nature of those boundaries and the conditions for entry by considering contrasts between those who are *just outside* the community and those who are *just inside* it. These will be people who are paradigm examples of neither fully responsible agency nor fully nonresponsible agency. They are, we might say, morally responsible sometimes and in some ways. But what could this mean? And what does it tell us about the nature of moral agency generally? There is a complicated story to tell here, and it is my task in this chapter to begin to tell it.

I will do so by contrasting mild mental retardation (MMR) with psychopathy, specifically among adults. For most of those who work with and know them, adults with MMR are thought to be obvious members of the moral community, albeit not full-fledged members. And for most of those who work with and theorize about adult psychopaths, they are *not* members of the moral community, albeit not in such a clear-cut fashion as the insane, say. Both psychopaths and adults with MMR have a *disability*, as we will see, and I am interested in how disability sometimes exempts one from the moral community and sometimes doesn't. More particularly, I am interested in exploring the tripartite relation between disability, responsibility, and moral community.

I will begin by discussing the nature of MMR, and I will then explain why *adults* with MMR constitute my focus. I will then discuss the nature of psychopathy and begin the contrast between adult psychopaths and those with MMR with respect to moral responsibility. It will then be through an examination of two associated puzzles that we will come to see the complicated tripartite relation at issue.

Adults with MMR

Being categorized as mentally retarded is primarily a function of scoring a 69 or lower on an IQ test. There are, roughly, three intellectual incapacities involved: (1) not being able to learn as much or as quickly as nonretarded people; (2) not being able to store information as well as the nonretarded; and (3) not being able to engage in abstract thought or to apply principles or information from one situation to another very well (Evans 1983, 7). These disabilities obviously come in degrees, so there are four categories of the mentally retarded, again based on IQ score: mild, moderate, severe, and profound. By far the largest subcategory is that of the mildly retarded, who make up 89 percent of the total mentally handicapped population (Evans 1983, 24). The range of IQ in this group runs from approximately 52 to 69, and its members have generally failed to arrive at—and will likely never arrive at—the fourth stage of Piagetian development—formal operations—at which one becomes capable of thinking abstractly, deploying deductive reasoning, "and perform[ing] logical operations on abstract ideas" (Castles 1996, 4–5).[3]

The mentally retarded are often thought to be "eternal children," and so discussions of moral responsibility that even mention them invariably lump them in with children and then suggest that, insofar as children aren't morally responsible, neither are the retarded.[4] After all, if what prevents children from being morally responsible are certain undeveloped cognitive capacities, and these capacities in the retarded are *perpetually* undeveloped, then it would seem obvious that the retarded are perpetually nonresponsible.

This comparison is seriously flawed, however, for there are physical and mental differences that emerge as those with MMR grow older that render them importantly distinct from children. Specifically, adults with MMR are typically more mature than children in three important ways.[5] The first is the most obvious: they are physically more mature, and this establishes the possibility for what Sigmund Freud thought to be the two most important characteristics for an emotionally healthy life: work and love (Castles 1996, 111). Approximately 50 percent of adults with MMR get a job (Castles 1996, 112), and because these adults have normal desires for sexual expression, many wind up leading full sexual lives, including dating, getting married, and having children (Castles 1996, 122–23).[6]

The love around which such relationships are typically built is an example of the second sort of relevant maturity, namely, emotional maturity. The emotional capacities with respect to a wide range of complex, mature emotions in adults with MMR are essentially the same as those of nonretarded adults; they have just developed more slowly (see, e.g., Kasari and Bauminger 1998, esp. 418). So adults with MMR are capable of romantic love, grief, despair, guilt, and remorse, which again distinguishes them from children.

The third sort of maturity is, perhaps surprisingly, cognitive. As already mentioned, adults with MMR essentially remain at the third stage of development—concrete operations—the stage in which they can nevertheless distinguish reality from the symbols representing it, engage in inductive reasoning, and see things from the perspectives of others (Castles 1996, 4). In normal development, children enter this third stage in their early elementary school years, and then enter the fourth stage (formal operations) in early adolescence. This is a relatively brief span in the course of their lives

---

[3] On the point that "[f]ew individuals with mental retardation achieve the cognitive stage of formal operations," see Castles 1996, 51.

[4] See, e.g., Wallace 1994, 167, n. 14. The degree to which children are or aren't responsible is actually, I believe, a vexed question.

[5] The ideas in this and the next two paragraphs are more developed versions of suggestions made in Shoemaker 2007.

[6] As Castles 1996 also notes (p. 126), there are occasionally those who are moderately retarded who get married, but "the vast majority" of marriages in the group as a whole come from those categorized as mildly retarded.

(lasting four to six years). Adults with MMR, however, remain more or less permanently in the concrete operations stage. Thus, they have had to negotiate their world (an *adult* world) with a limited set of cognitive tools for far longer than those who have developed normally. Ordinarily, children learn about their (childhood) world at the concrete operations stage for a short time before having to adapt to the adult world with a very different set of cognitive tools. They thus haven't had the opportunity to engage with the adult world in a way that those with MMR do on a daily basis. So the abilities of adults with MMR to live on their own, to work, to love, and to marry all indicate that they have learned how to adapt in the way we do to a world they don't fully understand, but they have done so in a way the rest of *us* can't fully understand. This sort of cognitive maturity is surely hard won.

Because of these key differences in maturity level, then, we shouldn't expect there to be an analogy between children and adults with MMR regarding moral responsibility. Indeed, these forms of maturity may compensate for or supplant their other cognitive disabilities sufficiently to bring them into the moral community. To appreciate this point fully, though, we need to explore the nature of another sort of disability.

Psychopathy and Disability

Among philosophical theorists, psychopaths are most often thought to be outside the boundaries of the moral community, ineligible for moral responsibility.[7] What is the source of their ineligibility, though? There are several competing theories of what counts as the psychopath's essential deficiency, some emphasizing an affective lack (for example, the inability to experience fear, empathy, or guilt, or to have a Violence Inhibition Mechanism [VIM]),[8] some emphasizing a cognitive lack (for example, the inability to grasp and apply moral reasons),[9] and some emphasizing a motivational lack (see Shoemaker 2007, 79–85). We need not take sides here, however, given the role that deficits in *all* these components play for the psychopath. After all, someone for whom the plight of others makes

[7] For a limited sampling of such theorists, see Strawson 2003, 79, 82; Wallace 1994, 177–78; and Kennett 2001, 189, 209–14. For more tentative stands on the psychopath's nonresponsibility (where the psychopath could be responsible if certain conditions obtained), see Darwall 2006, 88–90; and Fischer and Ravizza, 1998, 78–80. For the view that psychopaths *are* morally responsible, see Greenspan 2003; Talbert 2008; and, perhaps, the implications of Scanlon 1998, 287–90.

[8] For discussion of the psychopath's deficiencies of fear, see Eysenck 1977 and 1998; Fowles 1980; and Lykken 1995. For discussion of the psychopath's deficiencies in empathy and guilt, see Hoffman 2000. For a discussion of the psychopath's deficiencies in VIM, see Blair et al. 1995, and Blair 1995 and 1999b. For a summary discussion of this literature, see Fine and Kennett 2004, 428–30.

[9] For explicit statement and defense of this view, see Wallace 1994, 157. Beyond Wallace, those who accept some version of this sort of cognitive view include Darwall (2006); Fischer and Ravizza (1998); Kennett (2001); Arpaly (2003); Sher (2006); Watson (2004); and Wolf (1990).

no emotional dent surely lacks the capacity to be appropriately sensitive to the moral reasons deriving from their plight, and this deficiency in sensitivity is likely what grounds her failing to be motivated by such reasons as well (see, e.g., Russell 2004, esp. 297–99; also Watson 2008). Perhaps, then, the most plausible way to tell the psychopath's story is in terms of a *developmental intellectual disability*.[10] The capacity for certain sorts of emotional responses is necessary for the development of the intellectual capacity for sensitivity to, appreciation of, and responsiveness to moral reasons, and given that the psychopath lacks this emotional arsenal, her mechanism for understanding and being moved by the force of moral reasons has been permanently disabled. She has failed to develop true moral sensitivity, conscience, understanding, and motivation.

If the psychopath has a developmental intellectual disability, however, and is excluded from the moral community thereby, why isn't the adult with MMR, who also has a developmental intellectual disability, excluded thereby as well? To answer this question, we need to say more about the nature of the various disabilities and how they connect to moral responsibility and membership in the moral community.

MMR, Moral Responsibility, and Moral Community

There are at least three relevant differences between the paradigm psychopath and the typical adult with MMR. First, psychopaths show no arousal to the distress of others, whereas adults with MMR most definitely do.[11] This capacity is a key component of moral development.

Second, the adult with MMR has none of the emotional deficits of the psychopath.[12] While the psychopath may experience some feelings, as Fingarette points out, these feelings "are evanescent and 'superficial'. . . . [M]ature wholehearted anger, true or consistent indignation, honest, solid grief, sustaining pride, deep joy, genuine despair are reactions not found" (Fingarette 1967, 24–26). By contrast, these latter are all found in adults with MMR. What this means, then, is that the capacities for mature emotions—for example, guilt and remorse—that seem essential for the development of moral understanding, for the development of a *moral self*, are present in the adult with MMR.

---

[10] Cf. Greenspan 2003, 420, viewing psychopathy as a "kind of moral 'learning disability.'"

[11] See Blair 1996, 577. Blair also demonstrates that, despite what many might have suspected to the contrary, *autistic* children, from all along the autism spectrum, show sensitivity and "significant arousal responses to the distress of others" (577). See also Blair 1999a.

[12] In addition to the above citations on this topic, see Herpertz and Sass 2000.

The third difference is found in the instantiation, or lack thereof, of the capacity for a morally relevant type of *empathy*. Now the psychopath is capable of empathy of a certain sort, namely, being able to imagine (and perhaps even understand) what things are like from the inside for someone else, to represent internally what that person is thinking or feeling. This is presumably what some of the more notoriously violent psychopaths can do: they vividly represent the horrors their victims are going through in order to experience a kind of *delight* at their plight. Call this *detached empathy*. It is an ability to understand—cognitively—the feelings of another person without any emotional engagement with that person. This is also the sort of empathy practiced by the psychologist with respect to her patients. But it is different from *identifying empathy*, which, in addition to cognitive understanding of what things are like for another person, involves the capacity and disposition to *feel* what things are like for that person, to be in sync emotionally with that person's own emotional ups and downs.[13] To engage in identifying empathy with you is for me to be emotionally vulnerable to the up-and-down fortunes of the very objects to which you yourself are emotionally vulnerable. It is to be engaged with you emotionally (see Shoemaker 2007, 98). Because of his emotional deficits, this sort of emotional engagement is something of which the psychopath is incapable. It is, however, something of which the adult with MMR is clearly capable. Note, for instance, Castles's observation of interactions among adults with MMR in a workshop: "[W]ork-shop members are exquisitely sensitive to situations or remarks that might damage the self-esteem of their fellow workers. They protect one another from derogatory remarks and rush to provide comfort when a friend is upset. Indeed, people with mental retardation are often more sensitive to the problems and feelings of their peers than are even the most sophisticated and well-intentioned of nonhandicapped individuals" (Castles 1996, 80).

These three differences between the psychopath and the adult with MMR are closely related, and together they are sufficient to reveal why the former is typically excluded from the moral community while the latter is not: the psychopath's affective incapacities have rendered her incapable of genuine moral understanding and motivation, whereas the adult with MMR's intact affective capacities have enabled him to develop moral understanding and motivation (to some extent), which themselves must then be the key ingredients for membership in the moral community. The psychopath's developmental disability, in other words, is precisely a *moral* disability, whereas the adult with MMR's is not. Nevertheless, there are many complications here, brought out by consideration of two puzzles.

---

[13] Some psychologists have labeled the two types of empathy under discussion "cognitive" and "emotional." See, e.g., Dziobek et al. 2008.

The First Puzzle: Criminal and Moral Responsibility

By most accounts, the adult with MMR is a member of the moral community, eligible for assessments of moral responsibility, while the psychopath is not. But here is the first puzzle: when it comes to legal, or criminal, responsibility, the *psychopath* is typically thought to be eligible, whereas the adult with MMR is typically *not* (or if he is eligible, his responsibility is often thought to be diminished). Regarding the psychopath, for instance, Robert Hare notes, "[I]n most jurisdictions, psychopathy is considered to be an *aggravating* rather than a mitigating factor in determining criminal responsibility" (Hare 1998, 205; quoted in Fine and Kennett 2004, 425; emphasis mine). Regarding mentally retarded adults, however, their competence to stand trial may often be undermined by what is judged to be their inability to understand and participate in the trial process, and if they are judged competent, they may well meet the legal mitigating condition of insanity if they are found to have a "mental defect" that "interfered substantially with [their] ability to 'intend' to break the law" (Reid 1998, 374; see also Reid 2006, esp. 114–15). How, then, might we explain this mirror symmetry?

One way might be to try to point out various differences and discontinuities in the aims and functions of moral and criminal responsibility.[14] But let's suppose for the sake of argument that they're in fact continuous, that criminal responsibility is just one form of moral responsibility generally. Fine and Kennett, for instance, advocate such an approach. In articulating the broad functions of punishment, they identify a distinctively retributivist strand, one involving the community's expression of moral condemnation to the offender, and for such justifications the punishment itself must be morally deserved. Consequently, "it is crucial that the offender meets the conditions of moral responsibility" (Fine and Kennett 2004, 433). Such moral sanctions "must be directed only to those who meet some minimal requirements for moral agency. Moral address is not only wasted on nonmoral beings. It is unjust" (Fine and Kennett 2004, 434).

Fine and Kennett thus see true criminal responsibility as entailing moral responsibility. But because they view psychopaths as severely

---

[14] See, e.g., Shoemaker 2007, 81–82, n. 32. This strikes me as a rather plausible move. The world of moral responsibility, for instance, has all sorts of features that are absent in the world of criminal responsibility, including (a) positive attributions like praise, gratitude, and admiration, (b) assessments of character traits (e.g., "courageous," "generous," and "intemperate"), and (c) an emphasis on the responsible party's doing the right thing *for the right reasons*. One might well think, then, that disparate treatment of psychopaths and adults with MMR is just a function of there being two entirely different senses of "responsibility" in play here, that the conditions of moral responsibility are quite distinct from the conditions of criminal responsibility. Nevertheless, this seems a minority view, so I will set it aside in the text to explore how to deal with the puzzle on the more widespread assumption that criminal and moral responsibility are indeed continuous.

impaired in moral understanding and therefore susceptible to neither moral address nor moral agents, they maintain that "psychopathic individuals fall into the category of blameless offenders" (Fine and Kennett 2004, 436), and so *shouldn't* in fact be held criminally responsible or subject to punishment. Rather, they argue, psychopaths ought to be detained only for reasons of societal self-defense (Fine and Kennett 2004, 437–40).

Even if we accept the premises, however, there remains a gap between them and Fine and Kennett's conclusion about psychopaths. This is because it is possible that, while moral address is both wasted and unjust when directed to nonmoral beings, and while criminal responsibility indeed entails moral responsibility, one may be morally responsible in a sense that's legally relevant without yet meeting the conditions for sensible moral address. In other words, we have room—room we evidently occasionally exercise—to find *moral fault* with the psychopath without including her in the moral community.

To see how and why, we can draw on Gary Watson's important distinction between two faces of responsibility (Watson 2004, 260–88). These are the faces of attributability and accountability. To illustrate the distinction, suppose that I have injured you without justification or excuse. On the one hand, I have done something nasty, and so in judging me to be responsible, you fault me insofar as you attribute this action to a flaw in my character: I acted toward you with bad intent, so this action (and your subsequent moral predication) is thus importantly *mine*; it is properly attached to me and viewed as expressive of my character. On the other hand, you may go on to *hold me* responsible for this action, expressing a reactive attitude such as resentment, and in so doing you are holding me accountable to you (and others). I am thus here responsible on both faces. On the attributive face, my harmful action is attributable to my will, to my character (thus Watson also calls this the "aretaic" face [Watson 2004, 264]), and so, ultimately, to *me*. When you attribute a (moral) fault to me on this face, it is in virtue of the fact that I have revealed bad ends or aims in my action: I have expressed my *self* to you, and you like it none too much. On the accountability face, however, your blaming me via the expression of resentment or indignation is a matter of expressing a *moral demand* to me to treat one's fellows with goodwill (see also Darwall 2006, 74–90 and throughout). Such expression also serves other functions, including being an announcement that I have violated the basic demand for goodwill when harming you, an expression of your anger about it, and a request that I respond to this reminder, announcement, and expression by way of apology or other redress.

Consider now the fairness of the different appraisals. To judge me blameworthy on the attributability face is simply to attribute a (typically moral) fault to me; it is to judge that my conduct revealed, say, vicious intent or my commitment to some vicious end. I may thus be judged cruel, cowardly, manipulative, self-indulgent, or something else in light of what I have done. Such a judgment is unfair only if there is no such fault or if I lack the necessary intelligence and comprehension to apply such predications to my deliberations (Watson 2004, 282). Alternatively, to judge me blameworthy on the accountability face is to express some negative attitude toward me—resentment or indignation, say—which itself constitutes a kind of sanction. And such sanctions are unfair unless the targeted agent has had "*a reasonable opportunity to avoid incurring them*" (Watson 2004, 276; emphasis in original). On Watson's interpretation of the distinction, then, while the attributability face of responsibility is a necessary condition for the accountability face, it's not sufficient. The additional necessary component is that the target of assessment *deserves* both the negative attitudes and the further negative treatment that may be called for by those attitudes, and such desert seems to make sense only when that target has a sufficient degree of competence in grasping and responding to the basic moral demand that we make of one another.[15]

Both Patricia Greenspan and, very recently, Watson himself have applied this distinction to the psychopath. The trouble with the psychopath, according to Watson, is that while he's "constitutionally incapable of seeing moral demands as making any valid claims on" him, he can also be "brutally aggressive and nonchalantly dismissive of the interests of others" (Watson 2008). The first fact suggests the psychopath is not responsible, whereas the second suggests he is. One way to respond to the seeming tension between these facts, then, is to appeal to the distinction between the two faces of responsibility. On the one hand, the psychopath's behavior grounds many moral predications—"cruel," "callous," and "manipulative" among them—and when we respond to the psychopath as a result, with variations of scorn, disgust, or hatred generally,[16] we *attribute* the action to a fault in his character and hold him responsible thereby. By contrast, given that the psychopath isn't susceptible to hearing, understanding, or replying to moral demands, he cannot deservedly or even sensibly be *held* responsible on the accountability face. So while we may judge him responsible in the sense of finding fault with him, we cannot hold him responsible *to us*.

Appeal to this distinction helps explain away the first part of our puzzle, about why it is that the psychopath may be criminally responsible without being a member of the moral community. She may be criminally responsible in virtue of the fact that her harmful actions are properly

---

[15] Admittedly, there is much packed into this formulation. For further explication, see Shoemaker 2007.

[16] See Greenspan 2003, 423. Note that these are not the kinds of interpersonal reactive attitudes made famous and emphasized by Strawson and the ones relevant, I maintain, only with respect to accountability-responsibility (see Shoemaker 2007). Those consist instead primarily in attitudes such as resentment, indignation, guilt, gratitude, and forgiveness. See Strawson 2003, 75–77.

attributable to her: she intended to commit the harm for which she's accused, and insofar as she can understand that this sort of action has been deemed illegal—she has the capacity to apply the relevant abstract legal predicate to her deliberations in this concrete case—then that's all that's needed for a finding of (criminal) fault. Most psychopaths have no trouble at all understanding which actions have been deemed illegal—regardless of whether or not they can appreciate, understand, or respond to their moral bases—so insofar as they display bad intent, they warrant criminal blame (as well as certain negative moral predications, perhaps).

Something more is needed for membership in the moral community, however, and that something is eligibility for *accountability*. Here what's necessary is susceptibility to moral address; if one isn't so susceptible, the moral demands constitutive of expressions of this face of responsibility —resentment, indignation, and so forth—will be senseless, like resenting a dog for peeing in the garden.[17] And so it is senseless to attempt to engage in moral address with the psychopath: his particular developmental disability—his moral disability—prevents him from being accountable to us, and so prevents him from being a member of the moral community.

So much for the psychopath. How might we explain the mirror scenario for adults with MMR? While they do seem to be members of the moral community, they're often exempt from criminal responsibility. I believe applying the Watsonian distinction between the two faces of responsibility is helpful here also, although matters are more complex.

Start with accountability. How is it that adults with MMR are accountable to us? What's clear is that moral address is often perfectly sensible to them. This will be quite an obvious point for parents and caregivers of such adults. But the literature—what scant literature there is—hints at this as well.[18] What provides the conditions for accountability to us are precisely those capacities articulated earlier: sensitivity and arousal to the distress of others, emotional maturity, and empathy. To be accountable to others requires that one be susceptible to the moral demand expressed via various participant reactive attitudes, and this itself requires that one be able to (a) recognize and appreciate the distress associated with injuries and harms for what it is; (b) understand what it is like for the injured or harmed party; and (c) *feel* what the injured or harmed party feels in being so affected. These capacities are implicitly

---

[17] In both cases, certain expressions may serve to "correct" the offending behavior, but these will be variations of anger, not resentment, and anyway they will be ways of treating the offender with the "objective" attitude, intended solely to alter his future behavior through conditioning, rather than as a method of communicating with him as part of an interpersonal relationship.

[18] See Castles 1996, 78–79. Also see the examples given of interpersonal understanding in Heshusius 1981, 98–110.

assumed in the familiar moral prompt, "How would you feel if someone did that to you?"

Note that what it means to be accountable to someone does not consist in one's having a facility for applying abstract moral principles to concrete cases, as some have suggested (see, e.g., Wallace 1994, 157). This is, after all, a facility the nonretarded *psychopath* seems to have, for it's the defining capacity of the stage of formal operations at which she arrives right along with the rest of us. But insofar as the psychopath isn't morally accountable, but the adult with MMR—someone who never reaches the stage of formal operations—is, this abstract application capacity doesn't seem necessary to the accountability face of responsibility.

What does seem necessary is susceptibility to *emotional* address, the ability to appreciate and respond to the invitation to feel what one has done to another. And it is in taking up this invitation that one becomes emotionally engaged with the other person—one is drawn into identifying with him with respect to what he feels, after all—and it is the susceptibility to this sort of engagement, I suggest, that is the defining feature of the moral community. This means that the population of the moral community is made up of only those who are capable of meeting the accountability face of responsibility, those capable of holding, and being held, *accountable to* one another. And this is something of which adults with MMR are clearly capable (to some extent).

What, though, is the relation between the attributability face of responsibility and both the accountability face and the conditions of entry into the moral community? Here is where things get even more complicated. What I'm going to suggest is that responsibility-as-attributability is not in fact necessary for responsibility-as-accountability. Instead, they are actually quite distinct faces of responsibility, and this is brought out by deeper consideration of what makes blame of each sort unfair.

Judging you to be morally responsible in the attributive sense involves applying various moral predicates to you in light of your action. This is unfair if at least one of two conditions is met: (1) the action wasn't yours, or (2) you have no understanding of the predicate in question.[19] Set aside

---

[19] It's probably best to take these remarks as being primarily about blaming practices, rather than praising practices. After all, it sounds jarring, to say the least, to hold that it's *unfair* to judge someone praiseworthy in the attributability sense for a positive action (generosity, say) if that person doesn't understand the concept. It would likely be inappropriate or unwarranted, granted, but unfair? Now there *may* be some unfairness involved to others (cheapening their own praiseworthiness, perhaps), but surely it's not unfair to the target of the assessment. This is perhaps yet another illustration of a possible asymmetry between praise and blame. See Doris and Knobe forthcoming. Because we're talking about the relation of criminal to moral responsibility, however, and because criminal responsibility has little or nothing to do with praiseworthiness anyway, we can safely set aside this issue here.

the first condition and focus on the second. If someone doesn't even understand the concepts "manipulative," and "exploitative," and "cruel," then judging her as such is unfair insofar as it attributes qualities to her will or character that couldn't have been part of her deliberations.[20] This is a condition emphasizing a certain sort of *cognitive* competence, namely, the ability to comprehend the nature of certain concepts and be able to see how their various components might apply to one's own deliberations and actions in concrete cases. It is, in other words, a capacity enjoyed only by those who have developed to the stage of formal operations.

Contrast these conditions of unfairness to those relevant in holding others *accountable*. Here there are three general conditions: it is unfair to hold you responsible for some action on this face if (1) the action isn't yours, (2) what you did was unavoidable (in some sense),[21] or (3) you lack the relevant capacities for hearing and responding to emotional address. This last condition is the key. It is unfair to hold you accountable, and in so doing address you morally, if you are incapable of hearing, under-standing, or responding to such address. And as I have already argued, moral address consists primarily in *emotional* address, an invitation for you to make the empathetic leap, to feel what you've made me feel, to engage emotionally with me. If you are thus incapable of appreciating this sort of emotional address, it's not only unfair but it's *pointless* for us to hold you accountable.[22]

There are, then, different conditions for unfairness in appraisals of attributability and accountability. The crucial difference between them is, roughly, that what matters for appraisals of attributability is primarily a certain cognitive capacity—a facility with the components of moral predication—whereas what matters for appraisals of accountability is primarily a certain emotional capacity—sufficient emotional maturity to engage in the relevant empathy with others.

This means, therefore, that it's possible to be accountability-respon-sible without being attributability-responsible. This might occur when

---

[20] Cf. Watson 2004, 282: "In general, aretaic appraisal requires the intelligence and sensibility to comprehend at least the normative concepts in terms of which the relevant forms of appraisal are conceived."

[21] See Watson 2004, 276, for a somewhat similar condition.

[22] Two remarks. First, does the pointlessness of our holding you accountable mean you're in fact *not* accountable? This is an important question that I don't mean to be addressing here. My discussion is simply intended to be about our actual practices of responsibility-assessment, where such practices are also what determine the nature and boundaries of the moral community (whom *we take* to be included therein). Second, the worry about pointlessness isn't the consequentialist worry that our addressing you in this way will fail to have any good effects on your future behavior. Rather, the worry is that the reactive attitudes, say, will be pointless *as forms of moral address* if you can't hear, understand, or respond to them. For a similar point (albeit focused solely on moral understanding), see Watson 2004, 219–59.

one failed to understand certain abstract moral predications or their components, and yet was nevertheless susceptible to the sort of emotional address that could get one to appreciate that or how one had wronged another.[23] And this is precisely the situation that I believe is occupied by many adults with MMR. Certain attributability-judgments may be unfair with respect to them, given that they aren't able to understand certain abstract moral principles or predicates or their application to concrete cases (such as their own specific actions). Nevertheless, because of their emotional maturity and their well-seasoned cognitive facility with negotiating the world via only their capacities for concrete operations, they are susceptible to the emotional address at the heart of accountability's moral demand. So while the judgment that he was manipulative or exploitative, say, may be unfair to an adult with MMR, the demand that he "feel what he has done" may not be, precisely because it's a *concrete* appeal, one he is certainly capable of undertaking.

These remarks indicate how we might resolve our puzzle. To a significant degree, judgments of criminal responsibility emphasize the attributability face of responsibility, whereas holding people responsible and making judgments about membership in the moral community emphasize the accountability face of responsibility. Attributability-responsibility is of course about attribution, and so in the criminal arena it is first and foremost about attaching an illegal action to someone, in particular to someone's *will*. The crucial capacities here are thus primarily cognitive: if in voluntarily intending X you nevertheless know that X has been deemed wrong/illegal by the powers that be (and that the consequences of X-ing involve punishment), that is sufficient for attributing X to you for purposes of criminal responsibility.[24] In other words, if you are capable of understanding how various abstract moral/legal principles apply to your concrete actions, your actions are attributable to you (in both the criminal and the moral arenas). So while the psychopath may not know or appreciate that moral wrongness constitutes a normative constraint on her deliberations, she at least knows what's been *deemed* wrong by her society, and she also knows how to apply these abstract principles of societal wrongness to her own actions. In spite of this knowledge, however, she has deliberately, knowingly, and voluntarily aimed to hurt us, and so may be judged morally (and criminally) responsible. But more than this, attributability-responsibility (on the negative side) involves attributing some "bad" action to a *fault* in its agent, a judgment that the action was a concrete expression of a vicious aspect of his character, a product of either his skewed values/ends or his

---

[23] I have argued elsewhere that this latter capacity has to do with appreciating specifically *second-personal* moral reasons. See Shoemaker 2007, 85–92.

[24] It isn't necessary, though, given the possibility of "strict liability."

skewed ordering of those values/ends. Indeed, this is why psychopathy is often deemed an *aggravating* factor in criminal responsibility, for the psychopath's particular actions (and the ways he goes about performing them) reveal the thoroughgoing viciousness of his character, reveal just how against us he really is.

Nevertheless, the psychopath fails to be a member of the moral community because she lacks the mature emotional capacities necessary for accountability. She is incapable of the relevant sort of empathy, of feeling what another feels, and so she's incapable of being *held to account*, of entering into the types of interpersonal moral relationships that constitute those community ties. She is not *reachable*. What many have thought of as a moral blindness on her part, then, is actually an emotional deafness, an inability to hear or register the moral appeals of her fellows.

The adult with MMR has, in a way, the opposite problem. On the one hand, he is capable of the mature emotions necessary to the accountability face of responsibility, and so he is capable of empathy and entering into the relevant interpersonal moral relations. On the other hand, he may not have the kind of cognitive capacities necessary for criminal responsibility, insofar as what's required there is the ability to apply various abstract legal principles to one's concrete actions. This incapacity seems sufficient to meet the "insanity defense" provision of every state and federal jurisdiction.[25]

Let me explain this in a slightly different way by considering an objection.[26] Suppose that holding accountable does involve expressing reactive attitudes of some sort, and suppose further that these expressions are indeed modes of moral communication. Now when such demands are put to an agent, the *content* of what is expressed is meant to involve reference to the act of the agent that instigated the response, and the one holding responsible operates under the presupposition that the agent with whom she's engaging has the conceptual resources to grasp this content. One might worry, then, that even if the adult with MMR understands *that* she's being held accountable (given the excitation of emotions involved), this is insufficient for accountability: she must also understand the full point of what those holding her responsible are expressing. Otherwise, this would be a mere simulacrum of an exchange between members of the moral community. Yet it's doubtful from what I've said that the adult with MMR has the requisite conceptual grasp, and so it remains doubtful that one can decouple attributability from accountability in the way I have suggested. One could only be accountable if one had a conceptual facility sufficient to render one attributability-responsible as well.

---

[25] See, e.g., Reid 1998, 374. Note also Evans 1983, 241: "A person who does not abstract very well may not foresee the consequences of his deviant actions and is unlikely to be deterred by the abstract threat of punishment."

[26] My thanks to Michael McKenna for the objection and fruitful discussion of this point.

I think that this worry glosses an important distinction between the kinds of conceptual facilities called upon in the two faces of responsibility. We may plausibly suppose that the expression of reactive attitudes is an expression of the moral demand *that you not injure me in this way*. Now given that this is a demand—a demand that may be localized by the adult with MMR as having its source in the authority of the person standing before him—and insofar as the adult with MMR can ostensibly imagine and entertain this sort of concrete demand prior to his action (this is where his empathetic capacities come into play), he does seem capable of adhering to or violating such demands qua moral demands and thus understanding the full point of what those who are making such demands are expressing. Doing this doesn't require any abstract application or deduction capacities, and so it is not unfair to hold him accountable.

The fairness of responsibility as attributability, however, depends on different conditions; in particular, it depends on whether or not the targeted agent understands the components of the considered predicate and how it would apply here and now to her actions. Now the adult with MMR seems more or less incapable of grasping or applying the relevant concepts in *this* arena insofar as it requires understanding how these abstract concepts/components apply to one's concrete case, requires seeing how one's ends or values might best be expressed here and now. This ability is what's directly relevant to criminal responsibility (applying abstract rules to concrete actions), and it requires development to the stage of formal operations. So insofar as the adult with MMR is susceptible to the concrete moral demands of her range of intimates but may not be capable of applying abstract moral or legal concepts to her particular actions, she may be accountability-responsible without being attributability-responsible. She may thus recognize that something is demanded of her (by her caregiver, say) without fairly being judged to have expressed her ends or values in violating that demand.

The distinction between responsibility's two faces thus helps explain how the psychopath might have aggravated criminal responsibility without being in the moral community, while the adult with MMR might be in the moral community while having diminished or no criminal responsibility. Surprisingly, though, I think we can allow for this detachment of attributability from accountability without contradicting Watson's original, and quite intuitive, thought that attributability is *necessary* for accountability.

To see how, consider yet another distinction, focused now on the first condition of fairness for both faces. For me to be judged responsible *or* held accountable for some action, it must indeed be mine—the action must belong to me—but such ownership actually comes in two forms. On the one hand, there's a robust form of ownership in which an action is mine just in case it discloses or is expressive of my *self*, that is, it flows from one of my genuine character traits.[27] On the other hand, there's a very minimal form of ownership in which an action is mine just in case it depends on my will, regardless of whether or not it discloses my self (for example, this may be the case with actions performed on a whim). What is common to both faces of responsibility is just the latter, minimal form of attributability, which is also the only form necessary for accountability, it seems. After all, the person who steals on a whim may well be subject to the reactive attitudes, even if that action isn't traceable to some fault in his character.[28]

The former, more robust sense of attributability may not be necessary to accountability, however, as I have already suggested: that an action doesn't disclose one's self may be no bar to our expression of the moral demand that one nevertheless refrain from performing it. And again, this will likely be the case for adults with MMR: while their reduced facility with abstract, formal operations may prevent them from the sort of moral cognition necessary for the fault-finding of judgments of (attributability) responsibility, they may nevertheless be held accountable for their actions (actions dependent on their will), given the *concreteness* of the emotional appeals implicit in the moral demands "Can't you see how you've made me feel?" and "How would you feel if I did that to you?" This is precisely accountability with minimal attributability, but without robust attributability. We can thus account for the intuitive aspect of Watson's original thought by allowing that minimal attributability/ownership is necessary for both faces of responsibility, whereas robust attributability/ownership is necessary only for the attributability (aretaic) face itself.

The Second Puzzle: Degrees of Accountability

The second puzzle is solely about adults with MMR, and it is this: while such adults are members of the moral community, and so are eligible

---

[27] This is likely the form of ownership that theorists of *identification* are discussing, where theirs is an attempt to figure out the conditions rendering some action or psychological feature one's own, something with which one identifies and so renders it authoritative for self-determination. For the classic treatments of the issue, see Frankfurt 1988.

[28] For a very nice discussion of whims and identification, see Lippert-Rasmussen 2003. But what about the *psychopath* who steals on a whim? By stipulation his self/character isn't implicated in the action, which eliminates attributability-responsibility, and even though his action depends on his will he lacks the sort of moral understanding necessary for accountability-responsibility, so it looks as if he's left out of the responsibility loop altogether. While this result may strike some readers as odd, it actually seems right to me. If I were really to know that someone were a psychopath who stole on a whim, I would surely take up the objective attitude toward him and simply attempt to manage him and his thievery, without much by way of attaching any moral predicates to him either. Alternatively, one might attempt to insist on a *kind* of attributability-responsibility in this case by claiming that the psychopath's self/character is still implicated with respect to its *indulgence* or *neglect* over the doings of the "whimmer" within him, and this response seems plausible as well. Thanks to Michael McKenna for pressing me on this point.

for being held accountability-responsible for their actions, they are nevertheless typically thought to be *less* responsible than nonretarded members. But it seems as if membership in the moral community is all-or-nothing: either one is eligible for assessments of accountability or one isn't. How, then, do we make sense of the varying degrees of responsibility assessed in these cases?

There are two ways in which "responsibility" might admit of degrees. First, it could merely be a gloss on "blameworthiness" or "praiseworthiness," both of which clearly admit of degrees. So one agent might be less blameworthy than another for performing the same action as a result of various mitigating factors. This is quite familiar to us. Here one has met the general eligibility conditions for moral responsibility, but one is subject to varying degrees of blame or praise for specific actions. In other words, one is not *exempt* at all from moral agency and being appropriately assessed as blameworthy or praiseworthy; rather, such assessments are matters of degrees.

The second way in which "responsibility" admits of degrees is of more interest to us. It refers to degrees of *exemption* from the moral community. More specifically, one agent may be less responsible than another in virtue of being eligible *in fewer instances* for assessments of blame or praise. This agent is thus fully eligible for accountability-assessments in a range of cases, but that range is smaller than it is for other agents. In this sort of scenario, eligibility for assessment itself is still all-or-nothing with respect to specific actions, but with respect to *agents* it can be partial, such that they are exempt in certain instances but not exempt in others. This is the role I believe is occupied by adults with MMR.

What, then, defines the boundaries of the relevant range? Here I just want to offer a few speculative remarks, remarks that nevertheless strike me as quite plausible given the available evidence. It seems that adults with MMR, when they are eligible for accountability, are held to be so primarily just by those with whom they *already* find themselves emotionally engaged. That is, their accountability extends only to those with whom they are already in interpersonal relationships: family, friends, caregivers. And while their eligibility for such assessment may extend beyond this range, it likely does so in a nonstandard way. Let me explain.

Because their developmental capacities have been limited to the stage of concrete operations, adults with MMR may lack the capacity to recognize other unfamiliar members of the moral community *as* members of that community, and they may also not be susceptible to expressions of the moral demand when voiced by those unfamiliar others. This last is because they are likely unable to see or appreciate any sort of abstract principles about mutual recognition and accountability among fellow members of the moral community, nor are they likely to appreciate (without serious prompting) how the practices of mutual accountability with which they are familiar ought to be applied to unfamiliar agents. What they can and do appreciate, however, are concrete appeals from those they care about, those with whom they're already emotionally connected, and they also have no trouble holding such familiar agents to account as well (see, e.g., Castles 1996, 75–80).

Consequently, while they may be exempt from being held accountable in interactions with strangers, they are not exempt in interactions with their familiars (although they may well be excused, as are we all, in particular cases). This is borne out by considering how we ourselves react to both the nonretarded and the retarded. In our interactions with those we believe to be nonretarded, our default position is that of holding accountable: our reactive attitudes are at the ready, just in case the other person expresses good or bad will to us. Alternatively, when we find ourselves interacting with those we believe to be (even mildly) retarded, and with whom we are unfamiliar, our default position is to exempt from accountability, to discount any seeming expressions of ill will and so to suspend our reactive attitudes. For those in preexisting interpersonal relationships with mildly retarded adults, however, matters of accountability are almost exactly as they are with nonretarded adults. Labels are forgotten, and the gloves come off: praise and blame—from both parties—are full-throated (see, e.g., Taylor and Bogdan 1989, 29, 32).[29]

Of course, one of the ideals for many caregivers is to extend the range of accountability for their charges, and I have suggested elsewhere how this sometimes seems to take place (see Shoemaker 2007, 105–6). When the adult with MMR interacts with, and injures, a stranger, the caregiver may express a kind of resentment on behalf of the stranger (an exaggerated mimic, perhaps) followed by the familiar appeal, "How would you feel if someone did that to you?" In being susceptible to the reactive attitudes of the caregiver—someone with whom she is already in an emotional relationship—the adult with MMR may then feel the appropriate guilt or remorse. So far, however, she is merely identifying with, and responding to the demand made by, the caregiver. But through repeated encounters like this, the hope is that the adult with MMR will

---

[29] Could this full-throated sort of accountability-assessment be explained by the assessor's failure to retain a proper perspective regarding the retarded adult with whom she's in a relationship? This is surely possible in some cases, just as it is possible for someone to be so enthralled by a charismatic psychopath that she treats him as though he were a fellow member of the moral community. But in both cases a clear-eyed perspective on the agent in question will, I believe, yield the natural reactions I have suggested. For most of those in relationships with adults with MMR in particular, the evidence strongly suggests that their full-throated reactive attitudes are just as natural and proper-seeming (to both them and others) as their moral reactions to paradigm members of the moral community.

eventually come to see the face of the caregiver in the stranger and respond appropriately, without mediation or antecedent relationships. This is, no doubt, a nonstandard route to the extension of one's accountability relations, but the end result seems just as good as ordinary examples of these relations. And furthermore, to the degree that many adults with MMR are eventually capable of such an extension, it is once again a testament to their own nonstandard route to cognitive maturity, via exercise of concrete operations alone.

Conclusion

The idea here has been to get a clearer grip on the nature of the moral community by focusing on the nature of its boundaries. We have done so by contrasting agents who are just barely on opposing sides. But our investigation has revealed a number of complications, worth noting in the following summary of results.

First, the mildly retarded agents included within the moral community are *adults*, and they are distinct from children—whose status in the moral community is far more uncertain and unstable—in several key respects, being more mature socially, emotionally, and cognitively. These various forms of maturity are what in fact enable them to have the types of genuine interpersonal relationships constitutive of eligibility for moral responsibility, for they provide the essential conditions for developing moral sensitivity, understanding, and motivation. The psychopath, by contrast, lacks the relevant emotional and cognitive capacities to engage with others in this way.

Second, though, the psychopath is nevertheless held responsible in some arenas. More specifically, he is subject to certain moral predications and criminal responsibility. How do we make sense of this, then, if he's not a member of the moral community? The answer is that the moral community consists only in those agents eligible for being held *accountable* to one another, whereas the range of agents who are morally responsible generally may be wider than this. In particular, there may be those who are responsible in virtue of their actions disclosing some feature(s) of their selves, but not responsible in the sense of being accountable to others (because, say, they lack the capacities for moral sensitivity, understanding, and/or motivation). This is the location, I have suggested, occupied by the psychopath. But this sort of distinction also allows us to identify the location occupied by the adult with MMR, a location of accountability-responsibility (sometimes) but not attributability-responsibility (sometimes).

Third, even though she is a member of the moral community, the adult with MMR isn't a full-fledged, paradigm member. The way to explain this point is to note that what typically gets her into the moral community is her actual interpersonal relations with her familiars. The circle of her familiars, however, may effectively constitute the boundary of the range of those to whom she is accountable. But it also might not, given the possibility of the outward extension I suggested in the previous section. In any event, that the adult with MMR is a member of the moral community *to some extent* should be uncontroversial; attempting to articulate the nature of that extent is likely to be ongoing and perhaps more controversial.

I have of course been talking here in very abstract generalities about two different sets of agents, none of whom may very precisely or fully meet the membership conditions of their stated groups. So there may be some agents who aren't full-fledged psychopaths, meeting only some of the relevant conditions, and these agents may thus have some rudimentary capacities for accountability, or they may be accountable to *some* others *some* times. Alternatively, there may be some adults with MMR who aren't very accountable but who nevertheless meet some of the conditions for attributability-responsibility—there may, for instance, be retarded psychopaths. But these concrete examples serve, in a way, to illustrate my two primary points in the chapter. First, the nature of responsibility and the moral community is indeed quite complex, and we thwart an understanding of ourselves as moral agents when we pay insufficient attention to the relevant complexities. Second, and more important, our understanding of the nature of the moral community and our presence in it may be both enhanced and enriched when we move beyond the typical ruminations on "normal" agency to consider the wider panoply of human possibilities for engaging with both morality and one another.

Acknowledgments

This chapter benefited from so many sources that I surely won't be able to identify them all (but I'll do my best). For the initial invitation to contribute the chapter's ancestor to the Manhattan conference on ethics and the challenge of cognitive disability in fall 2008, I'm deeply grateful to Eva Feder Kittay. The conference itself was extraordinary, and I learned a great deal from it (and for that I'm also grateful to Licia Carlson, the co-organizer) as well as from the audience members at my talk. I subsequently delivered versions of the chapter in several forums, and I was helped by the audience members in attendance at each, so thanks to those audiences at Bowling Green State University, Florida State University, Princeton's University Center for Human Values, the University of British Columbia, and Tulane University. Finally, I'm most grateful to Michael McKenna, who offered extremely valuable advice and encouragement throughout the writing and editing of the chapter.

References

Arpaly, Nomy. 2003. *Unprincipled Virtue.* Oxford: Oxford University Press.

Blair, R. J. R. 1995. "A Cognitive Developmental Approach to Morality: Investigating the Psychopath." *Cognition* 57:1–29.

———. 1996. "Brief Report: Morality in the Autistic Child." *Journal of Autism and Developmental Disorders* 26:571–79.

———. 1999a. "Psychophysiological Responsiveness to the Distress of Others in Children with Autism." *Personality and Individual Differences* 26:477–85.

———. 1999b. "Responsiveness to Distress Cues in the Child with Psychopathic Tendencies." *Personality and Individual Differences* 27:135–45.

———, et al. 1995. "Is the Psychopath 'Morally Insane'?" *Personality and Individual Differences* 19:741–52.

Castles, Elaine. 1996. *"We're People First": The Social and Emotional Lives of Individuals with Mental Retardation.* Westport, Conn.: Praeger.

Darwall, Stephen. 2006. *The Second-Person Standpoint.* Cambridge, Mass.: Harvard University Press.

Doris, John, and Joshua Knobe. Forthcoming. "Strawsonian Variations: Folk Morality and the Search for a Unified Theory." *The Oxford Handbook of Moral Psychology.*

Dwyer, Susan. 2003. "Moral Development and Moral Responsibility." *Monist* 86:181–99.

Dziobek, Isabel, et al. 2008. "Dissociation of Cognitive and Emotional Empathy in Adults with Asperger Syndrome Using the Multifaceted Empathy Test (MET)." *Journal of Autism and Developmental Disorders* 38:464–73.

Evans, Daryl Paul. 1983. *The Lives of Mentally Retarded People.* Boulder, Colo.: Westview Press.

Eysenck, H. J. 1977. *Crime and Personality.* London: Routledge and Kegan Paul.

———. 1998. "Personality and Crime." In *Psychopathy: Antisocial, Criminal, and Violent Behavior*, edited by Theodore Millon, Erik Simonsen, Morten Birket-Smith, and Roger D. Davis, 40–49. New York: Guilford Press.

Fine, Cordelia, and Jeanette Kennett. 2004. "Mental Impairment, Moral Understanding and Criminal Responsibility: Psychopathy and the Purposes of Punishment." *International Journal of Law and Psychiatry* 27:425–43.

Fingarette, Herbert. 1967. *On Responsibility.* New York: Basic Books.

Fischer, John Martin, and Mark Ravizza. 1998. *Responsibility and Control.* Cambridge: Cambridge University Press.

Fowles, D. C. 1980. "The Three Arousal Model: Implications of Gray's Two-Factor Learning Theory for Heart Rate, Electrodermal Activity, and Psychopathy." *Psychophysiology* 17:87–104.

Frankfurt, Harry. 1988. *The Importance of What We Care About.* Cambridge: Cambridge University Press.

Greenspan, Patricia. 2003. "Responsible Psychopaths." *Philosophical Psychology* 16:417–29.

Hare, R. D. 1998. "Psychopaths and Their Nature." In *Psychopathy: Antisocial, Criminal and Violent Behavior*, edited by Theodore Millon, Erik Simonsen, Morten Birket-Smith, and Roger D. Davis, 188–212. New York: Guilford Press.

Herpertz, Sabine C., and Sass Henning. 2000. "Emotional Deficiency and Psychopathy." *Behavioral Sciences and the Law* 18:567–80.

Heshusius, Louis. 1981. *Meaning in Life as Experienced by Persons Labeled Retarded in a Group Home.* Springfield, Ill.: Charles C. Thomas.

Hoffman, M. L. 2000. *Empathy and Moral Development: Implications for Caring and Justice.* Cambridge: Cambridge University Press.

Kasari, Connie, and Nirit Bauminger. 1998. "Social and Emotional Development in Children with Mental Retardation." In *Handbook of Mental Retardation and Development*, edited by Jacob A. Burack, Robert M. Hodapp, and Edward Zigler, 411–33. Cambridge: Cambridge University Press.

Kennett, Jeannette. 2001. *Agency and Responsibility.* Oxford: Oxford University Press.

Lippert-Rasmussen, Kasper. 2003. "Identification and Responsibility." *Ethical Theory and Moral Practice* 6:349–76.

Lykken, D. T. 1995. *The Antisocial Personalities.* Hillsdale, N.J.: Lawrence Erlbaum Associates.

McKenna, Michael. 2005. "Where Frankfurt and Strawson Meet." *Midwest Studies in Philosophy* 29:163–80.

Reid, William H. 1998. "Evaluating Criminal Defendants: Responsibility and Competence to Stand Trial." *Journal of Practical Psychology and Behavioral Health* 4, no. 6:373–76.

———. 2006. "Sanity Evaluations and Criminal Responsibility." *Applied Psychology in Criminal Justice* 2:114–45.

Russell, Paul. 1995. *Freedom and Moral Sentiment.* Oxford: Oxford University Press.

———. 2004. "Responsibility and the Condition of Moral Sense." *Philosophical Topics* 32:287–305.

Scanlon, T. M. 1998. *What We Owe to Each Other.* Cambridge, Mass.: Belknap Press of Harvard University Press.

Sher, George. 2006. *In Praise of Blame.* Oxford: Oxford University Press.

Shoemaker, David. 2007. "Moral Address, Moral Responsibility, and the Boundaries of the Moral Community." *Ethics* 118:70–108.

Strawson, Peter. 2003. "Freedom and Resentment." In *Free Will*, 2nd edition, edited by Gary Watson, 72–93. Oxford: Oxford University Press. Originally published in *Proceedings of the British Academy* 48 (1962): 1–25.

Talbert, Matt. 2008. "Blame and Responsiveness to Moral Reasons: Are Psychopaths Blameworthy?" *Pacific Philosophical Quarterly* 89: 516–35.

Taylor, Steven J., and Gary Bogdan. 1989. "On Accepting Relationships Between People with Mental Retardation and Non-disabled People: Towards an Understanding of Acceptance." *Disability, Handicap and Society* 4:21–36.

Wallace, R. Jay. 1994. *Responsibility and the Moral Sentiments.* Cambridge, Mass.: Harvard University Press.

Watson, Gary. 2004. *Agency and Answerability.* Oxford: Oxford University Press.

———. 2008. "The Trouble with the Psychopath". Unpublished paper presented at the Center for Ethics and Public Affairs, April 25, at Tulane University, New Orleans.

Wolf, Susan. 1990. *Freedom Within Reason.* Oxford: Oxford University Press.

13

ALZHEIMER'S DISEASE AND SOCIALLY EXTENDED MENTATION

JAMES LINDEMANN NELSON

Where do minds end? When we think about Alzheimer's disease, this question might seem vaguely pertinent, perhaps, but hardly well put: to sort out worries about how best to trigger and direct proxy decision-making authority, as well as more existential anxieties about what progressive dementias do to people, "*When* do minds end?" would seem to be more to the point.

Yet "Where do minds end?" is a tolerably precise and certainly very live question in the philosophy of mind. Do our minds extend no further than the inside of our bodies—our central nervous system or some portion of it, as seems the default, even commonsensical view? Or might the content of our thoughts be individuated by features of the world outside our skulls? Might our sensations and our mental images super-vene on a wider range of reality than our own neural processes? Might our mental lives be best explained as some sort of dynamic interchange among the brain, the body, the natural and social environments, and time?[1]

These questions can be seen as part of philosophy's ongoing effort to contribute to our better understanding just what kind of beings we are, and surely that enterprise has value enough in itself to be going on with. But such efforts do, sometimes, have fairly direct implications for practical thought and life as well. Here, I hope to open up consideration of how somewhat iconoclastic answers to "Where are minds?"—so-called externalist positions in the philosophy of mind—might bear on how best to think about and respond to dementia. Ronald Dworkin (1993) and Agnieszka Jaworska (1999) have staked out positions in the debate about proxy decision making on behalf of demented people that are widely taken (rightly, as I see it) to set the broad contours of the problem. In so doing, neither thinker has had much to say about philosophical controversies about the mind's location, but this neglect could well appear altogether benign. The facts pertinent to philosophizing about

---

[1] For a clear, sophisticated survey, see Hurley forthcoming; for an admirably succinct account, see Levy 2007.

dementia and decision making look to be before us; they don't seem to
hinge on the resolution of disputes in philosophy of mind. I am, however,
inclined to think this appearance is misleading.[2] I'll flesh out this
inclination, first by considering Dworkin, whose position rests on his
well-known distinction between critical and experiential interests; critical
interests emerge from a person's reflective deliberations, and are (generally) to guide proxy decision makers even should they conflict with
interests emerging chiefly from how matters feel to a person. Naturally
enough, perhaps, Dworkin assumes that a person's critical interests are
fixed should she lose the cognitive abilities required to form or assess
them; I try to show that an externalist perspective would allow for
significant alterations in critical interests even should a person become
demented.

Next, and at some greater length, I turn to Jaworska, who has
distinctively argued that Dworkin demands too much of us, and that
people with moderate dementia are not restricted merely to having desires
but are well able to form values fully worthy of respect. A seeming
consequence of Jaworska's view is that the values espoused by a person
who currently enjoys the full use of his faculties may be displaced by
contrary values formed should he become demented. I try to show that on
an externalist view such contrary values might not simply supersede the
earlier values. Rather, the conflicting values may both have serious claims
to shape how caregivers should respond to people with dementia.

Unsurprisingly, acknowledging that the landscape of proxy decision making looks different if externalist perspectives on the mind
are part of the map does not mean that the ground is any easier to
traverse. The contrary is likelier to be true. What I provide is not a
detailed guide to getting around a reconfigured terrain; here, I just rough
out the contours.

Semantic Externalism: A Rough Sketch and a Gesture at Motivation

The 1960s and 70s saw the development of a picture of reference in which
the link between the speaker and the spoken of was provided not, or not
solely, by beliefs entertained by the speaker but by causal, historical, and
social relationships extending among the speaker and other members of
linguistic communities who established and sustained practices of using
certain terms in certain ways (Kripke 1980; Putnam 1975).

Thus, contrary to the tradition founded by Frege (e.g., 1892) and
Russell (e.g., 1905), and refined by Searle (e.g., 1958), a proper
name—say, Jane Austen—doesn't connect our thought to that woman

---

[2] Rebecca Dresser (1994) has also contributed importantly to this discussion, drawing at
times on specific conceptions of personal identity. I have considered her work in Nelson
1995.

by having the same meaning as any uniquely specifying definite description we might happen to know, such as "the author of *Emma*," or by meaning the same as a subset of a cluster of such descriptions ("the currently most prominent British female Regency author," or "Gilbert Ryle's favorite writer," or "the figure depicted by Anne Hathaway in the movie *Becoming Jane*"). Part of the evidence for this claim is the following observation: about *that very woman*, it is perfectly possible that she died of the typhus she contracted at seven; that would have precluded a career as a novelist, but it wouldn't have stopped her from being Jane Austen. Thoughts of this sort, properly expanded, indicate that the name Jane Austen is not synonymous with any uniquely specifying description; ergo, what accounts for my referential ability is not that I know something that picks her and her alone out of the crowd. The reference of the name is secured not by features thought to be "inside" me but by my participation in a certain kind of social network that connects my use of the name to its bearer. Similar conclusions, similarly motivated, have been put forward for natural kind terms as well as for proper names, and for many general referring terms.

Consider Putnam's classic discussion of water (1975). Suppose water is H_2O here on earth, but the phenomenally indiscernible stuff filling up the streams, ocean, lakes, rivers, and water coolers in an otherwise identical Twin Earth, although believed to be H_2O by speakers in that world, is actually something else ("XYZ"). The externalist intuition is that speakers in Twin Earth refer to something different by "water" from speakers around here, even though all the relevant beliefs held by speakers in each community are identical; the word as they use it picks out the stuff in their world, despite their false beliefs about it. Again, the conclusion is that the meanings of our words are determined, at least in part, by something other than features internal to our conscious lives or neural properties.

In the 1980s and subsequently, philosophers of mind began to explore the implications of semantic externalism. One seemed fairly straightforward: if the meanings of our *words* require an extensional connection to extramental objects, it seems that the same should hold good for the meaning of our *thoughts*.[3]

Interests, Values, and the Mind's End

Semantic externalism in the philosophy of mind brings with it the eye-catching suggestion that our relationship to our own mental

---

[3] If the meaning of, say, *chicory* is determined by relationships with items external to the mind, rather than by beliefs as traditionally (i.e., "internally") understood, someone who travels from the United States to the United Kingdom—where *chicory* refers to a perennial herb rather than endive—will eventually come to mean by *chicory* something quite different from what she takes herself to mean, without, perhaps, being herself aware of the shift, whether speaking aloud or *in foro interno* (Ludlow 1998).

contents—and therefore, in an important sense, to ourselves—is not immediate but travels through various social arrangements. Considerations of just this sort suggest that a feature of Dworkin's well-known views about critical interests may be insufficiently motivated (for more developed arguments to this effect, see Nelson 1995, 2003).

For Dworkin, human interests can be distinguished between experiential interests (those that are of value simply because they so strike the individuals who possess them) and critical interests, which are crucial to our integrity as persons, understood as continuous, temporally extended, self-understanding narratively structured beings. We value critical interests—or at least endorse our doing so—because normative reflection reveals them to be valuable. As Dworkin puts it, we "would be mistaken, and genuinely worse off," if we failed to recognize these interests; our "convictions about what helps make life good on the whole" are convictions that reflect our critical judgment (Dworkin 1993, 201–2). The authority wielded by critical interests does not depend on a person's ability at any given time to acknowledge or appreciate them; neither dementia nor even death can make our critical interests irrelevant to us. Our experiential interests are less robust; for them, insentience or nonexistence ends the story.

So much seems plausible. Yet Dworkin writes as though our critical interests are turned into stone once we lose certain cognitive abilities: once we can no longer reason autonomously, whatever constellation of critical interests we last competently endorsed retains its authority. If, however, the meanings of the terms that make up the content of our critical interests are at least partially determined by features of the natural and social world outside our heads, then our critical interests could shift: those external features might change after we become incapacitated, thus changing the content of our critical interests and, in turn, the appropriate course of action open to those who wish to respect those interests.

An illustration: imagine someone we'll call Martha, a moderately demented woman who is currently living a reasonably pleasant life.[4] Martha is a devout Jehovah's Witness. She develops a condition that is life threatening, but treatable with blood transfusions, a therapy famously forbidden by Witness religious understandings. Suppose, however, that since Martha became incapacitated, the Witness leadership has come to the conclusion that the biblical prohibition on "eating blood" was mistakenly taken to apply to transfusion; contrary to earlier authoritative understandings, then, the word *eating* does not include in its reference class being supplied with blood through a tube.

Should Martha receive the transfusion? For Dworkin, anything Martha herself might say here seems, ultimately, not to the point. As

---

[4] I think of her somewhat on the model of Andrew Firlik's well-known discussion of "Margo" (Firlik 1991).

she can no longer reflectively assess the arguments that support or challenge them, Martha's critical interests seem petrified.

Perhaps this is too strong. Dworkin might argue that Martha's proxies would best honor her critical interests by assuming, counterfactually, that, if Martha were aware of the change in Witness thought, she would accept the transfusion, and therefore it ought to be provided, as her fundamental critical interest is to live according to sound doctrine. On the other hand, he might claim that without an opportunity to reflect on the reasons for the change herself, Martha is not in a position to align the new information with her enduring critical interests, and therefore those interests are best respected by refusing the transfusion on her behalf. In my view, by way of contrast, either of these approaches assumes that the content of Martha's critical interests is fixed by features internal to her body and its history. An externalist perspective suggests, I think, that Martha should receive the transfusion, but not on the grounds that we ought to act as we have reason to believe the patient would autonomously decide now—that is, on the grounds that she would change or rerank her interests if she but could—but because the content of her critical interests has in fact *already* shifted with the change in the meaning of the word *eat* as understood by the linguistic community relevant to determining that content. In the relevant sense, *eat* is a technical term, whose reference is determined by experts, in accordance with what Putnam has called the Division of Linguistic Labor (1975).

On Jaworska's view, the cognitive abilities required to form critical interests are considerably less exacting than those required by Dworkin: no grasp of the connection between one's current evaluative posture and the shape of one's life as a whole is required. As Jaworska convincingly illustrates, many people with dementia can still affirm the correctness of their assessments, understand the relationship of those assessments to their sense of self-worth, and regard the importance of achieving what they assess to be worthy independently of their own experiences. Thus, despite lacking a grasp of the story of their lives overall, they value and do not merely desire. For Jaworska, people who have the capacity to express values in their decision making possess what is sufficient for those decisions to count as autonomous. As Martha, in virtue of her ability to value, is still an autonomous agent, we ought to ask her what she wants in the light of this doctrinal change, and then take her expressed views very seriously indeed, despite the fact that she is no longer in a position to provide the same kind of justification for them that once she could have done (see Jaworska 1999, 116).

However Jaworska's approach fares against Dworkin's alternative in general terms, it may seem less vulnerable to the concern that its practical conclusions presuppose an unargued internalist account of mental contents. Whether or not a person's mental contents shift due to changes in the external world, a person capable of making decisions presumably retains the authority to override those circumstances. It would seem an odd consequence of externalism indeed if it entailed that a Witness couldn't meet the new teaching with a contemptuous snort of "revisionist heresy!" and still conscientiously refuse transfusion. Such a person would in effect be withdrawing her endorsement of those posing as authoritative experts at the task of determining what the pertinent sense of *eating* denotes.

Suppose Martha is informed about the change in Witness practice but doesn't understand, or doesn't trust her informants. If Martha still is able to say, "I don't want a transfusion—it's not what a Witness does," it looks as though she passes Jaworska's test for distinguishing values from mere desires. In fact, Martha would then sound rather like Jaworska's own Mr. Burke, the moderately demented gentleman who shows up at home with a new truck, contrary to an earlier decision made jointly with his wife. As Jaworska sees it, Mr. Burke acts autonomously, as he is able to defend his action with the normative claim, "A man needs his truck" (1999, 107).

But, seen externally, "what a Witness does" doesn't seem to be the sort of thing that is altogether settled by what Martha says—or, to put the point more dramatically, Martha may not know her own mind here, since its contents aren't altogether determined by what is available to her immediately or introspectively. This indeterminacy isn't caused by Martha's dementia, of course—on the externalist picture, it is the case for us all. But it does suggest that Martha may need certain reflective capacities she now lacks to find a new basis for her reluctance to receive a transfusion that will make that reluctance a conscientious dissent from novel doctrine and not merely confusion about the content of her own beliefs. This is not to say that Martha's care providers would face no questions of judgment in deciding how best to help her in such circumstances. If transfusion and its aftermath would likely be lastingly traumatic to her, withholding that intervention might be the most defensible course of action. If so, her caregivers would not justify their action as an instance of deference to Martha's values. The judgment would stand on considerations of her welfare considered overall.

Beyond Externalism About Mental Contents

There's a good deal more that might be said about Martha's case. Yet even were one to be convinced that different views about where minds end have in-principle consequences for analyses of proxy decision making, it might also strike one that the practical implications are pretty recondite. After all, it took lots of fancy hypothesizing to generate an illustrative example. So let us consider a more commonplace situation: the perspective of people who are acquainted with these very debates. People like—well, many readers of these words. A possible consequence of

Jaworska's views—a consequence of which she is fully aware (see 1999, 137)—is that some of us may feel dementia to be an even more terrifying prospect than it is for people who do not trade in moral concepts for a living, one that threatens to estrange us even more completely from our futures. We must deal with the knowledge that our most cherished values, values that have emerged from our most mature and sophisticated reflections, might be ignored should they come into conflict with values we may espouse if we become demented—values whose implications we understand far less well, and whose coherence with our histories of evaluation may be much more fragmented. Defend me, some of us might think, from ever having an appeal to a normative understanding of what I am entitled to as "a man" accepted as an effective justification for any of my choices.

I will argue that if not only mental contents but also mental *acts*, such as endorsing a value and changing one's mind, are understood externally, accepting Jaworska's general view need not have such dire consequences. Famously (or perhaps notoriously) Andy Clark and David Chalmers (1998) have provided such a position, arguing that externalism extends beyond content to acts, motivating their "active externalism" not by claims about reference but in functional terms. They propose a *parity principle*: if some process plays a role in cognition such that were the process to go on inside the cognitive agent we would count it as part of her mind, then it is a part of her mind no matter where it is located.

Clark and Chalmers flesh out this claim by means of a story about one Otto, who, interestingly enough, suffers from a moderately advanced case of Alzheimer's. Otto, a fan of the Museum of Modern Art, can no longer recall where the museum is located without looking it up in a notebook he continually carries with him; in this, he differs from his friend Inga, who can remember the museum's location without benefit of a notebook. Yet, as Clark and Chalmers see it, the fact that Otto and Inga store their memories in different places is inconsequential. The proper way to understand Otto's story is that he does, in fact, have an accurate belief about the location of the museum—it's only that his way of remembering how to get to his destination involves inscriptions on a piece of paper to which he has reliable access. Understanding the matter otherwise is to make a fetish of the membrane that wraps up our bodies, rather than attending to the significance of what Otto can achieve via what Clark and Chalmers refer to as his "extended mind."

The philosophical literature is by now ornamented with many efforts to distinguish between Otto's notebook and the cranially located mechanism on which Inga relies to get to MOMA, efforts that in turn have prompted responses, typically provided by Clark (see especially his 2008, particularly chapter 5, for a series of objections and replies). Otto's belief about the museum's location is not immediately or continuously present to his consciousness, but if conscious awareness is a condition of having a belief, none of us has very many. Although Otto may have to do something different from what you do when you try to recall where the museum is, a fair amount of variety in mnemonic strategies seems tolerable. If, unlike you, I had to recite a rhyme to remember how many days hath September, we'd presumably still say that I was recollecting something that I believed. While Otto's notebook may not *always* be available to him, Alzheimer's itself, to say nothing of ordinary problems with memory, shows that constant coupling is not a reasonable requirement.

Much more, of course, needs to be said to defend active externalism adequately. If I am never without my iPhone, does that mean that I believe everything that's googleable? (Clark denies this, on the basis of considerations discussed below; Chalmers seems rather more impressed by his iPhone, as suggested by his foreword to Clark 2008).[5] Do mental states that are realized wholly internally have their content in some particularly direct way, while the content associated with external inscriptions flows, parasitically as it were, from that primary internal source? (See Adams and Aiwaza 2001; replied to in Clark 2008 and in Clark forthcoming.) My concern here is only to consider whether active externalism bears on our practical understanding of Alzheimer's and, in particular, on the specter of a kind of self-estrangement that Jaworska's view threatens to exacerbate.[6]

Now let's imagine not merely that Otto can't *remember* where the museum is without his notebook but that he continually comes up with *false beliefs* about MOMA's location. Active externalism will then say, presumably, that Otto entertains inconsistent beliefs. It would make sense for Otto to take steps to make the beliefs encoded in the notebook constitute his action-governing doxastic states. Similarly, or so I want to suggest, if I have reason to believe that I will come to decisions based on values of whose justification I have reason to be suspicious, I might take steps either to move those values out of the decision making loop or, perhaps, to try to find compromise courses of action. The reason is not that the values formed when I'm demented are not worthy of respect in their own right (Jaworska's analysis provides us with good reason to treat them as worthy of respect), but that they conflict with other values *that I continue to hold* (as per my reading of the Clark-Chalmers analysis.)

Let's return to Mr. Burke: Jaworska tells us that he suffers from moderate Alzheimer's disease, which leaves him still able to get around. The story continues: "One day he shows up at home, thrilled, driving a

---

[5] Chalmers there tells readers that his iPhone has "taken over some of the central functions of my brain ... replaced part of my memory ... harbors my desires ... settles disputes" (Clark 2008, ix).

[6] Nor am I riding any horse in the contest concerning the relationship between active externalism and what I call here semantic externalism. For a discussion, see Bartlett 2008.

brand-new red pickup truck that he has just bought at a local dealership. He has always wanted to own a truck like this, but he and his wife agreed long ago that they were not ready for the sacrifices in their lifestyle required by such a purchase. Their finances have not changed since. Mr. Burke's doctor, trying to help the family sort out the situation, asks Mr. Burke about his decision. 'A man needs his truck,' Mr. Burke explains" (1999, 107).

Why shouldn't we say that he has simply changed his mind about his earlier decision not to buy a truck? This seems to be Jaworska's own reading of the situation: "The demented person," she writes, "would be viewed as any other person whose values and commitments change over time" (1999, 112). But as idiomatically understood, changing one's mind is not the same thing as simply acquiring a new belief, even if that belief is inconsistent with what one otherwise takes to be true: one can acquire a new evaluative belief—for example, "men need trucks"[7]—without thereby rejecting inconsistent beliefs—for example, "as such, being a man doesn't entitle you to anything." Changing one's mind involves an elimination of an old belief as well as an acceptance of a new one.

After becoming demented, however, I may not be in a position to change my mind about my evaluative beliefs—that is, to see them as less worthy of acceptance than competitor values I once held and, on an externalist view, may continue to hold. Further, even if I am in principle in a position to change my mind, I may not have changed it. My previously formed evaluative beliefs may not be best thought of as having been relinquished so much as having faded into a region that I can't on my own recall to consciousness—a situation analogous in some respects to that in which anyone undergoing psychoanalysis might find himself. While it is true that I may no longer be inclined to affirm the correctness and significance of the earlier position, I did do so in the past, and it is, as Jaworska allows, characteristic of critical interests not to require con-temporaneous endorsement; they can, after all, survive even our deaths.

Admittedly, as the story is told, there is no reason in particular to think that Mr. Burke has done anything in particular to preserve his prior commitment. It would surely be tendentious to infer that a person has inconsistent beliefs if her current preferences differ from a previously held view simply because she has forgotten rather than relinquished that view (even if it is a critical interest). As Jaworska points out, the development of new values in dementia cases will often be a matter of shedding "more complex interests, so that in the new, simpler configuration the remaining interests gain import" (1999, 112). My point, rather, is that, had Mr. Burke been as distressed by the prospect that he might come to act inconsistently with the understanding achieved with his spouse, he might

---

[7] Enthymematic, no doubt, for, "Men need trucks and have a moral claim to what they need."

well have taken steps to preserve the continuing reality and effectiveness
of his evaluative beliefs at a given time in his history, with the result that,
should he lose the ability explicitly to reconsider and reject them, they
retain their force. If so, they are in conflict with subsequently formed
inconsistent views, not plainly superseded by them.

We tend to think of devices such as advance directives as "mere"
artifacts—and highly imperfect ones at that—which clearly have less
authority than contemporaneous decisions, at least if those decisions are
autonomous. As Jaworska point out, allowing advance directives to
prevail in such circumstances seems to require that we regard them as
"Ulysses contracts," with all their attendant difficulties: "My point is that
an advanced directive for a demented patient who is still a valuer is
equivalent to a Ulysses contract, and whether one thinks such directives
ought to be employed depends on one's take on the validity of such
contracts" (1999, 138). If, however, we think of advance directives in the
way Clark and Chalmers think of Otto's notebook, as parts of our minds,
parts of ourselves, rather than, say, as simply pieces of paper with various
inscriptions, then they become more akin to our (dispositional) memories,
in which are stored the contents of, not plainly superseded values, but
"uncanceled" acts of moral agency. What we have is not the past trying to
constrain the present, but a clash of contemporaneous states of the agent.

In his recent *Supersizing the Mind*, Clark discusses in some detail what
he regards as the criteria for accepting a nonbiological entity into an
organism's cognitive system. Slightly rephrased, the criteria are:

1. That the entity be readily available and typically invoked.
2. That any information thus retrieved be more or less automatically
   endorsed, rather than subject to critical assessment.
3. That information contained in the entity should be easily accessible
   as and when required.
4. That the information in the entity has been conscientiously endorsed
   at some point in the past, and, indeed, is there as a result of its
   previous endorsement. (2008, 79)

Clark thinks of these conditions as explicating the reluctance even of
proponents of extended minds (like, paradigmatically, himself) to regard
the books in his library or his iPhone-enabled constant access to the Web
as constituting parts of his mind; unlike Otto's notebook, the books and
the iPhone-Web connection fail conditions (2) and (4). In my view, these
conditions fall on the stringent side, as is suggested by the experience of
Alzheimer's disease itself: failing criterion (1), for example, seems almost
definitive of dementing conditions, but it would scarcely follow that if
Otto suddenly and atypically remembered where MOMA was located,
that memory would somehow not count as emerging from his mind. Yet
even given these conditions, advance directives seem to fare pretty well,

and certainly better than the books in Clark's library: condition (4) would seem met, and (2) at least presumptively, which is perhaps the most freedom from critical examination information should enjoy in general terms.

Conditions (1) and (3) also seem nicely accommodated by the advance directive, at least so long as the involvement of other agents is not seen as a defeating condition. Of course, to claim that the involvement of the agency of others is irrelevant to whether a source of stored information counts as part of a person's mind is hardly innocuous; however, it seems quite in the spirit of the extended mind hypothesis to allow it. It may, after all, take a skilled analyst's help for me to gain conscious access to beliefs I dispositionally hold, or to allow the beliefs I entertain to be reflected in my actions.

Further, externalism allows, at least in principle, that our minds may extend not only into artifacts but into other people as well (Clark and Chalmers 1998; see also Scheman 1993 for a politically more alert view of the subvenience base of mental states as encompassing other people, motivated by considerations of the sort advanced by Putnam and Burge). Some of my memories or my evaluative beliefs may have been stored not in a notebook or an iPhone but in another person; my achieving some of my most significant conclusions about myself may have recruited the judgment of others, particularly of intimate others with whom I have shared not only a life but a deliberative perspective (see Rovane 1998). Per Jaworska, a now-demented person may be autonomously forming or consolidating new evaluative beliefs that constitute respect-worthy responses to situations unanticipated earlier in her predementia life. Yet the demented person's previously formed, possibly inconsistent beliefs may well be as much a part of her mind as her recently formed views. Sorting out how to adjudicate the conflicting implications of those beliefs for practice will, of course, often require the most careful judgment—and in selecting judges, we would do well to bear in mind that we may have real-time access to some of the very same deliberative resources by which those undergoing the disease habitually achieved and sustained mature values, and sorted out their tangled practical consequences.

Acknowledgments

I am grateful for the opportunity extended to me by Eva Kittay and Licia Carlson to present these ideas at the conference "Cognitive Disability: A Challenge to Moral Philosophy," held at Stony Brook University in September of 2008, to the many conference participants who discussed them with me, to Agnieszka Jaworska in particular, who was searching and generous in her observations, and, as always, to Hilde Lindemann for many thoughtful philosophical discussions and her sharp editorial skills.

References

Adams, Frederick, and Kenneth Aizawa. 2001. "The Bounds of Cognition." *Philosophical Psychology* 14, no. 1:43–64.
Burge, Tyler. 1979. "Individualism and the Mental." *Midwest Studies in Philosophy* 4:73–122.
Clark, Andy. 2008. *Supersizing the Mind: Embodiment, Action, and Cognitive Extension.* New York: Oxford University Press.
———. Forthcoming. "Memento's Revenge." In *The Extended Mind*, edited by Richard Menary. Farnham, U.K.: Ashgate.
Clark, Andy, and David Chalmers. 1998. "The Extended Mind." *Analysis* 58:7–19.
Dresser, Rebecca. 1994. "Missing Persons: Legal Perceptions of Incompetent Patients." *Rutgers Law Review* 46:609–719.
Dworkin, Ronald. 1993. *Life's Dominion.* New York: Knopf.
Firlik, Andrew. 1991. "Margo's Logo." *JAMA* 265, no. 2:201.
Frege, Gottlob. 1892. "Über Sinn und Bedeutung." *Zeitschrift für Philosophie und philosophische Kritik* 100:25–50.
Hurley, Susan. Forthcoming. "Varieties of Externalism." In *The Extended Mind*, edited by Richard Menary. Farnham, U.K.: Ashgate.
Jaworska, Agnieszka. 1999. "Respecting the Margins of Agency." *Philosophy and Public Affairs* 28, no. 2:105–38.
Kripke, Saul. 1980. *Naming and Necessity.* Cambridge, Mass.: Harvard University Press.
Levy, Neil. 2007. "Rethinking Neuroethics in the Light of the Extended Mind Thesis." *American Journal of Bioethics* 7, no. 9:3–12.
Ludlow, Peter. 1998. "Social Externalism, Self-Knowledge, and Memory." In *Externalism and Self-Knowledge*, edited by Peter Ludlow and Norah Martin, 307–10. Stanford: CSLI Publications.
Nelson, James Lindemann. 1995. "Critical Interests and Sources of Familial Decisionmaking Authority for Incapacitated Patients." *Journal of Law, Medicine and Ethics* 23, no. 2:143–48.
———. 2003. "Agency by Proxy." In his *Hippocrates' Maze*, 29–52. Lanham, Md.: Rowman and Littlefield.
Putnam, Hilary. 1975. "The Meaning of Meaning." In his *Philosophical Papers*, vol. 2: *Mind, Language, and Reality*, 215–71. New York: Cambridge University Press.
Rovane, Carol. 1998. *The Bounds of Agency.* Princeton: Princeton University Press.
Russell, Bertrand. 1905. "On Denoting." *Mind* 14:4479–493.
Scheman, Naomi. 1993. "Individualism and the Objects of Psychology." In her *Engenderings*, 36–56. New York: Routledge.
Searle, John. 1958. "Proper Names." *Mind* 67:166–73.

14

THINKING ABOUT THE GOOD:
RECONFIGURING LIBERAL METAPHYSICS (OR NOT) FOR
PEOPLE WITH COGNITIVE DISABILITIES

LESLIE P. FRANCIS AND ANITA SILVERS

Introduction: Liberalism and Inclusiveness

Spacious Ideas of the Good

To accord persons (or other things or kinds) considerability is to acknowledge that they matter for moral, political, or other philosophical theorizing.[1] Liberalism does not deny considerability[2] to people just because of their unconventional values or views. Indeed, respect for different conceptions of individual good, even unconventional ones, is a hallmark of much liberal theory. This is inclusiveness about different conceptions of the good.

Another kind of inclusiveness, to which traditional liberal theory has been inattentive, also calls for respect for difference. People differ not only in the conceptions of the good they have but also in the cognitive processes whereby these conceptions are formulated and maintained. More specifically, people differ in their capacities to conceptualize, as well as in styles of conceptualization and skills in applying or realizing ideas. At one end of the spectrum are people appropriately characterized as cerebral who are proficient in, and profoundly involved with, conceptualizing. And at the other end are people so unable to express themselves in any way that we cannot be sure whether their behavior is mediated by concepts at all. Between these extremes people differ enormously in the degree and manner in which their thinking is abstract or concrete, coherent or disconnected, informed or naïve, as well as in many other aspects of cognition.

---

[1] For a discussion of metaphysical considerability and its connection with moral and political considerability, see Goodpaster 1978.

[2] On views such as Goodpaster's, appropriate respect is the outcome of considerability: "We need to understand better, for example, the scope of moral respect, the sorts of entities that can and should receive moral attention" (Goodpaster 1978, 309). On other views (e.g., Gibson 2007), considerability is thought to be entailed by or the product of respect. Our claims here about liberalism and considerability do not advance either of these interpretations of considerability over the other one.

Liberalism's toleration of differences in ideas about people's good should nourish a receptivity for inclusion of different kinds of people, including those whose proficiencies and styles of cognizing depart markedly from the norm. In previous work we included people like these among those we characterized as "outliers,"[3] namely, kinds of people who traditionally have been ignored by both theories and practices of justice.[4] Imposing views about how conceptions of the good are constructed that exclude outliers in this way is problematic, however. In light of its commitment to inclusiveness, it would seem as though liberalism should be as welcoming of unusual individuals as of ordinary ones. But contemporary critics (e.g., Nussbaum 2006; Kittay 1999; Mills 1997; Young 1990), including ourselves, think that liberal theory and practice have yet to meet this standard. Here we continue work on improving the inclusiveness of liberal theory.

Straitened Thinking About the Good

Humans differ in regard to their good, both in conception and in the process from which notions about the good emerge. An unexceptional extrapolation of liberal allegiance to pluralism of the good is that people are entitled to personalized accounts of their good. This corollary establishes liberal tolerance about the substance of the good, an acceptance that should hold for people regardless of who they are, how sharp their ability to reason and communicate their reasons is, and how dependent they are on facilitation by others.

Nevertheless, liberal theory often adds a different kind of condition, that individualized accounts of the good must have been arrived at independently. The constraint is applied not to substantive ideas of the good but instead to the process whereby those ideas have been formed. The proper process for arriving at and articulating the good specifies that individuals make determinations of their good on their own. Different ideas of the good acquire moral and political weight on the presumption that each is a person's own, formed autonomously.

From this comes the importance of testing claims about self for authenticity, which, as Charles Taylor (1992, 1989) has pointed out, is a notion associated with the advent of liberalism and which remains a criterion for much liberal theorizing.[5] The considerability that liberalism characteristically assigns to different ideas of the good arises from respect

---

[3] For a discussion of outlier status, see Silvers and Francis 2005; Silvers 2009.

[4] Helpful discussions relevant to the ideas of moral and political considerability can be found in Anderson 2004 and Diamond 2004; see also Dombrowski 2006. An underlying question here is whether there are relational aspects to justifying differential treatment based on species membership, see Francis and Norman 1978.

[5] See also the interchange between Charles Taylor and Anthony Appiah in Gutmann 1994.

accorded because each idea is a person's own. Such respect does not embrace anything anyone thinks about the good but extends only to views or values that persons embrace in the right way—that is, freely for themselves. Notions or preferences imposed or governed by external forces or authorities, or donned to become one of the crowd, are suspect because the subject who professes them is not truly their source.

Respect for views and values a person expresses but does not believe in neither translates into respect for the person herself nor establishes the person's claim to political and social participation. Nor does an idea of the good formed through adaptation to oppression, or manipulation by or imposition of the views of others.[6] To deserve moral weight as the product of a respectable process for construing personalized good, it has seemed, ideas of the good must be those of persons who think independently and can articulate the reasons that animate their thoughts. Thus, for much traditional liberal theorizing, broad tolerance of substantially different ideas of the good is abridged by an austere process for arriving at these notions. As we have observed in earlier writing on this topic, features of liberal theory meant to individualize and thereby promote diversity ironically produce the opposite outcome in the case of some outliers, for instance, individuals whose cognitive disabilities prevent them from independently constructing or communicating their own conceptions of the good (Francis and Silvers 2007).

Liberal theory traditionally looks for principles of justice at the intersection of individual rational agents' ideas of their good. For liberals like John Rawls, the view of individuals as self-originating sources of their good replaces foundationalist claims about the good. To achieve a common view of justice, people must be able to compare conceptions and converse (at least in principle or figuratively) about what is crucial to each of them, and to all as well. But people who have never been competent to decide on and express what is their own good are treated as though they have no entry into this theoretical conversation, nor can their points of view contribute to formulating the resulting principles of justice. And people who once were but no longer are competent also are accorded no direct entry and can participate only figuratively through extrapolations from their formerly articulated preferences and views.

Where there is no role for certain kinds of uncommon people in formulating justice, there also may be no protection through justice for them. Instead, conceptions of their goods may be misshapen to fit within a framework of justice constructed for others. Neither is their participation provided for at the level of practice. Generally, people with cognitive disabilities have been treated paternalistically, managed or governed

---

[6] E.g., Friedman 1999, 37. On Friedman's view, it should be noted, the critical self-reflection requisite for autonomy may include emotional as well as what she refers to as "narrowly cognitive" dimensions.

intrusively even when their management has been conducted under a banner of benevolence (Friedman 1995, 1285). Even those reformers who retrospectively are judged to be the most altruistic appear to have aimed at altering the conduct of people sent to institutions to comply with middle-class Protestant norms (Goodheart 2004).

Paternalism has skewed views about whether to encourage people with cognitive disabilities to live independently in the community, which education is appropriate, and what forms of work should be permitted or supported. Policy choices in these and other areas illustrate the practical impact of excluding people with cognitive disabilities from the ground floor of the theoretical enterprise of building justice and consequently denying them considerability, or at least attenuating their claim on considerability. If theorizing about justice takes place to a significant extent in the domain of what has been called partial compliance theory[7]— as we believe that it does—such exclusion results in a theory of justice without benchmarks against which remediation of injustices to people with cognitive disabilities can be gauged.

Liberalism: Political and Metaphysical

Cognitive Process and Human Nature

Liberalism embraces difference among accounts of the good by positing that such variety is central to the full expression of human nature. In supposing that conceptualizations of the good must be authenticated as products of individuals' independent thought, liberal theory constrains inclusiveness based on a theory of what humans who merit full moral respect ought to be able to do. Here we ask whether a metaphysics of human nature leads some formulations of liberal theory to marginalize, or altogether omit from considerability, individuals who are unable to cognize in the usual way.

Both John Rawls and Martha Nussbaum have explored developing theories of the good that do not invoke metaphysical views (Rawls 1985; Nussbaum 2006, 79, 186). Each is motivated by an underlying commitment to liberalism's respect for individual difference in conceptions of the good, but they approach the task quite differently. Rawls takes individuals to be self-validating sources of their good who thereby authenticate conceptions of the good. For Nussbaum, the good lies in provision for capabilities that at least reach the thresholds required for dignified human life. Each leaves room for anomalous conceptions of the good—but each does so in a way that is problematic for people who are anomalous in regard to conceptualizing their good.

[7] Partial compliance theory is theorizing about what justice requires under circumstances of injustice. The term was introduced by Rawls (1971).

Rawlsian Political Liberalism

As we shall show, Rawls's reliance on individuals as self-validating sources of their good turns out to be metaphysical, and in a way that excludes some or all people with serious disabilities from being part of the project of justice at its foundations. Rawls's move away from "metaphysics" is core to his claim that principles of justice can and should be justified to people with different overarching but reasonable conceptions of their good. After publication of *A Theory of Justice*, Rawls became convinced that attempts to rely on a single conception of the good to secure enduring social stability would be undermined by the multiple perspectives on the good that may occur within liberal societies.

In his later *Political Liberalism* (1996), Rawls explored defending a theory of justice that is both stable (in that it can claim ongoing allegiance for good reasons) and inclusive (in that it assumes a multiplicity of reasonable conceptions of the good).[8] The shift in Rawls's thinking from *A Theory of Justice* to *Political Liberalism* has been much explored, but its implications for inclusion of people with disabilities have been ignored. Rawls attempted to avoid reliance on a single overarching conception of the good (what he calls a "comprehensive" conception) by centering on persons as formulators of the idea of the good rather than on the idea of the good itself.

Political Liberalism thus advances a conception of the person as a self-originating source of claims. On this conception, all citizens are free and equal. "Free" means they are able to exercise powers of reason, thought, and judgment. They possess the moral power of commanding their own conception of their good, that is, the "capacity to form, to revise, and rationally pursue a conception of [their] rational advantage" (Rawls 1999a, 398). This is one of two moral powers that Rawls attributes to subjects of justice; the other is the capacity for a sense of justice. "Equal" means they can exercise these powers to a degree requisite for social cooperation. Those who cannot exercise either moral power to at least this extent lack the full capacity to participate as subjects of justice and experience justice only as dependent entities.

Subjects of justice differ in the conceptions of the good they formulate on their own. Ideas of the good on this theory (as well as some other paradigmatic versions of liberalism) have several different features. The good is plural: people differ. The good is not fixed, but revisable in response to circumstances, including the framework of justice itself. People's conceptions of the good are theirs, shaped to reflect what is valuable in their experiences and their lives: this is subjectivity. Finally, these conceptions of the good are arrived at by subjects reasoning on their own: the "independence" assumption (Francis and Silvers 2007).

---

[8]   Freeman (2002, 2) describes the Rawlsian project in this way.

How are these claims metaphysical? By his well-known catchphrase "political, not metaphysical," Rawls signaled his eschewal of assertions of universal truths, including those about "the essential nature and identity of persons" (Rawls 1999a, 388). But he did not give a full account of "metaphysical."[9] Observing in a footnote that "metaphysical" is deeply contested (1999a, 403–4 n. 22), Rawls sought to avoid this contentiousness by denying that he relied on metaphysical theses sufficiently strong to reintroduce the difficulties in justifying conceptions of the good that motivated his movement from *A Theory of Justice* to *Political Liberalism* in the first place. Specifically he asserted that "no particular doctrine about the nature of persons, distinctive and opposed to other metaphysical doctrines, appears among its premises, or seems to be required by its argument" (1999a, 403–4 n. 22). But is this claim true?

Here are some doctrines that are incorporated into the conception of people as self-validating developers of their ideas of the good. They are discrete entities with separate conceptions of their good. By exercising the moral power of constructing a conception of the good, those who hold these conceptions validate them. Their idea-building is accomplished in abstraction from interaction with others. Ontologically, everyone is an island with respect to constructing conceptions of the good.

Such self-validation is supposed to replace metaphysical modes of justifying conceptions of the good. But not just any conception of the good will do. Conceptions of the good must be "reasonable"—that is, must be consistent with justified principles of justice. To become and remain reasonable, conceptions of the good thus must be revisable—again, by individuals as self-validators who are willing to be bound by justified principles of justice. Other than reasonableness, there is no foundation for conceptions of the good.

This is itself an ontological view, but is it sufficiently robust to reintroduce the problems that dissuaded Rawls from metaphysics? Here are several reasons for thinking that it is. First, only those capable of being self-validating sources of claims can be on the ground floor of the project of justifying justice. Only those with the moral power to formulate their conceptions of the good independently command moral and political considerability in this sense.

Second, in portraying how people construct conceptions of their good, this picture abstracts from intersubjectivity and interpersonal interactions that shape both each individual's awareness of his subjectivity and other

---

[9] Given the history of Anglo-American philosophy at the time, we can see why this is very attractive to Rawls. Logical positivism and ordinary language philosophy didn't do ethics, much less political philosophy. So the strategy Rawls employed—moving from comprehensive conceptions of the good to self-authentication—was a successful way of reintroducing ethics and political philosophy, absent appeals to metaphysics that would turn off people at the time. Times have changed; metaphysics no longer gives people the chills or makes philosophers aspiring to a successful career take the Fifth.

people's understandings of that individual's subjectivity. If conceptions of the good are interactive and intersubjective products, this picture discards important features of our ontological landscape relating to what kind of social entities human beings are and how we interact with and understand each other.

Third, conceptions of the good must be alterable to fit within the framework of an account of justice justifiable to the people whose conceptions of the good they are. (This is crucial to the view that the right is prior to the good and to Rawls's view about the reasonableness of comprehensive conceptions of the good.) Conceptions are adjusted by individuals exercising moral powers of formulating and revising their conceptions of the good. Presumably, people with such powers can also challenge principles of justice, or the constitutional and statutory enactments selected in accord with them for a particular society.

The problem is to ensure that conceptions of the good that are adjusted to fit within the framework of justice are not skewed by problematic adaptive preferences. Self-validating agents, on the Rawlsian view, must guard against this for themselves. They are regarded as taking responsibility for their ends, including adjusting their ends by what they can reasonably accomplish and recognizing that their pursuit of ends must take place within a framework of justice (Rawls 1999a, 407).

But what of individuals who for reasons of biological or psychological limitation seem incapable of self-validation? How are judgments to be made to adjust their conceptions of the good to fit within an alleged framework of justice—or, on the other hand, whence could come assessments that the framework of justice is misshapen because it has been constructed through a process from which outliers such as themselves are excluded? Rawls has no theoretical resources to resolve these issues: this kind of individual is to be acknowledged only further along in the development of justice, at the legislative process, not at the more basic level of constructing justice.

Rawls's turn in *Political Liberalism* to self-validation as underwriting conceptions of the good relies on metaphysical assumptions that make commitments (supposedly avoided by Rawls) about the nature of persons and are strongly exclusionary. There are several respects in which the assumptions about fully considerable agents are not at all benign. The assumptions deny some kinds of individuals considerability as subjects of justice, or at least relegate responsiveness to their standpoints until after the basic principles of justice have been initially shaped. The assumptions deny them this standing even though, on an arguably liberal set of assumptions about the good, there are conceptions of the good that are theirs and can serve to benchmark fair treatment for them.

In *Political Liberalism*, Rawls maintained his view that certain goods are "primary" and should be available for every life. This view is not an empirical thesis about what goods would be necessary means for any life but a regulative view arising from "a particular conception of persons and their higher order interests" (Rawls 1999a, 388–89 n. 2). The goods postulated for all lives include liberty and opportunity, income and wealth, and the social bases of self-respect (Rawls 1999b, 54–55). Political liberties enjoy special priority because they are necessary for the exercise of the power of developing self-validating conceptions of the good. One argument for the priority of basic liberties rests on their importance for the exercise of the moral powers.[10] Another explanation lies in the definition of the worst off in terms of resources understood as primary goods in contrast to a welfarist or capability view (Freeman 2002, 7).[11] The result is a structure that sets protection of political liberties (if achievable) as lexically prior to economic goods.

This enshrinement of political liberties, while surely important for many lives and conceptions of the good, may prove problematic for others. Those who cannot exercise these liberties by themselves—as is true for many with significant cognitive impairments—may therefore be regarded as second-class citizens, or as noncitizens entirely. Their opportunities for expression of conceptions of their good may be abrogated, or they may be at the back of the line for specialized resources to realize their good if their standing emerges only at the legislative stage. Consider another possible formulation of a Rawlsian first principle: individuals should be supported with reasonable means to exercise moral powers and develop personalized conceptions of their good. Liberty is among those means, but so are the foundations for social trust that enable people to work interactively to build principles of justice together.

Nussbaum: From Capability to Functioning

In *Frontiers of Justice*, Martha Nussbaum defends a plural set of indices, a list of capabilities, as benchmarks for whether a society has delivered minimal justice to all of its citizens (Nussbaum 2006, 74). She emphasizes that the list is abstract, to be specified differently in different societies. And these are "capabilities"—what people can be and do—not "func-tionings" mandated for all lives. Without at least a minimal level of each

[10] See Freeman 2002, 5: "Because of their role in defining the conception of moral persons that underlies Rawls's view, justice as fairness assigns the basic liberties strict priority over other social goods."

[11] Here, more fully, Freeman (2002, 8): "It is because of his (Kantian) conception of agency that Rawls treats severe mental and physical handicaps as a special case. He abstracts from such handicaps in the initial argument for principles of justice, leaving special principles to be worked out for them to the legislative stage.... This ... does imply that for Rawls justice is not primarily about redressing inequalities imposed by nature or misfortune. Rather, justice is primarily about providing each person with resources that are sufficient to their realizing their 'moral powers' of free, responsible, and rational agency. As a result, Rawls (unlike Sen) does not give the naturally handicapped absolute priority in decisions of justice. He treats their situation similar to problems of partial compliance."

capability, Nussbaum says, any life will lack human dignity in that respect and thus will not be fully worth living, nor can a society in which some people are so bereft of dignity be just (2006, 78).

Like Rawls, Nussbaum considers her list as political, not metaphysical, "without any grounding in metaphysical ideas of the sort that divide people along lines of culture and religion" (Nussbaum 2006, 79). Contrary to Rawls, inclusion of people with cognitive disabilities, as well as other outliers, is central to the program of *Frontiers*. Nussbaum's vision is of a society that supports the development of people with cognitive disabilities with appropriate care (2006, 129) and acknowledges the importance of mutual respect for all (2006, 129).

Nussbaum brings metaphysics into her account of threshold levels of capabilities for people with significant cognitive disabilities. Like Rawls's, her account is more deeply pervaded by metaphysics than is initially apparent from the claim that it is political rather than metaphysical. The problem lies in the Aristotelian thrust of Nussbaum's view of capabilities and their realization.

Nussbaum's list of basic capabilities required for a dignified human life is supposed to be equally serviceable for assessing whether justice has been rendered to people with and without cognitive disabilities. There is a powerful strategic point here: society should not enable people who are unimpaired more generously than it affords those with cognitive disabilities. But the proposal has a second, more problematic prong: a shift from capabilities to functionings that brings its very liberalism into question.

Nussbaum's theory is influenced by the Aristotelian idea that specifiable goods are central to flourishing as a human being. The liberalism of capability theory lies in construing these goods as creating "space" for choices about lifestyles and plans rather than imposing a single model of flourishing (Nussbaum 2006, 182). Capability spaces, not functionings, matter: people should have the liberty to refuse to exercise capabilities such as freedom of conscience (e.g., 2006, 171). Only with dignity itself is "actual functioning ... the appropriate aim of public policy" (2006, 172).[12]

This liberal model—of available capabilities that people can choose to exercise or not to shape their own lives—is not extended fully to people with cognitive disabilities, however. Despite generous allocation and application of resources, some individuals may not be able to achieve even threshold levels of some capabilities. When people are not capable of making their own choices (about sex, or health care, and so on), Nussbaum concludes (2006, 173), the appropriate response is to treat

---

[12] Children are excepted: functioning may be the goal in education, health care, and bodily integrity, or other capabilities where choices in childhood might impair future exercise of the relevant capabilities.

functioning as the appropriate goal, "working tirelessly" to bring each up to the minimal level of functioning envisioned for citizens in a just society (2006, 190).

For Nussbaum, a life without several crucial capability spaces is to that extent "unfortunate" for its significant departures from human species norms (2006, 192). The shift from capabilities to functioning is not without costs, however. Like the Rawlsian list of primary goods, the shift imposes a "one size fits all" model for people with cognitive disabilities who cannot speak fully for themselves. There is a hint of the potential difficulty in Nussbaum's call for everyone to "work tirelessly to bring all children with disabilities up to the same threshold of capability that we set for other citizens" (2006, 190). Why not, instead, work tirelessly to bring each person with cognitive disabilities to the range of capability spaces constituent of their personalized good? The move from capabilities to functioning, in short, risks denying people with cognitive disabilities their fully personalized conceptions of the good, a result surely at odds with Nussbaum's own insistence on full inclusion. And the source of the imperative to do so is the ontologically preeminent status assigned to human species norms for basic capabilities.

Collaborating on Ideas of the Good

(In)Dependent Agents and Constructions of the Good

We take the principle that individuals must be free to embrace their preferred views and values as fundamental to liberalism's approach and equally important for people with and without cognitive disabilities. Individuals without cognitive disabilities usually do not lose their liberty from state or group intervention if their decision making is influenced or shaped by other people, even to a high degree. People with cognitive disabilities who depend on others to articulate conceptions of the good for them should not forgo this same liberty. Nor should these citizens be regarded as outliers with respect to participation in social contracting or other approaches to political justification that require individuals to have their own conceptions of the good.

We have argued elsewhere that people in general are cooperating agents in constructing their different goods and as such depend on each other in important ways (Francis and Silvers 2007). For all of us and not just for cognitively disabled people, conceptions of the good are socially scripted and interactively developed. People with cognitive disabilities do have subjective and personalized accounts of the good, albeit ones they have not constructed completely by themselves. People with cognitive disabilities can participate in practices that are centered on their own persuasions about their good, even though they may be unable to formulate, articulate, and communicate their awareness or feelings as ideas.

To sketch how to personalize ideas of the good for and with people with cognitive disabilities, we advanced a theory of trusteeship that provides for collaborative construction of the good for an individual subject. We delineated a role trustworthy assistance from others can play in building an understanding of the good for individuals who cannot form or communicate conceptualizations on their own. We now expand our account of trusteeship with more detail about how individuals with cognitive impairments may collaborate with trustees to build conceptions of their good that command considerability.

Prosthetics and Metaphysics

In the collaboration we envision, the trustee[13] does not step into the subject's role in shaping a personalized notion of the good. Instead, as a prosthetic arm or leg executes some of the functions of a missing fleshly one without being confused with or supplanting the usual fleshly limb, so, we propose, a trustee's reasoning and communicating can execute part or all of a subject's own thinking processes without substituting the trustee's own idea as if it were the subject's own. Prosthetics are operated by the subject, sometimes as automatically as fleshly limbs are moved, sometimes with conscious effort.[14] The mechanisms through which different prosthetics execute (some of) the functions of the absent biological component(s) will vary depending on the degree and location of loss. For example, there is a world of difference between what the subject does in operating below the knee and above the knee prostheses, or between prosthetics for amputations at wrist or shoulder. There are differences as well in what different designs can do. To illustrate, curved prosthetic racing feet and pegged bicycling feet are functional for running and pedaling, respectively, but neither works well for walking, which is better served by a different design of prosthetic foot. Despite these features, it is customary to attribute the functioning of prosthetics to the agent using them. The racer, not the metal foot, is taken to be running the race.

Individuals executing the trustee role, facilitating people with cognitive disabilities in the formulation and expression of personalized notions of their good, should be similarly responsive to their subjects' motivation.

[13] Although we will usually speak of "the trustee," we do not mean to suggest an account on which each individual with a cognitive disability is paired up with one individual who is that person's trustee. Our aim is to propose and sketch some features of an interactive process we are calling trusteeship. Someone with a cognitive disability may be engaged in this process of assistive thinking with one, several, or many people. As we explicitly eschew a surrogacy approach in which trustees are authorized to substitute or subrogate for disabled people, our account of trusteeship does not address assignment of a right to act or speak for cognitively impaired individuals.

[14] For a discussion of autonomy and cognitive prostheses, see Francis 2009.

Of course, individuals with different kinds and degrees of cognitive disability will benefit from different facilitations. The nature of the functional alternative to be supplied, and the auspiciousness of the functional outcomes achieved, will be affected by both the degree and nature of the subject's deficit and the effectiveness of the trustee's implementation. As with prosthetic mechanisms in general, differences will remain as well between nonprosthetic and prosthetic decision processes, just as there are differences between, for example, a racer's fleshly foot and a prosthetic racing foot (to propel the runner forward effectively, the latter is a metal arc somewhat longer than the typical human foot).

This last point introduces the matter of distinguishing between a prosthetic process that remains a simulation of a particular human capacity that the subject lacks and a prosthetic process that compensates with a different capacity. To illustrate this distinction, we turn again to the case of prosthetic racing feet. Faced with the prospect of prosthetic-using athletes with amputations proposing to compete against able-bodied runners, the International Association of Athletics Federations banned sprinters relying on assistive devices that roll on wheels. This is an understandable exclusion because running is not compatible with riding, and wheels typically indicate the availability of a ride. Prosthetic racing feet still require running on feet, whereas prosthetic lower limbs ending in wheels would compensate for the lack of fleshly feet by giving their wearer the capacity to roll rather than to run.

More controversial was the I.A.A.F.'s next ban, imposed on an athlete who uses prosthetic racing feet. Track officials proposed that to race on his metal racing feet was not to race at all, invoking such demurrers as that, without fleshly feet, prosthetics-users could not comply with one of foot racing's rules: that contact between foot and starting block must be maintained until the starter's signal. The International Court of Arbitration for Sport reversed the ban, declaring there was no evidence that running on metal feet takes less energy, effort, or skill, or was less legitimately competitive, than running on fleshly feet. In doing so, the court discarded an ontology at least some track officials had embraced, namely, an account of human development as an organic process that is striving toward natural perfection (Longman 2007). Individuals with artificial—that is, inorganic—limbs count *a priori* as defective on such a metaphysical view and consequently are not warranted the same con-siderability granted everyone else—inclusion based on achievement.[15] So, despite the availability of prosthetic conceptualization as proposed by our

---

[15] In the case referred to, I.A.A.F. officials have wished to confine any runners with a prosthesis *a priori*, regardless of ability, to the Paralympics and to deny them considerability in regard to elite competition.

account, might individuals with cognitive disabilities be similarly dismissed as defective by traditional liberal theory?

Powers of Self-Control

Relational Autonomy

Is there a response to meeting the liberal standard for the process of conceiving of the good that reaches to people with cognitive disabilities? Elsewhere we questioned liberalism's independence criterion, arguing that a plausible political philosophy cannot prohibit subjects from being assisted by and interacting with others in formulating ideas of the good without excluding us all (Francis and Silvers 2007). In this regard, some philosophers have recently observed that autonomy in practice is relational, not solitary (McKenzie and Stoljar 2000). In such a relational account, coaching or otherwise assisting people with cognitive disabilities in forming their notions of the good becomes simply a more extensive and enduring version of commonplace conceptual midwifery.

In itself, therefore, depending on others for guidance about the good should not undercut the legitimacy of the conceptual products of assistive thinking or reduce the respect that conceptualizations of the good formed through such prosthetic processes command. What remains to be shown, however, is that cognitively disabled individuals can receive effective assistance or accommodation so that the ideas of the good that emerge for them meet the foundational needs of liberal theory. Such assistance in thinking must function as a prosthesis, aiming at amplifying the functioning of the subject who is being assisted rather than being used as a tool of the assistant's, instead of the subject's, ends. Further, assistive thinking must be propelled by respect for the assisted person, to safeguard against substituting the assistant's standpoint for the person's own.[16]

We will now explore several proposals about capacities that have been cast as crucial to liberal thinking about the good. These are powers that people supposedly must possess to be full-fledged cooperators whose ideas of the good command considerability. Having these capacities has been associated with independence because they enable their possessors to bring to bear various kinds of self-control. We will ask whether individuals must be able to exercise these powers in isolation, or whether people still may be said to have such powers despite being unable to command them fully on their own.

Power of Reciprocity

Having the power to reciprocate—governing one's self to benefit others in return for being benefited oneself—and to understand that seeking and

---

[16] See Shiffrin 2000 for an expansion of this point.

achieving the good involves commanding this power, has been held to be essential to thinking properly about the good. Only individuals strong and smart enough to reciprocate benefits they receive, or to see themselves as committed participants in a mutually beneficial reciprocating scheme, are supposed to be able to envision intrinsically valuable ends at which cooperators properly can and should aim through their collaboration. But some disabled people are able to contribute reciprocally, although not always in all the usual ways, while some cannot do so at all. Disabled people as a class are not sought after, and sometimes are not permitted, to participate in arrangements for mutual benefit. Making the power of reciprocity so central introduces a bias against physically or cognitively impaired individuals whose limitations or dependency preclude their being viewed or valued, or viewing or valuing themselves, as contributing cooperators.

For Rawls, for example, the idea of the good needed to inform schemes of social cooperation "requires an idea of each participant's rational advantage"; to have an idea like this involves being able to see how one's own participation contributes to the other participants, from the others' standpoints (Rawls 1999a, 232). According to Rawls, having this power to do one's part in society as a person with "a capacity for a conception of the good" is crucial to being afforded full considerability (1999a, 333). Annette Baier (1986) and Martha Nussbaum (2006) think this reciprocity condition is fundamental to traditional social contract theory and both therefore condemn that theory for being exclusionary as a result.

In "Justice Through Trust" (Silvers and Francis 2005), we too criticized the importance traditional social contract theory has placed on the ability to reciprocate and to see one's part as doing so. We argued against this impoverished picture of the bonds that link people when they join in collective enterprises. To the contrary, cooperators do not always or even commonly condition their participation on being benefited as they benefit other participants. They do not even usually approach mutual action by bargaining with others to secure advantageous governance of their interactions. Connecting individuals with one another through mutual engagement in practices that nourish and build trust is more common and effective than bargaining for reciprocal advantage to link them cooperatively. Trust relationships are more inclusive because they do not require abilities to strategize or to be of use to others. Contrary to Rawls (1999a, 233), therefore, we do not believe that the status of full participant in social cooperation must be reserved for individuals able to see themselves, and be seen by others, as reciprocators.

Power of Responsibility

Another claim about the self-control that individuals accorded considerability should show relates to the power to exercise responsibility for one's moral and political aspirations. People must be able to understand that forming a conception of the good involves responsibility for pursuing and realizing that good.[17] For our ideas of the good to inform our conduct effectively rather than quixotically, our ends must be feasible to achieve or at least must be plausibly pursuable by whoever commits to them (Rawls 1999a, 243).

This is not to deny that thinking about the good may be aspirational, nor to detach ideas of the good from ideals. But forming ideas of the good functions both to formulate the aims one should pursue and to stimulate their realization. Effective thinking about the good envisions plausibly achievable goals, and thinkers about the good should be sufficiently immune to the attractiveness of fantasy to eschew barren because unrealizable ambitions. The effective thinker will reform extravagant thoughts by reference to practical possibilities for achievement in her own real world.

Responsibility is about control in the sense of self-determination: agents must be in control of determining their thoughts about the good rather than allowing an idea of the good to take control of them. But impairment of executive capacity often is an element of cognitive disability. Some people with cognitive disabilities do not have this capacity of reviewing their idea of the good to assess whether it is a proper aim for them, and some others have the power only to an attenuated degree (Francis and Silvers 2007).

Yet individuals with cognitive disabilities are neither the only nor the majority of people who are quixotic. And it is not unusual to assist such beguiled people, whether cognitively disabled or not, in refining their goals so they are achievable. We commonly advise or urge or even intervene to induce unmindful or feckless individuals to shift plans or adopt different projects. Most of us do not build responsible aspirations independent of our responses to other people, nor are we expected to do so. Nondisabled people are not held to an unmitigated standard of self-control in regard to the achievability of their conceptualizations of the good.

What is crucial when heuristic interaction is conducted by trustees is that the refinement or alteration of objectives becomes the subject's own. Trustees can simulate and thereby stimulate self-propelled critical revisioning, assisting people with cognitive disabilities to be in control of, rather than controlled by, where they want to go. Trustees for people with cognitive disabilities thus should provide prosthetic cognitive probing through a process of assistive thinking. Subjects' awareness of revamped aims or valuings need not reach the level of discursive activity, although it may. Nor need the interactions that constitute assistive thinking be

---

[17] Issues about the difficulty of trying to match one's actions, aspirations, and a reasonable knowledge of what is good have been discussed at least since the ancient Greeks.

conducted discursively, although they may be, depending on the usual ways the subject relates and responds to the world.

The power to disengage from inappropriate goals is important for both mental and physical well-being. Studies have shown, for instance, that "those who could not renounce hard-to-attain goals showed increased levels of the inflammatory molecule C-reactive protein, which is linked to such health problems as heart disease, diabetes, and early aging in adults" (Tugend 2008). Merely abandoning particular goal-directed conduct or spurning the erstwhile goal is not the answer, however. "Studies of older people found that they were happier if they found new goals to pursue once giving up on the old ones, in contrast with those who abandoned their previous aims without substituting anything new" (Tugend 2008). Trustees who interact with individuals with cognitive disabilities by providing prosthetic processes of thought therefore should not just draw their subjects away from pursuit of fantastical goals but should also be attentive to attracting them to more satisfying ones. Broadly, assistive thinking about the good for people with cognitive disabilities should be goal-appraising, with the trustee introducing calculation, reflection, extrapolation, focus, or other parts of the process the dependent cannot independently supply.

More specifically, people in general should look beyond desires in assessing whether the goals toward which they are drawn are fanciful or achievable. In doing so, they must do more than weigh practicalities. They must also transfer allegiances from conceptualizations that come to appear as chimerical to ones ready to be realized. Trustees charged with assisting people with cognitive disabilities in perfecting ideas of the good for them should be especially energetic in presenting and exploring alternatives through a revisionary process. Simply rejecting an idea does not do the job.

In addition, people should look beyond stereotypes in assessing whether their being drawn toward various goals is realistic for them. Too often, societal stereotyping makes aims toward which an individual feels affinity seem unrealizable when they are merely unusual, or when there is bias against people of the individual's kind realizing them. Less than half a century ago, it surely seemed unrealistic to aspire to a United States where an African American wins the presidency, or women pilot commercial airplanes, or a Carrie Buck can raise a family.[18] But those were thwarted

---

[18] Democratic as well as totalitarian states have prohibited people who have been diagnosed as disabled, especially cognitively disabled (but also in some cases blind, or deaf, or mobility impaired) from having children by sterilizing them. *Buck v. Bell*, 274 U.S. 200 (1927), is the infamous early twentieth-century U.S. Supreme Court case of a teenaged woman diagnosed as being cognitively disabled, where the diagnosis was attributed to heredity. This decision deprived the woman of reproductive freedom without regard for her own understanding of what was good for her. The rationale invoked by Justice Holmes was Buck's purportedly inherited inability to control her conduct-guiding aims and to reform

aspirations, not unrealistic ones—an important difference, as subsequent history shows. The lesson is that trustees who are charged with facilitating ideas of the good for people with cognitive disabilities should be especially careful to avoid importing societal biases that stifle rather than sustain ambitions for such opportunities as, for example, to be a parent and participate in a family of one's own making. This is just one aspect of the seriousness and skills pertaining to effective trusteeship.[19]

Powers of Self-Origination and Self-Authentication

This last point directs us to a third power some have thought crucial to right thinking about the good. Being self-originating is yet another kind of self-determination that individuals accorded considerability have been thought to need to command. According to Rawls, this is the ability of people to take themselves and their personally embraced ideas of the good, rather than the society external to themselves, as the source of their duties and obligations (Rawls 1999a, 242; Rawls 1980, 546). That is, their own reflection on values, rather than their reflection of society's values, controls what they believe they should do.

The sovereignty of self reflected by Rawls's notion of the liberal person as someone who regards himself as a self-validating source of moral claims turns out to be a kind of sovereignty over self. To separate one's own valuing from society's values, and to value one's self apart from how one is valued by society, calls for self-discipline and self-knowledge. One must be at liberty to ignore external pressures to conform to social norms, and also free from internal pressures compelling one to do so.

Stephen Darwall takes the attribution of the power of being self-originating to set constraints on whether and how one can be interfered with. Darwall contends that by extension and in a related way we owe respect to beings, including people with cognitive disabilities, who do not have the full capacities to exercise autonomy of the will (Darwall 2006, 271 n. 20). To discharge their duty in this respect, trustees for individuals with cognitive disabilities should proceed by recognizing that the subjects whom they assist must inspire the ideas of the good they are formulating. Neither the general society nor the trustees themselves may be the sources of, nor may they substitute their own, conceptualizations of the good for cognitively disabled people.

A further question may arise that we cannot resolve here. How do we know an idea that is the product of assistive thinking is authentically its

---

them to realistically reflect her prospects for respectable family life. (While the diagnosis of Buck as cognitively disabled now is understood to have been mistaken, this is not germane to our point about trustees freeing themselves of the societal biases that so often are imposed to reject disabled people's aspirations.)

[19] In our usage, the role of trustee is in principle not the role of caregiver. Although one person might fulfill both roles, the two roles are not necessarily compatible.

subject's own? To provide an answer requires deciding whether the concept of the authentic self incorporates, or instead detaches from, values drawn from the subject's group and culture. To decide between these ontological alternatives brings us back to the metaphysics of personhood.

Charles Taylor, for instance, believes that individuals are called on to be true to their personalized conceptions of the good, configured from community and cultural sources. Attachments to a community's normative framework are crucial to people's understanding who they are and to other people's understanding them. A lurking danger for cognitively disabled people comes from their internalizing their culture's devaluing of people like themselves. Such denigrating notions, if permitted to shape the consciousness of either a cognitively disabled subject or such a person's trustees, can shatter the person's possibilities for self-love and self-esteem. For Rawls, on the other hand, authenticity lies in independence, or the ability to detach reflectively, from community and culture. Here too lies a danger, however, for to detach cognitively disabled people so decisively from their social contexts risks isolating them and impoverishing their repertoire of valuings, especially where capacity for abstraction, extrapolation, or imagination may be absent.

This deep difference between two central philosophers of liberalism suggests self-authentication is no clearly understood power people can be expected to possess. Further, we may distinguish between two distinct objectives philosophers have in asking whether an idea of the good attributed to a subject is authentically that individual's own. These are so different as to result in two distinctly separate queries, despite their often being expressed in the same words. A moral and political interpretation of the question examines and therefore focuses on the possibility that what is represented as the person's good differs from what she actually values. A metaphysical interpretation of the question presumes the possibility of a divergence between what the good is thought to be for an individual, including what she herself may think it is, and what in reality is the good given the nature of individual she is.

As to the former, our account offers at least a partial standard for assessing the authenticity of a trustee's expression of the good for an individual with a cognitive disability. Such ideas cannot emerge authentically, we contend, except where the subject is the sole inspiration for the conceptualization the trustee advances. Every component of the idea of the good should be personalized to the subject and in this regard be singular. The conceptualization should be stripped of the personality of the trustee. A fit trustee also will be someone whose identity is not invested in executing the trustee role, so as to be able to abstract himself from the process and its product.

On our account, fulfilling the role of trustee is no casual occupation. Offering assistive thinking demands attentiveness and insight, as well as the imagination to see how to alter the world so the subject will flourish. If a trustee relationship issues in a conceptualization of the good for an individual with cognitive disabilities, an interactive process that refined the disabled subject's goals should be in evidence. Such a process might be discursive, but need not be so. Competent trustees should have communication skills adequate to elicit, and be guided by, responsiveness even from inarticulate subjects. Trustees do not represent their subjects as a result of this process. Rather, assistive thinking enables their subjects to configure ideas so as to represent themselves while the process unfolds through their use, via prosthetic functioning, of the trustees' cognitive and linguistic skills.

Parenthetically, our account should not be expected to serve as a prophylactic against people presenting themselves as trustees when they do not satisfy the standards of the role, or against people assuming the role to exploit rather than assist individuals with cognitive disabilities. No moral or political theory has such a directly protective impact on the world. Nor can theory alone guarantee the abolition of such problematic instances as when subjects are intentionally or inadvertently represented as if they would value what they actually would not. But the account supplies grounds for condemning pretenders to the role of trusteeship by delineating powers that genuine trustees assist their subjects in exercising, which powers are incompatible with the subject's being a means instead of an end.

The discussion through which we have just navigated responds to issues that arise when we ask moral and political questions about whether what is represented as the good for cognitively disabled people authentically conveys what they value. Metaphysical queries about authenticity differ by invoking claims about the nature of personhood and deriving direction for our moral and political conduct from this kind of claim. Metaphysical conceptualizations of personhood have been much invoked in debates about the value of individuals with cognitive disabilities, which is a very different matter from what individuals with cognitive disabilities value. We return to this metaphysical matter, although not to resolve it, in the concluding section.

Conclusion

We now have expanded prospects for full inclusion by liberal theory of people with cognitive disabilities through a practice of assistive thinking. This prosthetic practice differs in extent and implementation, but not in nature, from commonplace social interactions that facilitate people's development of their notions about the good. We have proposed that trustees' cognitive skills can be deployed prosthetically to enable conceptualizing and communicating an idea of the good by and for cognitively disabled subjects. To do so, the trustee interacts with the subject, enabling or facilitating exercise of self-determinative or self-controlling powers crucial to liberal thinking about the good.

The account contributes to a solution to exclusions advanced under the umbrella of liberalism by showing how cognitively disabled individuals may participate in certain kinds of processes related to cognition, and why liberal theory thus should not deny them full theoretical considerability. Our solution does not depend on the outcome of arguments for attributing moral personhood to them. Nor have we ventured into revising liberal metaphysics ourselves, although our approach at the very least introduces complexities and nuances into traditional views about how certain cognitive processes are at the core of human nature and are essential to moral personhood.[20]

While we describe some duties that accrue to those who accept or are thrust into the role of trustee, we refrain from proposing a further level of obligation that requires people to fulfill the functions of trustees. Some philosophers have argued that such a duty accrues to individual citizens and to society as a whole because all biological humans, including those with cognitive disabilities, possess personhood. Other philosophers, adopting instead a psychological criterion, have contended that serious deficit in the cognitive powers we have discussed disqualifies individuals for moral or political personhood.

Pressing metaphysical claims has the enormous attraction of appearing to provide a decisive *a priori* resolution for moral or political problems. And there is no doubt that metaphysical commitments can motivate social movements. What appears equally clear, however, is that in this case there is insufficient metaphysical momentum to move social change either way. To the contrary, debates about ontological groundedness tend to anchor the movement toward justice for cognitively impaired people in place, depleting progress toward inclusiveness.

We have tried to avoid metaphysical assumptions that cut either way, given what we have seen about both their intended and their inadvertent exclusionary effects. Rather, our focus is to show how people presumed to lack the requisite powers nevertheless might exercise them, even if not exactly in the usual way. As partial compliance theorists, we do not think we need to enter this metaphysical fray. Our question is how to build justice in the circumstances of the actual world, taking individuals as they are in all their variety. As we have pointed out elsewhere, realizing justice is an incremental process.

Does our proposal sufficiently safeguard those who are most vulnerable?[21] Quoting Patterson, Rawls describes slavery as "social death"

---

[20] Our hesitation in regard to entering the moral personhood debate concerns how well a metaphysical answer can resolve a moral and political question. See the debate between Eva Feder Kittay and Jeff McMahan in this collection.

[21] Some who embrace a biological or spiritual (as distinct from psychological or cognitive) definition of human personhood may object to our approach as neglecting entities who do not interact at all—for example, patients in deep comas. Writers of this persuasion, however, often invoke the criterion of interaction to argue for an attribution of personhood

because slaves were not considered capable of exercising any of the powers crucial to citizenship. Analogously, being diagnosed as cognitively disabled has had a similar result that we might call "social stillbirth." What remedy is available when a society neglects some kinds of individuals this way? As we elsewhere envisioned in discussing how to amplify consideration of the good for people with disabilities from the standpoint of liberal theory, "developing and expanding justice in a context of injustice is a process of working back and forth between the constraints of principles and the exigencies of nonideal circumstances" (Francis and Silvers 2007, 327).

We continue to explore how this incremental approach can involve people with cognitive disabilities in testing and revising ideals of the good and particular expressions of them. Recognizing that cognition is as at least as much a social as a solitary individual process helps guard against theories that dismiss the considerability of people with cognitive disabilities. For we have sketched out a process whereby the interaction between cognitively disabled individual and trustee reveals the personhood of the subject by putting it into action, somewhat as the interaction between an individual with an amputation and a prosthetic limb reveals the subject's capacity for mobility or manual function. Gaining an inclusive conception of personhood thus is posterior, not prior, to building out an adequately inclusive conception of justice. In other words, learning how to think more inclusively about personhood is an incremental benefit of building toward justice.

References

Anderson, Elizabeth. 2004. "Animal Rights and the Values of Nonhuman Life." In *Animal Rights: Current Debates and New Directions*, edited by Cass Sunstein and Martha C. Nussbaum, 277–99. Oxford: Oxford University Press.

Baier, Annette. 1986. "Trust and Antitrust." *Ethics* 96, no. 2:231–60.

Darwall, Stephen. 2006. "The Value of Autonomy and Autonomy of the Will." *Ethics* 116, no. 1:263–84.

Diamond, Cora. 2004. "Eating Meat and Eating People." In *Animal Rights: Current Debates and New Directions*, edited by Cass Sunstein and Martha C. Nussbaum, 93–108. Oxford: Oxford University Press.

Dombrowski, Daniel. 2006. "Is the Argument from Marginal Cases Obtuse?" *Journal of Applied Philosophy* 23, no. 2:223–32.

in particular cases; even when inconsistent with the physiological facts, a familiar claim in defense of the moral considerability of patients in persistent vegetative states is that the individual responds to caregivers' voices or seems to keep looking at them as they move around the room.

Francis, Leslie Pickering. 2009. "Understanding Autonomy in Light of Intellectual Disability." In *Disability and Disadvantage*, edited by Kimberley Brownlee and Adam Cureton, 200–215. Oxford: Oxford University Press.

Francis, Leslie Pickering, and Richard Norman. 1978. "Some Animals Are More Equal Than Others." *Philosophy* 53:507–27.

Francis, Leslie Pickering, and Anita Silvers. 2007. "Liberalism and Individually Scripted Ideas of the Good: Meeting the Challenge of Dependent Agency." *Social Theory and Practice* 33:311–34.

Freeman, Samuel, ed. 2002. *The Cambridge Companion to Rawls*. Cambridge: Cambridge University Press.

Friedman, Lawrence. 1995. "Review of James Trent, *Inventing the Feeble Mind*: A History of Mental Retardation in the United States." *American Historical Review* 100, no. 4:1284–86.

Friedman, Marilyn. 1999. "Autonomy, Social Disruption, and Women." In *Relational Autonomy: Feminist Perspectives on Autonomy, Agency, and the Social Self*, edited by Catriona Mackenzie and Natalie Stoljar, 35–51. Oxford: Oxford University Press.

Gibson, Suzanne. 2007. "Uses of Respect and Uses of the Human Embryo." *Bioethics* 21, no. 7:370–78.

Goodheart, Lawrence. 2004. "Rethinking Mental Retardation: Education and Eugenics in Connecticut, 1818–1917." *Journal of the History of Medicine and Allied Sciences* 59, no. 1:90–111.

Goodpaster, Kenneth. 1978. "On Being Morally Considerable." *Journal of Philosophy* 75:308–25.

Gutmann, Amy, ed. 1994. *Multiculturalism: Examining the Politics of Recognition*. Princeton: Princeton University Press.

Kittay, Eva Feder. 1999. *Love's Labor: Essays on Women, Equality and Dependency*. London: Routledge.

Longman, Jere. 2007 "Debate on Amputee Sprinter: Is He Disabled or Too Abled? *New York Times*, section A, column 2 (May 27).

McKenzie, Catriona, and Natalie Stoljar, eds. 2000. *Relational Autonomy*. New York: Oxford University Press.

Mills, Charles. 1997. *The Racial Contract*. Ithaca, N.Y.: Cornell University Press.

Nussbaum, Martha C. 2006. *Frontiers of Justice: Disability, Nationality, Species Membership*. Cambridge: Mass.: Harvard University Press.

Rawls, John. 1971. *A Theory of Justice*. Cambridge, Mass.: Harvard University Press.

———. 1980. "Kantian Constructivism in Moral Theory." *Journal of Philosophy* 77:515–72.

———. 1985. "Justice as Fairness: Political Not Metaphysical." *Philosophy and Public Affairs* 14:223–52.

———. 1996. *Political Liberalism*, revised edition. New York: Columbia University Press.

———. 1999a. *Collected Papers*. Edited by Samuel Freeman. Cambridge, Mass.: Harvard University Press.

———. 1999b. *A Theory of Justice*, revised edition. Cambridge, Mass.: Harvard University Press.

Shiffrin, Seanna. 2000. "Paternalism, Unconscionability Doctrine, and Accommodation." *Philosophy and Public Affairs* 29:205–50.

Silvers, Anita. 2009. "No Talent! Beyond the Worst Off: A Diverse Theory of Justice for Disability." In *Disability and Disadvantage*, edited by Kimberley Brownlee and Adam Cureton, 163–99. Oxford: Oxford University Press.

Silvers, Anita, and Leslie Pickering Francis. 2005. "Justice Through Trust: Disability and the Outlier Problem in Social Contract Theory." *Ethics* 116:40–76.

Taylor, Charles. 1992. *The Ethics of Authenticity*. Cambridge, Mass.: Harvard University Press.

———. 1989. *Source of the Self*. Cambridge, Mass.: Harvard University Press.

Tugend, Alina. 2008. "Winners Never Quit? Well, Yes, They Do." *New York Times*, section B, p. 5 (August 16).

Young, Iris Marion. 1990. *Justice and the Politics of Difference*. Princeton: Princeton University Press.

15

HOW WE HAVE BEEN LEARNING TO TALK ABOUT AUTISM: A ROLE FOR STORIES

IAN HACKING

Autism narrative is a boom industry. There are plenty of real-life stories of autism. I have written about autobiographies elsewhere; indeed, what I shall try out in this chapter is an extension of what I argue in connection with the role of what the autistic autobiographer Donna Williams has called autie-biographies (Hacking 2009a). I propose that the autobiographies are forging a language in which to talk about autism and in terms of which autistic people can think out their experiences. Biographies, in many cases written by a mother or father of an autistic child, are often of great interest in this respect. They tell us much about families with autistic children. Some of them are good representations of the child growing up. Some tell more about the parent, and her attempts to make sense of what has happened. No aspect of the phenomenon of autistic narrative is more influential than the Internet, a lot of which is biographical or autobiographical. It is a place for autistic people to "come out." But here I am concerned with make-believe, with old-fashioned story telling, with fiction, in short.

Why This Genre, the Autism Novel?

This is a chapter about mostly adult fiction, including novels, thrillers, science fiction, horror, harlequin romances, and all the other subgenres, such as plain old fantasy. "Mostly adult" is of course porous, and not only because teens who read, read stories for grownups. The best-known autism novel is *The Curious Incident of the Dog in the Night-Time* (2003). Its author, Mark Haddon, is a longtime professional writer of young adult fiction. His publishers had the wit to market the book in two formats, one directed at the public that reads middlebrow novels, and the other directed at reading teenagers. They hit the jackpot.

Why the present enthusiasm for telling stories, be they life stories or fictions, about people with autism? Why do people read them? What is the market?

There are some obvious answers. Some are not appealing. There is always a morbid fascination with the odd. But the situation is not like

that with Multiple Personality Disorder in its heyday, 1970–1995, when
that transient mental illness produced a glut of stories about multiples,
mostly trash.[1] They were a blend of voyeurism that used a sensational
behavior much in the news, in order to rework gothic themes.

Autism narrative seldom assumes that form. Autistic characters are
usually portrayed as people who are intrinsically interesting in their own
right and not just because they are strange, or worthy of the reader's
sympathy. Some fantasy sensationalism is inevitable, but fortunately
rubbish such as Brad Kelln's 2008 novel seems to be rare. Even in that
case, the autistic boy who is essential to the silly plot is a sweetie pie under
siege by (preposterous) villains, who are either alive (in the Vatican),
immortal (fallen angels), or in-between (lepers). This book, *The Tongues
of the Dead*, is a grim warning to writers in this genre. It is a ludicrous
exaggeration of the fable that autistic children have secret powers. It is
thus an unwitting parody of a dangerous falsehood. In this case the boy
turns out to be a fallen angel who not only can decode lost languages but,
like the other fallen, is also a body snatcher reincarnated, in the final
pages, in the body of an ordinary boy who falls prey to the plot.

Many people who read autism fiction are autistic individuals or their
families or friends. Then there is the larger class of readers who are
beginning to wonder if they themselves, or their family or friends, are
autistic. Let me warn here that by autistic I mean anywhere on the autistic
spectrum, including what is now generally and especially popularly called
Asperger's. There is, among other things, a scare about autism, and
people do read autism novels to get a sense of what it is about. That
unspoken fear cannot be gainsaid.

One may also venture a speculative functional explanation for the success
of autism fiction: it a mirror of the age. Autism has been called the pathology
of the present decade. It has been said that the very fact that it has become so
prominent so recently shows as much about our times as about the disorder
itself. I develop that theme in an essay, "Autism Fiction: The Mirror of an
Internet Decade?" (Hacking forthcoming). That, if it worked, would be an
external explanation of the success of autism fiction. In this chapter I suggest
a role for autism narratives internal to autism itself.

I believe that the genre is helping to bring into being an entire mode of
discourse, cementing ways in which we have recently begun to talk, and
will talk, about autism. It is developing a language, or, if you will, a new
language game, one that is being created before our eyes and ears. This

---

[1] There are plenty of examples in Hacking 1995. MPD was renamed Dissociative Identity
Disorder at the peak of this illness, 1994, when it was about to succumb to the scandals of
false memories encouraged by aggressive multiple therapy and the doctrine that multiple
personality was caused by forgotten child abuse. Transient mental illnesses (Hacking 1998)
are those that thrive at a place and at a time, in what I compare to an ecological niche. Need
I say that despite its recent leap to the center of public notice, autism is not a transient mental
illness?

speech is, in turn, creating or extending a way for very unusual people—namely, autistic ones—to be, to exist, to live.

This is precisely what I have argued in the case of autistic autobiography. I shall extend that proposal as a role for autistic fiction in the evolution of autism. The extension is imperfect, for autism fiction comes in many stripes, and only some of the stripes have the byproduct of facilitating ways to talk about autism.

A Role for Children's Autism Stories

Before we proceed, it is useful to have an aside on autism stories for children. One line of analysis is suggested by Douwe Draaisma (2008), who is especially useful on Haddon's *Dog*. Draaisma emphasizes the way in which Haddon has created a model in terms of which neurotypicals can think about an autistic adolescent; he fears, rightly, that this can lead to stereotyping. It can do so in another way too: Haddon's book is widely used in that segment of the teacher training syllabus devoted to special needs. Hence classroom teachers' notions of their charges are molded by what began as just a lively and well-written novel.

I propose an analysis of stories for children to supplement Draaisma's, one that is different from what I shall say about adult fiction. Not that the distinction is sharp: recall that Haddon's *Dog* was marketed to bridge both the Young Adult and the Adult categories. Despite such ambiguities, I believe that the role of children's autism stories is a little different from that of adult fiction, and that it is easier to understand. My proposal on this score will not be controversial in the way in which my views on adult fiction should be.

Autism stories for children go to great pains to describe how autistic children behave. They thereby serve as role models, sometimes for the children themselves, sometimes for other children relating to children with autism, and also for parents and other caregivers who read the stories aloud. The sibling format is quite common. Thus a twelve-year-old girl narrates her relation with her eight-year-old brother in the much-praised *Rules* (Lord 2006), intended for children aged nine to twelve. It won the Newberry Honor Award for best book for this age group. In the Juvenile category (which means ages five through eight), but with the same sibling format, there is the unusual English/Spanish bilingual book by Marvie Ellis (2005). Eight-year-old Thomas does not understand four-year-old brother Michael. A therapist teaches Michael how to play with Thomas, "making sibling time fun again." Many books in the young adult category serve the same function for older readers. In Caroline Ann Levine's *Jay Grows an Alien* (2007), an aspergic boy happens to meet a cyborg from outer space. Here, finally, is a being with whom he can communicate. Together they work out who neurotypicals are.

Jessica Kingsley Publishers in London publishes dozens or perhaps hundreds of autism-related books. Among them is a category of "Asperger Adventures," which include Kathy Hoopman's *Blue Bottle Mystery* (2000) and *Of Mice and Aliens* (2001), a mystery and its sci-fi sequel (more aliens). So underneath Haddon's *Dog* there are layers and layers of stories about autistic children that are directed at children. They are important to the evolution of autism because they so often tell neurotypical children how to accommodate to and respect autistic children—and how to love them, especially if they are part of your family. Or they help autistic children to understand themselves, or how to get on in a world of neurotypicals. Thus stories for children have a significant place in the culture of autism. They construct roles for children of all types to play. They implicitly teach what good behavior is. They preach what shall be normal, in the face of a child's own differences. A parent reading a story aloud to her child thereby learns what to expect of that child, and helps mold him to fit. Thus these stories not only share in the normalizing discourse of our times but also help to create the norms.

In one respect they strongly resemble Victorian morality tales for The Young. They are didactic. They are livelier or more amusing, to our eyes, than those treasures of a bygone era, but there is still a manifest Message. Do not forget, however, that morality tales for children can be moral fables for adults too: the most famous example is Charles Kingsley's *Water Babies* (1863). Like Haddon's *Dog*, it was intended for children but became a smash success with adults of the day.

The New Discourse

Some readers may recognize, in my thesis about creating a new discourse for autism, my old theme of "making up people" (Hacking 1986, 2007). But there is a special, possibly unique, feature here—namely, the language itself. Or rather, what amounts to making up language to give a voice to the people and thereby help determine who, or how, they shall be.

We take for granted that there is an immense and age-old language for human experience, emotions, and intentions, one that must go back to our most distant ancestors, and one that is being honed every day, in both the street and the garret. But a quarter century ago there was no language for autistic experience, emotions, and intentions.

Many people with autism have a great deal of difficulty in understanding what other people are doing, feeling, or thinking. The intentions of others are opaque. The situation is symmetric. Neurotypicals like me have a lot of problems understanding autistic individuals, even if they become quite articulate. The more severely affected among them, the ones who talk in strange ways or not at all, sometimes seem simply "other."

That is one reason for the trope of the alien that is so current both inside some autistic communities, to describe neurotypicals, and outside, to describe people with autism. That phenomenon is examined in my "Humans, Aliens, and Autism" (Hacking 2009b). We recall Temple Grandin's aphorism, immortalized by Oliver Sacks in his title *An Anthropologist on Mars* (1995). Grandin had said, when talking with Sacks, that much of the time, when interacting with neurotypicals, she feels like an anthropologist on Mars. She often experiences neurotypical actions and intentions as completely unintelligible. That's how neurotypicals often feel about autists. One is reminded of Ludwig Wittgenstein's aphorism: "If a lion could talk, we could not understand him" (2001, 190e). It is the very issue—of speech and the lack of it—that is the focus of my discussion.

You will have noted that I am using a recently made-up word for people who are not autistic: neurotypical. That is favored in some but only some autistic communities. Don't hear this as "neuronormal," as many neurotypicals are inclined to do. One point of the word is that there is no normal, there is just different.

A Caution

It is now a standard maxim, in many autism communities, that "if you know one person with autism, you know *one* person with autism." Within the autistic spectrum, there is a vast range of individuals. That is one reason I dislike the entrenched metaphor of an autistic spectrum. To the mind of a physicist or a logician—that's my own not very neurotypical mind—spectra are linear and autism is not. Autism is a many-dimensional manifold of abilities and limitations. I speak of autistic communities in the plural. There are many communities of autism activists who do not see eye to eye. Possibly—I am by no means sure of this—they attract, collect, and speak for different manifestations of autism, different fragments of the manifold.

An Invocation of Lev Vygotsky

It is reasonable to guess that as long as there has been human communication, there have been ways to describe emotions and intentions. I say *guess*, for maybe that is a mistake. Perhaps there is a long prehistory of human self-realization, in which a language for emotions came late. Lev Vygotsky (1896–1934) proposed that as children develop, they gradually internalize public, social, relationships, and generate conceptions of the intentions and feelings of other people (Vygotsky 1962). They start with their own family and with nearby children who are developing in the same way.

Vygotsky was concerned with children now, or rather children in the youth of the Soviet Union. But think of the human race in prehistory. I can imagine that the Vygotskian project, of crafting a language for the emotions of others and ourselves, may have taken many, many generations of our remote ancestors to complete. They arrived on the scene, like any primate, living in smallish groups, gradually evolving patterns of interpersonal behavior. But perhaps they had no inner life, no life that they expressed in words and thoughts (or what cognitivists call representations). In this scenario, the language that evolved for describing and expressing behavior would have been internalized very late in prehistory. What is now called "first person authority" over awareness of our own emotional states would, then, come into being slowly and late.

I am here making a familiar and widely discredited move: that of recapitulation. The development of the individual recapitulates, in small, the imagined development of the species. I use this not as a thesis about the facts but as a just-so story to think again about the inner life and the way we talk about it. It parallels what might be favored by evolutionary psychology, namely, that there is an innate Theory of Mind module, a product of natural selection, which enables us to understand other people. Despite the popularity of Theory of Mind, I am, like John Locke and Nelson Goodman, an inveterate skeptic about innate ideas, and see much of what is speculatively called innate as culturally acquired. I am comfortable with William James's statement, *"Our fundamental ways of thinking about things are discoveries of exceedingly remote ancestors, which have been able to preserve themselves throughout the experience of all subsequent time"* (James 1907, 65).

Incidentally, on this Vygotskian scenario, individuals with mild forms of autism would not have stood out, in the distant past, in the way that they do now. I am here speaking of prehistory, not of the quite different fact that compulsory universal elementary education was a prerequisite for noticing various kinds of cognitive difficulty in a systematic way.

An Invocation of Wolfgang Köhler

I have the bad habit of resurrecting thinkers who have faded into folklore. In "Autistic Autobiography" (Hacking 2009a) I draw attention to the insights found in the middle of Köhler (1929). He draws attention to the way in which we can so often tell from the look of another person what is going on in the mind. Wittgenstein coined a number of aphorisms on the strength of his reading that book; for example, "The human body is the best picture of the human soul" (Wittgenstein 2001, 152e). This was hardly original: Westerners have been saying that the eyes are the mirror of the soul at least from the time of Cicero's *De Oratore* (3.222; Cicero 2001, 294). One finds similar thoughts in other traditions. Neurotypicals can often see right off, from the look or gestures of another, what is intended, thought, or felt. They do not have to infer it or work it out. Many autistic people have great difficulty with this. Köhler (1929, 266) called the ability to see in the face and bodily movements of another person that person's state of mind "the common property and practice of mankind." It is not the common property and practice of people with autism.

So now I want to combine Vygotsky and Köhler, referring primarily to the former's definitive work published in 1934, but also to his earlier work on the role of play in child development. I suggest that autistic children are "non-Vygotskian." It has long been noticed that a great many autistic children do not pretend, and do not understand other people pretending. They do not play as other children play. They fail to understand what other people are doing. Yes, they lack a Theory of Mind, but I see that as secondary, not a cause but an effect. The primary fact is that autists do not interact with others in the way that neurotypicals do, and so they never go through the Vygotskian process of internalizing social relationships to form concepts of the mental. Autistic people are also "non-Köhlerian" in that they do not readily see, right off, what other people are doing. These two types of difference from neurotypicals are clearly interrelated.

The English language compilation of Vygotsky's many writings from 1925 to 1934 has the excellent title *Mind in Society: The Development of Higher Psychological Processes* (Vygotsky 1978). One might offer this as a sort of contrary to that title: Severely autistic minds are not minds *in society*, so they cannot internalize the behavioral concepts that cause neurotypicals to acquire ideas of what they call "higher psychological processes." They are not in society because they do not experience Köhler's phenomena. I believe you can readily continue these reflections, and work out for yourselves how this line of thought can be extended. I would repeat the caution, however, that people with autism are enormously various; I do not want to encourage such crass statements as "The autistic child is non-Vygotskian." I am merely offering a slightly nonstandard perspective on autism. It may make it easier to understand a role for autistic fiction.

Well-Established Language

Whatever evolutionary psychohistory we choose to fantasize, be it Vygotskian or that of a current crop of evolutionary psychologists, it is a fact that for all of historical time human beings have had public language in which to express the intentions, desires, and emotions of themselves and of other people. It was crafted by and for neurotypicals. We are only just beginning to adapt that ordinary language to the autistic life. In this we are much helped by autobiographies, novels, and the immensely rich world of autism lived on the Internet.

It is very common to say that autobiographies describe autism "from the inside." That suggests that there is a truth about autistic inner life that we are gradually revealing, and for which the truth conditions, even if as yet unknown, are fixed by psychological facts. I suggest there is little ready-made language to describe this inside, and that the autobiographies, the blogs, the novels, the movies, are creating it right now.

There are, I further suggest, no standing truth conditions for the mental life of autism. Whatever folderol you favor about the philosophical Problem of Other Minds, for example, knowledge by analogy as in John Stuart Mill and Bertrand Russell, or the (subsequent) inference to the best explanation account of Other Minds, or the present popular Theory of Mind theory—so popular that its adherents speak simply of ToM—the fact is that truth conditions for statements about what other people want or think or feel have been firmly entrenched in human life for as far back as we can honestly speculate. But there were no truth conditions for statements about what people with autism want or think or feel. Perhaps it is better to say that there were simply no facts of the matter until discourse about autism became established.

I think of this as an expression of common sense, cast into fancy language, but some will call it metaphysics or ontology. So let us make the usual escapist move of semantic ascent, moving up from facts and experiences to language. The autobiographies, novels, and blogs are entrenching a language in a domain where there was no language at all fifty years ago, and not much twenty-five years ago. We are participating in a living experiment in concept formation of a sort that does not come more than once in a dozen lifetimes.

It is to be expected that stories about people with autism may be at least as various as autistic people themselves. This is remarkably confirmed by autistic autobiography. The four exemplars used in Hacking 2009a—namely, Grandin, Williams, Mukhopadhyay, and Tammet—come from four continents. Their sexual orientation runs from nil, through monogamous gay, to multiply married. About all they have in common is autism and immense talent. Expect autistic fiction to be as various as autistic fact.

Incidental Autism

Autism is essential to some novels, but to others it is merely incidental. I do not wish to ignore the latter, so I shall mention a couple. Karin Fossum is a skilled contributor to the genre of Scandinavian "psychological police procedural" of whom Henning Mankel is, for English-speaking readers, the maestro. It is a feature of this genre that all the characters suffer from Non-Seasonal Affective Disorder, year-round gloom. Fossum is described as Norway's Queen of Crime. She really is good at her trade, and slightly less depressive than most writers in the genre. Her novels tend to involve a strikingly odd person with a diagnosable and usually diagnosed mental disorder. This character, perhaps a schizophrenic escaped from an asylum as in *He Who Fears the Wolf* (Fossum 2003), is presented sympathetically, but he is the prime suspect. Until five pages before the end, he is regularly proven guilty by circumstantial evidence until the denouement clears him.

Black Seconds (Fossum 2007) has an odd recluse who is more and more deeply implicated in the death of girl who just popped out for a moment on her bicycle. What we have known all along is confirmed on page 178: he is officially called autistic. I call this incidental autism because although the oddity of this man is central to the novel, it is not material to the story that his oddity is filed as autism. He has been a suspect from the start both for readers and for the police. In a sad final few pages, he turns out to be innocent and a victim only of his fear of neurotypicals.

Where Fossum let the autism out of the bag only near the end of the novel, Margot Livesey gives it away on page 2 of *Banishing Verona* (2004). There we learn that the hero, Zeke, was trained in recognizing neurotypical facial expressions from a poster given him at "the clinic." For those who missed the point, "Asperger's" is slipped in on page 27. Zeke is patterned on the son of a close friend of the author, and indeed the incident of the poster is based on a recollection of that young man (author's personal communication). Livesey writes old-fashioned romances. Twenty-nine-year-old Zeke earns his living as a decorator in London (viz., as an interior house painter and carpenter). He and an older pregnant woman whom he meets in bizarre circumstances fall in love. After the travails that befit romances, she cleaves to him. She comes from a world where deceit is the norm. She loves Zeke for his autistic traits, such as his inability to pretend or lie. Zeke's pathology in another register makes him innocent, honest, lovable, and, in comparison with Verona's usual habitués, sane. As you may expect, this is a pretty common device in autism novels.

Livesey creatively works with the ways in which she has heard her model speak, and gives him a rich emotional life. He has the ability finally to fall in love, and to hang on to Verona through thick and thin. Mostly thick, as befits an engrossing novel. It is true that Zeke's autism is only incidental, a convenient prop that makes his inability to deceive easy to put on stage. But perhaps partly because of this, it helps to entrench a way in which an autistic can be heard to feel, and can express what he feels.

One should notice that the autism of such characters is very often portrayed as a virtue that keeps the plot turning over. A thoroughly bad person with autism—or even a person in whom an autistic trait leads to vice—is missing from my reading.

The Child Biography Turned into Family Novel

I mentioned biographies of an author's own autistic child or children, books that occupy a serious niche in autism narrative. Some of these are very good, but critical response to weak autism biographies, from neurotypical reviewers, seems almost always too generous. The mothers have a hell of a time, and if they mostly manage not to be too sentimental, the books pass critical muster. This principle seems to apply to a less successful niche, the author who is a writer in her own right but who has an autistic child, and decides to write a novel rather than a biography around her experiences. It is clearly politically incorrect to pan these novels, but they do tend to be pretty weak, if judged as middlebrow fiction rather than as uplifting moral tales. Compared to the glowing reports on dust jackets and elsewhere, I am a grouch.

Thus there is Marti Leimbach's *Daniel Isn't Talking* (2006), about which only the *New York Times* managed to be a bit catty. Leimbach's first book, *Dying Young*, was made into a Julia Roberts movie. "In her new novel [writes the *Times*'s Eve Conant, 9 April 2006], the characters seem to be itching to get off the page and onto the set; layers of personality are sacrificed for plot expediency and straight-to-the-screen dialogue."

Leimbach is an American who has settled in England; she has an autistic son. There is every reason to believe she is doing a great job with her own child in real life. Her story is about an American heroine her own age, who is married to an increasingly awful English stuffed shirt, who fights bad practitioners in an inadequate National Health Service, and who lives in a country whose customs are foreign to her. She also has an autistic son. She finds a guru and a method of treatment and thus brings her son into humanity. Good for self-help, perhaps, but not for a novel. It is said that many people who have to deal with autism are exhilarated by Leimbach's tale. More power to her in the self-help department.

Two more remarks, one positive, one negative. Daniel is special and lovable because he is the heroine's complex son. Thank goodness he is not special because he has secret powers, the mystery of autism. Leimbach's novel is all to the good in combating that sort of popular legend. On the other hand, there is the hope of the magic cure out there, and I do not view this in a positive light. In this case it is the oversubscribed guru who goes against all the tired experience of the National Health Service doctors. An enormous number of parents of autistic children will try anything and everything; they are desperate. Many finally do settle on some regimen that seems better for their child than any other. They will see in this story a mirror of their own uphill battle, which can encourage people to hang in, but may lead to false expectations.

The Child Biography Turned into Mystery Story

Cammie McGovern is another writer of fiction with an autistic child. Her methods of educating her child have acquired disciples. My copy of her novel *Eye Contact* (2006) has eighteen enthusiastic puffs from reviewers and admirers. Were only half of them true, this would be the novel of the decade. And yes, the book has been optioned by Julia Roberts.

It is a thriller centered on an autistic boy who may, or may not, have witnessed the abduction and murder of a slightly older girl, also with special needs. There is a subplot that the boy's mother, when she was a girl, got a crush on a boy who was physically and cognitively disabled by a head injury. Plot and subplot weave around with many characters enmeshed in both. There are also amazing numbers of special needs children who shuffle through the plot, and who create a maze of false leads until the denouement.

This book is, in my opinion, bad writing and in particular bad suspense. The contortions of the subplot are too tedious to disentangle. Yet it is clearly "incorrect" to say so. I was unable to locate a single negative review. At least it should be pointed out that this mystery propagates the fiction of the autistic child who Knows What We Do Not Know. That's a great trick for suspense, perhaps. And in the end, only the Chosen can read the Child. I do not find this a good way to further autism discourse.

Neither of these books, Leimbach's and McGovern's, gives much language to the autistic boys who anchor the plots. What they do do, is to present the ways in which interactions between child and mother gradually evolve into communication. They also provide an image of the mother-child pair as being a unit coming to interact with the larger world. They thereby entrench ways of talking and feeling that simply did not exist some years ago. Thus although they are bad novels, they may serve the role I have proposed for autistic fiction.

Manga

Keiko Tobe's epic-length manga *With the Light* (2007–2009) is another story of a mother and her autistic child. It starts before the joyful birth, and charts the gradual discovery that the son is not developing like his peers, up to the ultimate diagnosis of autism. It deals with the incomprehension of family and neighbors. The father, at first in denial, is gradually weaned from his total immersion on the early rungs of the Japanese corporate ladder, becoming a father who cares for his wife and son. It is more overtly didactic than the two novels just discussed, and so is unlikely to be read in the West all the way to the four-volume end by any but the manga-hooked, or by the families of autistic children. Hence it may not contribute, in the West, to enlarging a discourse of autism, but it appears to be a vivid attempt to do just that for its Japanese readers. I do not know enough about the role of such fiction in the evolution of autism in Japan. I do regard this manga as a superb unfolding of the life of a "normal" severely autistic child, that is, one who has lots of difficulties and differences but no secret powers. The Japanese made-for-TV movie of the manga swept the Forty-first Television Drama Academy Awards, in 2004.

Overdoing the Inner

Elizabeth Moon is another successful novelist whose son is autistic, now an adult. *The Speed of Dark* (2002) is set some decades in the future. Neonatal gene therapy now prevents autism, but there is one last cohort of adult twenty-somethings that was never treated. A group of them is employed—grace of affirmative action law—by a megacorporation whose products I never did figure out, in order to detect patterns on computer screens. This skill is much valued by Megacorp for reasons that the author does not trouble to explain. The plot revolves around a new technique for brainwiping autistic people in order to make them neurotypical. Thus far it has been tested only on apes, but it is being marketed as foolproof, though first there must be trials on humans. The group employed by Megacorp is chosen for the experiment.

The hero wrestles long and hard: Will he submit himself to drastic brain alteration never before tested on human beings? Suppose it works; does he want to lose his old self and the emotions he has experienced up to now? I confess I was gunning for him to hang in and refuse, but at the end of the novel his opposition inexplicably collapses, and he agrees to treatment. He comes out of it a new man. He fulfills his dream of being an astronaut. One imagines that the author supports CAN: Cure Autism Now, rather than the neurodiversity movement.

Much of the story is told in the voice of the autistic hero. He falls in love with a neurotypical girl whom he meets in a fencing class, an event for which some in his autistic cohort despise him. There are endless inner monologues in which he goes through working out what other people are doing, or what they mean by their words. Of course he cannot tell how much Marjorie cares for him, or what behavior of his might help woo her.

Reading all this inner life feels like preparing for a test for neurotypicals enrolled in Autism 103, to be given in the spring semester of 2027 (Why Autistic People Have Trouble Figuring Us Out). Is the book thereby an exercise in creating a language for autistic expression? Well, it helps tell neurotypicals what autists find hard. The author presumably well knows some of the problems from the travails of her own son. Perhaps the book provides a tool for autistic people to convey to neurotypicals their difficulties in comprehension and in love.

The book goes closer than any of the other novels under discussion to reinforcing the stereotype of the autist as savant. Happily, novels do not seem to promote that wholly misleading feature. A few savants are indeed autistic, but hardly any autistic people are savants. Draaisma (2009) deplores the way in which so many autism movies follow *Rain Man* in casting their autistic characters as savants. Most novels do not do so, but Moon's does.

The folks in that last cohort of autism in what I am calling 2027— that is, the people who were born too early to be cured in the neonatal genetic clinic—do tend to have savant skills, along with their ability to detect stability in seemingly random patterns. Some of the patterns, for example, the pattern of play of a fencer, really are patterns, and an ability to detect them in one's opponent soon after the opening of a match would be a boon. Maybe the author knows of some such real-life example of reading the body of another person, but in general that is exactly what most autistic people are bad at. To treat fencing patterns and hidden patterns on a computer screen as on a par seems to me to be driving autistic fascination with "pattern" a bit hard.

In this novel, the stereotype of the moderately autistic individual as potential computer nerd shines through. The co-workers, who work in their own pod on the umpteenth floor in the Megacorp complex, have special powers that the corporation milks. That takes us to Douglas Coupland's *jPod* (2006).

Autism and the Nerd

The stereotype of the autist as savant may be rare in fiction as opposed to novels, but the picture of the computer geek as autistic is all too prevalent. Douglas Coupland himself says, in interviews, that he is mildly autistic, but a more plausible description of this bundle of creative energy is Hyper Artistic Activity Disorder. Not that the two diagnoses can't dwell in the same body. His sculptural work is increasingly well known, and he publishes many books, more than one a year, both fact and fiction. The title of his first novel (1991) gave us the expression "Generation X," as well as that word of our times, "McJob." The hero of his *Microserfs* (1995) opined that all techies are mildly autistic. His novel *jPod* expands on the theme. Coupland not only wrote *jPod* but also designed the printed book in the manner of what you encounter online. Some of it is e-mail, some more is what hits you with random googling; the whole is intended to make it the first Web 2.0 novel.

The eponymous jPod is a pod in a company that designs video games. All the young people in the pod have names that begin with *j*. Throughout the middle of the book, they are made out to have autistic traits, to the extent that one of them buys Temple Grandin's "squeeze machine." That's the home-made device that presses a person close and makes them feel less stressed out. It works on cattle, for which Grandin uses it after finding it worked for her own autistic and upset self. It works on neurotypical people too. It seems that when distressed we all need hugs, even wooden ones.

Despite the use made of autism to keep the plot rolling, or at least to keep the five hundred–odd pages rolling on, autism is not central to this book. Autism enters, plays for a couple of hundred pages, and exits. So this novel does nothing for *spoken* language in the world of autism. It is suggestive, perhaps, of autistic e-mail. That is something that autistic people discover for themselves, and they need no permission from

Coupland, nor do they need him as exemplar. What the book does, is to put this phenomenon into view as an object for all readers to experience and to reflect upon.

It also makes a quite different contribution to the so-called epidemic of autism. It licenses every single member of the burgeoning world of techs to think of himself as at least mildly autistic, and as sharing in the new expressive languages of autistic people.

Self-Discovery (My Son Is a Genius with Computers; I Must Have Some of His Genes)

The tech theme shows up in more modest proportions elsewhere. Clare Morrall's *Language of Others* (2008) puts my theme of language out front in the title, but it does not loom large in the text. Her first novel, *Astonishing Splashes of Colour*, was an astonishing mid-life success, short-listed in 2003 for the Booker Prize. She claims little first-hand experience with autism, but says she was much moved by all she was hearing about Asperger's. One suspects she had a moment of self-recognition, from which, we hope, she recovered.

Morrall has told an honest tale of a middle-aged middle-class English-woman muddling through on straitened means and limited emotional attachments. She has a pretty dreadful family—hardly her fault, methinks, that she can't understand them, and not a classic autistic trait of inability to understand the "language of others." She has a charmingly layabout son who spends all his time on computers. By the end of the book he invents brilliant video games and makes millions. Had she read Coupland, Morrall might have learned that video games are the product of teamwork and podwork, not of the single boy-genius. His diagnosis, which most readers will have guessed at since about page 10, is finally revealed to his mother. She realizes that she is genetically tarred with the same brush and comes to understand herself and her problems as the result of Asperger's.

That, of course, is another poignant theme in many autism novels: coming out. We are all kept in the brightly illumined dark, desperately waiting for the heroine finally to realize what is wrong with her. I hope this is a stage in the genre that will pass. Everybody knows now, so there is no suspense. Livesey was the better novelist when she told us on page 2.

From the Psychiatrist's Point of View

A Proper Knowledge (2008)—is that intended to recall Alexander Pope's "The proper study of mankind is man"? Presumably yes, for the author, Michelle Latiolais, is a literature professor at the University of California, Irvine. Her book is *written*, verging on overwritten. Nevertheless the complex prose held my interest a lot better than most of what I have been reading. Latiolais picked up autism from books, notably Uta Frith's 1991 *Autism and Asperger Syndrome*. Latiolais published her novel some years after she wrote it, and hence reflects autism lore of no later than 2000.

The hero is a psychiatrist who works with autistic children. His sister died of appendicitis when he was a smart-ass boy. He had told their mother that the appendicitis symptoms were due to the schizophrenia drugs she was taking (thanks to misdiagnosis). So this is a tale of guilt, which is fought by becoming an autism specialist in an expensive private practice. The guilt is healed by falling in love with a woman who is immersed in flowers, and who hardly needs to be told what ails him.

The children in his care are severe cases. Very occasionally in the past he has had a success, but mostly it is the hardest kind of uphill slogging. One child has echolalia to the *n*th degree, speaking only by citing, in apt situations, complete lines from old movies, mostly *The Manchurian Candidate*, in which, as you will recall, the commies planted a sleeper. Is there a hidden message, that this strangely gifted but otherwise impossible child is a sleeper? A more pertinent question is the real-life one: Are there known cases of echolalia this focused?

I doubt that many specialists would encourage the psychiatrist's techniques, but we know that dedication works wonders, no matter what the mode. There are no successes in this book, except the healing of the hero. The actual autistic children do not say anything at all, except the echolalia kid, so this is no contribution to new languages of autism.

Since Latiolais attributes much of her knowledge of autism to reading Uta Frith, I sent her a copy of *Autism and Asperger Syndrome*. She kindly read it and said that although the practice of the psychiatrist was sweetly described, she found that type of practice "abhorrent." She judges that the "talking cure" has no effect whatsoever on autistic children. She fears that the novel will perpetuate the myth of the autistic child as different but with strange gifts, a sort of superchild.

Latiolais and Morall seem to exemplify another aspect of autism novels. The authors' knowledge of autism is mostly book learning, often incomplete or out of date. These two talented writers are deeply respectful of the condition, and it is central to their plot, unlike the incidental autism mentioned earlier. The role of these novels in the evolution of autism might be called deliberate absorption into the mainstream. Some novels speak to the human condition. Nowadays we are less ambitious or more realistic. Our novels speak to particular conditions, and thereby make those conditions part of the larger tapestry of human life.

The Promise and the Danger

This partial survey of the genre will confirm that stories about autism are contributing to the formation of a discourse about autism. They suggest ways in which autistic people can choose to express their experiences. They suggest ways in which neurotypicals can think about the lives of others. Only in the past couple of decades have we begun to acquire such ways of speaking.

The novels will also blur the line between the autistic and the neurotypical. Few readers will fail to notice in themselves this or that autistic trait. (The ironist will observe that people, who are so blind to their own foibles that they cannot notice it, give evidence of an autistic symptom.) This may be a good thing, in enriching our own ways of thinking about ourselves. But it is a bad thing if it encourages a false sense of what autism is really like, especially in its more severe manifestations. And if all the techs in the world go around thinking they are mildly autistic, the richness, the depth, and the difficulty of the phenomenon of autism will be grossly misunderstood.

There is a greater danger to autism fiction. It can encourage the image of the autist as gifted with a secret knowledge or wondrous powers. It can lead to sliding from a genuine fact to a foolish fiction.

Yes, there is a simple fact, that some high-functioning autistic people are good at some tasks that many neurotypical people find arduous or boring. Paradoxically, the tasks are often the ones that may have special uses in our logocentric era, in which the formal codification and structuring of information plays an ever-increasing role. This fact contributes to the strength of the neurodiversity movement, for it enables members to say we are all different, can do our own things. But this fact, plus a lust for strangeness in stories, can lead some novelists in search of a plot to create the child, the adolescent, or the adult with whimsical or mysterious powers. That is a gross distortion of what autism is all about.

Curiously, the novels with which I began, the novels by Margot Livesey and Karin Fossum, in which autism is incidental and not central to the plot, may, after all, be the best of the genre. This is precisely because each of the two very different autistic characters on which the novels hinge is, in his own way, "ordinary." Not "normal" by any means, but, given who he is, an ordinary person making out in a very difficult world. This conclusion is not astonishing. Livesey and Fossum are both, in their respective genres, masters of their trade; honest tellers of stories, in short.

References

Bowler, Dermot M. 2007. *Autism Spectrum Disorders: Psychological Theory and Research*. New York: Wiley.
Cicero. 2001. *Cicero on the Ideal Orator*. Translated by James M. May and Jacob Wisse. New York: Oxford University Press.

Coupland, Douglas. 1991. *Generation X: Tales for an Accelerated Culture*. New York: St. Martin's Press.

——. 2006. *jPod*. New York: Random House.

Draaisma, Douwe. 2008. "Who Owns Asperger's Syndrome?" *Sartoniana* 21:23–48.

——. 2009. "Stereotypes of Autism." *Philosophical Transactions of the Royal Society, Biological Sciences* 364, no. 1522:1475–1480.

Ellis, Marvie. 2005. *Tacos Anyone?/¿Alguien Quiere Tacos? An Autism Story Book 2/Una Historia De Autismo Libro Dos*. Round Rock, Tex.: Speech Kids Texas Press.

Fossum, Karin. 2004 [1997]. *He Who Fears the Wolf*. London: Vintage.

——. 2007 [2002]. *Black Seconds*. London: Harvill Secker.

Hacking, Ian. 1986. "Making Up People." In *Reconstructing Individualism*, edited by T. Heller et al., 222–36. Stanford, Calif.: Stanford University Press.

——. 1995. *Rewriting the Soul: Multiple Personality and the Sciences of Memory*. Princeton: Princeton University Press.

——. 1998. *Mad Travelers: Reflections on the Reality of Transient Mental Illnesses*. Charlottesville: University Press of Virginia. Reprinted Cambridge, Mass.: Harvard University Press, 2002.

——. 2007. "Kinds of People: Moving Targets." *Proceedings of the British Academy* 151:285–318.

——. 2009a. "Autistic Autobiography." *Philosophical Transactions of the Royal Society, Biological Sciences* 364, no. 1522 (27 May): 1467–1473.

——. 2009b. "Humans, Aliens, and Autism." *Daedalus* (special issue on human nature).

——. Forthcoming. "Autism Fiction: The Mirror of an Internet Decade?" *University of Toronto Quarterly*.

Haddon, Mark. 2003. *The Curious Incident of the Dog in the Night-Time*. London: Jonathan Cape.

Hoopmann, Kathy. 2000. *Blue Bottle Mystery*. London: Jessica Kingsley.

——. 2001. *Of Mice and Aliens*. London: Jessica Kingsley.

James, William. 1907. *Pragmatism: A New Name for Some Old Ways of Thinking*. New York: Longmans Green.

Kelln, Brad. 2008. *The Tongues of the Dead*. Toronto: ECW Press.

Köhler, Wilhelm. 1929. *Gestalt Psychology*. New York: Horace Liveright.

Latiolais, Michelle. 2008. *A Proper Knowledge*. New York: Bellevue Literary Press (NYU).

Leimbach, Marti. 2006. *Daniel Isn't Talking*. New York: Random House.

Levine, Caroline Ann. 2007. *Jay Grows an Alien*. Shawnee Mission, Kans.: Autism Asperger Publishing Company.

Livesey, Margot. 2004. *Banishing Verona*. New York: Henry Holt.

Lord, Cynthia. 2006. *Rules*. New York: Scholastic Press.

McGovern, Cammie. 2006. *Eye Contact*. New York: Viking Penguin.

Mencius. 1960. *The Sayings of Mencius*. Translated by James R. Ware. New York: New American Library.

Moon, Elizabeth. 2002. *The Speed of Dark*. London: Orbit; New York: Random House, 2003.

Morrall, Clare. 2008. *The Language of Others*. London: Sceptre.

Sacks, Oliver. 1995. *An Anthropologist on Mars: Seven Paradoxical Tales*. New York: Knopf.

Tobe, Keiko. 2007–2009. *With the Light: Raising an Autistic Child*. New York: Yen Press (Hachette), 4 vols. Translated by Satsuki Yamasuta from *Hikara To Tomoni*, 8 vols. (Tokyo: Akito Shoten, 2001–2005.)

Vygotsky, Lev. 1962 [1934]. *Thought and Language*. Cambridge, Mass.: MIT Press.

———. 1978. *Mind in Society: The Development of Higher Psychological Processes*. Edited by Michael Cole. Cambridge, Mass.: Harvard University Press.

Wittgenstein, Ludwig. 2001 [1953]. *Philosophical Investigations*. Third revised translation. Oxford: Blackwell.

16

THE THOUGHT AND TALK OF INDIVIDUALS WITH AUTISM: REFLECTIONS ON IAN HACKING

VICTORIA MCGEER

The Clinical View Versus the Narrative View

Individuals with autism are very much in the public eye. These days, anyone versed in the comings and goings of everyday culture will have heard of autism (and/or Asperger syndrome)[1]—and doubtless knows something about it. Misconceptions also abound. But given that autism was only first described in the early 1940s (Asperger 1944; Kanner 1943), the subsequent development of clinical knowledge—and, with it, public awareness of the condition—has been quite remarkable. So remarkable, indeed, that certain clinical facts about autism are fairly well known—for example, that autism is a persisting neurodevelopmental disorder for which there currently is no cure; that it has a biological (and most likely genetic) basis, though environmental causes during foetal development are not ruled out; that it manifests behaviourally in very early childhood (around eighteen months), though is probably present from birth and shapes the entire trajectory of an individual's development; that it is a "spectrum" disorder, affecting individuals to varying degrees—severe cases involving significant cognitive and behavioural disability, less severe cases allowing for adaptive functioning in many domains (such individuals are often diagnosed with Asperger syndrome); that even in severe cases, there can be islets of good, even superior, cognitive-perceptual ability—for example, so-called savant talents (though this is rare); and, finally, that despite significant variation in symptoms, as well as in developmental progress and outcome, individuals with autism share some notable features in common on the basis of which diagnosis is made—to wit, a qualitative impairment in reciprocal social interaction, a qualitative impairment in verbal and nonverbal communication, and a notably restricted repertoire of interests and activities (DSM-IV-TR;

---

[1] Asperger syndrome is simply a milder form of autism, distinguished by no delay in language acquisition or in reasoning skills outside the social domain (Klin, Volkmar, and Sparrow 2000; Mayes, Calhoun, and Crites 2001; Mayes and Calhoun 2001; Ozonoff, South, and Miller 2000; Frith 2003). Henceforth, I will use the term "autism" nondiscrimately to cover Asperger syndrome as well.

ICD-10). (Needless to say, this list of basic facts is provisional. It will no doubt be revised as understanding of the disorder progresses.)

These clinical features support the public image of a socially awkward, isolated, or uncommunicative human being, with idiosyncratic needs and interests, and a very poor—often debilitating—understanding of what other people are up to, or of the kind of mutual expectations that govern our myriad forms of interpersonal life. To what extent is this public image being augmented—or even transformed—by paying attention to what individuals with autism say about themselves? To what extent is autistic experience itself being augmented or transformed by finding public ways to talk about it? These are the questions Ian Hacking takes up in a recently published article in the *Philosophical Transactions of the Royal Society*. His aim there is to explore the ways in which autistic autobiographies—and, in general, self-report—are contributing to "the ongoing social and cultural evolution of the autistic spectrum," which evolution will have significant transformative effects on the lived experience of autistic individuals themselves (Hacking 2009a, 1467).

But why just autobiographical reports? As Hacking points out, these reports are but one thread in a much larger tapestry of what he calls "autistic narrative." In the past thirty years there has been an explosion of works bringing an entirely new genre into being: "not expert reports by clinicians or reflections by theorists, but stories about people with autism, told by the people themselves, or their families, or by novelists, or by writers of stories for children" (Hacking 2009a, 1467). Such narratives occur in a variety of media: printed matter, DVDs, blogs, YouTube postings, chat rooms, and other Internet formats. And they have a wide range of objectives: self-help, advocacy, information dissemination, pedagogy, creative expression, entertainment, and so on. Yet taken as a whole, the genre attests to the fact that autism has escaped the bounds of the subcultural. It is no longer a vaguely known clinical condition, like Fragile-X or Williams syndrome, but has features that are familiar, recognizable, portrayable—so much so that "characters" with autism are now appearing in fiction, assuming a place in the common stock of personalities that walk through the pages of make-believe, however highbrow or lowbrow these may be.

Could all this writing and talking about autism, by experts and nonexperts alike, contribute to how autism is experienced by autistic individuals themselves? Taken literally, the idea seems far-fetched. But as Hacking points out, the cross-germination between different kinds of writing should not be underestimated: "Different kinds of items influence each other in complex ways. Novelists study autobiographies, whose authors learn from theorists. Parents pick up ideas from novels when they are thinking about their children. We all watch movies and documentaries" (2009a, 1467). Hence, in his contribution to this collection, Hacking invites us to consider a more inclusive thesis growing out of his speculations on the transformative power of autistic autobiographies:

"[T]he genre [of autistic narrative] is helping to bring into being an entire mode of discourse, cementing ways in which we have recently begun to talk, and will talk, about autism. It is developing a language, or, if you will, a new language game, one that is being created before our eyes and ears. This speech is, in turn, creating or extending a way for very unusual people—namely, autistic ones—to be, to exist, to live" (2009b).

In this short chapter, I explore how Hacking's thesis could be true. I do so by focussing not on the larger genre of autism narrative but on the smaller subset consisting of autistic autobiographies and other forms of self-report. I begin here for a number of reasons. (1) Autistic self-narratives are really at the epicentre of this phenomenon. While parents and other caregivers have written poignantly of their lived experiences with autistic individuals, it is the astonishing output of these individuals themselves that has really made an impact, both on the public imagination and on those who contribute to the genre of autism narrative from other perspectives. (2) Hacking has been deliberately inclusive in how he defines the genre of autistic narrative, including many fictional works that involve, through ignorance or creative licence, gross distortions of what autism is like. He rightly cautions about particular dangers that flow from the public dissemination of such mis-representations, even in their milder forms—viz., that "neurotypicals" (this term for nonautistics comes from the autism community) will simply miss the "richness, the depth, and the difficulty of the phenomenon of autism" (2009b). Of course, this is a delicate issue for Hacking, since his thesis is that the phenomenon of autism is evolving precisely under the pressure of how we all talk about it. So in what sense can these works of fiction encourage "a false sense of what autism is *really* like" (2009b, my emphasis)? I do not see an explicit answer to this question in Hacking's chapter. However, my hypothesis is that unless such representations actively engage those who have some first-hand experience with autism (including parents and caregivers, as well as autistic individuals themselves)—engage them, that is, by giving them a suggestive way of exploring their own experiences with autism—such representations will be completely idle from the point of view of performing the shaping role that Hacking envisions (that doesn't mean they can't work mischief, the possibility he warns against). If this is right, then the core phenomenon is, once again, how autistic individuals come to think and talk about themselves. Hence, it's worth exploring Hacking's transformative thesis in this narrower domain. Finally (3) for the reason just given, it seems Hacking's more inclusive thesis cannot be true unless the narrower thesis is true. This makes it a good starting point for critical discussion.

Informing Versus Transforming: Two Ways of Shaping the Autistic Spectrum

So far I have distinguished between narrower and broader versions of Hacking's basic thesis, which holds that the genre of autistic narrative is contributing to the "the ongoing social and cultural evolution of the autistic spectrum." The narrower thesis focuses on the effects of autistic *self*-narratives, the broader thesis on the effects of narratives that are about, or at least involve, autistic individuals. My immediate interest, as I have said, is in the narrower thesis, but the point I am about to make could apply to the broader thesis as well (though I'll not explore that possibility here).

There are two ways in which autistic self-narratives could have an impact on how autism is conceptualized and on how it is experienced. These ways are not mutually exclusive—indeed, I think Hacking has both in mind. However, the first way—which I call "informative"—is perhaps less controversial. This includes, for instance, giving nonautistic people or neurotypicals (whether they're parents, teachers, therapists, clinicians, academic psychologists, or simply members of the lay public) better insight into the subjective world of autistic individuals—so that they come to understand them as "thick," rather than "thin," people (to use Hacking's apt metaphor). It would also include giving autistic people themselves information that there are others out there like them, others with whom they may be able to connect (via the Internet and other forms of autism-friendly communication—Hacking mentions "texting" as an example) for purposes of friendship, information exchange, self-advocacy, and so on.

The second aspect of Hacking's proposal is perhaps more controversial; it's certainly more dramatic. It's that this relatively new and thriving genre of autistic self-narration has the power to *transform* how the autistic spectrum is constituted—as Hacking says—both "for those who inhabit [it] . . . and for those who do not" (2009a, 1467). The idea is that these self-narrations not only tell the nonautistic how autistic people experience their lives and the world around them but also help to create a framework, or "form of life," in terms of which their individual lives will be experienced—differently, as it may be, from how they would be experienced if this framework were not in place. I am attracted to this transformative thesis, but I also have questions about it, including how precisely to interpret it. I return to this issue later in the chapter. However, there is much to be said even about the less controversial aspect of Hacking's proposal, so I begin here: with the idea that autistic self-narratives can have a critical *informative* impact on how to understand individuals within the autism spectrum.

From Thin People to Thick People

These narratives have been—indeed, still are—regarded as amazing, even shocking (as Oliver Sacks says), given various assumptions that have prevailed about autism even among those who as parents, caregivers, and clinicians have the most familiarity with autistic individuals: assumptions about the "thinness" of their mental lives, supposedly consequent on their relative lack of self-conscious, reflective, and imaginative capacities. But how did neurotypicals form this mistaken impression of autistic sub-jective "thinness"?

There are, I think, two important sources of this mistaken impression, one more basic or "intuitive" and the other more "theoretical." Hacking focuses on the more basic, intuitive source of this impression by calling attention to what he terms "Köhler's phenomena," invoking the insight of Gestalt psychologist Wolfgang Köhler (Hacking 2009b; for more detail, see Hacking 2009a, 1470–71). This is such an important idea, it's worth dwelling on—and will lead, in any case, to my identifying what may be an important contributing factor to the mistaken impression of autistic subjective thinness: viz., the theoretical commitment that many cognitive psychologists have to a "theory of mind" deficit account of autistic social difficulties. Hacking himself professes no great enthusiasm for this approach, preferring instead a Vygotskian account of how we come to think of other people as having complex internal states (2009b). To my mind, however, there are dangers to the theory of mind approach that are not sufficiently highlighted in Hacking's passing remarks, so I shall try to make these more explicit. But first let me turn to Kohler's phenomena.

Hacking rightly emphasizes an absolutely basic feature of our percep-tion of other people, which he calls Kohler's phenomena (see too McGeer forthcoming): that, in many typical contexts, we don't *infer* the moods, thoughts, feelings, or intentions of others, we simply *see* such subjective or mental phenomena—such ways of being minded—directly *in their behaviour*, in the way they conduct themselves in relation to us or to other aspects of the world around them. We see it in their expressions, their gestures, their movements—and here Hacking gives some nice examples: seeing that a child wants to touch the dog, but doesn't dare; seeing that someone's upset at having to do a task he's just been assigned; seeing that someone's reluctant to keep a promise she's made.

Now this proclivity we have for seeing aspects of mind in everyday actions and expressions is so effortless and automatic that we even experience Kohler's phenomena in places where we know that no minds are really present at all. This was nicely demonstrated by the psycholo-gists Heider and Simmel in a simple experiment they conducted in the 1940s (Heider and Simmel 1944). They showed college students a short animated film (approximately ninety seconds long) of three geometric figures—two triangles and a circle—moving in and around a rectangular enclosure in a two-dimensional space (figure 1), and asked their subjects to describe what they saw.[2] The vast majority of viewers—thirty-four out of thirty-five subjects in the original experiment—are irresistibly drawn to

---

[2] The original Heider and Simmel animation can now be viewed on YouTube. Similar demonstrations are readily available on the Web by searching "Heider Simmel animation" (or demonstration).

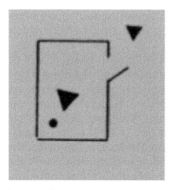

FIGURE 1. Still image from Heider and Simmel (1944) film clip

describe these movements in anthropomorphic terms. In fact, ordinary viewers are overwhelmingly consistent in their interpretations, perceiving in this film a stirring little drama involving two friends, one of which—a young Galahad—bravely tries to protect his small and terrified companion from the threatening attacks of a large and angry bully. There are a few close calls, but the story ends happily enough with our two friends trapping the nasty bully, delighting in their success, and making good their escape.

So what does this experiment demonstrate? That, for ordinary viewers, certain perceptual configurations (in this case, movements of figures in space in particular relations to one another) are sufficient to convey information of a specifically social—indeed, mentalistic—kind. But not so for individuals with autism; and this is true even if they are capable of passing quite sophisticated theory of mind tests, tests that are geared to measure their capacity to attribute and reason about others' mental states. In a recent study, the psychologist Ami Kin showed this film to a group of such high-functioning individuals and found that they did not produce the spontaneous social narratives so robustly offered by typical viewers. Indeed, if they used any mental state terminology at all (and many didn't), they did so infrequently and in a way that was often irrelevant to the social plot ordinarily discerned in the film (Klin 2000). In other words, these individuals failed to experience the Kohler's phenomena so evident to ordinary viewers.

Now we come to the key question: What explains the neurotypical's proclivity to experience Kohler's phenomena, both in everyday contexts and in these artificial circumstances designed to reveal the basic perceptual cues to which we're normally responding? More importantly for present purposes, what explains the *absence* of this proclivity in individuals with autism?

Two Hypotheses: "Theory of Mind" Versus "Form of Life"

The currently popular view among cognitive psychologists is that neurotypicals have a modularised (possibly innate) capacity for seeing others as possessing mental states, which states predict and explain their behaviour in systematic ways. This is the famed theory of mind (or ToM) hypothesis. Autistic individuals are said to have a ToM deficit—damage or dysfunction to this modularised system. And this explains why they are insusceptible to Kohler's phenomena, both in everyday contexts and with respect to the kinds of artificial stimuli created by Heider and Simmel. Now, as I've said, Hacking does not show any real enthusiasm for this view; indeed, he argues that the ToM approach "does not easily distinguish between, on the one hand, seeing what someone is doing right off and, on the other, inferring or working it out from clues" (2009a, 1470). It's worth pointing out, however, that ToM advocates do not see their approach as requiring explicit inferential processes. For many, this is the point of hypothesizing a ToM *module*: it performs its computations subpersonally, allowing those who possess such a module to see right off what others are "thinking, feeling, plotting, and so forth." If the ToM approach is off base, at least in this modular version, it must be for other reasons. Here I shall suggest two considerations that militate against it.

The first consideration is not compelling; still, I think it is worth noting. The ToM deficit hypothesis is supposed to explain why individuals with autism are insusceptible to Kohler's phenomena, including those that are robustly, if artificially, generated by the Heider and Simmel film. But the high-functioning individuals in Klin's study did not have a ToM deficit, at least as this is standardly tested and is standardly understood—namely, as a capacity to make mental state attributions for the purpose of explaining and predicting the behaviour of others. Recall that these individuals were quite capable of passing ToM tests (for example, a variety of false belief tasks). So ToM advocates must account for this dissociation. One possibility is that such high-functioning individuals do not pass ToM tests in the normal subpersonal way—that is, by grace of a properly functioning ToM module. Rather, they must rely on some explicit process of reasoning, something more like genuine theorizing, which is unlikely to be triggered by the kind of low-level perceptual cues present in the Heider and Simmel animation. In other words, the Klin study does not refute the ToM deficit hypothesis—indeed, it might be taken to argue in its favour, at least in its modular version.

A second consideration is far more compelling (for further discussion, see McGeer 2001). The ToM deficit hypothesis implies that the autistic inability to experience Kohler's phenomena is a disability unique to them, consequent on damage or dysfunction to their mind-reading system. But as Hacking points out, there's a crucial symmetry here: we do not experience any Kohler's phenomena in our interaction with autistic individuals any more than they experience such phenomena in their interactions with us. We do not directly perceive their subjective experiences as expressed in their behaviour any more than they perceive ours. They are blind to our minds, but so too are we blind to theirs. The ToM deficit hypothesis, by putting all the disability on the autistic side of the divide, does not seem to have the resources to explain why this should be the case. So we need an alternative hypothesis: call it the "form of life" hypothesis. (I take what follows to be roughly Hacking's view—and it's one I've defended myself, calling it, less elegantly, the "psycho-praxis" hypothesis [see McGeer 2001 and forthcoming].)

According to the form of life hypothesis, Kohler's phenomena are to be explained as a species of skilled perception that arises in conjunction with skilled performance in any norm-governed shared practice, or form of life. Consider a mundane example: learning how to play chess. In the beginning, the novice will make moves that mostly conform to the rules, although she may need some instruction in this. She knows what her objective is—to take the other's king and protect her own—but, not being very adept at making moves herself, she'll have little capacity to understand what her opponent is up to, and will mostly fail to perceive dangerous situations. But as her skill improves, she'll be able to strategize more effectively, and simultaneously she'll be better able to perceive her opponent's strategies as these unfold on the board in front of her. And if she persists in the practice, exposing herself to more matches and more styles of play, her performance will improve still further, encompassing both her ability to produce novel and interesting moves herself and her ability to perceive virtuoso play in the actions of others. As Gilbert Ryle so persuasively observed, skilled performance and skilled perception are two sides of the same coin (Ryle 1949).

Now consider the various social practices that make up what might loosely be called our "folk-psychology"—practices through which we regulate, share, or disguise our thoughts and feelings in order, among many other things, to ease or intensify social situations, to manipulate others to get what we want, to convey our faith or trust in them so as to encourage confidence in their own powers, to assure them of our dependability or our friendship. These practices, varied and complex though they may be, are deeply norm-governed. Take, for instance, what's involved in being a friend. Friends don't let each other down without good reason; they don't say malicious things behind one another's backs; they go beyond the call of duty for certain extraordinary demands; they laugh at one another's jokes (even if they're not very funny); they try to be honest with one another when it really counts; and so on. Anyone who's skilled in the practice of being a friend understands these things, and regulates himself accordingly, depending on the level of friendship he hopes to sustain in a particular relationship. Equally, anyone who's skilled in the practice of being a friend, recognizes when others are, through their actions and expressions, either trying to adhere to the norms of friendship, only paying lip service to these norms, or actively showing a disinterest in observing them.

How do we learn to be a friend—or, indeed, to be effective and skilled participants in the myriad complex practices through which we regulate, share, or disguise our thoughts and feelings in interaction with others? There's an elaborate developmental story to be told here, to be sure—one that psychologists are slowly beginning to unravel. But it's clear that our training in these folk-psychological practices begins in early infancy, as parents and other caregivers progressively scaffold our entry into more and more complex interactions that, thanks to them, bear the normative shape of recognizable social forms. Our thoughts and feelings develop likewise as we learn to form and regulate our own qualities of mind in ways commensurate with those of a "normal psychological agent" in the context of such interactions. There is, of course, plenty of room for play and manoeuvre, as there is in chess; but basic normative structures must be in place in all these varied practices if we are to make sense of one another's actions and expressions; if we're to share a form of life. That we experience Kohler's phenomena in interactions with one another is just the predictable outcome of our becoming skilled in the myriad practices that constitute our shared form of life.

Where does this leave autistic individuals? According to the form of life hypothesis, they are simply not skilled in the myriad practices that constitute our shared folk-psychological expertise. And why is this? Again, there will be a complicated developmental story to be told, one that reaches back into early infancy and identifies factors, both endogenous and exogenous, that disable autistic individuals from having their minds and actions moulded under the regulative regime of parental scaffolding. Hence, they will not become typical, recognizable psychological agents. They will not experience Kohler's phenomena in their interactions with us, and we—of course—will not experience Kohler's phenomena in our interactions with them.

But now, given that we do not experience Kohler's phenomena in relation to autistic individuals, they are bound to seem subjectively thin to us, as if they do not have complex or well-developed qualities of mind. This is one of Hacking's critical points. Moreover, this intuitive impression is likely to be considerably bolstered if we reflect on the fact that typical children only develop sophisticated qualities of mind, as they acquire language, through the continual give and take of regulative parental scaffolding—scaffolding that brings them into a communal language and a shared way of being minded. Thus, to be minded at all seems, for neurotypicals at any rate, to be irreducibly co-minded. So, how could autistic individuals develop any complex qualities of mind without participating in this shared practice?

Well, of course, autistic children do not grow up in utter isolation from other human beings. They are not, in that sense, deprived of parental scaffolding. Indeed, there are legion accounts, both heart-breaking and heart-warming, of continuous and exhausting effort on the part of parents, teachers, therapists, and caregivers to break through the barriers of autistic isolation and idiosyncrasy. And, of course, we now have many accounts from autistic individuals themselves of their equally heroic efforts to make sense and order out of a disturbed and disturbing universe. So somehow in this combined effort of insistent social and linguistic training, on the one side, coupled with the insistent need for routines, clear rules, soothing stereotypies, and other forms of environ- mentally managed sensory regulation, many autistic individuals develop extraordinary qualities of mind, even if some of these qualities of mind (some of their experiences, thoughts, and emotions) are strange and idiosyncratic and sometimes barely comprehensible to those of us who follow a more ordinary developmental trajectory.

And how do we know this? Well, as Hacking has argued, it certainly hasn't been, and indeed can't be, through reading their behaviour. This is just what we would expect if the form of life hypothesis is correct. So our only means of discerning the surprising fact that autistic individuals have much richer subjectivities than we might have thought possible is through their self-narratives. These narratives provide both an existence proof that their form of idiosyncratic linguistic and psychological development is possible and also gives us our best means of accessing what these minds, so differently developed from our own, can be like. Of course, such autistic narratives are likely to be odd and idiosyncratic and difficult to understand. And this is not just because the minds therein displayed are so unusual from a nonautistic perspective; it's also because the language available to display those minds is still our (nonautistic) communal language, a language geared, for the most part, to typical psychological experiences. As Hacking points out, autistic individuals will have their work cut out for them to adapt, manipulate, and perhaps outright distort the common meanings of our words in order to convey something of their own subjective experience. So we should be prepared for semantic oddities—and be prepared to accept as well that the experiences so conveyed may themselves shift and change under pressure from the language used to express them. I'll get to this possibility in a moment.

For now, let me simply agree with Hacking that this new and thriving genre of autistic self-narrative has a vital informative role to play in compensating, as he says, for the absence of Kohler's phenomena in the interactions between autistic and nonautistic people. This role makes sense if the form of life hypothesis is the right way to understand the disconnection between those with autism and those without it. But what can be said under the alternative hypothesis—that autistic individuals fail to understand neurotypical individuals because they suffer a ToM deficit?

Does according autistic self-narrative such a vital, informative role make equal sense on this conception of autistic disabilities? I think not. Indeed, cognitive psychologists who advocate this view have tended to be deeply suspicious of autistic self-narrative on theoretical grounds. That is, they regard autistic autobiographies as a particularly *misleading* source of information about autistic subjective experience. Why? Because reflecting on or talking about one's own subjective phenomena is reflecting on or talking about *mental* phenomena, precisely the kind of phenomena that autistic individuals are supposed, by their ToM deficit, to have real trouble understanding (see, for instance, Frith and Happé 1999). Hence, the very kind of reports that might encourage some serious rethinking of the ways in which a theory like the ToM deficit account misleads us as to the thickness of autistic mental life are, by virtue of that self-same deficit account, denied any real credibility. This is why I think the ToM deficit hypothesis is more troubling, and more important to question, than Hacking acknowledges.

Transforming the Autistic Spectrum

I have yet to comment on the more radical aspect of Hacking's proposal: that this relatively new and thriving genre of autistic self-narrative has the power not just to inform but to *transform* how the autism spectrum is constituted, both for those who inhabit it and for those who do not. As I said at the outset, I'm sympathetic to this thesis, at least in some respects. But I think there are different ways to understand it, and I have some doubts concerning at least one idea Hacking seems to have in mind.

So how might this genre of autistic self-narration have the power to transform the autism spectrum, by which I understand Hacking to mean: How will people's *experiences* with autism change, whether they are themselves autistic, whether they're nonautistic, or perhaps whether they're somewhere in between (we hear and talk a lot at the moment about family members, friends, or colleagues who have "autistic-like" characteristics)?

Here's one possibility that seems likely—in fact, I think there are plenty of signs that this is already happening. As autistic individuals talk and write more about themselves, and as these reflections become more widely disseminated through the medium of print, interview, self-made videos, blogs, and other rich resources now available through the Internet, our interactions with autistic individuals are bound to change in countless ways. This will be true mostly for people who work closely with autistic individuals—parents, caregivers, teachers, therapists, clinicians, social workers, colleagues, and even friends. But it may also be true for the wider public as well, as more room is made in social space for people with a now increasingly familiar suite of atypical behaviours and needs. The "odd" and "strange" and "better off avoided" will become, at least in some respects, more "normal," more accepted, more "worked with" than "worked against."

Of course, this is a slow process, but the practical consequences for autistic individuals will be of enormous importance. As their external environment changes—as it becomes more enriched from the perspective of offering more informed, and hence more suitable, kinds of emotional and physical support, teaching and therapy—so too will their own developmental prospects be transformed. In this autistic individuals are not unlike the rest of us. Their development will depend on the conditions they encounter on the long road to maturity, just as our development depends on the conditions we encounter. If autistic self-narratives have the power to change those conditions for the better, then autistic self-narratives have the power to transform what it is to be autistic. This idea seems entirely plausible.

However—and this is my last point—Hacking floats another suggestion for how autistic self-narratives can have the power to transform autistic experiences, and about this I'm a little more sceptical. He points (rightly) to the fact that autistic individuals are in touch with one another as never before. The Internet, in particular, provides a wonderful medium for such individuals to learn about one another, to share experiences, to discuss the challenges they face in dealing with neurotypicals and the world in general, and, of course, to form support and advocacy groups. Through all of this, Hacking suggests, norms are emerging—norms that reflect and perhaps constitute a sense of what it is to be autistic.

Now, in ordinary situations, when norms emerge for various ways of being—norms, for instance, concerning what it is to be a friend, or a good neighbour, or a patriot—there's a very strong tendency among neurotypical individuals to shape and regulate their attitudes and behaviour in accord with these norms, and thereby to reinforce them. (Hacking has called this a "looping effect" in other writings; in this chapter, I call it a susceptibility to "co-mindedness".) As I pointed out earlier, this susceptibility to co-mindedness is, in fact, the way neurotypicals come, in the course of ordinary development, to develop minds at all. But what about autistic individuals? The surprising, even shocking, discovery has been that they have become minded in quite sophisticated ways without ever becoming co-minded, without sharing in our normative ways of being a psychological agent. So this raises a question. How do autistic individuals relate to norms, even norms that emerge (so to speak) in the context of their own discussions?

Words for neutotypical human beings are powerfully social; they are a primary means by which we become and remain co-minded with one another. Will autistic individuals come to relate to words in the same way, as they discover and build a community of others? Will they feel compelled to live up to certain ideas that get expressed of what it is to be autistic? Or will they be less moved, less influenced, by reflections that may in some sense resonate with their own experience, yet fail to suggest to them a normative way of being? In short, will they ever become co-minded with one another, or will they just remain differently minded? I don't have strong views about this one way or the other; but I think there's reason to suspect that their relationship to language will never be quite what it is for neurotypicals, even as they develop a language that is more satisfyingly their own. As one such individual, Amanda Baggs, says, "My language is not about designing words or even visual symbols for people to interpret. It is about being in constant conversation with every aspect of my environment" (Baggs 2007). So I end with the following thought: Hacking cautions us about using phrases like "*the* autistic mind"—"as if 'the autistic mind' were a species of mind" (2009a, 1470). Ironically, I think this observation may be truer than he suspects—indeed, if I am right, *neurotypical* minds are more likely to constitute *a* species of mind; autistic minds are more likely to remain exceptionally multiple and idiosyncratic.

References

Asperger, Hans. 1944. "Die autistichen Psychopathen im Kindesalter." *Archiv fur Psychiatrie und Nervenkrankheiten* 117:76–136.
Baggs, Amanda M. 2007. "In My Language." (Video.) YouTube.
Frith, Uta. 2003. *Autism: Explaining the Enigma*. Oxford: Blackwell.
Frith, Uta, and Francesca Happé. 1999. "Theory of Mind and Self-Consciousness: What Is It Like to Be Autistic?" *Mind and Language* 14, no. 1:1–22.
Hacking, Ian. 2009a. "Autistic Autobiography." *Philosophical Transactions of the Royal Society B: Biological Sciences* 364, no. 1522:1467–73.
———. 2009b. "How We Have Been Learning to Talk About Autism: A Role for Stories." Included in this collection.
Heider, Fritz, and Mary-Ann Simmel. 1944. "An Experimental Study of Apparent Behavior." *American Journal of Psychology* 57:243–59.
Kanner, Leo. 1943. "Autistic Disturbances of Affective Contact." *Nervous Child* 2:217–50.
Klin, Ami. 2000. "Attributing Social Meaning to Ambiguous Visual Stimuli in Higher-Functioning Autism and Asperger Syndrome: The Social Attribution Task." *The Journal of Child Psychology and Psychiatry and Allied Disciplines* 41, no. 7:831–46.
Klin, Ami, Fred R. Volkmar, and Sara S. Sparrow, eds. 2000. *Asperger Syndrome*. New Haven: Yale University Medical Center.
Mayes, Susan D., and Susan L. Calhoun. 2001. "Non-significance of Early Speech Delay in Children with Autism and Normal Intelligence and Implications for DSM-IV Asperger's Disorder." *Autism* 5, no. 1:81–94.

Mayes, Susan D., Susan L. Calhoun, and Dana L. Crites. 2001. "Does DSM-IV Asperger's Disorder Exist?" *Journal of Abnormal Child Psychology* 29, no. 3:263–71.

McGeer, Victoria. 2001. "Psycho-practice, Psycho-theory and the Contrastive Case of Autism." *Journal of Consciousness Studies* 8, nos. 5–7:109–32.

———. Forthcoming. "The Skill of Perceiving Persons." *The Modern Schoolman.*

Ozonoff, Sally, Mikie South, and Judith N. Miller. 2000. "DSM-IV-Defined Asperger Syndrome: Cognitive, Behavioral and Early History Differentiation from High-Functioning Autism." *Autism* 4, no. 1:29–46.

Ryle, Gilbert. 1949. *The Concept of Mind.* Chicago: University of Chicago Press.

17

THE ENTANGLEMENT OF RACE AND COGNITIVE DIS/ABILITY

ANNA STUBBLEFIELD

The majority of contemporary social theorists, including philosophers, endorse the view that the concepts of race, class, and gender and sexuality are social constructions, although they frequently disagree about the details. The idea that a society's understanding of intellect—who is regarded as cognitively able and cognitively disabled and on what basis—is also a social construction is less widely considered by the same social theorists, although this idea has been explored by a small number of disability studies scholars for more than thirty years. Taking their work as a starting point, I have argued elsewhere (Stubblefield 2007) that in order to fully understand the history of the conception of intellect in the United States and our present-day usage of that concept, we must understand the ways in which our construction of intellect has developed in concert with and is inextricably entwined with our concepts of race, class, and gender.

To illustrate this entanglement through a brief exploration of one aspect of it, I focus in this chapter on the concepts of blackness and cognitive disability. To consider blackness and cognitive disability together is para-doxical. On one hand, supposed black intellectual inferiority was used by Europeans and white Americans to justify the enslavement, colonization, and exploitation of people of African descent, and black people have reasonably responded by demonstrating that they are not lacking in intelligence. Intelligence testing has been held up by white elites as scientific proof that black people are intellectually inferior to white people, and black scholars and their allies have responded by pointing out the cultural biases in the tests and the ways that test data have been manipulated to support false claims of black intellectual deficit. Black students in racially desegregated schools are disproportionately labeled as having mild mental retardation or emotional impairment and are placed in special education and remedial classes on the basis of standardized test scores, other academic skills measures, and teacher referral. This resegregation of desegregated schools has been decried by theorists and political activists as both an effect and a reinforcement of erroneous white beliefs about black intellectual inferiority.

On the other hand, as I discuss in detail in this chapter, black children who are struggling in school are less likely than their white counterparts to access the services they need or receive the least restrictive school placement (as mandated by the Individuals with Disabilities Education Act). Compared with white American children, and due to disproportionate poverty rates, black American children are disproportionately subject to inadequate prenatal health care, to lead poisoning, and to various environmental factors that are causes of brain damage. Furthermore, black adults labeled as cognitively impaired are less likely than their white counterparts to access the best services and support available. For example, due to receiving disproportionately poor health care, black people with Down syndrome live significantly less long on average than do white people with Down syndrome.

An explanation for this deplorable state of affairs is captured in the following set of propositions. (1) The concept of measurable intellect is a social construction. (2) In the United States, the concept of intellect as a measurable quality of individuals was developed by white elites in a racialized way as both a rationalization and a tool of antiblack oppression, and white elites use it in the same way today. (3) Although black students are disproportionately subject to environmentally caused health problems (due to disproportionate poverty resulting from our nation's history of antiblack oppression) that may result in developmental challenges, black students who fail in school do not get the support they need, because most school authorities perceive students' struggles as the result of individual "intellectual impairment" that has been constructed as described in (1) and (2), while black adults who face developmental challenges are less likely than their white counterparts to obtain the services they require, due to the disproportionate poverty and difficulty in accessing white-dominated support and health care services that are the results of antiblack oppression justified historically, as described in (1) and (2).

These problems cut across a commonly drawn—but, I argue, artificial and erroneous—divide between the "judgment" categories of mild cognitive impairment into which black children are disproportionately placed and the "organic" categories of severe cognitive impairment. This division is itself part of the contemporary collective denial of the racialized history and construction of our notion of intellect that ends up harming black Americans. To maintain the objectivity of intelligence testing and labeling when speaking of "profound" impairment, while admitting that intelligence testing is racially biased when it is used to attribute mild cognitive disability, implies that racial bias is a contingent feature of an otherwise objective intelligence assessment process. I argue that the concept of measurable intellect itself is racialized and suspect on a number of grounds and cannot be redeemed.

My skepticism concerning the use of intelligence testing and the dichotomy between the judgment and organic categories is not a denial that there are genuine challenges—of various degrees, various sorts, and various origins—that many individuals face with respect to cognitive skills. Rather, my position is that we should not foreclose anyone's possibilities with labels and presumed deficits and that we should instead provide support in self-development to anyone and everyone by finding ways to help all people meet their developmental challenges. My aim is to show that the historical legacy and current practice of intelligence testing reveal that the dichotomy between judgment and organic disability categories not only is not helpful in securing the services that people require but also cannot be logically sustained.

The only way out of the conundrum of the overrepresentation of black Americans in the judgment categories of cognitive disability and the underrepresentation of black Americans in inclusive education and therapeutic and support services regardless of the disability categories into which they are placed is to dispense with cognitive ability labeling. There is simply no way to revise the usage and process by which the labels are applied that will render them anything other than a tool of racial (and other forms of) oppression, and, as I discuss in this chapter, we can provide both children and adults with the support they require to flourish without first labeling them based on a supposed measurement of their "intelligence" level. Indeed, as I will demonstrate, we can support people much better when we do not get caught up in the process of labeling them. This is a point that has been made by various education scholars, although more frequently about "judgment" labels than about all cognitive ability labels. But it is a point that philosophers must be fully cognizant of, lest we compromise the validity and relevance of our philosophical projects. We err when we speak of cognitive ability and disability as if these concepts represented an essential, natural distinction between human beings and as if they had no connection to social oppression.

Understanding Intellect as a Social Construction

The idea of intellect as a social construction has been advocated for many years by a number of scholars, including Sarason and Doris (1979), Gliedman and Roth (1980), Bogdan and Taylor (1982), Biklen (1992), Ferri and Connor (2006), and Kliewer (2008). It is not within the scope of this chapter for me to make a full-blown case for why intellect is a social construct, and I refer the reader to the excellent work of these scholars and those cited throughout this section.

To say that intellect is socially constructed is not to say that there are no differences in cognitive development. But just as we have come to under- stand that we do not derive attributions of race straightforwardly from skin color or other physical differentia, unmediated by our socially constructed perception of these characteristics, so we do not derive attributions of intellect straightforwardly from cognitive skills, unmediated by our socially constructed approaches to measuring them. Indeed, cognitive skills are as elusive as skin color and evade measurement just as much. The notion of a measurable "intelligence quotient" or the idea that any test of specific skills can measure intellect in some general sense is itself part of how our contemporary understanding of intellect has been constructed.

There are many people who find it very hard to reason, to employ logic, to problem solve, to grasp abstract ideas, and/or to perform academic skills. But we must be cautious in drawing conclusions about the intellectual abilities of others from their apparent difficulty in demonstrating a particular set of cognitive skills. We can see if someone is able to demonstrate specific skills in the way we demand in a specific test, but we cannot legitimately jump from that to judgments about her overall "intelligence" (McClennen 1991, 48–50). Furthermore, we have to be aware of ways in which we are drawing conclusions based on tasks requiring specific motor skills (McClennen 1991, 42). For example, we may assume that moving blocks is a basic motor skill, so we test for an understanding of quantity by asking someone to pick out three blocks from a pile. But if the motor skills involved are too difficult for that person and he does not do as we request, then we assume that he does not know how to count. We have to eliminate many other possibilities before we can accurately conclude that a person does not know how to count. And then we cannot assume that it is "impossible" for him to learn to count until we have tried many different approaches, not just the "typical" approach, to helping him learn.

We also have to recognize ways in which the skills we look for are culturally and socially specific and understand that not having certain skills is only a problem in certain contexts. Many students waste hours of time learning to tie shoes (a difficult motor operation that is often used as a measure of intellectual accomplishment) in an age of Velcro fasteners. And we have to avoid jumping to conclusions about someone "never" being able to learn a certain skill. If it is a skill that is useful for her to learn, we should keep trying to help her learn it, but we also should not delay introducing other skills on the basis that "she'll never be able to do this if she hasn't learned to do that" (you do not need to know how to read in order to work on developing problem-solving skills, for example). We also have to be careful about assumptions about what skills are useful for a particular person: for example, if we have already decided that a person has little cognitive ability, we may assume that he does not "need" to learn to read, but this is again bringing in questionable assumptions (Chandler-Olcott 2003). And if someone is having a difficult time reading (which is often due to motor and sensory-processing difficulties, as reading requires a lot of effort in these areas, so much so that for many people no energy or attention remains to appreciate the meaning of the text), then it does not follow that she will not enjoy or be able to make academic use of text in audio form.

Furthermore, the construction of intellect is bound up with the construction of what counts as "communication." People who consider themselves to possess intelligence attribute intellect to others based on the ways in which the latter communicate. When a person cannot understand another easily or follow his thought processes, or a respondent does not give a questioner the answers she expects to certain kinds of questions, she concludes from this that the respondent has cognitive deficits. Yet if she recognized the ways in which she is failing to communicate with him—by not adapting herself to his mode of communication, his language use, and his pace, or by failing to appreciate his behaviors, gestures, and glances as communications—she might find that he is not so unable to communicate after all. She might realize that what she took as his lack of communicative skill—and hence evidence of his cognitive deficit—is really her lack of communicative skill (Lovett 1996, 6–7; Rapley 2004).

Once we grant that the notion of intellect is constructed through assumptions about what counts as communication and what skills people must demonstrate before they are granted access to opportunities for development, we can understand that what disables people who are labeled as "intellectually impaired" is (1) an environment in which a successful or full life is defined in limited terms, based on notions of independence from others and competitive accomplishment, and (2) an environment in which people who are not independent or successful in these narrowly defined ways are therefore deprived of the opportunity to challenge themselves developmentally, participate as citizens, use their skills and talents to make contributions to society in ways that are beneficial and meaningful to them, and enjoy full protection of their rights.

Psychologists and educators commonly draw a distinction between "organic" and "judgment" categories of intellectual impairment. The organic categories of cognitive impairment indicate "moderate" or "severe" intellectual impairment that is in some but not all cases the result of an accompanying diagnosable physical anomaly. The judgment categories (in the terminology typically used in the United States) are "educably mentally impaired," "emotionally impaired," and "learning disabled." They are referred to as "judgment" categories because there is no accompanying physical diagnosis that can account for or confirm the judgment of the evaluating psychologists that the child is intellectually impaired. These are also categories of what is called "mild" cognitive impairment: children placed in these categories are expected to continue to learn academic skills, but with support and at a slower pace than "typical" students. Children are assigned to these categories on the basis of classroom performance (teacher referral) and psychological evaluation.

The concern with the disproportionate placement of black children in special education is with disproportionate categorization of black children into the judgment categories. The suspicion is that, in the absence of a diagnosable physical anomaly, they are being labeled as cognitively impaired due to racially skewed judgments on the part of teachers and psychologists within a network of school structures and policies that are stacked against nonwhite children. Statistics indicate that black children are not disproportionately labeled with "organic" cognitive impairment labels. This leads social critics who are concerned about antiblack oppression in cognitive disability labeling to accept the dichotomy between judgment and organic cognitive impairment. For example, Harry and Klingner acknowledge cultural differences in how a wide variety of disabilities—including organic disabilities like deafness, blindness, physical deformities, and epilepsy—are perceived, but do not acknowledge that perceptions of "gross mental or physical impairments" might also be socially constructed (Harry and Klingner 2005, 8).

In order to fully understand the entanglement of race and intellect as social constructions, however, we must call into question the judgment/organic distinction. The so-called organic categories are not as objective as the term "organic" and the distinction from judgment categories might lead us to believe. First, even when a person has a physical anomaly that has been associated with developmental disability, the way in which he experiences developmental challenges (if he experiences any) is very individualized and depends upon how he is treated by others. Until the 1970s, for example, the assumption made by professionals about children with Down syndrome was that they would never learn to talk, walk, take care of themselves, or perform academic skills. They were therefore confined to institutions where they were not given the opportunity to learn these skills, thus turning the assumption into reality (Trent 1994, 267). But when given the opportunity, people with Down syndrome are capable of much more than was previously believed (Kingsley and Levitz 1994; Bérubé 1996).

Second, while there are causes of brain damage that are known, such as lead poisoning and phenylketonuria, we must separate out the existence of a cause of brain damage from gross generalizations about the cognitive results. For example, John Lorber, an expert on hydrocephalus, identified a number of cases of adults who had hydrocephalus that had not previously been diagnosed, because it did not cause noticeable developmental challenges, even though they had only a small percentage of the brain of typical individuals (Lewin 1980). This suggests that neither known exposure to causes of brain damage nor anomalous brain development visible on an MRI scan indicates with certainty how a person will function cognitively. This does not mean that we should not try to prevent brain damage from lead poisoning or from phenylalanine. But we must be careful that we do not compound damage that has occurred by making gross generalizations about a child's ability that lead us to treat her as less able, or less able to become able, than she is, thereby turning our assumptions into reality.

Third, some disability categories that are considered to be organic—implying that there is a physiologically identifiable organic condition that is the cause of or is reliably associated with the presence of intellectual impairment—are categories in which there is no known etiology and in which intellectual skills (for example, reasoning and abstract thinking) may not be among the developmental challenges faced by the individual placed in the category. Cerebral palsy, for example, does not have a clear etiology. The attribution of cerebral palsy indicates only that certain physical traits, like ataxia and spasticity, have been observed. A current reference article for pediatricians states that two-thirds of people with cerebral palsy experience intellectual impairment (National Institute of Neurological Disorders and Stroke 2002), a claim that is presumably based on intelligence test results. And it has typically been assumed that inability to speak, a symptom displayed by some people with cerebral palsy, is an indicator of intellectual impairment. Yet some people with cerebral palsy who cannot speak have demonstrated, when given access to an alternative method of communication, that their challenges do not include struggles with intellectual skills. We have a history of confusing physical challenges with intellectual challenges. For example, Anne McDonald, an Australian woman who has cerebral palsy and cannot speak, lived in an institution until she was eighteen years old. Based on an intelligence test administered when she was three years old, she was labeled as severely mentally retarded. When she was provided with access to a means of communication via typing with one finger, she successfully sued the state to regain her own guardianship and went on to graduate from college and become an international advocate for disability rights. In a newspaper piece McDonald observes that she has the body of a three-month-old—she cannot walk, talk, or feed herself—and that led doctors, psychologists, and institution staff to perceive her as having the mind of a baby as well (McDonald 2007).

Similar misattributions of lack of intellectual skills occur in the cases of people labeled with autism who cannot speak (autism is another disability label that is not based on a known etiology but rather is attributed when people have a collection of "symptoms"). Nick Pentzell (2003, 2004), Sue Rubin (2003, 2004), Amanda Baggs (2007), Lucy Blackman (2001), Jenn Seybert (2003), Sharissa Joy Kochmeister (2003), and Jamie Burke (2003) are among a number of people labeled with autism who were considered to be "severely retarded" until they obtained access to typing.

Currently, we decide if a person with autism or a person with cerebral palsy or a person with lead poisoning or a person with phenylketonuria or a person with Down syndrome is intellectually impaired and the "extent" of his impairment by administering an intelligence test. But "intelligence" is not an objective quality: it is not an attribute that can be verified independently of the use of intelligence tests, with the result that the tests are defining what they supposedly are discovering. As Edmund Boring, a Harvard psychologist and psychometrician, noted (seemingly without recognizing that the circularity of his claim undermined the objective grounding of intelligence testing): "Intelligence as a measurable capacity must at the start be defined as the capacity to do well in an intelligence test. Intelligence is what the tests test" (Mensh and Mensh 1991, 47).

Furthermore, the original Stanford-Binet intelligence test was constructed through a process in which questions were included in or excluded from the test based on how well the performance of sample test takers on those questions correlated with previous beliefs about how those individuals would perform. As Richard Lewontin observed, "In order for the original Stanford-Binet to have won credibility as an *intelligence* test, it necessarily had to order children in conformity with the *a priori* judgment of psychologists and teachers about what they thought intelligence consisted of. No one will use an 'intelligence' test that gives highest marks to those children everyone 'knows' to be stupid" (Mensh and Mensh 1991, 65)

As I have already discussed, however, we have a history of presuming that people with the bodies and speech capacities of three-month-olds, in Anne McDonald's words, also necessarily have the intellectual skills of three-month-olds, but this is incorrect. And as I will discuss in the next section, Henry Herbert Goddard, Lewis Terman, and other developers of intelligence testing shared the widespread presumption that women, black and other nonwhite men, and people living in poverty were intellectually inferior to elite white males. A test for which there is no other means of validation other than its conformity to prior assumptions is not an objectively valid tool of measurement. Furthermore, intelligence tests have always been constructed so that the scores in the sample population used to validate the test conform to a bell-shaped curve, based on the theory that the frequency distribution of real characteristics always takes this form, although this has been shown to be the case only under certain circumstances (Mensh and Mensh 1991, 75–76).

Current intelligence tests are validated using four criteria: *face validity, concurrent validity, predictive validity*, and *construct validity*. None of these renders current tests any more objective than the originals. *Face validity* means that the test must appear to do what it claims to do, namely, consistently pick out as having or lacking in intelligence those subjects who seem to have or lack intelligence, but validation under this criterion simply maintains the original flaw of circularity (proving what is already assumed) that undermined the objectivity of intelligence tests from the beginning. *Concurrent validity* means that the test results correlate with other tests of its kind: by this criterion, a newer test is validated by assuming the validity of at least one of its predecessors, which does not ensure the objectivity of newer tests if we know that earlier tests all lacked an objective basis, as argued above. *Construct validity* means that there is a high correlation between overall scores on the test and each of its subtests and between overall scores on the test and scores on individual items. But high correlation within the test begs the question of what the test is actually measuring. *Predictive validity* means that performance on the intelligence test predicts the scholastic performance of the individuals tested. This might seem at first glance to be the most objective of the four criteria, but it does not hold up either. The measure of scholastic performance used in predictive validity checks for intelligence tests is based on standardized scholastic achievement tests. As Judah Schwartz has argued, "Group achievement tests [scholastic achievement tests] and group ability tests [intelligence tests] are sufficiently similar that without labels, one has difficulty telling which is which," which renders scholastic achievement tests useless for objectively validating the results of intelligence tests (Mensh and Mensh 1991, 62–64).

We can assess people for performance on specific tasks, but all we can learn for sure by doing so is whether or not they can perform particular operations in the exact way that it is demanded by the test at the time they took the test. And we should assess how well people perform specific tasks, so that we can identify specific skill areas in which they need assistance to improve their cognitive development (keeping in mind, of course, that difficulty with a particular task might indicate difficulty with peripheral skills, such as motor skills, rather than with the cognitive skill supposedly being tested for) (McClennen 1991, 48–49). But we cannot legitimately infer a more general conclusion about the overall intelligence or intelligence potential of people to whom we administer tests, and to do so is to bring in judgment, as much in so-called organic cases as in so-called judgment cases.

Thus, the claim that there are two contemporary problems involving race and cognitive disability—one in which black children are disproportionately "erroneously labeled" as intellectually impaired and a separate one in which black children who are "really" intellectually impaired do not receive the services they are due—is based on erroneous beliefs about the measurability of intellect. Once we set aside our flawed assumptions about intellect, we can see that the two problems involving race and cognitive disability are actually differing manifestations of a single problem. That problem is that the concept of intellect that we continue to employ in the United States was constructed by white elites to provide a scientific justification for racism (and classism and sexism).

Measuring Intellect as a Racialized Project

To understand the deep entanglement of the constructions of race and intellect in the modern period, we must begin by examining how the idea of scientifically measuring intellect developed. The modern notion of race developed from the early 1600s through the 1800s, as differences in human appearance began to be understood in terms of anthropology and natural science rather than religion. As a crucial part of this project, eighteenth- and early nineteenth-century European and American scientists undertook research designed to prove white intellectual superiority. For example, Dutch anatomist Petrus Camper (1722–1789) attempted to analyze racial differences in intelligence by measuring and comparing human and animal skulls. He argued that African skull measurements were closer to those of apes than were Caucasian skull measurements (Graves 2001, 40–41). In the 1840s, Samuel Morton, a Philadelphia physician, assessed the cranial volume of different races by the amount of birdseed or lead shot that different skulls could hold. He concluded that African skulls held less than Caucasian skulls and hence that black people were intellectually inferior to white people (Graves 2001, 45–46).

During the same time that Morton was measuring skulls, however, the rationale behind research into intelligence and race began to shift. The aim of research up to and including Morton's was to establish scientifically that nonwhite races were intellectually inferior to the white race. The primary question was, Is the white race intellectually superior? The accuracy of the methods used to measure intelligence—by reference to skull size, for example—was not in question. The goal of the new research (called "psychometrics") was to find the most accurate method for measuring intelligence. This research began with the assumption of the intellectual superiority of the white race. The truth of this assumption was the basis for evaluating different approaches to measuring intelligence. For example, when Paul Broca began experimenting in the mid-1840s he reasoned as follows: White people are more intelligent than black people. Therefore, to determine if brain size is an accurate measure of intelligence, one must evaluate how white subjects and black subjects compare using this method of measurement. If black people turn out to have larger brains, this must not be an accurate measure of intelligence, because if it were, then black people must be more intelligent than white people. Because we know that black people are not more intelligent than white people, this shows that the measurement technique is inaccurate (Gould 1981, 84–85). Another example is found in the work of Robert Chambers, who in 1844 proposed a recapitulation theory of human development, arguing, "Our brain goes through the various stages of a fish's, a reptile's and a mammifier's brain, and finally becomes human. There is more than this, for after completing the animal transformation, it passes through the characters in which it appears, in the Negro, Malay, American, and Mongolian nations and finally is Caucasian" (Kliewer and Fitzgerald 2001, 460).

Research into how to measure intelligence required defining intelligence and intellectual deficit. Thus, beginning in the mid-nineteenth century, research into both normal and defective brain development flourished. For example, J. Langdon Down, whose name is still invoked in the classification "Down syndrome," based his understanding of intellectual deficiency on theories like Chambers's. Expounding upon his original 1866 publication, "Ethnic Classification of Idiots," Down wrote: "I was struck by the remarkable resemblance of feeble-minded children to the various ethnic types of the human family." He proceeded to discuss white feebleminded children who "from some deteriorating influence" had been "removed into another ethnic type" and therefore resembled so-called Negro, Malay, North American Indian, or Mongolian people (Down 1990, 4–6). What is striking here is that the initial identification of white children with Down syndrome—a cause of "organic" cognitive impairment—was understood in terms of racial deteriorization. And it is worth keeping in mind, when I discuss ways in which black Americans with developmental challenges experience discrimination in provision of support services, that Down syndrome in black children was not of interest to J. Langdon Down: his concern was with white children who had experienced racial deteriorization. Given his definition, it was not possible for a black child to have Down syndrome, as it was not possible for a black child to deteriorate racially: there was no lower rung on the racial ladder.

The thoroughgoing equation of cognitive deficit with nonwhiteness continued in the early twentieth century in the theories of intelligence put forward by Henry Herbert Goddard and Lewis Terman, the designers of the first American versions of the IQ test. Defending tests of invention and tests of mathematical abilities as useful indicators of general intelligence, Terman argued that "we have only to compare the negro with the Eskimo or Indian, and the Australian native with the Anglo-Saxon, to be struck by an apparent kinship between general intellectual and inventive ability," and "ethnology shows that racial progress has been closely paralleled by development of the ability to deal with mathematical concepts and relations" (Gould 1981, 175).

In 1917, Robert Yerkes, Harvard psychology professor and president of the American Psychological Association, received approval from the U.S. military to test draftees. Working with a team including Terman and Goddard, Yerkes developed IQ-type tests that were administered to 1.75 million soldiers. In 1921, the National Academy of Sciences published a statistical analysis, edited by Yerkes, of scores from 160,000 of the tests. According to this analysis, the average white American draftee had a mental age of thirteen years. Eighty-nine percent of black draftees, most of the draftees who were recent immigrants from southern and eastern Europe, and 37 percent of the white American draftees were categorized as "morons" (with a mental age of between eight and twelve years) based on the tests (Mensh and Mensh 1991, 31).

Yerkes had covered up data, however. A review of the entire set of scores by psychologist Ashley Montagu in 1945 revealed that black recruits from four Northern states performed better, on average, than white recruits from nine Southern ones, and that black recruits from Ohio had scored better on average than had white recruits from nine Northern states (Montagu 1945).

Research into race and intellect that presupposes that intellect is in fact measurable and that there may in fact be a link between race and intellect—which presupposes an essentialist understanding of race—continues. *The Bell Curve*, by Charles Murray and Harvard professor Richard Herrnstein, and J. Phillipe Rushton's *Race, Evolution, and Behavior*, both published in 1994, are two examples of this work. The problem with these and similar works goes beyond the conclusions drawn by the researchers: it lies in the motivation behind the research itself. As long as we persist in thinking useful information might come from trying to measure "intelligence," and as long as we think that useful information might come from comparing "intelligence measurements" from members of different races, we have not escaped from the entanglement of race and intellect in which the construction of intellect is rooted.

The Impact of the Social Construction of Race and Intellect in the Lives of Black Americans Labeled with Cognitive Disability

A particular source of ongoing concern for those who struggle against antiblack oppression in the United States has been the disproportionate placement of black children into the judgment categories of "educable mental impairment" and "emotional impairment." In addition to the stigma of bearing a label of intellectual impairment, these children are disproportionately relegated to separate special education classrooms. In supposedly racially desegregated schools, this practice re-creates segregation on the basis of race.

As Ferri and Connor have argued, this contemporary form of segregation based on linking blackness and cognitive disability is an extension of American educational policy from the years before the 1954 *Brown* decision. From its inception in the late 1800s, public education in the United States has been based on the premise of keeping students who are perceived as less educable or not educable separate from "normal" students. And because the white understanding of blackness as essentially intellectually inferior was reinforced from the same period through the emergence of the "science" of intelligence testing, to be black was by definition to require "special education." Ellwood Patterson Cubberley—dean of the School of Education at Stanford at the time of his retirement in 1933 and a founding figure in the field of education administration—placed literature on "Negro education" in the same category as literature on the education of blind, deaf, "crippled," and "feebleminded" children (Tyack 1993, "Race" section).

Impressive efforts by Southern black civic leaders to create a system of quality public education for black students following the Civil War came to an end with the demise of Reconstruction (Stubblefield 2005, 48; Tyack 1993, "Race" section and note 43). Despite the ongoing protest of black scholars and civic leaders such as W. E. B. DuBois and Anna Julia Cooper, public education for black children throughout the nation remained separate, underfunded, of inferior quality, and inconsistent throughout the first half of the twentieth century. White politicians and educators apparently took this state of affairs to be so acceptable that they included almost no discussion of it in debates or scholarship about school reform (Tyack 1993, "Race" section).

The developments in public education that institutionalized inferior, segregated schooling for nonwhite children also institutionalized inferior, segregated special education classes for white children labeled as "feeble-minded" (Trent 1994, 144–55). Following World War I, educators began to use intelligence testing to track white students into different academic programs (special education, vocational, academic). These tracks corresponded with class background, keeping students from working-class backgrounds out of academically oriented education. After 1954, the use of tracking based on intelligence tests also became a means to continue racial segregation within supposedly desegregated schools. U.S. Circuit Court Judge Skelly Wright ruled against this practice in *Hobson v. Hansen*, a suit brought against the Washington, D.C., school system in 1967. But the practice continues de facto under the guise of providing special education for children labeled as being in the judgment categories, who continue to be disproportionately black (Mensh and Mensh 1991, 56–59; Ferri and Connor 2006, 25; Losen and Orfield 2002; Harry and Klingner 2005).

The association between blackness and failure in school settings continues even in contexts in which the focus is on intelligence understood as the result of environment ("nurture") rather than heredity ("nature"). For example, the Moynihan Report in 1965 suggested that the continued lack of success of black students at the time (as based on standardized test measurements) was the result of past social inequality that had rendered black people educationally disadvantaged (which meant that the quality of education being provided to black students at the time of the report was not to blame). The Coleman Report a year later linked poor school performance by black students (again measured by standardized test scores) to educationally deprived ("culturally deprived") family environments (Mensh and Mensh 1991, 93–94). Furthermore, cultural and accumulated environmental deficit models, developed during the 1960s, continue to be a mainstay of contemporary educational policy, now grounding the perception of the "at-risk" child. These approaches locate the cause of black children's struggles in school within the child and the child's family, rather than in the failure of schools to provide appropriate learning experiences for all children (Pearl 1997; Valencia and Solórzano 1997).

As Harry and Klingner argue, the disproportionate labeling of black students and their subsequent placement in special education classrooms is not, in general, a simple matter of overt racism on the part of teachers, psychologists, and school administrators. Rather, it is the result of the history I have just summarized, in which notions of intelligence and how to measure it that were designed to support racist beliefs about black inferiority became institutionalized in school policy in ways that have warped our entire educational system. Intellectual disability labels and typical special education programs, Harry and Klingner demonstrate, do not help students who are struggling to improve their skills. Rather, they provide a means of shifting the blame for failure in school to something perceived as inherently wrong with the child, away from the failure of schools to provide appropriate environments and instruction.

The argument Harry and Klingner put forward can only be strengthened by challenging the distinction that they themselves accept between the judgment and organic categories. Although black children are not overrepresented in the organic categories of "trainable" and "severe" mental impairment, there is cause for concern about the quality of services that black students in all special education categories receive in comparison with white students. In a study of special education students in Michigan during the 1999–2000 school year, the researchers found that only 22 to 24 percent of all nonwhite special education students were in inclusive education placements (defined as less than 21 percent of the school day spent outside the regular classroom) rather than in segregated special education classrooms, compared with 37 to 39 percent of their white counterparts (LeRoy and Kulik 2001). Data from the U.S. Department of Education from 2002 showed that nationwide 37 percent of all black students labeled with disabilities were in inclusive settings, compared with 55 percent of all white students labeled with disabilities (Fierros and Conroy 2002, 45). Federal law since 1997 mandates inclusive education, acknowledging that "over 20 years of research and experience has demonstrated that the education of children with disabilities can be made more effective by ... providing appropriate special education and related services and aids and supports in the regular classroom to such children" (Individuals with Disabilities Education Act). A growing body of research indicates that inclusive education correlates with gains in development and positive postschool outcomes for students with significant developmental challenges and increased levels of employment for youth with milder developmental challenges (Leroy and Kulik 2001, 3–4).

Furthermore, studies have shown that black Americans either with Down syndrome or labeled with severe mental retardation fare worse in various ways than their white counterparts. While shortened life expectancy is an outcome of Down syndrome, black Americans with Down syndrome die significantly younger, on average, than white Americans with Down syndrome. In one study (Yang et al. 2002), researchers documented the average age of mortality for people with Down syndrome from 1983 to 1997 by studying U.S. death certificates. They examined the death certificates of 17,897 people listed as having Down syndrome (87 percent white, 11 percent black, 2 percent other). During these years, the average age of mortality for people with Down syndrome from all racial groups in the study increased dramatically. But in 1997, according to the Yang study, the average age of death for white people with Down syndrome was fifty, while for black people with Down syndrome it was only twenty-two.

In another study (Day et al. 2005) tracking mortality rates during approximately the same time period (between 1988 and 1999) among 14,781 people with Down syndrome in California who were receiving services from that state's Department of Developmental Services, the average life expectancy for black people with Down syndrome was forty-nine years, compared with fifty-five years for their white counterparts. This 9 percent earlier mortality rate for black people with Down syndrome mirrors the general difference between white and black American mortality rates (Day et al. 2005, 174). The differences between the two studies suggest that black people with Down syndrome in the Day study, who were all receiving state services, lived significantly longer on average than black people with Down syndrome in general.

Similarly, a study on the quality of state developmental disability services provided for black adults compared to their white counterparts showed no difference in outcomes of service provision, but the authors cite evidence that black people labeled with developmental disabilities have less access to those services (Stancliffe and Lakin 2006, 180).

In other research, however, black adults labeled as severely mentally impaired were less likely than their white counterparts to achieve steady employment, even when they received comparable vocational rehabilitation (VR) services (Moore et al. 2002). This study found that out of 188 consumers of VR services, 126 of whom (67 percent) were white and 62 of whom (33 percent) were black, 87 achieved employment for 90 days or more, of whom 68 (78.2 percent) were white, while 19 (21.8 percent) were black.

In addition, another study demonstrated that racial bias (not necessarily conscious) influenced VR counselors' perceptions. Two groups of counselors were given otherwise identical cases, but for one group the client was identified as black, while for the other group the client was identified as white. The counselors evaluating the case they believed to be a black person rated the client as having a lesser chance of achieving employment success (Rosenthal 2004).

These studies are too few and too small in scope to support strong general conclusions. But they do suggest that, as a society, we need to pay closer attention to ensure that black adults labeled with developmental disabilities are actually accessing available support services and that ongoing racism is not undermining the quality of service they receive.

Finally, lead poisoning is a known cause of developmental delays, and black children in the United States are disproportionately likely to suffer from exposure to lead, because they are disproportionately likely to live in old and run-down housing with lead pipes and peeling lead paint. According to a Centers for Disease Control study from 2001, out of nearly 2.5 million children tested nationwide, 74,887 had confirmed elevated levels of lead in their blood. Race was only recorded for 63.6 percent of these children. Of those whose race was recorded, 17 percent were non-Hispanic white, 16 percent were Hispanic, and 7 percent were other races, while 60 percent were non-Hispanic black (Centers for Disease Control 2003). Exposure to toxic waste is another suspected cause of developmental delays (both prenatally and postnatally), and black Americans are disproportionately likely to be exposed. More than fifteen million of the twenty-five million black residents of the United States live in communities with uncontrolled toxic waste sites. The nation's largest hazardous waste landfill, which houses toxic waste from forty-five states, is located in Emelle, Alabama, with a population that is 79.9 percent black. The greatest concentration of hazardous waste sites in the United States is in the South Side of Chicago, the population of which is predominantly black and Hispanic. In Houston, Texas, six out of eight municipal incinerators and all five city landfills are located in primarily black neighborhoods (Warren 2000, 13).

These and similar health problems, disproportionately experienced by black Americans as the result of antiblack oppression, make it disproportionately more likely that black children will struggle in school, which feeds them into the loop of not getting the support they need, either as children or as adults. This is the unsurprising outcome of a social system that embraces a concept of measurable intellect that was developed specifically to justify the segregation and exclusion of nonwhite people. Intellectual labeling in the United States was developed to oppress people, not to help people. Because it does not yield useful information about what people need when they are struggling in school and in life, it simply justifies and reinforces practices like segregated special education that do not meet the needs of people who are struggling, while leaving unchallenged the oppressive circumstances which cause people to struggle, and which intellectual labeling was constructed to rationalize.

To attack this injustice in its totality, we must move beyond labeling children who struggle in school as intellectually impaired on the basis of intelligence tests. Rather, we can assess what kinds of support children need by observing—through ongoing evaluation of their development in natural contexts of home and school—what they learn easily and in which areas they struggle. In a genuinely inclusive school, educational strategies like cooperative and experiential learning enable groups of children with differing skills to learn from and with each other, using a mix of resources (such as printed text, recorded text, pictures, field trips) and projects (written assignments, visual or tactile displays, presentations) that meet the individual learning needs of each participant. Teachers model social skills and educational approaches, such as how to communicate with a student using a communication board, how to interpret what might have caused a student to become upset (rather than attaching blame), and how to support a student. Accommodations for students' disabilities are introduced only as necessary and are accomplished naturally and unobtrusively to minimize the identification of students with disabilities as significantly different from other students. Teachers create opportunities for students with disabilities, like other students, to fill leadership roles in their classes and schools (for example, a student who is not ready to learn to alphabetize can lead an alphabetization game for other students by selecting the words they will put in order). The school evaluates programs for their effectiveness in integrating students with differing skills, and educators revise instructional approaches on the basis of these evaluations. Consulting teachers assist in observing students in their classrooms and in developing curricula and suggestions on troublesome situations. The educational community sets high expectations for all students, based on knowledge of their skills and school programs. Finally, the school uses a common language for describing students, curriculum content, classes, teachers, and other aspects of schooling, abandoning the medical and psychological language that permeates the field of special education (Biklen 1992, 177–78). Schools that follow these principles are better schools for all their students and represent a vast improvement over the low quality of education typically found in impoverished, urban school districts that serve mostly black and Hispanic populations.

In *The Miner's Canary: Enlisting Race, Resisting Power, Transforming Democracy*, Lani Guinier and Gerald Torres (2002) use the miner's canary—the bird whose death from poison gas warns miners that they must evacuate—as a metaphor for impoverished nonwhite Americans. These Americans, according to Guinier and Torres, are the most vulnerable members of our society, and when they fare poorly—when they suffer from inadequate education, inadequate employment, and inadequate health care—we should recognize that as a sign that our society is failing. To Guinier and Torres's account, I add *all* Americans with disabilities, regardless of race. But furthermore, nonwhite Americans with disabilities are the canary's canary: the most vulnerable of the vulnerable, the people whom we push so far to the margins of our society that most of us do not even notice when they fall off the edge. In a truly equitable and just society, we would all hold on to each other, and no one would fall.

References

Baggs, Amanda. 2007 "In My Language." (Video.) January 14. http://
www.youtube.com/watch?v = JnylM1hI2jc (last accessed March 12,
2009). See also "Ballastexistenz" (blog), http://ballastexistenz.autistics.
org/(last accessed March 12, 2009).
Bérubé, Michael. 1996. *Life as We Know It: A Father, a Family, and an
Exceptional Child.* New York: Random House.
Biklen, Douglas. 1992. *Schooling Without Labels.* Philadelphia: Temple
University Press.
Blackman, Lucy. 2001. *Lucy's Story: Autism and Other Adventures.*
London: Jessica Kingsley.
Bogdan, Robert, and Steven Taylor. 1982. *Inside Out: The Social
Meaning of Mental Retardation.* Toronto: University of Toronto Press.
Burke, Jamie. 2003. "Life's a Beach." In *Sharing Our Wisdom*, edited by
Gail Gillingham and Sandra McClennen, 109–12. Durham, N.H.:
Autism National Committee. Available from http://www.iodbookstore.
org/categories/Autism-National-Committee/(last accessed July 6, 2009).
Centers for Disease Control. 2003. *Surveillance for Elevated Blood
Lead Levels Among Children—United States, 1997–2001. MMWR*
[Morbidity and Mortality Weekly Reports] 52 (SS-10) (September
12): 1–21.
Chandler-Olcott, Kelly. 2003. "Seeing All Students as Literate." In
Access to Academics for ALL Students, edited by Paula Kluth, Diana
M. Straut, and Douglas P. Biklen, 69–84. Mahwah, N.J.: Lawrence
Erlbaum Associates.
Day, Stephen M., et al. 2005. "Mortality and Causes of Death in Persons
with Down Syndrome in California." *Developmental Medicine and
Child Neurology* 47:171–76.
Down, J. Langdon. 1990 (1887). *On Some of the Mental Affections of
Childhood and Youth.* London: MacKeith Press (Blackwell Scientific
Publications).
Ferri, Beth, and David Connor. 2006. *Reading Resistance: Discourses of
Exclusion in Desegregation and Inclusion Debates.* New York: Peter Lang.
Fierros, Edward Garcia, and James Conroy. 2002. "Double Jeopardy: An
Exploration of Restrictiveness and Race in Special Education." In
Racial Inequity in Special Education, edited by Daniel Losen and Gary
Orfield, 39–79. Cambridge, Mass.: Harvard Education Press.
Gliedman, John, and William Roth. 1980. *The Unexpected Minority:
Handicapped Children in America.* New York: Harcourt Brace Jovanovich.
Gould, Stephen Jay. 1981. *The Mismeasure of Man.* New York: W. W.
Norton.
Graves, Joseph L., Jr. 2001. *The Emperor's New Clothes: Biological
Theories of Race at the Millennium.* New Brunswick, N.J.: Rutgers
University Press.

Guinier, Lani, and Gerald Torres. 2002. *The Miner's Canary: Enlisting Race, Resisting Power, Transforming Democracy.* Cambridge, Mass.: Harvard University Press.

Harry, Beth, and Janette Klingner. 2005. *Why Are So Many Minority Students in Special Education?* New York: Teachers College Press.

Kingsley, Jason, and Mitchell Levitz. 1994. *Count Us In: Growing Up with Down Syndrome.* New York: Harcourt Brace.

Kliewer, Christopher. 2008. *Seeing All Kids as Readers.* Baltimore: Paul H. Brookes.

Kliewer, Christopher, and Linda May Fitzgerald. 2001. "Disability, Schooling, and the Artifacts of Colonialism." *Teachers College Record* 103, no. 3:450–70.

Kochmeister, Sharisa Joy. 2003. "To Have a Voice." In *Sharing Our Wisdom*, edited by Gail Gillingham and Sandra McClennen, 117–32. Durham, N.H.: Autism National Committee. Available from http://www.iodbookstore.org/categories/Autism-National-Committee/ (last accessed July 6, 2009).

LeRoy, Barbara, and Noel Kulik. 2001. "The Demography of Inclusive Education in Michigan: State and Local District Findings." Detroit: Developmental Disabilities Institute, Wayne State University. Available from http://ddi.wayne.edu/publications.php (last accessed July 6, 2009).

Lewin, Roger. 1980. "Is Your Brain Really Necessary?" *Science* 210, no. 12 (December): 1232–34.

Losen, Daniel, and Gary Orfield, eds. 2002. *Racial Inequity in Special Education.* Cambridge, Mass.: Harvard Education Press.

Lovett, Herbert. 1996. *Learning to Listen.* Baltimore: Paul H. Brookes.

McClennen, Sandra. 1991. *Cognitive Skills for Community Living.* Austin: Pro-Ed.

McDonald, Anne. 2007. "The Other Story from a Pillow Angel." *Seattle Post-Intelligencer* (June 15). Available at http://seattlepi.nwsource.com/opinion/319702_noangel17.html (last accessed March 12, 2009).

Mensh, Elaine, and Harry Mensh. 1991. *The IQ Mythology.* Carbondale: Southern Illinois University Press.

Montagu, M. F. Ashley. 1945. "Intelligence of Northern Negroes and Southern Whites in the First World War." *American Journal of Psychology* 58, (April): 161–88.

Moore, Corey, et al. 2002. "VR [vocational rehabilitation] Services for Persons with Severe/Profound Mental Retardation: Does Race Matter?" *Rehabilitation Counseling Bulletin* 45, no. 3:162–67.

National Institute of Neurological Disorders and Stroke. 2008. "Cerebral Palsy: Hope Through Research." Available at http://www.ninds.nih.gov/disorders/cerebral_palsy/detail_cerebral_palsy.htm (last accessed March 12, 2009).

Pearl, Arthur. 1997. "Cultural and Accumulated Environmental Deficit Models." In *The Evolution of Deficit Thinking*, edited by Richard Valencia, 132–59. London: Falmer Press.

Pentzell, Nick. 2003. "Three Presentations." In *Sharing Our Wisdom*, edited by Gail Gillingham and Sandra McClennen, 44–51. Durham, N.H.: Autism National Committee. Available from http://www.iodbookstore.org/categories/Autism-National-Committee/ (last accessed July 6, 2009).

———. 2004. "Fools of God." *The Other Side* 40, no. 2:36–38.

Rapley, Mark. 2004. *The Social Construction of Intellectual Disability*. Cambridge: Cambridge University Press.

Rosenthal, David. 2004. "The Effects of Client Race on Clinical Judgment of Practicing Vocational Rehabilitation Counselors." *Rehabilitation Counseling Bulletin* 47:131–41.

Rubin, Sue. 2003. "FC: The Key to Success." In *Sharing Our Wisdom*, edited by Gail Gillingham and Sandra McClennen, 133–42. Durham, N.H.: Autism National Committee. Available from http://www.iodbookstore.org/categories/Autism-National-Committee/ (last accessed July 6, 2009).

———. 2004. "Autism Is a World." (DVD.) CNN Productions and State of Art, Inc. Available from http://www.iodbookstore.org/categories/Autism-National-Committee/ (last accessed July 6, 2009).

Sarason, Seymour, and John Doris. 1979. *Educational Handicap, Public Policy, and Social History*. New York: Free Press.

Seybert, Jenn. 2003. "Inclusion ... Finally!". In *Sharing Our Wisdom*, edited by Gail Gillingham and Sandra McClennen, 101–8. Durham, N.H.: Autism National Committee. Available from http://www.iodbookstore.org/categories/Autism-National-Committee/ (last accessed July 6, 2009).

Stancliffe, Roger J., and K. Charlie Lakin. 2006. "Minority Status, Consumer Outcomes, and Service Inputs in Four States." *Mental Retardation* 44, no. 3:165–83.

Stubblefield, Anna. 2005. *Ethics Along the Color Line*. Ithaca: Cornell University Press.

———. 2007. "'Beyond the Pale': Tainted Whiteness, Cognitive Disability, and Eugenic Sterilization." *Hypatia* 22, no. 2:162–81.

Trent, James. 1994. *Inventing the Feeble Mind*. Berkeley: University of California Press.

Tyack, David. 1993. "Constructing Difference: Historical Reflections on Schooling and Social Diversity." *Teachers College Record* 95, no. 1; online article number: 01614681.

Valencia, Richard, and Daniel Solórzano. 1997. "Contemporary Deficit Thinking." In *The Evolution of Deficit Thinking*, edited by Richard Valencia, 160–210. London: Falmer Press.

Warren, Karen. 2000. *Ecofeminist Philosophy*. Lanham, Md.: Rowman and Littlefield.

Yang, Q., et al. 2002. "Mortality Associated with Down's [*sic*] Syndrome in the USA from 1983–1997: A Population-Based Study." *Lancet* 359, no. 9311:1019–25.

18

PHILOSOPHERS OF INTELLECTUAL DISABILITY:
A TAXONOMY

LICIA CARLSON

This chapter grows out of my preoccupation with three questions: How do philosophers talk about intellectual disability? To what end? And at what price? The breadth of the chapters in this collection suggests that there can be no single, clear answer to these questions, and that it is impossible to discern a univocal philosophical voice concerning intellectual disability. There are, however, certain general tendencies that become apparent if one looks at the place of intellectual disability in philosophical discourse. There seem to be two broad approaches: direct and indirect. In some cases, the "intellectually disabled" are direct objects of philosophical inquiry that centers on a variety of ethical and bioethical questions regarding their moral status, personhood, and treatment. Yet the "intellectually disabled" are also addressed indirectly, appearing as an excluded group, a passing thought experiment, or serving simply to bolster the case for another group of individuals (Carlson forthcoming).

Rather than simply presenting various examples of these as a way of addressing my opening questions, I would like to engage in a reversal of sorts, whereby the philosopher, rather than the "intellectually disabled," becomes the object of study. In asking, "Who is the philosopher of intellectual disability?" I would like to raise critical questions regarding the multiple positions that philosophers can and do occupy in relation to intellectual disability. To do so, I will draw upon both historical and contemporary figures, and ask: What parallels can be drawn between these roles and the philosopher of intellectual disability? And what can these figures reveal to us about our own philosophical projects regarding intellectual disability?

The Expert or Gatekeeper

In his history of the modern prison, Michel Foucault writes: "The penitentiary technique and the delinquent are in a sense twin brothers. . . . They appeared together, the one extending from the other, as a technological ensemble that forms and fragments the object to which it applies its instruments" (1979, 255). Similarly, the American institutions for the "feebleminded" (a term that came to encompass all grades of intellectual disability, including "idiots," "imbeciles," and "morons") that appeared in the mid- to late nineteenth century carved out a new professional space. The various instruments that were applied to the individuals within these facilities (called schools or asylums) generated new typologies and constituted a new class of "experts" in the field. As one examines the many taxonomies of feeblemindedness, one finds a series of internal tensions that speak to the complexity and the contestations that surround this group of human beings: qualitative and quantitative portraits of feeblemindedness; descriptions of curable/educable cases and custodial/incurable cases; and competing philosophies of treatment and institutional design that echoed these designations. And amid this plethora of classificatory systems and categories, we find complex power dynamics between expert and inmate, and between professionals themselves. In this sense, the broad category of feeblemindedness was both internally and externally heterogeneous: internally, it contained numerous subcategories based on various criteria; externally, it was defined as an object of knowledge by multiple disciplines whose representatives often vied for the legitimacy of their particular definition or theory (Trent 1995; Carlson forthcoming, chap. 1).

In defining and treating these various types of individuals, the experts also constructed certain prototypical cases that became representative of the group as a whole. These prototypes shifted: at one time, the educable case was emphasized so as to get funding for new "schools" for the feebleminded; with the rise of the IQ test and the eugenics movement, concern with "invisible" cases of feeblemindedness led to the emergence of a new prototype: the "moron" (perceived as most dangerous because of his or her moral degeneracy and ability to "pass" as normal and reproduce). This points to another feature of this broad category: its instability and the permeability of its boundaries. The various definitions of feeblemindedness were profoundly affected by changing assumptions about heredity, race, morality, sexual deviance, and degeneracy (Carlson forthcoming, chaps. 2–3; Stubblefield 2009).

But what does this complex history have to do with the ways in which philosophers speak about intellectual disability? How can these historical examples be instructive in a contemporary philosophical context? Intellectual disability as a category continues to be internally and externally heterogeneous, and there is no reason to think that it is any less complex today than it was in the past. In fact, in the wake of genetic advances and a robust disability rights and advocacy movement, one could argue that it is even more so. As philosophers we too are experts of a sort. We draw up classificatory systems around the "intellectually disabled" and devise mechanisms to define and differentiate forms of intellectual disability. In ethical arguments, the concern may be less with the specifics of the conditions and more with how we draw our moral boundaries. Thus, as many of the chapters in this collection reveal, philosophers ask: Are the "severely intellectually disabled" persons? Are they owed anything in terms of respect, justice? Can we distinguish them from animals, morally speaking? As we engage in our labor of developing what Hans Reinders (2008) has referred to as our "moral taxonomies," however, a number of questions arise: To what extent do philosophical discussions reflect this complexity? What definitions of intellectual disability do philosophers provide? Are they explicit, or simply assumed to be self-evident? How do philosophers and bioethicists perpetuate certain prototypes of intellectual disability? (For example, philosophical discussions seem far more often to center on the most severe cases.) And how does this discourse shape the ways of speaking and thinking about intellectual disability? While one can imagine the potentially liberatory and transformative effects that certain philosophical views might have, it is equally important to seriously consider how philosophical discourse can also perpetuate certain forms of oppression.

Iris Marion Young defines marginalization as one face of oppression (1990, chap. 5). The institutions for the "feebleminded" in many ways contributed to the marginalization of persons with intellectual disabilities, insofar as they removed them from communities and placed them at their margins. And one could say that within philosophy, too, the "intellectually disabled" have occupied a marginal place, both insofar as there is relatively little said about them and insofar as what *is* said often places them at the far edges of our moral boundaries. Yet these forms of literal and conceptual marginalization can be accompanied by another form of oppression—exploitation—which, in Young's words, "occurs through a steady process of the transfer of the results of the labor of one social group to benefit another" (1990, 49). Within the institutions themselves, for example, there were many "feebleminded women" who were defined as such and institutionalized because they had more than one illegitimate child (violating dominant Victorian sexual norms). Once marginalized in society and safely confined within the institution, however, they served as an unpaid maternal labor force to care for the more severe cases, with their feminine virtues presumably intact (Carlson 2003; forthcoming, chap. 2). This is but one of many examples of exploitation in the history of intellectual disability (Trent 1995). But is there such a thing as conceptual exploitation? And what might that mean in a philosophical context?

Consider the following example. It is quite common to find references to intellectual disability in discussions of the moral status of animals, specifically in critiques of speciesism (understood as an arbitrary and unjustified preference for members of our own species). Peter Singer's discussion in this collection offers a good example of such arguments, whereby the "severely intellectually disabled" are invoked in large part to challenge what Singer views as the commonplace assumption that human lives of any kind are more valuable than animal lives, simply by virtue of being *human* (Singer 2009). While it is clear why the connection is drawn between the moral status of nonhuman animals and the "intellectually disabled" when cognitive ability, rather than species membership, is used as a moral yardstick, my concern is that the "intellectually disabled" are performing a kind of philosophical labor in the service of enhancing our concern for nonhuman animals, without any benefit in return (Carlson forthcoming). In fact, in some cases philosophers conclude that individuals with severe intellectual disabilities should be accorded a moral status on a par with or even below the status of certain nonhuman animals. For example, in his book *The Ethics of Killing*, Jeff McMahan writes: "It seems that our traditional beliefs about the special sanctity of the lives of severely retarded human beings will have to yield. How much they must yield depends on how drastically we are willing to revise traditional beliefs about the permissibility of killing animals with psychological capacities comparable to those of cognitively impaired human beings. Killing animals, and allowing them to die, are morally far more serious matters than we have supposed. But allowing severely retarded human beings to die, and perhaps even killing them, are correspondingly less serious matters than we have believed" (2003, 230).

It is not my aim in this chapter to engage in a debate about the moral status of nonhuman animals or individuals with intellectual disabilities. Rather, I point to these examples to raise a number of critical questions concerning the use of intellectual disability as an example, a marginal case, in philosophical discourse. Is it necessary, for example, to use the case of intellectual disability in order to make the case against speciesism and to define the moral status of nonhuman animals? To what extent *must* discussions about intellectual disability rely upon appeals to nonhuman animals?[1] Must we view animal interests as being in conflict with the interests of the "severely intellectually disabled"? If we take seriously the potential for conceptual exploitation and the current marginalization of intellectual disability in philosophy, we must critically consider the roles that the "intellectually disabled" have been assigned to play in this discourse.

It is equally important to ask what effects our philosophical claims might have beyond our discipline. Just as the superintendents' role was to both define and treat, it is important to recognize the profound impact that philosophizing about intellectual disability (particularly in a bioethical context) can have on concrete lives. Peter Byrne writes, "The theorizing of moral philosophers may seem harmless enough were it not for the fact that such reasoning about the handicapped is reflected in

---

[1] I have argued elsewhere, along with others, that they need not. See Carlson 2007; forthcoming; Diamond 1991.

aspects of clinical practice. Indeed, the worlds of contemporary medicine and moral philosophy now interconnect, thanks to the rise of bioethics" (2000, 13). It seems, in fact, that the stakes are quite high.

Adopting the expert role also means being a gatekeeper of knowledge, determining what counts as a legitimate knowledge claim and who is granted the authority to speak about a particular subject. If we look back through the history of intellectual disability, we find many gatekeepers: the superintendents of the schools/institutions; the psychologists who implemented mental tests; the women field workers who determined someone's family pedigree and traced generations; and feminist reformists who had a hand in defining the boundaries of womanhood and motherhood (Carlson 2001; forthcoming). Yet philosophers, too, can act as gatekeepers when it comes to knowledge about disability. To illustrate this, let me begin with two examples of this role—one past and one present.

Among the fascinating features of the history of intellectual disability is the way in which gender norms have played a part in defining and treating the "feebleminded." While most superintendents of institutions were male, there were hundreds of nondisabled women who were mobilized as "field workers," whose job it was to go out and conduct interviews in order to find cases of feeblemindedness. It was thought that because they were women they were more intuitive by nature, and better suited to perform this task (Rafter 1988). What this meant, however, was that despite the fact that they were not considered experts in the way physicians and psychologists were, they were endowed with significant power to direct the lives (and in some cases determine the fate) of their "feebleminded" counterparts (Carlson 1996; forthcoming, chap. 2). In a contemporary context, we can see that genetic counselors have become the new gatekeepers of knowledge about intellectual disability. Given the fact that prenatal screening for conditions like Down syndrome is now routine (and was recently endorsed for *all* women, regardless of age), the responsibility and potential impact of the role played by genetic counselors cannot be underestimated (Rapp 2000; Patterson and Satz 2002).

So what do field workers and genetic counselors have to do with philosophers engaging intellectual disability today? The gendered nature of their roles raises interesting questions in the context of feminist bioethics and feminist disability theory. For example, what power dynamics are established between feminist philosophers and women with intellectual disabilities? When feminist philosophers speak about "women" as a group, to what extent do they include women with intellectual disabilities? Given the pernicious historical associations between women and intellectual disability more generally, to what extent do contemporary feminist theorists who address disability attempt to distance themselves from the issue of intellectual disability? Do appeals to the burdens of having a child with an intellectual disability in feminist discussions of reproductive freedom perpetuate yet another kind of conceptual exploitation? (One thinks of Margaret Sanger here, and her exhortation against perpetuating feeblemindedness as she articulated her feminist agenda: "Imperfect fruit comes from imperfect trees" (Sanger 1920, 233). We can also ask in what ways the philosopher, like the genetic counselor, performs a gatekeeping function with respect to the *kind* of knowledge claims that are put forth regarding intellectual disability, and the *ways* in which this condition is depicted. For example, is it assumed to be "objectively bad or undesirable"? Is it presented in a way that captures the complexity of this category and the realities of those who experience it?

Being a gatekeeper also means that one plays an important part in determining *which* knowledge claims are valued, accepted, and included. In a philosophical context, it is crucial to explore the mechanisms by which some perspectives are dismissed, refuted, or excluded. Not surprisingly, the most profound silence surrounds persons with intellectual disabilities themselves. While one can understand that individuals with severe intellectual disabilities may be incapable of entering into the conversation, there is a paucity of work that engages the voices of persons with mild intellectual disabilities.[2]

Compounding the problem of exclusion are assumptions regarding the lives that persons with intellectual disabilities lead. Just as the testimonies of persons with physical disabilities are often discounted when they claim to lead lives that are far richer than ones of "minimal satisfaction" and when they speak about the positive dimensions of having a disability, we can ask: To what extent does the assumption that persons with intellectual disabilities cannot lead meaningful lives underlie our philosophical discussions?[3] The normative assumption that having a condition like mental retardation is "objectively bad" can be found in even the most committed work on justice for persons with intellectual disabilities (Veatch 1986).

While it is perhaps understandable (though not necessarily justifiable) that the voices of persons with intellectual disabilities are omitted from philosophical discourse (particularly insofar as they are consistently defined as lacking the capacities that would render them "knowing subjects" in any sense), there is a more complex dynamic with respect to the voices of those who are in a close relation to persons with intellectual disabilities: parents, family members, advocates.

---

[2] For methodological discussions of how one might incorporate these perspectives, see Rioux and Bach 1994.

[3] For a discussion about the normative assumptions underlying such definitions and the dismissal of claims by persons with disabilities that they do in fact experience a high quality of life, see Wasserman, Bickenbach, and Wachbroit 2005.

Family Member or Advocate

Anyone familiar with disability history knows the profound effect that advocacy (by parents and other family members, friends, and allies) has had in shaping the disability rights movement and institutional, social, educational, and legislative reform for persons with intellectual disabilities. And in an academic context, the work of Eva Kittay, Sophia Wong, and Michael Bérubé provides powerful examples of how one can speak simultaneously in an academic and in a personal voice (Kittay 1998; 2002; 2005; Wong 2002; Bérubé 1998). However, while many would say that their position "from within" grants them a certain degree of authority to speak about intellectual disability, this is by no means a universally shared assumption. These voices are often left out of philosophical discussions of intellectual disability, and when the parents or family members *are* included they play a somewhat paradoxical role: they are not granted epistemic authority as "experts" but *are* deemed important insofar as their relationship to the intellectually disabled person actually *confers* moral status upon the disabled individual.

In some ethical discussions about intellectual disability, there is a presumption of authority on the part of the disengaged moral philosopher, and a corresponding dismissal of the authority of those who are in embodied, concrete relation to persons with intellectual disabilities. This dissonance can be seen in statements that dismiss certain attitudes toward the "intellectually disabled" as unduly sentimental and/or altogether misplaced. In defending the title of his article "Do the Mentally Retarded Have a Right Not to Be Eaten?" for instance, Jeffrie Murphy says, "Too much well-meaning sentimentality is allowed to pass for thought in discussion of the retarded, and I want to shock my way through this" (1984, 43).

What assumptions lie behind such concerns? First, these concerns erroneously assume that this unduly sentimental attitude is in fact widespread. This worry seems misplaced on two counts: in concrete terms, one need only look at the disturbing history of intellectual disability and contemporary cases of abuse to see that this is far from the case; and the repeated marginalization and dehumanization of this group of "nonpersons" in academic discourse leaves one wondering where in fact these sentimental, heartfelt but "misguided" portraits are. Second, calls to distance ourselves from any kind of sentiment, attachment, or emotion rely on the assumption that any legitimate work in ethical matters rests on the disengaged, detached subject, a point that many scholars in feminist ethics and epistemology have challenged (Carlson forthcoming, chap. 4). In fact, it is precisely in constructing the "other" position as epistemically compromised by virtue of sentiment and proximity that the normative assumptions that underlie more "objective" accounts are masked.[4] In his critique of the ways that Jonathan Glover and James Rachels invoke examples of the "severely disabled" in their moral theories, for example, Byrne exposes "an implicit, rhetorical contrast between an extant set of moral convictions which is to a large degree made up of inherited prejudices and a new, critical morality which has passed through the mill of rigorous argument" (2000, 46).

The assertion of moral authority on the part of the disengaged, unsentimental philosopher can also place those scholars who *do* have connections with persons with intellectual disabilities in a sort of double bind, whereby their perspectives can be rendered invalid or invisible. In advocating for an individual close to them, and challenging the associations between the "severely mentally retarded" and nonhuman animals, for example, their positions may be explained away by virtue of their relation to that individual and thus be rendered invalid. Yet if the requirement for participation in moral discourse is a dispassionate, disengaged "objective" stance, then the voices of those close to persons with severe disabilities may be silenced or excluded altogether. The irony, however, is that while their *voices* may not have a place in moral discourse, the individuals themselves do not disappear altogether (Carlson forthcoming, chap. 4).

Some have argued that the "severely intellectually disabled" do not possess any intrinsic worth or dignity, that they are deserving of moral consideration only by virtue of the fact that they matter to someone who *is* a full person (McMahan 2003). Does it follow from this that if I am *not* connected to individuals with intellectual disabilities in any way, then they do not have any direct claim upon me? What is at stake in adopting this position? And does it restrict the realm of concern simply to those for whom intellectual disability is a lived reality? What if we were to reverse the assumption, and treat the parental or familial relationship as a model for what it would mean to be in ethical relation to an individual with an intellectual disability? If the parental-familial formulation seems too problematic for some, what about the concept of friendship, as Reinders advocates? He writes, "We cannot seriously maintain that we seek the inclusion of people with ID in their capacity as fellow citizens without considering whether we want to include them in our own lives as our friends. I propose that this is the real challenge that people with ID pose for us, i.e. not so much what we can do for them, but whether or not we want to be with them. Ultimately, it is not

---

[4] Jeff McMahan expresses concern about our "commonsense" sentimental view of the severely cognitively disabled (2003). For an incisive critique of McMahan's work, see Kittay 2005.

citizenship, but friendship that matters" (2002, 5).[5] Perhaps this provides a new role for the philosopher as meaningfully engaged, rather than as profoundly disengaged.

The Nonhuman Animal

Foucault has said that madness "took its face from the mask of the beast," and in many ways the same can be said of intellectual disability (Foucault 2006, 147). The relationship between intellectual disability and animality has a long history. Historically, "idiots" and the "feeble-minded" were often described in terms of their animal-like appearances (for example, Samuel Gridley Howe (1848) spoke of the idiot's peculiar "monkeyish" look) and were defined in comparison to other non-humans. For instance, in appeals to the Pennsylvania government to open a school for "idiots" the following claim was made: "Even idiots can be raised, from a condition lower than that of brutes, to the likeness of men" (quoted in Carlson forthcoming). Yet these were more than mere theoretical associations: the institutional history of intellectual disability points to numerous instances where the treatment of persons with intellectual disabilities was justified on the basis of their animal-like nature. Wolf Wolfensberger examines the "subhuman," animal-like status that persons with mental retardation have historically been accorded, and explains the belief that the "retarded" were insensitive to heat and cold justified their being denied heat in their cells in the winter (Wolfensberger 1972, 14–15). And as late as a few decades ago in places like Willowbrook we find individuals with intellectual disabilities kept in conditions that can only be described as "subhuman."

But what of philosophical associations between intellectual disability and animality? They are not hard to find. As I mentioned earlier, numerous references to the "intellectually disabled" (usually "severe" cases) can be found in animal rights literature, primarily as a means of arguing against certain forms of speciesism. But references to nonhuman animals are also found in discussions specifically about persons with intellectual disabilities, where analogies and comparisons to nonhuman animals are often used to characterize them (Carlson 2003; forthcoming). While there is good reason to ask what impact the continued animalization of intellectual disability can have, both on our philosophical approaches to this group and in perpetuating concrete forms of dehumanization, there may be ways that taking our own animality seriously might open new paths for the philosopher of intellectual disability. What would it mean to think of the philosopher-as-animal in the context of intellectual disability?

---

[5] Many of the chapters in this collection point to more robust and capacious ways of defining the role of the advocate, citizen, and friend, suggesting that we may be able to view friendship and citizenship as complementary. See Nussbaum 2009; Silvers and Francis 2009; Wong 2009.

Increasing attention has been paid to the failure of philosophers to acknowledge that we are *human animals*, raising critical questions regarding the ways in which the philosophical celebration of reason and the denigration of the body have contributed to the disavowal of our animal nature. In his book *Dependent Rational Animals*, Alisdair MacIntyre argues that it is in recognizing certain animal features in disabled individuals that we are able to view them (and ourselves) as most clearly human. In addition to the virtues of independence, we must acknowledge "the virtues of acknowledged dependence" (MacIntyre 1999, 120). For MacIntyre, it is precisely in recognizing that "we never completely transcend our animality" that we might more fully realize an ethical relationship with individuals who have intellectual disabilities, and broaden our conception of human flourishing (MacIntyre 1999, 8; see Carlson 2003).

The notion that "reasserting our animality" can both serve to critique certain problematic conceptions of disability and offer a liberatory philosophy within which to attend to the moral status and respect owed to persons with "intellectual disabilities" is an intriguing one. First, this approach is *inclusive* rather than *exclusionary*: far from the margins, the individual with severe intellectual disabilities represents features that are most centrally human—vulnerability and dependence. Second, the recognition of ourselves *as* animals may serve to dislodge the central place that has been accorded to our rational capacities for so long (Carlson forthcoming, chap. 5). Opening a dialogue with theorists in ecofeminism and environmental philosophy might provide new ways of reconceiving ourselves as human animals that inhabit a shared world regardless of our cognitive capacities.[6] This, in turn, might allow us to reconfigure the ways in which associations have traditionally been drawn between disability and animality, and move beyond stark divisions that serve to distance the rational, able-bodied philosopher from these marginalized groups.

While this may offer a new role for the philosopher of intellectual disability, however, I must sound a cautionary note. In proceeding along this path, it seems crucial to keep the following questions in view: How is the long history of animalizing disability (and literally *de*-humanizing the "intellectually disabled") relevant to a reassertion of animality? What are the potential consequences—theoretical and practical—of philosophers continuing to associate intellectual disability with animality? What does it mean to reassert animality for a group of individuals who have historically been defined in those very terms, and whose own humanity has been denied? (Carlson 2003; forthcoming)

---

[6] For some examples, see Painter and Lotz 2007; Atterton and Calarco 2005; Warren 1996.

The "Intellectually Disabled"

I would like to conclude with a brief consideration of how the very concept of intellectual disability might be instructive in the practice of philosophy. What might it mean to consider the philosopher-as-disabled in this context? First, as many disability theorists and philosophers of disability have pointed out, there are ways in which we are all "temporarily able," and there is great value in acknowledging the human vulnerability and dependence that we *all* experience as human beings (Wendell 1996; Kittay 1998). While this recognition may guard against the many forms of exclusion, marginalization, and exploitation that have characterized both the history and the many philosophies of intellectual disability, however, there may also be conceptual, political, and practical reasons to be wary of placing persons with intellectual disabilities in this mirror role (Carlson forthcoming, chap. 7).

If the philosophical impetus to examine the nature of intellectual disability grows out of the fear or acknowledgment that "that may someday be me," there is the danger that the interests of persons with intellectual disabilities will be obscured by the fears and assumptions that shape the nondisabled person's own reflection. And while there may be strong ethical grounds for recognizing what the person with an intellectual disability shares with the nondisabled person, there may also be important political reasons to maintain the distinction between "disabled" and "nondisabled." Given the structural nature of oppression, and the necessity of recognizing certain forms of difference to secure social and economic support, some make the case that there may be harmful practical consequences in trying to erase these boundaries. As disability theorist and activist Simi Linton argues, "I'm not willing or interested in erasing the line between disabled and nondisabled people, as long as disabled people are devalued and discriminated against, and as long as naming the category serves to call attention to that treatment" (1998, 13).

As the philosopher of intellectual disability moves from questions of classification and identification with the "other" to the task of *self-*definition in the face of intellectual disability, new challenges emerge. What does it mean to leave the roles of expert, gatekeeper, and classifier aside, to focus squarely on one's own limitations and consider the ways in which the philosopher himself or herself is a subject with limited knowledge? In "The Speculum of Ignorance," Nancy Tuana offers a taxonomy of ignorance, and while her analysis centers on examples from women's health, her categories generate provocative questions for philosophers of intellectual disability (Tuana 2006; Carlson forthcoming).

First, are there deliberate or unintentional efforts to remain ignorant? In the context of intellectual disability, this can manifest itself in a number of ways: the philosopher's lack of interest in the specific nature of the condition; an ignorance about the lived realities of the individuals being discussed; and the failure to acknowledge the historical basis of this category and the history of oppression and mistreatment of persons with intellectual disabilities. Thus one can ask whether the history and complexities of intellectual disability simply fall below the radar of philosophical interest, or whether there is a more palpable sense in which philosophers maintain a posture of willful ignorance.

Second, what kinds of epistemological barriers confront the philosopher in analyzing intellectual disability? To borrow Tuana's phrasing, perhaps "We do not even know that we do not know." This speaks to my reaction upon reading philosophical work on intellectual disability that so profoundly strips persons in this group of any recognizable *human* characteristics, work that describes them as unrecognizable, as radically *other*. What rich dimensions of these supposedly impoverished lives are being missed by those for whom "the intellectually disabled" are nothing more than abstract thought experiments? (Kittay 2005; Carlson forthcoming)

Finally, the complexity of intellectual disability as a lived experience suggests that some barriers to knowledge for those who are not defined as intellectually disabled may be insurmountable, either temporarily or perhaps permanently. The mysterious dimensions of another's existence, particularly in cases where traditional forms of communication are limited, speak to the possibility of what Tuana calls "loving ignorance," whereby we "accept what we cannot know" (Tuana 2006, 15–16). This form of acceptance, articulated by many who share their lives with persons with severe intellectual disabilities, points to the necessity for humility and epistemic responsibility in our philosophical discussions (Kittay 2005; Reinders 2008).

These final points prompt me to reflect on the nature and limitations of the very project I have undertaken in this chapter. Any attempt to pin down or define "the philosopher of intellectual disability" seems as misguided as trying to sum up "intellectual disability" or "the intellectually disabled" in facile, simplistic terms. Many philosophers (including those represented in this collection) may not identify with any of the roles I have defined. Moreover, one could legitimately argue that in offering this taxonomy of philosophers of intellectual disability, I have simply constructed a series of abstract "kinds" that fail to capture the nuance and depth of our philosophical discourse. This suggests that the richness and complexity of both objects of knowledge, of both *subjects*—the person with an intellectual disability and the "philosopher of intellectual disability"—may very well exceed any neat labels pinned on them. Perhaps it is here, then, that we can begin to recognize the value and possibility of moving beyond an attenuated philosophical portrait of intellectual disability.

References

Atterton, Peter, and Matthew Calarco. 2005. *Animal Philosophy: Essential Readings in Continental Thought*. London: Continuum.

Bérubé, Michael. 1998. *Life As We Know It: A Father, a Family, and an Exceptional Child*. New York: Vintage.

Byrne, Peter. 2000. *Philosophical and Ethical Problems in Mental Handicap*. New York: St. Martin's Press.

Carlson, Licia. 2001. "Cognitive Ableism and Disability Studies: Feminist Reflections on the History of Mental Retardation." *Hypatia* 16, no. 4 (Fall): 124–46.

———. 2003. "Rethinking Normalcy, Normalization and Cognitive Disability." In *Science and Other Cultures: Issues in the Philosophy of Science and Technology*, edited by Sandra Harding and Robert Figueroa, 154–71. New York: Routledge.

———. 2007. "The Human as Just an *Other* Animal: Madness, Disability and Foucault's Bestiary." In *Phenomenology and the Non-Human Animal*, edited by Christian Lotz and Corinne Painter, 117–33. Dordrecht: Springer.

———. Forthcoming. *The Faces of Intellectual Disability: Philosophical Reflections*. Bloomington: Indiana University Press.

Diamond, Cora. 1991. "The Importance of Being Human." In *Human Beings*, edited by David Cockburn, 35–62. Cambridge: Cambridge University Press.

Foucault, Michel. 1979. *Discipline and Punish: The Birth of the Prison*. Translated by Alan Sheridan. New York: Vintage Books.

———. 2006. *The History of Madness*. Translated by Jonathan Murphy and Jean Khalfa. New York: Routledge.

Howe, Samuel Gridley. 1848. "On the Causes of Idiocy." In *The History of Mental Retardation: Collected Papers*, edited by Marvin Rosen, Gerald Clark, and Marvin Kivitz, 1: 31–60. Baltimore: University Park Press, 1975.

Kittay, Eva. 1998. *Love's Labor: Essays on Women, Equality and Dependency*. New York: Routledge.

———. 2002. "When Caring Is Just and Justice Is Caring." In *The Subject of Care: Feminist Perspectives on Dependency*, edited by Eva Feder Kittay and Ellen K. Feder, 257–76. Lanham, Md.: Rowman and Littlefield.

———. 2005. "At the Margins of Moral Personhood." *Ethics* 116 (October): 100–13.

Linton, Simi. 1998. *Claiming Disability: Knowledge and Identity*. New York: New York University Press.

MacIntyre, Alisdair. 1999. *Dependent Rational Animals*. Chicago: Open Court.

McMahan, Jeff. 2003. *The Ethics of Killing*. Oxford: Oxford University Press.

Murphy, Jeffrie. 1984. "Do the Mentally Retarded Have a Right Not to Be Eaten?" In *Ethics and Mental Retardation*, edited by John Moskop and Loretta Kopelman, 43–46. Dordrecht: Reidel.

Nussbaum, Martha. 2009. "The Capabilities of People with Disabilities." Included in this collection.

Painter, Corinne, and Christian Lotz, eds. 2007. *Phenomenology and the Non-Human Animal*. Dordrecht: Springer.

Patterson, Annette, and Martha Satz. 2002. "Genetic Counseling and the Disabled: Feminism Examines the Stance of Those Who Stand at the Gate." *Hypatia* 17, no. 3:118–45.

Rafter, Nicole Hahn. 1988. *White Trash: The Eugenic Family Studies, 1877–1919*. Boston: Northeastern University Press.

Rapp, Rayna. 2000. *Testing Women, Testing the Fetus: The Social Impact of Amniocentesis in America*. New York: Routledge.

Reinders, Hans. 2002. "The Good Life for Citizens with Intellectual Disability." *Journal of Intellectual Disability Research* 46, no. 1:1–5.

———. 2008. *Receiving the Gift of Friendship: Profound Disability, Theological Anthropology and Ethics*. Grand Rapids, Mich.: Eerdmans.

Rioux, Marsha, and Michael Bach. 1994. *Disability Is Not Measles*. North York: L'Institut Roeher.

Sanger, Margaret 1920. *Woman and the New Race*. New York: Brentano's.

Silvers, Anita, and Leslie Pickering Francis. 2009. "Thinking About the Good: Reconfiguring Liberal Metaphysics (or Not) for People with Cognitive Disabilities." Included in this collection.

Singer, Peter. 2009. "Speciesism and Moral Status." Included in this collection.

Stubblefield, Anna. 2009. "The Entanglement of Race and Cognitive Dis/ability." Included in this collection.

Trent, James W. Jr. 1995. *Inventing the Feeble Mind: A History of Mental Retardation in the United States*. Berkeley: University of California Press.

Tuana, Nancy. 2006. "The Speculum of Ignorance." *Hypatia* 21, no. 3:1–19.

Veatch, Robert. 1986. *The Foundations of Justice: Why the Retarded and the Rest of Us Have Claims to Equality*. New York: Oxford University Press.

Warren, Karen J., editor. 1996. *Ecological Feminist Philosophies*. Bloomington: Indiana University Press.

Wasserman, David, Jerome Bickenbach, and Robert Wachbroit, editors. 2005. *Quality of Life and Human Difference: Genetic Testing, Health Care and Disability*. Cambridge: Cambridge University Press.

Wendell, Susan. 1996. *The Rejected Body: Feminist Philosophical Reflections on Disability*. New York: Routledge.

Wolfensberger, Wolf. 1972. *Principles of Normalization in Human Services*. Toronto: National Institute on Mental Retardation.

Wong, Sophia Isako. 2002. "At Home with Down Syndrome and Gender." *Hypatia* 17, no. 3 (Summer): 89–117.

———. 2009. "Duties of Justice to Citizens with Cognitive Disabilities." Included in this collection.

Young, Iris Marion. 1990. *Justice and the Politics of Difference*. Princeton: Princeton University Press.

19

SPECIESISM AND MORAL STATUS

PETER SINGER

Introduction

This chapter derives from a talk presented at the conference "Cognitive Disability: A Challenge to Moral Philosophy."[1] As that title suggests, cognitive disability does present a challenge to moral philosophy. I focus here on the challenge it presents to views about moral status that are widespread both among moral philosophers and in the wider community. However, the reverse is also true: moral philosophy can and ought to challenge how we think about people with cognitive disabilities and about the value of human life. I want to enlarge the sphere of discussion, so that we are looking not just at people with cognitive disabilities but also at the way in which our thoughts about moral status relate to beings who do not have the cognitive abilities that normal humans have. Although there is among some who write on cognitive disability a strong aversion to comparing humans with nonhuman animals, these comparisons are unavoidable if we are to clarify the basis of moral status.

Hence I begin with some examples of cognitive abilities that show significant overlap between some nonhuman animals and some human beings. I then discuss the widely accepted ethic of "the equal value and dignity of all human life," and the various grounds—religious, speciesist, cognitive-ability-based, and "slippery slope"—on which people have attempted to support this ethic. I argue that this view of universal and equal human dignity cannot be supported without a drastic revision to aspects of our morality, which most people do not want to make. As an alternative, I present a graduated view of the moral status of humans and nonhuman animals.

[1] The conference was held at Stony Brook University in New York City in September 2008. I dedicate these thoughts to Harriet McBryde Johnson because my presentation at the conference was the first time since she died that I spoke on issues of intellectual disability. In recent years, while she lived, whenever I spoke or wrote about intellectual disability, I could expect an e-mail from her telling me where I was wrong. Knowing that my work would receive her sharp scrutiny was a spur to defending my views as well as I could. Sadly I'm not going to hear from her this time.

Cognitive Abilities in Humans and Animals

Let us consider a few examples of the capacities and cognitive abilities of nonhuman beings, with regard to IQ and language comprehension. I specifically want to consider research done on great apes, border collies, and grey parrots.

Great apes: Francine Patterson of the Gorilla Foundation claims that the gorilla Koko scored between 70 and 95 on human IQ tests and understands about a thousand signs. Though this finding is controversial, there is a substantial amount of uncontroversial research suggesting that many of the great apes, including gorillas, chimpanzees, bonobos, and orangutans, can use human sign language and can develop a fair range of comprehension.[2] At least, it is clear that they understand a number of signs, and they use a kind of structured syntax. The question of whether or not we should call this "language" is not my concern here. What is relevant for this discussion is comparisons with humans with cognitive disabilities; the point being that if we raise the standard for language to exclude the signs used by Koko, Kanzi, Washoe, Chantek, or some of the other signing apes, then we would have to say that some humans at profound and severe levels of cognitive disability don't have language either. We must keep a level playing field for comparisons between species—in this case between some humans with cognitive disabilities and great apes.

Dogs: There's been some interesting recent work on dogs' abilities to recognize human spoken language. Border collies, when presented with a collection of hundreds of different toys with different names, are able to respond and fetch a particular named object. Tests have demonstrated that they can comprehend two hundred to three hundred human words.[3]

Grey parrots: Remarkable work was done by Irene Pepperberg with Alex, an African grey parrot, who died recently. Alex grasped about a hundred words; of course, parrots are actually grasping spoken human language and responding to it in the same spoken language—no sign language here. Alex—and this also goes for other grey parrots that are being studied—was shown to be not just "parroting," because he could answer novel questions. Furthermore, his answers to the questions showed a grasp of concepts. For example, if Alex was shown a yellow sphere and a yellow cube and was then asked, "What's the same?" he would answer, "Color." When shown a red sphere and a yellow sphere and asked, "What's the same?" Alex would say, "Shape." So it seems clear that Alex

---

[2] See, for example, the essays in part 2 of Paola Cavalieri and Peter Singer, eds., *The Great Ape Project: Equality Beyond Humanity* (New York: St. Martin's Press, 1994).

[3] See the research by Juliane Kamiski and Sebastian Tempelmann, cited by Virginia Morell in "Minds of Their Own," *National Geographic*, March 2008.

understood what was going on with these basic concepts, and he had modest numerical ability as well, being able to count up to seven.[4]

Having considered these examples of nonhuman animal cognitive ability, let's look at some human beings with cognitive disabilities. I'm focusing here on the very bottom of the range: those with profound mental retardation, and I acknowledge that this is a very small percentage of people with intellectual disabilities. In fact, the American Association for Intellectual and Developmental Disabilities says it's 1 percent. Other statistics are available that vary slightly on this, but the point is not so much how many human beings there are in this category but rather the fact that there are some, for they form the basis on which I will later raise arguments about claims that *all* human beings have a certain kind of moral status. I recognize that for those with a particular concern for people with cognitive disabilities, this may make what I'm saying less interesting because I am going to make an argument that concerns the moral status of human beings in general, as compared to nonhuman animals. There may also be some who are working with people with disabilities or who are caregivers or relatives of people with cognitive disabilities who will look at my examples of severe and profound cognitive disability and say to themselves that I am not discussing people who are like the people that they work with or care for. I acknowledge, of course, that people with cognitive disabilities are not easy to categorize. Obviously the issues are different depending on the severity of the cognitive disabilities. But let me reiterate that for the moment I have in mind those with profound mental retardation as defined below, and the definition is not mine.

According to the American Association on Intellectual and Developmental Disabilities, people with profound mental retardation

- have an IQ range below 25;
- will always require much supervision, though they may acquire some self-help skills;
- have an ability to understand that exceeds their ability to speak;
- may have little or no speech;
- may be capable of following simple directions;
- have no academic skills;
- may be unable to perform any useful work, though with training may be able to achieve a work-activity level of productivity;
- may appear socially isolated and pay little attention to others except as it relates to their own needs.[5]

---

[4] See Irene Pepperberg, *The Alex Studies: Cognitive and Communicative Abilities of Grey Parrots* (Cambridge, Mass.: Harvard University Press, 1999).

[5] Quoted from Taskforce Independence, "Supported Accommodation for All Who Need It: A Reality, Not a Dream," available at www.nds.org.au/nsw/Conferences/2007annual/papers/3.1b_Discussion%20Paper_Australia.doc. I have been unable to trace the original source.

Now let us think about nonhuman animals in terms of these capacities.

- IQ: Some nonhuman animals, such as the gorilla Koko, have IQ ranges significantly above 25.
- Supervision: Animals don't require much supervision—many of them get on and always have got on with their lives perfectly well—often better—without human interference.
- Speech: It is generally true that nonhuman animals have little or no speech, or what we would call speech, although, as we have seen, there are exceptions.
- Following simple directions: Many animals, including dogs, can follow simple directions. Can they acquire skills? Dogs, horses, dolphins, pigeons, and several other animals can be trained to perform useful work. In fact, one of the reasons why it is thought that border collies are good at following human commands is that traditionally they have been bred to work with sheep and to respond to commands to separate some sheep from others.
- Social isolation: We are not the only social animals; there is clearly a wide range of social mammals for whom sociability is very important. All of the great apes, primates generally, dogs, and many other nonhuman animals are social beings and develop in society, respond to the needs of other beings in their group, communicate with them, reciprocate certain kinds of behavior, and so on.

Given that there are some humans who are profoundly mentally retarded and have the characteristics listed above, it is clearly not the case that *all* humans have cognitive ability above *all* nonhuman animals. On the contrary, we have many nonhuman animals who are significantly above some human beings in their level of cognitive ability: in particular, they are above those with profound mental retardation. Our question is: What ethical significance can we draw from this?

The Equal Value of All Human Life?

Consider this statement by Pope John Paul II: "As far as the right to life is concerned, every innocent human being is absolutely equal to all others. . . . Before the moral norm which prohibits the direct taking of the life of an innocent human being there are no privileges or exceptions for anyone. It makes no difference whether one is the master of the world or the 'poorest of the poor' on the face of the earth. Before the demands of morality we are all absolutely equal."[6] This represents a widely held ethical position, not merely the position of a religious leader or of someone with a Christian or, more specifically, a Roman Catholic viewpoint. It expresses a kind of "official morality" that is often applied in statements about people with

[6] John Paul II, *Evangelium Vitae*, 1995.

cognitive disabilities. Most people pay lip service to it, though I'm not sure how many really hold it when it comes to the crunch. I will argue that this doctrine cannot be sustained in the light of the facts that I have been referring to—or at least not without a very drastic revision to aspects of our morality, which most people don't want to make.

Here is the problem: Can we justify attributing equal value to all human lives, while at the same time attributing to human life a value that is superior to all animal life? Of course Pope John Paul II's statement does not say, "All human life is absolutely equal but all humans are superior to animals," but obviously that is implied by the statement, and by the fact that while popes very frequently denounce abortion and euthanasia, no pope has yet denounced the unnecessary killing of animals for food, although such killing takes place on a vastly larger scale than abortion and euthanasia. (The number of animals killed for food each year is in the tens of billions, vastly greater than the entire human population of the planet, and that does not include fish and other marine creatures.) Clearly, Pope John Paul II and those who accept his position on this issue think not only that all humans are equal to each other but also that they are far superior to nonhuman animals. The philosophical problem is whether we can justify that view.

In what follows, I briefly discuss three general attempts to ground such a view, dividing them into three categories: religious, speciesist, and those that depend on cognitive abilities.

Religious Grounds

As Pope John Paul II's statement indicates, obviously there is a variety of religious grounds upon which people might attempt to justify the doctrine of both the equal worth of all human life and human superiority over nonhuman animals. For example, religious grounds might include the following:

1. We are made in the image of God, and animals are not.
2. God gave us dominion over animals.
3. We have immortal souls, and animals do not.

I do not think there is any good evidence for any of these claims. I regard them all as false. Some people may believe that these are true claims. I would argue, however, that even if they are true, such claims should not be the basis of law or public policy in a society that is not based on a religious creed or religious profession. The desirability of keeping church and state separate is sufficient basis for saying that even those who accept these religious claims should agree that in a pluralist society they should not suffice for making laws that regulate how we treat human beings and nonhuman animals.

Speciesist Grounds

I use the term "speciesism" deliberately, to make a parallel with other "isms" that we are familiar with, particularly racism and sexism. There are a number of arguments that fall into this general category. Sometimes they are made by quite respectable philosophers—for example, Bernard Williams, who defends the view that since we humans are doing the judging, we are entitled to prefer our own kind.[7] In response to an example in his article about an imaginary situation in which humans are being conquered by aliens, and the aliens defend their conquest by claiming, truthfully, that they are intellectually superior to us and have better, richer, and fuller lives than we do, Williams replies that if any human accepted such an argument, we could respond by saying simply, "Whose side are you on?" Williams then applies this to the case of animals, arguing that we are entitled simply to say, "We're humans here, we're the ones doing the judging; you can't really expect anything else but a bias or prejudice in favor of human beings." This seems to me to be a very dangerous way to argue, precisely because of the parallel to which I adverted above. I do not see that the argument is really different from a white racist saying, when it comes to a question about how one should treat people of different races, "Well, whose side are you on? We're the ones doing the judging here, why don't we simply prefer our kind because it is our kind?"

We cannot claim that biological commonality entitles us to superior status over those who are not members of our species. In the case of applying this to people with severe and profound cognitive disabilities, there is also a problem about saying who the "we" are. What is really important about saying "us?" Is it that we are all capable of understanding language, and perhaps even rational argument? In that case, I am not addressing those who are profoundly mentally retarded. Or is it that I am addressing all those who are members of my species? I think it is much more important that the "we" of this statement are beings of at least a certain level of cognitive ability. So, if it happens that one of you is an alien who has cleverly disguised yourself in a human shape, but you are capable of understanding this argument, I am talking to you just as I am talking to members of my own species. In important respects, I have much more in common with you than I do with someone who is of my species but, because he or she is profoundly mentally retarded, has no capacity for verbal communication with me at all. In other words, if we take Williams's question "Whose side are you on?" to refer to being on the side of those who share our species membership (as he presumably intended it), it is a bad argument. If on the other hand we take it to refer

[7] Bernard Williams, "The Human Prejudice," which appears, along with a response from me, in *Peter Singer Under Fire*, edited by Jeffrey Schaler (Chicago: Open Court, forthcoming).

to being on the side of those capable of sharing in discussions of right and wrong, it clearly does not support the claim that all humans are equal.

There is another claim that one often hears: that humans and no others have intrinsic worth and dignity, and that is why humans have superior status. This is really just a piece of rhetoric unless it is given some support. What is it about human beings that gives them moral worth and dignity? If there is no good answer forthcoming, this talk of intrinsic worth and dignity is just speciesism in nicer terms. I do not see any argument in the claim that merely being a member of the species *Homo sapiens* gives you moral worth and dignity, whereas being a member of the species *Pan troglodytes* (chimpanzees) does not give you worth and dignity. Something more would need to be said.

Superior Cognitive Abilities

Some have attempted to justify superior moral status for humans on the basis that humans have superior cognitive abilities. Many people refer to Immanuel Kant's moral philosophy as providing justification for the claims that human beings are ends in themselves, and that humans have both worth and dignity, while animals do not. In Kant's view, "Animals are not self-conscious and are there merely as a means to an end. That end is man."[8] Kant's argument for why human beings are ends-in-themselves is that they are autonomous beings, which, in terms of Kantian philosophy, means that they are capable of reasoning. Note that Kant goes from defending the value of autonomy or self-consciousness to maintaining that "man" is the end. If we really take his argument seriously it means that human beings who are not self-conscious—because perhaps they are so profoundly mentally retarded that they lack self-consciousness or self-awareness— are also merely means to an end, that end being autonomous or self-conscious beings. So the Kantian approach is not going to help those whose objective is to demonstrate that all human beings have superior status to nonhuman animals.

Those who see morality as a social contract are also likely to link moral status to higher cognitive capacities. According to this view, the core of morality is that I agree not to harm you, in return for your agreement not to harm me.[9] Some cognitive abilities are required to be capable of forming and adhering to an agreement of this kind. If you are profoundly mentally retarded, you may not have those abilities. You certainly are not likely to have them to an extent that is superior to that of some

[8] Immanuel Kant, *Lectures on Ethics*, translated by Louis Infield (New York: Harper Torchbooks, 1963), p. 239.

[9] The social contract view can be found in ancient Greece, for example in the position of Glaucon, as represented in Plato's *Republic*. Its most famous exponents are Thomas Hobbes, John Locke, and Jean-Jacques Rousseau, and in our own era, John Rawls and David Gauthier.

nonhuman animals, who have been shown to be capable of reciprocity. As with the Kantian argument, therefore, a contractarian account of morality is unable to justify granting all humans a moral status superior to that of any nonhuman animal, though it may justify granting some humans a moral status superior to that of some humans and of any nonhuman animal.

So to reiterate: because of the overlap in cognitive ability between some humans and some nonhuman animals, attempts to draw a moral line on the basis of cognitive ability, as Kant and the contractarians try to do, will require either that we exclude some humans—for example, those who are profoundly mentally retarded—or that we include some nonhuman animals—those whose levels of cognitive ability are equal or superior to the lowest level found in human beings. Hence we have to conclude that the standard ethical view that we find expressed in the statement by John Paul II—the view that all human beings, irrespective of their cognitive abilities, have equal moral status, and that this status is superior to the moral status of the most intelligent nonhuman animals—cannot be defended. We find ourselves in need of an alternative to the status quo.

An Alternative View

There are a number of possible alternatives to the view that all human life is of equal value, and this value is superior to that of any nonhuman animals. We could:

1. preserve equality by raising the status of animals, granting them the same status we now grant to humans; or
2. preserve equality by lowering the status of humans to that which we now grant to animals; or
3. abandon the idea of the equal value of all humans, replacing that with a more graduated view in which moral status depends on some aspects of cognitive ability, and that graduated view is applied both to humans and nonhumans.

I assume that we can all agree in rejecting (2). I am to some extent sympathetic to (1) but not in every respect. Alternative (3) remains a possibility; let us consider how we might go in that direction.

Long before most people were contemplating any serious degree of concern for animals, Jeremy Bentham, the founding father of the English school of Utilitarianism, wrote, "The question is not, 'Can they reason?' nor, 'Can they talk?' but, 'Can they suffer?'"[10] That is indeed a crucial question to ask whenever we are talking about beings who are capable of suffering and one that is clearly relevant to how we should treat both

---

[10] Jeremy Bentham, *Introduction to the Principles of Morals and Legislation* (1789), chap. 17.

humans and nonhuman animals. Can they suffer? Can they enjoy life? If so, they have interests that we should take into account, and we should give those interests equal weight with the interests of all other beings with similar interests. We should not discount their interests in not suffering because they cannot talk or because they are incapable of reasoning; and we should not discount their interests in enjoying life, in having things that are fulfilling and rewarding for them, either. The principle of equal consideration of interests should apply to both humans and animals. That's the sense in which I want to elevate animals to the moral status of humans.

I imagine that many people who care for profoundly mentally retarded humans would support Bentham's idea that the ability to talk or to reason is irrelevant to the importance of avoiding suffering and facilitating an enjoyable life. But Bentham's principle many not apply to all aspects of human or animal life. Consider a comment from Roger Scruton, a conservative British philosopher who defends the killing and eating of animals, although only if they are well treated during their life and not, for example, reared on modern intensive farms. Killing animals is not, Scruton says, wrong in itself, because "there is a real distinction, for a human being, between timely and untimely death. To be 'cut short' before one's time is a waste—even a tragedy. ... No such thoughts apply to domestic cattle. To be killed at thirty months is not intrinsically more tragic than to be killed at forty, fifty, or sixty."[11]

One of the reasons Scruton thinks that "untimely death" is a tragedy for a human being is that if a human being is killed before his or her time there are likely to be achievements that this human being may have accomplished which he or she will not accomplish. So, if you like, there is a failure to carry out plans that had been made, and to achieve what the person wanted to achieve. Cattle, on Scruton's view, have no plans for the future, and no accomplishments that they would have achieved, had they been able to live long longer. We could debate this factual claim, but I accept the normative view that there is greater significance in killing a being who has plans for the future—who wishes to accomplish things— than there is in killing a being who is incapable of thinking about the future at all but exists either moment to moment or within a very short-time horizon (for example, a time horizon limited to thinking about eating something in the near future). It is, other things being equal, much less a tragedy to kill that sort of being than to kill someone who wants to live long enough to do the sorts of things that humans typically want to achieve over the course of their lives. But, of course, if this reason is invoked to justify killing well-treated animals for food, then this has implications for the question of whether one can justify ending the life of

[11] Roger Scruton, "The Conscientious Carnivore," in *Food for Thought*, edited by Steve Sapntzis (Amherst, N.Y.: Prometheus, 2004), pp. 81–91; the passage quoted is on p. 88.

a profoundly cognitively disabled human being. One could, after all, rewrite Scruton's statement as follows: "There is a real distinction, for a cognitively normal human being, between timely and untimely death. To be 'cut short' before one's time is a waste—even a tragedy.... No such thoughts apply to a being unable to make plans for the future. For such a being, to be killed at an early age is not intrinsically more tragic than to die in old age." Of course, this challenges a widely accepted human ethic. So if you thought that Scruton provided you with a sound justification for continuing to enjoy steak for dinner (as long as you get humanely raised, grass-bred beef), you need to think whether you are prepared to accept the argument in a nonspeciesist way and apply it to all beings who are unable to make plans for the future.

That there is *some* significance, as far as the wrongness of killing is concerned, in whether the being killed can think about the future, seems to me defensible. *How much* significance there is in this is a more difficult question, to which I have no clear answer. But I think we can conclude that pain and suffering are equally bad—and pleasure and happiness equally good—whether the being experiencing them is human or nonhuman, rational or nonrational, capable of discourse or not. On the other hand, death is a greater or lesser loss depending on factors like the extent to which the being was aware of his or her existence over time, and of course the quality of life the being was likely to have, had it continued to live.

The Views of Parents

The parents of children with cognitive disabilities differ greatly in their attitudes to their children. Consider some comments parents have made about children born with disabilities considerably less severe than those I have been considering. Here is a highly positive view:

> Those of us with a Down's Syndrome child (our son, Robert, is almost 24) often wish that all our children had this extraordinary syndrome which defeats anger and malice, replacing them with humor, thoughtfulness and devotion to friends and family.[12]

And here is one of the contrary opinions that I've had expressed to me:

> My son, John [not his real name] was born almost $2\frac{1}{2}$ years ago 11 weeks premature and weighing only 1 lb. 14 oz. . . . John has spastic diplegia cerebral palsy with underlying right hemiplegia . . ., has sensory problems, and has speech delays. . . . My husband and I love our son (middle of three), but had someone told me, "Mrs B. your son will have numerous disabilities down the road. Do you still want us to intubate him?," my answer would have been no. It would have been a gut wrenching decision, but it would have been for the

---

[12] Quoted from Ann Bradley, "Why Shouldn't Women Abort Disabled Fetuses?" *Living Marxism* 82 (Sept. 1995).

best. It would have been in the best interest for John, for us, and for our children. I am saddened beyond words to think of all he will have to cope with as he grows older.[13]

I don't have enough data to venture a conclusion as to which view is the more prevalent among parents of children with disabilities, and even if I did, that would not resolve the ethical question one way or another. Rather, we should consider parental choice as a factor in its own right, and one that ought to have an important role in decisions about whether to prolong life or whether to end it. (I would add here that if the parents of John would have been justified in refusing life-prolonging treatment shortly after his birth, then in my view they would also have been justified in taking active steps to end his life at a later stage, if they still believed that that was in his best interests, and he was incapable of expressing any view on such a matter.)

Who Has Dignity?

Before closing, I will comment briefly on a case that received extensive publicity in 2007. At the time of the procedure I am about to describe, Ashley was a nine-year-old girl living with her family in Seattle. There was some dispute about how profound her disabilities were. It was reported that she was unable to walk or talk, keep her head up, roll over, or sit up by herself; that she was fed with a tube, and that she could not swallow. After discussion with her parents, doctors administered hormones to prevent normal growth. The aim of this growth attenuation was to keep Ashley small and make her easier to care for. The parents said that this was in Ashley's interests, as it would make it possible for her to continue to travel with the family on vacation. Ashley's doctors also, again in accordance with her parents' wishes, performed a hysterectomy and removed her breast buds—the hysterectomy so that she would not have problems with menstruation, and the breast bud removal, they said, once again to keep her lighter and easier to care for, but also to reduce the likelihood that if she had to be placed in an institution, she would be a victim of sexual assault.

During the controversy that arose after Ashley's treatment was publicized, an article in the *Los Angeles Times* said: "This is about Ashley's dignity. Everybody examining her case seems to agree about that."[14] But "dignity" is a vague term. We are prepared to use the term "best interests" for animals without too much hesitation; we know what that means. We are less willing to speak of an animal's dignity, because it

---

[13] From a letter sent to me in 1999 after publicity about my views on euthanasia for severely disabled infants (name withheld).

[14] Sam Verhovek, "Parents Defend Decision to Keep Disabled Girl Small," *Los Angeles Times* January 3, 2007.

is not clear what cognitive capacities might be required for a being to have dignity. The same problem arises for someone as developmentally disabled as Ashley. It isn't clear how she could possess dignity. If we say that she does, are we also prepared to grant dignity to nonhuman animals at a similar cognitive level?

In my view, whether the treatment to which Ashley was subjected was justifiable depends primarily on whether it was in her best interests, rather than whether it befitted her dignity.

"Slippery Slope" Arguments

Some people may object that even if the position I am taking is completely logical, in the abstract, it is nevertheless dangerous in the real world, because it leads to a slippery slope. We should, these people are likely to say, affirm the dignity and worth of the human person precisely because in the past century we've come through the scourge of wars and genocides that have been based on failure to respect human dignity and worth. So the question arises: Even if it is not philosophically defensible by any other means, is it still sound policy to maintain that all human beings have dignity and worth, in order to avoid a recurrence of the tragedies that occurred during the Nazi era and afterward?

This so-called slippery slope argument is often made specifically with regard to the need to protect the status of those with intellectual disabilities. For example, a fact sheet from the American Association on Intellectual and Developmental Disabilities refers to the "long history of oppression and the callous disregard for the lives of individuals with mental retardation" and offers this as a reason why we "must be especially vigilant to protect the autonomy and the right to equal protection under the law of individuals with mental retardation." I agree that there has been a long history of oppression and callous disregard for the lives of individuals with mental retardation.[15] I also agree that we should do our best to avoid such oppression and callous disregard.

But should we accept the slippery slope argument as a reason for not making any changes in the ethic that we currently have? Here we need to ask some questions. First, in terms of the danger of a repeat of the Holocaust, how significant are the particular historical circumstances in which those events took place? That is a question we can debate, a historical question as to whether we are likely to go down that slope again, given very different historical circumstances. But second and very important, if it is only the slippery slope argument that justifies our talk about the equal value of all human life, what is the cost of maintaining this fiction?

---

[15] This was amply documented in Douglas Biklen's presentation at the conference at which the original version of this chapter was presented.

One cost of adhering to the slippery slope argument is the cost to nonhuman animals of the continuation of the view that they are inferior in moral status to all human beings. If we are moved by pictures of institutionalized and physically confined children with intellectual disabilities, as we should be,[16] then surely we should be equally moved by photographs of animals on factory farms, kept in even closer confinement—especially when we know that the latter situation, but not the former, is still the rule in the United States. For example, the breeding sows that produce almost all of the pork, bacon, and ham sold in this country are so tightly confined in metal crates that they cannot walk a single step or turn around. And yet, pigs are animals who compare quite well in terms of cognitive abilities with human beings who are profoundly mentally retarded. I doubt that it would be possible for people to treat pigs in this way, if they did not put them in a moral category that is far inferior to that in which they would place any human being. For hundreds of millions of sentient beings, the cost of the barrier that we draw between human and nonhuman animals is immense.

The other cost involved in maintaining the belief in the equal value of all human life falls on those parents who feel like John's mother, whom I quoted above. If some parents believe that it is in the best interests of their profoundly mentally retarded child and of their family that their child should not live, then they should not be compelled, because it is important for us all to maintain the fiction that every human life is of equal value, to accept medical treatment for their child in order to make that child live, and in some circumstances—especially if the child is suffering—they should have the option of euthanasia to end the child's life. To force the parents to bring up the child, neither for their own benefit nor for the benefit of the child but so that we do not slide down an allegedly possible slippery slope into a repetition of the Holocaust, is, ironically, to do just what Kantians normally object to doing: treating the child (and the parents) as merely a means to an end. The cost, financial, physical, and emotional, of bringing up a profoundly mentally retarded child is great even when parents positively want to bring up their child. It will clearly be much harder to bear if the parents never wanted to bring up the child but were not able to make that choice.

In any case, is it even possible, in the long run, to maintain the ethical stance that is supposed to prevent us sliding down the slippery slope? I mentioned above that this idea of the equal value of all human life is part of "official" morality. Then I added a qualification: *it's the morality we pay lip service to*. If we look at what people *do*, when they have a choice, as distinct from what they say, we can see that the idea that all life is of equal value is not the morality that people in fact act on. Consider

---

[16] I am referring here to a photograph that Dr. Biklen showed of a child confined in a cot that looked more like a cage.

pregnant women who are told their child will have a cognitive disability—and of course the cognitive disability that most pregnant women are told about is a relatively mild one, Down syndrome. And yet we know that 85 percent of the women who are told that their fetus carries the extra chromosome that causes Down syndrome elect to terminate the pregnancy. Presumably for women who are told that the child would have a more severe form of mental retardation, that number is, if anything, still higher. So when it comes to making choices for what kind of child we want to have, very few among us believe that all human lives are equally worth having, and that it doesn't really matter what level of cognitive ability your child will have. Most of us prefer to have a child with normal cognitive abilities when we have that choice. When it comes to the crunch, the fiction that we believe in the equal value of all human life breaks down, here as in other areas of life-and-death decision making.[17]

There is also the question of allowing severely disabled infants to die. In many hospitals—perhaps most hospitals today—this is, in certain cases, a part of normal practice. I sometimes take my Princeton students to the nearest neonatal intensive care unit, which happens to be a Catholic hospital—Saint Peter's Hospital in New Brunswick, New Jersey. When we are there, the director of that neonatal intensive unit is prepared to tell my students quite openly—he has done it with a video camera rolling in front of him, and in front of the hospital's Catholic chaplain as well—that there are some cases where he withdraws treatment and allows a baby to die. If an extremely premature baby is on a respirator and has had a massive bleeding in the brain, and the physicians agree that the child is going to be so cognitively disabled as to be unable to do anything but lie in bed without responding to his or her parents, the director will suggest to the parents that treatment be withdrawn. The parents almost always accept that suggestion, and the baby dies. So even in a Catholic hospital decisions about life and death are not really based on the equal value of all human life.

Conclusion

In closing, let me say that I am aware that this is a large topic, and I make no claim to be expert on all aspects of it. I hope I have nevertheless said enough to challenge two closely related views: that species membership is crucial to moral status, and that all human life is of equal value. If I am right, this makes a difference to the ethical options available to us when we consider decisions we are called upon to make for those who are profoundly mentally retarded.

---

[17] For discussion of other areas, see Peter Singer, *Rethinking Life and Death* (New York: St. Martin's Press, 1995).

20

COGNITIVE DISABILITY AND COGNITIVE ENHANCEMENT

JEFF MCMAHAN

Introduction

At the conference from which this collection of chapters is derived, I was asked what my purpose has been in writing about the moral status of human beings with extreme forms of cognitive limitation. The question arose because some of what I have written challenges certain assumptions we tend to make, yet these challenges can be painful, particularly for relatives of those with severe cognitive limitations and for people who themselves have milder forms of cognitive disability. There is, moreover, a risk that raising questions about the moral status of those with severe cognitive limitations could ultimately lead to their receiving worse treatment—a real danger given the neglectful and cruel treatment to which they have been and sometimes continue to be subjected. So why raise the issue of their moral status? What can this accomplish, I was asked, other than to promote an "ethics of exclusion"? This chapter is in part an answer these questions, though its broader aim is to contribute to our understanding of the moral status of those with severe cognitive limitations.

To avoid the use of terms that may have different connotations to different people, I refer to human beings in the category with which I will be concerned as the "radically cognitively limited"—though here, for the sake of concision, I will abbreviate "radically cognitively limited" to "cognitively limited." These are human beings who are capable of consciousness but whose cognitive capacities and congenital cognitive potential are no higher than those of the most highly psychologically developed nonhuman animals.[1]

Animals

The moral status of cognitively limited human beings first became a topic of philosophical discussion in the writings of philosophers whose aim was

---

[1] Eva Kittay raises questions about what it means to suppose that there are such human beings in "At the Margins of Moral Personhood," *Ethics* 116 (2005): 130. For a short response, see McMahan 2009, 241–42.

to challenge complacent beliefs about the morality of various harmful uses of animals, such as raising and killing them for food. These philosophers recognized that most people, when challenged to defend their view that human beings are inviolable in ways that animals are not, typically cite certain superiorities of human psychological capacity, such as self-consciousness, the ability to act on the basis of reasons, and so on. They also noticed, however, that some human beings *lack* these capacities. Fetuses and infants, for example, are neither self-conscious nor autonomous. Yet there are obvious responses to the concern that our beliefs about the permissible treatment of animals are inconsistent with our beliefs about the permissible treatment of fetuses and infants. One is that most of us do in fact accept that even those fetuses with the capacity for consciousness are not morally inviolable in the way that adult persons are. Most people accept that it can be permissible to kill a conscious fetus via abortion for reasons that would be insufficient to justify the killing of an adult person. Moreover, even though fetuses and infants are not capable of self-consciousness or action on the basis of reasons, they nevertheless have the potential to develop those capacities. Similarly, persons who have become irreversibly demented or comatose may also lack these capacities and even the potential to have them in the future, but they differ from animals in having had them previously.

To challenge people's complacency about harming animals, therefore, it was necessary to press them to defend the consistency between their beliefs about animals and their beliefs about the permissible treatment of human beings who not only lack certain psychological capacities but also, like animals, lack the potential to have them, as well as a history of having had them. How could people cite certain psychological capacities as morally differentiating human beings in general from animals, yet treat animals in ways in which they recognized that it would be wrong to treat human beings who lack those capacities?

The aim of those philosophers who introduced the cognitively limited into the discussion about the moral status of animals was to use the common belief that the cognitively limited share the inviolability of cognitively normal human beings as a fixed point in the set of our moral convictions in order to criticize common beliefs about animals as inconsistent with it. While some may have believed that the cognitively limited have a lower moral status, or came to believe this in the course of thinking through the argument, it was no part of their motivation to question the status of the cognitively limited.

The challenge these philosophers posed has never, in my view, been satisfactorily answered.[2] Most people believe that it would be permissible, and perhaps morally required, to kill an adult chimpanzee if the

---

[2] For criticism of the responses with which I am familiar, see McMahan 2002, 203–32, and McMahan 2005.

transplantation of its organs could save the life of an adult human being. Yet no one in our society has suggested, or would suggest, that it could be permissible to kill a cognitively limited human being, even if his or her psychological capacities were lower than those of a chimpanzee, and even if his or her organs could be used to save the lives of *several* cognitively normal human beings. And probably no more than a few people believe that it could be permissible even to allow a cognitively limited human being to die for this purpose. Indeed, most people accept that it would be impermissible to allow such a human being to die for *any* reason other than one that would also justify allowing a cognitively normal human being to die. Most people believe instead that we ought, as a society, to devote significant resources to life-sustaining medical treatments for cognitively limited human beings, including those with no living relatives. Yet no one has yet shown how the belief that chimpanzees are sacrifice-able can be reconciled with the belief that human beings with comparable psychological capacities and potential are not.

Saving people's lives is of course one of the most important aims one can have. But our harming and killing of animals very seldom serves that end. The reason for which people in the United States slaughter billions of animals each year, causing most of them long periods of suffering beforehand, is to enjoy the difference in pleasure between meals with meat and meals without meat. I believe that this difference is trivial and that those who sincerely believe otherwise have a distorted sense of what significant deprivation involves. Thus, when combined with the demand for moral caution, the challenge to consistency posed by the comparison between the cognitively limited and animals with comparable cognitive endowments ought, as a matter of moral and intellectual integrity, to move those who argue and campaign for the rights of the cognitively limited to accept the inconveniences of being vegetarian.

Fetuses

Perhaps the main reason I began to think about the moral status of the cognitively limited is that I realized when I began to study the morality of abortion as a graduate student that liberal beliefs about the morality of abortion are doubtfully consistent with common beliefs about the moral status of the cognitively limited. It seems likely that most of those who have offered secular arguments for the view that the cognitively limited are morally inviolable also accept that abortion can be permissible in a wide range of cases, even after the onset of fetal consciousness. Yet because some cognitively limited adults have cognitive capacities no higher than those of a conscious fetus, these people cannot consistently believe that psychological capacity is the basis of inviolability; therefore they cannot believe that the permissibility of late-term abortion depends on the psychological nature of the fetus. It cannot, on their view, be connected with the fetus's lack of the capacity for self-consciousness, or with its lack of the ability to care about its own future, or with the fact that even if it were to live it would be psychologically related to itself in the future in only the most attenuated ways. For many cognitively limited adults also lack these properties.

Liberals naturally assume that a permissive view of abortion must be compatible with a strong duty of care for the cognitively limited, who are among the most vulnerable of all the disabled. Yet at least in the case of fetuses with the capacity for consciousness—and in this discussion I will be concerned solely with fetuses that have this capacity—the relevant facts suggest otherwise. Like a cognitively limited child, but unlike an animal, a conscious fetus is both a member of the human species and the biological offspring of human parents. And because the capacity for consciousness arises after the current point of viability, such a fetus is capable, with medical assistance, of independent life in the external world. It is, of course, both true and important that most cognitively limited human beings have cognitive capacities higher than those of any con- scious fetus. But what seems necessary for a liberal view of abortion to be compatible with the view that cognitively limited human beings are inviolable is that there should be a threshold on the scale of psychological capacity that separates the violable from the inviolable and that conscious fetuses should be below it, while most older cognitively limited human beings are above it. That such a significant threshold would neatly divide conscious fetuses from most cognitively limited human beings would be highly serendipitous. More importantly, there would be unacceptable intuitive costs to finding the threshold at this point; for premature infants, whose psychological capacities are no higher than those of fetuses at the same stage of development, would be below this threshold, while higher animals with capacities comparable to those of cognitively limited adults would be above it.

One intrinsic difference between almost all conscious fetuses and all cognitively limited human beings is that while the former have the potential to develop high cognitive capacities, the latter do not. Because most people tend to attribute moral significance to potential, and because conscious fetuses share with the cognitively limited other properties to which our intuitions respond, such as membership in the human species and kinship with persons, it seems that the comparison between fetuses and older cognitively limited human beings, in conjunction with the assumption that the cognitively limited share our inviolability, challenges the liberal view of abortion. Unlike the comparison between animals and the cognitively limited, which challenges the traditional view of the moral status of animals, the comparison between fetuses and the cognitively limited *supports* the traditional, conservative view of the moral status of the fetus. If liberal defenders of the inviolability of the cognitively limited are unable to identify a morally highly significant difference between the cognitively limited and conscious fetuses, consistency may require that they abandon their permissive view of abortion. If psychological capacity is irrelevant to an individual's status as inviolable, the idea that abortion is permissible may seem to be a widely accepted and therefore conspicuously successful dimension of the "ethics of exclusion."

Those familiar with the philosophical literature on abortion may be undismayed by this problem of consistency. For they may expect to be able to solve it by availing themselves of some version of Judith Jarvis Thomson's argument for abortion, which makes no appeal to assumptions about the moral status of the fetus but instead seeks to justify abortion by claiming that, at least in most cases, the fetus has no right to draw life support from the pregnant woman when this requires that it occupy her body. Since it has no right to the use of her body, she does not violate its rights by expelling it from her body, even if this requires killing it in the process, as abortion sometimes does.[3] Many people have seen it as an advantage of this argument that it demonstrates the permissibility of abortion without entailing or even supporting the permissibility of infanticide, even if there are no intrinsic differences between a late-term fetus and a premature infant at the same stage of development. But it could also be invoked to show that a liberal, permissive view of abortion is compatible with recognizing the inviolability of *all* human beings with the capacity for consciousness: conscious fetuses, infants, and all cognitively limited human beings. For what it purports to show is that conscious fetuses can share our status as inviolable yet still not be morally protected against abortion, since inviolability of the sort that we possess does not guarantee immunity from lethal expulsion if we invade or trespass upon another person's body.

This would be a happy solution to the problem of consistency if Thomson's argument had no unacceptable implications. But I believe that it has an implication that no one can reasonably embrace. This is that the infliction of grievous but nonlethal prenatal injury could *in principle* be justified whenever abortion is. Imagine a case in which a pregnant woman has an interest that is frustrated by the fetus's presence in her body and that is sufficiently important that, according to Thomson's argument, she would be justified in having an abortion to satisfy the interest. Yet suppose she could also satisfy the interest in a way that would merely injure the fetus, causing it to suffer moderate pain intermittently throughout its life, but allowing it to have a life that, despite the pain, would be well worth living. In these circumstances, in which the woman's interest could be satisfied either by having an abortion or by doing what would injure her fetus, and in which it is better for the fetus to be injured than killed, she ought to do what will injure the fetus rather than kill it. In

---

[3] Judith Jarvis Thomson, "A Defense of Abortion," *Philosophy and Public Affairs* 1 (1971): 47–66.

injuring it, she would not, according to Thomson's argument, be wronging it. Since she has no duty to allow the fetus to remain in her body, the fetus may continue to live only on her sufferance. An injury may simply be the cost it must bear for the sake of the benefit of using her body for life support.

This conclusion is unacceptable. It is false that a woman may permissibly injure her fetus, thereby causing it to suffer lifelong problems, whenever (1) it would be permissible for her to have an abortion, (2) her aim in having the abortion could be equally well served by an act that would injure the fetus but not kill it, and (3) it would be better for the fetus to be injured than to be killed. This is not only counterintuitive but also misunderstands the moral difference between killing and injuring a fetus. Killing a fetus via abortion frustrates only those interests it has at the time, which are weak for reasons that I explain in the following section. Nonlethally injuring a fetus, by contrast, may frustrate not only those weak interests but also the stronger *future* interests of the adult into whom the fetus will develop.[4] Because Thomson's argument has unacceptable implications for prenatal injury, it cannot provide the moral justification for abortion, which must instead appeal to facts about the nature and status of the fetus. Hence the problem remains of achieving consistency between a liberal view of abortion and common beliefs about the status of the cognitively limited.

There are of course various possible ways of resolving the apparent inconsistency: one can abandon the liberal view of abortion, retain the liberal view but reject the inviolability of the cognitively limited, make less substantial adjustments to one's beliefs about the moral status of *both* fetuses and the cognitively limited, or find an alternative argument for the liberal view of abortion that neither appeals to the nature of the fetus nor implies the permissibility of causing prenatal injury. I will offer no recommendations here. But unless we can resolve this apparent inconsistency, we cannot claim to understand the basis of our own moral status.

Cognitive Enhancement

This problem of consistency can be rendered even more acute by considering the possibility of genetic cognitive enhancement. Most people seem wary of genetic cognitive enhancement. They seem to believe that there is no moral reason to enhance the future cognitive capacities of a

---

[4] For further discussion, see McMahan 2006. One might argue that the proponent of Thomson's argument could consistently rule out the permissibility of causing prenatal injury on the ground that the strong and enduring interests of a person that the injury would frustrate can override the right of the pregnant woman to deny a fetus unimpaired access to the use of her body. But those interests do not provide a reason that is stronger than one's reason not to kill a fetus *if* it is inviolable.

cognitively normal fetus, and perhaps even a reason *not* to, at least by genetic means. Yet even those who claim that disabilities are not misfortunes tend to concede that there is a moral reason, if possible, to enhance the cognitive capacities of a fetus that would otherwise be cognitively limited, and to do so *for its own sake*. Here as elsewhere in debates about genetic enhancement, many people attribute great significance to the distinction between therapeutic enhancement, or enhancement that brings an individual up to the norm, and enhancement beyond the norm.

Many of those who believe that there is a moral reason to provide cognitive enhancement for a cognitively limited fetus also believe that it can often be permissible to kill a cognitively limited fetus, or indeed a cognitively normal fetus, via abortion. But are these beliefs compatible? If we examine the considerations that might favor cognitive enhancement, we can determine what they imply about the morality of abortion.

The intuition that there is a moral reason to provide cognitive enhancement for a cognitively limited fetus might be explained and justified in three possible ways. The justification might appeal (1) to the present interest of the fetus, (2) to the interests that the individual affected would have later in life, or (3) to the idea that it would be better in impersonal terms for there to be a cognitively normal adult rather than a cognitively limited adult in the future.

Consider first the present interest of the fetus, on the assumption that the fetus and the adult into whom it will develop are identical—that is, one and the same individual at different times. (Assuming that the fetus has the capacity for consciousness, this assumption is plausible on most views of our identity.) There are two general ways in which the fetus's life might proceed. Without enhancement, it will become a cognitively limited adult. With enhancement, it will develop normal cognitive and other psychological capacities. Because it will later have more dimensions of well-being accessible to it if it develops normal cognitive capacities, it will be better for it, considering its life as a whole, to receive cognitive enhancement.

Most people assume that the difference in value between the two possible lives determines the strength of the individual's present interest in the better of the two, even when the individual is a fetus. If this is right— that is, if the cognitively limited fetus has an interest in having the better of the two possible types of life that is proportionate in strength to the extent to which a life with normal cognitive capacities would be better— then its present interest in receiving enhancement must be exceedingly strong. And to the extent that the strength of moral reason to satisfy an individual's interest varies with the strength of the interest, the reason to provide the enhancement must be correspondingly strong.

If, however, a cognitively limited fetus has a strong interest in having a future life with normal cognitive capacities rather than a life with radically limited capacities, it seems that a normal fetus must have a comparably strong interest in having a future life with normal cognitive capacities rather than no future life at all. If we compare the two possible types of life it could have, depending on whether or not an abortion is performed—that is, a life of normal length with normal cognitive capacities and a life that ends prior to birth—it is obvious that the former is the better of the two. Assuming that the extent to which the longer life would be better is the measure of the strength of the fetus's present interest in having the longer life rather than the shorter, its interest in avoiding an abortion must be exceedingly strong. And to the extent that the strength of the moral reason to satisfy an individual's interest varies with the strength of the interest, the reason not to perform an abortion must be correspondingly strong.

Indeed, a normal fetus's interest in continuing to live should be even stronger than a cognitively limited fetus's interest in receiving cognitive enhancement. This is because a future life with radical cognitive limitation is significantly better than no future life at all; hence a future life of normal length with normal cognitive capacities is better than no future life at all by significantly more than a life of normal length with normal capacities is better than a life with radical cognitive limitation. Considering only reasons derived from fetal interests, therefore, the reason not to kill a normal fetus via abortion should be significantly stronger than the reason to enhance a cognitively limited fetus. There are, moreover, other considerations that may widen this gap even further. For example, abortion is an instance of *doing* harm, while the failure to enhance a cognitively limited fetus merely *allows* an undesirable condition to persist.

I have argued elsewhere that this way of understanding the strength of the fetus's interest in continuing to live is misleading. The strength of the fetus's interest in continuing to live *at the time*, and thus the strength of the moral reason to preserve its life *for its own sake*, depends not only on how good its future life would be but also on the extent to which it would be psychologically related to itself in the future were it to live. The strength of what I have called its "time-relative interest" in continuing to live is, in other words, discounted for the degree of psychological discontinuity between itself now and itself in the future, were it to live.[5] Given the tenuousness of the psychological relations between a conscious fetus and itself at any time after its birth, death would not be a great misfortune for it. It is this, together with the nature of the fetus as a being lacking the capacity for self-consciousness and other higher psychological

---

[5] McMahan 2002, 80 and 269–80. In this book, I understand psychological continuity as admitting of degrees. In Parfit's canonical understanding of the notion, it is not a matter of degree. (See note 7 below.) For reasons of brevity, I will refer here simply to interests rather than time-relative interests.

capacities, that makes the killing of a fetus substantially less serious morally than the killing of a person.

But if this is correct, it undermines not only the view that fetuses have a strong interest in continuing to live but also the view that a cognitively limited fetus has a strong interest in being cognitively enhanced. For a cognitively limited fetus would be no more closely psychologically related to itself as an enhanced, cognitively normal adult than a normal fetus would be to itself as an adult. So just as a normal fetus's comparatively weak interest in continuing to live grounds only a weak moral reason not to kill it, so a cognitively limited fetus's comparatively weak interest in having normal cognitive capacities as an adult grounds only a weak moral reason to provide it with cognitive enhancement. In short, what seems to me to be the best defense of the liberal view of abortion implies that the moral reason to enhance the cognitive capacities of a cognitively limited fetus for its own sake—that is, the reason deriving from its own interests—is even weaker than the comparatively weak moral reason not to have an abortion. (It is weaker because the alternative to enhancement—a life of cognitive limitation—is better than the alternative to not having an abortion: no life at all.)

One might respond to this point by noting that whereas abortion prevents further interests from arising, and thus affects *only* the interests that the fetus has at the time, which may all be quite weak, the failure to provide cognitive enhancement for a cognitively limited fetus not only affects its present interests but also will affect the *future* interests of the adult it will become. While there might be only a very weak reason not to kill a cognitively limited (or cognitively normal) fetus via abortion, since that would frustrate only its weak present interests, there might nevertheless be a strong moral reason to provide it with cognitive enhancement *if* it will live, since the failure to do so would doom many of its future interests to frustration.

This is in fact the correct way to distinguish morally between abortion and most forms of prenatal injury. It may seem paradoxical that considerations that could justify *killing* a fetus via abortion might not be sufficient to justify injuring it in some nonlethal way. But there is no paradox if one realizes that while abortion frustrates only the present interests of a fetus, which may all be weak, prenatal injury can frustrate the interests of a later adult, which may be significantly stronger and more enduring. And one might think of the failure to provide cognitive enhancement for a cognitively limited fetus as a passive form of prenatal injury—a form of injuring via allowing rather than by doing.

The problem with this appeal to future interests, though, is that the interest of a cognitively limited adult in having normal cognitive capacities is not significantly stronger than the interest of a cognitively limited fetus in becoming a cognitively normal adult. For whenever an individual with initially very low psychological capacities develops high capacities, whether through artificial enhancement or natural maturation, there is necessarily substantial psychological discontinuity between the two phases of the individual's life—just as there is when brain damage or progressive dementia causes a parallel decline from high capacities to low. If, moreover, the strength of an individual's interest in some future good is discounted for psychological discontinuity between that individual now and itself at the time it would experience the good, then there can be no point in the life of a cognitively limited adult at which he or she has a strong interest in having greatly enhanced cognitive capacities. It follows, therefore, that it cannot be a strong moral reason to provide cognitive enhancement for a cognitively limited fetus that the failure to provide it would frustrate the much stronger future interests of the adult into whom it would develop.

Failing to provide cognitive enhancement for a cognitively limited fetus—or indeed *causing* a normal fetus to become cognitively limited—is therefore relevantly different from most other forms of harmful prenatal neglect or prenatal injury. Action or omission that arrests the development of the fetus's psychological capacities at or near their initial level thus precludes the kind of psychological continuity over time that is a necessary condition of a strong present interest in having normal adult psychological capacities. This is not true, however, of prenatal injuries that result in physical impairment. These may make the life of the person into whom the fetus develops more difficult and less fulfilling than it would have been without the impairment. And, although the injury occurs while the victim is a fetus, the harm is suffered later, when the victim is a person; thus the injury frustrates the strong interests of a person rather than just the weak interests of a fetus.[6]

In summary, the appeal to interests, both present and future, when discounted for psychological discontinuity, yields the following conclusions. The interest of the fetus in continuing to live is comparatively weak and grounds only a weak objection to abortion. The interest of a cognitively limited fetus in receiving cognitive enhancement is similarly weak and grounds only a weak reason to provide it with cognitive enhancement. The future interests of the person into whom a normal fetus will develop, if it lives, are likely to be strong and to ground a strong reason not to cause most forms of prenatal injury. Yet the interest of a cognitively limited adult in acquiring normal cognitive capacities is weak for the same reason that the interest of a fetus in developing adult cognitive capacities is weak. Because of this, one cannot argue in favor of cognitive enhancement for a cognitively limited fetus on the ground that the failure to provide the enhancement will frustrate that individual's future interest in having normal rather than radically limited cognitive

---

[6] For an important complication that I cannot pursue here, see Robert M. Adams, "Existence, Self-Interest, and the Problem of Evil," *Noûs* 13:317–32.

capacities. Assuming that there is a morally significant difference between doing and allowing, there is a stronger moral reason not to cause a normal fetus to become cognitively limited than there is to enhance the capacities of a cognitively limited fetus; but even that reason is not as strong as commonsense intuition supposes that it is, *if* it is assumed to derive from the present interest of the fetus or the future interest of the cognitively limited adult. Finally, it is worth noting that another implication is that there is no significant reason to enhance the cognitive capacities of an animal for its own sake—again because of the psychological discontinuity there would be between the unenhanced and the enhanced animal.

Some of these implications of focusing on interests will be pleasing to many people. Many will welcome the liberal implication about abortion, most will welcome the basis for objecting to most forms of prenatal injury, and virtually all will welcome the conclusion that there is little or no reason to enhance the cognitive capacities of an animal. But the other implications—that there is only a weak reason to enhance a cognitively limited fetus or adult, and that there is only a somewhat stronger reason not to cause a normal fetus to be cognitively limited—are highly counterintuitive.

Perhaps the best option for avoiding the unwanted implications is to abandon the focus on interests—that is, to abandon the effort to account for and justify our intuitions about cognitive enhancement by appeal to "individual-affecting" reasons, or reasons concerned with what is better or worse for individuals. We might instead seek to defend our intuitions by appeal to "impersonal" reasons—that is, reasons that, though they may be concerned with considerations of well-being, need not make any essential reference to what is better or worse for individuals. To borrow the kind of example that Derek Parfit made famous in his seminal work on the Non-Identity Problem, suppose that one has a choice between having a child now, when any child one might have would be cognitively limited, and waiting some months, after which one could have a *different* child with normal cognitive capacities. And suppose, for the sake of argument, that one's choice would be on balance neither better nor worse for other existing and future people. Most of us believe that one nevertheless has a strong moral reason to postpone having a child. Yet this cannot be explained by reference to what is better or worse for individuals. If one has a cognitively limited child now, that will not be worse for that child, or even noncomparatively bad for it, if its life will be worth living. Similarly, if one waits to have a child with normal cognitive capacities, that will not be better for that child than never existing would have been. For if that child had never existed, there would have been no one for whom that would have been worse. And because "better for" and "worse for" are essentially comparative terms, existing cannot be better for an individual if never existing could not have been worse for that individual. It seems, therefore, that one's reason to have the cognitively normal child rather than the cognitively limited child is an impersonal reason. This reason is related to the fact that a cognitively normal child can reasonably be expected to have a richer, better life than a cognitively limited child, but the reason cannot be that the cognitively normal child's life would be *better for it* than never existing would be.

If, however, there is a strong impersonal reason to cause a cognitively normal child to exist rather than a different cognitively limited child, it seems there must also be at least as strong a reason to provide cognitive enhancement for a cognitively limited child, so that, again, a cognitively normal life will be lived rather than a cognitively limited life. Consider, for example, the following two choices.

(1) One can cause a cognitively limited individual to exist or cause a *different* cognitively normal individual to exist.
(2) A fetus that does not now exist but will exist will initially be cognitively limited. One can act now to ensure that this fetus will receive cognitive enhancement that will enable it to have normal cognitive capacities; otherwise it will remain cognitively limited. Whether one acts now to ensure that it will be enhanced will not affect its identity, or the identity of the adult into whom it will develop.

In case 1, one's choice will determine whether a cognitively limited individual or a different cognitively normal individual will exist. In case 2, one's choice will determine whether a particular future person will be cognitively limited or have normal cognitive capacities. (I have stipulated that the individual in case 2 is not a currently existing individual in order to avoid engaging intuitions about the distinction between existing and future individuals, which I suspect are more influential than most of us realize.) In both cases, the choice is between there being a life with radical cognitive limitation and a life of cognitive normalcy. The difference is that in case 1 these would be lives of different individuals, while in case 2 they would be alternative possible lives of the same individual.

According to Derek Parfit's No-Difference View, this difference between the two cases is of no significance.[7] Parfit introduces this view in a discussion of two hypothetical medical programs, one of which would cure a thousand fetuses that will later exist independently of whether the program is implemented and will have a certain disability if it is not implemented, while the other would enable a thousand women to have a child without that disability rather than a *different* child with it. Parfit suggests that, if we can implement only one of these programs, it makes no difference which we choose. What matters is that there should be a

⁷ Derek Parfit, *Reasons and Persons* (Oxford: Oxford University Press, 1984), 366–71. Also see his *On What Matters* (Oxford: Oxford University Press, forthcoming), chap. 22.

thousand future lives lived without rather than with the disability; it makes no difference whether these will be the lives of future people who would have been disabled if a different program had been adopted or whether they will be the lives of people who would never have existed (so that different people with the disability would have existed instead) if a different program had been adopted. If one agrees with this conclusion, one might take this to show that, in some cases at least, impersonal reasons can have the same weight as individual-affecting reasons.

The comparison between cases 1 and 2 suggests a different conclusion (not one that is incompatible with Parfit's but merely different). As in the choice between medical programs, the possible outcomes in each case are, under certain descriptions, the same: either a life will be lived with radical cognitive limitation or a life will be lived with normal cognitive capacities. In case 1, the impersonal reason to cause the cognitively normal life to be lived seems quite strong. And intuitively the reason to cause the cognitively normal life to be lived in case 2, via cognitive enhancement, seems equally strong. Yet I have argued that the *individual-affecting* reason one has to provide enhancement—that is, the reason to enhance the fetus for its own sake—is comparatively weak. I do not think, however, that the comparison between these cases requires the retraction of that claim. That the individual-affecting reason to ensure enhancement for the fetus is weak is compatible with its being true that the reason to ensure enhancement is as strong in case 2 as the reason to cause a cognitively normal individual rather than a cognitively limited individual to exist is in case 1. For the strong reason to ensure enhancement could be, like the reason to cause a cognitively normal individual to exist, *impersonal* in character.

This is in fact the conclusion I think we should draw. Even though the fetus will, because of its psychological isolation from its future self, have only a weak interest in cognitive enhancement, and even though this would remain true if it were to develop into a cognitively limited adult, there is nevertheless a strong reason to ensure that a life will be lived with normal rather than radically limited cognitive capacities. One ought to ensure that the enhancement is provided not so much for the sake of the fetus itself as simply to ensure that a better life is lived rather than a worse life. It seems that Parfit is right that it makes no difference whether or not this is the life of an individual who would otherwise have been cognitively limited.

It is worth noting that although there *is* a weak individual-affecting reason to ensure enhancement in case 2, it does not combine with the impersonal reason to form an overall stronger reason. If it did, one's reason to ensure enhancement in case 2 would be stronger than one's reason to cause a cognitively normal rather than a cognitively limited individual to exist in case 1. But that seems implausible. I infer from this that, at least in this case, the individual-affecting and impersonal reasons are not additive.

I earlier claimed that the interests that ground an individual-affecting reason to enhance a cognitively limited fetus also ground an individual-affecting reason of at least equal strength not to kill a normal fetus via abortion. But I then argued that both those reasons are quite weak. I have now suggested that there is an impersonal reason to enhance a cognitively limited fetus that seems quite strong—at least as strong as the impersonal reason to choose to have a cognitively normal child rather than a cognitively limited child. This raises the question of whether the considerations that ground the impersonal reason to ensure cognitive enhancement for a cognitively limited fetus also ground an equally strong impersonal reason not to kill a normal fetus via abortion. If they do, it will be difficult, if not impossible, to defend a liberal view of abortion, assuming that the failure of Thomson's argument shows that the moral case for a liberal view has to rest on claims about the lower status or weaker interests of the fetus. For if the reason to have a cognitively normal rather than a cognitively limited child is strong, and if the impersonal reason to provide cognitive enhancement for a cognitively limited fetus is at least equally strong, and if, finally, there is an impersonal reason not to kill a normal fetus that is as strong as the reason to enhance a cognitively limited fetus, then it seems to follow that there is a strong impersonal reason not to have an abortion.

At this point, however, it must remain a matter of speculation what the implications are for the morality of abortion of the claim that there is a strong impersonal reason to enhance the cognitive capacities of a cognitively limited fetus, so that it would develop normal cognitive capacities. For at this point we do not know the content of the relevant impersonal moral principle. It might plausibly be claimed that if there is a strong impersonal reason to choose that a life will be lived with normal cognitive capacities rather than that a life will be lived with radical cognitive limitations, there must also be a strong impersonal reason to choose that a life will be lived with normal cognitive capacities rather than that no life will be lived at all. If that is correct, the impersonal reason to enhance the cognitive capacities of a cognitively limited fetus may well imply that there is an impersonal reason of comparable strength not only not to kill a normal fetus but also to cause individuals to exist with normal human cognitive capacities rather than not to cause such individuals to exist. An impersonal reason to enhance a cognitively limited fetus might, in other words, imply both an objection to abortion and a further impersonal reason to cause new individuals with lives worth living to exist.

But while it is possible that the considerations that ground the impersonal reason to enhance the cognitive capacities of a cognitively limited fetus also ground an impersonal reason not to kill a normal fetus, it is also possible that they do not. To explain why, it will be helpful to review the argument for thinking that if there is a strong reason to enhance a cognitively limited fetus, it must be an impersonal reason. The presupposition of that argument is that the relation between a fetus and its future self is psychologically so tenuous that the choice between providing and not providing cognitive enhancement for a cognitively limited fetus is relevantly like a choice between causing an individual with normal cognitive capacities to exist and causing a cognitively limited individual to exist. The explanation of why the reason to provide enhancement is impersonal rather than individual-affecting is thus that the two possible futures that the fetus might have are relevantly like the possible lives of different individuals. Mere identity without any significant psychological continuity cannot ground a significant individual-affecting reason for enhancement.

The psychological discontinuity between a normal fetus and its future self is just as great as that between a cognitively limited fetus and its future self (with or without enhancement). Abortion is, therefore, relevantly similar to preventing an individual from ever existing, and a choice not to have an abortion is relevantly similar to allowing an individual to come into existence.[8] (Note that I say "relevantly similar" rather than "exactly like" or "equivalent to.")

With this as background, it seems, intuitively, that one ought to be able consistently to hold both of the following views:

(1) If one or the other of two different individuals will exist, there is a strong impersonal reason to choose that it be the one who would have the better life. Hence if either a cognitively normal or a cognitively limited individual will exist, there is a strong impersonal reason to choose that it be the one with normal cognitive capacities.

(2) There is no significant impersonal reason to cause that same cognitively normal individual to exist rather than not to cause anyone to exist.

The parallel claims concerning fetuses, cognitive enhancement, and abortion are these:

(3) If the cognitive capacities of a cognitively limited fetus can be enhanced to the normal level, there is a strong impersonal reason to enhance them so that the fetus's future will be that of a cognitively normal individual rather than that of a cognitively limited individual.

---

[8] For a detailed defense of these claims, see McMahan 2002, 169–71. If we thought that there was an *individual-affecting* reason to enhance a cognitively limited fetus that was as strong as the impersonal reason to have a cognitively normal rather than a cognitively limited child, that *would* seem to imply that there is an even stronger *individual-affecting* reason not to kill the fetus.

(4) There is no significant impersonal reason to preserve that same cognitively limited fetus's life rather than to have an abortion.

It may be that the impersonal reason to enhance the cognitively limited fetus's capacities is conditional on the decision to allow it to live. That is, there may be no significant impersonal reason not to have an abortion, though *if* an abortion is not performed, there is then a strong impersonal reason to provide enhancement, so that the life that will be lived will be one of cognitive normalcy rather than radical cognitive limitation.

I mention these possibilities without knowing how to proceed to determine which is correct, or closer to being correct. The second possibility—that the strong impersonal reason to enhance a cognitively limited fetus is compatible with the absence of a strong impersonal reason to preserve a fetus's life—is considerably more intuitive, at least for those who think that psychological capacity is relevant to moral status, but that alone does not guarantee that is correct, or even coherent.

This is one of two problems—or, rather, of at least two problems—that I will leave unresolved. The other concerns the cognitive enhancement of nonhuman animals. Assuming that the reason to enhance a cognitively limited fetus is impersonal in character, there seems to be no ground for supposing that it is only in the case of *human* lives that it is impersonally better for a life to be lived with higher rather than lower cognitive capacities. One response to the problem of defending the intuition that there is no impersonal reason to enhance the cognitive capacities of an animal is that the level of psychological capacity that it is good for an individual to have is a function of that individual's essential *nature*, which is determined by its *species*. I have, however, argued extensively against this view in various places and will not rehearse those arguments here.[9]

Supra-persons

According to commonsense morality, it is a defining feature of our moral status that we are *inviolable*. This means, among other things, that we cannot permissibly be sacrificed for the benefit, even the greater benefit, of others. Most people, or at least most people with secular moral views, now accept that fetuses are in certain ways violable, and thus do not share our moral status. These people accept that a fetus may be sacrificed if its presence becomes seriously burdensome to the woman carrying it. This suggests that the basis of our inviolability cannot be species membership alone.

There are, however, certain forms of sacrifice to which more people think that even fetuses are not morally vulnerable. No society, to my knowledge, accepts the permissibility of killing a fetus in order to *use* it in some opportunistic way—for example, to use its organs for transplanta-

---

[9] See, for example, McMahan 2002, 145–49; McMahan 2005; and McMahan 2009.

tion. Yet even here many people distinguish between embryos, which they think may permissibly be used, and older developing human organisms, which again suggests that mere membership in the human species is not the basis of our status as inviolable (assuming that embryos are members of our species).

Yet most people believe that animals are violable. Most people have no qualms about using them for food, clothing, sport, experimentation, and many other purposes. By contrast, few would accept that it could be permissible to sacrifice a cognitively limited human being, even one whose psychological capacities are uniformly lower than those of some animals we sacrifice for certain purposes, irrespective of whether the sacrifice would be to eliminate a burden this individual imposed or to provide a benefit to others. Most accept, as I have noted, that post-fetal cognitively limited human beings share our inviolability, which suggests that most do not accept that psychological capacity is the basis of moral inviolability.

This leaves us with strong intuitions without any apparent foundation. We do not appear to have a coherent understanding of the basis of our own inviolability. What is more, most people do not really believe that we are literally inviolable. Most people—or at least the great majority of people whose moral views are not dictated by ancient religious texts—are not moral absolutists. They accept that all substantive moral principles may be overridden in conditions of extremity. For example, most of us who believe that it is wrong intentionally to kill an innocent person nevertheless accept that it would be permissible to kill an innocent person if that were necessary as a means of preventing a very large number of other innocent people from being intentionally killed by others.

We are right to reject absolutism, which necessarily bases momentous all-or-nothing moral judgments on considerations that are intrinsically morally trivial. Consider, for example, the only type of act that many contemporary liberals claim is absolutely prohibited: torture. For it to be true that torture is absolutely prohibited, there must be a determinate distinction between acts that constitute torture and those that do not. Consider, then, the kind of act among all those that count as torture that is least bad for the victim. If there is an absolute prohibition of torture, there is no goal, however important, that could justify committing an act of that sort against another. Next consider an act that is only slightly less bad for the victim that does not constitute torture and, though generally wrong, is not absolutely prohibited. The difference between this act and the least bad act of torture may be trivial. Yet this act can, by hypothesis, be justified in certain conditions—for example, if it is necessary to prevent a great catastrophe. Yet, according to absolutism, an act that is only trivially worse for the victim will count as torture and thus cannot be justified even to prevent a catastrophe that would be *vastly* worse. This is arbitrary.

This objection to absolutism is quite general. For every important concept that figures in an absolute prohibition, and thus must have a determinate extension, there are phenomena that lie just outside the extension of the concept and differ only trivially from ones that lie just inside. If, for example, certain acts of killing are absolutely prohibited, there must be acts that are outside the scope of the absolute prohibition that differ only trivially from some of those within—because, for example, they do not count as instances of *killing* because the causal path from the act to the death is slightly less direct. Or if what is absolutely prohibited is the killing of the *innocent*, there will be some acts of killing that are just outside the scope of the prohibition, but differ only trivially from some that are absolutely prohibited, because, for example, the victim just barely fails to satisfy the criteria for innocence.

What most people really believe, therefore, is that all individuals are morally violable, but to greatly varying degrees. Judging by their behavior, most people believe that animals are sacrificeable for almost any reason that would serve human interests, however trivial, such as the interest in having a meal with meat rather than a slightly less appealing meal without it. Normal adult human beings, by contrast, are almost universally regarded as having an extremely low degree of violability. The sacrifice of an innocent person can be morally permissible only if it is necessary to prevent a substantially greater harm to many other people. Commonsense morality seems to assign fetuses an intermediate degree of violability, yet attributes to cognitively limited human beings beyond the fetal stage a low degree of violability comparable or identical to our own.

Assume, for simplicity, that we have identified a single property as the basis of our moral status, and that this property is possessed to varying degrees by different individuals. Suppose, for example, that that property, which we can call the "base property," is the capacity for autonomy. People clearly vary in the extent to which they are capable of autonomous action. Some are more reflective, better able to understand the reasons they have for acting in certain ways, and more capable of controlling themselves, so that they are better able to act on the basis of the reasons they perceive themselves to have. In these conditions, one way to understand variations in moral violability would be to suppose that the degree to which an individual is violable is proportionate to the degree to which that individual possesses the base property.

I know of no one who holds such a view. Most people's beliefs are considerably more egalitarian—at least within the human species. Yet, as I have doggedly and tiresomely endeavored to show, the consistency of this general egalitarianism is challenged both by animals outside the species and by fetuses within it. One challenge emerges from the possibility of cognitive enhancement for cognitively limited fetuses. In exploring that challenge, I considered only cognitive enhancement up to the normal level for adult human beings. But perhaps consideration of the possibility of both cognitive and overall psychological enhancement beyond that level might stimulate our thinking about what we rather inaccurately refer to as human inviolability.

Suppose it were possible for us to create and coexist with individuals whose psychological capacities were genetically enhanced to such an extent that they would exceed ours *by more* than ours exceed those of the highest nonhuman animals. Call such individuals "supra-persons." Reflection on these hypothetical individuals might reinforce commonsense beliefs about the moral status of the cognitively limited. If we think that we would have the same moral status as these beings, or that they would be no less violable than we are, this could support the view that the cognitively limited have the same moral status that we have. For it would provide another instance in which we accept that a difference in psychological capacity that is as great as that between the cognitively limited and ourselves does not entail a difference in moral status, or violability. Yet reflection on supra-persons could exert pressure in the other direction. For if we would have the same status as supra-persons and the cognitively limited have the same status that we have, it follows that the moral status of supra-persons would be no higher than that of the cognitively limited, despite the fact that the differences of psychological capacity between the members of the two groups would be more than twice as great as those between ourselves and higher animals.

That would be unsurprising if moral status were entirely unconnected with psychological capacity. But what else could be the basis of our high moral status? What else could it be that makes lower animals more violable than we are? As I noted earlier, if fetuses and embryos are also more violable than we are, the relevant difference between animals and ourselves cannot be merely a matter of species membership. Indeed, if species membership were relevant to moral status, that could provide a basis for the view that supra-persons would have a higher status, or lower level of violability, than we have. For the differences, both of genotype and phenotype, between them and us might be so great that they would constitute a different species. It would be odd, however, to suppose that to determine their moral status we would need to determine their species membership—that is, that the question of their moral status could be answered only with the assistance of a biologist.

Intuitively, it does not seem entirely implausible to suppose that supra-persons could have a lower degree of violability (or, if one prefers, a higher degree of inviolability) than we have. Recall that one important dimension—almost certainly the most important dimension—of relative violability is the extent to which an individual may justifiably be sacrificed for the sake of others. I have suggested that most people accept that a single innocent person may permissibly be sacrificed for the sake of a sufficiently greater number of other innocent people. There is, presumably, wide variation in what people would regard as sufficient to override the relevant moral constraint. But suppose, for the sake of argument, that we all agree on a rough threshold for the sacrifice of an innocent person: namely, that it would be permissible to sacrifice the life of one innocent person if that were the only means of preventing not significantly fewer than a thousand other innocent people from being wrongfully killed. Next suppose that supra-persons would not only exceed us in psychological capacity by more than we exceed the highest nonhuman animals but would also, and as a consequence, have a substantially higher capacity for well-being, both synchronic and diachronic, than we have. Finally, suppose that they would also have significantly greater average longevity. Given these assumptions, it does not seem implausible to suppose that it could be permissible to kill one innocent person as a necessary means of saving significantly fewer than a thousand supra-persons—perhaps 950, or nine hundred. Nor does it seem implausible to suppose that it would *not* be permissible to sacrifice one innocent supra-person to save a thousand ordinary innocent people. It might take the saving of eleven hundred, or even two thousand innocent people to override a supra-person's right not to be killed, or not to be sacrificed.

One could accept these claims without embracing the view mentioned earlier according to which an individual's violability varies proportionally with the extent to which the base property or properties are realized in that individual's nature. It might instead be that the existence of supra-persons would introduce a new moral threshold, above which all individuals would have a higher status than all those below.

The structure of commonsense morality is best explained by the assumption that there is at present a single threshold that divides all post-fetal human beings from all nonhuman animals as well as from most, and possibly all, human fetuses. According to this view, all post-fetal human beings are violable only to a very low degree, while animals and fetuses have a higher degree of violability. While most people seem to accept that there may be varying degrees of violability below the threshold (for example, it may take more to justify the killing of a conscious fetus than the killing of a nonconscious fetus, and more to justify the killing of a chimpanzee than the killing of a mouse), the general view is that all individuals above the threshold are violable, or inviolable, to the same degree. This view is, in other words, egalitarian in the status it assigns to all those above the threshold.

Some philosophers, myself included, have argued for a more Kantian conception of the threshold, according to which only *persons*—that is, individuals with certain higher psychological capacities, such as self-consciousness, the capacity for caring, or the capacity to act on the basis of reasons—have a higher degree of inviolability. But these philosophers have tended to agree that all persons are violable or inviolable to an equal degree.

The existence of supra-persons might complicate this conception of moral status—a threshold defined by some base property or properties, above which all individuals have a higher degree of inviolability than any individual below it—by introducing a second, higher threshold. In a world with supra-persons, it might remain that all post-fetal human beings, or all persons, would have the same degree of inviolability, which would be greater than that of any animal, or any other individual below the relevant threshold. Yet it might also be that all supra-persons (or at least all *normal* supra-persons, for a severely cognitively impaired supra-person might be psychologically indistinguishable from a normal adult human being) would be inviolable to a higher degree than any unen-hanced person. Presumably all supra-persons would be inviolable to an equal degree—that is, there would be equality of moral status beyond the second threshold as well. But we can leave that issue aside. The important point for our purposes is that there is some plausibility, and no incoherence, in the supposition that just as there is a moral threshold between ourselves and animals, so there would be a parallel threshold between supra-persons, who would differ from us psychologically by more than we differ from animals, and ourselves.

Allen Buchanan has recently argued forcefully against this suggestion.[10] "Merely augmenting the characteristics that make a being a person," he observes, "doesn't seem to be the sort of thing that could confer higher moral status. If a person's capacity for practical rationality or for engaging in practices of mutual accountability or for conceiving of herself as an agent with interests persisting over time were increased, the result presumably would be an enhanced person, not a new kind of being with a higher moral status than that of person" (Buchanan forthcoming, pp. 11–12 of the manuscript). He points out that there are already significant and well-appreciated differences in cognitive and general psychological capacity among existing persons, but these do not tempt us to abandon our egalitarianism about moral status above the threshold. "Equality of moral status of the sort we associate with personhood," he concludes, "can accommodate many inequalities, including inequalities in the very characteristics that confer moral status" (Buchanan forthcoming, p. 12 of the manuscript).

I suspect that Buchanan is right about this. After all, virtually everyone accepts that there is a threshold between animals and ourselves and, although there are disagreements and uncertainty about what the basis of our being above it is, there is general agreement that it is not a property that we share with animals but simply possess to a higher degree. Suppose, for example, that the basis of our higher status vis-à-vis animals is some psychological capacity or set of such capacities. Even though

---

[10] Buchanan forthcoming. I have benefited in my thinking about these issues from my access to various drafts of Buchanan's paper. Frances Kamm offered similar grounds for skepticism about the possibility of a higher threshold in discussion at Harvard Law School following the presentation of an earlier version of this paper.

these capacities may have emerged over the course of evolution through the gradual development and refinement of capacities already found in our animal ancestors, they are nonetheless now different in kind, rather than merely in degree, from those of animals.

But even if Buchanan is right that mere enhancement or augmentation of our existing capacities would not be sufficient to yield a new and higher moral status, it seems possible that the genetic enhancement of a variety of psychological capacities that we possess could produce new, *emergent* capacities in posthumans that would plausibly ground a higher degree of inviolability. Indeed, all the psychological capacities that *we* have that are reasonable candidates for the basis of *our* higher inviolability—self-consciousness, the ability to act on the basis of reasons, and so on—seem to be emergent properties that have arisen from the combined enhancement of capacities found in animals.

A major problem, of course, is that it is difficult to imagine an emergent psychological capacity that we do not possess but that would be relevant to moral status if it existed. But here is one suggestion. Many people, and some philosophers, have claimed that one morally significant difference between ourselves and animals—one that is clearly relevant to our higher moral status—is that we possess free will while animals do not. Perhaps most of those who have made this claim have had in mind a robust conception of libertarian free will rather than the weaker notion embraced by compatibilists. Yet this weaker conception is more commonly accepted by philosophers now, since many philosophers have become convinced that we do not actually have libertarian free will. Indeed, many believe that we cannot have libertarian free will because the notion itself is incoherent. But suppose that the notion of libertarian free will is actually coherent. And suppose further that those who have asserted that libertarian free will is what distinguishes us morally from animals are right that it is a sufficiently significant capacity to ground a difference in moral status, but wrong to believe that we actually possess it. But suppose, finally, that supra-persons *would* have it. They would have a psychological capacity that we lack but that most people have believed that we have and that is what distinguishes us morally from animals.

Here is another suggestion. It is widely held that empathy is relevant to, and perhaps even necessary for, moral agency, and many philosophers have held that the capacity for moral agency is necessary for the higher form of moral status. Suppose, then, that supra-persons would have a capacity that would be better for moral agency than mere empathy. Suppose they could actually *experience* other individuals' mental states while simultaneously reflecting on those experiences in a self-conscious manner from their own point of view. This would require a divided form of consciousness, but that would be only a rather extreme instance of the fragmentation of consciousness of which we are increasingly aware in ourselves.

One could speculate about other possibilities. But these examples are sufficient to show that it is conceivable that supra-persons could have emergent psychological capacities that we lack and that would be recognizably relevant to moral status and relative inviolability. The view that even in a world that contained supra-persons, it would be the case that there would be only a single threshold for a higher moral status, that all those above that threshold would be of equal moral status, that we ourselves and all post-fetal cognitively limited human beings would be above it along with posthumans, but that all animals would be below it— this seems too congenial to be true. It looks suspiciously like a product of self-interest, or conceit, or favoritism toward our own.

I concede, however, that these speculations about supra-persons prove nothing. They are meant only to be suggestive. They do not, in particular, seem to have any obvious implications for the status of the cognitively limited, except perhaps this: *if* one finds it plausible that supra-persons, as I have defined them, would have a higher degree of inviolability, in that it would take more to justify sacrificing one of them than to justify sacrificing one of us, this strongly suggests that differences of moral status are grounded in differences of psychological capacity.

Acknowledgments

I am greatly indebted for comments on an earlier draft of this chapter to John Basl, Allen Buchanan, Eva Kittay, Derek Parfit, and Melinda Roberts.

References

Buchanan, Allen. Forthcoming. "Moral Status and Human Enhancement." *Philosophy and Public Affairs*.

McMahan, Jeff. 2002. *The Ethics of Killing: Problems at the Margins of Life*. New York: Oxford University Press.

———. 2005. "Our Fellow Creatures." *Journal of Ethics* 9:353–80.

———. 2006. "Paradoxes of Abortion and Prenatal Injury." *Ethics* 116:625–55.

———. 2009. "Radical Cognitive Limitation." In *Disability and Disadvantage*, edited by Kimberley Brownlee and Adam Cureton, 240–59. Oxford: Oxford University Press.

21

CARING AND FULL MORAL STANDING REDUX

AGNIESZKA JAWORSKA

A being has moral standing if it or its interests matter intrinsically, to at least some degree, in the moral assessment of actions and events. For instance, animals can be said to have moral standing if, other things being equal, it is morally bad to intentionally cause their suffering. This essay focuses on a special kind of moral standing, what I will call "full moral standing" (FMS), associated with persons. In contrast to the various accounts of what ultimately grounds FMS in use in the philosophical literature, I will propose that the emotional capacity to care is a sufficient condition for the FMS that we ascribe to persons. I will develop this account by exploring intuitions about the moral standing of various imaginary nonhuman species, modeled on existing nonstandard human agents.

It is commonplace in ethical theory and standard moral practice to hold that ordinary adult human beings have an exalted moral standing—that we owe them special concern and respect. A core constituent of FMS is a kind of inviolability: roughly put, we are prohibited from destroying and from interfering in various other ways with a being with FMS for the sake of another being, or for any other value. For instance, we are prohibited from killing an innocent human being for the sake of saving one or several others, or even, perhaps, for the sake of justice and world peace; but we are allowed to kill a chicken for the sake of justice and world peace, or to save a human being, or even, perhaps, to save five other chickens.[1] Furthermore, all creatures with FMS are thought to possess such inviolability in equal degree.[2]

Full moral standing also encompasses weighty positive moral claims. These are harder to isolate, since factors such as special relationships, or the agent's projects and commitments, may override them. Still, other

---

[1] The last example is borrowed from Thomson 1990, 292. To put the point in the text differently, persons have special rights of noninterference, the content of which is specified by the correct theory of rights.

[2] If A and B are both inviolable, how could they be unequally inviolable? It could be worse to violate A than to violate B in the same way. FMS rules out such comparative variations: if A and B have FMS, otherwise equivalent violations of each are equally bad.

things being equal, beings with FMS are paramount in the calculus of positive duties—their interests matter much more than the interests of other types of beings. When faced with a choice of saving a human person or a chicken from a severe ordeal, barring further reasons that may complicate the moral picture (indirect consequences of saving the chicken for other people, and so on), one is required to pick the person—simply because of the kind of creature it is.[3] Further, ceteris paribus, like interests of all creatures with FMS matter equally in moral decisions, giving rise to the requirements of fairness. For example, when distributing goods among creatures with FMS (who could all benefit similarly), barring special purposes, relationships, or independent claims on the goods, we ought to distribute equally.[4] By contrast, beings lacking FMS are outside the scope of the considerations of fairness. (A state policy that takes no account of the welfare of chickens living in the state is not deemed unfair.) Third, it is morally costly to forgo support of vital interests of a being with FMS, even when it is morally justified. For example, if in distributing scarce resources among creatures with FMS (think of famine relief) one lacks enough to protect the vital interests of all affected, this is a moral misfortune of the gravest kind.

Commonsense morality seems to dictate that membership in the human species, regardless of capacities, guarantees FMS (at least for independently subsisting beings; the standing of fetuses is indeed disputed). Infants and severely cognitively impaired humans are normally taken to have FMS, while nonhuman animals of the very same or even higher mental capacities are not. This commonsense approach, whose advocates I'll call "preservationists," is contested by theorists I'll call "revisionists."[5] Both preservationists and revisionists standardly back their positions by appealing—albeit in rather different ways—to valuable mental capacities that underlie FMS. Let me elaborate.

Revisionists see the commonsense view as unjustifiably inconsistent: moral standing must be a response to some valuable properties of the being in question, and similarly endowed beings should have similar standing. To fill in their theory, revisionists need to specify which capacities give rise to FMS.

On the other side, preservationists do not simply claim that membership in the human species as such confers FMS. They typically keep firmly

---

[3] Admittedly, privileging the person in such cases does not necessarily imply that the person as such matters more than the chicken: it is also possible that each creature matters morally just as much, but the person's interest at stake turns out to be more compelling. After all, the same level of pain may have more severe and lasting consequences for the person, given her ability to remember the pain, to attribute various meanings to the pain, to fearfully anticipate further pain of this sort, and so on. Thus, great care must be taken to keep the relevant factors equal.

[4] Ideas from Broome 1990–91 helped me in this paragraph, although not all I say is consistent with Broome.

[5] For a prominent example of a preservationist view, see Scanlon 1998, esp. 177–87. For a prominent example of a revisionist view, see McMahan, 2002, esp. 203–32.

in view the valuable traits of nonimpaired adult humans,[6] which account for FMS in these uncontroversial cases. They then explain the special standing of humans in the nonstandard cases roughly in two ways. For infants and children, they appeal to the potential to acquire the relevant capacities in normal development. And they cover severely cognitively impaired human beings by appeals to the species nature, membership in a kind, the characteristic form of a species or a kind, or the like,[7] that is, to some sort of complex (presumably biological) mode of organization that, barring defects, makes the emergence of the relevant properties possible. Clearly, then, preservationists also have to rely on an account of valuable capacities that *ultimately* underwrite FMS.[8] (Note, too, that their approach leaves theoretical room for the possibility that nonhuman species and/or individuals possess FMS.)

My goal is to develop an alternative to the available accounts of the mental properties that *ultimately* justify the special moral requirements of FMS, relevant for both camps. I propose to consult our intuitions about the moral standing of adult unimpaired members of various imaginary nonhuman species, modeled on existing nonstandard human agents. The transposition from nonstandard humans to adult unimpaired members of alternate species is meant to ensure as much as possible that the intuitions about moral standing are based on the actual abilities of the creatures in question, and not *merely* on membership in a species or on potential abilities. Examining our intuitions in such imaginary cases, unconfounded by possible appeals to potential or species capabilities, can be particularly helpful in uncovering what capabilities *ultimately* underlie FMS. Intuitions about alternate species may not be firm enough to settle the question, but when combined with further arguments, they can help establish the capacity to care as a very plausible ground of FMS.

Admittedly, a new account of what attributes ultimately underlie FMS— and specifically my appeal to the capacity to care—will not resolve the debate between preservationists and revisionists. Preservationists can still insist, against their revisionist opponents, that all human beings have FMS because humans as a species possess the capacity to care—or indeed any attribute plausibly deemed relevant. On this issue, I will remain agnostic.

---

[6] There are important exceptions here—views that emphasize the role of relationships and of the possibility of the being in question sharing a form of life with us. See, e.g., Diamond 1991 and Byrne 2000, chap. 3.

[7] I list these different formulations since different proponents of the views in this category phrase their positions slightly differently. Sorting out whether these different formulations amount to substantive differences is beyond the scope of this essay.

[8] As Byrne 2000, chap. 6, perspicuously exhibits, even theological accounts, which ground FMS in humans' unique relation to God, when fully worked out, are typically forced to appeal to the very same valuable properties of humans invoked by the secular accounts: if you don't believe that God acts arbitrarily, something must explain why God cares about all human beings.

But it still matters a great deal that both sides correctly identify the ultimate basis of FMS: that they zero in on the right explanation of why we owe special moral duties to persons. Such a sound theoretical foundation will also allow the two approaches to delineate more accurately their disagreements and perhaps even discover previously unforeseen common ground.

1. Testing the Received Wisdom About the Basis of FMS

Full moral standing is usually thought to be grounded in the ability to reason. But there is much variation in how this ability is understood and which aspects of it are taken to confer FMS. I will first show that when the ability to reason is interpreted in standard ways, it is either insufficient or unnecessary to ground FMS. Ultimately, I hope to isolate attributes not previously recognized as sufficient for FMS, which may even turn out to be necessary as well.

A. Are Minimal Rational Capacities the Basis of FMS?

On many views, very minimal rational capacities, such as the ability to use language, manipulate abstract concepts, or form a conception of oneself, are sufficient to ground FMS. Is this plausible?

Imagine a species of talking catlike creatures, Verbcats, who possess minimal rational abilities—they can talk sensibly, say, about the weather or food, and competently employ self-reflexive pronouns, for example, in sentences like "I have white fur"—but these abilities don't lead them to develop any corresponding motivations and don't affect at all how they initiate action and how they conduct their lives. They live exactly like cats we know. Their desires and corresponding interests are consistently confined to sensual and bodily appetites. Their lives revolve around eating, sleeping, basking in the sun, and the like. Their memory and interest in their own future are no different from those of ordinary cats.[9] Just because they talk, we shouldn't imagine them pleading "I don't want to die!"—their lack of concern for their future precludes this plea.[10] They are like our cats in every way, except for the added elementary ability to comment on the world around them and on themselves. It is implausible that this addition, which has no effect on what matters to them, would

---

[9] As I see it, severe impairment of cognitive development and severe dementia can reduce the capacities of a human being to an analogous or even lower level.

[10] Many animals, including even insects, exhibit in their behavior aversions to pain, physical damage, or attack, which some might construe as pleas not to be hurt, damaged, or attacked. I believe this reading implicitly imputes too much sophistication to the animal, since a plea not to be hurt, damaged, or attacked requires a conception of oneself as the one who is not to be hurt, damaged, or attacked. But even if these pleas could be attributed to an animal, they are still not equivalent to a plea to let one live, which requires something a notch more sophisticated: a conception of one's own future. (Thanks to Eva Kittay for prompting this clarification.)

drastically change these creatures' moral standing as compared to actual cats. For instance, we would presumably still be willing to sacrifice them in medical experiments that would help prolong the lives of humans. Given the rudimentary level of these creatures' interests, which remain catlike, we would not grant them moral standing equivalent to ours.

I take this admittedly fanciful example to support the view that moral standing is grounded on practical rather than theoretical abilities: on the kinds of interests a creature is able to generate, and not on what it is able to know or understand. Minimal rational abilities don't seem to be sufficient for FMS.

B. Is the Faculty of Practical Reason the Basis of FMS?

Next, consider the influential view associated with Immanuel Kant, according to which the distinctive mark of persons, and the consequent ground of FMS, is the ability to employ reason in the practical domain, the domain of action. Persons use reason in order to figure out what ends to pursue, what ends are good to have,[11] and also to figure out how to realize those ends in the concrete circumstances of their lives. In this sense, persons are able to live their lives by their own lights: through the use of reason, they can set their own standards, their own values, and then lead their lives according to those self-imposed standards. Persons can live by laws they impose on themselves—they can be autonomous.

This may be interpreted as a very demanding set of requirements. In order to figure out what ends are good to pursue, one needs, at a minimum, sophisticated conceptual abilities to grasp various ends; one needs to be able to compare and contrast, weigh pros and cons, and understand the consequences of various options. One may also need to be able to grasp (at least implicitly) and to apply the very complex concept of justification.[12]

Are these sophisticated abilities necessary to ground FMS? Imagine a species called Befuddled, whose unimpaired members may be physically quite different but in terms of their psychology closely resemble mildly demented human individuals, people we know in early stages of Alzheimer's disease. They all have cares and values like those of ordinary humans, but they are somewhat disoriented and forgetful and cannot keep track of facts relevant for their choices. They are constantly overwhelmed by complex arrays of options for action, each with its advantages and drawbacks, and so forth. These creatures lack the ability to make their own decisions in most circumstances, so they lack a crucial

[11] For a Kantian, these two tasks amount to the same thing, but I leave room for the possibility that they might be distinct.

[12] Note that even the most minimal requirements of practical reason are much more cognitively demanding than the "minimal rational capacities" (language use, self-awareness, and so forth) discussed in the previous section.

aspect of Kantian autonomy. Luckily, in the alternative world we are imagining, many humans enjoy taking care of the Befuddled and helping them figure out how to make decisions that would best serve what they value and care about. The Befuddled's lack of decision-making capacity, being simply due to mild confusion and forgetfulness, does not seem to affect their moral standing in comparison with ordinary humans. Given that their mental capacities are only slightly different from mine or yours, and that, with help, they can lead lives very similar to our own, it seems that the Befuddled would possess FMS. They lack crucial aspects of Kantian autonomy, and yet we are inclined to attribute FMS to them.[13]

Imagine also a species called Kiddies, whose normal adult representatives are psychologically very much like human children between the ages of two and four. Our children do not develop the abilities required for Kantian autonomy at least until the age of eight or nine, and some think that even adolescents don't adequately command them (Schapiro 1999). But it seems implausible to claim that the Kiddies would lack FMS. Our intuitions about the Befuddled and the Kiddies cast doubt on the view that the capacity for autonomy, as traditionally understood, is necessary to ground FMS.[14]

2. The Capacity to Care as an Alternative Basis of FMS

So far, I have suggested that minimal rational capacities are insufficient to ground FMS, while robust Kantian autonomy is unnecessary. We are looking for an alternative set of mental attributes sufficient for FMS, and perhaps even necessary as well. As a first step, I will develop observations about the nature of children and the moral standing of Kiddies into the hypothesis that the capacity to care is sufficient for FMS.[15]

I focus on the case of the childlike Kiddies because here the ability to care stands out as crucial in the assessment of FMS: young children have not yet developed a lot of other abilities traditionally thought to underlie FMS, including most elements of Kantian autonomy, and yet we would attribute FMS to the Kiddies. (By contrast, the case of the Befuddled—

---

[13] A robust capacity for Kantian autonomy does ground some moral restrictions on what can be done to an individual, such as restrictions on paternalism. And these restrictions apply only to individuals who possess FMS. But none of this should mislead us into thinking that a robust capacity for Kantian autonomy also grounds FMS itself.

[14] Note that we cannot rule out the capacity for autonomy as the ultimate ground of FMS by examining the moral standing of human children or human Alzheimer's patients. Even if these individuals (who lack the capacity for autonomy) possess FMS, this doesn't show that the capacity for autonomy cannot ultimately ground FMS: in these special cases, FMS could be due to past, potential, or species capacity for autonomy.

[15] My discussion of the nature of caring and the internality of caring, here and in sections 2A and 2C, including several examples of caring in children, is borrowed, sometimes verbatim, from Jaworska 2007.

while effective in showing that full Kantian autonomy is unnecessary to ground FMS—cannot be used to showcase the ability to care as the most likely explanation of FMS, since mildly demented folks retain many abilities that could be thought to explain FMS, including some individual elements of Kantian autonomy, such as the ability to make evaluative judgments.)

Consider this description of the concerns of a young child, from the earliest memories of Sergei Aksakov:

> My little sister I loved at first more than all my toys, more than my mother; and this love took the form of a constant desire to see her, and a feeling of pity for her: I always fancied that she was cold or hungry and in want of food, and I wished constantly to give her my food and dress her in my clothes; of course I was not allowed to do this and that made me cry. . . . I could not bear to see her tears or hear her cry without beginning at once to cry myself. . . . I lay whole days in my crib with my sister beside me, amusing her with different toys or by showing her pictures. (Aksakov 1983, 1–6)[16]

We readily interpret little Sergei's concern for his sister as a form of caring. And we marvel that a young child may be capable of such a sophisticated attitude. Intuitively, something notable, something quintessentially human, is manifest here.

There is ample evidence that children as young as two and three are capable of caring. Developmental psychology research shows that at around one-and-a-half years children begin to "act constructively to relieve another's distress," both at home and in laboratory playrooms (Thompson 1987, 131; Zahn-Waxler et al. 1992). In a study of early sibling relationships, by the time the older siblings were thirty months, at least 30 percent were observed expressing empathic concern for the younger child, typically through helping gestures, such as "offering toys or food when the sibling was crying" (Dunn and Kendrick 1982, 114). There is also anecdotal evidence that two- and three-year-old children exhibit other forms of caring, caring about objects or ideas.[17] Consider a prototypical toddler who consistently insists on doing many routine tasks—from eating to tying her shoes—by herself. The child can usually convey just how important being in charge is to her: she attempts to take charge in novel ways and in novel circumstances, she communicates joy at her successes, she gets angry at a parent who doesn't let her try, and so on. Or take the story of a colleague's son who took very seriously the task of blowing out all the candles on his third birthday: he prepared for the event, got very frustrated with his initial not-so-successful attempts, triumphantly announced his eventual success, and reminded his parents about the feat for days.

---

[16] According to the recollections, Aksakov would have been around three at the time.

[17] I am assuming that caring about things and ideas and caring about people have core features in common. The basis of this assumption will become clear shortly.

There is something compellingly human in these displays of caring, a special form of motivation expressed in action. These children do not engage in the complex reasoning required for Kantian autonomy, and they surely lack the necessary capabilities. And yet if the Kiddies are truly like these children, capable of caring, we would be inclined to attribute FMS to them. For example, we would find it morally abhorrent to sacrifice the Kiddies in medical experiments designed to prolong the lives of humans.

At first, it may appear that a modest modification of the Kantian account of FMS could accommodate the intuition that caring attitudes of the Kiddies are the source of FMS. After all, caring attitudes may be thought of as the starting points of the ability to reason about goals and actions—as inputs into decision making—and this might qualify them as appropriate bases for FMS on the Kantian picture. Developing this idea, one could think that caring about something must involve positively evaluating the object of care, so that evaluative judgment or evaluative conviction of some sort is part and parcel of caring.[18] Such an evaluative judgment need not draw on the ability to form a conviction on the basis of reasoning or justification. A rudimentary judgment that the object of care is good could consist merely in properly applying the normative concept "good" to the object. This, at a minimum, requires only a commitment (albeit implicit) to the correctness or appropriateness of the judgment—a conviction that one is right. For example, the judgment holder must understand and (at least provisionally) accept that if she were not to hold the judgment—say, if she were to change her mind in the future—she would be making a mistake, or that other people in relevantly similar situations would be mistaken if they didn't hold the judgment.[19]

Are young children capable of evaluative judgments in this thin sense? Developmental psychology provides convincing evidence to the contrary: two- and even three-year-olds don't understand the idea of correctness as it applies to beliefs, including their own beliefs. Hundreds of studies corroborate this conclusion. These are variations of the so-called false belief tasks, which test children's predictions about how a deceptive

[18] What follows is a quick sketch of my argument against this interpretation. For details, see Jaworska unpublished.

[19] This is a requirement for evaluative beliefs, not meant to apply to other beliefs (about tables and chairs, and so on). For a belief to have evaluative content, the belief holder must understand the evaluative concept evoked in the belief. And one does not really understand the evaluative concept one purportedly employs in one's belief unless one would recognize the lack of such a belief—especially one's own former, future, or counterfactual lack—as a mistake. Believing that my chair is blue does not immediately involve me in imputing error to anybody (including a counterfactual me) who lacks this belief—my chair-related belief is not inherently tied to considerations about believing, my own or others'. But if I believe one ought to help others in need, or that it's good to have fulfilling personal relationships in one's life, I do implicitly hold that those who lack this belief (especially my past or projected self who lacks it) would be importantly mistaken.

object will appear to others. In one scenario, children are presented with a familiar candy box, which, they soon find out, is filled with pencils. "They are asked what someone else will think when they first see the box. Three-year-old children consistently say that the other person will think there are pencils in the box. They apparently fail to understand that the other person's belief may be false" (Gopnik 1993, 4). In other experiments, they make the same errors even when they are asked about *their own* immediately past false beliefs (Gopnik 1993, 4). They simply don't understand that beliefs are representational states that can be correct or incorrect.

Two- and three-year-olds are thus incapable of being committed to the correctness of their own convictions, and so they cannot hold evaluative judgments of even the most rudimentary sort. If carings of these children are starting points of reasoning about goals and actions, this cannot be because they incorporate evaluative judgments even in the weakest form. Furthermore, we do not lose our conviction that Kiddies have FMS even when we explicitly accept that Kiddies, like human children, lack even the most rudimentary capacity to judge evaluatively. A more radical rethinking of the Kantian view is needed to accommodate the intuitions suggesting that carings of Kiddies can be the source of FMS.

Of course, FMS of young human children is easy to explain by appeal to their (or their species') potential to develop sophisticated mental capacities, including the capacity for Kantian autonomy. But these explanations do not apply to the Kiddies. How, then, do we explain the FMS of the Kiddies? The idea that the source of FMS is caring itself—independent of judging evaluatively—offers a plausible answer.

A. A Closer Look at Caring

To appreciate the relevant features of carings, we need to see them first and foremost as emotional attitudes. An emotional episode is a particular pattern of thoughts, feelings, bodily states, involuntary facial expressions, predispositions to act, perceptual selectivity, direction of attention and imagination, and so forth, which amounts to a person being, for example, angry, or fearful, or ecstatic at a particular time. By contrast, what I mean by an emotion is a more enduring state, an ongoing psychic orientation, composed of various interrelated emotional episodes and dispositions to experience subsequent concurring emotional episodes, unfolding intermittently over time, waxing and waning, at least partly in response to the context at hand.[20] For example, the emotion of grief typically involves episodes of recurring painful thoughts concerning the lost person or object, especially the recollection of the circumstances of the loss; a tendency to imagine how things could have gone differently; a predis-

---

[20] See Goldie 2000, esp. chap. 2. What I say here is indebted to Goldie's work, but it is not meant to be a full or fully faithful representation of his views.

position to notice and dwell in one's thoughts on objects, events, or locations that remind the bereaved of the lost figure; a predisposition to hold onto the mementos of the lost figure; and so on. Other combinations of gradually and intermittently evolving elements, structurally linked in a similar fashion, constitute anger, fear, joy, disgust, jealousy, pity, and so forth.

In this way, emotions are constituted by conceptual connections among various elements of a person's psychology occurring at different points in the history of her mental life. Emotional episodes have conceptual content, they are about something, and the contents of episodes of the same emotion are tied to one another. Sometimes one episode of an emotion directly refers to another: as when a bereaved person recalls the experience of putting away the mementos of the lost figure. But otherwise, most of the episodes are interconnected referentially by virtue of referring in a consistent way to the same figure or to the same circumstances; for grief, the connected episodes are those of recalling, imagining, wishing something about, and associating one's current experience with the lost figure and the circumstances of the loss. That is, the episodes are various ways of being mentally agitated by the thought that the lost figure is missing.

Now, caring has an even more complex structure than most ordinary emotions—it is best understood as a structured compound of various less complex emotions, emotional predispositions, and also desires, unfolding over time in response to relevant circumstances. Typical components of caring include joy and satisfaction when the object of one's care is doing well and advancing and frustration over its misfortunes or setbacks, anger at agents who heedlessly cause such misfortunes or setbacks, pride in successes for the object and disappointment over its defeats or failures, the desire to help ensure those successes and to help avoid the setbacks, fear when the object is in jeopardy and relief when it escapes untouched, and grief at the loss of the object and the subsequent nostalgia.[21] Not all of these elements must always occur in a given case of caring, but if enough of them are missing in the relevant circumstances, talk of caring is not warranted.

Such component emotions, emotional predispositions, and desires all construe the same object—a person, an animal, an ideal—as a source of importance commanding emotional vulnerability. This object, as a steady focus of emotional attunement, conceptually connects all the components to one another and gives the ensuing complex emotion its structure. The complex emotion is, as a result, *about* the object, for example, a caring about Mom.[22]

---

[21] This aspect of my understanding of caring is indebted to Bennett Helm's work. See, e.g., Helm 1996, 76–77.

[22] For a very helpful elaboration of this idea, see Nissenbaum 1985, esp. chaps. 5–7.

The connections between the components of caring are not limited to a shared reference to a common object. A complex pattern of rational requirements is involved, so only certain emotions concerning the object and only certain sequences of such emotions qualify as part of caring about that object.[23] Joy at the successes of the object of care rationally requires sadness at the object's failures; if things go well for the object, fear or hope are rationally required to turn into an emotion such as relief; and so forth. Thanks to their rational and referential interconnection, the individual caring emotions are intelligible as mental states of one agent.[24] But, more important, by virtue of his steadfast emotional attunement to the ebb and flow of the fortunes of the object, the caring subject imbues the object with importance. A subject cognitively sophisticated enough to employ, at least implicitly, the concept of importance would *comprehend* the object's importance, and this can inspire further cognitive activity, for example, further inquisitiveness about the object, or the formation of stable intentions, plans, and policies concerning the object. This cognitive sophistication is necessary for genuine caring.[25]

Findings in developmental psychology suggest that complex emotional structures of the sort just described do indeed lie behind the caring behaviors of young children. A longitudinal study of "concern for others" in the second year of children's lives reports "consistently observed linkages between prosocial actions, expressions of concern, and verbal attempts to comprehend the nature of distress events that children cause and witness" (Zahn-Waxler et al. 1992, 134). The studied children exhibit consistent caring behaviors toward the same person (usually their mothers) over a period of time. When the person is in distress, they provide verbal and physical comfort, offer advice, try to help in various ways, or at least to distract the person to make her feel better; they also try to protect her from injury or distress. These actions are accompanied by "emotional arousal that appears to reflect sympathetic concern for the victim," as evidenced by "facial or vocal expressions (e.g. sad looks, sympathetic statements ... in a soothing or reassuring tone of voice, or gestures such as rushing to the victim while looking

---

[23] For a more detailed discussion, see Helm 2001, 67–69.

[24] The connections don't guarantee that the individual caring emotions belong to the same agent. But they contribute to the overall psychological unity and so, on the neo-Lockean picture, to the unity of agency over time.

[25] There may be a weaker notion of caring for which such conceptual sophistication is not necessary: the subject could imbue the object with importance by virtue of his emotional reactions, without having a conceptual grasp of the object's importance. In fact, animals such as cats and dogs seem capable of "caring" in this weaker sense. However, I focus on caring of the more sophisticated kind described here because, on my view, only this kind of caring can be the basis of FMS. As I will explain in section 2C, by virtue of inspiring further cognitive activity (for example, the formation of stable intentions, plans, and policies), this kind of caring helps to support the unity of agency over time and thereby helps to fashion a self worthy of special respect.

worried)." The children also focus their attention in a manner characteristic of caring: they attempt "to label or understand the problem," asking
"What happened?" or trying to diagnose the problem on their own,
sometimes making "complex inferences" (Zahn-Waxler et al. 1992,
129).[26] As I read it, they use their emotional sense of the mother as
important to guide their reasoning and behavior.[27] While the study did
not record the full gamut of caring emotions, and while perhaps some
relevant emotions may have not yet had a chance to arise in the short time
span of early childhood, it is hard to interpret the documented combination of reactions as anything other than the beginnings of a pattern
of caring.

My anecdotes about individual children make better sense in light of
these more systematic findings. Knowing that two-year-olds do begin to
develop the complex emotional structures characteristic of caring, we can
more justifiably assume them as background to the individual episodes of
caring behavior. Besides, the anecdotes do contain enough interrelated
elements evolving over time so that the emotional structure of caring is
somewhat explicit. In the story about the birthday candles, witness the
boy's frustration at his original failures to accomplish the task he cared
about, elation at his eventual success, and pride in the accomplishment, as
evidenced by his repeated reminders about the incident to his parents.
And we can see the relevant structure in Aksakov's recollections about his
sister: as I see it, he uses his emotional sense that his sister is important to
guide his reasoning and behavior.

So long as the complex emotional structure of caring can be found in
young children who, as we have seen, are incapable of the most
rudimentary evaluative judgment, this emotional structure is a plausible
candidate for the source of FMS of the childlike Kiddies. The complex
emotional ability to care remains standing as a viable explanation of the
Kiddies' FMS once even the least demanding variant of the main rival
explanation—the one citing a rudimentary capacity to make evaluative
judgments—has been ruled out.

B. Is the Capacity to Care Necessary to Ground FMS?

With the above detailed picture of caring in the background, the
importance of the ability to care for FMS can be further corroborated
by examining cases in which this ability is absent.

Consider Elliot, a patient described by Antonio Damasio. Elliot, who
sustained brain damage in the ventromedial prefrontal cortices, performed normally or even superiorly on a full battery of psychological

---

[26] I omitted a confusing use of brackets from the original.

[27] It is important to note that we can be at least confident, based on their linguistic
capabilities, that young children could grasp the concept of importance. This point will be
relevant again in my discussion of great apes below.

tests (tests of intelligence, knowledge base, memory, language, attention, basic reasoning, and so forth), and yet he was an extremely poor decision-maker in everyday life. He was unable to work, maintain personal relationships, or stick to a plan or task: he was incapable of sustained goal-directed behavior in any aspect of his life. And yet he was remarkably emotionally unaffected by his tragic life history. He would recount the story of his failures "with a detachment that was out of step with the magnitude of the events. ... Nowhere was there a sense of his own suffering, even though he was the protagonist" (Damasio 1994, 44). Elliot did not seem to care about himself. He did not experience joy or satisfaction when he was flourishing or frustration over his misfortunes; no anger at agents who caused his misfortunes; no pride in his successes or disappointments over his failures. He had no sustained desire to help ensure those successes or to help avoid the failures. He did sometimes experience fear when he was in danger, especially in response to stereotypical danger clues, such as a loud noise (Damasio 1994, 138–39). But this is not enough to constitute a pattern of caring about himself. Caring about oneself is such a basic form of caring that we wouldn't expect someone incapable of caring about himself to be able to care about anything else. And so it was with Elliot.

Elliot showed no abnormalities in means-ends reasoning and problem solving; he was perfectly able to come up with a full array of options for action in a particular situation as well as to work out the consequences of each option. Yet his ability to choose was impaired. After a full analysis of all the options, he would comment: "I still wouldn't know what to do!" (Damasio 1994, 39). His emotional responses and feelings were severely blunted, and this "prevented him from assigning different values to different options, and made his decision-making landscape hopelessly flat" (Damasio 1994, 51). He was no longer sufficiently invested in anything; he simply ceased to care.

This is not to say that Elliot had no interests stemming from the part of his life after the brain injury. He was still, of course, a sentient creature and had interest in avoiding physical pain and in mental and physical comfort. He had likes and dislikes and habitual pastimes such as collecting. Most important, he did find things captivating "in the moment." What he lacked was sustained and caring interest in anything, a pattern of emotional investment retained over time.[28] His fleeting impulses, motivations, and attractions constantly took him off track, so he couldn't maintain job commitments or personal relationships. Consequently, his interests did not revolve around relationships and commitments, but for that, they were not any less defined.

---

[28] Note that, given my analysis of caring as a complex of emotions, "momentary caring" is not a possibility. Caring is a structured compound of various emotions and emotional predispositions, unfolding over time in response to relevant circumstances (see section 2A).

A condition such as Elliot's has been called "acquired psychopathy" because the psychiatric profile of patients with those brain injuries is strikingly similar to the well-studied profile of a psychopath. While the popular image of psychopaths emphasizes their brazen lack of concern for other people, the psychiatric diagnostic criteria have recognized the much broader scope of their deficit: their underlying problem is a lack of deep emotional attachment to anything, including other human beings and even their own long-term welfare. Like Elliot, they merely get caught up in the desires of the moment and switch pursuits according to what grabs their attention.[29] Here is a psychiatrist's narrative of the motivational pattern of one psychopath.

Milt volunteered to drive his ailing mother on an errand. Their car broke down on a bridge, leaving them stranded in a dangerous spot as darkness fell. Milt offered to walk to a nearby garage to replace a blown-out fuse, the cause of the mishap. He promised to return within fifteen minutes. The mother waited, worried, for about an hour, until a passerby drove her home. When Milt eventually returned, he

> showed . . . a bland immunity to any recognition that he had behaved irresponsibly or inconsiderately.
>
> Milt had begun his trip to the garage with commendable haste. Shortly after leaving the bridge, he passed a cigar store. Noting . . . the afternoon's football scores . . . posted on a blackboard, he lingered for ten or fifteen minutes to check results.
>
> During this interval he recalled that a girl he knew lived . . . in this neighborhood and decided to drop in on her. . . . He spent approximately an hour in her company. There is no evidence that any sudden sexual urge or any other strongly tempting impulse diverted our patient. He had no special liking for the girl, and no attempt was made to gain even the mildest erotic favor.
>
> Milt chatted with the girl . . . desultorily about trifling matters. His departure followed the arrival of her date for the evening, whose rights to her company he acknowledged after a pleasant exchange of courtesies. . . .
>
> . . . This conduct did not result from absent-mindedness, from specific amnesia or confusion. . . . He was quite aware . . . of his mother waiting on the bridge and seems to have been free from any grudge or other impulse that would influence him deliberately to offend her or cause her hardship. Missing from his realization, apparently, was the evaluation of her emotional reactions that would in another have outweighed a whim so petty as that which in Milt gained easy ascendancy. (Cleckley 1988, 160–62)

[29] If the desire of the moment happens to persist, a psychopath may pursue something for an extended period of time and give the impression of being devoted to a goal. This, I think, is what happens with psychopaths we tend to hear about in popular culture: they have strong and persistent desires and, since no deep concern about anything puts a check on their activities, they can end up doing terrible things to others in the process of pursuing what captivates their current attention. But monomaniacal attention to a goal is not the same as caring.

Hard as it is for us to enter into the frame of mind that generates such a motivational sequence, we see here a creature with interests, only interests considerably different in kind from our own. However fleeting and shifty, the motivations, desires, and impulses of individuals like Elliot and Milt determine the content of their interests.

Let us imagine, then, a species called Pathians, whose unimpaired members may be very different physically but psychologically are like Elliot and Milt. In intellectual abilities, and much of what we think of as "the ability to reason," Pathians are similar to us. Yet nothing seems to matter deeply to Pathians, and their choices simply express whims of the moment. Even their own fate doesn't deeply concern them. So, it's difficult to invest in much on their behalf, or for their sake. On these grounds, they may reasonably appear to lack the kind of interests that call for full moral respect. On this reading, it seems morally permissible to sacrifice the interests of a Pathian in the name of sufficiently weighty value-based interests of ordinary humans. The requirements of fairness would not apply to them. The death of a Pathian would not be a loss comparable to the death of an ordinary human being. Perhaps we could even kill a Pathian or subject him to medical experiments for the sake of sufficiently weighty benefits to humans. In short, the possibility emerges that Pathians lack FMS, due to their lack of (current, former, potential, or species) capacity to care.[30] The capacity for caring would then appear necessary as the ultimate ground of FMS.[31]

We have now seen two important cases pointing to a crucial role of the ability to care in FMS. The Kiddies seem to have FMS due to their ability to care, strongly suggesting that the ability to care is sufficient for FMS. Further, it may also be that the Pathians lack FMS because they (not just as individuals but as a species) lack this ability, and this would indicate that the ability to care is necessary to ultimately ground FMS. In each case, we can be reasonably confident that the ability to care makes the crucial difference in the assessment of FMS because the ability stands out in the relevant way: in the case of the Kiddies, a lot of other abilities traditionally thought to underlie FMS are missing, and yet we grant FMS; conversely, in the Pathians, many of the same abilities are present, and yet we deny FMS. If I am right that the ability to care makes this crucial difference, it must make the difference even in cases in which other plausible explanations are also available and the actual

---

[30] The Pathians certainly have some moral standing, at least due to their capacity to suffer, and the exact level of their moral standing remains an open question. The beings who lack FMS are not all on par, and the moral standing of Pathians could still be higher compared to most known animals, for example.

[31] Again, in the case of Elliot or Milt, our intuitions may well be different, since we may well attribute FMS to them based on their former or species ability to care. It is precisely to set such factors aside that we are testing our intuitions about moral standing on imaginary species.

basis of FMS is harder to pinpoint. Thus, presumably, only the presence of the ability to care explains why the Befuddled have FMS, and only the lack of the ability to care would explain why the Verbcats, creatures resembling our cats with the added ability to talk, lack FMS; but neither claim can be easily confirmed in a direct way.[32] Most important, if the ability to care is necessary and sufficient for FMS of paradigmatic members of a species, this would begin to establish the presumption that it ultimately grounds FMS.[33] Yet, so far, these are somewhat tentative results, since our intuitions about FMS in imaginary cases are not clear-cut. To boost these intuitive results, I'll now argue more directly that the ability to care is a plausible candidate for a foundation of FMS.

C. Theoretical Considerations That Favor Caring as the Basis for FMS

It seems difficult and even paradoxical to distance oneself from one's carings, to view them as foreign or external, to feel oneself taken over by them. It is common enough to experience a strong desire that one fights off like a foreign intrusion or to have an outburst of anger with respect to which one is a "mere passive bystander" (Frankfurt 1988b, 59). But being a "passive bystander to one's caring attitude" is an oxymoron. Granted, it is not so hard to evaluatively distance oneself from one's carings. We do, not so mysteriously or infrequently, consider our own carings mistaken or misplaced, but even in those cases we don't normally view them as alien forces or as attitudes that we simply "find occurring within us."[34] If our ordinary subjective identifications are to be trusted, we cannot but be identified with what we care about. Carings always represent one's point of view as an agent: in Harry Frankfurt's terminology, they are internal to the agent. (One can, of course, give up on one's caring—decide to cease to care and follow through. What is ruled out is caring and being dissociated from what one cares about at the same time.)[35]

Consider a person fully and explicitly convinced that a particular caring is bad for her. She really doesn't want to care and even begins to take steps to bring herself to stop caring—because, let us suppose, the individual she cares about routinely harms her. Even in her case, so long

---

[32] I used the case of the Befuddled to show that full Kantian autonomy is unnecessary to ground FMS, and I used the case of the Verbcats to show that minimal rational capacities are insufficient. I picked these cases because they involve just the right set of capacities to help us determine what is not the basis of FMS, but they are not well calibrated to positively pinpoint what such a basis in fact is.

[33] In other words, if the ability to care is necessary and sufficient to grant FMS to adult unimpaired members of alien species, it seems to be a ground of FMS in those cases. And we can then presume that this ability also ultimately grounds FMS of humans, in both standard and nonstandard cases.

[34] Phrase borrowed from Frankfurt 1988b, 59.

[35] Thanks to Michael Bratman for prompting this clarification.

as she has not yet succeeded in ceasing to care, she would be making a mistake if she viewed the caring as a mere happening in her psychology, not integral to who she is. This is why the predicament of a woman who wants to leave an abusive husband whom she still loves is especially tragic. The conflict she experiences runs deep—it is a conflict within her identity. (Indeed, her own identification with the caring is likely to play a large role in why she judges the caring inappropriate or pernicious.)[36] By contrast, the conflict experienced by an unwilling addict intent on overcoming his addiction may be harder to resolve in practice, due to the sheer strength of the desire at issue, but because the addict doesn't care about the drug, the conflict does not "tear him apart."[37]

The built-in internality of our carings is particularly conspicuous when we find ourselves caring about things we never suspected we cared about, things that don't fit our prior self-image. One experiences such revelations as finding out something important about oneself, as discovering a stance toward the world that is truly one's own, and not as observing a mere occurrence in one's psychic life.

The detailed account of caring I gave earlier can help elucidate why carings are the sort of attitudes with which agents are always identified. By combining various individual emotions into a complex rational and reference-based structure, carings forge a network of rational and referential connections that support the agent's identity and cohesion over time.[38] Further, as we have seen, by being steadfastly emotionally attuned to the changing fortunes of the object of care, the caring subject imbues the object with importance. And once the subject cognitively grasps the object's importance, this can inspire further psychological alignments: for instance, the formation of stable intentions, plans, and policies concerning the object, which keep the subject on track and thus weave the web of unified agency. (It is therefore no accident that individuals unable to care, like Elliot, break down as unified agents

---

[36] I thank Gary Watson for this way of putting the point.

[37] What if a person is both overcome or swept away by a caring, so that she has no control over it, and also judges it bad to care? Is she still identified with the caring? The abused woman in our example may be precisely in this predicament: she is caught up in her love for her husband, and yet she thinks she ought to cease to love him. This doesn't make the conflict she experiences any less deep; we would trivialize her problem if we invited her to view her love for her husband as a mere happening in her psychic life. (I am grateful to David Hills, Sibyl Schwarzenbach, and Allen Wood for pressing me to elaborate on these examples.)

[38] Carings are constituted by complex rational and referential connections, which synthesize and organize disparate elements of one's psychic life, allowing for convergence of several psychological elements into a coherent cluster. In this sense, they support the agent's identity and cohesion over time. Note that, to play this role, carings need not be consistent with each other. Love and hatred of the same person, so long as each is constituted by an entire network of its own emotions and emotional episodes, will each function to support the agent's ongoing identity.

over time.) Because they connect various aspects of our psychology together and support our psychological unity and continuity over time, carings are tied to our sense of self more closely than other attitudes—they are more strongly our own.[39]

Once we recognize that carings are invariably internal attitudes, our intuitions about their role as grounds for FMS gain theoretical backing. It makes sense that a creature who possesses a sense of self— enough of a self that the distinction between motivations that merely occur within him and those that are truly his own applies to him—would have the underpinnings of a higher moral standing than a creature who lacks such self-delineation. The latter creature, who is simply a substratum of events occurring within the history of his mental life, and who doesn't have enough mental organization for any of these events to be truly his own, would be appropriately considered a wanton rather than a person.[40]

(Note that, for the relevant sense of self-delineation, the creature need not explicitly recognize attitudes as his own. Internality is not a matter of how the agent feels about aspects of his psychology and how his attitudes appear to him. Specifically, carings are invariably internal by virtue of the kind of attitudes they are, due to their structure and the consequent role they play in forging the agent's Lockean identity and cohesion over time, and not by virtue of some special additional act or attitude of identification that all agents invariably apply to their carings. The claim that carings are invariably internal is not meant as a prediction that all agents will recognize their carings as internal; it simply identifies a class of attitudes that always represent one's point of view as an agent. As such, it can apply to creatures incapable of taking their attitudes as objects of reflection, let alone of recognizing attitudes as their own or alien.)[41]

Because carings are very deeply our own, thanks to their role in structuring the unity and continuity of our psychology over time, they are

[39] For a fuller exposition of this point see my 2007.

[40] My use of the term "wanton" here is somewhat different from that familiar from Frankfurt's work. According to Frankfurt, a wanton is a creature who does not assess his own desires in any way, who is "not concerned with the desirability of his desires themselves" (Frankfurt 1988a, 17).

[41] Healthy agents, not alienated from themselves, will usually explicitly identify with aspects of their psychology that are truly their own and will not identify with the external aspects. Hence, we can usually tell that an attitude is internal to the agent if the agent experiences the attitude as his own, or at least if he doesn't dissociate himself from the attitude and doesn't see it as alien. Our patterns of associating ourselves with some attitudes and dissociating ourselves from others are vital inputs into any workable theory of internality, and I relied on them at the beginning of this section. Such a theory is meant to delineate which attitudes are truly the agent's own, and not merely when an agent would feel that this is the case. Once we construct the theory based on paradigm cases of agents identifying themselves with some attitudes and distancing themselves from others, we can apply it to instances in which the agent is not explicitly aware of her fully internal attitudes, and even to agents outright incapable of such awareness, as is likely the case with young children.

appropriate sources of principles of action that are authentically our own, principles according to which we can govern ourselves as truly autonomous decision makers. In this way, carings function as the most elemental building blocks of the capacity for autonomy: a caring agent at least has the beginnings of a self with which to engage in self-legislation. And caring attitudes' role as starting points of autonomous decisions adds further plausibility to the idea that they are the bases for FMS. The intuition that the capacity to care may be sufficient for FMS was at first, recall, a source of difficulties for the Kantian approach. But now we see how the claim that the capacity to care is a foundation of FMS can be incorporated into a view that preserves the fundamental connection between autonomy and FMS, and so remains, in this sense, Kantian in spirit. If we amend the Kantian picture to the (sizable!) extent of accepting carings rather than evaluative judgments as the more fundamental starting points of autonomy, it will accord perfectly well with our intuitive assessments of FMS in the Kiddies and the Pathians.[42]

The discussion of the connection between caring and internality and autonomy may help clarify how difficult it is to meet the criterion of caring in actual cases. The caring criterion is weaker than the evaluative judgment criterion, so many cognitively impaired humans, including some of those classified as severely impaired, may well meet this less demanding criterion. However, this will surely leave many human beings, including infants and some subset of severely demented humans and humans whose cognitive development is severely impaired, below the threshold of caring.[43] Caring is much more cognitively and emotionally demanding than mere desiring. It requires sufficient emotional capacity to generate a sophisticated pattern of rationally interconnected emotions focused on a specific object. And it requires a cognitive capacity to grasp the concept of importance so as to be able to further structure one's activity, or at least one's psychic economy, around the importance of the cared-for object. I have only argued that attitudes with this emotional and cognitive depth have an automatic claim to be genuinely the agent's own

[42] Note that, on my proposal, the capacity to care is the foundation of FMS, where caring is a type of attitude, not necessarily associated with a specific object or content. Similarly, as I read it, the standard Kantian view treats the capacity to value as the foundation of FMS, without requiring the agent to hold specific values. In particular, just as on my proposal the capacity for altruistic caring is not necessary for FMS, so the Kantian view doesn't require the specific ability to recognize moral reasons as a precondition for FMS—the more general ability to engage in evaluative reasoning is sufficient. Thus, amoral agents and other agents whose concerns may be misguided or mistaken are handled similarly by both approaches. (Thanks to the anonymous associate editors of *Ethics* for prompting this clarification.)

[43] Empirically, it may be very hard in a specific case to determine whether an individual is above or below this threshold, but there is no reason to believe that, simply in virtue of being human, we must all be capable of caring, regardless of the severity of the cognitive impairment.

and hence to be appropriate starting points of autonomy. Some human individuals lack the requisite emotional and cognitive capacities and thus do not qualify as carers. I am allowing, for the purposes of the present argument, that such individuals may have FMS due to their potential or species capacity to become carers. But if so, the capacity to care is still the ultimate ground or explanation of their FMS, even though they themselves don't currently possess this capacity.

3. Further Implications

The view I have developed here is meant to elucidate, in the first instance, by virtue of what capacities, be they actual, species, or potential, we can take human beings to have FMS. But the view is also of consequence for our judgments about FMS of some nonhuman creatures in our world. Those who have worked with or extensively observed great apes would readily testify that these are animals capable of the cognitively sophisticated kind of caring described in this essay. The minute details of chimpanzees' and gorillas' long-term intimate bonds with one another probably provide the best evidence of this, but even less comprehensive accounts are very telling.

Consider Koko, a gorilla conversant in American Sign Language, made especially famous by a *National Geographic* cover, in which she, a 230-pound intimidating-looking animal with gigantic hands, is gently cradling a tiny kitten. The sheer fact that Koko could even go near the kitten without trampling him is remarkable enough, but there is much more to the story. Koko developed a long-term bond with the kitten, whom she named All Ball. She was able to play with Ball without frightening or injuring him, caressing him gently even though he habitually bit her following his kitten ways. She dressed him in linen napkins and hats, and signed phrases like "Koko love visit Ball" and "Soft good cat cat" (Vessels 1985).[44] Most remarkably, she went into what could only be understood as deep mourning after Ball escaped one day and got run over by a car (Patterson and Gordon 1994, 67–68). She "cried shortly after she was told of his death." Three days later, in response to her caretaker's questions about the cat, Koko signed "Cry" and "Sleep cat." "When she saw a picture of a cat who looked very much like All Ball, Koko pointed to the picture and signed, 'CRY, SAD, FROWN.'" Three months later, when asked, "How did you feel when you lost Ball?" Koko signed "Want," "Open trouble visit sorry," and "Red red red bad sorry Koko-love good." Even after several years she still signed "Frown" and "Sorry" upon seeing pictures of Ball.[45]

---

[44] There are many accounts of the remarkable abilities of the great apes: see, e.g., de Waal 1996. However, Koko's relationship with All Ball provides the clearest illustration I am familiar with of animal caring.

Koko's gentle handling of Ball shows that she was able to understand his needs and interests—very different from her own—to a remarkable degree and to respond to them adequately. A full gamut of her emotions was focused on Ball, including joy in his company, fondness, excited anticipation of his visits, and, most remarkably, grief over his loss. Unlike many other animals who may also seem to "care"—about their young, about their owners, and so forth—this gorilla's attitudes and reactions are not stereotypical. They go far beyond a rudimentary pattern of attachment found, for example, in dogs: protest at the perceived threat of separation from the object of attachment, sadness when separated, elation at reunion. Koko's reactions track the distinctive needs and interests of the kitten, to which Koko could not respond so well merely through biologically prescribed instincts. Rather, Koko appears to be knowingly attuned to All Ball's needs. Given Koko's elementary mastery of language, it doesn't seem far-fetched to presume that she has enough cognitive ability to form the concept of importance and that her nonstereotypical responses and actions toward All Ball are dictated by her implicit perception of All Ball, the focus of her emotions, as important. By the criteria advanced here, Koko is a carer and therefore a person worthy of full moral respect.

Accordingly, the recognition that FMS ultimately rests on the capacity to care requires revisions in both currently established approaches to FMS. The preservationist approach holds that all humans have FMS and nonhuman animals do not, but once we see that the basis of FMS is less demanding than traditionally thought, it turns out that some nonhuman animals have FMS.[46] Similarly, the established revisionists must now draw moral boundaries in a new place and accept that we have special duties toward all individual beings (human or not) that have the capacity to care and that we lack such duties to beings (human or not) incapable of

[45] A journal entry more than five years after All Ball's death: "Koko comes across a picture of herself and All Ball in a photo album. K: THAT BAD FROWN SORRY [emphatic] UNATTENTION [Koko's negation of the sign for attention, covering her eyes with her hands—clarified in the internet version of the article]" (Patterson and Gordon 1994, 68).

[46] Since I labeled this view "preservationist," it appears odd to suggest that the view can be revised and still remain preservationist. My idea is this: the goal of preservationists is to justify the commonsense approach to FMS, and especially the conviction that all humans have FMS. In doing so, they typically adopt a certain theoretical strategy: they appeal to valuable capacities of unimpaired adult humans and to the value of potential and/or species possession of such capacities. I have tried to show that, once we attend to intuitions about the moral standing of imaginary species, this preservationist approach can be sustained only if we recognize the capacity to care as an ultimate ground of FMS. The resulting view preserves the key element of common sense: the idea that all humans have FMS. But it forces some revisions of common sense; namely, animals capable of caring, such as great apes, now also turn out to have FMS. (Note that by suggesting this revision I do not side with revisionists in their core debate with preservationists: I still remain neutral on whether potential and/or species capacities can ground FMS.)

caring. True, as I forewarned, my proposal does not settle the entrenched debate between the two camps. The revisionists will deny FMS to human beings who lack the capacity to care, while the preservationists will continue to insist that such humans have FMS owing either to their potential for caring or to the human species' capacity to care. Still, their disagreement has been bridged to some extent, since both camps now at least have to agree on one set of cases that has hitherto exacerbated their debate: nonhuman animals capable of caring, such as the great apes, must be treated with respect normally accorded to persons.

Acknowledgments

Thanks to Jodi Halpern, Matthew Liao, Maggie Little, Eva Kittay, Debra Satz, Neven Sesardic, JulieTannenbaum, anonymous reviewers at *Ethics*, the members of the Fellows Seminar at the Center for Human Values at Princeton University, the audiences at the Bay Area Forum for Law and Ethics at the University of California at Berkeley, the Symposium on Evil and Psychopathy at the University of San Francisco, the Ethics Reading Group at the University of California at San Diego, the International Workshop "Human Nature and Bioethics" at the Governance in Asia Research Centre at the City University of Hong Kong, and to my students in Philosophy 378 at Stanford for helpful comments on earlier drafts. I am especially grateful to Jeff McMahan for extensive comments and for numerous very helpful conversations; to Cole Leahy, Melissa Fusco, Govind Persad, Caleb Perl, and Daniel Halliday for research assistance; and to the Center for Human Values at Princeton University for sabbatical support. This essay is a shorter and substantially altered version of my article "Caring and Full Moral Standing" published in *Ethics* 117 (April 2007): 460–497, © 2007 by The University of Chicago.

References

Aksakov, Sergei. 1983. *Years of Childhood.* Oxford: Oxford University Press.
Broome, John. 1990–91. "Fairness." *Proceedings of the Aristotelian Society* 91, no. 1:87–102.
Byrne, Peter. 2000. *Philosophical and Ethical Problems in Mental Handicap.* New York: St. Martin's.
Cleckley, Harvey. 1988. *The Mask of Sanity.* Augusta, Ga.: Emily S. Cleckley.
Damasio, Antonio R. 1994. *Descartes' Error: Emotion, Reason, and the Human Brain.* New York: Putnam's.

de Waal, Frans. 1996. *Good Natured: The Origins of Right and Wrong in Humans and Other Animals*. Cambridge, Mass.: Harvard University Press.

Diamond, Cora. 1991. "The Importance of Being Human." In *Human Beings*, edited by David Cockburn, 35–62. Cambridge: Cambridge University Press.

Dunn, Judy, and Carol Kendrick. 1982. *Siblings: Love, Envy, and Understanding*. Cambridge, Mass.: Harvard University Press.

Frankfurt, Harry. 1988a. "Freedom of the Will and the Concept of a Person." In his *The Importance of What We Care About*, 11–25. Cambridge: Cambridge University Press.

———. 1988b. "Identification and Externality." In his *The Importance of What We Care About*, 58–68. Cambridge: Cambridge University Press.

Goldie, Peter. 2000. *The Emotions: A Philosophical Exploration*. Oxford: Oxford University Press.

Gopnik, Alison. 1993. "How We Know Our Minds: The Illusion of First-Person Knowledge of Intentionality." *Behavioral and Brain Sciences* 16, no. 1:1–14.

Helm, Bennett W. 1996. "Freedom of the Heart." *Pacific Philosophical Quarterly* 77, no. 2:71–87.

———. 2001. *Emotional Reason: Deliberation, Motivation, and the Nature of Value*. Cambridge: Cambridge University Press.

Jaworska, Agnieszka. 2007. "Caring and Internality." *Philosophy and Phenomenological Research* 74, no. 3:529–68.

———. Unpublished manuscript. "Moral Psychology in Practice: Lessons from Alzheimer's Disease and the 'Terrible Twos'." Department of Philosophy, University of California, Riverside.

McMahan, Jeff. 2002. *The Ethics of Killing: Problems at the Margins of Life*. Oxford: Oxford University Press.

Nissenbaum, Helen. 1985. *Emotion and Focus*. Stanford, Calif.: Center for the Study of Language and Information.

Patterson, Francine, and Wendy Gordon. 1994. "The Case for the Personhood of Gorillas." In *The Great Ape Project: Equality Beyond Humanity*, edited by Paola Cavalieri and Peter Singer, 58–77. New York: St. Martin's Press.

Scanlon, T. M. 1998. *What We Owe to Each Other*. Cambridge, Mass.: Harvard University Press.

Schapiro, Tamar. 1999. "What Is a Child?" *Ethics* 109, no. 4 (July): 715–38.

Thompson, Ross A. 1987. "Empathy and Emotional Understanding: The Early Development of Empathy." In *Empathy and Its Development*, edited by Nancy Eisenberg and Janet Strayer, 119–45. Cambridge: Cambridge University Press.

Thomson, Judith Jarvis. 1990. *The Realm of Rights*. Cambridge, Mass.: Harvard University Press.

Vessels, Jane. 1985. "Koko's Kitten." *National Geographic* 167, no. 1:110–13.

Zahn-Waxler, Carolyn, Marian Radke-Yarrow, Elizabeth Wagner, and Michael Chapman. 1992. "Development of Concern for Others." *Developmental Psychology* 28, no. 1:126–36.

22

THE PERSONAL IS PHILOSOPHICAL IS POLITICAL: A PHILOSOPHER AND MOTHER OF A COGNITIVELY DISABLED PERSON SENDS NOTES FROM THE BATTLEFIELD

EVA FEDER KITTAY

Introduction

An op-ed piece in the *Washington Post*, written in the wake of the Baby Doe case, began: "The one thing a child does is make a philosopher out of a parent" (Cohen 1982, B1).

Well, what if you already are a philosopher and are raising a child with severe physical and cognitive disabilities? As a philosopher who is the mother of a wonderful woman with severe intellectual disabilities, I finally determined that I should subject philosophical treatments of cognitive disability to a critique based on my knowledge and personal experience as a mother. It is this experience that has informed much of my writing already. The work that I had done on an ethic of care and the practice of caregiving comes out of my personal engagement with the care for an entirely dependent person. Furthermore, my teaching of ethics and social and political thought always ran up against an untruth: that all humans were such and such, where this "such and such" did not at all match what I learned in caring for and loving my daughter. In fact, much of philosophy depends on being able to make such claims about distinctive human capacities, and many claims of political ideals of justice, autonomy, and equality are grounded on a set of competences or potentials, many of which my daughter most likely does not possess. As a critique of philosophy based on my experience as a mother of a cognitively disabled daughter is a critique that touches on foundational concerns, I could expect that this road would be full of land mines, some of which could be anticipated. Others would be discovered only after I had already stepped on them. Unsurprisingly, I have stepped on several, and it has at times prompted me to ask the question: Should I continue? What is to be gained?

I want to defend the idea that stopping is a poor choice—for me, for the profession, and for people with cognitive disabilities. I will do so even as I exhibit some of the difficulties of being a mother trying to philosophize on a matter so close to my heart. Furthermore, taking on

this project is of a piece with the "invisible labor" that is done by people
with disabilities and their families to allow those without disabilities to
understand and interact with people with disabilities. It is, in fact, a form
of caring that families do when they include a family member with
disabilities. Finally, I will point to the idea that there is an inextricable
relationship between the personal, the political, and the philosophical.
And I will be appealing to this relationship as I seek to justify my
philosophical claims, ones whose important political implications are
based on the personal knowledge gleaned from a close relationship to a
person with severe cognitive disabilities. I begin with an anecdote.

So there I was. In a roomful of distinguished philosophers at a workshop
in Atlanta, Georgia, trying to convince the attendees and philosopher-
bioethicist Jeff McMahan that an argument he launched in his monumental
Ethics of Killing (McMahan 2003) is not only philosophically flawed but also
based on totally inadequate familiarity with the population that is adversely
affected by the arguments he put forward, which are at once philosophically
problematic and potentially dangerous to a highly vulnerable population.[1]
The population in question is a group he calls in that work "the congenitally
severely mentally retarded" and in later work, the "radically cognitively
limited." His thesis is that the moral status of this group should be demoted
below that of all other human beings (at least those beyond the stage of
infancy), and that the appropriate comparison group is nonhuman animals,
whose moral status should be appropriately elevated.

McMahan argues for a two-tiered morality, one for persons, and one
for nonpersons. Persons include all human beings who function at a
certain (unspecified) cognitive level and possess certain psychological
attributes that allow them a variety of functions that we recognize as
distinctively human. Nonpersons include all other sentient beings—the
sorts of beings that vegetarians typically do not eat. In the nonperson
category, he argues, we may or may not include human beings whose
cognitive capacity has not yet developed, such as fetuses and infants, and
those children and adults whose cognitive capacities have been so
diminished—through illness or injury—that they can reliably be said to
have neither a strong continuity of self, nor a capacity to project
themselves into the future, nor an ability to appreciate the higher
pleasures we associate with being human, and so forth. In the case of
infants, we recognize a capacity to develop these intrinsic properties that
will allow us to see these individuals as potential persons. In the case of
those who have lost the capacities, their former possession of properties
that made us once recognize these individuals as persons may arguably
give them the right to the same moral standing as persons.

There is one category of human nonpersons whose inviolability and
right to justice we cannot argue for on the basis of their potential or on

---

[1] This paper was eventually published as Kittay 2005.

the basis of their former personhood, and that is the "the congenitally severely mentally retarded." Therefore this group presents itself as a seemingly less difficult group to cite when arguing that moral status should be assigned not on the basis of species membership but on the basis of intrinsic psychological capacities, foremost among which is higher-level cognition. It is these capacities, McMahan argues, that should determine whether an individual is due justice and whether it is as bad to kill that individual as it is to "kill one of us." My daughter, according to this reasoning, has no grounds to claim justice, and it is less bad to kill her than to kill "one of us."

In making my case against a conclusion that seems to me so self-evidently abhorrent—the basis for an argument *ad absurdum*, not a thesis to maintain—I try to keep my arguments tight, my interpretations clean and correct, my reasoning clear of the emotional turmoil I feel as I read McMahan's words. McMahan responds. He thinks that we are arguing past each other; that I have missed what his arguments are meant to show; that I have taken things out of context. But fundamentally he isn't backing away from the central thesis I am attacking. He just thinks that I have failed to show where the argument goes wrong and that my admittedly provisional and tentative alternative will not hold up. (Although his criticism is as sketchy as is my offering.) Most of the others sit silent. Those who do speak up do so in order to defend McMahan and attack me for attacking McMahan. I had, in fact, made the inflammatory claim that McMahan's arguments exemplify how philosophical bioethics can itself be unethical in its methodology and import. (Something I return to below.)

Where were my defenders? As I left the meeting, I thought, "What am I doing in this profession?" What, I wondered, was I doing in a discipline that thought it appropriate to question the full worth of a portion of humanity, one that happened to include my own daughter? A discipline whose practitioners sat on the sidelines as I fought to defend her moral worth and that of those like her?

By the time I got on the plane, I was determined to resign at the semester's end. By the time I got off the plane, I had decided not to leave but to attempt to change this venerable hoary profession—at least to give it a good try.

This current collection of chapters is the culmination of the ensuing Stony Brook conference on cognitive disability and philosophy that I helped organize. This chapter, however, was written after the conference. It is a meditation on the conversation that closed the conference, and it is a reflection on my dual role: philosopher, and also stakeholder in the philosophical debate—though not just any stakeholder, but a mother. Can one do good philosophy, be practically efficacious, and keep intact the relationship of mother and child, or are the difficulties in this project insurmountable? Are there philosophical and practical payoffs in making philosophy this personal—and do they justify the personal costs of the effort?

What Is the Problem? Why Try to Change the Profession?

What is it philosophers have said about cognitive disability that I found so appalling that I was ready to jettison a career of more than thirty years? Here is how Licia Carlson summarized her quest, while still an undergraduate volunteering at a local center for people with intellectual disabilities, to discover what philosophers had to say on the topic: "Plato decreed that 'defective babies' should be left to die. Locke and Kant defined those who lack reason as less than human. And most troubling of all, when I looked for contemporary discussions about this group, most of the references I found were in discussions of animal rights, asking pointedly whether the 'severely mentally retarded' could be distinguished from non-human animals in any meaningful sense" (Carlson forthcoming).

A passage in Jeff McMahan's work illustrates some of these disturbing claims:

> It is arguable, however, that a further effect of our partiality for members of our own species is a tendency to decreased sensitivity to the lives and well-being of those sentient beings that are not members of our species.
>
> One can discern an analogous phenomenon in the case of nationalism . . . [where] the sense of solidarity among members . . . motivates them. . . . But the powerful sense of collective identity within a nation is often achieved by contrasting an idealized conception of the national character with caricatures of other nations, whose members are regarded as less important or worthy or, in many cases, are dehumanized and despised as inferior or even odious. . . . In places such as Yugoslavia and its former provinces—the result is often brutality and atrocity on an enormous scale. . . .
>
> I believe our treatment of the severely retarded and our treatment of animals follows a similar pattern. While our sense of kinship with the severely retarded moves us to treat them with great solicitude, our perception of animals as radically "other" numbs our sensitivity to them. . . . When one compares the relatively small number of severely retarded human beings who benefit from our solicitude with the vast number of animals who suffer at our hands, it is impossible to avoid the conclusion that the good effects of our species-based partiality are greatly outweighed by the bad. (McMahan 2003, 221–22)

Again, imagine being the mother of a child with severe intellectual disabilities reading within the pages of a philosophical text such statements as: "I have argued that the cognitively impaired are not badly off in the sense relevant to justice and indeed do not come within the scope of comparative (and, by extension, noncomparative) principles of justice. Not only do they not have special priority as a matter of justice, but their claims on us seem even weaker than those of most other human beings" (McMahan 1996, 31). After outlining three possible conclusions to his argument, McMahan gives as the third "that the treatment of animals is governed by stronger constraints than we have traditionally supposed, while the treatment of the cognitively impaired is in some respects subject to weaker constraints than we have traditionally supposed." And he concludes: "The third seems the only reasonable option" (McMahan 2003, 31). Reasonable? To whom? Certainly not to me.

For a mother of a severely cognitively impaired child, the impact of such an argument is devastating. How can I begin to tell you what it feels like to read texts in which one's child is compared, in all seriousness and with philosophical authority, to a dog, pig, rat, and most flatteringly a chimp; how corrosive these comparisons are, how they mock those relationships that affirm who we are and why we care?

I am no stranger to a beloved animal. I have had dogs I have loved, dogs I have mourned for. But as dog lovers who become parents can tell you, much as we adore our hounds, there is no comparison between the feelings for a beloved child of normal capacities and those for a beloved canine. And I can tell you that there is also no comparison when that child has intellectual disabilities.

If the demands of philosophical inquiry are so painful in this respect, why continue to engage the issue? Why not just quit—or quit working in this area of philosophy? Why try to change the profession with respect to issues of cognitive disability? To respond, it is useful to draw an analogy with the situation of women who entered the field of philosophy in the heady days of the women's liberation movement. These women were intellectuals who wished to align their intellectual pursuits with the persons they are and with the position they occupy in the world. The political atmosphere made especially evident sexist presumptions that have long been predominant in philosophy, but these women chose not to pass over these presumptions as aberrations, holdovers from more patriarchal times. Instead, they—much like Mary Wollstonecraft and Simone de Beauvoir before them—asked how philosophical inquiry itself might be distorted by the false beliefs about women. They believed that limiting a field to those who live similar lives diminishes its truth and usefulness, yielding at best partial truths, at worst distortions of central concepts. For those of us who have fallen in love with philosophy, turning away without falling out of love seems a poor way of treating a lover.

Moreover, by tackling problematic assumptions of philosophy, those previously underrepresented in the field help to clarify and unmask political views that predominate beyond philosophy. In matters dealing with cognitive disability, philosophical positions formed in the absence of any representation either by people with disabilities or by their families find their way, via bioethics, into health-care and policy decisions. Such positions have posed the possibility of truly deleterious consequences. Finally, philosophy, when approached critically, may have something important to offer in the striving for the just and caring treatment of those who have been outside its scope. If you think that philosophical inquiry is both intrinsically and instrumentally important, then to leave it to its ignorance and prejudices is a poor option indeed.

But there is another reason as well. When Sara Ruddick describes the practice of mothering, a central feature is socializing the child for acceptance into society. The mother with a disabled child hears this requirement somewhat differently from most (Ruddick 1989). For her, socialization for acceptance means that you have both to help the child make her way in the world given her disabilities *and* to help shape a world that will accept her. My daughter, Sesha, will never walk the halls of academe, but when what happens within these halls has the potential to affect her, then I as an academic have an obligation to socialize academe to accept my daughter. Such "care" may seem to be far from the daily care that her fully dependent body requires, and it may appear to be far-fetched to call this "care," but it is part and parcel of that labor of love that we do as parents, especially parents of disabled children—more still in the case of those who are so disabled that they cannot speak for themselves, a defining condition for those who are severely intellectually disabled.

The disability scholar and biomedical ethicist Jackie Leach Scully speaks of a form of discrimination against people with disabilities that resists legislative measures. For this she uses the term "disablism" and says, "People who are nonconsciously or unconsciously disablist do not recognize themselves as in any way discriminatory; their disablism is often unintentional, and persists through unexamined, lingering cultural stereotypes about disabled lives" (Scully 2008, 2).[2] She shows how disabled people cope, "manage," or even in some cases are forced to "manipulate" these less-than-conscious forms of disablement in their daily interactions, and she calls this "management" the "invisible labor of disabled people." Family members of disabled people also do such invisible labor. It is part of the labor involved in the socialization for acceptance that mothers of disabled children do when they work to socialize the world to meet their child. In deciding to write about my disabled daughter in the context of philosophy, I not only am engaged in this labor but am working to make some of this labor visible. My efforts deploy philosophical reasoning and are directed at philosophers and philosophical texts, but they are also part of mothering, of doing that otherwise invisible work managing "the disablist" so that those who live with disability can live better.

The Challenges

What are the specific challenges facing someone in my position? There are essentially two. The first is to overcome the anger and revulsion that one feels when encountering the view that one's disabled child—or child with

---

[2] "Disabilist" should include those who try to sharply distinguish an impairment and a disability, as does McMahan when he claims that the "radically cognitively limited" are not disabled, for social conditions have nothing to do with this limitation (see McMahan 2009, included in this collection). For a critique of such a reading of the social model of disability by one of its formulators, see Shakespeare and Watson 2001.

a particular disability—is less worthy of dignity, of life, of concern or justice than others. What does this labor look like? As I was writing the paper that I delivered at that philosophical workshop of which I spoke at the start of this chapter, a paper that required a very careful reading of McMahan's *Ethics of Killing*, I would return to my daughter, Sesha, and find myself trying to analyze the features that differentiated her from the nonhuman animals with whom she was being compared, features that would make her worthy of personhood. As I did so, I would simultaneously shrink away in disgust from such reflection.

Now consider what it means to make these comparisons. Comparisons always involve the positing of at least a partial identity. We compare by matching up features or aspects of something, and then regard those features that do not align themselves as the differentia. In scientific inquiries we do compare humans and nonhuman animals, matching humans and animals feature by feature, either to differentiate what is definitively human or to ascertain what we share with fellow animals. But such comparisons exist against an understanding that man and beast are distinct—however alike we may be in certain respects. When, in contrast, comparisons are made with pernicious intent, as when African Americans are compared to apes, or Jews are analogized to parasites or called dogs, the object is to reduce the human to the nonhuman, to strip away those aspects of human beings that connect these human beings more closely to other human animals than to nonhuman animals. As the cognitive psychologist Amos Tversky pointed out, the predicate "is like" is not symmetrical (Tversky 1977). When we assert that A is like B, we take B as the template—its features are salient—and the features of A not found in B lose their salience. That is, if B is characterized by the features x, y, and z, then we come to see A only in terms of its similarity with respect to x, y, and z, even if in other contexts A's features, a, b, and c, are the salient ones. The pernicious reductive comparisons between humans and nonhuman animals take such an asymmetrical form.

Thus, to respond to the challenge to articulate the differences between a human animal with significantly curtailed cognitive capacities and a relatively intelligent nonhuman animal means that one first has to see the former as the latter. That is the moment of revulsion. Relating with that stance to my daughter as my daughter is an impossibility. Note that this response has little to do with the affection one might feel for a nonhuman animal. Remember that the Nazis expressed a great affection for nonhuman animals and were deeply attached to their dogs. But that did not keep them from calling Jews "*Hunde*."

Imagine, if you can, taking the person that you love as much as you love anything in this world, your beloved child, and looking at her with the comparative measure of a dog or a rat or a chimp or a pig. This thought is still worse than Bernard Williams's famous "one thought too many"—that is, the thought of the husband who thinks he needs a justification to save his own wife when faced with the choice of saving her or someone else (Williams 1976, 214). And I had to fight that one thought, one thought too many and too hideous, interposing itself between my daughter and me in order to preserve the fulgent sweetness of her being.

But without that thought, how could I answer the skeptics? And if *I* sensed the comparison cutting me off from my own daughter, then imagine the wedge the process of juxtaposing the cognitively disabled and the nonhuman animal would place between a person with severe cognitive disabilities and those who lack any familiarity with such individuals. In the case of the theorist the wedge may be merely conceptual, but it has the potential to translate into one with horrific consequences on a practical level.[3]

Of course, a part of the experience I am describing involves the paradox of trying to study another subject, and in so doing turn a subject into an object. I was studying my daughter and my relationship to her, and such study does seem to require an objectification that is at odds with the relationship of two subjects. But what makes this particular case so toxic is that the relentless comparisons of my daughter to a nonhuman animal, this dehumanization, is in itself the objectification of her, and it is I who am required to be the objectifier in order to see how to refute the offensive claims.[4] No one who aspires to be "a good parent," to fulfill the basic duty of a parent, can but revolt against the dehumanization or the moral demotion of one's own child. Added to this insult is the fact that, historically, giving the cognitively disabled the "face of the beast" has permitted so much abuse and neglect (even of people whom we would not today treat as cognitively disabled) (Carlson forthcoming). Such abuse continues unabated in some quarters even today.[5] The history comes alive each time the comparison gets made.

Epistemic Responsibility and Credibility

It might be supposed that I have just demonstrated the impossibility of a mother being able to ascertain objectively the truth about the moral status of her own child, where that moral status is not one she would want to affirm. But is it possible to say that the intimacy of parent and child and

[3] I thank Licia Carlson for this point.
[4] Addressing me, Licia Carlson has made the following insightful point: "Though unlike in *your* case (having to turn a subject into an object), in philosophical discourse she's never been a subject. It's almost a different *kind* of objectifying when one confirms an object of study as an object (and whose subjectivity has been dismissed, and really never posited in the first place)" (personal communication).
[5] The state of Texas continues the practice of employing state institutions to warehouse mentally disabled individuals. According to an Associated Press article reported by MSNBC, "In Texas, officials verified 465 incidents of abuse or neglect against mentally disabled people in state care in fiscal year 2007. Over a three-month period this summer, the state opened at least 500 new cases with similar allegations, according to federal investigators" (Associated Press 2009).

the parent's caring labor gives us not a lesser grasp of the moral truth but a greater one—a truth born of the labor of the hand and heart as well as the mind (Smith 1987)? I believe it can.

In another work I have argued that Peter Singer and Jeff McMahan fail to adhere to what I take as fundamental ethical precepts that philosophers need to uphold in their philosophizing (Kittay 2008). These are, first, *epistemic responsibility*: know the subject that you are using to make a philosophical point; and, second, *epistemic modesty*: know what you don't know.[6] These two principles serve to indicate the paradoxical position of a philosopher with affinitive relations to a cognitively impaired individual who inquires into the validity of morally demoting such individuals to nonpersonhood.

Epistemic Responsibility: Empirical Adequacy

As I have already noted, if *anyone* might be accused of epistemic irresponsibility, it may seem to be the mother, not the philosophers, whose conceptual and personal distance from the subject matter lend them a degree of objectivity. After all, it is the mother whose emotional investment may skew her judgment. But let us think again. Let us ask: Of whom are philosophers such as Singer and McMahan actually speaking when they invoke the "severely mentally retarded" or the "radically cognitively impaired"? To whom do they refer?

Singer (1996) asks us to think about a "special institution" for the retarded that is found in the Netherlands. Here mentally retarded individuals are confined, but live a life without many of the usual constraints of such institutions. They are free to wander about, form associations with one another, engage in sexual activity, and have and raise children who result from sexual encounters. Residents indicate their desires and wants with grunts and gestures, raise their children, pick leaders, get elderly females to help with raising the little ones. From Singer's description it appears that they possess no physical problems, other than their cognitive deficits. Close to the end of the description, he notes that when one of the residents kills another, the death is not treated as would be the death of a nonresident, and the killer is not thought to have done the same sort of injury. This "special institution" for the retarded, it turns out, is not for people at all, but (gasp!) for chimpanzees. From the description we are meant to think that the behavior of the chimps is adequate to a description of a group of retarded persons, and so to conclude that both populations share the same morally relevant attributes.[7]

---

[6] The others are *humility*: resist the arrogant imposition of your own values on others, and *accountability*: pay attention to the consequences of your philosophizing (see Kittay 2008).

[7] Incidentally, it seems that chimps do not take the killing of one of them as lightly as Singer implies. See the description by Frans de Waal (2006, 47) of the murder of Luit at the

The description, however, is suspect because human impairments are multiple, so one rarely sees a population of people with intellectual disabilities as uniform as those of the chimpanzees in Singer's zoo. While deficits in a population of retarded persons would vary considerably, the residents of Singer's community are pretty much alike and function at the same level. Singer can paint such a picture precisely because he is speaking of chimpanzees without the deficits characteristic of the severely cognitively impaired human. To borrow from Tolstoy, "All unimpaired humans are alike; each human with a severe impairment is impaired after its own fashion."[8] We can retain some characteristically human capacities and lose others. What's lost and what is retained constrains the extent to which, and how fully, we are able to partake in scope of human existence and the panoply of human possibilities.[9]

It is most unlikely that one could have a community of humans who all have the same cognitive impairments, who all function at the same level, and who together can function as a community without the assistance of humans without such impairments.[10]

The empirical inadequacy of this example feeds a conceptual fallacy. It is as if one were to say that an automobile that has lost a wheel, and hence is three-wheeled, is functionally (and in the case of the human-chimp example morally) equivalent to a motorized tricycle. Both, after all, are motorized vehicles with three wheels, except, of course, that cars were designed to function with four wheels, and the loss of a wheel is a significant impairment. Without at least a minimal acquaintance with cars and tricycles, a conceptualization of the two vehicles as functionally equivalent seems reasonable enough. With the appropriate knowledge the error is self-evident.

I point to this example of Singer's "community for retarded people" because it indicates that its author has very little knowledge of people with the sorts of impairments about whom he purports to speak. Now this is a thought experiment, and so it can surely include counterfactual elements. What is counterfactual, however, is exactly what is at stake in

Arnhem zoo in the Netherlands. This inaccuracy should make us wary of the empirical adequacy of Singer's account of both chimpanzees and humans with retardation (see below).

[8] The original passage from Tolstoy is of course: "All happy families are alike but an unhappy family is unhappy after its own fashion" (1954, 13).

[9] It is worth observing that what one considers as falling within the scope of human existence is not a notion that is clearly defined. Some may consider the dependency of infancy, significant disability, illness of frail old age as conditions that are part of our "animal" and not our human existence. See Kittay 1999, MacIntrye 1999, and Nussbaum 2006 for an opposing view.

[10] This would be true even if all the residents had the same syndrome, say Down, as Down will not express itself to the same extent and in the same way in each case. The scenario also presumes the children of residents would have the same genetic condition. Even in the genetic syndromes like Down, although a higher than usual proportion of Down parents will have Down children, most will be unaffected (Bovicelli et al. 1982).

the example—that is, whether chimps are functionally indistinct (in ways that count morally) from mentally retarded humans. So it cannot be effective in proving that very point without begging the question. As Singer is an astute philosopher, it is probably more likely that he erred in the empirical claims embedded in the example than in the form of argumentation. Moreover, the example *depends* on the ignorance of what mental retardation in humans looks like.

The sense that it is unnecessary to acquaint oneself sufficiently with the empirical realities of mental retardation is no less evident in the work of McMahan. McMahan defines the severely mentally retarded (in a note, he excludes the mildly and moderately retarded and those whose incapacity is a result of brain injury after birth) as human beings "who not only lack self-consciousness but are almost entirely unresponsive to their environment and to other people" (1996, 5). He also says, "The profoundly cognitively impaired are incapable . . . of deep personal and social relations, creativity and achievement, the attainment of the highest forms of knowledge, aesthetic pleasures, and so on" (1996, 8).

This is seriously misinformed. Most severely retarded people can speak at least a few words and can be and are involved in activities and relationships. Even "profoundly mentally retarded" individuals are far from being unresponsive to their environment and to other people. My daughter, Sesha, was diagnosed as having severe to profound retardation. She is enormously responsive, forming deep personal relationships with her family and her long-standing caregivers and friendly relations with her therapists and teachers, more distant relatives, and our friends. I have written quite a bit about her love of music, especially but not exclusively classical symphonic music, with the master of this form, Beethoven, being on the top of her list. So much for the assertion that persons with severe mental retardation cannot experience aesthetic pleasures![11]

Since writing the article in which I counter McMahan's claims and arguments, I experienced one of the most profound learning experiences of my life. My daughter now lives in a group home with five other people who are all considered to be severely mentally retarded, and have been so since birth. Two of her housemates lost their fathers within the period of a month. One, a young woman diagnosed with Rett's syndrome, would be found sitting with tears streaming down her face after she was told that her father was extremely ill and would die. In the case of the other, a young man who invariably greets me with a huge smile, I was witness to the howling, wailing grief minutes after his mother and sister informed him of the death of his father. He waited till they left before he began his heart-wrenching sobbing.

[11] McMahan (2008) raised the bar for the appreciation of aesthetic pleasures where he identified these as capacities such as the ability to understand the "complexity of a Bach fugue." I worry that many who would otherwise make it over the bar easily might now find themselves among the radically cognitively impaired.

They most likely left not knowing what he had understood, and only learned of his response when they later spoke to the staff.[12] We are speaking here of the capacity to understand the very abstract concept of death, the death of a beloved person. So much for cavalier claims that the severely retarded cannot form profound attachments.

McMahan has other characterizations of the congenitally severely mentally retarded. In *The Ethics of Killing* he sometimes speaks of them having the capacities of a chimp, in other places he maintains that they have psychological capacities equivalent to those of a dog.

What Sesha can do, she does as a human would do, though frequently imperfectly; but it is humanly imperfect, not canine perfect. However, even with all Sesha cannot do and seems not to be able to comprehend, her response to music and her sensitivity to people are remarkably intact—or more correctly, quite simply remarkable. What a discordant set of abilities and disabilities she exhibits!

Epistemic Modesty: Know What You Don't Know

The lack of epistemic modesty on these issues was on exhibition at the Stony Brook conference in an interchange between Singer and me. It came at the end of a talk where he argued that many nonhuman animals have cognitive capacities that exceed those of people with severe cognitive disabilities, and that for this reason the two groups are morally on par. He also maintained that he would have more in common with an alien from outer space who was sitting here cleverly disguised as a human than with someone with severe cognitive disabilities. At the end of his talk I noted that he had taken his students on a field trip to a neonatal unit in New Brunswick, which is approximately half an hour away from Princeton University where he teaches, presumably to learn that physicians quietly believe that they should not be keeping some of these neonates alive. Here all one sees of cognitive disability is a tiny creature, more fetus than infant, lying in a bubble-like environment, with tubes coming out of all the infant's orifices and monitors ringing, clinking, and clanging. To offer a different picture, I invited him to come and visit the Center for Discovery, a community composed of group homes for people with very significant and multiple disabilities approximately two hours from New York City (and an hour and a half from Princeton, New Jersey), which is now home to my daughter, Sesha. Here people with cognitive disabilities live flourishing lives, work, and are well cared for, not warehoused. The ensuing conversation went like this:

> *Eva Kittay:* Peter, next time you take your students on a field trip, won't you bring them to the Center for Discovery?

---

[12] It is not unreasonable, in the case of this young man, that he held back his grief to spare his mother and sister.

Peter Singer: It's a little further than New Brunswick.

EK: It can be arranged, and I would be happy to personally arrange it. I don't know how much you can see in one visit. I want you to see some of these people that you are talking about. You bring your students to the neonatal unit; I would just like equal time for the Center for Discovery. . . .

PS: . . . I would like you to tell me what it is—just in terms of the argument that I presented—what it is that I would see there that would challenge the argument that I presented.

EK: Well, where do I start? You would see, for one thing, the difference between . . . what you have in common with the folks who live there and—what was the comparison that you made?—with a Martian, or with a pig, or a chimpanzee. (I have to say chimpanzee is the most flattering of the comparisons that are made.) That's what you would see. How much you see is also what you bring to the situation. I'm not sure what you'd see. But it would at least be a beginning.[13]

What is especially salient in our exchange is that in all their writings about people with significant cognitive impairments, philosophers such as Singer and McMahan presume to know the cognitive capacities of the people they write about, when, as I have attempted to demonstrate, they know virtually nothing at all. And they fail to acknowledge their ignorance. They do not know what they do not know, nor do they appear to take any concrete steps to rectify the situation, because they presume that they have nothing to learn that is of moral significance. It suffices, they believe, to know some bare facts about the deficits in question.

Now what cognitive capacities Sesha possesses *I* do not know, nor do others. And it is hubris to presume to know. I am often surprised find out that Sesha has understood something or is capable of something I did not expect. These surprises can only keep coming when she and her friends are treated in a manner based not on the limitations we know they have but on our understanding that *our* knowledge is limited. If my daughter's housemates had not been told of their fathers' death on the premise that they cannot possibly understand the concept of death, we never would have known that they could have a grief as full and as profound as any I have seen or experienced.

It is easy enough to say that I am "blinded by love," that because of my attachment to my daughter and to her friends I fail to see these folks as the sad specimens they are. I fail to appreciate how superior apes or pigs

---

[13] Quoted from the transcript of the conference proceedings, available at https://podcast.ic.sunysb.edu//blojsom_resources/meta/phicdc/16-PETER_Singer_Q%26A.mp4. Singer counters that if he visits the center, then I should visit a place where chimpanzees employ sign language. I respond that I am willing, and invite us each to find ways of defending the moral status of those we care passionately about without diminishing the moral standing of the other group.

are in terms of any relevant moral characteristics. But it is because I see Sesha close up, because I have a deep and intimate relationship with her, that I am able to see what is hidden from those who are not privileged enough to see her when she opens up to another. It is because I was in her group home that I could witness the young man's overwhelmingly clear expression of his grief when he heard of his father's death. As critics of an unadulterated objectivity, a view from nowhere, have repeated, there is no view from nowhere. If my position as Sesha's mother skews my epistemic relation to questions of cognitive disability, the distance that McMahan and Singer maintain skews it in another direction.

Evelyn Fox Keller, in her study *A Feeling for the Organism*, discusses the methodology of the Nobel-winning scientist Barbara McClintock, who made startling discoveries concerning the transmission of genetic material in maize:

> Inevitably, "seeing" entails a form of subjectivity, an act of imagination, a way of looking that is necessarily in part determined by some private perspective. In ordinary life, these private perspectives seldom emerge as discrepancies; the level of shared vision required of people to cooperate is usually met. But science and art alike make tougher demands on intersubjectivity [than does ordinary life, where intersubjectivity merely requires that we cooperate]: both are crucially dependent on internal visions, committed to conveying what the everyday eye cannot see. (Keller 2003, 150)

Keller goes on to argue that McClintock's "feeling for the organism," the close personal attentiveness that McClintock devoted to the entities that she studied, allowed a personal internal vision to see what the "everyday eye," which in some cases are the eyes of other scientists as well as lay people, could not perceive. One can say the same of someone who is in close contact with a dependent person, especially a person who is limited in his or her communicative skills. The close attentive eye needed to care for the dependent individual gives rise to perceptual capabilities that are not shared by those who have at best a glancing acquaintance.

In primatology, the value of subjective interaction with the individuals studied made the work of Jane Goodall seem hopelessly naïve. She writes in her memoir: "As I had not had an undergraduate science education I didn't realize that animals were not supposed to have personalities, or to think, or to feel emotions or pain. I had no idea that it would have been more appropriate to assign each of the chimpanzees a number rather than a name by which I got to know him or her" (Goodall 2000, 14). Today, of course, it is standard practice to name chimpanzees. If Goodall had not lived with her chimps and given them proper names (and for both she was at first condemned and ignored), we would have continued with the poor understanding we previously had of these beings. Note that these are discoveries that Singer and McMahan depend on and do not seek to impeach. Yet it is no less true that without a strong affective bond with people with severe cognitive disabilities, we often fail to get a glimpse into the lives of these persons.

The epistemic position I am relying on maybe be called, with Sandra Harding, "strong objectivity," which, she says, "starts thought in the perspective from the life of the Other, allowing the Other to gaze back 'shamelessly' at the self who had reserved for himself the right to gaze anonymously at whomsoever he chooses.... Strong objectivity requires that we investigate the relation between subject and object rather than deny the existence of, or seek unilateral control over, this relation" (Harding 1991, 150, 152). It is this relation between "subject" and "object" which is at the heart of the inquiry I have here embarked upon, and which, as Harding's rhetoric suggests, has important political implications. The question is whether my knowledge can be recognized as such, whether my voice can be heard, or whether a patronizing response to the injured mother absolves the parties of any damage that may result from policies formulated on the basis of the denial of the moral personhood of individuals who do not have a place at the table where their fates may be decided.

As we will see in the following section, my own authority (as a philosopher and as one knowledgeable enough to speak about the moral status of people with severe cognitive impairments) is effectively questioned even as recognition is accorded the "special relationship" of mother and child. I hope to provide an argument that takes this recognition and turns the tables on opponents of the moral personhood of people with severe cognitive disabilities. Such recognition, I will argue, effectively settles the case in favor of the moral personhood of people with severe cognitive disabilities.

Why the Personal Is Philosophical Is Political

Now should anyone think that no one—not even a philosopher—would pointedly ask a parent how his or her child differs from a nonhuman animal, say a pig, with respect to the child's moral status, let us look at this interchange between Singer, McMahan, and myself, in the last session of the last day of the Stony Brook conference.

Peter Singer (directed at Eva Kittay): ... You've said a couple of times and you said it just again in response to the last question that you think that Jeff [McMahan] doesn't have the empirical stuff right, and you also said that in response to my comparison between humans and nonhuman animals. You put up Jeff's comments [in which McMahan puts forward a list of comparisons between "radically cognitively impaired" humans and nonhuman animals and then says] and so on and so forth.... [T]hen you said that "we can't wave our hands and then say and so on, because there is so much more to what it is to be human." You've said that a couple of times. So I am just wanting to ask you:

Well, can you tell us some of these morally significant psychological capacities in which you think that human beings, and let's talk about real ones, so the ones who are "profoundly mentally retarded," to use that term, in which they *are* superior to . . . you sort of said, maybe chimpanzees and great apes are different . . . so let's say in which they are superior to pigs or dogs or animals of that sort. (*Eva Kittay responds by shaking her head.*) It's a factual question. You can't just shake your head. You have to put up or stop saying that.

EK: Peter, . . . you asked me how is Sesha different from a—what did you say— a pig? And [when I shook my head] you said, well, it's a factual question, "put up or shut up." The first thing I have to do when you ask me that question, is I have to get over . . . a feeling of nausea. It's not that I'm not able to answer it intellectually, it's that I can't even get to the point emotionally, where I can answer that question. (*Pause.*) Most of the time. When I say you can't just wave your hand and say "and so on," it's because there is *so much* to being human. There's the touch, there's the feel, there's the hug, there's the smile, . . . there are so many ways of interacting. I don't think you need philosophy for this. You need a *very good writer.* . . . [T]his is why I just reject . . . [the] . . . idea that you [should] base moral standing on a list of cognitive capacities, or psychological capacities, or any kind of capacities. Because what it is to be human is not a bundle of capacities. It's a way that you are, a way you are in the world, a way you are with another. And I could adore my pig; I could dote on my pig. It would be something entirely different. And if you can't get that; if you can't understand that, then I'm not sure exactly what it is that you want to hear from me that I could tell you. . . . I'll keep trying because I think this is a very important.

Jeff McMahan: Let me say something on behalf of Peter's [Singer's] point of view here. . . . Peter has not said anything to deny the significance of a mother's relation to her own child. Nothing, as far as I can tell. The question here is a question about what moral demands there are on other people. And the fact that you, Eva, have a relation with your daughter doesn't necessarily give other people the same set of reasons that you have to respond to your daughter in certain ways and to treat your daughter in certain ways. The question is what is it about people like your daughter that makes moral demands on other people that nonhuman animals cannot make on any of us. That is the question that Peter is asking. He's not denying that you have a special relation to your daughter and that that is very significant for you in your life, significant for her, and so on, and that that's true of many other people. Or again to get you to look at George Pitcher's book [Pitcher 1997] or many other books (*EK:* I've read it; in fact it's a very good book) that indicate that these relations—some attenuated version of these relations—I wouldn't claim and I'm sure George Pitcher wouldn't claim that his relation to his dogs was as deep or as significant or as objectively important as your relationship to your daughter. Nobody's saying that. I will also say, though, that (*long pause*). You know, Peter and I didn't come here to hurt anybody's feelings. We're here to try to understand things better. I think that Peter and I engage in a fair amount of voluntary self-censorship. I'm trying very hard not to say anything offensive, something hurtful. I'm profoundly averse to making people miserable.

EK: I know you're not trying to hurt anyone's feelings. I know Peter isn't trying to hurt anyone's feelings. That's not what it's about. For me, it's not what I am experiencing, it's what your writings might mean for public policy. That's what concerns me. And that's not just about my daughter.[14]

Before I turn to my conclusion, it is worth observing a number of points about the dialogue I have just recounted. My comments about what it is to be human are cast entirely in relational terms. I am attempting to steer the discussion away from the only criteria of moral worth that Singer and McMahan are willing to hear—namely, "a set of morally significant psychological properties" possessed by all humans and not by nonhuman animals. My point of contention is with the very idea of a list of attributes as the basis of moral personhood, and although it is one that I repeat in my writings, in the commentary I gave at the conference, and in my responses during the Q&A session, that contention is never joined. Granted that I may not have made my case well. But that was not at issue for Singer and McMahan, because they could not be dissuaded from the idea that there *must* be such a list of morally significant psychological properties and were not willing even to engage the question.

The second point worth noting is that the discussion is hijacked, in a sense. It is turned away from the genuine point of contention to a cloaked and patronizing apology for hurting the feelings of a mother: "Of course you love your child, and we do a great deal of 'self-censorship' to avoid making any one 'miserable.'" Perhaps I courted this response by speaking of finding the comparisons that Singer was asking me to make nauseating and speaking of the psychological cost of engaging in this debate. To conclude this chapter, then, I want to justify these sorts of statements by explaining why they are not thinly veiled attempts to censor Singer, McMahan, and others who hold this position, and why they are not pleas for apologies from those who induce these strong responses.

In fact, in responding, McMahan, unwittingly I believe, comes to grant a consideration which is indispensable to my own argument and in which these bits of self-confession actually play a part. Consider one of the last remarks that McMahan makes. He maintains that his and Singer's aim is not to deny the special relationship between my daughter and me, or the claims she has on me as her mother. It is rather to ask why she has any claims on "the rest of us" that other nonhuman animals fail to have.

I now see how I must reply. If McMahan and others acknowledge the special relationship that is constituted by parenthood, and if they can grant that the parent of a child with the severe cognitive impairments has a deeper and morally and objectively more significant relationship with that child than does a pet owner with his beloved pet, then I believe that a number of

[14] Quoted from the transcript of the conference proceedings, available at https://podcast.ic.sunysb.edu//blojsom_resources/meta/phicdc/36-KITTAY%3AMcMAHAN_Q%26A.mp4

implications suggest that the recognition of the child as possessing moral personhood must follow.

I as a parent have obligations to fulfill toward any child of mine. Following Sarah Ruddick, we can say that what a child "demands" of its parent is to assure that the child's life is protected, that the child's development and growth are fostered, and, as I have already pointed out, that the child can find social acceptance. Now, no parent with a child of typical capacities can do this in a vacuum. All parents need access to certain resources to fulfill their obligations to their child, ones that are at least partially supplied by the larger society. Every parent needs schools and other social institutions to ensure that her child can develop her capacities, whatever those capacities may be. Every parent needs to work with both the child and the social world that the child enters to ensure that the child will grow into a member who is granted respect and who can develop a sense of self-respect. No child is simply the parent's own private matter. If McMahan and Singer claim to honor my relationship to my child and to grant its moral significance, then they cannot with any consistency grant the means to fulfill parental obligations to one parent and deny them to another parent based on some set of features of the child, for these are what all parents need to fulfill their ethical responsibilities to their children regardless of their capacities and needs.

Now what sorts of things are important to the parent qua parent? Foremost is the need that the wider society recognize the worth and worthiness of the child. It is incoherent to grant the special relationship I have with my daughter and then to turn around and say, "But that daughter has no moral hold on anyone but her parent." Her parent cannot fulfill her role as parent, unless others also have an acknowledged moral responsibility to the child—a moral responsibility on a par with the one it has to anyone's child. But it is not for *my* sake that I want my child recognized. It is for *her* sake. That is the nature of the parental relationship. It's not that I want people to care about Sesha because I care about her. It's that I cannot give her the care it is my duty to provide if others do not respect her as a being worthy of the same care as is due to any child.

Reflecting on this last point reveals part of my motive—one that may even have been hidden to myself—in laying bare the intensity of my relationship to a daughter who has such profound intellectual disabilities, and the depth of my revulsion to the sorts of arguments made by Singer and McMahan. I am effectively *showing* what it is impossible to argue. That Sesha is as much a daughter as is any other beloved daughter to a loving parent. That in showing this, I am carrying out my role as her primary caregiver, because I am attempting to win for my daughter the respect and regard that other mothers try to secure for their children. When McMahan directed his distress at making someone miserable to me, the apology misfired, because it was not for my sake that I wanted the mother-child relationship acknowledged. It was for my daughter's sake. What our morally significant relationship and my caring work reveals is that whatever is due to the child of another mother is due to my child, regardless of any of her particular features or "morally significant psychological properties." Whether or not she possesses these, or possesses them in excess of those of a pet dog, McMahan himself grants that the relationship between my daughter and me is present only in an attenuated form in the case of a dog owner who has the deepest affection for his pet. In carrying out a public display of caring in the philosophical context, I am engaged in a philosophical disputation, a point that was actually conceded when McMahan granted the difference between my relationship with my daughter and George Pitcher's relationship to his dog.

In addition, in carrying out this public form of personal caring I am engaged in an act with potential political consequences—attempting to secure for my daughter just treatment and moral protection. For moral personhood is, as many of the chapters in this collection demonstrate, importantly connected with ability to make claims of justice and receive the resources and protections that justice is meant to guarantee. The strategy is then evident, for I have been attempting to affirm in this chapter that the personal is philosophical, and the philosophical is political. The "philosophical" is the unacknowledged middle term in the equation that feminists have championed, namely, "the personal is political."

The personal is political in still another sense in the case of my project. For if I as a mother require that my work of mothering is only possible when the wider society can grant the moral worth of my child, then this is no less true of any child, regardless of his capacities and, importantly, regardless of whether a person with severe cognitive disabilities is still being cared for by his mother, or was ever raised by his biological mother. Each child needs to be cared for by some mothering figure(s), and so the requirement is no less true.

Philosopher Naomi Scheman, after the discussion between Singer, McMahan, and myself has taken place, states what I as a mother cannot say: "It's not just that Eva cares about Sesha, *I* care about Sesha . . . and I don't *know* Sesha. . . . Sesha is Eva's daughter and that is a fact about her that affects the sort of being *she* is." She continues: "I adopted a feral cat. Once I adopted the cat she is no longer a feral cat, she is a different sort of being. It is not that you cannot now do certain things to her that you couldn't do before because it would hurt me, it's because you can't do certain kinds of things to her because *now she is a different kind of being*" (emphasis in the original).[15] The difference between Naomi Scheman's cat

---

[15] Quoted from the transcript of the conference proceedings, available at https://podcast.ic.sunysb.edu//blojsom_resources/meta/phicdc/36-KITTAY%3AMcMAHAN_Q%26A.mp4

and Sesha or any other human with cognitive disabilities, however, is that human beings do not long survive as feral beings. We human beings are the sorts of beings we are because we are cared for by other human beings, and the human being's ontological status and corresponding moral status need to be acknowledged by the larger society that makes possible the work of those who do the caring required to sustain us. That is what we each require if we are some mother's child, and we are *all* some mother's child.

References

Associated Press. 2009. *Texas Lambasted over Care of Mentally Disabled: Justice Department Accuses State of Violating Patients' Constitutional Rights*. MSNBC 2008 (cited June 8, 2009). Available at http://www.msnbc.msn.com/id/28036793#storyContinued

Bovicelli, L., L. F. Orsini, N. Rizzo, V. Montacuti, and M. Bacchetta. 1982. "Reproduction in Down Syndrome." *Obstetrical Gynecology* 59 supp., no. 6:13S–17S.

Carlson, Licia. Forthcoming. *The Faces of Intellectual Disability: Philosophical Reflections*. Bloomington: Indiana University Press.

Cohen, Richard. 1982. "It Depends." *Washington Post*, April 20, B1.

Goodall, Jane. 2000. *Through a Window: My Thirty Years with the Chimpanzees of Gombe*. Reissue, illustrated edition. New York: Houghton Mifflin Harcourt.

Harding, Sandra G. 1991. *Whose Science? Whose Knowledge? Thinking from Women's Lives*. Ithaca: Cornell University Press.

Keller, Evelyn Fox. 2003. *A Feeling for the Organism: The Life and Work of Barbara McClintock*. New York: Macmillan.

Kittay, Eva Feder. 1999. *Love's Labor: Essays in Women, Equality and Dependency*. New York: Routledge.

———. 2005. "On the Margins of Moral Personhood." *Ethics* 116: 100–31.

———. 2008. "Ideal Theory Bioethics and the Exclusion of People with Severe Cognitive Disabilities." In *Naturalized Bioethics: Toward Responsible Knowing and Practice*, edited by Hilde Lindemann, Marian Verkerk, and Margaret Urban Walker, 218–37. Cambridge: Cambridge University Press.

MacIntrye, Alasdair. 1999. *Dependent Rational Animals: Why Human Beings Need the Virtues*. Peru, Ill.: Open Court Press.

McMahan, Jeff. 1996. "Cognitive Disability, Misfortune, and Justice." *Philosophy and Public Affairs* 25, no. 1:3–35.

———. 2003. *The Ethics of Killing: Problems at the Margins of Life*. Oxford: Oxford University Press.

———. 2008. "Cognitive Disability, Cognitive Enhancement, and Moral Status." Paper presented at the *Cognitive Disability: Its Challenge to*

Moral Philosophy conference, Stony Brook Manhattan, New York, September 20, 2008.

———. 2009. "Cognitive Disability and Cognitive Enhancement." Included in this collection.

Nussbaum, Martha. 2006. *Frontiers of Justice: Disability, Nationality, Species Membership.* Tanner Lectures on Human Values. Cambridge, Mass.: Belknap Press of Harvard University Press.

Pitcher, George. 1997. *Dogs Who Came to Stay.* London: Orion.

Ruddick, Sara. 1989. *Maternal Thinking.* New York: Beacon Press.

Scully, Jackie Leach. 2008. "Hidden Labour: Disabled/Nondisabled Encounters and Agency." Paper delivered at the *International Journal for Feminism and Bioethics Inaugural Conference.* Stony Brook Manhattan, New York.

Singer, Peter. 1996. *Rethinking Life and Death: The Collapse of Our Traditional Ethics.* New York: Macmillan.

Shakespeare, Tom, and Nicholas Watson. 2001. "The Social Model: An Outdated Ideology?" In *Exploring Theories and Expanding Methodologies: Where We Are and Where We Need to Go,* edited by Sharon N. Barnartt and Barbara M. Altman, 2:9–28. Amsterdam: JAI Press.

Smith, Dorothy E. 1987. *The Everyday World as Problematic: A Feminist Sociology.* Boston: Northeastern University Press.

Tolstoy, Leo. 1954. *Anna Karenin.* Translated by Rosemary Edmonds. New York: Penguin Classics.

Tversky, Amos. 1977. "Features of Similarity." *Psychological Review* 84, no. 4:327–52.

Waal, Frans de. 2006. *Our Inner Ape: A Leading Primatologist Explains Why We Are Who We Are.* New York: Riverhead Books.

Williams, Bernard. 1976. "Persons, Character, and Morality." In *The Identities of Persons,* edited by Amelie Rorty, 197–253. Berkeley: University of California Press.

INDEX

Note: an "n" and a number after a page reference number refers to a note number on that page.

AAIDD (American Association on Intellectual and Developmental Disabilities), 37, 39, 42, 58, 60, 333, 342
abortion, 19, 335, 344, 346–55, 358–60
    and prenatal injury, 348–55
    selective, 106 *see also* infancy and prenatal screening
    therapeutic, 32
abstract reasoning, 47, 61, 372
abuse of people with disabilities, 8, 15, 69, 126, 153, 183, 321, 385, 400
access to resources and services, 8, 57, 85, 89, 94, 105, 133, 137, 138, 151, 156, 294, 297, 299, 307–8, 410
Adams, Robert, 354n6
adaptive/social model, defining ID, 40 *see also* social model of disability and defining intellectual disability
adaptive preferences, 116, 243
advance directives, 234–5
advocacy, 4, 5, 15, 30, 199, 280, 290, 316
    self-advocacy, 4, 5n4, 15, 280,
    and self-narrative, 288–90
advocates, 4, 5, 16, 29, 30, 42, 100, 103, 154, 198, 280, 299, 320–23
Africa, 47, 199
African Americans, 11, 293, 304–5 *see also* race
    rates if ID, 40
    children placed in special education, 297, 304–6
    IQ/intelligence testing and, 40–3, 300
    overrepresentation in "judgment" categories of cognitive disability, 130, 294–5, 298, 301
    life expectancy with Down syndrome compared with whites, 306–7
agency, 1, 6, 10, 12–14, 17, 99, 120, 157, 234, 235, 365, 386
    caring and, 10–11, 379n24, 384–6, 387

collaborative conception of, 14, 177
    and enabling conditions, 134–5
    and moral responsibility of people with ID, 2, 12, 67, 68, 167, 170–81, 174, 200–20, 234, 366
    and narrative identity, 163, 165, 167
    and quality of life, 177–81
    rational, 8, 9, 111–12, 114, 117–23, 172, 194, 239
    semantic, 11, 137, 171, 175–80, 268
Aid to Families with Dependent Children (AFDC/TANF), 45
Aksakov, Sergei, 375, 380
Alex (parrot), 332–3
Alexander, Duane, 32
Alzheimer's disease, 1n1, 2, 3, 11, 141, 171, 174–5, 176, 373, 374n14 *see also* dementia
    and identity holding, 165
    personhood of people with, 11
    and socially extended mentation, 225–35
American Association on Intellectual and Developmental Disabilities (AAIDD) (was AAMR) *see* AAIDD
American Association of Mental Deficiency, 188
American Association on Mental Retardation, 37, 42, 58
American Journal of Psychiatry, 55
American Psychiatric Association, 37, 58
American Psychological Association, 303
American Sign Language, 388
Americans with Disabilities Act (1990), 5, 7, 49, 89, 105, 141
animals, nonhuman, 2, 8, 16, 77, 98, 323–4, 394
    cognitive abilities compared to humans, 330, 332–4, 334–6, 345–8, 396–412
    and cognitive enhancement, 355, 360
    and dignity, 337, 341–2
    equal consideration of interests of, 339
    killing of, 335, 339–40, 346–7, 368